# ST. PETERSBURG

# ST. PETERSBURG

Madness, Murder, and Art on the Banks of the Neva

## JONATHAN MILES

PEGASUS BOOKS
NEW YORK LONDON

St. Petersburg

Pegasus Books, Ltd.
148 West 37th Street, 13th Floor
New York, NY 10018

First Pegasus Books hardcover edition March 2018

ISBN: 978-1-68177-676-7

10 9 8 7 6 5 4 3 2 1

Printed in the United States of America
Distributed by W. W. Norton & Company, Inc.

*for Katiu*

# CONTENTS

# ST. PETERSBURG

*Impressionistic panorama of St Petersburg around the middle of the nineteenth century.*

BIRD'S-EYE VIEW

1. Okhta.
2. Smolnoi Convent.
3. Taurida Palace.
4. Arsenal.
5. Public Gardens.
6. Champ de Mars.
7. Hotel of the Sappers.
8. Michailoff Palace.

9. Souvoroff's Monument.
10. Marble Palace.
11. Theatre of the Hermitage.
12. The Hermitage.
13. Imperial Palace.
14. Admiralty. [the Great.
15. Equestrian Statue of Peter
16. English Church.

17. English Church.
18. English Quay.
19. The New Admiralty.
20. Isaac's Square.
21. School of Equitation.
22. St. Isaac's Cathedral.
23. Court House.
24. Hotel de l'Etat-Major.

25. Alexander's Column.
25*. The Nevskoi Prospekt.
26. Foundling House.
27. Kasan Ch. of the Virgin.
28. The Great Bazar.
29. The Michael Theatre.

30. Con
31. Hay
32. St. 
33. The
34. Sun
35. Tri

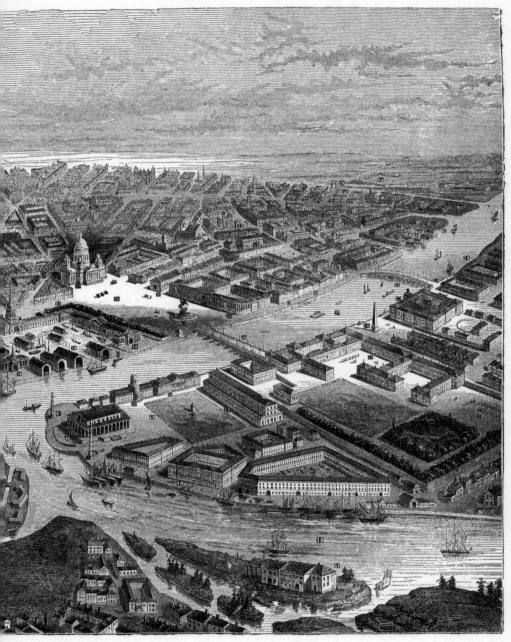

ST. PETERSBURG.

Stories circulate about about a man born in St Petersburg, who grew up in Petrograd, who grew old in Leningrad and was asked where he'd like to die.

He replied, 'St Petersburg.'

# 1

# TWILIGHT ON THE NEVSKY

*1993*

In October 1917, a blank fired from the battleship *Aurora* signalled the start of the Russian Revolution. Three-quarters of a century have passed and, once again, there is chaos and change. It is an eerie 3 a.m. on a summer's morning in 1993. I am standing on a balcony overlooking the Nevsky Prospekt, the once-great avenue of the once-great city of St Petersburg. There is something surreal about the perpetual twilight of these so-called 'White Nights'. The French novelist Alexandre Dumas, visiting the capital at the height of its glory, suggested that, at such a moment, the silence makes you wonder if you 'hear the angels sing or God speak'.[1] For me, there are no angels, and the silence is disturbed by the rattle of antique traffic. When Dumas wrote, the splendid metropolis was a powerful magnet for the greatest European architects, writers and thinkers. In the early 1990s, having flourished for much of its 300-year history, St Petersburg is visibly crumbling. The street below me is pot-holed, the façades on the far side of the Prospekt are cracked, their stucco flaked and their windows mired. There is no money or any adequate agency to protect and care for a city created as a spectacular setting for its own great drama. After three riveting acts – 1703–1825, 1825–1917 and 1917–1991 – I wonder if this is the final curtain.

I look down on a scatter of thugs as they swiftly close in on a well-dressed man and beat him up. People on the street shuffle by. Somewhere a shot rings out. Another. It strikes me as odd that a city whose past has been dominated by the struggle between the revolutionary intellectual and repressive authority should now resemble a lawless frontier town – but maybe it always has. The deft hoods leave their victim in a heap. Nobody seems to care. As the man tries to stagger up, I can't help thinking that violence is endemic to the city. It was conceived in violence as the capital of a new Russia – an attempt to yank the country from its isolated past by a megalomaniac Europhile. Peter the Great set his will not only against nature, but also against the practices of a vast country stretching from the borders of Poland and Germany across almost 13,000 kilometres of northern Asia to the Pacific Ocean. Although it was sited on Russia's western edge, Peter's 'window onto Europe' has been slammed shut again and again, the city abandoned to tyranny and coercion, the spirit of the population perpetually torn between extravagant hope and hopeless deprivation. Even in the first years of the twentieth century – when the city centre was bright with bourgeois opulence – the five-kilometre stretch of the Nevsky Prospekt, from the magnificent government buildings at the historical heart of the capital to the muddy slums on its outskirts, dramatised the persistent gulf between dazzling wealth and dire poverty and between the new and old Russia. St Petersburg is both confrontational and contradictory.

Compare the swift creation of its magnificent physical structure – an architectural and engineering achievement unparalleled in modern times – with the sloth of a paralysing bureaucracy that stifled the lives, but not the souls, of its inhabitants. The city is schizophrenic: pushed and pulled by dramatic changes of identity and name. It has been expeditionary, imperial, enlightened, repressive, dissolute, revolutionary, communist and chaotic. It has been called St Petersburg, Petrograd, Leningrad and, once again, St Petersburg. On this visit, I can see that whatever joy the inhabitants feel in shaking off the yoke of seventy-five years of communist rule is negated by the material difficulties of a society unprepared for radical change. That is typical St Petersburg time-warp – politically, everything happens too quickly or too slowly and the population is left stranded. The frustrations that compromise innovation, and the recurring and unresolved tensions, make the story of Petersburg as maddening as it is exciting.

As the sun rises on another difficult day I go down onto the Nevsky Prospekt, on which so much of St Petersburg's history has occurred. The Nevsky is the central nervous system of the city. There has been no greater display of its modernity. By 1830, it had become the most important avenue, the longest, widest and best-lit thoroughfare. In its heyday the Nevsky was a polyglot consumer showcase. Sadly, as I walk down the Nevsky in the dying years of the revolutionary twentieth century, I see broken cars and abandoned trucks shrouded by muck left from the late-spring thaw. And yet strange new illuminations glint through the stagnation of this brown-wrapped world: an aluminium hamburger stand, with its acid lights, breaks the neoclassical decorum of Arts Square. The logos of Lancôme, L'Oréal and Baskin-Robbins shine through the gloomy dawn, hinting at the shape of things to come. Although ten years on there will be a surge of confidence in the rouble, in 1993 these Western consumer outposts only tease the population with dreams. The Philips shop trades solely in dollars, and a middle-range hi-fi costs what an average citizen earns in many months. A supermarket on the Nevsky Prospekt fronted with garish neon, and filled inside with rows of glaring white freezers, has only apples for sale. The queue and the empty shelf are the two givens of any shopping trip – just as they were under communism. It is tragic to see how one of the world's great social thoroughfares is so broken. But this new dawn is only a moment in the story of the swift rise, difficult life, rapid

decay and agonised rebirth of the glorious city of St Petersburg. The vandalised phone kiosk that I pass is a witness to
what must be the defining notion of this city: absurdity. When
you can find a booth that is not battered into oblivion, you
discover that the public telephone takes a fifteen-kopek piece.
But fifteen-kopek pieces are scarce and can only be obtained
from cunning racketeers for fifty times their face value.[2] The
closer you get to what passes for normal in St Petersburg, the
more irrational the place becomes. The writer Nikolai Gogol
knew this. The composer Dmitri Shostakovich contended with
it. There was folly in the choice of the site. There was madness
in the excesses and fetishes of its early rulers. And yet, if you
look at a plan of St Petersburg, there is logic. There is order.
There is intention.

   In 1839, the Marquis de Custine observed that St Petersburg
was undoubtedly one of the wonders of the world, and yet, it was
a folly without measure – a Greek city improvised for Tartars
like some theatre set, a site where hordes of peasants camped
in shacks 'around a pile of ancient temples'.[3] This juxtaposition
of order and chaos was a source of great tension in the nineteenth century and a major theme in the literature of that period.
St Petersburg writers created the figure of the 'little man' adrift,
struggling against the injustices of officialdom. In the shadowy,
post-communist city, it is once again the ordinary, honest citizen
who is suffering. On my previous trip – just after the break-up of
the Soviet Union – I happened upon impromptu markets where
desperate people tried to sell one shoe, one boot, a lock without
a key, a key without a lock. When I talked to dancers from the
Mariinsky Theatre, they attributed a decline in the standard of
their performances to worthless wages and malnutrition. The
market was de-regulated at the beginning of 1992 and prices
doubled, then trebled. For vast sectors of the population with
no access to hard currency, the situation became extreme. The
problem of under-developed modernisation, which had assailed

the population for 300 years, was still – in a newly reincarnated St Petersburg – claiming innumerable victims.

Continuing down the Nevsky Prospekt, I step into the underpass by *Gostiny Dvor* metro station. Some buskers are punching out 'Blue Suede Shoes'. Only years before, such freedom was forbidden. But accompanying such vital performances are wildly misguided visions of life in the glittering, gilded West; St Petersburg is – and always has been – a city in which dreams are big, and information and truth are in short supply. I spoke to a friend who, as a child, had been sent with her school choir to sing in Kiev soon after the Chernobyl disaster. When they returned to what was then Leningrad, the children were told simply to throw away their shoes. Restriction of information – the chilling scale of official secrecy – runs through the history of the city and has given rise to a rich and dynamic underground culture.

I walk into the heart of historical Petersburg on the banks of the Neva, where I am struck by the majesty of the Admiralty and the Headquarters of the General Staff – buildings which remind me that Peter the Great's original intention was to build a fort to protect a port. But the siting of a naval and trading base on the banks of a river that freezes up for eight months every year was absurd or, perhaps, desperate. Craving access to the Baltic trade route, Peter situated his new capital on Russia's vulnerable north-western frontier. The risk was at once made obvious by the Great Northern War against Sweden, which disturbed the first years of the city's construction.

As I stand before the magnificent parabola of official buildings that embraces Palace Square, I am reminded of what the French writer André Gide said when he visited in 1936: 'In Leningrad it is St Petersburg that I admire.'[4] I glance across at the turquoise, gilt and white façade of the Winter Palace, where the 1917 Revolution began – a historical 'moment' emasculated by the ease with which the revolutionaries entered the building. The only shooting in Palace Square, observed the poet Joseph

Brodsky, was done by Soviet film-maker Sergei Eisenstein in his
celebration of the Revolution: *October*.[5]

Between 1711 and 1917 the Winter Palace, in one or other of
its incarnations, has been the residence of so many larger-than-
life personalities – epic figures who played their extravagant part
in the folly and bravura of St Petersburg: the impulsive and despotic founder, Peter the Great; the indolent and sadistic Anna I;
the hedonistic Elizabeth I; the culturally and sexually voracious
Catherine the Great; mad Paul I; repressive Nicholas I. Add to
these rulers the subversive writers Alexander Herzen and Nikolai
Chernyshevsky; the flamboyant showman Sergei Diaghilev; the
disturbed dancer Vaslav Nijinsky; the priest-turned-celebrity-
protester Father Gapon; the pilgrim-turned-debauched-con-man
Rasputin; the uncompromising revolutionary Vladimir Ilyich
Lenin. Add to those the many writers, artists and musicians
whose innovative and often-preposterous creations have captured the spirit of an improbable capital in which a resilient
and resistant population has battled every kind of adversity.
Beyond this incredible cast of extraordinary characters stands
the grandest and most interesting of them all: the awe-inspiring,
dysfunctional city itself, risen from the mists and – at this point
in 1993 – in danger of sinking into the mire.

# PART I

# EMPERORS

*1698–1825*

# 2

# HAVOC IN LONDON

## *1698*

Wearing simple clothing, he left his diplomatic 'Great Embassy' when it reached the Rhine, boarded a small boat and sailed towards Zaandam on the Ij. At the beginning of a grand adventure that would change his nation's destiny, he was nearing that Dutch port on a Sunday in mid-August 1698, when he suddenly yelled across the water at a man spending quiet hours with his eel traps. Disturbed by such sudden, wild clamouring, Gerrit Kist glanced up from his catch, astonished to see his old master – tsar of that distant and exotic country, Russia – dressed in working man's clothes and sailing a humble skiff. Kist had worked as a blacksmith for Tsar Peter in Moscow and was, at once, sworn to secrecy: the tsar was travelling to Zaandam disguised as a simple artisan to learn the Dutch manner of ship-building from the keel up.[1]

Motivated by his urge to understand how things worked, the two-metre-tall twenty-six-year-old tsar shunned pomp and ceremony. His Great Embassy, headed by his unquenchable drinking buddy François Lefort, acted as a decoy. As the Russians crossed Europe, Lefort drew the diplomatic heat, leaving Peter free to satisfy his curiosity. But for all his precaution, the tsar's purpose and reputation preceded him. In England, the Bishop of Salisbury spoke of 'a mighty Northern Emperor' who, 'to raise his Nation, and enlarge his Empire . . . comes to learn the best methods of doing it'.[2] And there were other, less flattering impressions coming out of Moscow. The tsar, it seemed, forced nobles to skid, bare-arsed, on the ice. He enjoyed seeing his favourites shoot at one another. He was delighted by the sight of houses burning and by fireworks and other explosions. During *Svyatki* – or Yuletide – Peter forced 'the fattest Lords' to sledge over cracks in the ice where many tumbled into the freezing water and drowned.[3] Prince Kuratkin, later the Russian Ambassador to Holland, recalled how Peter and his friends stuck a candle in Prince Volkonsky's anus and chanted prayers over him. They 'tarred and pitched people and made them stand on their heads'. On one occasion they 'used a bellows to pump air into Ivan Akakievich's colon', horseplay which resulted in the man's immediate death. Such scenes – worthy of Brueghel or Bosch – suggest a world of carnivalesque irreverence, a world turned upside down. *Maslenitsa*, the Butter Week revelry preceding Lent, was a time when people abandoned themselves to the devil, in a gluttonous obliteration of winter.[4] It was a festival celebrated with a merciless thirst and by roughhousing, sanctioned by the fact that no Russian ruler had ever gained a new perspective on things by visiting a Western land. To Europe, at the dawn of the Age of Enlightenment, such romps seemed like pagan antics from a land that time forgot. For Russia, Tsar Peter's behaviour carried a sting in its tale. His tomfoolery was not merely carnival freedom, but an assertion that the tsar could do absolutely as he pleased because he was an autocrat.

In 1671, Peter's father, Tsar Alexei, married a nineteen-year-old black-eyed beauty called Natalya Naryshkin, ward of his friend and adviser Artamon Matveyev.[5] The match ignited a feud between two clans vying for control of Russia: the Miloslavskys, who were the family of Alexei's deceased wife, and the

Naryshkins, the family of his young bride. Natalya brought a breath of fresh, gently Westernising air to the court and, in May 1672, produced a robust male heir who was christened Peter Alexeivich Romanov.

As a young boy, Peter enjoyed toy soldiers and guns. His staff of dwarfs were both servants and playmates. Strong, capable and inquisitive, Peter was adored by his loving parents until – in early 1676 – the healthy and happy Tsar Alexei caught a chill while blessing the waters of the Moscow River. A month later he was dead, and Peter became subject to a new tsar, his fifteen-year-old half-brother, Fyodor III – a Miloslavsky. When Fyodor III died in 1682 without a male heir, protocol dictated that his sixteen-year-old brother, Ivan, should rule. But Ivan was lame, almost blind and battling a severe speech impediment.[6] By contrast, his strapping ten-year-old half-brother, Peter, seemed a popular and prudent choice. Many of Moscow's senators or privy counsellors – the *boyars* – wanted the strong young Naryshkin to rule under the regent, Natalya. Thus Peter was declared tsar. But the Miloslavskys protested: Ivan was older, Ivan was next in line. The Naryshkins and the Miloslavskys embarked on a savage power struggle, which became entangled with the discontent of the *streltsy*.

Moscow's all-purpose emergency guard was an underused, overpaid grab-bag of 22,000 gaudily uniformed men who were also traders pampered by the state. They were rich and idle, but their very name, *streltsy* – 'musketeers' – hinted at their trigger-happy tendency. When the rank and file of one of their regiment accused their colonel of corruption, the allegation proved infectious. The inexperienced and ill-advised Natalya unwisely yielded to their demands, thereby giving them a taste of power. The Miloslavskys were swift to exploit this and persuaded the *streltsy* that the Naryshkins had murdered Ivan, in an attempt to secure the throne for Peter. As bloodthirsty *streltsy* surged into the Kremlin, Artamon Matveyev persuaded Natalya to appear before them with both Ivan and Peter. Prince Michael Dolgoruky, son of the *streltsy* commander, rashly chose that precarious moment to reassert military discipline, and the *streltsy* pressed up the stairs to where he stood, seized him and flung him down onto the pikes and halberds of their comrades below. Skewered, Dolgoruky's body was then butchered and the *streltsy* went for Matveyev. They prised the old man from Natalya's arms and – in front of her wide-eyed ten-year-old son, Peter – flung him onto the blades below. It was at this moment that Sophia, the dynamic older sister of Fyodor and Ivan, intervened. Peter and Ivan would rule jointly and Sophia would become regent.[7] Her seven-year tenure as the first woman to control Russia had begun.

Young Peter, traumatised by the undisciplined behaviour of the *streltsy*, turned his back on the capital. He didn't go far to begin with – only a few kilometres along the Yauza River to the hunting lodge at Preobrazhenskoe, where he once again played soldiers, this time using real ordnance and a swelling number of sympathetic noblemen and commoners. If the child is father to the man, then Peter's delight in building earthworks and fortresses can be seen as the first intimation of his obsession with the construction of what would become St Petersburg. As his military installation grew and his war games became more sophisticated, he began to shape the new Russia by forming the celebrated Preobrazhensky and Semyonovsky Regiments of the imperial guard. Showing an early inclination to learn matters from the ground up, Peter enlisted as a drummer boy.[8] As he rose through the artillery, he shared the humble duties of a foot soldier, revealing his deep-seated understanding that a modest will to learn was more useful than an inherited title.

Sophia's regency was finally compromised by two failed military campaigns and her relentless passion for their ill-chosen leader, the married Prince Vasily Golitsyn, who managed to lose 45,000 men in four months without even engaging the enemy in battle. After being mendaciously hailed as a hero in Moscow, the prince was chosen to mis-lead another campaign in which he lost a further 35,000 men to death or capture. Some of the most powerful families – among them the Rodomanovskys, Shereme-tevs and Dolgorukys – rallied around Peter and his mother and, when Ivan V died in 1696, Peter became tsar. Ivan had failed to produce a male heir, but Peter – married to Evdokia Lopukhina since he was seventeen – had two sons. One of them, Alexei, survived to become a perpetual source of irritation throughout most of Peter's reign.

Prince Golitsyn, with his keen appreciation of Europe and his interest in science, was a key figure in preparing Russia for reform. He owned clocks, Western portraits and Venetian plate. His Moscow house was influenced by European architecture.[9] He should have been an ally to Peter rather than an enemy, but he was exiled to Siberia for his sympathies and failures. When Sophia attempted to engineer another *streltsy* uprising, Peter crushed it – incarcerating her in the Novodivechy Convent and branding, breaking, beheading and hanging the conspirators. The Prussian Ambassador Printz recalled that the tsar ordered twenty prisoners to be brought before him. He took a shot of vodka and then beheaded one. He took another shot, then hacked the next prisoner to death, and continued thus until he had dis-posed of the traitors. Then he invited the terrified ambassador to match him.[10]

Among the foreigners living in Moscow's 'German Suburb' Peter found a good number of people who shared his enthusiasm for soldiery, ships and debauchery. First among these was the hard-drinking Swiss mercenary François Lefort – almost twice Peter's age and nearly as tall. Lefort's house hosted an ongoing party where revellers were 'locked in for three days at a time'.[11] In 1692, the married tsar fell for one of Lefort's mistresses, Anna Mons, the sassy, hard-drinking daughter of a German wine mer-chant, who would become Peter's mistress for the next eleven years. Filippo Balatri, the Italian *castrato* brought to Russia in

the autumn of 1698, saw Peter playing chess at Anna's house and
was told, 'This is the place where Peter Alexeivich can be found
when he wants to leave the tsar at court.'[12]

Peter's early enthusiasm for sailing on the lakes and rivers near
Moscow persuaded him to travel to Arkhangelsk, Russia's northern White Sea port, where he was captivated by tales of Dutch
shipbuilding. Despite a successful military adventure against
the Turkish garrison at Azov, Peter knew he needed to improve
Russian naval capability by observing and emulating Western
models. So the overgrown boy, driven visionary and calculating
buffoon cunningly went off to Europe incognito.


Despite the presence of foreigners in Moscow, the essential ignorance of Peter's Embassy concerning foreign modes and manners
became apparent early in its progress. At a dance given by the
widowed Electress of Hanover, the Russians mistook the whale-
bones of German corsets for ribs, and Peter himself commented
that 'German ladies had devilish hard bones.'[13] For Peter – gauche
and in obvious need of being brought up to date – Holland was
a useful destination. The Dutch dominated international trade,
and their nautical expertise and maritime prowess attracted the
tsar. Holland, master of the oceans, was also at war with a sea
that threatened to wipe parts of its territory from the face of the
earth. Throughout the early seventeenth century there had been
frequent and violent flooding, and the Dutch were now skilled in
canalisation, sluicing and drainage. As for shipbuilding, Dutch
maritime trade was so brisk that between 1625 and 1700, the
Republic constructed between 400 and 500 sea-going vessels per
year.[14] Zaandam alone boasted fifty shipyards.

Arriving in that port, Peter registered at the Lynst Rogge
shipyard and set to work. However, with his impressive height
and often unruly manner, his presence began to draw unwanted
attention. Crowds began to pursue the tsar and, when he went

sailing on the Ij, he angrily flung two bottles at the captain of a mail boat who steered a gaggle of inquisitive ladies too close. The situation in Zaandam became intolerable and, after one hectic week, Peter was forced to flee to cosmopolitan Amsterdam. From September 1697 to early January 1698 Peter laboured in the East India Docks at Ostenberg,[15] while other Russian apprentices were scattered around Amsterdam learning different aspects of the shipbuilding art.

Sited from a combination of hubris and necessity, Amsterdam was testimony to man's triumph over nature. Houses and commercial properties were constructed along a system of five concentric canals intersected by narrower radial channels. At the height of its power during Peter's visit, Amsterdam was the wealthiest city in the world, with palatial government buildings and thriving commerce. Its waterways were clogged with boats, ships and barges on which people lived. Its narrow streets offered a veritable cornucopia of raw materials and merchandise. On the Nieuwe Brug Peter found bookshops, sea charts, sextants and ironmongery. On Bickers Island there were chandlers. In the Warmoesstraat there were exotic fabrics, Nuremberg porcelain, Italian majolica and Delft faience. But above all, the ambitious young tsar would find the city itself a particularly instructive model, for he too would wage war on the sea.[16]

While the shipyards in the Dutch Republic retained a time-honoured, artisanal approach, the country also embraced the latest scientific learning. Amsterdam alone boasted around a hundred printers and publishers, making it one of the most important centres for book production in Europe. Higher education prospered and a flexible attitude towards learning – coupled with the arrival of exotic natural specimens unearthed by Dutch explorers and traders – resulted in an environment predisposed to scientific investigation. Displayed in cabinets, curiosities attracted many visitors – Peter among them. The tsar met Anthonie van Leeuwenhoek, a barely educated draper whose hobby was to search out the hidden secrets of decay. The first person to observe bacteria through the lenses of a microscope, Leeuwenhoek would pick food from his teeth and examine it, collect his own excrement to study, and monitor the fungal life that grew between his toes when he neglected to change his stockings for a period of weeks. He also examined his own semen and was one of the first people to describe the activity of 'little animals' or spermatozoa.[17]

The skilled dissector and embalmer Frederik Ruysch invited Peter to his Anatomy Theatre, which presented 'anatomical revelation' as a spectacle lit by candlelight and accompanied by music. The tsar, fascinated by disembowelment, shared Ruysch's particular interest in freaks of nature. He was so taken by Ruysch's collection of 2,000 embryological and anatomical specimens, assembled over half a century, that he eventually purchased it for 30,000 guilders in 1717.[18] When not in the shipyard wielding his axe, or drinking in Dutch *musicos* where men gambled and whored, Peter was busy searching out the latest Dutch inventions and techniques. He met Jan van der Heyden, the inventor of the pressured fire hose, whom he tried to lure to Russia to assist in the fight against the blazes which frequently raged in Moscow's congested wooden alleys. The tsar became interested in paper-making, printing, engraving, architecture and botanical gardens. The modernity of the Dutch Republic stimulated a monarch who would, up to a point, break with old ways.

Peter found himself in a land where the countryside was flat, and the bodies fat. Like Russians, the Dutch had gargantuan appetites – one contemporary observer described the Dutchman as 'a lusty, fat, two-legged cheese-worm'. They had 'so many rules and ceremonies for getting drunk' that formal dining became a secular religion.[19] By contrast, Peter's self-styled 'All-Mad, All-Jesting, All-Drunken Assembly' descended into anarchy and brutality. The tsar reportedly drank thirty to forty glasses of wine a day and still remained sharp. Stories claim that, even in his early teens, Peter drank a pint of vodka and a bottle of sherry over breakfast, followed by about eight more bottles of wine before going out to play[20] – exaggerations with some basis in fact. Moscow banquets began around noon and lasted into the next morning. They started with vodka, followed by strong wines and beers served in massive glasses. There were speeches and toasts, heralded by trumpet blasts or artillery salvoes. If anyone found disfavour during these feasts, they were punished with the Great Eagle: a massive, ornate double-handled goblet filled with a litre and a half of vodka – all to be downed in one gulp.

When England's King William III invited Peter to dine near Utrecht, the London *Post Boy* reported that 'the tsar of Muscovy was so highly pleased with the magnificent dinner . . . he merrily invited himself again'.[21] In fact, Peter's thoughts were already turning towards England, where his study would be serious, his behaviour outrageous. On 7 January 1698, he boarded HMS *Yorke* and – resolutely remaining on deck to brave a terrific storm – crossed the Channel to England where, in the Pool of London, he hoped to learn more about England's scientific approach to shipbuilding.

If Amsterdam was wealthier in 1698, London was larger. Although – only three decades before Peter's visit – it had suffered a devastating plague and fire, the capital now boasted a population of nigh on half a million. With post-fire reconstruction, the English capital was experiencing a period of tremendous change, fusing its 'mosaic' of neighbourhoods into one physical and commercial entity. It was being transformed from a warren of medieval wooden buildings into a modern metropolis of bricks and stone.[22] But while the devastation of the Great Fire had made way for wider streets, the opportunity to restructure the layout of the city was largely wasted, and the creation of modern London was evolutionary rather than revolutionary.[23] Instead of 'a convenient regular well built city,' wrote the architect Nicholas Hawksmoor, we have 'a chaos of dirty rotten sheds, always tumbling', with 'lakes of mud and rills of stinking mire running through them'.[24] During the 1690s the streets were crowded with beggars, and even those squares which had been laid out for light and airy recreation attracted gamblers, vagabonds and thieves. The diarist John Evelyn – who spent much time ordering his own house and garden at Sayes Court in Deptford – was so worried about the chaotic way in which the capital was developing that he suggested a precautionary green belt to protect the city from a stifling collar of dark satanic mills and factories.[25]

Instead of practical strategies for the planning of a modern city – like those drawn up for St Petersburg, Washington DC or Baron Haussmann's Paris – priorities for London reconstruction centred on church-building. This resulted in a veritable forest of spires: an antiphon to the jungle of masts clogging the River Thames. Dominating this multitude of parish churches was the dome of Christopher Wren's St Paul's Cathedral. There is no evidence that Peter met Wren, but the architect's works lay spread at the tsar's feet when he climbed the Monument to the Great Fire in early April 1698.[26]

Arriving in London, Peter was lodged – at the expense of the Crown – at 21 Norfolk Street in the elegant network of recently built houses south of the Strand. Along with Fleet Street, Cheapside and Cornhill, the Strand was one of the finest commercial centres in London – a shopping thoroughfare outshining anything in Louis XIV's Paris. So Peter went shopping. His forays were reported in the London gossip sheets in the manner that a star's spree would be splashed across the tabloids today. From John Carte, a watchmaker in the Strand, the tsar purchased a geographical clock, which told the time in all parts of the world as well as marking the different sunrises and sunsets. It cost £60. Peter also spent £50 on a gold watch, £250 on medical instruments, telescopes, quadrants and compasses.[27] He purchased an English coffin – amazed that such a receptacle was swiftly assembled from planks of wood, instead of being laboriously hollowed from an entire tree trunk, as was the custom in Russia.[28] The tsar also bought black servants for £21, 'a negress' for £30, along with '18 pairs of stockings for the blacks' at a shilling a pair.

While in London, Peter attended concerts and Temple masquerades – on one occasion disguised as a butcher.[29] He was also – in the words of the hydraulic engineer John Perry – 'prevail'd upon to go once or twice to the play', which 'he did not like'.[30] However, there was something about the theatre Peter clearly did enjoy. Since the Restoration in 1660, women played women's roles on the London stage, and Peter was attracted by the young Letitia Cross, who had recently made her name playing 'Miss Hoyden . . . daughter to Sir Tunbelly Clumsey' in John Vanbrugh's *The Relapse*. The degree of her intimacy with the tsar is a matter for speculation, although Andrei Nartov, Peter's instrument-maker, claimed that his master 'became acquainted, through Menshikov, who was drowned in luxury and sensuality, with an actress, named Cross, whom sometimes during his stay in England he took for amorous dalliance'.[31] The low-born, semi-literate Menshikov – who worked his way up through the ranks in the Preobrazhensky Regiment to become the tsar's right-hand man – shared Peter's ability to drink and party. In 1698, the year that began with Peter's sojourn in London, a Russian merchant was arrested for suggesting that Peter took Menshikov to his bed 'like a whore'.[32] Giving possible credence to such an accusation, John Perry – describing the debauchery in Moscow – maintained that 'the horrible sin of sodomy . . . which they are very much addicted to in their drink' is hardly considered a crime in Russia.[33] Rough-hewn Peter, with his Dutch workman's clothes and consummate lack of etiquette, provoked rumours and outrage wherever he went. At a meeting with King William in Norfolk Street, the tsar's pet monkey suddenly leapt at the monarch. Visiting Anne, the future Queen of England, Peter refused an armchair and sat on a stool at the feet of the princess.

When the Earl of Macclesfield called unexpectedly, the tsar suddenly rose from the table, went upstairs and locked himself in his bedchamber.[34] But despite appearing petulant and unruly, Peter agreed to sit to Rembrandt's pupil, Sir Godfrey Kneller. The resulting portrait of a saucy military commander, whose small head sits a little uneasily on his huge body, now hangs in the King's Gallery of Kensington Palace. Comparing the image with a 1670s painting of Tsar Alexei, we see how unequivocally Kneller thrust Peter into the Age of Enlightenment. While Alexei is depicted with his traditional crown, the Cap of Monomakh, Peter is firmly placed in a Western context with ermine, armour, classical architecture and an impressive naval presence, which – in terms of Russia in 1698 – was pure fantasy.[35]

That was about to change. Peter was lured to England by the gift of the *Royal Transport*, the first schooner-rigged ship in the British Navy. It was a present that came with a bonus – its designer, Admiral Carmarthen,[36] who became the tsar's London drinking companion, guide and mentor. In between quantities of sherry, Carmarthen counselled Peter on how to set up a Russian navy along English lines. In return for the Russian tobacco monopoly, Admiral Carmarthen also advanced Peter £12,000.[37] Despite this windfall, Peter's entourage left unpaid bills at taverns, inns and guest houses – and there was worse to come. In February, Peter moved to Deptford on the south side of the Thames, where the King's Dockyard stood beside the splendid house he rented. It was owned by the very man who had expressed concern about the industrial threat to London, the diarist John Evelyn. The tenancy proved to be an owner's nightmare. The occupants left a trail of vomit, a urinous stink in wet beds. As the severe winter gave way to the mild English spring, the ongoing bash sprawled out into the garden. The catalogue of breakages included twenty fine pictures torn and their frames broken, carpets stained with grease, paintwork damaged, chairs ripped apart and windows broken. Evelyn's flowerbeds and bowling green were devastated, the kitchen garden wasted. His servant wrote to his master describing 'a house full of people, and right nasty'. A government survey concurred, observing that the 'indoor habits of Peter and his retinue were . . . filthy in the extreme'.[38]

In nearby Greenwich, Peter took elementary lessons in navigation. He met the first Astronomer Royal, John Flamsteed, at the Royal Observatory. He also visited the Arsenal at Woolwich, where he shared his interest in fireworks with the Master of Ordnance, Henry Sidney, First Earl of Romney. He toured the Mint several times, and visited the Tower of London and the Royal Society.[39] Perry recorded that 'the King was pleased to send Admiral Mitchell down with him to Portsmouth, to put the fleet that lay at Spithead to Sea, on purpose to show him a sham Engagement'.[40] Delighted by the sophistication of the manoeuvres in the mock-battle, Peter apparently did not fare so well on the Thames. The small yacht in which he practised sailing collided with the bomb ship *Salamander*, and, on another occasion, the tsar rammed an eight-gun yacht, the *Henrietta*.[41]

The English found it somewhat odd that Peter should travel to England while there was friction in Moscow and an ongoing 'Great War against the Turks and Tartars'. In fact, 'oddness' seemed to sum up this young giant, who was given to fits and seizures in which his head twitched suddenly and violently towards his right shoulder. He appeared a rattled, chaotic soul in search of order and precision. Painted by Kneller with the accoutrements of a Western king, upon his return to Russia, Peter was represented as a ruler in his father's mould, wearing the Cap of Monomakh. In yet another image, he was decked with the laurels of a Roman emperor.[42] The conflict of these images – the pull between archaic Russia and enlightened Europe, not to mention a dream of imperial grandeur – suggests something of the confusion in the young tsar's mind. Peter was an expeditionary who, during his drunken roll through Amsterdam and London, acquired sufficient architectural inspiration and engineering skill to return home and decide that it was possible to build a dream city on a reclaimed swamp.

When Peter left English waters on 25 April 1698, the Austrian representative in London reported on Peter's visit to his government: 'They say that he intends to civilise his subjects in the manner of other nations. But from his acts here, one cannot find any other intention than to make them sailors; he has had intercourse almost exclusively with sailors, and has gone away as shy as he came.'[43]

Even before his premature return to Russia, Peter instructed the sadistic and drunken governor of Moscow, Fyodor Romodanovsky, to be ruthless in his reprisals against the newly rebellious *streltsy*. When Peter arrived, he supervised the public executions himself. However, the gruesome scenes described by 'civilised' foreign visitors should not have shocked or even surprised them. Along with ideas about science and shipbuilding, Peter brought back from Europe personal experience of the Western tradition of execution as public spectacle – in December 1697, the City Fathers of Amsterdam had invited the tsar to witness a public branding, beating, hanging and beheading.

During the month of October 1698, 799 *streltsy* were executed.[44] At Preobrazhenskoe, fourteen chambers were set up where the leather whip, or knout, was used to beat rebels, who were then slow-roasted over a fire. As Johan Korb, secretary of the Austrian Legation observed, 'Peter himself cut off five heads', and went on to note that other executioners were so ham-fisted that the axe fell in the middle of a miscreant's back rather than on his neck. Rebels were 'tied alive to the wheel'. There were 'horrid lamentations throughout the afternoon and the following night' as they ended 'their miserable existence in the utmost agony'. Reflecting on the scope of all the punishments, Korb noted that the exterminations hardly seemed draconian, 'considering the daily perils to which the Tsar's Majesty was hitherto exposed'.[45]

# 3

# DANGEROUS ACCELERATION

## *1700–25*

By the tsar's decree, the Russian year 7208 became 1700. It was a leap back to the future and a dangerous acceleration. Peter knew that in order to become great, Russia should trade with the progressive yet incessantly warring nations of Europe. He needed to export Russian goods, and import ideas and expertise. So rather than calculating from Russia's choice for the creation of the world all those 7,208 years earlier, Peter decided to date events – as in Europe – from the birth of Christ and end Russia's 'banishment outside the passage of time'.[1] But when he adopted the Julian Calendar in 1700, the trend elsewhere was to convert to the Gregorian Calendar. His choice made him out of date. Russia lagged behind until some three months after the revolution when – if you blinked on 1 February 1918, – it became 14 February, the day the Bolsheviks went Gregorian.

Peter declared that, on 1 January 1700, when Red Square would be illuminated, 'everyone who has a musket or any other fire arm should either salute three times or shoot several rockets'.[2] Russia's new age would begin with a bang. Securing a temporary peace with the Ottoman Empire, the tsar promptly declared war on Sweden. At first things went badly and the Russians lost the Battle of Narva in November 1700. Exhilarated by his success, Charles XII of Sweden turned his attention towards Poland, leaving Peter free to modernise his army and manoeuvre against the poached Russian lands of Karelia and Ingria.

Modernisation had been the priority since Peter returned in 1698 from his Great Embassy. The focus was on 'one of the darling delights of this monarch'[3] – the navy. Built by foreign experts and manned almost entirely by foreign sailors, it succeeded in frustrating a Swedish attack on the White Sea port of Arkhangelsk in 1701. In the same year, the Moscow School of Mathematics and Navigation was set up under the direction of the Scot Henry Farquharson and two graduates of the Royal Mathematical School at Christ's Hospital, Richard Grice and Stephan Gwynn.[4] Peter's key shipyard at Voronezh on the Don was placed under the direction of Dutch, Danish and English craftsmen – among them Richard Cozens, whose child, Alexander – sometimes rumoured to be the tsar's own son – grew up to become the first notable British landscape painter, and father of the most talented of picturesque watercolourists, John Robert Cozens. The importance of the English contribution to Russia's navy is confirmed by the *castrato* Filippo Balatri, who witnessed Peter at Voronezh, axe in hand, building a sixty-gun ship under the guidance of an Englishman.[5] The sea captain John Deane wrote to Lord Carmarthen, 'I'll assure Your Lordship it will be the best ship'[6] among the large number being built.

Muscovites, known to be 'great enemies to all innovation', reacted strongly when they were compelled to adopt European dress. Russian diplomatic representatives were despatched to European capitals – not without an inevitable culture clash. Likewise, when foreign envoys were received in Russia, the outcome was not always happy. In 1702, Herr Königseck, the representative from Saxony, fell from a drawbridge and drowned. While his effects were being gathered, a portrait of a lady fell from one of the dead man's pockets. To the tsar's astonishment, the likeness was that of his own long-term mistress, Anna Mons. When several letters were discovered written in Anna's hand, in 'the tenderest style' and addressed to the envoy, the ever-promiscuous tsar placed Anna and her relatives under house-arrest. During their interview, which could have ended with Anna being sentenced to death, Peter 'melted into tears' and empathetically forgave her, 'since he so severely felt how impossible it was to conquer inclination'. He vowed: 'you shall never want, but I will never see you more'.[7]

In the summer of that same year, an orphaned Livonian kitchen and laundry maid called Martha Skavronskaya married a Swedish trumpeter in Marienburg. Their union lasted all of eight days, until the trumpeter left with his retreating regiment.[8] The Russians, under Field Marshal Boris Sheremetev, advanced on the town and Martha was taken. Bright-eyed and lively, she attracted male attention and was passed up the Russian chain of command until she was registered as a laundress in the household of the corrupt Alexander Menshikov. He introduced Martha to Peter, who was immediately captivated by her vulgar sense of humour, her capacity for drink and her lust for life. He fell desperately in love.[9] Martha changed her name to Catherine and secretly, then later publicly, married the married tsar.

In the late sixteenth century, when Ivan the Terrible set up trade with England through the port he established at Arkhangelsk, the voyage to and from that often ice-bound haven involved perilous navigation round the far-flung North Cape of Norway. Aware that Russia had much to sell abroad – grain, hemp, hides, tar, timber, rhubarb, caviar and isinglass – Peter sought a more accessible sea port.[10] His thoughts turned to the mouth of the short River Neva, which ran seventy kilometres through the sodden clays and marshy wilderness between Lake Ladoga and the Gulf of Finland. The choice was, in many respects, ridiculous. Nearly sixty degrees north, the site was – as the poet Anna Akhmatova later put it – 'particularly well suited to catastrophes'. For half

*The River Neva in the early 1700s showing St Petersburg, Nyenskans and Shlüsselberg at the mouth of Lake Ladoga.*

*The undeveloped Neva Delta.*

the year the Neva delta was ice-bound, and for the rest, the 'newa' – Finnish for swamp – was a mosquito-ridden marsh. Understandably, the region was almost uninhabited. Apart from Swedish invaders in their fort at Nyenskans, there was only a scatter of lost little fishing villages on the shores of Lake Ladoga and along the banks of the Neva. In order to secure the site, Peter had to break the Swedish stranglehold on Karelia on the northern bank of the Neva, and on Ingria to the south. By 1 May 1703 the tsar had captured the fort at Nyenskans and moved about four kilometres downriver, to where the Neva branched around several small islands.

This was the story: Peter came ashore on Yanni-saari – Hare Island – near the mouth of the Neva. In that wilderness he hacked out some turf from Mother Earth, then shaped it into a cross, beneath which he buried a stone casket containing relics of St Andrew. Peter declared, 'Here will be a city,' and, to mark this new beginning, built a gateway out of birch[11] – a tree symbolising light and fertility. As the tsar passed through the arch, an eagle descended to settle on his arm. He then cut down two magic willows, one to mark where the Cathedral of the Trinity would be sited and the other to indicate where his humble log cabin would stand.

Such hokum smacks of the charged climax of a symbol-fraught opera, and not as a record of the almost chance landing of a tsar at war, in a wet and windy marshland – if he landed at all. On the Feast of the Trinity, 16 May 1703 – the significant date chosen for the founding of St Petersburg – the tsar may have been in the shipyards on the shores of nearby Lake Ladoga. But there was craft behind this cosmic public-relations exercise. St Andrew was the patron saint of Russia who – according to tradition – had visited and planted a cross in the country. The interment of the saint's relics provided excellent credentials for Peter's unlikely city. The bones of St Andrew were the first of many on which Petersburg's foundations were to be laid. Three centuries later,

this city built on the skeletons of its first labourers would bury
yet more bones – victims from Stalin's purges, dumped in mass
graves on the very island where Peter, founder of the Russian
secret police, was believed to have come ashore.

The date chosen for Peter's advent was riddled with Christian
significance. St Nicholas of Mozhaisk – patron saint of seafarers
and the protector of northern Russian lands – was favoured in
having not one saint's day, but two. One of these occurred in early
May, and in 1703 it fell within the octave of the moveable Feast
of the Trinity.[12] Looking beyond Christianity to local Finnish
folklore, we find the tale of a giant who created a city instantly.
Such myth-making and symbolism were politically useful to a
tsar rumoured by his enemies to have been a changeling, plucked
from the German Suburb of Moscow – a European substitute for
the girl born to Tsar Alexei and Natasha.

The tsar's first choice for his fort was on the dagger-shaped
island of Kotlin, thirty kilometres out in the Gulf of Finland.
A contemporary sketch plan – possibly in Peter's hand – shows a
grid of streets and canals that looks surprisingly like a map of
modern-day Manhattan. But while Kotlin was a reasonably strategic choice for a naval base, nobody showed much enthusiasm
for settling on a cold, windy island in the middle of the sea.[13]
Not that they were much more excited by the soggy mainland
round about. Visitors from Europe were appalled by the 'vast
and horrid forests and deserts' of a region where, during summer
months, 'the sun raises the vapours' from 'the low and marshy
ground' and 'the sun hardly sets'. As for winter, the days were
short and the sun was seldom seen, because of 'thick fogs with
which the air is filled and darkened'.[14] But there were some assets.
The Neva was – according to the Scottish traveller John Bell –
'a noble stream of clear, wholesome water' containing 'a great
variety of excellent fish', including abundant salmon. The woods
on either bank were 'stored with game such as hares, which are
as white as snow in winter, and turn brown in summer'.[15]

For the scattered peasants and fisherfolk, life was measured by cyclical, seasonal time – spring followed winter, which followed autumn, which followed summer, which followed spring. Suddenly it was 1703, European-time, as Peter imposed an urban chronometer on his outpost. As 1703 became 1704, then 1705 and 1706, life became scheduled and hectic, as the population was urged to beat the clock in an endless scurry of meetings and encounters. The tsar of an antediluvian and introverted country yoked necessity to impossibility and established a fort and a port that rapidly evolved into a capital. It would be a new type of city in an old country – a fact that would play havoc with its identity and its inhabitants throughout its first three centuries. It was the absurdities and obsessions of this remarkable tsar that gave birth to St Petersburg, a city created by a drunken man trying to walk a straight line. His feverish imposition of change created a time-warp – absurd juxtapositions of the modes and habits of different ages – which has remained a feature of St Petersburg since the moment the tsar stamped 1703 on time out of mind.

The first phase of building corresponded to the period of the Great Northern War, during which Peter was on the defensive. General Kronhjort's large Swedish force was camped threateningly on the northern side of the Neva, while Vice-Admiral Nummers – commanding a flotilla – lay at anchor in the bay. The Russians soon gained a foothold on Kotlin and started to construct the fort of Kronstadt to guard the approaches to the delta. Despite gains against the Swedish, there was no escape from the bitter south-west wind that blew up the Gulf of Finland towards 'St Petersburg' – first mentioned as such in a letter written to the tsar towards the end of June 1703. Two months later, the settlement suffered its first flood. With such natural and human adversaries, the outlook was bleak.

Peter's priority was to engineer a fort to protect the settlement. Styled on the impressive citadels devised by Louis XIV's celebrated military engineer, the Marquis de Vauban, the Peter and Paul Fortress was – in the first instance – constructed of earth and wood. St Petersburg's handwritten newspaper, the *Vedomosti* reported that 20,000 sappers toiled to build the fort during that first summer.[16] Add the hundreds of fellers and loggers floating tree trunks to the site and you had – in the middle of a barren wilderness – a population explosion. The tsar summoned Russian, Tartar, Cossack, Kalmuk, Finnish and Ingrian labourers, who were joined by Swedes and Livonians fleeing towns devastated by the war. Peter sent an order to Prince Romodanovksy – 'Mock-tsar' in Peter's All-Drunken Assembly, and head of the newly created Secret Office – to reassign 2,000 criminals destined for Siberia to St Petersburg to work on the fort. Toiling 'in the utmost misery', labourers lacked food, housing and even adequate tools. Without wheelbarrows, they transported earth – scarce thereabouts – in the 'skirts of their clothes and in bags made of rags and old mats'.[17] The fortress was completed in five months. The bodies of workers killed by malaria, scurvy, dysentery or Swedish attack were wrapped in muslin sacks and packed into cavities in the foundations. Reasonable estimates for the human cost of the initial building of St Petersburg run to 30,000 deaths. The fort was the impressive beginning of a settlement that was officially named St Petersburg – after the tsar's patron saint – on the Feast of St Peter, 29 June 1703. Informally, it was referred to as 'the capital' by September of the following year.[18] Upon hearing the news, Charles XII of Sweden declared, 'Let the tsar tire himself with founding new towns, we will keep for ourselves the honour of taking them later.'[19]

By 1704 dockyards were operating on the opposite side of the river, on a site that would – within five years – become the Admiralty. Craftsmen, mechanics and seamen came to settle with their families. Labourers who survived malaria and frostbite during the first year stayed on to build houses for the nobility and the traders summoned by the tsar to people his city.[20] As early as New Year's Day 1705 there were fifteen substantial wooden houses on Petersburg Island to the north of the fortress, a number that increased tenfold in the next five years. In autumn, isolated by the rising waters of a flood, the clusters of houses became a miniature archipelago. During winter freezes – with a sound like gunshot – their wooden beams cracked and snapped. Wandering freely through this uncertain community were stray wolves, wild dogs and unattended cattle. But most strangely – striding through groups of sackclothed workers – were men in full-skirted knee-length, shot-silk coats, matching breeches and spattered stockings. These were Dutch, German or Italian artisans, with their balletic gesticulations, surveying the scene, attempting to wrest some kind of order out of chaos.

Among those trying to impose sense and elegance was Domenico Trezzini, the first of many major European architects whom Peter and his successors engaged to shape St Petersburg. Born to a humble family in Lugano, Trezzini had worked in Copenhagen, where he absorbed the sober, northern Protestant form of the baroque style of architecture. Encouraged to employ the Dutch principles that Peter so admired, Trezzini worked in Petersburg from 1703 until his death in 1734 – three remarkable decades, during which a wooden settlement, rashly and rapidly thrown up in a wilderness, was haltingly transformed into a bustling capital. Working in collaboration with the tsar, Trezzini imposed ratios of 2:1 or 4:1 for street width to building height. The houses of the wealthy – their façades aligned along straight streets – began to be constructed from bricks and tiles. Canals and sluices were planned, so that the settlement came to be known as the 'Amsterdam of the North'. But while the countryside of Holland could be secured by its dykes, a French visitor to Petersburg commented that it was impossible to escape impromptu flooding from the Neva. Three years after it was founded, the community suffered its third sizeable flood, with water rising more than two and half metres. Nevertheless, construction proceeded ambitiously and obstinately, and Peter created a Chancellery of Urban Affairs headed by Trezzini. Its purpose was to monitor and coordinate projects – particularly useful when Peter was off fighting on several fronts. Beside the ongoing Swedish struggle, he fought the Ural Bashkirs between 1705 and 1711 and, in 1706, faced down a revolt of the *streltsy* in Astrakhan, over compulsory German dress and the removal of beards.[21] The tsar's dream for St Petersburg was born of his desire to create a civilised peace.

Since the concept of an ordered garden or park in which to promenade was unknown in Russia, the planning of St Petersburg's Summer Garden was a novelty. To supplement the endeavours of 400 labourers, there were 100 carpenters, sixty masons, sixteen plumbers along with a further sixty workers required to work on the fountains.[22] With the aid of his Garden Office, the tsar collected European treatises and plans and personally made a large and often-outrageous contribution to the project.[23] In 1708, with the city barely established, he sent to Moscow for '8,000 singing birds of various sorts'. In 1712, 1,300 mature linden trees were imported from Holland, along with chestnuts from Hamburg, cypresses from southern Russia, oaks from Moscow, and lime and elm trees from Kiev. The Dutch gardener Jan Roosen, who developed the scheme in 1712–13, incorporated the first masonry structure in the city – Peter's small Summer Palace.[24]

A grotto was added to the garden by Andreas Schlütter, who was lured to St Petersburg in 1713 after one of his buildings collapsed in Berlin. Consisting of three small rooms, the grotto was embellished with exotic shells and coloured stones, which kaleidoscopically flashed and reflected its interior pools. Built alongside the Fontanka River – so named because it fed the fountains of the garden – the grotto was destroyed by major flooding in 1777.[25] Schlütter also embellished the Summer Palace with twenty-nine bas-reliefs punctuating the spaces between the ground-floor and first-floor windows and celebrating Russian victories in the Great Northern War. French flourish and affectation – trees pruned geometrically, and gravel paths curving past ornamental flowerbeds – were added to the prevailing Dutch style of the garden, after Jean-Baptiste Alexandre Le Blond arrived from France in August 1716.[26] Le Blond brought intimate knowledge of the schemes and ideas of his master, André Le Nôtre, the doyen of French gardeners and the man responsible for the formal gardens at Chantilly, Fontainebleau and Versailles. With the involvement of the Italian Niccolò Michetti – the hydrodynamic engineer who lost out on the commission for Rome's Trevi Fountain – the Summer Garden was becoming a truly pan-European achievement. It was Michetti who scoured Italy for the classical statuary that graced the alleyways, his choices often shocking visitors of a conservative, orthodox sensibility. Peter had a labyrinth created containing sculptures of the animals found in Aesop's Fables. He would conduct small groups to these carvings and explain their significance. Most importantly, the gardens became a place for fun after dark. Peter hosted outdoor parties where people would mix informally, play games and drink his health from a communal tub.[27] Guests were locked in and were expected to get drunk and marvel at the fireworks and music. While it was the tsar's habit to rise early and work hard, the afternoon and a good part of the night he gave to pleasure, taking 'to his bottle heartily'.

By 1708, of all the territory the tsar had reclaimed, only the environs of St Petersburg remained in his hands and Peter was obliged to go on the offensive, devastating Ingria to make forage difficult for his adversary. Then, after a particularly severe winter, when Charles XII's army laid siege to the town of Poltava in April 1709, the Swedish were routed by the Russians. Although fought ten years before the Treaty of Nystadt ended the Great

Northern War, the Battle of Poltava decided its outcome. In fact the
Swedish Army surrendered to the 'Mock-tsar', Romodanovksy,
while a very tall officer – Peter, incognito – looked on, amused.
Peter often played with role and rank, raising those who were
unsuitable, incapable or self-interested to positions of shadow
power. He elevated a humble youth like Menshikov to a prince-
dom, turned a landlubber like Fyodor Apraksin – a man credited
with consuming 180 glasses of wine in three days – into an
admiral.[28] They were all part of Peter's mirror-image mock-
court, a sleight-of-hand that allowed the tsar – while seeming to
play the fool – to keep a tight grip on the reigns of power.[29]

Success at Poltava was celebrated first in Moscow, as facilities for formal pageants were still minimal in Petersburg. It was
June 1710, fourteen months after the battle, before a regatta and
fireworks finally commemorated the victory in the new capital.
It was a signal moment, confirming what Peter had boasted to
Admiral Apraksin, 'Now, with God's help, the final stone in the
foundation of St Petersburg has been laid.'[30]

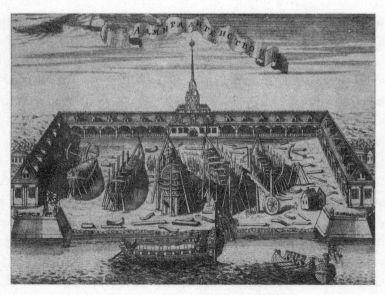

*View of the Admiralty in 1717.*

On the site of the early dockyards, an area shored-up with thousands of piles and filled with rubbish, earth and corpses, the Admiralty was built.[31] Entered over a drawbridge, it was a large wooden complex of sail- and rope-makers, carpenters and caulkers – all of whom contributed to the men-o'-war being built on the scaffolds and launched from the slips. Yet in 1710, of the tsar's twelve frigates, eight galleys, six fire-ships and two bomb-vessels, only three frigates were ready for service.[32] Developing the Admiralty was therefore essential, if Peter was to realise his ambitions for a Baltic fleet. During the following decade more than 50,000 shipwrights and craftsmen arrived to materialise his dreams.

In spring 1710 Petersburg's population of around 8,000 was doubled by the seasonal labourers who, once again, arrived to continue the frenetic building programme.[33] As dry terrain was at a premium, they were obliged to live and build on marshland, which resulted in 'streets exceeding dirty'. Nonetheless, the first stone houses began to give a sense of permanence to the settlement. A mansion for the Governor General of St Petersburg, Alexander Menshikov, and Peter's Summer Palace were both begun. The tsar also decided to rebuild the Peter and Paul Fortress in stone, using material taken from the captured Swedish settlement at Nyenskans.[34] Bastion walls were built nearly twenty metres thick and, in the extensive inner ward, the wooden cathedral was demolished to make way for Trezzini's flat-fronted masonry structure, topped by a towering golden spire, which was eventually completed in 1733. When struck by lightning almost a quarter of a century later, the 123-metre tower burned down. A decade after that, Catherine the Great ordered an identical spire, which was finished in 1776 and has since remained one of the capital's most visible landmarks.

Menshikov's palace, fronting the Neva on Vasilevsky Island, was built 'of stone after the Italian manner, three stories high'.[35] Grander than the tsar's Summer Palace, it suited a man

*Peter the Great overseeing the construction of St Petersburg.*

*Festivities for the marriage of the Royal Dwarf, Yakim Volkov,
at the Menshikov Palace in 1710.*

'possessed with a boundless ambition' and insatiable avarice. Menshikov began life either as a pastry cook's street-vendor or as a stable boy – a good number of contemporary commentators favouring the vision of him crying, 'Puffs!' and selling 'cakes made of minced meat . . . about the streets of Moscow'. The story goes that Peter heard him singing in a lane and, when he asked if he could buy the basket as well as the pies, Menshikov demonstrated the cunning that would carry him to the top. His 'business was to sell pies, but he must ask his master's leave to sell his basket; yet as everything belonged to his prince, his majesty had only to lay his commands upon him. The tsar was so pleased with the answer, that he immediately ordered him to court.'[36] Menshikov rose rapidly to become Peter's right-hand man, the quintessential manipulator in the subversive mock-court. Stealing voraciously from both the state and the people, Menshikov became a formidable kleptocrat.

Ironically, Menshikov's mansion was not completed until 1727 – just in time for its owner's fall. But one room that was finished early on was the 'spacious hall' for 'great entertainments', where the tsar – who delighted in his small-roomed, low-ceilinged Summer Palace – was obliged to hold receptions and celebrations. When, in 1710, Romodanovksy commanded dwarfs from across Russia to attend the marriage of the Royal Dwarf, Yakim Volkov, it was celebrated in the Menshikov Palace. The seventy dwarfs who attended were placed at miniature tables in the hall, overlooked by the court guests, who much enjoyed watching them get drunk.

Menshikov's palace was used for another marriage that autumn: the negotiated union of Peter's niece, Tsar Ivan's daughter, Anna Ivanova, to Frederick William, Duke of Courland. This time, the dwarfs played a more active role in the entertainment. In the days before the marriage, two of them drove about the city issuing invitations. On the wedding day, the smallest dwarf acted as Master of Ceremonies, leading the bride and groom to the celebrations. At the dinner, a huge pie was served from which two female dwarfs sprung, attired in the latest French fashion, to sing, dance and recite verse. Female guests were compelled to drink to excess, but it was the groom who came off worst. Less than a month after the wedding, he died on the road to Courland – quite possibly from alcohol poisoning.

The tsar used drink in order to intimidate. The Danish envoy, Just Juel, attempting to escape the punishment of downing one and a half litres of vodka from the notorious Great Eagle, hid in the rigging of a tall ship, only to find the tsar – Eagle between his teeth, and his pockets stuffed with bottles – scrambling up the ratlines after him.[37] Juel expressed scant respect for Peter's attempts at refinement, recording that his rabble 'shrieked, bellowed, guffawed, puked, spat' as they pelted handfuls of food at one another in a greasy dining-room brawl.[38]

In 1711, another important arranged marriage took place. This time it was between the indolent *tsarevich* Alexei – the son Peter despised – and the seventeen-year-old Charlotte of Brunswick-Lüneburg who imported many German names and habits into the Romanov court: the Chief Steward became the *Ober-Gofmeister*, and the powerful Groom of the Chamber became a *Kamer-Junker*. German was employed at court – Peter was pretty adept, and 'even the illiterate Menshikov spoke and understood' the language. Of Peter's bosom companion, Catherine, the Frenchman François Villebois observed that she 'spoke fluently' in four languages, 'namely Russian, German, Swedish and Polish and to those it may be added that she understood some French'.[39]

It was only after the victory at Poltava that Catherine was brought to Petersburg from Preobrazhenskoe to live permanently with the tsar. But her life in the new capital was upset in 1711 when Peter left on a campaign against the Turks.

Catherine accompanied him, leaving their children in the care of Menshikov and his wife, Daria. In *The Maid of Marienburg* – a seventeenth-century play of less-than-modest literary merit – a character suggests that 'Heaven gave to Catherine the charms of a fine person, wit and vivacity, a feeling heart and masculine understanding.'[40] When, in July 1711, the Russian Army was surrounded by Turkish forces on the River Pruth in Moldavia, it was rumoured that the seductive and determined Catherine met the commander of the Turkish forces and sued for peace.[41] Robust and gutsy, she was a worthy match for Peter.

In February 1712, dressed in the uniform of a rear admiral, the tsar publicly married his beloved in a simple ceremony at the Menshikov Palace. Two of their children – Anna Petrovna, aged four, and Elizabeth, hardly old enough to walk – briefly carried their mother's bridal train. Peter and Catherine sat at a table shaped like a crown, and Charles Whitworth, England's 'Ambassador Extraordinary' to Russia, observed that the 'most pleasant' aspect of this nuptial was that 'no one was forced to drink to excess'. Catherine, a commoner and a foreigner, was now married to the Tsar of Russia, whose first wife, Evdokia, still lived, incarcerated in the convent at Suzdal, then moved to a more remote nunnery on the shores of Lake Ladoga. The union Peter made with his second wife was not a marriage designed to stabilise and strengthen the state, but a declaration of earthy, passionate love.[42] As Peter's character observes in *The Maid of Marienburg*, 'Happy is the Prince who has discovered a woman's mind that loves not the Prince in the man – but who loves the man in the Prince.'[43]

People persisted in their reluctance to settle in St Petersburg. Upper-class Russians complained that the upstart city was 700 kilometres from their favourite merchants in Moscow, and from their comfortable estates in the rolling countryside around the old

capital. Peter threatened the Muscovite nobility with the alternative of moving to his city or losing their titles. Not surprisingly,
they relocated and the merchants followed. But they grumbled.
Around Petersburg not much could be grown in soil that was wet
and cold – turnips, white cabbage and cucumbers were possible,
but little else.[44] There were mushrooms in the woods and some
game and fish, but otherwise food had to be brought in by sledge
in the winter and carried by lake and river during the summer. If
settlers found themselves travelling through a fen as they neared
their destination, the city itself was no less boggy. Any seemingly
dry ground for a kitchen garden proved impractical for digging,
as the water came in 'at a two foot depth'.[45]

Under such conditions, it is not surprising that people needed
to be coerced to settle. In late 1712, Peter sent for more merchants and craftsmen to serve the city, to which he had summoned
another thousand of the best noble families. When, in 1714, he
ordered yet another thousand of the wealthiest families to come,
some spent 60 per cent of their savings on what was clearly a
costly move.[46] With losses of such an order, potential settlers
showed continued reluctance to relocate, forcing Peter to declare
that if 'Russians of the old stamp' had not moved to his city by
1725, they would have their houses demolished and would be
forced to live in huts in the marshes of the undeveloped parts
of Vasilevsky Island. Meanwhile, the all-important workers
appeared similarly unenthusiastic. In 1712 and 1714, one-third
of the conscripted workforce simply did not show up.[47] It was
not until 1717 that Prince Cherkassy, Head of the Chancellery
of Urban Affairs, suggested to Peter that forced labour was less
efficient, and ultimately more costly, than hired labour.


Arriving in St Petersburg in 1714, Friedrich Weber – the Hanoverian representative to Russia – 'was surprised to find instead
of a regular city as I expected, a heap of villages linked together,

like some plantation in the West Indies'.[48] Certainly, many visitors from Europe would have had the impression of arriving in a colonial capital, with its bizarre reinvention or parody of the occupying culture. By contrast, when John Bell arrived in Petersburg in July 1715 to join an embassy that Peter was sending to Persia, he found the capital 'well peopled, and had not the appearance of a city so lately founded'. These two contradictory impressions combine to give a just picture of the city's erratic early development. Kilns and furnaces were baking bricks at an incredible rate. However, the soundness of much construction work was compromised by poor mortar and the cavalier habit of working through the cold winters. Repairs to buildings lately finished were necessary immediately. Though encircled and congested by the foul camps of its ill-treated workforce, a social life and a season began to establish themselves in a capital which – after a decade of construction – took on some semblance of grace. Masquerades and musical evenings were enjoyed in the grander residences. Peter's sister, the amateur playwright *tsarevna* Natalya Alekseevna, gave Weber the chance to attend the kind of European-style entertainment to which the fledgling court aspired. After the obligatory vodka, guests sat down to a first course consisting of 'hams, sausages, jelly-broth, and divers sorts of meat dressed with oil of olives, onions and garlic'. After a good hour, 'the soups, roast meat, and other hot victuals, which make up the second course' were served, followed by dessert. The 'beauties of Petersburg' were desperate to adopt French fashion, and Weber noted that they struggled awkwardly with their hoop-petticoats. But it was their painted or decayed black teeth that gave them away – 'sufficient proof, that they had not yet weaned themselves from that notion so fast riveted in the minds of the old Russians, that white teeth only became blackamoors and monkeys'.[49]

In the year in which the Hanoverian representative arrived, Peter came sailing up the Neva in triumph, having beaten the Swedish fleet at Hangö, in July 1714. In that summer, as the

Venetian polymath and anglophile Francesco Algarotti later wrote, to the English courtier Lord Hervey, the tsar 'really beheld the completion of his works'.[50] The house-count tallied 34,550,[51] but as the city expanded on various islands and on either bank, the Neva delta became more problematic. Well over a kilometre across at its widest point, the major branch of the river separated the different quarters of the city at a time when only the small waterways were spanned by fixed bridges. The sole method of crossing the *Bolshaya Neva* was by one of the twenty state-controlled ferry boats, which charged a modest two to four kopeks[52] and promised a dangerous voyage in the turbulence of spring thaws and autumn floods. Furthermore, Peter – who would only allow the nobility to arrive at court by barge – wanted his subjects to sail. From 1718 he provided the boats on which they could learn. New arrivals from land-locked Moscow felt much intimidated when they were forced to undertake Sunday excursions in the gulf, and were irate when they were punished for missing two Sundays in a single month. Members of the highest ranks were expected to maintain their own vessels and to participate in naval celebrations. When the river was frozen, special craft were built for skating or sail-boating across the ice.[53] Indeed, communication in the city, as throughout the region, was much improved by cold weather, when boggy roads hardened to enable carts and baggage trains to travel without floundering in the mud. In summer months, sandbars at the mouth of the Neva meant that ships drawing above seven feet of water were unable to dock. The deep-water port at Kronstadt provided one solution. Another was the discharging of cargo from ships anchored in the bay, which resulted in a congestion of small craft and flat-bottomed lighters.

Such inconveniences, coupled with the annual blockade by the winter freeze, made it clear why the city was struggling for credibility. Crazy Peter misruled his mock-court in a capital that seemed, to many practical people, to be nothing but a mock-port.

To them, St Petersburg was an ongoing and inconvenient prank, played out in the wilds of the Ingrian marshes. The river was, however, the city's *raison d'être* and took on a sacred significance. An important annual celebration was the Consecration of the Waters, which took place at Epiphany. Headed by the tsar, the Preobrazhensky Guard marched to the middle of the frozen river, where they formed a square and watched as a hole was cut, through ice more than half a metre thick, to the river below. An arched shrine was constructed out of cut blocks of ice, as the bells of St Petersburg pealed and priests processed to the impromptu shrine, celebrated Mass and consecrated the water flowing beneath. Cannon fired, muskets discharged, and mothers brought their babies to be baptised. Those who survived the freezing water were promised a blessed life. When the priests and the guards withdrew, the people – including the sick and the lame – flocked to the opening and filled buckets and cups with the restorative water, which would not be seen again until May.

Some ten days after the Consecration of the Waters in 1715 there was the burlesque wedding of Nikita Zotov, an eighty-four-year-old drunkard and ex-tutor to the tsar, who occupied the throne of 'Prince Pope' in Peter's All-Drunken Assembly. His bride was a 'buxom widow of 34'. The wedding procession was led by 'Mock-tsar' Romodanovsky, who reclined in a sledge attended by four bears on their hind legs, which were prodded and goaded to make them roar. As they processed towards the fort, snare-drums battered out a welcome. Everyone in the procession was encouraged to make a noise, and wild animals roaming close by began to bellow. A Scot, Peter Henry Bruce, recorded that the functionaries appointed to welcome the company 'were four of the greatest stammerers in the kingdom; the four running footmen were the most unwieldy, gouty fat men that could be found; the bride-men, stewards, and waiters were very old . . . and the priest that joined them in marriage was upwards of one hundred years old' and blind. The grotesquery continued for ten days, as the revellers progressed from house to house, drowned in the bacchanalia of past ways. There were also lavish and anarchic festivities in November 1715 for the birth of Catherine and Peter's child, Peter Petrovich. Again, dwarfs were an important part of the entertainment. On the table where the men sat, a huge pie was placed. A 'well-shaped woman dwarf' emerged 'stark-naked, except' for 'her head-dress and some ornaments of red ribbons'. She made a speech and filled her audience's glasses from wine bottles stashed inside the pie. Before the ladies, on their tables, a naked male dwarf performed a similar service. There were toasts and fireworks, and everyone ended up paralytically drunk.[54]

In the very month that Peter Petrovich was born, the tsar began manoeuvring against the son he had had with Evdokia Lopukhina, the *tsarevich* Alexei. Bruce had met the young man in Moscow and found him 'slovenly' and surrounded by 'debauched ignorant priests', who – if he mounted the throne – would help him 'restore Russia to its former state'. Peter wrote in anger to his son, who refused to join the military effort against Sweden asking, Who can I leave my country to, when I die? 'To a man, who like the slothful servant, hides his talent in the earth . . . You do not make the least endeavours, and all your pleasure seems to consist in staying idle and lazy at home.'[55] Having set out his concerns, Peter waited a little longer to see if the *tsarevich* would mend his ways. 'If not, I will have you know that I will deprive you of the succession.' Alexei's drinking intensified and, when his father ordered him to join a monastery, he fled to Europe.

In September 1715, the Petersburg flood waters rose so high that a two-masted ship was swept against a house and beached on a boggy street as the waters receded. Cattle were drowned, people were lost and fortifications, built at a high human cost, were washed away. Despite such setbacks, the following month

Peter sent out an order across Russia for 12,000 more families to settle in his capital.[56] During 1716, there were grandiose plans for enlarging the areas close to the Peter and Paul Fortress – on Petersburg Island to the north, on the tip of Vasilevsky Island to the south-west and around the Admiralty on the opposite bank of the river. These appear on a map of the city produced in Nuremberg in 1720, based on a German original made two years earlier. While the plan is a reasonably accurate record of the state of building around the Admiralty and near the Fortress, the gridding of marshy Vasilevsky Island was as much a fantasy as the insert drawing of the lighthouse fort of Kronstadt,[57] which appears like something cooked up by Jules Verne.

In 1717, Le Blond produced a more sophisticated and typically French plan for Vasilevsky Island. Owing much to the fort designs of Vauban and the gardens of Le Nôtre, it placed the imperial palace at its heart. Both the layout of Versailles and Le Blond's scheme for Petersburg would inspire his compatriot, Pierre-Charles L'Enfant, in his planning of the new American capital, Washington DC – although Le Blond's scheme remained unrealised.

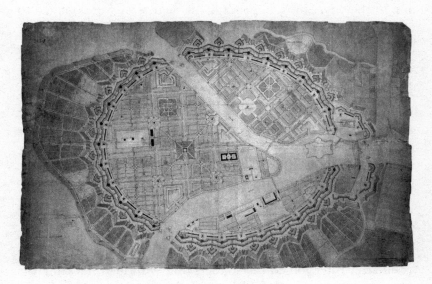

*Le Blond's plan for St Petersburg.*

Several edicts, aimed at making the city safer, warned residents not to allow livestock to wander the streets, unless
accompanied by a herdsman. Nonetheless, packs of marauding
wolves, thirty to forty strong, were seen in broad daylight. In
1715, a woman was devoured by a pack within sight of Prince
Menshikov's palace. A sentry guarding the Foundry on the south
bank was attacked and, when another soldier went to his aid, he
was mauled and torn to pieces.

The transformation of a frontier settlement into a Dutch-style
baroque city was accelerated by the 1714 ban on construction in
wood in certain sectors.[58] Wattle-and-daub walls raised on stone
foundations and roofed with tiles became the norm for humbler
dwellings, while stone was used for the houses of the rich. A
countrywide shortage of masons prompted a ban on building in
stone elsewhere in Russia and – as the material was scarce in the
marshy environs of St Petersburg – people coming to the city by
sea or land were required to bring stone with them, as a contribution to the construction. The duty levied from 1714 required
three stones of no less than two kilos each, from every cart arriving in the city. Ships, depending on their size, were obliged to
deposit between ten and thirty stones.

The scale, style and ambition of a house were determined by
the social rank of its owner. Humble taxpayers lived in one-storey
houses. Those who were better off added dormer windows in the
roof. Le Blond designed two-storey mansions with dormer windows and œils-de-bœuf for the elite.[59] However, in the poorer
quarters, wooden houses were crammed so close together that
a fire breaking out in one would easily ignite its neighbour
and rapidly fan into a conflagration. When a spark was spotted, watchmen rang bells and drummers circulated, beating the
alarm. Carpenters and soldiers of all ranks hastened to the blaze
and isolated the fire by pulling down adjacent houses. When in
residence, Peter joined the soldiers and workmen, tackling the
blaze, hatchet in hand.[60]

The settlement's main tap-house stood close to the bridge connecting the Peter and Paul Fortress with Petersburg Island. Owned by the tsar, it sold wine, beer, spirits, tobacco and cards. The beer brewed there was too strong to be thirst-quenching and Weber found the hygiene wanting. Beer stood in an open tub and people ladled it into their mouths, some running down their dirty beards and back into the tub. If day-labourers were short of money, they would pawn some item of clothing, which was then hung around the brim of the vat – often dipping into the liquid, sometimes tumbling in – until, at the end of their day, the workmen returned with their wages to redeem their sodden rags.[61]

Near the tsar's tap-house and to the north-west of the wooden Trinity Church was the Great Market, a vast square timber building with four gates leading to an interior yard. Around this space ran two levels of shops, with galleries to protect customers from snow and rain.[62] On the eastern edge of the nearby Tartar quarter was the Rag Fair, a crowded and dangerous flea-market:

A certain officer of the Grenadier Guards, who is German, once returned from that Place without either hat or peruque, and the very same day a woman of fashion had the like

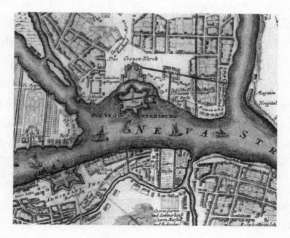

*The centre of early St Petersburg showing the Tartar Market.*

misfortune in losing her head-dress there. Two Tartars on horseback had met the said two persons at different places, and, whipping off their respective head-ornaments with great agility, left them exposed to the laughter of the mob, and even within their sight offered their spoil to sale.[63]

To the south of the Tartar quarter, near the banks of the Neva, was the new slaughter house, and a market where pots and wooden utensils, lentils, oatmeal and the wheat and rye used for making bread were to be found.[64] Supplying the city with sufficient flour was a problem that would not be solved until the reign of Catherine II. Indeed, shortages of food in the city led to the implementation of price controls in April 1722, giving way to a more sophisticated regulation of profits the following year. Peter curbed abuses in the cereal markets and – in one of his last acts before his death in January 1725 – forced local producers to bring their goods to market early and sell to the public in small quantities at the price posted each morning. Only after midday could they negotiate wholesale prices with retailers. Flour was thenceforth sold by weight rather than volume, and fluctuations in price were monitored in order to control the cost of baked goods. Cheats were publicly flogged by a knout and their goods were confiscated and donated to the hospital.[65] Travelling along one of the main thoroughfares of the city in 1726, the French traveller Aubry de la Mottraye saw the three heads of Victualling Commissaries impaled on stakes. Guilty of mis-administration, they were beheaded after a public flogging with the knout, the standard punishment in Russia at that time. Not unlike a cat-o'-nine-tails, the knout had whip ends that were produced from strips of ass's skin boiled in vinegar and mare's milk. The guilty were led onto a wooden scaffold, where their feet were fastened to the ground. Men were stripped to the waist, and women to their petticoats. First one shoulder was lashed, then the other. With a moderate punishment, de la Mottraye reported that there was 'an abundance of blood' streaming from the victim's back. With a severe penalty, one saw 'small pieces of his flesh flying out'. If it was 'ordered to the utmost rigour, it becomes generally mortal'. The executioner strikes the criminal on his sides 'under the ribs and cuts the flesh to the very bowels.'[66]

As a stimulus and strategy for embellishing St Petersburg, the journeys abroad made by the tsar in 1712–13 and 1716–17 were vital. The timing of the earlier trip suggests that there was an element of swagger in the enterprise. Russia was perceived as a new and major force in the European balance of power, following its triumph at Poltava. Certainly the iconography associated with the tsar changed after that victory – the god's face in *The Triumph of Mars*, painted on the ceiling of the Menshikov Palace, resembled Peter's face.[67] Peter now travelled to Europe not as a humble shipwright, but as a powerful monarch seeking glorification through art and science. He visited Dresden and Vienna. He saw Versailles. He studied the declaration of regal power manifest in the grandiose landscaping of palace gardens.

The French king Louis XIV, like Peter, had been scarred by violence when he was a child. As a result, he decided to quit his capital and establish a new one. Less radically than Peter, he chose a site only fifteen kilometres from Paris, at Versailles. Finished in 1682 after fourteen years of construction, it was the jewel in the French crown, the envy of the civilised world. The impact of its geometrical terraces, vast walks, pools and fountains was prodigious. It was achieved – as St Petersburg would be – with an enormous workforce at a sizeable human cost. The logistics were not as challenging as those at the mouth of the Neva, but workers at Versailles likewise lived and laboured in miserable conditions, and malaria claimed many victims. However, while Louis XIV built securely on the bedrock of European tradition, in Russia Peter effected a stylistic volte-face. While the method of St Petersburg's construction was unreservedly Russian, the emerging rectilinear and geometric pattern of Peter's city was Western.

In Paris, Peter bought Gobelin tapestries and invited some of the weavers to settle in his capital. He was painted by the French portraitist Hyacinthe Rigaud.[68] Pictures were purchased – mainly Dutch works by painters such as Rubens, Van Dyck, Jan Steen – along with the first of many Rembrandts acquired by Russian monarchs, *David's Farewell to Jonathan*. Peter also collected painters such as the Frenchman Louis Caravaque, who settled in St Petersburg in 1716 and stayed until his death in 1754. The purchasing of Western art, and the presence of European painters and craftsmen, had lasting repercussions for the development of Russian culture. As with the study of navigation, Peter also sent Russian painters abroad to learn.[69] The 'founder of Russian portraiture', Ivan Nikitin, was among the first to spend a few years abroad and return to deflect the course of Russian painting from the icon and the stylised portrait, or *parsuna*, towards a manner reflecting the trends and movements of European art.[70]

Peter was an eighteenth-century Citizen Kane, ransacking western Europe for treasures to fill his newly established Xanadu. His curiosity knew no bounds. Book-buying played an important part in these extended shopping trips. Peter's library – a large proportion of which was devoted to architecture, gardening and shipbuilding – included an edition of Vitruvius's *De architectura* (*The Ten Books on Architecture*), the only major surviving work on the subject dating from classical antiquity.[71] In Holland, Peter purchased a large collection of natural specimens from Albertus Seba, an apothecary in Amsterdam, along with the Ruysch collection, which he had first seen in 1697. In Calais, he engaged a man called Nicolas Bourgeois, who stood well over two metres tall. Plagued by terrible headaches, Bourgeois died in Petersburg, where his body was dissected.[72] As de la Mottraye recorded when he saw the remains in 1726, Bourgeois had a 'very big heart and large stomach and his privy part was very small'.[73] Today, Bourgeois's impressive skeleton is standing on exhibition in the Kunstkammer.

While many people were impressed by the Russians in Europe, the precocious ten-year-old Markgravine Wilhelmina of Bayreuth gave a scathing account of Catherine in Berlin in 1718:

> It's enough to look at her to see her humble origins. Her tasteless dress seems to have been bought at a junk dealer's; it is old-fashioned and covered with silver and dirt. A dozen orders are pinned on her and the same number of small icons and medallions with relics; all these jingle when she walks so that you have the impression that you are being approached by a pack mule.[74]

Not content just to wage war on nature by building on the banks of the Neva, Peter also set about creating a constellation of palaces around his capital: Oranienbaum for Menshikov; Tsarskoe Selo for his second wife, Catherine; Strelna for his daughter, Elizabeth; and Peterhof for himself. In engravings, Oranienbaum appears bombastic, as if clamouring for attention – effects altogether suited to its first owner, the ostentatious nouveau-riche 'prince pie-seller'. But despite being the work of architects sprung from conflicting traditions – the Italian, Giovanni Fontana, and the north German, Gottfried Schädel – the result is, in fact, harmonious and sober. Seen from the sea side, Oranienbaum stands a commanding three storeys high, with extensive semi-oval wings on either side. A grand staircase descends to the formal French garden and a small canal leads to the harbour on the Gulf of Finland. Built on a bank, the façade turned inland presents a more modest single storey in which most rooms were small, but richly furnished.

In May 1710, during that more secure time after Poltava, the tsar chose a site and began to plan his palace at Peterhof. The modest main building, which was begun in 1714, stood on a hill twenty metres high, nearly a kilometre from the coast. It comprised a ground floor destined for servants and a first floor, with sweeping views of the Gulf of Finland, for the tsar's family – Kronstadt to the left and Petersburg to the right. In terms of the difficulty of building, it was St Petersburg all over again. Much of the land had to be drained, layers of clay removed and earth and fertilisers imported by barge. Tens of thousands of maples, lindens, chestnuts, fruit trees and bushes were lugged and ferried from Europe. The Grand Cascade, a magnificent complex of fountains, was constructed under the supervision of Russia's first hydraulic engineer, Vasily Tuvulkov, who used more than 4,000 sappers to construct the intricate canalisation which fed the cascade from springs on the Ropsha hills, more than twenty kilometres away. The workers, like those who constructed the capital, lived in appalling conditions, ate miserable food and were prey to steamy heat, bitter cold and disease. Many died onsite.

Peter valued the understated power of northern baroque architecture complemented by magisterial gardens. He possessed an album of views of Versailles and, at Peterhof, he ambitiously ordered Le Blond to make the park finer 'than the French King's'. Indeed, so impressed had Peter been by Versailles that he gave the pavilions at Peterhof French – rather than German – names: *Marly, Monplaisir and Hermitage.* As with his concept for the capital, Le Blond devised an imperial scheme, a stage for the spectacle of sovereignty.[75] His garden subdued nature by subordinating it to his artistry and declared Peter's ambition, refinement and power. To this end, Le Blond established nineteen specialised workshops filled with master craftsmen, whom he brought with him from France, but he died of smallpox in the winter of 1719, two years before the first phase of building was complete. Peterhof's fountains, terraces, grottoes and cascades were more than a match for Versailles – an expression of Peter's triumph over the northern marshes, an elegant vindication of his folly.[76] By importing classical statuary, the Russian tsar accessed a new fund of mythology and a new order of learning. However, by allowing Versailles to influence the gardens at Peterhof, the tsar turned away from the republican restraint of the Dutch style, towards the assertion of the kind of power associated with France and its Sun King. Eluding progressive enlightenment, Peter was moving forward and yet stepping backwards. The ensemble was a declaration of a new scale of power, an attempt to create an earthly paradise, even though Peterhof became just another ordered setting for wild release. The Hanoverian representative, Friedrich Weber, was invited to a lunch at which he and the other guests were 'so plied with *tokay* wine . . . that at our breaking up, we were hardly able to stand'. Nevertheless, the guests were each obliged to empty another quart bowl offered by Catherine, 'whereupon we quite lost our senses, and were in that pickle carried off to sleep, some in the garden, others in the wood, and the rest here and there on the ground'. The drunken company was, at length, woken by the tsar, who gave seven of them hatchets and led them to a wood, through which he marked out a 100-metre passage leading to the sea. Peter began to clear the bracken at once, but his hungover workforce 'found so unusual a drudgery very hard for people, who had not half recovered their senses'. They struggled as best they could, only to be rewarded at supper by 'such another dose of liquor as sent us senseless to bed'. After an hour and a half, they were roused to drink the night away until, at breakfast, they were welcomed with large cups of brandy and invited to take the air on a hill near the palace.[77]

At Peterhof, as with Oranienbaum, a small canal ferried visitors to a protected harbour in which a boat would be waiting to return them to Petersburg. At the base of the Grand Cascade, two diagonal avenues spread out towards the pavilions of Monplaisir – crammed with newly acquired paintings – and the Hermitage, which took the overflow. During the next 200

*Peterhof: the Marly Pavilion after the Nazi occupation and restored since the war.*

years Peterhof was embellished by the architects who made St Petersburg great: Francesco Bartolomeo Rastrelli, Andrei Voronikhin and Giacomo Quarenghi. The ultimate absurdity is that the palace was only finally completed in the early twentieth century – just in time for there to be no royal family left to occupy it. To heap tragedy on the oddness of such timing, two decades later, Peterhof was occupied by Hitler's troops for twenty-seven months. They wrecked the interior, destroyed the fountains and statues and chopped down some 14,000 maples, lindens, chestnuts and fruit trees – many of which had been imported from Germany at enormous cost and effort by Peter the Great. As a result, in 1944 Peterhof became Petrodvorets, in order to obliterate the German association. Today, while the park appears much as it did at the end of Peter's reign, the palace has been restored to reflect later embellishments.

A decree of 1714 established compulsory education for the children of the nobility, government clerks and lesser officials. Children between the ages of ten and fifteen were to be taught mathematics and geometry. Foreigners were employed as tutors, and the offspring of the upper classes soon became familiar with German and French. But the quality of the education varied enormously. People who had been actors, *valets-de-chambre* and hairdressers passed themselves off as teachers – the dazzle of a foreigner was sufficient to ensure that no references were checked.[78]

Despite the ongoing problem of alcoholism, which blurred Weber's visit to Peterhof, there were attempts to order and control behaviour. The first Russian book of etiquette was published in 1717. Originally with a print run of 100 copies, this guide book prepared young men for polite society and instructed the opposite sex in the ways of modesty and chastity. It proved so popular that 600 copies were printed two years later, and 1,200 more in 1723. For the young men, conversation – particularly in a foreign tongue – along with fencing and horseriding were de rigueur.[79] Ignoring the example set by the *tsarina*, young women were expected to behave demurely and to avoid frivolity and pranks. Dancing was encouraged, to promote genteel interaction between the sexes and develop finesse in control of the body. At table, diners were to refrain from licking their fingers or picking their teeth with a knife, and using the back of the hand was prohibited when wiping the mouth. Napkins appeared, to replace the long beards once used.[80]

In the new Europeanised milieu, women were coaxed from the obscurity of their homes. This occurred through the *assemblée*, an informal gathering at which people from the upper echelons of society – from the tsar, down to master craftsmen and rich merchants – would meet and converse. *Assemblée* started at four in the afternoon and did not continue beyond ten in the evening. There were games of chess, cards and elegant European dances. Fashionable women were squeezed into corsets in order to maximise the allure of their new, low-cut gowns. As this fashion spread beyond St Petersburg, the conservative Daria Golitsyna complained that she was 'reduced to showing my hair, arms and uncovered bosom to all of Moscow!'[81] Naturally drawn to more raucous and riotous entertainments, Peter and Catherine nonetheless danced on at *assemblée*s when others collapsed in exhaustion.[82]

For other sections of the population, enjoyments such as drinking and gambling came under the control of the Police Chancellery, set up in 1718 in a determined attempt to control unruly behaviour. Despite the example of Peter's All-Drunken Assembly, riotousness and lewdness in the capital were regulated. The tsar instructed the police to close all 'suspicious houses' and 'obscene establishments'. Prostitutes were banned from mixing with the army, and those who disobeyed were driven naked from the capital.[83] At festive times, people were drawn to popular entertainments by quick-witted barkers, who sat them down on rough wooden benches in front of makeshift booths to gawp at puppets enacting old Russian folk tales.[84] On the south bank of the Neva, in the fields beyond the settlement, pugilism was tolerated – even promoted – by the authorities. It was seen not only as a social safety-valve, but also as a way of making 'better soldiers'. Baths, or *banya*, were a source of relaxation for the Russians and a curiosity to foreigners. After a beating with birch branches, which stimulates 'the circulation of the fluids, gives elasticity to the organs, and animates the passions', bathers sweated out the grime of their rough life in a steamhouse, before plunging into the chilly waters of the river. Weber was astonished 'to see not only the men, but also the women unmarried as well as married . . . running about . . . stark naked without any sort of shame'.[85]

The pan-Russian census of 1719 revealed that, on Petersburg Island, nearly one-fifth of the inhabitants were under sixteen. This was the first generation born in the newly created city. Among them were orphans, many of whom were taken on as servants. Children as young as ten were purchased from those sheltering them, and were lucky to be offered some kind of employment, as begging was banned in the capital. Anyone caught giving alms to the poor received a five-rouble fine. Life was undoubtedly tough for those not born into privilege, and even as St Petersburg was enjoying its first flush of splendour, the seeds of later revolt were being sown. Ivan Pososhkov was the enterprising son of a silversmith who worked his way up the social ladder, all the while observing and considering the realities of life in Russia. The upshot was his sociological study, *On Poverty and Wealth*, written in 1724 and intended for the tsar. In the tract, Pososhkov declared that the 'tsardom is wealthy when all the people are wealthy according to their own standards' – in other words, society is safe and sound when members at every level prosper. Disparaging excess and indifference, Pososhkov criticised tax evasion, the selling of shoddy goods, the superstitions of the clergy, corruption at the court and the illiteracy of peasants. He suggested that, for 'the sake of national preservation, both monks and merchants should be kept away from excessive drinking and luxurious life', and that it would 'be desirable to introduce among merchants the idea that they should aid and not ruin one another'.[86] Such 'worldly asceticism' proved unacceptable to the more rapacious authorities.[87] Pososhkov was arrested soon after Peter's death and imprisoned in the Peter and Paul Fortress, where he died in 1726. *On Poverty and Wealth* remained unpublished until 1842, when its observations impressed the intelligentsia of a generation who, having witnessed the initial tremors of revolt, were taking the first steps towards priming the country for revolution.

Nevertheless, the new Police Chancellery was, in part, created to control some of the very abuses identified by Pososhkov. Set up under the supervision of a Portuguese sailor, Anton de Veira, whom Peter had met in Amsterdam, the under-resourced office had wide responsibilities. It controlled crime prevention and law enforcement, fire-fighting, waste-disposal, street upkeep and canal maintenance, as well as the promotion of hygiene and the control of disease.[88] It was, in fact, the task of the Police Chancellery to transform a wild frontier town into an orderly court city. In 1721, a regular rubbish collection was implemented, with carters and vagrants detailed to gather refuse placed outside houses. Hygiene improved. Streets were cleared of unattended cattle. Dirty, smelly market stalls stitched together out of old rags were replaced by new canvas constructions. House owners were expected to make a contribution to the environment by planting trees and shoring up their portion of the embankment, if they fronted a river. Peter ordered 600 street lights to be hung, so that his city was becoming a tolerable place in which to live – but at a cost. It was estimated that the Petersburg Chancellery of Urban Affairs was spending nearly 5 per cent of Russian state revenue.[89]

For serious criminal offences, the tsar often meted out the punishments himself. When Peter returned from sixteen months in Europe in October 1717, the English writer John Mottley recorded that he 'found the complaints of his people very high against the Ministers with whom he entrusted the government'. The tsar spent the rest of the year 'in redressing, with indefatigable application, the great disorders committed in the state and in punishing the authors of them'. He was in the Senate every morning at four o'clock, hearing and examining cases. But these were complex, and an extraordinary Court of Justice was established and administered by officers of the guards. 'So absolute was the power of the tsar,' Mottley suggested, 'that he obliged the members of a venerable Senate, composed of the heads of the greatest families in Russia, to appear before a lieutenant as their judge'.[90] To combat malevolent court intrigues, the tsar had his own special agents. Yuri Shakhavskoy was awarded the Order of Judas in Peter's mock-court as his family had, once upon a time, betrayed the Romanovs. Given that legacy, it was amusing that he was appointed as Peter's informer. Shakhavskoy spied on senior officials and plied his suspects with drink. He taunted them and broke them, thus earning himself the title of Peter's Chief Executioner.[91]

In 1718, Peter lured his son, the *tsarevich* Alexei, back from exile and promptly imprisoned him in the Peter and Paul Fortress. During his interrogation by torture, the tsar, who made quite a hobby of pulling teeth, personally tore off his son's nails. A 'confession' was extracted, which reads like a prototype of those presented in the Stalinist show trials of the mid-twentieth century:

> . . . my inclinations run solely upon bigotry, idleness, frequenting priests and monks and drinking with them . . . by degrees I came to abhor not only my father's military affairs and his other actions, but even his very person . . . unwilling to imitate my father in anything, I endeavoured to obtain the succession by any other method whatsoever than what was fair.[92]

While the authorities were unanimous in finding 'that the *tsarevich* Alexei Petrovich deserves death for his crimes',[93] the tsar wanted to leave nothing to chance. Peter Henry Bruce, the tsar's Scottish artillery commander, was present at the Fortress on the afternoon of 7 July 1718 when 'his majesty, attended by all the senators and bishops' visited the apartment in the fort where Alexei was being kept prisoner. The 'violent passions of his mind . . . had thrown the *tsarevich* into an apoplectic fit'. Three messengers had been despatched to the palace to inform Peter that Alexei begged to see his father and seek forgiveness. Peter arrived, reiterated the *tsarevich*'s crimes, forgave and blessed him and then departed. After that, Marshall Weyde of the Russian Army sent Bruce on an errand to 'Mr Bear, the druggist, whose shop was hard by'. Bear's dispensary was smart and well stocked, its shelves lined with pots of fine Chinese porcelain.[94] When Bruce handed Weyde's message to the chemist, the man 'turned quite pale'. A little while later, the marshal arrived to collect a covered silver cup, which he carried into the prince's apartments, 'staggering all the way . . . like one drunk'. Shortly afterwards, a messenger was sent to inform the tsar that the prince, 'after great agonies, expired at five o'clock in the afternoon'. Bruce ended his eyewitness account with the ominous coda: 'few believed' that Alexei 'died a natural death, but it was dangerous for people to speak as they thought'.[95] Such danger would haunt St Petersburg for three centuries.

Apart from being the offspring of Peter's detested first wife, Evdokia, Alexei's biggest error had been his desire to return the court to Moscow and to the old style of government. Moscow was still an important administrative centre, and the relocation of the government to the new capital was only slowly realised. Moscow was also much larger and continued to play a crucial role in Russian ceremonies and pageants. Coronations took place in its Kremlin until the Revolution. Yet in the early eighteenth century the old capital was a jumble of monasteries, taverns and dense, winding streets.[96] To improve its situation, Peter began to impose some of the guidelines that governed building in St Petersburg, and Moscow thus benefited from initiatives in the new capital. Slowly the 'post-Byzantine Mannerism' of Moscow's sixteenth- and seventeenth-century architecture was replaced by the Russian 'imperial' style, which took its lead from northern European baroque. St Petersburg, however, remained the centre of Westernisation, a place where high winds carried the groans of dying Russian labourers and the lilt of European minuets.

When John Bell returned to Peter's city in December 1718 after a three-year absence, he found it much changed. During the previous year, 6,000 wooden houses had been built on the outskirts – 'beam upon beam, rough without, and smoothed within by the help of a hatchet', roofs being constructed with thin strips of fir laid on flammable birch bark or topped with turf.[97] Shipbuilding had progressed astoundingly, with thirty ships of war and 300 galleys completed. Necessary but disagreeable abattoirs at the mouth of the Moika River were concealed by false residences with fake windows – the first instance of a

kind of deception, or 'Potemkinisation' – that was to become
so familiar in Russia and the Soviet Union. By 1720 there were
about 60,000 houses, including ever more 'magnificent palaces'.
Weber noted that conditions had changed so much since his
arrival in 1714 that a visitor would 'think himself in the midst of
*London* or *Paris*'.[98] Much the grandest project at this time was
the designing of the Kunstkammer, to house the anatomical collections purchased in Europe and the minerals and fossils found
in Siberia. The tsar's private midnight visit to a Dresden cabinet
of curiosities made a big impression on him, and a Dresden-born
architect, Georg Mattarnovy, began designs for Petersburg's
own Kunstkammer. Like Schlüter and Le Blond, Mattarnovy
died after a short time in the Russian capital and the building
was developed by another German, Nicolas Herbel, by the Russian, Mikhail Zemtsov and by the Italian, Gaetano Chiaveri,
who produced elaborate ideas for the tower dividing the immense
two-winged building, which was not finished until 1727.[99]

The foundation of schools and academies, along with the construction of buildings to house such august bodies, accelerated
towards the end of Peter's life. The Engineers School was founded
in 1719, the Artillery Laboratory in 1721. A decree of 28 January 1724 announced the Academy of Sciences. The German
philosopher Gottfried Wilhelm von Leibniz had urged the tsar
to establish such an institution, in order to train men to carry
out God's will that 'science should encompass the globe'.[100] The
Academy of Sciences comprised three departments: mathematics,
physics and the humanities. It was to be run by researchers and
teachers who would discuss learned issues, instruct pupils and be
responsible for assembling a library. It would open officially on
2 November 1725 – ten months after Peter's death.

In 1718, Peter created the first three administrative colleges:
War, Foreign Affairs and the Admiralty. By 1722, there were
eight more.[101] Trezzini won the competition for the building in
which to house the colleges – a 500-metre-long edifice that owed

much to the architect's experience of Copenhagen. Designed by
1724, the exterior was finished eight years later. The interior was
completed in 1742, by the first Russian architect to qualify in
that profession, Mikhail Zemtsov, who had been sent by the tsar
to study in Stockholm and whose Petersburg practice trained the
first generation of Russian architects.[102]

Of course Peter interfered in the day-to-day running of the
colleges and had agents in place to lobby and report on any corruption or malfunctioning.[103] Given Petersburg's latitude, winter
days were short, and the tsar was onsite before dawn. If the officials weren't hard at work, the tsar 'would thrash them soundly
with his cane, a thing that he has done a hundred times to the
great Prince Menshikov'.[104] Captain John Deane observed that
after early-morning visits to the colleges, Peter would hurry to
the Admiralty to consult with shipbuilders and work 'hard with
the axe or adze, scarce allowing himself time to eat'.[105]

If the tsar, his architects and his planners were triumph-
ing, St Petersburg's biggest adversary refused to yield. In early
November 1721, the French envoy, La Vie, watched the water
in his lodgings rise to a level of one metre. For Russia's religious
conservatives, who found St Petersburg unnatural, if not dia-
bolical, it seemed as if nature had come as an avenging angel.
The 1721 flood caused a huge amount of damage, but it was
nothing compared to the great flood of October 1723. In that
ninth flood since Petersburg's founding, the waters rose to what
would be the seventh-highest level of the 300 floods suffered by
the city throughout its entire history. Yet the construction continued. A playhouse was opened on the Moika in 1723. The
tsar's art collection – growing too sizeable for Peterhof – was
shown in the first public picture gallery in Europe, which opened
in St Petersburg in 1724. On display were 120 mediocre Dutch
and Flemish canvases.[106] The end of the Great Northern War
facilitated an intense phase of construction, as Russia confirmed
possession of Karelia, Ingria, Livonia, Estonia and Courland.

Ironically, it gave Peter three very workable Baltic ports at Narva, Riga and Reval – present-day Tallinn. But by then the tsar's 'paradise' was beginning to thrive, and the opening of a 2.8-kilo-metre canal between Tvertsa and the Tsna at Vyshnii Volochek meant that cargo could be carried up the Volga from the Russian heartland to St Petersburg without portage. Suddenly it seemed as if Peter's choice of capital was not completely absurd.

The city was a busy naval base, accommodating forty-eight ships of the line and 300 galleys manned by more than 7,000 Russian sailors.[107] The head of this Russian Navy was Ivan Mikhailovich Golovin. Without enthusiasm or skill, Golovin had proved a duff craftsman during his sojourn in Holland, so Peter sent him off to Venice to study shipbuilding. Once in the Republic, Golovin hardly left his lodgings and, when he returned to Russia, Peter was so impressed by the man's confession of indolence that he made him Chief Surveyor and Supervisor of the Fleet. According-ing to the German diarist Friedrich Wilhelm von Bergholtz, at the wedding of Golovin's daughter to Prince Trubetskoy, Peter approached the 'prince master-craftsman', Head of the Fleet, who was greedily gobbling jelly, and rammed more and more

*The Twelve Colleges designed by Trezzini – as seen in 1753.*

down his throat as if he wished to stifle him.[108] Peter often
humiliated those close to him, behaving like an immature tsar
superstar, abusing his followers. Exercising absolute power,
Peter's whims and wishes galloped out of control. He stubbornly
gave a heavily pregnant woman a punishment drink for missing
a victory parade. Bergholtz records that the woman later sent
the corpse of her stillborn child – pickled in alcohol – to the tsar.

Peter's All-Mad, All-Jesting, All-Drunken Assembly was an
affront to the rituals of Orthodox Christianity, an attack on
respectability. There were drunken orgies at which a naked
Bacchus appeared, wearing a bishop's mitre. At the marriage celebration of one of their number, Peter Burturlin – who replaced
the ageing tutor Nikita Zotov as 'Prince Pope' – the newly-weds
drank vodka from vessels in the shape of outsized genitals: male
for the bride, female for the groom. After the feast they made
their way to a specially constructed pyramid sprinkled with spy
holes, which allowed the revellers to ogle the nuptial mating.
Opposite 'Prince Pope' Burturlin's house, members of the British
colony set up the Bung College in imitation of Peter's mock-
court. College officials carried titles such as 'Prick Farrier' and
'Cunt Peeper', and their antics included basting a penis with egg
and oatmeal and setting two hungry ducks on it.[109]

On 22 November 1721, shortly after the marriage of Burturlin
and the celebration of the Peace of Nystad, Peter was proclaimed
Emperor. It was decreed that 'through his own guidance only . . .
he has brought the state of all Russia into such a strong and prosperous condition and his subjects such glory in the whole world'
that they must 'beg His Majesty, in the name of the whole Russian people, to accept from them . . . the title of "Father of the
Fatherland", Emperor of all Russia, Peter the Great'. The images
used in the coronation panegyrics – as with the myths surrounding the remarkable origins of St Petersburg – invoked a movement
from darkness to light, from nothingness to being.[110] These representations and allegories were not unlike those used by the

'Sun King', but while Louis XIV's persona was artifice, Peter's glorification was closely based on his exceptional courage and acumen, which had brought his country, quite suddenly, to prominence.[111] Although other nations were slow to acknowledge the newly elevated status of the Russian ruler – Britain and Austria recognised the title of 'Emperor' only in 1742, Spain and France two years later – Peter had gained an enormous victory over the old Russia. Orthodoxy was subdued and the emperor took his place among the pantheon of classical gods. Secular pageants eclipsed liturgical celebration. The divine order ceded to imperial prowess. The secularisation of the Russian state had begun.

In order to consolidate his new order, at the outset of 1722 Peter decreed the Table of Ranks, based on a system used in Prussia. The fourteen grades equated the status of occupations in the civil service, the military and the court. For instance, the fifth rank in the civil service was a State-Councillor, the equivalent of a Brigadier in the army or a Master of Ceremonies at court. Peter hoped that his system would neutralise the privileges of inheritance. A person born noble would receive no recognition of that fact until he achieved a service rank that entitled him to nobility. But the tenacity of privilege is revealed by the fact that thirteen families in the top four ranks – the Burturlins, Cherkasskys, Dolgorukys, Golitsyns, Golovins, Kurakins, Plescheevs, Romodanovksys, Saltykovs, Shcherbatovs, Sheremetevs, Veliaminovs and Volynskys – were among the twenty-two families comprising the Boyar Duma 150 years earlier.[112] The nobility would not let go. Furthermore, commoners rising through the ranks became protective of their new position, their mixture of pride and paranoia providing the material for a good deal of the comedy in nineteenth-century Petersburg literature.

In 1722, Peter turned fifty and his thoughts focused on the succession. He had eliminated his son in 1718 and issued a Charter on the Succession to the Throne consolidating that action: 'It will always be subject to the desires of the ruling monarch to appoint whomsoever he wishes to the succession or to remove the one he has appointed in the event of unseemly behaviour.' Accidents of birth and aberrations of character were thereby subordinated to the will of the tsar. Attempting to disentangle the Russian monarchy from the intrigues and inbreeding of noble families, and launch it into the orbit of the politically motivated match-making of the West, Peter declared that members of his family should marry Europeans. He was, in effect, preparing for Catherine's succession – something that almost didn't happen.

To judge by her rapid rise, Catherine was ambitious and politically adept. When Peter was attacked by muscular spasms which gave him a 'wild and terrible air',[113] it seemed that Catherine alone was able to calm him. She personally selected Peter's mistresses, and he wrote to her openly about them. For her part, she assured the tsar that when courtiers came to dine with her while he was away, they were men of advanced age. His letters were full of jokes and innuendoes, anxieties about possible infidelities, and despair at being separated for long periods. Above all, they reveal a relationship that was both robust and tender. When Peter was in Brussels in 1717, he wanted to send Catherine some lace and wrote to her asking for a pattern to give the lace-makers. Catherine replied sweetly, if not cunningly, that she required nothing special, 'only that there should be two names worked into the lace, yours and mine, interwoven together'.[114]

Catherine was crowned the first Empress of Russia in Moscow's Assumption Cathedral on 7 May 1724 – a foreign-born Cinderella inaugurating seven decades of female rule. Catherine was already *imperatritsa* by marriage so this unnecessary ritual, can only have served to consolidate Peter's intention that she should succeed. The Archbishop of Novgorod, Feofan Prokopovich, delivered a strange sermon. Seemingly laudatory, upon closer scrutiny it was clearly barbed. Feofan placed Catherine in an apparently impressive context, among some of the most powerful women of myth and history. But oddly – and perhaps necessarily, in order to flourish in a man's world – these women all had darker sides. Semiramis of Babylon, noted for her sexual energy, was granted her wish of ruling for five days, during which she had her husband, Ninus, put to death. The Amazon, Penthesileia, was another odd choice, as she killed her sister. Among the three Roman empresses cited, Helena, Pulcheria and Eudokia, the last was a jarring choice, as Peter's first wife, Evdokia, still lived.[115] Grouping Catherine with women whose fame rested on their lust for power and sinister deeds, Feofan was either expressing covert displeasure at Peter's choice of empress and successor, or warning Peter about some aspect of her character or activity.

Just five months after Catherine's coronation, the William Mons embezzlement scandal broke – quite possibly a cover for the fact that 'the handsome and stately' Mons, who was head of Catherine's Estates Office, was also her lover. Peter's Procurator General, Pavel Yaguzhinsky, spread stories at court, so that when the tsar saw Catherine and the man she 'much loved' alone in a garden or dining together, he could only imagine the worst.[116] Mons was knouted and axed to death in Trinity Square and his head was impaled on a post, past which the tsar drove Catherine day after day.[117] Subsequently it was pickled, to become an admonitory exhibit in the Kunstkammer. But as Peter's rage over the Mons affair subsided, he seemed happy for his second wife to be his successor. Perhaps the touching testimony to shared tastes was not lost on the tsar – he had fallen for Anna Mons, and Catherine for Anna's brother.


On the morning of 28 January 1725, Peter the Great died in the Winter Palace, and Catherine Skavronskaya became Empress of All Russia in her own right. Peter lay in state in the palace for almost six weeks, as the inhabitants of the city that he had spent the previous two decades building filed past. Edward Lane, the talented Welsh engineer who worked on the fortifications and harbour at Kronstadt for a decade,[118] called to pay his respects to the tsar who had masterminded the enterprise. Often seen grieving beside the coffin was Catherine, whose youngest daughter, Natalya, died on 4 March, aged seven – her tiny pall placed near that of her father.

On 10 March, the funeral train of 166 different groups of mourners slowly processed through the snow flurries dusting the path marked out across the frozen Neva. Choristers sang as Catherine, weak from weeping, followed the coffin. Cannon fired, trumpets blew, tympani boomed with a sound like the ice on the Neva cracking. Regimental drums beat the steady funeral march to the unfinished Peter and Paul Cathedral. The elegy by Feofan Prokopovich was unequivocal in its praise: 'What he made of his Russia, thus it shall remain: . . . He made it frightening for enemies, frightening it shall remain; he made it glorious throughout the world, then it shall never cease to be glorious.'[119] The man who thought it possible to build a city on a marsh was being buried. The glorious city he imagined had yet to be built.

The French philosopher Jean-Jacques Rousseau observed that Peter wanted to civilise the Russians 'when he should only have checked their brutality. He wanted to make them at once, Germans and Englishmen, whereas he ought to have begun by making them first Russians.'[120] Alexander Sokurov's 2002 film *Russian Ark* is a stroll through Petersburg's Hermitage Museum in a single 96-minute shot that carries the viewer through 300 years of Russian history. Its central character, based on the acerbic early nineteenth-century Marquis de Custine, asks, 'Why borrow Europe's mistakes?'[121]

Peter the Great was not only the author of St Petersburg, but also of its subsequent afflictions, which stemmed from a dangerous acceleration revving up in the back of beyond. Yet against the backdrop of war with Sweden and much domestic unrest,

Peter created a shipyard, a naval base, a port, an administrative centre, a court, a capital increasingly marked by solid and elegant stuccoed buildings, ordered gardens and straight, clean streets – the first pan-European city created by architects from Italy, Switzerland, France, England, Germany and Russia – a 'paradise'.[122] Building was driven by hubris, its mythology mired in misinformation. In 1720, Weber recorded the already-exaggerated 'one hundred thousand souls'[123] who perished in the construction of the capital. By 1733, when Sir Francis Dashwood visited, gossip had already flown well ahead of credibility – in 'laying the foundation of this town and Kronstadt, there were three hundred thousand men perished by hunger and the air'.[124] And all for a second choice. Peter's original intention had been to construct a new capital on the Black Sea – a place more suited to the exotic birds that the tsar imported to Petersburg, only to watch them die. In the event, he had been forced to create a capital with naval access on Russia's Baltic shore, a site vulnerable to invading enemies and unforgiving nature. Ominously, Peter the Great set his imperial will against nature, historical precedent and the practices of an entire nation.

Some thought of the capital as a new Rome – if so, it was brought into the world by Caesarean section. The city was the upshot of an unparalleled act of megalomania. A Finnish legend spoke of the many kings of different countries who tried to build on Neva's marshes but it was the vision, volition and technical accomplishment of Peter the Great that successfully brought such attempts to fruition. The poet Joseph Brodsky, who grew up in the sad, standard 'room and a half' of a Leningrad family flat, summarised Peter the Great's achievement: 'This ruler used only one instrument while designing his city: a ruler.'[125]

# 4

# OBLIVION AND REBIRTH

*1725–40*

There was a rumour circulating that Catherine poisoned Peter in revenge for the murder of her lover.[1] Medical opinion has it that the founder of St Petersburg died of prostate adenoma or stricture of the urethra, resulting from an inflammation frequently caused by badly treated gonorrhoea.[2] Drink must have also played its part. Catherine, meanwhile, made great demonstration of her grief and took steps to secure her succession. As it was a novelty for a woman to be anointed sovereign, Archbishop Feofan used great skill and a certain audacity to ease matters. He addressed Catherine in his funeral oration for the emperor: 'The whole world sees that your female flesh does not prevent you from being like Peter the Great.'[3] A coin was struck. On one side, there was a bust of Peter. On the other, a likeness of Catherine surrounded by accessories suggesting that indeed she was worthy to take Peter's place – a globe, sea-charts, plans and mathematical instruments.[4] Thereafter she would often appear as an Amazon, a 'warrior queen' – a potent tactic to mollify traditionalists, who believed that only a man should rule Russia. On the ceiling of her throne room, *The Triumph of Catherine* showed the empress in a sumptuous and revealing gown, holding the figure of a warrior.[5]

Yet Catherine's right to the throne was disputed and there were murder threats. Two reckless con-men emerged – one in the Ukraine, the other in Siberia – both claiming to be the dead *tsarevich* Alexei. They were arrested, sent to St Petersburg and beheaded.[6] Catherine's more serious rival, the nine-year-old son of the murdered Alexei, was in a strong position. Grandson of Peter the Great and Evdokia Lophukina, he had the support of the powerful Golitsyns and Dolgorukys. Yet when voices in the State Assembly started to clamour for the boy, the late tsar's Preobrazhensky and Semyonovsky Guards – generously lubricated by Catherine – arrived in full dress uniform, their drums menacingly beating out their support for their bounteous lush.[7] By the following morning Catherine was confirmed as empress and the guards were given more vodka. In Alexander Borodin's opera, *Prince Igor*, a character suggests that 'no one will serve a ruler who is stingy with drink'. To reward the army as a whole, Catherine pledged to honour arrears in pay.[8]

But if Catherine had the guards in the palm of her hand, Menshikov had the empress in his grasp. Owing her advancement to the prince, Catherine acted as his protector. Whenever accusations of theft and extortion had compromised Menshikov's relations with the late tsar, Catherine had interceded. This occurred in 1711, 1715 and 1719 and climaxed in 1723, when Peter became so furious about the corruption surrounding him that he urged the immediate execution of all officials found stealing from the state. He was dissuaded by his Procurator General, Pavel Yaguzhinsky, who declared that 'we all steal. Some take a little, some take a great deal, but all of us take something.'[9] Just over a century later, Nikolai Gogol's swindling hero, Chichikov, candidly explained, 'I helped myself to the surpluses . . . had I not, others would have taken them instead.'[10] Another century on, under the Soviets, comrades wryly observed that Russia was the richest state on earth because people had been stealing from it for years, and there was still more to pilfer.[11] Protecting Catherine on the throne, Menshikov protected himself, while nurturing a scheme to further the fortunes of his own house. If Alexei's son,

Peter, could be married to one of his daughters, then Menshikov's grip on the country would be secure for years. Not surprisingly, the prince had powerful enemies with similar ideas.

It was, in fact, another marriage that – by hook or by crook – was to secure the Romanov succession. In the late spring of 1725, Catherine and Peter's seventeen-year-old daughter, Anna Petrovna, was married to Charles-Frederick, Duke of Holstein-Gottorp. To honour the occasion, the duke gave a superb dinner in his Petersburg palace and the crowd of spectators gathered outside was invited to join the celebrations by drinking as much as they wanted, a generosity that resulted in ten deaths. The duke was given a place in the Supreme Privy Council, formed in February 1726. Although Catherine was the nominal leader of this small policy-making body, after several appearances she seemed to lose interest, stopped attending, and for the rest of her reign allowed Menshikov to dominate.[12] The Council had its work cut out – simplifying Peter's reforms, reducing the size of the army and abandoning imperial projects in order to slash taxes. Several years of bad harvests and a high poll tax were crippling Russia's rural population at a time when the elite was spending exorbitantly.[13] Under the influence of Catherine and Menshikov, the court was becoming noted for its extravagance. The empress – happy to obliterate all memory of her humble past – spared no expense in the pursuit of imperial splendour. In her first year on the throne, her lust for luxury disposed of 450,000 roubles, nearly 4.5 per cent of state expenditure.[14] *Assemblées* were replaced by lavish balls and more formal receptions at court. At these grand dinners, guests were forced to drink toasts from a communal cup that was in constant circulation. The feasting was followed by the dancing of popular sarabandes, allemandes and gavottes. Pierre Deschisaux, a French physician and botanist, noted that the empress arrived and departed to a fanfare of trumpets and kettledrums. During the evening – which lasted until 2 a.m. – she changed several times and ordered glasses to be filled and refilled so that the assembled company could drink her health, which, after years of boozing with Peter, was rapidly deteriorating.

Deschisaux arrived in St Petersburg in 1726 to find splendid ships in the harbour and an extremely well-ordered Admiralty, which his compatriot, Aubry de la Mottraye, likened to the Arsenal of Venice. The Winter Palace, built after designs by Mattarnovy, was being refurbished, but – according to Deschisaux – was 'nothing remarkable'.[15] In fact, the state of the city remained precarious. The Peter and Paul Fortress with its church by Trezzini lay unfinished, for want of money. Evidence of crime and punishment was everywhere: bodies decomposed on the wheel, others dangled rotting from the gibbet, and spiked heads provided stark warnings to all passers-by.[16] In the summer heat, the smell of rank human flesh merged with the butchery of the abattoir.

An English visitor suggested that Petersburg had been 'built in spite of all the four elements . . . the earth is all a bog, the air commonly foggy. The water sometimes fills half the houses, and the fire burns down half the town at a time.' Despite short summers, sodden soil and long, dark winters, Catherine encouraged

*The Kunstkammer.*

the development of the city's gardens. De la Mottraye paid tribute
to the achievement, asserting that 'if there is a tolerable piece or
spot of ground that can be called pleasant or fertile it is entirely
owed to art'.[17] Yet violent contrasts persisted in a city where clusters of intense activity were tenuously connected by man and kept
apart by nature. After admiring the Dutch-style gardens with
their trellises and bowers, Deschisaux could not help noticing the
'monstrous' animals and strange vegetation in adjacent fields. The
city's first overwhelming flood brought home to its inhabitants –
once again – the absurdity of their predicament. The flash flood
of November 1726 was even larger than the great flood of 1721.
Taking refuge in his attic, Deschisaux was convinced that the
tidal bore that broke the banks of the Neva was powerful enough
to sweep away the foundations of his lodgings.[18] Distinct channels of the river united in one vast sea, from which the tops of
buildings emerged like lighthouses. The swell engulfed the city
and boats were carried where, hours before, people had strolled.
Muck was swept up by the swell and deposited as the surge
receded, leaving a grey, mud-coated metropolis. Such were the
scale and damage caused by this flood that Catherine redoubled
efforts to shore up the banks of the river with timber pilings.

The empress also encouraged two projects dear to the late tsar's
heart.[19] The first was the search for a north-east passage to reach
and establish trading ties with North America, which they knew
as 'New Spain'. Catherine equipped an expedition that departed
in 1725 under the Danish explorer Captain Bering, but she would
be dead before there was any news of the explorer. It was during
his second expedition in 1741 that Vitus Bering reached the coast
of North America – a discovery which led to Russia's annexation
of what is now Alaska and the Pacific Northwest.[20] The second
project was the landmark opening of the Academy of Sciences and
the 'rarity chamber', or Kunstkammer. The first truly monumental
structure completed in St Petersburg, this 100-metre-long building
impressed a French visitor as 'one of the most superb edifices of

its kind in Europe'. The collection it housed included plants, animals and instruments, as well as Turkish cannonballs from Peter the Great's Pruth River campaign. Among the anatomical displays was a sequence showing the progress of the embryo from one week to nine months, assembled by Ruysch in Amsterdam.[21] It was the kind of exhibit prohibited by the Orthodox Church, which feared that a soul could rise from rest to reclaim its physical body – the kind of exhibit that would thus contribute to the promotion of a scientific way of thinking.[22] Freaks were well represented: a two-headed calf, 'a lamb with eight legs', another 'with three eyes', a dubious 'flying dragon'[23] along with a 'serpent with wings', both generally thought to be the devil incarnate. De la Mottraye was amazed by the 'generative parts of an hermaphrodite . . . an human foetus of a she Moor four months old the clitoris whereof was come out as long as the privy member of a boy of that age' and by a 'Calmuck child of about nine months with two bodies and two heads with all their respective parts well formed'.[24] The size and particularity of such a collection were a reflection of a ruler's status, and Peter the Great had sent Johann Schumacher – librarian and curator of his cabinet of curiosities – all over Europe to gather such exhibits. Schumacher was instructed to bid in auction and buy, buy, buy. The Kunstkammer opened to the Petersburg public at no charge. Indeed, visitors were offered coffee, wine or vodka, but even such blandishments did not stimulate much local interest.[25]

The Academy of Sciences, established in the palace of the deceased widow of Ivan V, stood adjacent to the Kunstkammer. Catherine often sat empty-eyed or dozing through its learned discourses, which were frequently presented in Latin. In any case, Catherine – midway through her short reign – was tumbling headlong into oblivion. She sustained Peter's regimen of hard drinking without taking much time out for ruling, although she did preside over what was left of the All-Drunken Assembly, at which Princess Nastasha Golitsyna, Catherine's ageing jester, out-drunk everyone. Natasha guzzled through

the night and into the next day, until she collapsed in a heap
under the table.[26]

Catherine became so persistently intoxicated that she would
pass out while having sex with her lovers.[27] When her legs were not
so swollen that she was unable to rise from her bed, she enjoyed
appearing in the trappings of an empress. Her riding habit was of
silver cloth, her robe fretted with gold Spanish lace, and a white
plume swayed seductively above her hat. She often mixed the
soldier with the sexpot, wearing low-cut dresses beneath a regimental jacket when reviewing her guards. On one such occasion,
in February 1726, a bullet from a gun salute narrowly missed
the empress's head and killed an unlucky merchant standing
nearby – perhaps an accidental discharge, perhaps attempted
murder.[28] There were certainly indications of discontent. In a
contemporary woodcut, Catherine was pictured as the repulsive
and cannibalistic folkloric figure Baba-Yaga, riding on a pig to
attack Peter the Great.[29] Previously supportive of the empress's
succession, the archbishop now made critical public statements
about her lifestyle. After he was sentenced to death, Catherine
commuted the penalty to incarceration in an underground cell
in Arkhangelsk. Half starved and fouled by his own excrement,
Feofan died there in 1726.

As Catherine's health continued to degenerate and life began
to blur, she appointed the dead *tsarevich*'s son, Peter, to be her
successor, intending him to make a match with Menshikov's
daughter. Weakened by alcohol poisoning, asthma and venereal
disease, Catherine caught a chill in that habitual death-trap of
Russian rulers, the Blessing of the Waters on the Feast of Epiphany. After a prolonged illness, she died on 6 May 1727. Her reign
had been too short and too dissolute to have accomplished much
and, without Menshikov, it would have amounted to very little
indeed. Catherine's most important contribution to the state
had been as Peter's soulmate. She matched him drink for drink
and went with him on campaigns. Enduring the rough, she also

enjoyed a tumble. John Mottley suggested that her lowly origins, 'so far from being disgraceful to her', reflected a 'greater lustre upon her own merits'.[30] Voltaire even claimed that Catherine was 'as extraordinary as the tsar himself'. Regarded by many as a peasant fertility goddess, the empress was the mother of the fatherland.[31] Ironically, this mother gave her name to Ekaterinburg in the Urals, where the Romanovs – the dynasty into which she miraculously married – would one day be anihilated.

Within a month of Catherine's death, Menshikov was appointed to the highest possible rank – *Generalissimus* – and his daughter, Maria, became engaged to the twelve-year-old tsar.[32] Predatory and puffed up with power, Menshikov began to act ever more outrageously. He appropriated gifts intended for Peter II. He invited the ruler to Oranienbaum and, when the boy snubbed the invitation, 'Menshikov stupidly sat in the throne prepared for Peter – an act that did not go unmarked' by his enemies. When he later travelled to Peterhof to speak to the young ruler, he was, once again, snubbed. The boy refused to stop his hunt and receive his guest. Ignored, Menshikov returned to Petersburg to prepare a reception for the emperor, only to be confronted by General Saltykov, who had orders to repossess furniture and convey it to the Summer Palace. That same evening the general returned to arrest Menshikov. For offences both 'criminal' and 'political', the most powerful man in the land was stripped of his titles and exiled to Siberia, where he died in 1728.

While this drama was unfolding, the most significant change to St Petersburg was the creation of a pontoon bridge that crossed the Neva to connect the Menshikov Palace on Vasilevsky Island to the Admiralty. Vulnerable to the freeze and turbulent thaw, the bridge had to be repositioned every spring until, in 1850, a permanent structure was at last put in place. But the floating bridge came too late to serve the capital, as Peter II decided to establish

his court in Moscow, after his coronation there in January
1728. This delighted the many traditional families who detested
Petersburg – particularly the all-powerful Dolgorukys who, like
Menshikov, fostered dynastic ambitions.[33] In 'Petropolis' building slowed, factories closed and merchants lost money, as the
exodus cut the population to a half of what it had been when
its founder died. The splendid capital-in-the-making rapidly
became a provincial city in decay. St Petersburg seemed ready to
take its place in history as the most evanescent of any major city.
While many of its mansions became uninhabited and many of its
unfinished buildings deteriorated to the point of collapse, there
was one significant project that had been commissioned by Peter
the Great and which came to fruition while his grandson's court
was in Moscow.

The iconostasis for the Peter and Paul Cathedral was commissioned in 1722 and begun in the autumn of that year in
Moscow by a team of more than fifty carvers, carpenters and
gilders. Completed in January 1727, segments were transported
by sleigh or barge to St Petersburg, where it proved impossible
to install them, as the cupola of the cathedral was still open to
the sky, and the plastering – a problem at the best of times in
Petersburg's damp climate – consequently remained unfinished.
The iconostasis was a remarkable departure from Russian tradition. In place of a screen separating the sanctuary from the
congregation, the structure was based on the triumphal arch and

*Pontoon Bridge across the Neva, 1753.*

was probably so ordered by Peter the Great, in imitation of those temporary structures erected to celebrate his victories. Above all, implicit in the concept of the iconostasis as triumphal arch was the apotheosising of Russia's first emperor. Peter was – as the polymath and poet, Mikhail Lomonosov, later claimed – 'an incarnation of God on Russian soil'.[34]

The subjects depicted on the panels were as innovative as the structure itself. The Romanovs were placed alongside more conventional Christian iconography, and Peter the Great is seen against a Dutch baroque façade, celebrating the architectural style of his capital. St Alexander Nevsky – patron saint of both Peter and his city – is depicted as a secular prince, wearing the style of clothing the tsar himself would have worn.[35] By the time the cathedral was at last ready for the mounting of the iconostasis, the furious tempest of September 1729 had all but submerged St Petersburg and confirmed to the pro-Muscovite faction that Peter II had been wise to abandon such a vulnerable capital.[36] And so the gilded proclamation of Peter's triumph was installed in an abandoned city that seemed destined to become a ghost town.

In Moscow, the powerful Prince Alexei Dolgoruky drew the young tsar into his circle and indulged him with endless hunting parties. He presented his seventeen-year-old daughter, with whom Peter fell in love.[37] Thus Catherine Dolgoruky replaced Maria Menshikov as Peter II's bride-to-be, but the triumph of the Dolgorukys was short-lived. Only days before the solemnisation of the marriage – after blessing the waters during the Epiphany celebration in the River Moskva in January 1730 – Peter II caught a chill, just as his great-grandfather Tsar Alexei had, and 'on the nineteenth, the day appointed for his marriage' he died.[38] Peter left no heirs, had made no testament, and the Dolgorukys' dreams all but evaporated. Emerging from the bedchamber in which Peter II lay dead, Prince Ivan Dolgoruky – in a desperate

attempt to salvage the grab for power – drew his sword and proclaimed, 'Long live the Empress Catherine!'[39] To no avail. Prince
Dmitry Golitsyn proposed summoning the daughter of Ivan V,
the infirm tsar who had briefly co-ruled with Peter the Great.

The plan was that Anna Ivanovna, Duchess of Courland,
would be obliged to accept the rule of the eight members of a
Supreme Privy Council, without whose permission she would
remain powerless to levy taxes or declare war. When she arrived
in Moscow, a document was produced stating that, if she did
not comply with the conditions laid down by the Privy Council,
she would be denied the accession. Supported by guards officers
and about 600 nobles who were worried that 'instead of one
autocratic sovereign', they would face 'tens of absolute and powerful families', Anna refused.[40] She declared instead that, as her
subjects had 'all unanimously begged' her 'to deign to assume the
autocratic power in our Russian Empire as it had been held of
old by our forefathers, we have, in consideration of their humble
pleas, deigned to assume the said autocratic powers'. Anna had
proclaimed herself empress.

'They say the court will go to Petersburg this winter,' wrote Mrs
Rondeau, wife of the British Consul:

> if so, my affairs will oblige me to follow them . . . The Dol-
> goruky family are all banished and the poor empress of the
> day with them. They are gone to the very place where Prince
> Menshikov's children are. So the two ladies who were suc-
> cessively contracted to the young tsar may chance to meet
> in banishment. Would not this make a pretty story for a
> tragedy?[41]

The population that had left the city with Peter II returned with
Anna, who intended to make St Petersburg her court for nine

months of each year. The architect Trezzini was to prepare the palaces for her arrival in mid-January 1732. Commerce would thrive, building would recommence and Anna, with her whims and her passion for freaks, would rekindle something of the spirit of the city's founder.

The moment she set foot in her capital, there was spectacle and theatre – everything from her dazzling entry procession, to Italian opera, ballet and her favourite grotesque farces. The arrival cavalcade took Anna through five elaborate and specially constructed triumphal arches. Although these had become politically less appropriate in Europe by 1732, the Romanovs were still in the halting process of establishing the majesty of their court, and such structures suggested Petersburg's notional descent from the power and the glory of ancient Rome. Their theatricality echoed extravagant and fashionable stage settings by designers such as Giacomo Torelli and Inigo Jones. As she passed through the first arch, the empress – like an ancient conqueror – arrived to take possession of St Petersburg. The procession began at 1 p.m., before the arch erected at the Anichkov Bridge. The city's postal director led off, his staff fanfaring their post horns. Foreign merchants, mounted dragoons and foreign diplomats followed. On one side of the empress's carriage rode Karl Gustav von Löwenwolde, commander of Anna's newly formed Izmailovsky Guards. On the other side rode the empress's adviser and lover – grandson of a stable boy and a married father of three – Count Ernst Johann von Biron. The procession followed the city's longest and straightest thoroughfare, the Great Perspective Road, passed through another arch beside the Admiralty and marched on to the St Isaac of Dalmatia Church to hear Mass. At every halt or new stage of the parade there were cannon volleys and musket salutes. At length the empress reached the Winter Palace, which had been refurbished for her arrival.[42] There was a ball, followed by fireworks, while a multitude of soldiers on the frozen Neva manoeuvred themselves into a giant pattern spelling

A H H A.[43] The capital had been well groomed and, all through the day, crowds celebrated the fact that their city was waking from four years of slumber.

During St Petersburg's 'interregnum' there had been three important improvements. The first was development of the press. The *Vedomosti* – the newspaper that had appeared in one form or another since the founding of the city – had folded in 1727. For months the capital remained without a paper and then, just as the court deserted the city, the *St Petersburg Vedomosti* appeared as a larger, twice-weekly publication with a print run of 300. Reaching a circulation of 2,000 by the end of the century, it published in Russian and German until the Revolution.[44]

The second development was the opening of an important stretch of the Ladoga Canal, which ran along the southern shore of the lake from Shlüsselberg on the Neva and gave shipping a safe alternative to Ladoga's sudden squalls and dangerous silting.[45] Such a protected passage for goods from the Russian heartlands lessened the likelihood of famine in the capital.

The third development was the creation of the Cadet Corps in 1731, housed in the Menshikov Palace, which had been empty since the prince's exile. Francesco Algarotti observed that providing accommodation for 200 students made better use of the space 'than the displaying to the eyes of the nation the luxury of a favourite'.[46] Cadets began their course at thirteen, with classes in calligraphy, Russian, Latin and arithmetic. In their second year they learned geometry, geography and grammar, before passing on to more focused subjects in their penultimate year: fortification, artillery, history, rhetoric, jurisprudence, ethics, heraldry and politics. Students would then spend their final year specialising in the subjects in which they excelled, though they continued German and French, which were obligatory at every level. The majority graduated to military and civil ranks, while the most brilliant went on to further studies at the Academy of Sciences.

The Cadet Corps became the unlikely setting for early

developments in an art that St Petersburg would make its own –
ballet. In the first instance, a dance school had been established
to instruct the daughters of the aristocracy. The French ballet
master Jean-Baptiste Landé was hired by – and taught – Peter the
Great's daughter, the crown princess Elizabeth. Landé was given
a salary of 300 roubles and rooms in the Winter Palace.[47] Shortly
afterwards he started to instruct boys at the Cadet School, in
order to provide the court girls with dancing partners.[48] So successful were both endeavours that in 1738 the ballet master
offered to take on six boys and six girls under twelve and teach
them for a three-year period.[49] Thus was founded the St Petersburg Classical Dance and Ballet School. It went on to admit
children from the orphanage, train the first Russian soloists, and
grew into the Imperial Ballet School.

In 1708, before St Petersburg was secure, Peter the Great had
ordered Tsar Ivan's widow, Praskovia Saltykova, and her children to move from Moscow to his new settlement. If a good
number of Muscovites found it hard to adjust to Peter's city, then
Praskovia was no exception. Her 'barbaric' household – peopled
with grotesques and soothsayers – sat uncomfortably with the
hopes that Peter had for his new Russia.[50] When, in 1710, the
tsar started forging links with European powers by searching
for a Russian bride to marry the impoverished, hard-drinking Frederick William, Duke of Courland, Praskovia proposed
her least-loved child, Anna Ivanovna. When Anna eventually
returned to St Petersburg in triumph after years of impoverished
widowhood in Courland, she brought back with her both a taste
for oddity and a delight in Europeanised entertainment.

Empress Anna's bizarre retinue was a grab-bag of 'freaks'
who looked like the most disturbing exhibits from the Kunstkammer sprung to life. There were midgets, giants, hunchbacks,
cripples – a damaged entourage that made visiting Europeans

blanch. Freaks, of course, had been common in European courts, but as rulers became less rough around the edges, deformity ceased being a means to offset the majesty of kings. Anna's attraction for the ugly was perhaps an expression of her physical and intellectual discomfort. Natalia Sheremeteva, Prince Ivan Dolgoruky's bride, described the empress as 'taller than every-one by a head and unusually fat'.[51] The wife of the British Consul agreed that Anna was 'a very large made woman', but added that she was 'very well shaped for her size'.[52] Others recorded her sombre, short-necked masculine bulk, with a face lightly pockmarked and a voice that was high-pitched and strident.[53] At Anna's court, outlandish burlesques, cruel displays and the indecent pranks of a multitude of jesters and dwarfs became commonplace. As the court emerged from Mass on Sunday, her six favourite jesters, their faces blacked by coal, would line up in a row and imitate hens laying eggs. They would also enact cockfights, clawing viciously at one another and drawing blood. At the sight of their contortions and bloodshed, Anna and her lackeys shrieked with laughter. As for the empress herself, she was often vicious – grabbing courtiers, tweaking and pinching them, and slapping those who both pleased and displeased her. It was, perhaps, more hazardous to be at court than in the meanest shack in the least salubrious quarter.

Sir Francis Dashwood travelled to St Petersburg with George, Baron Forbes, envoy extraordinary to the court of St Peters-burg, the man who negotiated the Anglo-Russian treaty of 1734 – Russia's first commercial accord with a European power. Arriving in June 1733 on one of the ninety English ships that sailed to St Petersburg that year, Dashwood's first impression was that Kronstadt was built 'upon marsh and bog in the sea'.[54] There was a fine forge, but the haven and the brick houses on the island were 'gone very much to decay' through neglect and 'the violence of the cold'. Arriving in the city, the visitor found both the Peter and Paul Fortress and the Alexander Nevsky Monastery unfinished, and much evidence that work had halted during the absence of the court. On Vasilevsky Island 'long rows of large houses, that look well on the outside' were 'almost all unfinished, and most uninhabited'. Later in the year, Dashwood found those that were occupied 'exceeding cold' and damp, despite being heated by sizeable ovens faced with Dutch tiles. As for the one-storey wooden houses, each crack and crevice in the walls was sealed with tow by professional 'corkers' who moved through the city from house to house.[55]

At the time of Dashwood's arrival, even the empress was living in a hastily built wooden Summer Palace. The visitor marvelled at its speedy construction, which had only taken six weeks, commenting that 'they make nothing here of employing two thousand men at work upon the same building'.[56] Under more protracted construction was the third Winter Palace. Work started during the year Anna returned the court to St Petersburg and lasted until 1735. The result, according to Mrs Rondeau, was 'nothing remarkable either in architecture, painting, or furniture', for it comprised 'a great number of little rooms ill-contrived'.[57]

A vivid picture of life in St Petersburg midway through Anna's reign is given by the ironically named Elizabeth Justice, who – after being ill-used by her husband and the British legal system – went to Russia in 1734 as a governess to an English family. She arrived in August, the season of thunder and lightning, 'which often causes damage and frightens her majesty'. Despite the poor soil around and about, Justice gave the impression that horticulture had advanced since the early days of the settlement. While cherries were 'scarce and very bad', the inhabitants enjoyed good strawberries, gooseberries and a kind of 'transparent apple' that – when ripe – 'is so clear that you can see the kernel through it',[58] and which tasted superior to any variety she had eaten in England. Apart from an abundance of the predictable crops such as turnips, carrots and cabbages, the local farmers also grew asparagus, French beans and lettuce. As for fish, Elizabeth Justice saw:

> finer smelts . . . than ever I did in England; and twenty of them sold for a kopek, which is equal to a penny. The price of salmon is three kopeks each pound . . . But what appears to me the most valuable, is what they call the Sterlate. They cost five or six roubles, which amount to nearly thirty shillings a-piece. They are very luscious and the water in which they are boiled appears yellow as gold. They eat them with nothing but vinegar and pepper and salt.[59]

While Petersburg exported a great deal of caviar to England, it was not to be compared with that on offer in the capital itself, where it was eaten upon 'toasted bread with pepper and salt and has the taste of a fine oyster'. Dining with Russians during Lent, Justice watched them 'eat heartily of a jole of salmon raw'. They removed the skin, cut it into large pieces and marinated it in 'a great deal of oil, vinegar, salt and pepper'. They also made fish soup and prepared 'small fish, very like our shrimps which are fried and served up in the dish they are cooked in. The nicety of them is to have them hot and crisp.'

As for meat, 'mutton is but small, very sweet and fat. There's very good veal but it's scarce. The beef is excellently good and cheap. They have also fine pork and are very fond of kids which they have in great plenty.' Methods of preparation included frying, boiling, baking and marinating, and the locals made broth with lean meat flavoured with herbs and onions. There were also turkeys, chickens, pigeons, rabbits, partridges, wild fowl and snowbirds – the now-outlawed ortolan – costing ten kopeks a pair. With such a cornucopia, it is hardly surprising that Justice claimed that 'I believe there is no part of the world where the English live better than they do at Petersburg.' As for the poorer Russians, 'they can make an hearty meal on a piece of black sour bread, some salt, an onion or garlic'.[60]

Elizabeth Justice's obvious talent as a travel writer provides us with vivid pictures of different times of year. In summer – during which ships are launched in the presence of the empress – people idled on the Neva in barges to the accompaniment of live music. They went fishing upriver and built fires on which to cook their catch. In winter, no expense was spared on illuminations and yet more firework displays, as 'rockets and bombs . . . played off before the Palace'. In one display the figure of 'Plenty' was traced in the night sky beside a likeness of Anna, adorned with the motto 'Beyond Praise' – the kind of crude tribute so beloved, two centuries later, by Joseph Stalin. There were sophisticated firework effects, such as 'a garden so natural, that you would imagine you might gather oranges from the trees'. During the Butter Week carnival there was sledging on nearby hills – a great source of broken arms and legs. This was a time of 'regaling', when revellers ate and drank until Shrove Tuesday. On that day they would kiss and 'bid adieu, saying "Tomorrow I die" and mortify themselves to Easter'. During fasts, Justice observed, the Russians were very good at abstaining from food, but not from drink. They 'love the strongest liquor they can get; and if they cannot obtain it honestly, they will steal it'. On one occasion, attending a christening, she recalled that the celebrant 'was very drunk'. When Easter arrived, guns and cannon around the citadel were fired at one or two o'clock in the morning and, later in the day, the wealthier people exchanged elaborately decorated Easter eggs with 'figures that move'.[61]

Meanwhile, at court Anna abolished the Supreme Privy Council in response to their interference at her accession and restored the status of the Senate, setting its membership at twenty-one. The German presence at her court was considerable, but influential figures formed no unified group because of their diverse origins: the ambitious von Löwenwolde came from Livland; the uncompromising Count Münnich from Oldenberg; the industrious Andrei Osterman from Westphalia; and Anna's favourite, Count Biron, from Courland. This young man 'got deep into the favour of the Duchess, who took such delight in his company, that she made him her confidant'. Biron married one of Anna's maids of honour, but had by then become Anna's lover. Later, in St Petersburg, the empress effectively became a member of the Biron family. She openly held hands with the count and it was even rumoured that she was the mother of Biron's youngest son.[62] If the count was ill, the empress would attend him and, towards the end of her reign, Biron always slept in her rooms. According to General Manstein, Münnich's adjutant, Biron was 'haughty and ambitious beyond all bounds, abrupt, and even brutal . . . He took a great deal of pains to learn to dissemble, but could never attain any degree of perfection in it, comparable to that of Count Osterman, who was master of the art.'[63] Yet, with a little learning and a modicum of good sense, Biron ruled 'with perfect despotism over the vast Empire of Russia'. Anna – having little interest in the affairs of state – entrusted the task to her lover, while she turned her attention not only to the animals that she delighted in riding, killing and torturing, but also to her freaks, jesters and servants. Prince Mikhail Golitsyn was appointed 'Prince Kvasnik', the imperial cup-bearer, and Princess Volkonskaya was entrusted with Anna's pet rabbit.[64]

With her youth having passed in impoverished provincial obscurity, nothing seemed too beautiful or too expensive to satisfy the 'capricious, passionate and indolent' empress. In this she was matched by Biron, who adored pomp and magnificence. They shared a great love of horses – Anna, it is said, kept a different horse for each day of the year, and Biron owned 200 jewel-studded saddles. Inspecting her stables every morning, Anna rode whenever the weather permitted. She also loved hunting and shooting and was a crack shot with the rifles that were beautifully fashioned for her in the imperial workshops. During 1739 it was recorded that Anna shot no fewer than nine stags, sixteen wild goats, four wild boars, a wolf, 374 hares and 608 ducks – without counting all the birds she blew to bits. The cruellest manner of killing involved the *Jagdwagen* into which animals would be herded, only to be picked off at point-blank range by smug hunters sitting comfortably, waiting for each batch to arrive. The empress had zoological gardens and aviaries installed at Peterhof so that she could wander through Le Blond's park, killing at will. Dangerously – in a country in which there was a perennial threat to the throne – loaded rifles were placed all over the Winter Palace, so that Anna, on a sudden whim, could fling open a window and pick off the sparrows, cranes and magpies soaring overhead. She would then invite her maids of honour to try their luck. After her exertions, the empress would invite the court to feast on what she had shot.[65]

The empress rose before eight in the morning, and by nine she was dealing swiftly with despatches. At midday she dined with Count Biron and his family on simple food, drinking beer or Tokay in moderation. When there were no functions at court, she had a light supper and retired between eleven and twelve. Cards were played privately and were also part of the evening's entertainment at a ball. Although gambling was banned in 1733, General Manstein observed 'deep play at court: many made their fortune by it in Russia and many others were ruined'. He witnessed as many 'as twenty thousand roubles lost in one sitting at Quinze or at Pharoah'[66] – and there was also a social cost. The wife of the British Consul observed, 'I fancy, one might find agreeable conversation, if cards were not known in Russia.'[67]

Chatter – rather than conversation – was an important diversion for Anna, who was always searching out new companions: 'Princess Viazemsky, a young girl, lives at the home of the widow Zagriazhskoy . . . Locate her and send her here . . . I want her for my own amusement as they say she talks a great deal.'[68] In the search for companions, the empress ordered General Saltykov to find her tall, clean Persian or Georgian girls who were not stupid. She preferred garrulous companions of about her own age and needed new supplies to replenish her dwindling stocks – Tatiana Novokshchenova would 'die soon and I want someone to take her place'.[69] With her strange passion for the croaking of frogs, when human voices ceased to entertain her, Anna sat at a window in the palace just above a specially stocked well and enjoyed the laryngeal mating calls.[70]

Although she recoiled from the sight of cripples or paupers on the streets of St Petersburg, Anna spent a good deal of time with old, amputated and crippled servants from her mother's court. Among them were to be found storytellers, bedtime heel-scratchers and a lively band of six jesters. Two of these were foreign: a Portuguese Jew named Jan d'Acosta and a Neapolitan violinist, Pietro Mira, nicknamed Pedrillo. When Pedrillo – for a lark – married a goat, Anna was beside herself when he took it to bed. Pranks delighted the empress. She thought there was nothing funnier than to ring the city fire bells in the middle of the night and rouse the inhabitants of the capital, who came stumbling half-dressed out into the dark streets, only to realise that as the hands of the clock passed midnight, it became 1 April 1735 and they were April Fools. When, several days later, a church steeple was struck by lightning and set on fire, people claimed it was God's judgement against Anna's folly.[71]

Despite its unsettling roughness, in its more public guise the court under Anna took on a fresh level of brilliance. Women were required to have a new dress for each holiday. The uniforms of officers were trimmed with gold, their cockades knotted with broad white ribbons and red feathers. Anna avoided sober colours on public occasions,[72] and the total effect was summed up by a foreign envoy: 'I have never seen such a brilliant gala and first-class supper. You cannot imagine the splendour of this court', its 'luxury and magnificence surpasses even the most opulent ones, including the French'. The city hosted frequent masquerades, both at court and in the houses of the nobility, for which, despite a general 'want of money, great sums' were 'laid out by all courtiers to get magnificent habits'.[73]

The garden of the Summer Palace hosted sumptuous dinners, followed by dancing in a huge tent in the cool of the evening. Ladies appeared in diaphanous gowns of white gauze decorated with scatters of silver flowers. On one occasion during the War of the Polish Succession, French prisoners taken at Danzig in June 1734 were introduced to the company in what – at first sight – seemed to be a cruel act of humiliation on the part of the empress. However, Anna 'called to several ladies, who she knew spoke French, and desired them to do all they could to make the gentlemen forget they were prisoners, at least for the evening'. The wife of the English Consul was among those chosen, but – feeling too weak to dance – acidly observed that she

*Masquerade at the court of Anna I, c. 1736.*

'passed the evening in chat' with a French officer, experiencing 'a pretty strong dash of that redundancy of rhetorical expression so inherent to his country'.[74]

In the cold months, balls were held in an indoor winter garden containing 'orange trees and myrtles in full bloom'. The consul's wife was present at one and observed that the 'fragrance and warmth of this new formed grove, when you saw nothing but ice and snow through the windows, looked like enchantment'. Indeed, 'the music and the dancing in one part, and the walks and trees filled with beaux and belles . . . made me fancy myself in Fairy-land'.[75]

Russian reality was not so fabulous. Outside in the streets – as in the country at large – there was aching poverty. Even the nobility had been much impoverished by the cost of incessant wars and their enforced toing and froing between Moscow and St Petersburg. At court, the pinch was visible. Manstein records that the 'richest coat would sometimes be worn together with the vilest uncombed wig; or you might see a beautiful piece of stuff spoiled by some botcher of a tailor; or if there was nothing amiss in the dress, the equipage would be deficient. A man richly dressed would come to court in a miserable coach.'[76] Like the buildings of the city that crumbled because of the cost of incessant repairs, many minor nobles could not sustain the financial burden of extravagant display, and the effect was somewhat like a Soviet-era opera, where economic constraint was visible in the tattiness of a wig or the crudity of faded drapes painted on rickety theatre flats.

In apparent contrast to her delight in the barbarity of her entourage and the slapstick savagery of wild burlesques, Anna possessed a keen interest in opera and ballet. She rifled the treasury in order to sponsor visiting European musical talents, opera companies and *commedia dell'arte* troupes. In 1733, Anna appointed the Venetian Luigi Madonis as concert master of her court orchestra. Most probably a student of Vivaldi, Madonis dedicated his Twelve Diverse Symphonies for Violin and Bass to Anna. While these were firmly anchored in the traditions of Venetian baroque, Madonis took the novel step of incorporating Russian and Ukrainian folk songs into his violin sonatas.

In 1735, an Italian opera company arrived, featuring the celebrated singer Zanetta Farussi, the mother of Giacomo Casanova, who would, when grown up, visit St Petersburg during the reign of Catherine the Great. The following year another company, directed by the Sicilian composer Francesco Araja, performed his celebration of the power of love and hate, *La forza dell'amore e dell'odio*. Gaudy and increasingly embellished by mechanical marvels, the effects in these operas – like sugar in a multicoloured sweet – compensated for their lack of substance. The ballet interludes were an important ingredient and were choreographed by fellow Sicilian Antonio Rinaldi, who rapidly became the rival of the French choreographer and ballet master Jean-Baptiste Landé. Under his stage name of Fusano, Rinaldi took over as director of the ballet school after Landé's death and laid the foundations for the Italianate phase of Russian ballet. Anna's passion for the dance made her a harsh critic. Like a severe ballet mistress, she took the habit of slapping performers if they did not please. Vasily Trediakovsky, the translator of *La forza dell'amore e dell'odio*, was rewarded 'with a most gracious slap in the face' after 'reading verses for the *tsaritsa*, sitting by the fireplace'. One of Trediakovsky's tasks was to write and read dirty poems to the empress.[77]

During Anna's reign a 1,000-seat theatre was built to present operas – a good number of them written by Araja, who created the lavish production of *Semiramide* in 1737 to celebrate the empress's forty-fourth birthday. The 'large and lofty' theatre was heated by eight ovens, and performances open to all but drunkards and those in working clothes were given twice a week. Anna sat in the middle of the parterre with the princesses, Anna Leopoldovna and Elizabeth Petrovna, on either side. Typically

Princess Anna was observed with her hair curled, wearing 'crimson velvet, embroidered richly', while Elizabeth was decked in silver and gold.

Straight theatre – with a lack of Russian material, and without the mechanical thrills of the operatic spectacles – was slightly less popular. Elizabeth Justice noted that there were 'sometimes Dutch plays; but I think nobody would choose to see them twice'.[78] However, at the court of Anna's cousin, the crown princess Elizabeth on Tsaritsyn Field, the medium was used privately and politically. A drama written in 1735 by one of Elizabeth's ladies-in-waiting, Mavra Shepeleva, was critical of the empress.[79] Elizabeth's circle were, at that time, in their mid-twenties and they delighted in subversive drama, which acted as an emotional release. During the 1730s the crown princess felt far from secure. General Manstein records that 'the Empress had a great mind' to shut Elizabeth up in a convent and 'deprive her of any hopes of ever ascending the throne of Russia'.[80] The crown princess found her sojourns at Tsarskoe Selo – inherited from her mother, Catherine I – unsettling. On one occasion she sent to Petersburg for ammunition because bandits were 'roving and skulking to hurt me'.[81] Under considerable strain, Elizabeth took refuge in drama, drinking and dance.

Among those enlisted in the Ukrainian Cossack choir established at Elizabeth's court was a farmboy from Chernihiv, Alexei Rozum, who had been spotted by one of Anna's courtiers singing in his village church. Alexei became a favourite of the sweet-voiced Elizabeth Petrovna and – perhaps – even her secret husband. Under the name of Alexei Razumovsky, he rose to the rank of general field marshal and resided in the Anichkov Palace. Surpassing even this rapid rise from rags to riches is the meteoric story of Alexei's brother, Kyril. At sixteen he was brought to court and despatched to study at the University of Göttingen for two years, before returning to be appointed President of the Academy of Sciences in St Petersburg at the age of eighteen. He then went on to become the Hetman of the Ukraine by the age of twenty-two.[82] If St Petersburg transfigured an obscure delta, it also transformed many lives.

In the summers of 1736 and 1737 large fires raged through the central part of the city near the Admiralty. Behind the stone edifices lining the banks of the canals and rivers, ramshackle wooden houses crammed too close together provided dangerous tinder. In August 1736, the new British Consul, Claudius Rondeau, counted 1,000 houses 'consumed to ashes'.[83] The suspected cause of the fire was arson and, as a result, a woman was beheaded and two men were burned to death – rather slowly, as the wind that day was wayward.[84] In the fires of June 1737 the Millionnaya, where some of the grandest houses stood, the Palace Embankment and the palace of the crown princess Elizabeth were touched, while hundreds of lesser buildings were completely destroyed.[85] The upshot of these conflagrations was the creation, in 1737, of a Commission for Construction, set up under Peter Eropkin. It established five administrative areas in the city, regulated building and planned an ordered expansion of the left bank of the Neva – an important departure from the Trezzini/Le Blond way of thinking, which had centred the capital on the Peter and Paul Fortress and Vasilevsky Island. By focusing on the mainland instead of the islands, Eropkin made for limitless expansion along three avenues radiating from the Admiralty.

Among the young men whom Peter the Great had despatched to Europe to learn their profession, Eropkin had returned – after seven years in Italy studying the villas of Andrea Palladio – to become the architect of this definitive phase of St Petersburg's expansion. Eropkin worked with Mikhail Zemtsov, Ivan Korobov – a Dutch-educated architect employed at the Admiralty – and Domenico Trezzini's relative, Pietro Antonio Trezzini. Under Eropkin, they created a masterpiece of urban planning: three diverging avenues – Nevsky, Gorokhovaya and Vosnezensky – connected by a succession of semicircular streets.[86] Although few architectural landmarks remain from Anna's reign, the creation of this street plan, fanning out from the Admiralty, marks the main axes of the central city as it stands today. Rapidly constructed unbroken façades lined these avenues, along which the empress loved to race in wintertime. For others, speed restrictions were introduced.

The first stretch of Petersburg's central prospekt, the Great Perspective Road, already existed, paved by Swedish prisoners and hung with lights along its short length. With their ambitious plans to enlarge the city, the Commission for Construction extended this prospekt all the way to the still-unfinished Alexander Nevsky Monastery. Although he was focused on Europe, Peter the Great did not neglect the memory of great Russians, especially when he perceived similarities between a historical figure and himself. Such was the case with Alexander Nevsky. Both men were accomplished generals, and both raised Russia to a new position of importance. It is therefore not surprising that, as early as 1704, Peter promoted the cult of Nevsky and that – in July 1710 – he had founded the Alexander Nevsky Monastery, in honour of the man who had beaten the Swedes in 1240 and the Teutonic Knights in the celebrated battle on the frozen Lake

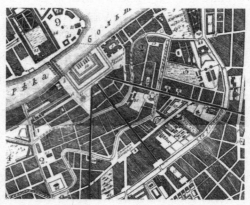

*Eropkin's three diverging thoroughfares, the Nevsky, Gorokhovaya and Vosnezensky, fanning out from the Admiralty.*

Chudskoe in 1242. Peter brought the general's remains from Vladimir to the new monastery. After Eropkin's extension of the thoroughfare in 1738, the Great Perspective Road was renamed the Nevsky Prospekt in honour of the venerated general.

If Eropkin's greatest contribution to the future of St Petersburg was the result of fire, then his most bizarre commission involved ice. The puffy-faced, barrel-stomached empress could be particularly spiteful. When Prince Mikhail Golitsyn married a non-Orthodox Italian woman, Anna was furious and made Golitsyn – who held the rank of lieutenant – her jester. The Italian bride died shortly after the marriage, and the empress thought it just and funny to force the widowed Golitsyn to marry one of her servants, a shrunken, hunchbacked old lady, Avdotya Buzheninova, whose ugliness frightened even the priests. When Avdotya confessed to Anna that life without a husband was like a hard frost, she planted an idea.

February 1740 was registering a drastic cold rarely seen in Petersburg, and the empress decided to construct a mansion out of ice on the banks of the Neva between the Winter Palace and the Admiralty. The luckless newly-weds would spend their wedding night in a baroque igloo. Throughout each winter the poor were routinely employed to break the river ice in order to obtain water. Now they were cutting blocks for artisans to sculpt an elaborate palace, designed by Eropkin. The sixty-metre-long, six-metre-wide, six-and-a-half-metre-high structure was held together by water which froze as it was poured between the blocks of ice. The edifice was decorated by an ice balustrade at ground level and by a gallery with statue-capped columns of ice on the roof. Its windows were ornamental, their frames painted in mock green marble. Except for a few real cards frozen into a table, everything inside was ice: ice beds, ice blankets, ice goblets, even ice candles that burned a reservoir of oil briefly, but not long enough to cause them to melt. Outside, an ice cannon capable of shooting ice cannonballs guarded the structure. An ice dolphin and ice elephant

spouted water during the day and burned oil at night.[87] The bride
and groom – in a cage mounted on an elephant – processed at the
head of the 300 wedding guests, summoned from all corners of
Russia. Some were in sledges drawn by reindeer, goats or hogs,
others mounted on camels. The participants paused for a meal
and a ball at the Duke of Courland's old riding stables, then the
party moved on to the Ice Palace, where the bride and groom
spent the night almost perishing on their frigid marriage bed.[88]

The whole prank was typical of autocratic excess. But Anna –
like those who came before and followed after – was guilty of
a worse kind of excess. In 1740, Eropkin was implicated in a
plot against Anna's lover, Count Biron. Organised by Eropkin's
brother-in-law, *Ober-Jägermeister* Artemy Volynsky, the plot-
ters were caught and severely punished. Volynsky had his hand
cut off, followed by his head. Eropkin – whose work on St Petersburg much pleased the empress – was also beheaded, while the
other conspirators were knouted, tortured and exiled to Siberia.[89]

As Anna's reign progressed, arrests and executions increased.
Her 'natural inclination . . . to tattling and inquisitiveness' kept
her well informed, and in dealing with threats to the state, the
empress made good use of gossip. To help her with 'dirty' political work, she used the President of the College of War, General
Burkhard Christoph von Münnich. This general, 'more feared
than loved by the troops',[90] was a practised dissembler. Mrs
Rondeau described him as 'one of the most gallant men of this
court', who, when he was 'amongst the ladies . . . affects a gaiety
and tenderness that are to me very disagreeable'. Seen 'in the
papers as slaying his thousands and ten thousands, how would
you be surprised to see him hearken to your voice with dying
eyes, on a sudden snatch your hand and kiss it in raptures! But
how much more would you be surprised to find he thought it
necessary to do so to all women!'[91]

Anna created the Chancellery for Secret Investigatory Affairs
in April 1731 under Andrei Ushakov, a man who had cut his

teeth in Peter the Great's secret police.[92] Ushakov's department was a terrifying place, with racks for torture and red-hot irons to coax stubborn suspects. Tongue-cutting was the punishment for those who spread malicious gossip and was much used at a time when 'insulting the Imperial Person of Her Majesty' constituted a major offence. If anyone was suspected of antipathy towards Anna, or was heard tattling about the exact nature of the relations between the empress and her married favourite, Count Biron, they would be detained by Ushakov. When someone informed against a person, they too were arrested.[93] If the suspect didn't crack, then the informer was probed, and so the methods of Ushakov's department became the terrible prototype for the Cheka and the KGB. Under Anna – who enjoyed sharing all the dirt that Ushakov collected – the eyes, ears and paranoid misgivings of a police state were already on the streets of St Petersburg.

In August 1740, the empress's niece, Anna Leopoldovna, gave birth to a boy called Ivan. The twenty-two-year-old mother, granddaughter of Ivan V, had lived in the empress's palace until her 1739 marriage to Anthony Ulrich, Duke of Brunswick-Wolfenbüttel. Unprepossessing, bashful and – according to Münnich – 'naturally lazy', Anna Leopoldovna lacked the dynamism to rule. But she offered a way for the empress to block Peter and Catherine's popular daughter, Elizabeth, and secure the Romanov line through the descendants of her father, Ivan V. The birth of Anna Leopoldovna's son was timely, as Anna's health was failing. She had gout. She was fainting frequently and spitting blood.

In mid-October, a huge and exotic procession of 4,000 foreigners appeared on the streets of Petersburg. There were camels and mules bearing gifts, along with fourteen elephants to be presented to the newborn, Ivan. This was the embassy of the Shah Nadir, who had conquered India and wished to woo the crown princess, Elizabeth. The industrious Ostermann, one of the power-sharers at court, refused to allow her to meet the ambassador, and Elizabeth – furious to be treated thus by a man whom her father had raised from the position of scribe – vowed revenge.

Several days later – having nominated the baby Ivan as her successor, and her favourite, Count Biron, as regent – Empress Anna died. Charles Cottrell, son of the Master of Ceremonies to George III, was in St Petersburg at the time of the empress's funeral and adds an eerie footnote to the life of a woman renowned for her ghoulish curiosity. Anna lay 'in state a month but not having been rightly embalmed was almost fallen to pieces before her burial'.[94]

In November, Münnich – in a bid for power – marched on the Summer Palace with his adjutant, Manstein, and eighty soldiers. When they entered the regent's bedchamber, Biron tried to hide under the bed, but Manstein grabbed the bellowing man, gagged him, bound his hands and dragged him off. When brought before the notorious Ushakov, Count Biron was exiled to Siberia and Anna Leopoldovna became regent.

About St Petersburg during the reign of Ivan VI there is almost nothing to say, as he acceded to the throne at just over two months old and was deposed when he was three months past his first birthday. His mother – a gloomy regent – had little appetite for ruling and spent all her time with her maid of honour, Julia Mengden. According to Edward Finch, the English minister plenipotentiary who played cards at court, 'Anna loved Julia as passionately as only a man could love a woman', noting that 'they often slept together'. When, on 25 November 1741, Crown Princess Elizabeth staged a coup, Mengden was in Anna Leopoldovna's bed. Johann Friedrich Ostermann and Münnich had been outmanoeuvred by the group supporting Elizabeth. Exiling Ostermann and the entire Brunswick family, the drink-loving, man-iser Elizabeth Petrovna returned the succession to the descendants of Peter the Great.[95]

Despite the excesses and indolence of her court, city life had been calmer and cleaner under Empress Anna. More streets were paved, more river banks reinforced. With expansion to the south, new markets had opened in different parts of the city – including a central market between the Fontanka River and the Catherine Canal. Those able to work were kicked out of almshouses, to make way for the truly destitute.[96] However, the secretary of the Prussian Legation observed that 'no advantage has been obtained by the country from St Petersburg which would not have been had in far greater measure at Moscow, had the government been left there'.[97] Furthermore, appraisal of the country as a whole was far from positive. Edward Finch said of Russia in mid-1741, 'I must confess that I can yet see it in no other light, than as a rough model of something meant to be perfected hereafter.' But it is remarkable to observe how a court and a city had so rapidly shaped their particular approximation of European style and taste. When Anna died, she may have left no heir, but the city to which she returned the court had been reborn.

# 5

# DANCING, LOVE-MAKING, DRINK

## *1741–61*

H er father, Peter the Great, intended her as a bride for the French king, Louis XV. To that end, Elizabeth had a French dancing master, learned European languages and was painted stark-naked as 'a young Venus' by Louis Caravaque.[1] According to the Spanish envoy, at eighteen she was a beauty 'such as I have rarely seen . . . exceptionally lively . . . gracious and very flirtatious'.[2] These were qualities that made Elizabeth popular, upset the Empress Anna and fueled gossip: she took lovers, held orgies, drank like her parents – qualities and behaviour that ensured informers were planted, while the police hired cabmen to watch the crown princess's palace.

Elizabeth's rollicking lifestyle made her the darling of the regiments. When she seized power with a pre-dawn coup in 1741, she was dressed in the uniform of the Preobrazhensky Guards. The soldiers were glad to be ousting the foreigners who wielded so much power – Münnich, Ostermann and von Löwenwolde.[3] But despite their removal and an upsurge of nationalism, St Petersburg was stimulated by unending and ever more elaborate European influences during Elizabeth's twenty-year reign. The arts thrived, and the city – animated by a newly sensual style of architecture – grew.

As the annual thaw liberated winter's stranglehold on the Neva delta, foreign ships arrived and visitors came ashore to marvel at the ravishing young city that spread before them. Elizabeth's chief architect, Francesco Bartolomeo Rastrelli, was creating a series of elaborate baroque buildings that answered her desire for vivacious ornamentation to animate the practical, rectilinear city established by her father and developed by Eropkin under Anna. When Elizabeth returned to St Petersburg after her Moscow coronation on 25 April 1742, her triumphal entry – grander than Anna's a decade earlier – consolidated her usurpation of the throne. The daughter of Peter the Great was claiming Peter's burg.

While a legitimate male tsar lived, Elizabeth's rule was illegal and there were plots to assassinate her and put Ivan VI on the throne. A conspiracy by a palace servant and two members of the guards was uncovered. They were knouted, their nostrils were slit, the leader's tongue was cut out and they were exiled to Siberia.[4] Although Elizabeth abolished capital punishment, torture was still used. Two society ladies involved in a 1743 plot to crown Ivan were also knouted and had their tongues branded. Another conspiracy that same year resulted in the knouting and exiling of four members of the Lopukhins, the family of Peter the Great's first wife. Ushakov – who remained in place as Head of the Secret Chancellery – was kept busy, as Elizabeth's position remained precarious.[5]

Having concluded a war with Turkey in 1739, Russia was, once again, fighting Sweden. At court, Elizabeth strove to econ-omise. Silk was to be cut according to rank, and there was a limit on the amount of lace that was worn. Gold and silver were temporarily forbidden. Fireworks – increasingly sophisticated displays, emblazoning patriotic allegories against Petersburg's night sky – were restricted to the New Year and the empress's birthday and name-day.[6] Yet Elizabeth's craving for luxury and lavish display meant that restraint was soon abandoned as she spent excessively on the glorification of herself, her court and her city. St Petersburg became more ostentatious and more comfortable. Gone was the unruliness of previous decades, although there were still outbreaks of rowdy behaviour. To reward their help during her coup, Elizabeth promoted and ennobled an entire company of the grenadiers. According to General Manstein – who, as adjutant of the banished Münnich, may not be the most unbiased witness – they 'ran through all the dirtiest public-houses, got drunk and wallowed in the streets. They entered into the houses of the greatest noblemen, demanding money with threats, and took away, without ceremony, whatever they liked.'[7] The company was promptly disciplined.

When English philanthropist Jonas Hanway arrived in June 1743, he found St Petersburg 'so open, airy, and regularly built in many places'.[8] However, the mansions that displayed the city to advantage were mere havens in a sea of crowded shacks. When a nobleman left the comfort of a court building, the precariousness of a makeshift, hand-to-mouth life was at the gate. At the limits of the city, sodden land defied the desire to expand. Yet Elizabeth continued the efforts of her predecessor to ameliorate the capital. Francesco Bartolomeo Rastrelli's architectural frills and furbelows adorned buildings fit for a fun-loving empress. Son of the sculptor and architect Carlo Bartolomeo Rastrelli, who had been summoned to St Petersburg in 1716 by Peter the Great, Francesco was responsible for nearly all the major construction in the city and its environs during Elizabeth's reign. He was undoubtedly a virtuoso, and his very name conjures up the most overblown excesses of the baroque style. The interiors of his palaces – through persistent patterning, mirroring and gilding – create a flowing, frolicsome effect that match the fluid grace of his monumental, yet ostentatious exteriors. Rastrelli's froufrou grandeur captured the spirit of a tremendously feminine empress who wore masculinity as a badge of office. His extensive

*Rastrelli's repetitions – the façade at Tsarskoe Selo.*

façades of the Winter Palace and at Tsarskoe Selo harnessed the delicacy of contemporary courtly dance to the rigour of a march. And if his effects appear to belong to a style of decoration that is not much valued today, it is perhaps in the rhythm of his repetitions that he can appeal to the modern eye. If gilt embellishment has been ruined for us by sham gold glued to cheap reproduction furniture, then the gilded arabesques of Rastrelli's palaces are the real thing: the dancing indulgence of a spoilt court, a declaration of a newly enriched and empowered monarchy. Rastrelli's Winter Palace – built between 1754 and 1762 – was the fourth version of that residence and the one which stands today. Its 250-metre-long façade overlooking the Neva is one of the abiding symbols of St Petersburg. With its turquoise-coloured walls punctuated by white pilasters and more than 2,000 windows, it was completed just after Elizabeth's death, during the short reign of Peter III.

Mikhail Zemtsov was commissioned to design the Anichkov Palace for Elizabeth's favourite, Alexei Razumovsky. When

Zemtsov died in 1743, Rastrelli took over the project. He remained relentlessly in demand throughout the 1740s and '50s. In revolt against the flat façades of earlier Petersburg buildings, Rastrelli constructed the gracious, curving Vorontsov Palace for the chancellor, its interior spaces resounding with gold. He built the now-demolished Summer Palace and a mansion for Sergei Stroganov, whose salt-mine monopoly made him one of the richest men in Russia. Meanwhile, Rastrelli's designs for buildings such as the church at Petersburg's Smolny Convent and the independent chapel at Peterhof revealed his ability to blend native traditions – acquired while working in Kiev and Moscow – with his signature Italian baroque. The fusion of styles responded to Elizabeth's desire to acknowledge Russia's heritage.

The Smolny Convent was begun in 1748 on the site of Peter the Great's tar yard, where '*smola*' was stored for rigging and caulking. Although named the New Resurrection Convent of the Virgin, the association with tar stuck and it became known as the 'Smolny'. Inspired by Moscow's Orthodox architecture, its central church was built in the shape of a Greek cross, surmounted with five onion-dome cupolas. A rectangular perimeter building housed cells and – in each of the four corners – there was a cupola-capped chapel. Savva Chevakinsky's Maritime Cathedral of St Nicholas was likewise indebted to earlier Russian churches. It took nearly a decade to build and was finished two years before the Smolny, in 1762. In refusing to ignore Russia's artistic heritage, St Petersburg was signalling a certain maturity.[9]

Despite her desire to promote native architectural traditions, Elizabeth was ultimately dazzled by European style, and Rastrelli's design for her palace at Tsarskoe Selo was a proclamation of Italian baroque extravagance. Completed in July 1756, it became Elizabeth's principal residence while the Winter Palace was under construction. Its luminous and animated interiors created a splendidly theatrical milieu for masquerades and lavish receptions. The early twentieth-century artist Alexandre Benois noted: 'from the first hall, there opened an endless enfilade of gilded and densely decorated rooms'. Reflection was vital to the titillation of this interior space and, in the Great Hall alone, there were 300 large mirrors. The French diplomat de le Messelier recalled the sublime moment when 'the blinds were drawn and daylight suddenly was replaced by the brilliance of twelve hundred candles', their flames multiplied in the reiterating mirrors. When an 'orchestra of 80 musicians began to thunder . . . The doors suddenly opened wide and we saw a splendid throne, from which the Empress descended surrounded by her attendants.'[10] Sheer autocratic opulence. The palace gardens with their amusements – the swings and Great Slide in the summer, ice hills in the winter – became a playground for the nobility. The winding garden paths, threading between the games and grand pavilions, extended the rococo rhythms of the palace out into nature.

The colours used in Rastrelli's interiors – pastel shades of light blue, turquoise and rose – were, Théophile Gautier observed, the very tints which shone in the sky above the city when the cold was 'dry and the snow cracks under the feet like glass powder'.[11] They were also found in the colours of court dresses, although Elizabeth herself preferred to wear white and silver and to stud her hair with diamonds, out-dazzling the jewelled snow of sunlit days. The empress adored clothes, craved accessories and had a pre-emptive monopoly on all the accoutrements of beauty that arrived in her capital. Ships offloading fabrics and dresses were not allowed to sell their wares publicly until Elizabeth had scrutinised the cargo.[12] The empress bought wholesale and – by royal command – cheaply. The privilege of having anything she wanted became a habit of taking everything. She bought sixty-three pairs of dogs from the British Prime Minister, Robert Walpole, and found a mansion to house the hounds and their handlers. She had twenty-five wooden 'rest' palaces built along the route between St Petersburg and Moscow, some of which were used only once.[13] She acquired a superabundance of lace, bijouterie, buckles and bolts of fabric – cascades of Indian cottons, satins, shot-silk taffetas, ribbed silks – mordant-dyed and gold-spotted. There were chintzes, brocades, damask moiré: hundreds of metres of the finest stuff. White Chinese silks, along with crimson and scarlet satins, came overland from Peking, as ever more opulent items were amassed to camouflage Elizabeth's lack of substance as a ruler. Like some eighteenth-century Imelda Marcos, she owned several thousand pairs of shoes and trunks full of silk stockings. Despite the loss of some 4,000 dresses in a Moscow fire of 1747, Peter III discovered a further 15,000 dresses in the Summer Palace after Elizabeth's death[14] – impressive for an empress who spent a good deal of time in uniform.

In Peter the Great's day, Russian envoys to foreign courts had been ordered to bid for biological curiosities to display in the Kunstkammer. Elizabeth used her agents as fashion scouts to find and purchase the latest and the best. Like a star of the silver screen with an exclusive lighting cameraman, she controlled the hierarchy of beauty at court and would never allow others to be seen to equal advantage. The empress would think nothing of cutting ribbons from a lady's hair or even savaging the hair itself, if it threatened to eclipse her. The Grand Duchess Catherine – young wife of Elizabeth's nephew, Peter – noted that Elizabeth reduced the ladies of the court to tears when she commanded them to shave their heads and sent them, by way of compensation, badly made black perukes.[15] Catherine's attitude towards Elizabeth's vanity was caustic. Informed that the empress 'had forbidden the ladies to include in their finery many kinds of ribbon and lace', she remarked that Elizabeth need not have bothered to tell her, as she never made 'beauty or finery the source' of her merit – 'when one was gone, the other became ridiculous'.[16]

In 1753–4 alone, Elizabeth's court spent 230,000 roubles on imported luxuries such as canes, fans and snuff boxes – Field Marshal Apraksin possessed a different jewelled box for each day of the year.[17] Gems were 'much in use', noted the Englishman

John Richard, and the Russian court was the sole market for large blemished jewels, 'as they regard more the size than the quality'.[18] Similar sham and bluff were evident in the equipage of the minor nobility. The coach might be drawn by horses of different colours and driven by a coachman in peasant dress, yet three or four well-dressed footmen would dance attendance.[19] Minor nobles struggled to keep up, while the richest dazzled with excess. Sergei Naryshkin wore a uniform embroidered with silver, gold and jewels; and it seemed as if the glittering contents of a large jewellery box had been shaken over Count Peter Sheremetev when he appeared at court. Even the liveries of the pages from the richest families were of cloth of gold. Given the peasants on the streets beyond the palace, itching and sore in coarse cloth and wrapped in folds of woollen stuffs to keep them alive, it is clear that Elizabeth's court was a bubble. While the nobility tripped the light fantastic, the poor dwelt in the gloom of Petersburg's damp and dismal air. Beyond the capital, small groups of peasants scattered through Elizabeth's empire – serfs owned by their masters – rose up in arms against their inhuman treatment and the mismanagement of their lords. Dragoons were despatched to quash the disturbances.

Allegory supported Elizabeth's dubious claim to the throne, but – in many painted images – the empress stood alone, unsustained by the iconography that had been used to buttress Catherine I. Even in Louis Caravaque's startlingly naked image of Elizabeth aged seven, she is seen without gods in attendance and is merely holding a miniature likeness of her father as proof of her identity. Intended to seduce the King of France, the young Elizabeth is seen against an ample ermine fur with its subliminally vaginal markings – a sexual message underscored by the cleft between her toes. In mature portraits, fashion created Elizabeth's majesty. As she got older, the empress suffered from that eternal conspiracy against women: the falsehood that they lose their looks and should make every effort to compensate.

A French diplomat noted that, after spending much time adjusting her appearance, the empress became angry with the mirror, ordered the removal of her headdress and accessories and postponed her engagement. Pauzié, the court jeweller, recalled that she 'never retired earlier than six o'clock in the morning and slept until noon or later'.[20] Like her parents, Elizabeth was an alcoholic, frequently drinking so much that she fainted and had to be cut out of her dress and corsets by her maids.[21]

The drink helped her flee from the terror that stalked her. Fear of a coup or assassination kept Elizabeth awake at night and on the move. She constantly had locks changed and slept in different rooms. She would suddenly decide to leave Petersburg at a moment's notice. Or she would suddenly depart from Peterhof with a carriage full of palace cleaners, or take supper with maids and lackeys. The English traveller John Richard observed that 'Elizabeth was a person of amorous turn, and she indulged her passions without ceremony or restraint, nor was her choice always from the nobility, persons of very mean rank had sometimes the good fortune to please her.' The empress took many lovers, and 'foreign courts made a point of sending as their ambassadors, men, whose persons and address might assist their negotiations' – among them the French envoy, the Marquis de la Chétardie. This 'Blazing Star' found Elizabeth 'debonaire', but he proved indiscreet. A letter was found in which the marquis wrote 'in such unreserved terms, that he was directly recalled'.[22] In fact, Chétardie's crime was not only sexual swaggering, but also double-dealing diplomacy. He encouraged Turkey to attack Russia while the empress was preoccupied with Sweden. Another French diplomat, Jean-Louis Favier, noted Elizabeth's ability to dissemble. The 'secret folds' of the empress's heart remained 'inaccessible even to the oldest and most experienced courtiers, with whom she is never so gracious as at the moment she is deciding their disgrace.'[23] Subject to convulsions and fits of terror, Elizabeth was capricious and violent, sometimes beating her chambermaids and thus earning the nickname *Khlop-baba*, 'the woman who beats people'. Her last-minute reprieve of Münnich when he stood on the scaffold, and of Ostermann as his head lay on the block, also suggests a sadistic streak.[24]

Elizabeth used the festivities at court to sound out visiting diplomats and keep tabs on changes to the European balance of power.[25] After the victories of Frederick II of Prussia during the 1740–48 War of the Austrian Succession, Russia played an important role in urging France and Austria to become allies and restrain Prussian ambition. During the Seven Years War, which began with Frederick's provocative attack against Saxony in 1756, the Russians won important victories against Prussia and thus – during Elizabeth's twenty-year reign – her empire became established as a powerful diplomatic and military player in European politics.[26] Some measure of this new importance is suggested by the fact that Great Britain began to spy on Russia. John Maddison, a collector of Russian books, was commanded by George III to learn Russian and, to that end, travelled to St Petersburg. When he returned home, he was assigned to the British Secret Office to intercept and translate letters and crack Russian ciphers.[27]

The problems of internal government were not – as with her predecessor – of much interest to Elizabeth. After attending the Senate fifteen times in her first three years on the throne, she went only three more times during the remaining seventeen years of her reign. The British envoy to Russia, Lord Hyndford, complained bitterly of Elizabeth's 'backwardness in all sorts of business or anything that requires one moment's thought or application'.[28] The empress preferred the gossip of her confidantes, whom she employed in her own domestic intrigues. Stroganov wittily called one of them – the ageing and disreputable Elizabeth Ivanova – '*Le ministère des affaires étranges*'.[29] For matters of state, Elizabeth was content to sustain the ideas and policies of her father, reminding the Senate that, during his reign, one of its most important tasks had been to collect as much revenue as possible.[30] Ideas for modest reforms came from her inner circle of favourites, a group ranging from the handsome but uneducated to the shrewd and innovative. The sweet-voiced Cossack Alexei Razumovsky was unable to read or write and so he was made 'Grand Master of the Hunt'.[31] During the summer months, Elizabeth hawked and hunted with him – riding fast and wild.

During the 1740s, the vain and ostentatious Peter Shuvalov began his ascent. An enlightened thinker, Shuvalov tried unsuccessfully to persuade the empress to introduce 'fundamental and permanent' laws to protect her subjects, laws that would apply to the monarch and people alike – an attempt to transform autocracy into enlightened monarchy. Shuvalov increased import and export duties, abolished internal customs and switched from unworkable direct taxation to indirect ways of gaining revenue for the state by taxing salt and alcohol. In the process he made himself enormously wealthy from monopolies and franchises. When he died in 1762, he was so unpopular that people gathered to hurl insults at his funeral procession as it moved from his mansion on the Moika to the Nevsky Cloister. Others with access to the empress – courtiers such as Alexander Shuvalov, Roman Vorontsov, Ivan Chernyshev and Sergei Yaguzhinsky – were given huge enterprises on advantageous terms. The free labour of serfs, along with vast deposits of untapped natural resources, gave these men an oligarchic potential.[32]

Under Elizabeth, theatre did not exist simply for the glittering nobility to be seen and admired while onstage the actors struggled on unheeded. Drama was taken seriously and, just as her father had fined residents for missing Sunday nautical excursions on the Neva, Elizabeth was capable of fining court ladies fifty roubles if they missed a performance. In the summer of 1751, an unusually small attendance at a French comedy prompted the empress to open up her theatres outside the court to suitably attired merchants and their wives. Thenceforth, a paying audience would help to fill St Petersburg's growing number of playhouses. A new comedy theatre opened in 1743 on the site of former stables on the Nevsky Prospekt and remained active until it burned down six years later. Beside the temporary wooden Winter Palace – swiftly erected to serve while the site on the Neva was being rebuilt – a new opera house was constructed, while Rastrelli designed yet another theatre in the Summer Garden that opened in 1750.

The head of the Cadet Corps, Prince Yusupov, encouraged his pupils to perform Russian as well as French plays. In 1746, a merchant from Yaroslavl was so taken with one of these perform-ances that he returned home to set up a troupe. It developed such a reputation that – ten years later – Elizabeth decreed:

> We have ordered that there be established a Russian Theatre for the presentation of tragedies and comedies; we assign for its use Golovin's stone house on Vasilevsky Island near the House of the Cadets. Actors and actresses are to be engaged for this theatre: actors, from among the student singers and members of the Yaroslavl troupe who are now at the Corps of Cadets, as well as others who are not in the service – as many as are needed; likewise, let a sufficient number of actresses be engaged. For the maintenance of the said theatre . . . the sum of 5000 roubles shall be paid yearly . . .[33]

Thus a permanent Russian state theatre was founded and directed by the politically progressive playwright Alexander Sumarokov. There were performances, in patchy and guttural French, of Racine, Molière and Corneille, and the prolific Sum-arokov produced a steady supply of the moralistic tragedies that were popular at Elizabeth's court.[34] The empress, who had used subversive drama as an emotional safety-valve during her years of tension with Anna, was now grateful for Sumarokov's adaptation of Shakespeare's *Hamlet*, which foregrounded the hero's sense of duty to the state rather than his obsession with revenge.[35] Sumarokov's own sense of duty was called into question when he was fired from his directorship by Ivan Shuvalov in June 1761 for mismanagement and, perhaps, embezzlement. After the incident, the director was able to dedicate himself to his first love, poetry. He wanted to be recognised and valued as a professional poet – a novelty in St Petersburg.[36]

If theatre went public during Elizabeth's reign, so did concerts. In July 1746, a promoter charged one rouble for admission to a recital by a foreign bass, given in the house of General Artemy Zagriazky. Permission for the performance was sought from the Police Chancery and posters pasted about the city advertised the concert. Two years later, early-evening Wednesday concerts began in the house of Sergei Gargarin – entrance, once again, was one rouble. While merchants and townspeople were welcome in the audience, drunken servants and 'unsuitable' women were not. In addition to such presentations, a musical curiosity invented for Sergei Naryshkin by a Bohemian member of Elizabeth's court orchestra was seen and heard both at court and out and about on the city streets. It was a 'living organ', which required a group of twenty-five to forty performers – clearly an invention for a society in which labour was cheap. Every pipe was blown by a different player, and the result was that this absurd-looking contraption could perform 'the completest symphonies of every kind, from the slowest *largo* to the quickest *prestissimo*'.[37]

The sweet-voiced Elizabeth loved court chapel-singing and often stood in the shadows and sung along. It was to the ranks of these court singers that St Petersburg owes a patron saint. When the singer Colonel Andrei Petrov died, his wife, Xenia, gave away their possessions, dressed in his old clothes and wandered the streets of the capital for the next forty years, aiding and praying for the poor. People came to love her, and her otherworldliness proved of commercial benefit to those who were kind to her. Merchants giving her food or cabmen offering her free rides attracted custom, their kindness rewarded by a population grateful for their generosity to a holy fool. After Xenia's death, her grave in the Smolenskoe Cemetery became a place of pilgrimage, attracting upwards of 5,000 people a day in the first years of the twentieth century. In 1988 – towards the end of the communist era – she was canonised by the Orthodox Church as St Xenia of Petersburg.[38]

Opera as a court entertainment had been well established under Anna, and after Elizabeth took the throne, more Italian troupes with increasingly elaborate stage effects delighted court audiences. Giovanni-Battista Locatelli's travelling company arrived at the end of 1757 and presented *opera buffa*. Locatelli was a great publicist for his art and gave lectures at his house while his chief dancer, Niodini, taught the court ladies how to improve their dancing.[39] Increasingly, Russian-trained performers were seen. The first Russian female opera singer was heard on the Petersburg stage during the 1740s, and the first dancer whose

*The 'living organ'.*

career was recorded was Aksinia Sergeeva, who had been chosen to dance at Elizabeth's coronation.[40]

Francesco Araja created about thirty operas during Elizabeth's reign, including *Scipio*, written in 1745 for the sumptuous marriage of the empress's seventeen-year-old nephew, Grand Duke Peter Fedorovich, to his sixteen-year-old German fiancée, Sophie Friederike Auguste von Anhalt-Zerbst-Dornburg. Sophie had converted to the Russian Orthodox Church a year earlier, taking the name Ekaterina Alekseyevna, and would play a significant role in Russia's future. The marriage involved ten days of celebration, during which there were services, gun salutes and banquets. Court guests dined around large tables 'incorporating fountains, cascades and pyramids of candles' while, out in Palace Square, the populace was treated to wine fountains and roasted meat.[41] The dandy Sergei Naryshkin was applauded for arriving at the marriage wearing a jewelled kaftan and travelling in a carriage inlaid with glittering mirrors.[42] Festivities culminated in a huge and highly elaborate ball of masked quadrilles, after which the Grand Duchess Catherine settled into the boredom of her new life.[43] She left a detailed but not impartial account of her youth at Elizabeth's court, presenting herself as too intelligent and energetic to be stifled by an unfortunate marriage to an imbecilic man, the future Peter III.

Easily bored by the luxurious court, wary of its manipulative empress – yet all the while learning how to negotiate the complicated power struggles of an ambitious nobility – Catherine took refuge in reading. She consumed everything from cutting-edge philosophy to the classics. One day it was Montesquieu's *De l'esprit des lois* or Voltaire's *L'histoire universelle*, the next it was Tacitus or Cicero. Although the grand duchess detested hunting, she developed a love of riding, straddling the horse like a man – much to the consternation of the empress, who felt the position might compromise the grand duchess's ability to produce an heir.[44] Indeed, it seemed as if Elizabeth's anxieties were founded when – after nearly a decade of marriage – Catherine and Peter produced no offspring and were both sanctioned to take lovers. During 1752, Sergei Saltykov was known to be making overtures to Catherine so that, when she gave birth to the Grand Duke Paul Petrovich on 20 September 1754, people speculated that Peter was not the father. The French Ambassador, the Marquis de L'Hôpital, noted curtly in his despatches that the child 'belongs to Monsieur Saltykov'. Nevertheless, the birth empowered Catherine, who was now not only the wife of the heir apparent, but also the mother of a future emperor. After Elizabeth confiscated the baby Paul, to supervise his upbringing, Catherine went on to have children by a number of lovers – a daughter, Anna, by the Polish Count Poniatowski; and a son, Count Brobinsky, by Gregory Orlov. These lovers and pregnancies helped the rapidly maturing grand duchess understand that, at court, everything private was public, and a secret was what a good number of people made it their business to know. As for Peter, he didn't seem to be a party to court intelligence[45] – 'God knows where my wife gets all her pregnancies. I really do not know if this child is mine and if I ought to recognise it.'[46]

If the birth of Paul weakened Elizabeth's position in relation to Catherine,[47] it did little to curb her exuberant displays of power. Although the number of guests at court balls seldom exceeded 200, the feasts were extravagant. One particular delicacy, *pâté de Périgueux truffé – foie gras en croûte* – was carried overland to Elizabeth in crates of ice on carriages given diplomatic immunity as they passed through hostile Prussia. At court, a perennial favourite was the 'Empress Roast': a culinary *matryoshka* doll in which a lark was stuffed with olives and then stuffed into a quail, which was stuffed into a partridge, which was stuffed into a pheasant, which was stuffed into a capon, which was stuffed into a suckling pig – all intended for a single guest. There were four courses to a dinner, but each course contained between two and fifteen dishes. Such a selection was only meant to be sampled, and functioned primarily as a display of imperial wealth. Elizabeth had a sweet tooth and the tables were piled with pyramids of sweets surrounded by sugar ornaments or 'subtleties' for decoration – often small-scale versions of Petersburg landmarks.[48]

When the empress left the capital, the court went with her and St Petersburg became silent. When she returned, the capital became a theatre in which the saga of autocracy was played out and – under Elizabeth – kaleidoscoped into make-believe. The seductive deception of cross-dressing added one more strategy for escape and pandered to Elizabeth's vanity. The empress awarded herself the male Order of St Andrew, appointed herself colonel of five regiments, and captain of a grenadier company of the Preobrazhensky Guards.[49] Lord Hyndford witnessed her wearing the uniform of the guards and marvelled at the transformation: 'I am persuaded that those who had not known her, would, by her air, have taken her for an officer.'[50] Jonas Hanway observed that the empress appeared particularly impressive when sitting 'at the table with her officers, in regimentals as their colonel'.[51] The Grand Duchess Catherine recorded in her *Memoirs* that during transvestite masques:

> Most of the women resembled stunted little boys, and the eldest had fat, short legs that hardly flattered them. No women looked truly and perfectly good in men's clothing except the Empress herself; since she was very tall and had a somewhat powerful build, men's clothes suited her marvelously. She had more beautiful legs than I have ever seen on any man and admirably proportioned feet.[52]

With uncharacteristic generosity, Catherine added that Elizabeth 'dressed to perfection and everything she did had the same special grace whether she dressed as a man or a woman'.

During her reign, cross-dressing became implicated in a controversial diplomatic intrigue. A lawyer by training, Charles Geneviève Louis Auguste André Timothée d'Eon de Beaumont – Chevalier d'Eon for short – was a military officer, a skilled fencer and an authority on history, economics and politics. He was also recruited to the *Secret du Roi*, a group of agents employed by Louis XV of France. Above and beyond all that, the Chevalier d'Eon was one of the most infamous transvestites in history. He spent his first five decades largely as a man and his remaining thirty-two years largely as a woman, and he claimed that he used his feminine self – Lia de Beaumont – in espionage against Russia and England.

What a self-mythologising spy presents as truth is obscured by layers of deception, and d'Eon's autobiography plays with the ambiguities of transgendered life. One purpose behind his tale was to justify cross-dressing by demonstrating how it served the interests of his country. The chevalier concocted the story that he disguised himself as one of Empress Elizabeth's maids in order to gain access to her and inveigle her into making a secret alliance with France against Austria. When he was dining with Chancellor Vorontsov at Tsarskoe Selo during his first 'secret' mission to Russia, his host informed d'Eon that a French tutor in the empress's service was convinced that 'she knew you when you stayed with the Benedictine Sisters in the Royal Abbey of Noëford in Meaux' and that she remembered earrings and 'a small wine-coloured birthmark on the left cheek'. D'Eon record-ed, 'I blushed to the roots of my hair', sensing 'that this discovery would make my dragoon uniform lose its lustre'. Vorontsov confessed that he and his wife had spotted the birthmark and noticed d'Eon's pierced ears. Quick in his defence, d'Eon protest-ed that he had lately thrashed several German fencing masters and suggested that it is unlikely he developed such a skill with the sisters of Noëford. The French tutor, he added, was 'a drowsy, flighty girl who dreamed that the moon was made of green cheese'. Vorontsov was undeterred: 'If these suspicions are correct, as I suspect they are, you have nothing to fear in spite of your disguise . . . Your circumspection and knowledge would be very useful to the empress. Wear a dress once again and go off for only a month or two to the convent for well-born girls . . . and the position of reader will be yours.'[53] In fact d'Eon's work at the Russian court was straightforwardly diplomatic. During his two trips to St Petersburg he had three roles: political observer, agent of the *Secret du Roi* attempting to frustrate the impractical Anglo-Russian Subsidy Treaty, and secretary to the embassy. Nowhere in the French diplomatic archives does it state that d'Eon ever posed as a transvestite reader to the empress.[54]

Although Elizabeth was modestly educated and preferred dazzle and debauchery over scholarship, St Petersburg was becoming a centre for learning. The first Russian study of the city – a lengthy topographical description with illustrations – was produced between 1749 and 1751 by Andrei Bogdanov, assistant librarian at the Academy of Sciences. It claimed that Elizabeth's capital was so 'adorned and exalted with such glorious new buildings' that it was superior to many European cities 'renowned for their antiquity'. A growing nationalism was palpable. At the outset of Elizabeth's reign, Mikhail Lomonosov celebrated the overthrow of German influence with the kind of images that had been used to apotheosise Peter the Great. Son of an upwardly mobile fisherman from Arkhangelsk, Lomonosov became St Petersburg's leading *savant*, a giant of science and letters. He was, suggested Pushkin, 'our first university' – a chemist, geologist, grammarian, playwright, poet and creator of literary Russian. Centuries after his arrival in western Europe, Renaissance man appeared in Russia. Lomonosov founded the journal *Monthly Compositions* in 1755, in order to discuss issues raised by the Enlightenment – ideas that might help contour the kind of rationalised state of which Peter the Great had dreamed. Although Elizabeth could take little personal credit for these intellectual advances, in her capacity as a 'protector of science' she was held to embody the qualities of Minerva. During her reign the city was no longer just 'Petropolis', but – according to a panegyric written for her name-day in 1759 – 'ancient Rome, and ancient Athens'.[55] The dawn of a new and great culture broke while the court was hungover from the night before.

Anna had supported plans for an Academy of Arts, but these were rejected by the Academy of Sciences in 1733. It was only when Lomonosov fought for its creation that the Imperial Academy of the Liberal Arts of Painting, Sculpture and Architecture came into being in 1758. Part of Moscow University, the Imperial Academy was situated in St Petersburg – absurd as that may seem, the capital was where artists of calibre obtained commissions and where the best instructors could be found. Despite the institution's nationalistic aspirations, its first three teachers were a French painter, a French sculptor and a German engraver. Of its initial intake of thirty-eight pupils, eleven were from the nobility and twenty-seven were from the lower court and governmental ranks.[56] The 1750s saw other important developments in learning directed by Peter Shuvalov's cousin, Ivan, who became a kind of Minister of Education. Paving the way for Russia's military successes in the second half of the century, a second Cadet School was opened to replace the Naval Academy in 1752, and the Artillery and Engineers' schools were amalgamated in 1758. There was also an attempt to improve the quality of service at court when, in 1759, the Corps of Pages was set up to train young nobles.[57]

The city's sixth-largest flood occurred in October 1752, followed by a second, less dramatic one a few days later. That year, when Count Choglokov invited Catherine and her lover,

Sergei Saltykov, to hunt on his island in the Neva, the party had
just sat down to supper when 'a great wind arose at sea, which
made the water rise so considerably that it reached the bottom
of the stairs, and the island was covered in several feet of sea-
water'.[58] During Elizabeth's twenty-year reign, the city suffered
one-tenth of its total number of major floods. 'Sooner or later,'
suggested the Marquis de Custine when he visited early in the
following century, 'the water here will get the better of human
pride.'[59] There were also major fires in the poorer quarters during
the 1740s, clearing more slums. But for all the natural and man-
made catastrophes, the streets were becoming safer. Before
Empress Anna returned the court to St Petersburg there had been
a move to shut the brothels that did such a lively trade in a city
full of soldiers and sailors. But the problem had not been solved,
as the prostitutes merely plied their trade in taverns instead. So,
under Elizabeth, taverns were closed on the main thoroughfares
as part of the continuing fight against the sale of sex.[60] In 1750,
the city was rocked by a scandal in which a German madam,
Anna-Cunegonda Felker – known as 'Dresdensha' – bribed an
official in the Police Chancellery in order to run prostitution
outlets across the city: hot-spots offering music, dancing and a
selection of girls. Dresdensha attracted important clients such
as Prince Boris Golitsyn, Count Fyodor Apraksin and a number
of court officials. The investigation against the racket, led by
State Councillor Demidov, ended with 250 arrests. The guilty
were knouted, the prostitutes were sent to work in mills and
the foreigners were deported. After the success of his operation,
Demidov remarked how quiet the streets had become at night.[61]

During the day, however, there was steadily increasing activity.
The early-morning streets saw the arrival of maids from neigh-
bouring villages carrying their milk in cool, decorated birch-bark
and earthenware pots. In the cold weather, hawkers roamed the
streets selling *zbiten*, a cheap, steaming drink made from honey,
spices and hot water.[62] All over the capital, merchants set up

*View down the Nevsky from the Fontanka in the mid-eighteenth century.*
*The Anichkov Palace is on the left.*

small tables and sold soup, *pierogis, blinis* and *kvas* – that working man's brew of fermented meal, malt and bread.[63] Markets were operating in different quarters, and the wholesale flour trade operated from barges moored on the outskirts of the city near the Alexander Nevsky Monastery.[64] From there, flour was reloaded onto smaller boats for distribution to the large number of shops or stalls selling loaves, buns and pastries. Fish barques – with reservoirs for fresh fish in their holds – were moored on the Neva and along the canals.[65] In the coldest months, fish pulled from the water would freeze within seconds.

The city's industry, which had previously been devoted to the manufacture of indifferent building material, began to produce luxury items when the Lomonosov Imperial Porcelain Factory opened in 1744. It produced tableware for the court with monochrome motifs, and used gold leaf beaten down from coins in the imperial treasury. The empress became anxious about the number of hazardous factories in the centre of her capital – among them an armaments foundry and a munitions plant, which she banished to the outskirts in the mid-1750s.[66] Elsewhere in the empire, heavy industry and manufacturing grew prodigiously, using the involuntary labour of serfs or assigned peasants; but in St Petersburg it was trade with Europe that continued to dominate business.

As Elizabeth approached fifty, the age at which her father had died, the blur of glitter and gossip was taking its toll. She was in constant abdominal pain. Her face was swollen. She was seen less and less. Ravaged by sex, superstition and drink – self-indulgence on a grand scale – she died in December 1761. Although the centre of St Petersburg had been mapped out, many of its landmark buildings had yet to be built, and the next stage of this city's precocious development would be accomplished under the influence of a prodigious empress who would refine the court and capital.

The Grand Duchess Catherine had a vested interest in painting a particularly dire portrait of her husband – the heir apparent – in her *Memoirs*, yet much of what she wrote was confirmed by others. Catherine judiciously understood that life presented her with the choice of 'perishing with him, or by him, or else saving' herself, her children, 'and perhaps the state from the disaster that all this Prince's moral and physical faculties promised'. From the age of ten, Peter had been fond of drink and swiftly became an incurable alcoholic. Attendants found it impossible to prevent him drinking and, in his debilitated state, the only teacher to make a mark was 'Landé who taught him to dance'. Peter loved toys and dolls, and mounted 'insipid' spectacles with marionettes. Catherine noted that he arranged all his toy soldiers on very narrow tables to which pliable brass strips were fixed. When these were twanged, they sounded like gunshots, and Peter celebrated 'court ceremonies by making these troops shoot their rifles'. He enacted a changing of the guard with these toys every day, attending the parade – Catherine wrote – 'in uniform with boots, spurs, high collar, and scarf, and those servants admitted to this lovely exercise were obliged to dress in the same manner'.[67] At Oranienbaum in the summer, Peter drilled servants in Holstein uniforms and expressed a dangerous admiration for Russia's enemy, Frederick the Great of Prussia.[68]

Sexually cold towards Catherine, Peter developed a great lust for the Countess Elizabeth Vorontsova, who spat, stank, had a squint and was covered with smallpox scars. More positively, she loved to drink and exhibited a great eagerness for sex with the high-pitched, lank-haired grand duke. When she was replaced by Madame Teplova, Peter stuffed his rooms with military paraphernalia, in a desire to give the new woman pleasure. He also proved to be something of a voyeur, drilling holes through a locked door so that he could enjoy Empress Elizabeth's amorous moments with Razumovsky and invite his entourage to share in 'this indiscreet pleasure'.[69]

Clearly, Peter was to make an unworthy occupant of the throne of All Russia. For one whole winter he became absorbed by plans 'to build a country house near Oranienbaum in the form of a Capuchin monastery', where he, Catherine and their court would dress as monks and nuns. When Catherine discovered a large rat that Peter had 'hanged with all the ceremony of an execution', and asked what it meant, the grand duke replied that the 'rat had committed a criminal act and merited the ultimate punishment according to military laws . . . it had climbed atop the ramparts of a cardboard fortress on a table in this room and eaten two papier-mâché sentries standing watch on one of the bastions'. Catherine could not keep herself from 'bursting with laughter for the extreme folly of the thing'.[70]

Russia was to be saved from its disastrous new tsar by a political act that was becoming so familiar it could almost be taken as a new norm: the coup. Meanwhile, Peter – plastered at Elizabeth's funeral – kept interrupting the service by shrieking with laughter and sticking his tongue out at the priests.[71]

# 6

# THE CITY TRANSFORMED

## *1762–96*

'We have eight months of winter, and four months of bad weather,' quipped Russia's fourth empress, Catherine[1] – called 'the Great' not only to mark her flirtation with the Enlightenment and her impressive territorial gains, but also to stamp her in the same mould as the founder of St Petersburg. Peter's greatness broached the improbable. Catherine's greatness emblazoned the capital's first unsteady century. Yet, however much the fortunes of the city had ebbed and flowed since Peter's first landfall, its weather remained constant: – 'rude . . . unsettled and unfriendly'. A cold wind blew up the Gulf of Finland, only to be ambushed by the savage blast that came howling out of Siberia. Winter could start on 1 November and not abate until mid-April. 'Cold! Desperately cold!' grumbled William Richardson, who was travelling with Lord Cathcart, England's Ambassador Extraordinary to the Empress of Russia. Richardson recorded a temperature of −32° on the Réaumur Scale in March 1771 – a challenging −40° Celsius. With a low so extreme, in a month associated with the spring equinox, it is hardly surprising that the writer took pains to emphasise the brevity of Petersburg's mildest season: 'the weeks, you will observe I don't say months, of the summer'.[2] Short perhaps, but intense, and the mosquitoes were 'agonising'. Knowledgeable travellers offered advice on the subject: when 'the gnat is fixed, it is better to allow it to take its belly full of blood, and go away. If it is killed upon the spot, some part of the proboscis frequently remains in the wound, and causes more acute pains than would be felt otherwise.' But the insects were soon gone. Winter – at that latitude – came with 'awful rapidity': 'you take farewell of Summer at night and hail the grim tyrant in the morning'. The Neva delta became 'one crystalline mass', and a visitor from the capital could speed to Kronstadt along the carriage road marked out over the frozen gulf on ice as 'smooth and level as a bowling green'. Once there, he would find the Russian Navy 'firmly bound in the harbour, dismantled of its rigging, and hung round with icicles'.[3]

In St Petersburg, pedestrians skidded on the slippery cobbles in hasty and 'perpetual flight' from the wild driving of more than 4,000 winter cabbies – a rough and rowdy bunch of peasants from the surrounding countryside – who, unable to work their frost-bound land, brought horses into Petersburg to drive the droshkies they hired out for a mere kopek a ride. Passengers were smacked and sliced by the sharp air, as the drivers raced against their competitors. Ladies did benefit from the protection of 'paint inch thick', which – if it did nothing for their beauty – prevented 'them from being frost-bitten'. Male vanity, by contrast, almost doomed those who were afflicted: 'A Russian beau of the first magnitude despises warm dress, as it spoils his shapes – he struts in silk stockings, a hat and cockade; and, as often as the cold will permit, he throws his fur coat aside, to display his silk breeches, and satin vest.'[4] During the freeze, the nobility and the grandest merchants placed their coaches on special 'sledge-frames', the number of horses in harness determined by the owner's rank – from six for a chancellor or field marshal down to one for a humble merchant. Dignitaries would keep their attendants waiting out in the arctic air for ten hours, huddled over braziers

*Ice hills on the frozen Neva and 'whirligig chairs' at a summer fair, c. 1807.*

which scorched their hands and faces and left their limbs numb. During the winter of 1781, two coachmen died while awaiting their master.[5]

On the frozen Neva at Epiphany, a carpeted walkway led from the Winter Palace to a temple made of gilded wood and crowned with a cross. It was there that Casanova saw children being baptised in a hole cut through the ice below. He watched, horrified, as a baby slipped through the priest's hands into oblivion, and was much surprised to find the parents in 'an ecstasy of joy . . . certain that the babe had been carried straight to heaven'.[6] The ice-crusted Neva also hosted huge and splendid fairs where people hurtled down steeply angled ice-hills, ten metres tall. Lying in the lap of a practised guide who leaned back with his arms outstretched, the intrepid skittered down the glassy surface on a round toboggan, gathering speed, yelping with fright trying to catch a gulp of gelid air. Between these artificial hills there were railed-in race courses where punters placed bets.[7] The Empress Catherine, escorted by hussars, drove through the crowd in a sledge to observe her subjects, too busy 'drinking, singing and laughing' to fight. Constrained by the extreme cold, the revellers did 'not tipple for hours', but swallowed 'as much in two or three minutes as completely does the business they came about'[8] and then went on their way.

Such festivities enlivened the long winter months for the many workers who kept the city going – the *dvorniki* and the *budochniki* being among the most visible. The *dvornik* was an essential factotum for all prosperous families. He would fetch water, clean the yard, open the gate, light the lamps, turn the spit and, in cold weather, chop wood and monitor the ovens that warmed the house. These heaters were vast contraptions four metres high by two metres wide and worked by virtue of a valve that was closed when the wood burned down to charcoal. If a careless servant shut this valve before the wood had fully charred, then, as Casanova observed, 'the master sleeps his last sleep, being suffocated in three or four hours. When the door is opened in the morning he is found dead, and the poor devil of a servant is immediately hanged, whatever he may say . . . a necessary regulation, or else a servant would be able to get rid of his master on the smallest provocation'.[9]

The responsibilities of the *dvornik* did not end with his domestic chores. It was also his duty to assist in fighting city fires, sweep the streets around his master's property and inform the police when a guest arrived – either from the country or from abroad.[10] *Dvorniki* were aided in their civic duties by the *budochniki* – watchmen armed with halberds – who manned circular wooden shelters on major street corners and struck the half-hours on a board or triangle of iron. In winter, such booths provided little protection against the piercing wind. Outside major establishments, guard boxes were altogether warmer, being built of granite and roofed with iron.[11]

In 1763, a small fire-fighting branch of the police force was established, but home owners were still obliged to provide fire-watchers and fighters from their domestic staff when the need arose. Indeed, throughout the 1760s and '70s, proprietors had a multitude of civic responsibilities, as there were few policemen patrolling and civic funding was erratic. That changed somewhat in 1780, with a report entitled 'Concerning the City of Petersburg', a precursor of the important 1785 Charter of the Towns, which recommended management of urban affairs by representative bodies. However, St Petersburg's City Council or Duma, which first took office in 1786,[12] gained full control of the city's finances only in 1803, and until that time diverse sources of income were sought. A portion of customs revenue, as well as taxes on craftsmen, alcohol and public bathhouses, were used to finance improvements to the city streets, maintain the canals, build new sewers and clean and light important thoroughfares. By 1785 there were more than 3,000 globular lamps fixed on wooden posts in the centre city, and military recruits, seconded to the police, swelled the ranks of the lamplighters.[13]

Chimney sweeps moved from house to house. Dog-catchers scoured the streets. Coopers circulated and – using only a hatchet – repaired the casks and utensils of householders. *Kalatchniks* wandered through the city, selling bread made from the superior 'Moscow flour'.[14] Farmers journeyed to the city to sell their goods directly, although there was no shortage of middle-men keen to muscle in and rake off a profit. Since Anna's reign, each quarter of the capital had enjoyed its own market, but the city's most important bazaar remained the *gostiny dvor* – or 'merchant's yard' – near the Admiralty. Destroyed by fire in 1782, it was rebuilt on the Nevsky as a two-storey brick and plaster structure, containing many shops under its pillared galleries. With the concentration of trading came the problem of monopolisation. Among the traders, twenty-two men owned 451 of the 1,204 stalls in the *gostiny dvor*. During the 1780s one man – Savva Yakovlev – owned 9 per cent of all outlets.[15] In an echo of her father's encounter with Menshikov, Elizabeth had been so entranced when she heard the sweet cries of Yakovlev selling meat pies that she ordered him to make pies for the palace, thereby launching his business empire.

Each spring, peasants arrived from far afield to hire a piece of land on which to cultivate vegetables to sell to the city.[16] Blocks of ice from the winter freeze were installed in house cellars to store fresh produce purchased during the summer. In the winter, greens, fruit, meat and fish were sold frozen at the Great Market on the newly commercialised section of Nevsky Prospekt stretching towards the Alexander Nevsky Monastery. Thousands of skinned, rock-hard animals were piled according to their kind, with a sample carcass left standing to indicate the identity of each frozen heap. Others were packed tightly together, on their hind legs, as if the beasts were rearing, desperate to flee after being flayed alive. In complete contrast to these scalped carcasses, a gaudy throng of vibrantly dressed patrons – everybody from the imperial family right down to simple merchants – came to purchase frozen food that was one-third cheaper than the fresh produce offered in other markets.[17] If a customer wanted only a portion of the beast, the vendor would hack it off with a hatchet, sending splinters of frozen flesh flying in all directions.[18] Customers returned home with their frozen purchases and thawed them in cold water prior to cooking.

Early on in Catherine's reign, luxury items began to be sold in private shops and houses.[19] The legality of this practice was questionable, but when a prosecution was brought against a Frenchman in 1766, he won the right to trade from home. About a hundred merchants swiftly followed suit. Craftsmen and vendors advertised in the *Vedomosti* and word-of-mouth also carried news of talented artisans and well-stocked shops. Signs, regulated in size and style, were permitted in the better streets and – with artisans allowed to live and work near their wealthy clients – the city centre became more commercial. By 1789 it was estimated that there were more than 1,000 tailors – 840 of them Russian. There were 149 barbers to trim the whiskers of the vain young men, and sixty-four hairdressers to tend the ever-complicated locks of the ladies.[20] Independent vendors scattered across the city began to compete successfully with the monopolies and bazaars. But in these early days of commercialisation there were confusions. During the 1790s there were four independent establishments trading under the name 'The English Shop' – their business booming, after Catherine's ban on the import of post-Revolution French goods in May 1793. One of the shops was run by Mrs Sarah Snow, who advertised her wares in the *Vedomosti*: English fabrics, millinery and notions, as well as household items, toys, 'sporting weapons' and 'the latest editions of English books'. Other English shops sold brass and pewter, as well as wall clocks that were advertised as 'playing various attractive arias'. Merchants from all over the world settled in

St Petersburg, but the British were predominant, satisfying the craze for English products. Indeed, demand was so great that unscrupulous tradesmen tried to pass off Russian imitations, just as street vendors do today with Asian Hermès fakes. Hatchett's of Long Acre in London was appointed imperial coach-maker and supplied not only Catherine, but also members of the nobility, such as the spendthrift Prince Grigory Potempkin.[21] There were English grooms to teach the English style of riding, as hundreds of English horses were imported each year. Anglophilia spilled over into entertainment when Mr Fisher's Company of English Actors performed in the Russian capital from the autumn of 1770 until early 1772. With 'great diligence and much tinsel', the players refurbished an old barn beside a merchant's house on the Moika and made it into 'the likeness of a theatre', in which they acted Shakespeare as well as popular contemporary plays. Catherine herself made an impromptu visit to watch the company,[22] which sadly broke up when the actors started quarrelling. There was also an English Inn, which offered that rare treat, coffee; an English Club, where billiards and cards were played; and the esoteric and erotic Most Puissant Order of The Beggar's Benison and Merryland – a select British club indulging in salacious readings, voyeurism and masturbation.[23]

In 1762, the capital had witnessed yet another dynastic drama when Catherine, exasperated by the drunken foolery of her husband, Peter III, felt compelled to reign in his place. She had the nerve, the will and the support to rule. But there were, against any claim she might make, two legitimate heirs to the throne: Peter III and Ivan VI, both grandsons of Russian tsars. Catherine – from Anhalt-Zerbst-Dornburg – was merely the niece of Empress Elizabeth's long-dead fiancé. She had, however, been living in St Petersburg for seventeen years by the time her unsound, pro-Prussian husband became Peter III. While he wished to get rid of Catherine and her son, Paul, there were powerful factions at court who baulked at the idea of being ruled by someone considered, in many quarters, to be a treacherous ninny. Catherine's lover, Grigory Orlov – aided by his brothers – won the crucial support of the Preobrazhensky and Izmailovsky Guards, and the action began. The empress described the manoeuvre in a letter to her former lover, Count Stanislas Poniatowsky of Poland – written to dissuade him from coming to the Russian capital while matters were 'in a state of ferment':

> Peter III lost what little intelligence he ever had. He shocked and offended everyone . . . I was sleeping peacefully at Peterhof at six in the morning of the 28th. Alexei Orlov came in very calmly and said, 'All is ready for the proclamation, you must get up.'[24]

The conspirators proceeded to the Winter Palace, where the Senate and Synod were assembled along with 14,000 troops, while Peter – as Catherine informed Poniatowsky – 'abdicated in perfect freedom at Oranienbaum'. Yet, even before that letter was written, 'We Catherine II by the grace of God, Empress', gave out the following statement:

> The 7th day after our accession to the throne of all the Russias, we received information, that the late Emperor Peter III by means of a bloody accident in his hinder parts, commonly called piles, to which he had been formerly subject, obtained a most violent, griping, cholick . . . to our great regret and affliction we learned yesterday evening, that by the permission of the Almighty, the late Emperor departed this life.[25]

'Bloody accident'? Allegedly without Catherine's knowledge, Peter was strangled and poisoned by the Orlovs.

Having dealt with Peter in 1762, there was another skeleton in the closet. Ivan VI had been imprisoned at Schlüsselberg since 1756 and Catherine visited him when she took the throne. How great, she wrote, 'was our surprise! When, besides a defect in his utterance, that was uneasy to himself, and rendered his discourse almost unintelligible to others, we observed in him a total privation of sense and reason.'[26] She decided to leave him where he was. Two summers later, in 1764, when there was a plot to put him on the throne, Ivan was murdered.[27] The court behaved as if nothing had happened – apart from arranging the suppression of a play written in Hamburg, *Innocence Oppressed, or The Death of Ivan, Emperor of Russia*.[28] Yet usurpation would haunt Catherine throughout her reign, despite much support and soft words. The Senate – five years after her coup – pressed her to accept the titles 'the Wise, the Great, and Mother of the Fatherland'. Catherine replied with characteristic wit and acumen, 'only God is Wise; my progeny will appraise my greatness; as for the Mother of the Fatherland? I would rather say: I love you and want to be loved.'[29]

In Catherine's devious, self-justifying and thrice-revised *Memoirs* the Russian court appears as a place of bickering and politicking. As grand duchess, she was constantly bowed at, bobbed at. Her statements were endlessly dissected by mischievous courtiers, and her every movement scrutinised by foreign diplomats. But while there were customs and ceremonies that could not be escaped, there was a marked change in the tone of the court when she took the throne. The excessive indulgence of Elizabeth's reign was replaced by a measured grandeur and a tacit assertion of Catherine's industry and devotion to the intellectual prosperity and administrative well-being of Russia. Her coronation may have outdone that of her predecessors, and her triumphal arrival in St Petersburg in 1763 may have been extravagant,[30] but thenceforth there was a noticeable relaxation of pomp in Catherine's court, though it remained 'vast and colossal'.

The empress rose at six, lit her own fire and had a modest breakfast of toast and strong coffee *mit schlag*. She read and wrote till eight, when an adviser came to read her the news. After numerous court interviews, Catherine ate lunch.[31] As she preferred fatty foods, gastronomes were reluctant guests. Then, after a little private time with her current favourite – an interval known to court gossips as the 'Time of Mystery' – the empress worked on diligently through the afternoon. One face of the commemorative medal struck to mark her accession showed Catherine in the double capacity of warrior and wise woman – a helmeted Minerva. The medal's obverse showed the empress taking her crown from a kneeling figure representing St Petersburg.[32] By 1770, secretly disparaging Peter the Great's achievements, her own spectacular transformation of his city was taking on mythical status. She amassed a treasure trove of art and commissioned magnificent buildings. In a translation of Virgil's *Aeneid*, Vasily Petrov – follower of Lomonosov and librarian to Catherine II – evoked 'miserable hovels' being replaced by 'the splendour of the city'. Virgil was talking about Dido's triumph at Carthage. Petrov was talking about Dido *and* Catherine. The capital became the most visible manifestation of her greatness, as Catherine's 'splendour' trumped Peter the Great's 'hovels'. The Cameo Service that Catherine ordered for her favourite, Grigory Potempkin, included a table decoration with a bust of the empress, again as Minerva, goddess of wisdom. For his part, Potempkin gave Catherine a service in which she was celebrated as Dido.[33]

Catherine's disarming desire to bridge the gap between court and capital was visible in her habit of driving about St Petersburg after dark in an open sledge, virtually unattended.[34] Subjects – if they were suitably dressed – were welcome to visit imperial parks. The Summer Garden was open to people from the upper levels of society, who could enjoy its tree-lined alleys and fountains and consume the non-alcoholic juices on sale.[35] Towns-people were also invited to share in the celebrations of the court. Balls on public occasions staged 'separate entertainments to different classes; to the first class of nobility, then the second, the military . . . and the merchants last'. Catherine was indefatigable. The French Ambassador, the Comte de Ségur, observed her flaming pink cheeks – the consequence of kissing the over-rouged faces of merchants' wives.[36] When Casanova rented accommodation in the smart Millionnaya, his landlord gave him a ticket to a court reception – a masked ball for 5,000 people, which lasted no fewer than sixty hours. He was impressed by Russian court spectacles and marvelled at the huge amphitheatre designed by Antonio Rinaldi for a medieval joust in Palace Square, which took place in June and July 1766. It was opened by Russian Amazons – ladies from all the best families – in chariots.[37] As the empress observed the pageant from the palace, spectators crowded into the amphitheatre or crouched on nearby rooftops. And on the occasion of an imperial marriage, a *'cocagne'* was set up in the same square. It consisted of two reservoirs holding 36,000 litres of red and white wine, which fountained into huge basins. Above, scaffolding pyramids supported shelves laden with loaves 'of bread, roasted fowls, geese, ducks, hams, &c.' and 'at the top of the pyramid, a whole roasted bullock' covered with crimson damask, so that only its head and gilded horns were visible. Guarded by police until the moment the imperial family appeared on the balcony of the Winter Palace, the cordon surrounding the *cocagne* was then dropped. From that moment, the bullock's head was targeted with food and the first person to hit home won a prize. Ammunition that missed its mark fell and bobbed in the wine until it was consumed, sodden with alcohol.[38]

In political terms, Catherine fell far short of her expressed desire to be an empress for the people. The nineteenth-century thinker Alexander Herzen noted sharply that 'Russia and the people' were absent from her *Memoirs*.[39] But Catherine possessed

the talent – witnessed by numerous observers, including
Casanova – for 'pleasing by her geniality and her wit, and also
by that exquisite tact which made one forget the awfulness of the
sovereign in the gentleness of the woman'.[40] Care replaced empty
ostentation, as the maternal love of the empress for her subjects
became the avowed measure of the new reign.

There was, nonetheless, a good deal of licentiousness at a court
where liaisons were either politically motivated or mere sport.
The Earl of Pembroke wrote in a letter from the capital that 'the
Narishkin girls are married ere this and fucking about Petersburg like rabbits'.[41] The preference for intrigue and dalliance
over tenderness and affection is recorded in the sensational and
anonymously published memoirs of Charles François Philibert
Masson: 'Almost all the ladies of the Court kept men, with the
title and office of favourites. I do not say lovers, for that would
imply sentiment, while theirs was merely gross desire'.[42] The
visitor John Richard observed that circulating libraries, 'those
seminaries of gallantry' were 'as yet unknown here, nor are love
letters the study of *beaus* or *belles* . . . In short, love seems here
a passion of instinct.'[43]

To an extent, this was the case with Catherine, who took an
undetermined number of lovers – somewhere between twelve and
fifty – all of whom were judiciously examined by her physician.[44]
Catherine was an exceptional woman in an exceptional position, and her cravings were perhaps driven by pressure as much
as by desire. In flight from a loveless marriage, she indulged in
the delights and anguishes of a succession of affairs. She was
devastated by the infidelity of men such as Sergei Saltykov and
Grigory Orlov, her lover for twelve years.[45] In 1773, she began
her brief but supremely important liaison with Grigory Potempkin, ten years her junior. Potempkin was more than a favourite,
and Catherine relied on him until his death in 1791.[46] Possibly
her secret husband, the prince became viceroy of southern Russia
and one of the country's great military statesmen. The empress

obviously enjoyed the intrigue of their affair: 'Behave cleverly in public, and that way no one will know what we are thinking. I so enjoy being crafty!'[47]

Catherine wanted to improve the infrastructure of her capital and initiate architectural projects that would add to its majesty. She had early experience of the dangerous deficiencies of local building when, as a nineteen-year-old guest of Alexei Razumovsky at nearby Gostilitsa, she was almost killed. Lodged on the third floor of a wooden outbuilding, the grand duchess awoke to find the stone foundation blocks giving way and – as the building began to shake and totter – she was lifted to safety by a human chain of servants.[48] Not so lucky were the twenty domestics and workers who were killed. After such a scare, Catherine energetically addressed the problem of building in the capital, with legislation and cash. Thirty thousand roubles were given to rebuild the hemp warehouse that was destroyed in the year before she took the throne.[49] In December 1762, the Commission for the Masonry Construction of St Petersburg and Moscow was created, to make these cities more solid and habitable. At the outset of Catherine's reign, wooden houses outnumbered masonry structures by nearly nine to one. By the time Catherine died, the ratio was just two to one, with the highest concentration of stone structures near the centre – close to the Winter Palace in the First Admiralty Quarter, where three- or four-storey structures were becoming common.

The canals and a large stretch of the Neva's bank were clad in granite to help the city rise above the perpetual flooding. Eight vaulted bridges over the Fontanka replaced the previous wooden structures,[50] but there was almost no building in the boggy lands to the north of the city or on the western end of Vasilevsky Island. As for the built-up eastern portion, the Scottish traveller Andrew Swinton found the canals, which still ran through the middle of

some streets in the late 1780s, to be foul in the summer, just as
they had been forty years earlier.[51] As for the surrounding houses,
those that had burned down in the great fire of 1736 had not been
rebuilt – desolation compounded by another fire, which destroyed
a further 140 houses on the island in May 1771. St Petersburg
was still far from being the uninterrupted urban mass that we
recognise as a city. There were many open spaces for kitchen gardens, and about 20,000 cows grazed in the capital.

Under Catherine, a number of new, intelligently situated factories were established and private ownership began to replace
some state monopolies. Manufacturing processes that were
highly flammable were sited on the outskirts, and tanneries
were moved downriver so as not to further pollute the Neva.
There were closures due to lack of funding, stock surplus and
because Russian produce was considered inferior. The College
of Medicine – which supervised apothecaries and hospitals –
demanded that instruments be made of English or German steel.
The city was controlled by such bodies: the College of Commerce
monitored honesty and hygiene in the markets; the College of War
supervised the sentry booths on street corners; and the Admiralty
was responsible for that impossible task – flood prevention.[52]

A foundling home was set up in the capital in 1770. Corporal
punishment was forbidden and, despite high rates of infant
mortality, eyewitnesses testified to the fact that pupils of both
sexes emerged with vastly increased prospects. France and
England provided models for noble and charitable education,
while the Austrian system became the model for a proposed
national school system during the 1770s and '80s, when Russia
took its first tiny steps towards general education. Teachers
were trained and textbooks produced, but the number of pupils
remained low. In the capital, interest among the city's artisans
and minor officials – a group whose children would have most to
gain from such an education – was slight. However, the boarding
establishment for noble girls that Catherine established at the

Smolny survived until the Revolution, and a sister school was attached to it for girls from the lower orders, who were provided with twelve years of lodging and education. The satirist and philanthropist Nikolai Novikov, a tireless publisher of abrasive magazines, launched one to help fund a charity school in the capital. Ironically, the school attracted more funding and ended up paying for the periodical[53] – one of the many publications that enabled satirical voices to be heard for the first time in Russia. Remarkably, one such voice belonged to the empress herself. Catherine secretly supported, subsidised and even wrote for these fly-by-night journals, which were loosely modelled on Addison and Steele's London *Spectator*. As a result of Catherine's approval of private presses in January 1783, around 400 Russian-language books and periodicals were published each year – more than one-third of them by Novikov.[54] During the early 1790s, in the wake of the French Revolution when written attacks on autocracy were less welcome, Novikov was incarcerated without trial and his presses shut down. But during the twenty-year heyday of Catherine's 'enlightenment', intellectual renegades had a certain freedom to attack the injustices of Russian life and – being hot-headed young men – each other.[55] However precariously, Grub Street had come to St Petersburg.

Apart from her mocking and subversive squibs, Catherine was a prodigious writer. Fluent in German, French and Russian, she compiled a secular *Russian Primer for the Instruction of Youth*, which became a best-seller. She was a tireless correspondent with some of the finest minds of the century, including Voltaire, Diderot and Baron von Grimm – editor of the French *Correspondance littéraire, philosophique et politique* – who became Catherine's informant in Paris.[56] Early on in her reign she funded the Society for the Translation of Foreign Books. Among the volumes published in Russian there was a spectacular absence of theology and a predominance of classics, English literature and works of political science, which were so important to Catherine's avowed desire for reform. Russia's first dictionary began to appear in 1788[57] – only three decades after Dr Johnson published his groundbreaking work in London.

Catherine's intellectual sweep was wide, if not always profound. Like the thriving international port that was her capital, she was a channel through which the best of contemporary civilisation and culture came to Russia. Within two weeks of ascending the throne, the empress invited Denis Diderot to Petersburg to finish his great *Encyclopédie*. German writers such as Gotthold Lessing and Christian Gellert were widely read.[58] Sheridan and Molière were performed. French, Italian and Scottish architects arrived. European paintings were bought in bulk, ideas and artefacts were amassed, and a growing network of connections abroad helped secure the men and masterpieces necessary to make the Russian capital great among the cities of the world. One significant early translation was Jean-Jacques Rousseau's huge success, *La Nouvelle Héloïse*. In this epistolary novel the hero, Saint-Preux, writes to his alpine sweetheart about the frisson he experiences as he plunges into the bewildering spin of Paris. He becomes lost in a whirl of conflicting opinions, where 'nothing is shocking because everyone is accustomed to everything'. He is disturbed by 'all the things that strike' him, yet finds that nothing holds his heart. He seeks something tangible, but finds only phantoms.[59] It is telling that Heinrich von Storch, in his lengthy survey of St Petersburg at the end of Catherine's reign, should talk about the Russian capital in terms clearly borrowed from Rousseau's vision of Paris: 'Even those unsettled characters who attach themselves to everything and adhere to nothing, who detest today what filled them with transports yesterday, who are pleased everywhere and nowhere – even these find their proper station here.'[60] Both writers were describing the upsetting sensation of 'modernity'. As with Paris, the speed, noise and challenge of modernity would rattle St Petersburg over the course of the next 150 years, as the driving energy of the city moved from the court to the street.

Diderot travelled to Petersburg in 1773. Alexei Naryshkin had met him while taking the waters in Aix-la-Chapelle and flattered the philosopher into sharing his carriage all the way to the Russian capital. It proved to be an unhappy visit. Diderot's politics had become more radical, while Catherine's monarchy had been challenged by rebellion. Nonetheless, daily meetings were scheduled for three in the afternoon, during which the empress and the Frenchman discussed literature, philosophy and economy as well as social and legal questions. Diderot was pushing 'enlightenment', but Catherine exercised – as Voltaire put it in a letter to the mathematician and physicist Jean le Rond d'Alembert – 'the most despotic power on earth'. She was not about to relinquish one iota, on the urging of a dangerous French *philosophe*. To add to his ideological frustration, Diderot was out of sorts – a victim of the cold and the infected water of the Neva, host to the parasite *Giardia lamblia*, which has given cramps and diarrhoea to generations of the city's visitors and inhabitants. No ambassador for French fashion, Diderot seemed uncomfortable at court balls in his single mean black suit, and became the butt of jokes. On one occasion he was approached and asked, 'If a plus b to the power of n over z equals x – therefore God exists. Reply!' Diderot declined.[61]

The *encyclopédiste* performed one important service for Catherine, which left its mark on her capital. Diderot recommended his friend Étienne Falconet to sculpt what has become the iconic image of St Petersburg.[62] The project revealed Catherine's wish to associate herself publicly with Peter the Great, and it was her good fortune that Elizabeth had cut the funding for a proposed equestrian statue of her father by the Rastrellis.[63] Their project, which leaned too heavily on traditional civic monuments, would have been academic and unremarkable. By contrast, Falconet wrote to Diderot that he didn't wish his monument to express 'the victor over Charles XII but . . . the person of the founder, legislator, benefactor of his country'.[64] Falconet's aim was to express the youth of an emperor who proclaimed a new era in Russian history – an era that Catherine was busy consolidating. As the empress wanted not only to celebrate Peter, but also to boost her own image, she carefully monitored the evolution of Falconet's thinking[65] and brought together the names of Peter and Catherine on the brief legend that she composed for the statue's wild and unusual plinth.

The fifty-year-old sculptor travelled to St Petersburg with his eighteen-year-old pupil, Marie-Anne Collot. Possibly his mistress and certainly the wife of his son, Collot was an accomplished sculptress who was credited by Falconet himself with being responsible for the head of what has become known as *The Bronze Horseman*[66] – perhaps a ploy to silence scandal, by suggesting that Collot was a collaborator and not just Falconet's alarmingly young lover.

When a model for the statue was exhibited in 1770, Falconet became concerned by the cross-winds in Senate Square, where his commission was to be sited. The snake was added at this point to provide another stabilising contact between the pedestal and the statue.[67] Seven years later the actual bronze was successfully cast, but the following year Falconet returned to France and never saw his statue in place. The plinth on which it stood was a mammoth rock found in the Karelian wastes, over which Peter had exerted his mastery when he established Petersburg. The transport of the rock was itself a triumph of science over nature. Ivan Betskoy – director of the Bureau of Imperial Buildings and Gardens, who was in charge of the statue project – had a Greek aide-de-camp, Captain Marin Carburi de Ceffalonie. This man, who would be murdered by embittered workers on his native island of Cephalonia, had been forced to flee Venice in 1759 for slashing the face of a woman who resisted his advances and came to St Petersburg possibly as a spy for the Venetian Republic.[68] When a suitably impressive stone was found about thirteen kilometres from the capital, it was Carburi de Ceffalonie, aided

*Transporting the 'thunder rock', 1777.*

by the architect Yuri Felten, who engineered its shipping to Senate Square. The 138-tonne rock had to be excavated and then hoisted onto a rolling platform, to carry it down to the shore of the Gulf of Finland. By March 1770, after some false starts, it was rolled onto a huge raft, which was towed by two ships to the quay fronting Senate Square. Absurdly, after all the effort, the rock – originally twelve metres long and six metres high – was chiselled away until it was nearly halved. Contemporaries found it 'a little rock under a great horse',[69] 'almost too small for proportion'.[70] In fact the relationship is perfect, and skilful cutting made it appear like a wave. With its forward and upward thrust, the rock propels the emperor – poised with latent power on his horse – into action.

The statue was unveiled in August 1782, the year that marked the centenary of Ivan and Peter the Great's joint accession. The city shook with gun salutes, drum rolls and trumpet voluntaries. As the scaffolding that had concealed the statue clattered to the ground, a figure darted out from the crowd and fell prostrate before the rearing figure. Catherine was alarmed by the athletic intruder until it was discovered that he was an octogenarian who had served under Peter and – with his old naval uniform flapping loose from his ageing body – had come to pay his last respects.

The man was given a pension by the empress and died when he reached 100.[71]

The motto – 'To Peter I from Catherine II' – appeared in Latin on the western side and in Russian on the eastern side of the 'thunder rock', so-called because it was said to have been split by lightning. The outstretched arm of the emperor expressed 'parental affection for his people',[72] a sentiment that was pleasing to Catherine. In a letter to Melchior Grimm she observed that Peter 'had a look of contentment which . . . encouraged me to do better in the future'.[73]

As the cultural and political significance of *The Bronze Horseman* remains unsurpassed by any other Petersburg monument, it is both predictable and apt that such a defining symbol of the city was created by a foreigner. A few years after its inauguration, Eleanor Cavanagh, an Irish maid to the visiting Catherine Wilmot, was not the first nor the last person to be terrified by Falconet's work: 'I thought the screech wou'd have choak'd me when turning round my head what wou'd I see leaping over a rail rock but a giant of a man on the back of a dragin of a horse.'[74]

*Falconet's* The Bronze Horseman, *detail.*

The impact of the statue reverberated through the lives and works of poets, novelists and activists, who explored the positive and negative repercussions of Peter the Great's act of hubris. The 1825 Decembrist revolt against tsarist absolutism would take inspiration from Falconet's vision of benevolent might. A decade later Alexander Pushkin praised Peter while questioning his legacy, in a vision of *The Bronze Horseman* come alive and riding rough-shod over the lives of Petersburg's inhabitants. Seventy years on, the novelist Andrei Biely would use the statue as a symbol of the dangerous divisions facing Russia in 1905. Falconet's *Bronze Horseman* patrolled 'the borders not only of political fact but also political imagination'. The statue was part of the capital's 'official architecture', which reinforced a 'police state in the mind'.[75]

As part of Catherine's cultural putsch, the Academy of Arts was established in 1764. The annual intake was of sixty boys between the ages of five and six, who were mainly drawn from the lower classes, although 'unhealthy or deformed children' were excluded. Pupils were 'clothed and kept' and their education was broad. The most talented proceeded 'to instructions in the Arts', the rest to 'mechanical trades'. Students with real artistic talent studied life drawing, perspective, anatomy, iconology and mythology. Once every three years, twelve prize-winning students were sent abroad. There was a theatre department filled with boys and girls taken from the foundling hospital, who were taught 'declamation, music, dancing, gesticulation and mimickry'.[76] Elizabeth had launched the project, but her 'untimely death prevented her from completing the necessary regulations'. Eager 'to perfect an undertaking so advantageous to the interests of our subjects',[77] Catherine was left to provide the institution with statutes and adequate funding – both for its premises and for its day-to-day functioning. Ivan Shuvalov chose Jean-Baptiste Vallin de la Mothe to be the architect and the

*Jean-Baptiste Vallin de la Mothe's Academy of Arts.*

Frenchman produced a monumental, rectangular building faced with Doric columns and pilasters. The foundation stone was laid in the summer of 1765 and Catherine hoped it would set the style for a more ascetic architecture in her capital. De la Mothe was consequently named court architect in 1766 and appointed the first Professor of Architecture at the Academy. The sober style followed when De la Mothe designed the imposing new *gostiny dvor* on the Nevsky Prospekt. Later he built the powerful New Holland Arch with its stark Tuscan Doric columns, an austere order which – following excavations at Paestum, Pompeii and Herculaneum – attracted architects and their powerful clients. Catherine became empress in the year before the Pompeii excavations got under way, and only a few years after Johann Joachim Winckelmann – the German archaeologist and art historian – publicised the new fascination with classical art. The intention behind neoclassicism, wrote Winckelmann was to achieve 'noble simplicity and calm grandeur'.

Reflecting the tastes of the Empress Elizabeth, Antonio Rinaldi had been appointed as the architect of Peter and Catherine's young court. He designed an elegant rococo bolthole for the grand duchess in the southern corner of the park at Oranienbaum, along with an all-weather tobogganing pavilion in powder-blue and white. Rinaldi, following shifts in taste, moved on from Elizabethan baroque towards the lucid neoclassicism of Catherine's reign. For Grigory Orlov – Catherine's early favourite – he designed the Marble Palace in a sober neoclassical style. Begun in 1768, the palace overlooks the Neva on one side and Tsaritsyn Field on the other, and today it functions as extra exhibition space for the Russian Museum. It was also for Orlov that Rinaldi built the magisterial, yet austere palace at Gatchina. Catherine delighted in the complex and, when Orlov died in 1783, bought the palace for her son, Paul.

Sometime during 1772 Falconet – whose *Bronze Horseman* offered economical energy and poise in place of baroque flamboyance – showed Catherine a sketchbook full of designs and decorations based on classical forms. Intrigued by their restraint, she was considerably less impressed by Falconet's plans for an enormous mock-Roman palace in the grounds of Tsarskoe Selo. Although he lost a commission, Falconet helped the empress engage with the quiet power of the neoclassical style.[78] Its forthrightness appealed to her, despite the fact that it became strongly associated with republican ideals, after Jacques-Louis David's neoclassical painting *The Oath of the Horatii* was heralded as a republican call to arms in France. Catherine realised that the essential strength of neoclassicism could purify the frippery of Elizabethan baroque and architecturally align the capital with the new European mainstream. Baroque and rococo were clearly falling out of fashion. During Catherine's reign, a visitor called Rastrelli's palace at Tsarskoe Selo a 'triumph' of the 'barbarous taste I have seen in these northern kingdoms'.[79] By the time the Reverend Edward Daniel Clarke visited in the early nineteenth century, tastes had shifted so much that he cited the palace as 'a compound of what an architect ought to avoid'.[80]

So, having invited a cosmopolitan array of architects to improve building procedures and amplify the stylistic scope of architecture in and around St Petersburg, Catherine fixed on the restrained order of neoclassicism and the feigned informality of the English garden. To realise her vision, the empress first turned to a Scot, Charles Cameron – an architect, interior designer and landscape gardener who had studied antiquity in Italy. Later she turned to the Italian Giacomo Quarenghi, whose considerable architectural contributions to St Petersburg continued during the reign of Alexander I. Cameron arrived in the late 1780s and went to work just outside the capital at Tsarskoe Selo. He began by replacing some of Rastrelli's assertive palace interiors with more intimate themed rooms, designing every detail of the ensemble, right down to the locks, keys and door handles. There were medallions bas-reliefs, niches with vases and statues, friezes incorporating mythological scenes and variously coloured marbles. While Cameron's exteriors tended to clean lines and economy, his interiors were ordered but often intense.

Sitting in a somewhat strange relationship to Rastrelli's palace, the open colonnade, or Cameron Gallery, was a covered walkway supported by Ionic columns, with an enclosed space running through the centre. The loggia provided Catherine with a place to promenade on the frequent rainy days, a belvedere from which to enjoy her steadily evolving park. There were bronze

*The Cameron Gallery at Tsarskoe Selo.*

busts of ancient philosophers to stimulate reflection, and one of a contemporary politician, Charles James Fox, leader of the British Parliamentary opposition, whom Catherine credited with preventing war between their countries.[81] At one end of the gallery there was an imposing staircase. When the empress became too elderly to climb it, Cameron added a ramp. There was a tactful majesty about the ensemble. It was no baroque allegro, like the gilded façade of Rastrelli's palace, but – as the contemporary poet Gavrila Derzhavin suggested – 'the temple where the graces dance to the sound of the harp'.[82]

In order to carry out these Russian projects, Cameron advertised in the *Edinburgh Evening Courant*: 'For Her Majesty the Empress of all the Russias – Wanted – Two clerks, who have been employed by an Architect or very considerable Builder . . . Two Master Masons, Two Master Bricklayers', and for many more 'masters of the above work' who can 'bring with them proper certificates of their abilities and good behaviour'. One hundred and forty masons, plasterers, wives and children made the journey. However, after they arrived, their hosts were not impressed by their capacity for work. Used to commanding an unreservedly obedient native workforce, the Russians found the foreigners lazy. Arriving late for work, the British left early. Not only did they celebrate their own holidays, but they also took the opportunity to enjoy Russian ones as well. Consequently Catherine demanded stricter controls, and some Britons decided to return home. Those prepared to work hard stayed until the gallery, cold baths and Agate Pavilion were finished in 1787. The cost of these works – the lavish use of precious materials such as malachite, lapis lazuli, jasper and agate – was enormous.[83] As Catherine put it to the Scot, when she viewed their achievement at Tsarskoe Selo, 'It is indeed very handsome *mais ça coute* .'[84]

Gardens were supremely important to Catherine. As a grand duchess, she had sought their seclusion as a temporary respite from the pressures of the court.[85] As an empress, she cherished their solitude for personal reflection and privileged tête-à-têtes, where green and shady spaces permitted a focus that was not always possible amid the hubbub at court. In a letter to Voltaire, Catherine declared, 'I profoundly despise straight lines and paired paths. I hate fountains which torture water'[86] and Charles Cameron – collaborating with the gardener John Bush of Hackney – avoided the strictness of the French garden. When, at the end of the 1770s, the empress became influenced by the neo-Gothic style emanating from England and expressed her passion for curving alleys, lawns and picturesque groupings of trees, it reflected a political and cultural realignment.[87] The decadence and dangerous unrest in France prompted a move towards the quiet respectability of the English heritage. Catherine's enthusiasm for the controlled freedom of the English garden was an indication of her willingness to employ intimacy and apparent spontaneity as disarming political tools. The English Ambassador, Sir James Harris, noted that the empress 'considered joint walks through the garden as a sign of great distinction'.[88]

Bush not only gardened at Tsarskoe Selo, but was also partly responsible for maintaining the huge greenhouses that permitted exotic fruits – oranges, lemons, peaches and nectarines – to be grown at that latitude. Théophile Gautier later observed that such fruit is 'one of the great manias of Northern peoples' and added that hothouses 'half buried in the snow' were not what they were cracked up to be, a 'stove, however well heated, never quite makes up for the sunshine'. There was, he suggested, a resulting coarseness of taste.[89]

Catherine's passion for things English was revealed in an order for a 944-piece, fifty-place dinner service from Josiah Wedgwood, featuring 1,222 hand-painted panoramas of English castles, country houses and landscape gardens. While it was undeniably prestigious for the English potter to produce such a large service for the empress, Wedgwood was worried by the investment required to fulfil the order: 'Do you think the subjects must all be from *real views* and that it is expected from us to send draftsmen all over the Kingdom to take these views?'[90] But the commission was too grand to refuse, even though the Green Frog Service – one of the most sober and homely to be owned by the Romanovs – was originally ordered for the unimportant, neo-Gothic Kekerekeksinen, or 'Frog Marsh' Palace. This stood on swampy ground between the capital and Tsarskoe Selo, hence its croaking name and the green frog emblem to be found on each piece of the service. For Catherine, the palace was a staging post, and she only used its tableware on rare occasions when the establishment – renamed Chesme Palace in 1780 – hosted official functions. Despite the fact that Wedgwood baulked at the size of the enterprise, fifty covers proved inadequate for imperial banquets, and imitation items had to be produced in St Petersburg's Imperial Porcelain Factory.[91]

The Green Frog Service featured English castles and country estates, while Cameron's new garden around the Great Pond at Tsarskoe Selo was inspired by Lancelot Capability Brown's gardens at Stowe.[92] Monuments set up in the park to celebrate the people dear to the empress, or the victories of her busy armies against Turkey and Persia, were either improvisations on follies in that English garden or based on designs by Palladio, who exerted great influence on Cameron, and therefore on St Petersburg and its environs.

Built between 1781 and 1796, the Palace of Pavlovsk was Catherine's gift to her son Paul and his consort, the Grand Duchess Maria Feodorovna, in honour of their son Alexander, who had been born in 1777. The estate was landscaped by Charles Cameron, who dammed the River Slavyanka to form a lake. He scattered a good variety of shrubs and trees in copses and clumps, informally framing the house and disclosing the occasional folly. The main building had been conceived by him as a villa rather than a palace. Its central section recalls Palladio's Villa 'Capra' outside Vicenza, and its stunted cupola, sitting on a circle of thin, tightly grouped columns, is reminiscent of Rome's Pantheon.[93] On either side of the three-storey central building, semicircular colonnades embrace the spacious front courtyard, which is approached along the lime-tree avenue that Cameron also created. Behind the villa the ground falls away, affording an imposing view of the central structure from across the small river. The original ensemble proved insufficient for Paul and Maria, who had Cameron's mansion enlarged and the interior redecorated by Vincenzo Brenna, their court architect. Cameron, weary of interference with his ideas, withdrew and – for the rest of his life – undertook prosaic projects in the capital.

Without making such an impact as the foreigners Cameron and Quarenghi, Russian architects were coming into their own and were now making an important and lasting contribution to the St Petersburg cityscape. Nikolai Lvov was a Renaissance man whose talents included not only architecture, but also engineering and poetry. He compiled a seminal volume of folk songs, which has been mined by Russian and foreign composers – Beethoven drew on it for themes in his Razumovsky Quartets.[94] Lvov's impressive neoclassical Central Post Office on Pochtamtskaya Street is one of the few administrative buildings constructed in the eighteenth century that still serves a similar purpose today.

Yuri Felten was the son of Peter the Great's head chef and there is something of the wedding cake or sugar subtlety about some of his buildings. St Catherine's Lutheran Church, which Felten built on Vasilevsky Island, has an iced, almost over-decorated façade, and his tendency towards confection is most successful when at its most extravagant – as in the unrestrained excess of his St John the Baptist Church at Chesme. Named after the successful 1770 naval battle against the Ottoman Empire, Catherine's country palace and church have long since been absorbed by the expansion of St Petersburg to the south. Felten's exuberant early work reflects not only his father's creations for the table, but also his apprenticeship under Rastrelli. His mature work, however, reflects a developing neoclassicism: the wrought-iron gate and railings around the Summer Garden, the exterior of the Zubov Wing of the Catherine Palace at Tsarskoe Selo, and his important contribution to the evolving Winter Palace complex – the Large Hermitage.

Ivan Starov successfully designed palaces at Bogoroditsky and Bobriki near Tula for Catherine's illegitimate son by Grigory Orlov. As a result, he won important commissions in the capital. The Cathedral of the Trinity in the Alexander Nevsky Monastery is fronted by a robust Tuscan portico while its colonnaded cupola closely resembled Jacques-Germain Soufflot's Church of Sainte-Geneviève – Paris's present day Panthéon. Starov's masterpiece was Catherine's gift to Prince Potempkin, the Tauride Palace, built between 1783 and 1788. Catherine generously repurchased her gift from the prince so that he could cover his debts and then presented it to him again in 1790, only – absurdly – to buy it back from his heirs after his death in 1791. Sited so as to overlook the Neva, its view was spoiled in the mid-nineteenth century by a huge water tower and its adjacent buildings. The vast neo-Palladian palace, one of the largest in St Petersburg, was celebrated by the poet Derzhavin for its simplicity and sublimity. The extensive park was the work of Capability Brown's pupil, William Gould, who imported trees and shrubs from England and produced a twenty-four-hectare park, creating an impression of delicately ordered rurality in the Russian capital. After working for Potempkin to such stunning effect, Gould was appointed Imperial Gardener in 1793.

Giacomo Quarenghi's early exposure to Palladio remained an influence on his life's work and, therefore, upon St Petersburg. Born in Bergamo, Quarenghi studied in Rome, first with the German-born painter Anton Raphael Mengs, and then with Antoine Decrezet, a friend of Winckelmann. Spotted by a Russian nobleman who was scouting for Catherine, Quarenghi arrived in St Petersburg in 1780 and became responsible for much of the neoclassical city that we know today. Distinguishable by his huge, bruised bulbous nose,[95] which made it seem as if the northern climate had either given him an incurable cold or driven him to drink, Quarenghi was appreciative of his contemporaries. He raised his hat when passing Rastrelli's Smolny complex, and called Cameron's buildings 'as splendid as they are original'. Quarenghi's Currency Bank between Sadovaya Street and the Catherine Canal is a horseshoe-shaped Palladian structure embracing a simple, six-pillared central building enlivened by precariously placed statues, mounted at the apexes of the pediment. Altogether more sober is the unadorned Ionic portico of the Academy of Sciences building, which stands adjacent to the Kunstkammer on Vasilevsky Island. Quarenghi was prolific. He built the English Reformed Church and the Institute for the Education of Noble Girls in the Smolny and designed houses for the nobility, such as the Gargarin Palace on the Neva and the Yusopov Palace on the Fontanka. Catherine wrote to Grimm that 'the whole town is stuffed with his buildings'[96] – not least among them, the important Hermitage Theatre, which was clearly influenced by Palladio's late Teatro Olimpico in Vicenza.

If *The Bronze Horseman* has become a manifestation of the spirit of St Petersburg, no building is more expressive of the city's ostentatious majesty than the Winter Palace, which – like the capital itself – developed, in fits and starts, to become the composite structure that stands today. Between the founding of the city and the end of Catherine's reign there were five incarnations of the Winter Palace standing on the site of Rastrelli's impressive edifice. After his completion of the landmark structure, several architects worked to enlarge and refine the complex. De la Mothe and Felten designed the Small Hermitage and decorated its apartments overlooking the Neva, where Catherine and her twenty maids of honour lived – rooms that were lost in the great fire of December 1837. Most importantly, a gallery overlooking the interior hanging garden was constructed for Catherine's rapidly enlarging trove – a picture collection which would grow to become one of the most significant in the world.

Despite his preference for scientific artefacts and specimens, Peter the Great had started an imperial picture collection in the first decades of the century, prompted by his understandable enthusiasm for Dutch marine artists. Fifty years later, Catherine decided to enlarge the collection substantially with a streak of extravagant, high-profile and often politically pointed purchases. The empress began in 1764, with the 255 canvases belonging to Johann Ernst Gotzkowsky, a Berlin art dealer. The Russian Ambassador to Berlin secured the collection that Frederick the Great desired, but had been unable to purchase. The Seven Years War had left him impoverished, and Catherine's ease of acquisition was something of a snub.[97]

Just as *philosophes* like Diderot amassed an encyclopaedia full of knowledge, so Catherine wished to accumulate art. With agents scattered all over Europe and an imperial purse, the empress gratified her dreams of cultural grandeur. She was perfectly candid – 'It is not love of art, it is voracity. I am not an *amateur*, I am a glutton.'[98] With feigned humility, she classed herself as a professional ignoramus and admitted that she relied on the taste of people such as Melchior Grimm and her ambassadors in Europe. She depended on connoisseurs such as Count Stroganov and her Grand Chamberlain, Ivan Shuvalov, who – Catherine said – 'are both members of at least 24 academies'.[99] Stroganov owned one of the best art collections in Europe, as well as a library of 10,000 volumes. These were available for loan, a scheme that led to the building of the Imperial Russian Public Library on the Nevsky Prospekt between 1796 and 1801. Its collection of more than half a million volumes and manuscripts opened to the public in 1814.

Purchasing art in Paris towards the end of the eighteenth century depended on influence and inside information, for there were no commercial galleries – only an intermittent Salon of Living Artists held in the Louvre. Between 1759 and 1771 Diderot was the critic of those Salons, and his knowledge and connections helped Catherine obtain works by Jean-Baptiste Greuze, Claude-Joseph Vernet and the great still-life and genre painter, Jean-Baptiste-Siméon Chardin.[100] Her ambassador to France, Prince Dmitry Golitsyn, visited studios, commissioning new works as well as acquiring existing paintings. It was through such a network that – in 1766 – Catherine obtained paintings left by a close friend of Chardin, the painter Jacques Aved, whose success as a portraitist had given him the wherewithal to assemble a good collection of Flemish and Dutch art. From Louis-Jean Gaignat – the renowned collector and secretary to Louis XV – Catherine's agents bought forty-six paintings, including five Rubens. Once again the empress outbid the cash-strapped Frederick the Great when she purchased 6,000 drawings and some Dutch and Spanish canvases at a sale of the Count Karl Cobenzl collection in Brussels in 1768. The following year, Catherine acquired 600 Flemish, Dutch and French paintings from the Polish-Saxon diplomat and collector Count Heinrich von Brühl – the haul including Rembrandt's *Portrait of a Scholar* and Watteau's *An Embarrassing Proposal*, along with works by Rubens, Cranach and Tiepolo.

Collecting with a vast purse was not difficult, but the logistics of acquisition sometimes were. In July 1771, Catherine obtained items from the estate auction of the deceased Dutch distiller, timber merchant and collector Gerrit Braamcamp, including some important Dutch paintings by Paulus Potter, Philips Wouwerman and Gerard Terborch. These and other artefacts were loaded aboard a Dutch two-master, the *Vrouw Maria*, which set sail for St Petersburg on 5 September 1771 – part of a cargo that included a vast quantity of sugar, cotton, indigo, thread, mercury and madder. A month later, seemingly carried off-course by a storm, the ship ran aground off the Finnish island of Jurmo. She managed to refloat, but was beached again, this time losing her rudder. The *Vrouw Maria* was then dislodged by a large wave and started taking water. At dawn on 4 October, the crew abandoned ship and were rescued. They tried to salvage what they could, but were hampered by spillage from the cargo clogging the bilge pumps. Five days later, the *Vrouw Maria* sunk in forty-one metres, with Catherine's canvases on board. The fact that the Russian Foreign Minister, Nikita Panin, despatched Major Their to attempt a salvage suggests that the canvases were known to have been rolled and sealed before the ship set sail. Major Their returned without the paintings. In fact it was not until 1999 – with modern archival research, side-scan sonar and divers using compressed air and trimix breathing gas – that the sunken wreck was located. Obviously benefiting from its sojourn at the bottom of the Baltic Sea, with its low levels of corrosive salt, the hold was found to be full of cargo and the hull intact. In 2008, there were Russian and Finnish plans to mount a salvage operation, but – so far – there has been no recovery of the twenty-seven paintings on board.[101]

They were a mere drop in the ocean. A year earlier Catherine bought 100 paintings from the Swiss banker François Tronchin in Geneva and in 1772 took delivery of seventeen packing cases full of 400 paintings, which Dmitry Golitsyn bought for the empress on Diderot's advice. This was the collection of Pierre Crozat who died in 1740, and which came on the market after the death of his nephew, Baron de Thiers.[102] It included two *Danaës* – one by Rembrandt, one by Titian – a *Bacchus* by Rubens, Giorgione's *Judith* and Raphael's *Holy Family*, which was later sold to the United States by a cash-strapped early Soviet government.[103] As for Rembrandt's *Danaë*, that was slashed and doused in sulphuric acid by an embittered Lithuanian in 1985. The acid dissolved the glazes, obliterating detail[104] but after twelve years of restoration, the painting was hung once again on the walls of the Hermitage Museum.

To consider the rapid manner in which the Hermitage Collection was put together is to plunge into the kind of statistical vaunt beloved of tour guides, although even Catherine was delighted by the magnitude of her acquisitions. Writing to Grimm in 1790, she boasted, 'My museum in the Hermitage – not counting the paintings and the Raphael loggias – consists of 3,800 books, four rooms filled with books and prints, 10,000 engraved gems, approximately 10,000 drawings and a natural science collection that fills two large halls.'[105] A Soviet-era guide bragged that on 1 January 1972, the 'museum's displays and store rooms contain about 2,650,000 works of art and other objects'.[106] Today the figure is placed at around three million items. If you were to spend a meagre minute with each exhibit, it would take you 50,000 hours, or 2,000 days, or more than five and a half years of viewing – and that's without counting the time for moving about the museum's 353 halls. Italian art alone occupies thirty-seven of those rooms.

The first step towards the creation of this great institution was taken in the 1770s, when it became clear that space was needed to display Catherine's rapidly expanding collection. Building along from the Winter Palace towards the Winter Canal, Yuri Felten designed the three-storey Large Hermitage, which was completed in 1776. Viewing the collection at this stage, the Dutch physician Pieter van Wonzel noted that there 'was a good deal of mediocrity'[107] – understandable when you bulk-buy. The French chargé d'affaires, the Chevalier de Corberon, found Catherine's gallery 'too narrow' and a good number of the pictures 'badly displayed' – not that the hanging in the Louvre during the late eighteenth century was exemplary, with paintings skied and crushed side by side.

In the late 1770s, after George III sent a gift of Benjamin West's portrait of the Prince of Wales and his brother, Catherine acquired English works by Joseph Wright of Derby, Godfrey Kneller and the portraitist and Principal Painter to the Court of

Charles II, Sir Peter Lely.[108] Then – once again proving herself an opportunist in the face of the financial misfortune of others – Catherine purchased, for £43,000, Sir Robert Walpole's old Houghton Hall collection from the ex-prime minister's impoverished nephew. People were up in arms, just as they had been in France over the Tronchin sale. 'Russia is sacking our palaces and museums,' complained Josiah Wedgwood. Dr Johnson petitioned Parliament to block the export of a collection which included Poussin, Rubens and Rembrandt.[109] Parliament – exhibiting its chronic talent for philistinism – refused John Wilkes's proposal that the works be purchased by the state to form the foundation of a national collection. Thus Catherine added, among many other paintings, twenty Van Dykes, nineteen Rubens, eight Titians, three Veroneses, two Velázquez, a Raphael and a Poussin to her collection.[110]

At the beginning of the 1780s, the empress was advised that space and funds were becoming a problem and she curtailed her cupidity. Golitsyn's last purchase on her behalf was in 1781 when he obtained 199 Dutch, Flemish, French and Italian paintings from the collection of Count Baudouin. By her death in 1796 Catherine possessed nearly 4,000 paintings, which were hung – according to the German academician Johann Gottlieb Georgi – not 'in keeping with schools or painters', but according to their emotional impact.

The empress collected painters as well as paintings. As Grand Duchess, she and Peter were painted many times by the German portrait painter Georg Christoph Grooth, who arrived in the Russian capital the year before Catherine and worked there until his death in 1749. Pietro Rotari was invited to paint at the Russian court, at a cost of 1,000 gold roubles in travelling expenses alone. After a brief visit in 1756, he returned to St Petersburg the year Catherine became empress, but died shortly after his arrival. Nonetheless, the imperial collection boasted 863 paintings by Rotari – many merely small portraits of coquettish young girls. Much later in Catherine's reign, Elisabeth Vigée-Lebrun fled the French Revolution and installed herself temporarily in Petersburg, where she produced a good number of portraits of the nobility in what could loosely be termed the English style.

An area of the Hermitage's Pavilion Hall was set aside as a space where Russian artists such as Dmitry Levitsky and Vladimir Borovikovsky studied and copied the masters. Levitsky presented twenty canvases at the first exhibition of the Academy of Fine Arts, including a portrait of Diderot, who sat informally without a wig. This secured Levitsky's reputation, a teaching post, and won him imperial commissions. As Professor of Portraiture at the Academy, he taught Borovikovsky, who in 1794 painted a portrait of the intelligent, no-nonsense Catherine walking a whippet in the park at Tsarskoe Selo. It presented an empress indulging the newly discovered love of nature in a landscaped park, in which a monument to Count Rumyantsev's successes in the 1768–74 Russo–Turkish War is visible. Borovikovsky painted variations on this image, which became the source of a frequently reproduced engraving.

While painters were establishing a secure base for a Russian school, topographical engraving had come into its own during Elizabeth's reign, when Mikhail Makhaev produced views and maps of St Petersburg in the early 1750s in honour of the fifty-year anniversary of the city's founding. Makhaev's raised points of view, and his use of an optical 'camera' with a wide-angled lens, intensified his perspective and dramatically dynamised and flattered the city.[111] As a result of his success, a special class in topographical engraving was established at the Academy. Towards the end of Catherine's reign, topographical painting came into its own – notably in the work of Fedor Alekseev, who had been influenced by the views of Canaletto and other *vedutisti* during a sojourn in Venice. In Petersburg he painted the sweep of a surprisingly calm and uncluttered Neva lined with granite banks and impressive neoclassical buildings.

As Catherine's enthusiasm for painting cooled, so her passion for the theatre increased. The building of Quarenghi's Hermitage Theatre stimulated activity and, during the last decade of her life, she wrote six opera libretti, aided by her personal secretary, Krapovitsky. The new theatre was used both for *Grands Hermitages* – splendid performances for visiting dignitaries – and for the more modest *Petits Hermitages*, for the empress's close friends. The elaborate spectacle of all-singing, all-dancing Italian opera was gradually being displaced by a taste for French *opéra comique*, in which the score was less important than the libretto. Catherine's own plots were wide-ranging and were set by celebrated foreign composers, such as the handsomely paid Spaniard, Vincente Martin y Soler, as well as by native composers who rose to the challenge. Vasily Pashkevich produced an impressive Mozartean score for Catherine's *Fevey*, which tackled the theme of filial responsibility and was presented in a lavish production at the Hermitage Theatre in April 1786. The empress addressed the necessity for strong leadership in *The Brave and Bold Knight*, and, in *Kosometovich, The Woeful Knight* she penned a satire on Gustav III of Sweden, with whom, in 1789 – the year of the opera's creation – she was at war. In other works the empress used Russian fairy tales and folklore, a decision that appears to have influenced the evolution of Russian opera.[112] Had Potempkin succeeded in his attempts to persuade Mozart to work in St Petersburg, the future of Russian opera might have been profoundly changed.[113]

By 1790, St Petersburg was larger than Moscow.[114] Without a Kremlin and concentric rings of buildings encircling it, the capital was expanding in a manner that was different from any other Russian city. The legacy of Eropkin's three-pronged attack on the undeveloped environs meant that areas housing the poor were forever being pushed further outwards. Filthy, cramped and temporary, they were densely populated by state-owned peasants who were often grouped according to occupation. Crowding was inflated by vagabonds – peasants without passports issued by a lord or village official – who came to the capital for seasonal employment or fled from the poverty of the countryside, only to die in greater misery in city slums. Among those legally allowed to work, miserable wages or insufferable conditions led to the first stirrings of labour unrest. In 1771, eleven spinners downed tools in protest over the low quality of the raw materials they were expected to use.[115]

The police opened two workhouses in which to detain the strays and drunkards who were no longer tolerated on the streets, but Petersburg's jails left much to be desired. When the English prison reformer John Howard visited in 1781, he was appalled by an enthusiastic demonstration of the sadistic instruments owned and used by the chief of police – the knout, branding irons, nostril-cutters and medieval bone-breaking equipment. Six years later, a new two-storey pentagonal prison with a covered exercise yard was built on the Moika Canal, and did meet with Howard's approval. Each cell had a stove, a stone chair and table, and a pipe that relayed religious services, in an attempt to reform inmates. As a tribute to the modest crime rate, this new prison remained quite empty, although a separate detention centre for petty criminals pending trial was well used.[116]

The police presence was strengthened modestly during Catherine's reign. The night watch numbered 500, with an army backup, and people felt they could walk in safety at any hour – though some men took the precaution of putting an officer's cockade in their hats as a deterrent against attack. The Winter Palace, however, fell victim to a gang of robbers operating among its numerous interior decorators. While reported crime remained low for a sizeable city, wealthier people started to keep guard dogs and lock their doors.[117]

Central streets were largely paved, but a good number of

others were only timbered over. The best-kept thoroughfares were the main prospekts and major roads leading out of the city. Drainage and refuse remained a problem. On a prestigious part of the Neva Embankment near the Winter Palace, piles of discarded building materials and trash were heaped up, even though Catherine had intended to improve the environment.[118] In the late 1760s, the empress promised Voltaire, 'I will do everything possible to enhance the quality of the air . . . We have been draining the marshes around the city for three years already and we cut the pine forests that cover it in the south. And now there are already three extensive areas inhabited by settlers where one used to be unable to walk without sinking in water to the waist.'[119]

In 1780, the Fontanka Canal was dredged and lined with stone. The project for cladding the banks of the Neva in granite, begun under Felten in 1763, was far from complete in September 1777, when the river rose nearly four metres. A ship from Lübeck was carried into the woods on Vassilevsky Island.[120] Others were swept onto the embankment in the middle of the night by waters that broke the basement windows of the Winter Palace and flooded its cellars.[121] Catherine started to pray while people died in their beds, as more than 100 small houses were washed away. After that disaster, a more comprehensive warning and rescue system was put in place. When the water rose to a dangerous level, cannon would be fired, flares ignited and drummers despatched to beat the alarm throughout the city. Two oar-powered lifeboats were commissioned.[122] Yet in September 1792, when a flash flood swelled water above the Neva banks, the granite lining had still not been finished.

Peter the Great's hopes for a powerful navy and a thriving merchant marine had all but evaporated by the mid-eighteenth century. Out of the 425 trading ships sailing into St Petersburg in 1752, only five were Russian.[123] During Elizabeth's reign impressive work by hydraulic engineers at Kronstadt created a canal well over a kilometre long, capable of admitting ten stricken ships of the line. But it was hardly used and Kronstadt's dry dock, capable of servicing twelve ships, remained idle.[124] It was only by virtue of a complete refitting of Russian ships at England's Portsmouth shipyards that Catherine's navy was able to sail into the Mediterranean in 1770 and win the major victory over the Turks at Chesme. British Admiral Sir Charles Knowles was persuaded by the empress to come to Petersburg, overhaul Russian shipbuilding and revive Kronstadt.[125] Catherine was Peter the Great's worthy heir and, in the last years of her reign, the empress sat confidently in her palace, while the cannonading between the Swedish and rehabilitated Russian fleets off Kronstadt rattled the windows and rifled her ears.[126]

Military victories in the south increased Russia's cereal production, and thousands of barges and corn barques carried harvests north to Petersburg. Access to Black Sea ports meant that exotic items from Mediterranean lands – olive oil, almonds, capers and raisins – were transported by inland waterway to the capital. As for Baltic trade, without a stock exchange and with ineffective attempts to set up Russian banks during the 1750s, Petersburg merchants were obliged to borrow money in Holland. To help remedy the situation, in 1787 Catherine set up the Imperial Loan or Assignation Bank, the first institution in Russia to promote the circulation of money and stimulate commerce.[127] Shortly afterwards, nearly one-tenth of the ships sailing into the mouth of the Neva carrying delicacies such as oysters, cheeses, coffee, chocolate and gingerbread were Russian.

The Neva, however, carried more than delicacies. Drinking water taken from the river was considered safe – particularly if it was drawn from midstream – but it contained the parasite that had proved so unwelcoming to Denis Diderot, *Giardia lamblia*, which had first been observed under the microscope of Peter the Great's Amsterdam acquaintance, Anthonie van Leeuwenhoek. The parasite is spread by animal faeces, so it is hardly surprising that the Neva was infected, as it drains water from north-west

Russia and south-east Finland, regions rich in wildlife. Water taken from the Moika – severely polluted through the dumping of waste and human excrement – was boiled to kill germs and flavoured with vinegar to disguise its taste. Domestic sanitation was primitive, even in the wealthiest establishments. When John Parkinson, Fellow and Bursar of Magdalen College, Oxford, paid a visit to Count Osterman, he recorded that he was 'almost poisoned by the stench of the necessary', adding that in spring, 'when it begins to thaw, the nuisance is insufferable'.[128] Even when the first drains were dug in 1770, they only carried refuse by the shortest route to the Neva. It was not until a few years later that a system transported sewage much further downriver in conduits dug almost a metre below the surface.[129] Suffering from frequent stomach aches and with two mortal diseases threatening her subjects, Catherine began to pay great attention to the question of health.

Peter II had died of smallpox. Empress Elizabeth had lost her fiancé to smallpox, and it had disfigured the already unprepossessing Peter III. A folk remedy known as variolation – in which someone was immunised against the disease by rubbing fluid from the pustules of the infected into superficial scratches made on the skin of a healthy person – was widely practised in China as well as on the southern borders of Russia. Although Catherine had slight regard for doctors – echoing Rousseau in calling them 'charlatans' and preferring a spartan diet and fresh air to medical interference – the threat of smallpox was so daunting that, in 1768, she summoned the Englishman who had perfected the process of variolation in the West, Dr Thomas Dimsdale. He variolated the empress and the Grand Duke Paul. Catherine fell ill immediately. After she slowly recovered, a thanksgiving service celebrated Dimsdale's success;[130] and Derzhavin, in a forgettable poem of 1789, praised Catherine's courageousness: 'To save the health of her world, / She drinks the poison without fear.'[131] Nobles followed the empress's example and St Petersburg's Inoculation Hospital opened to treat the children of the nobility, officers and artisans, not to mention serfs – 'property' that their owners wished to protect. Dimsdale was made a Baron of the Russian Empire and returned to the capital in 1781, to variolate Catherine's grandson, Alexander.[132] Success in St Petersburg set the example, and hospitals opened in towns and cities across Russia. Science was beginning to triumph. A court pageant was staged – *Prejudice Overcome*, in which Minerva (Catherine), Ruthenia (Russia) and the Genius of Science conquered Ignorance and Superstition.[133]

The second major threat to health was the plague, which was carried to Moscow in 1770 by soldiers who had served in the south. As it crept closer to the capital, with suspected outbreaks near Pskov and Novgorod, the authorities were quick to react. Checkpoints were established on the main roads to monitor those travellers – post men, tax collectors and government officials – who were obliged to make the journey between the old and new capitals. A quarantine house was set up in St Petersburg, and incoming goods were treated with fire, smoke and vinegar. As the authorities watched anxiously, autumn dragged towards winter and the deepening cold kept the plague at bay.[134] By the end of the 1770s the first general public hospital was established in the capital, financed by the Crown. It was located south of the Fontanka. Close by, Russia's first mental institution opened and operated under an enlightened regime.[135] Another 300-bed hospital was built in stone during the 1780s, with an annex opening in 1790 providing a further 260 places in wooden dormitories, erected in the grounds of the College of Medicine. There were nine beds in each airy ward. There was hot and cold water, and patients enjoyed sheets that were changed regularly, water jugs and hand bells on their bedside tables.[136]

In a publication which riled Catherine – *Voyage en Sibérie* – the Abbé Chappe d'Auteroche attacked Russian sexual habits. He suggested that venereal disease was widespread and that 'unlawful' sexual relationships threatened the well-being of the state.[137] Catherine took the first steps in combating the situation by setting up a sixty-bed hospital for men and women near the Kalinkin Bridge on the Fontanka, dedicated to the treatment of sexually transmitted diseases. It was a discreet hospital,[138] to which patients were admitted without revealing their identities, and in which they wore a cap inscribed with the word 'secrecy'.[139] Catherine also made it illegal to use a house for 'indecency' or to live off immoral earnings and yet Russia's first great social critic, Alexander Radishchev, wrote of 'painted harlots on every street' in Petersburg and Moscow.[140] Prostitutes caught plying their trade would be sent to factories and, if it was ascertained that they had given venereal disease to a soldier, they would be treated and then sent to work in the mines in Siberia.[141]

One major source of cleanliness and well-being that continued to intrigue and outrage foreigners – Chappe d'Auteroche among them – was the *banya*. The Reverend William Tooke, who published his *View of the Russian Empire during the Reign of Catherine the Second* in London in 1800, noted that ordinary Russians took few medicines, but rather frequented 'the sweating bath', which was 'so much a part of the system of living, that it

*Ivan Letunov's* Banya, *1825.*

is used by people of every age and in all circumstances . . . as often as possible', which meant at least once a week. Poorer people visited communal baths set up beside streams or rivers, while those 'of the middle station . . . and the great' constructed 'vapour-baths . . . in their own houses'. The interior heat of 40–50° Celsius was maintained 'by the throwing of water every five minutes on the glowing hot stones in the chamber of the oven'. The bathers lay 'stark naked', and numerous foreigners were outraged.[142] Nathaniel Wraxall's letter of July 1774 reported a scene of 'promiscuous bathing of not less than 200 persons of both sexes', where men and women paid little heed to the segregated spaces and sat 'in a state of absolute nudity' among one another.[143] If they did respect the segregation of the bathhouse, then 'both men and women' ran out 'perfectly naked to plunge together into the river'.[144] The reaction of visitors had changed little since the first reports of *banyi* filtered back from Peter the Great's court – except that, as the Russian capital became increasingly Westernised, the indignation intensified.

The sexual mores of Russia in the late eighteenth century were, however, vastly different from those of western European countries. When Casanova visited, he was sold Zaira, a fourteen-year-old maidservant whom he was forced to examine in order to verify that she was a virgin – a state which would justify her father's 100-rouble price tag. In return for her undivided loyalty, Casanova was to feed her and let her to go to the *banya* and the church once a week. When he asked if he was obliged to take Zaira with him when he left St Petersburg, the Venetian was told that should he wish to do so, permission would have to be sought, as Zaira was also 'a slave to the empress'.

Apart from the girl's superstitious nature and jealous tendencies, the relationship was seemingly a good one, and Casanova delighted in Zaira's increasing use of scraps of Venetian dialect. Indeed, he confessed that the girl permitted him to live 'soberly' all the time he was in St Petersburg, even though he almost succumbed to the charms of an effeminate young officer, who felt called upon to prove – in no uncertain terms – that he was not a woman, and who then proceeded to offer that proof for the pleasure of the visitor. When Casanova left the city, he was refunded the 100 roubles that he had paid for Zaira and – on condition that she was willing – wished to pass her on to the aged 'but still vigorous and sensual' architect Antonio Rinaldi, who was smitten with the girl. Zaira stated that if Rinaldi really loved her, he could talk things over with her father. The architect wasted no time, and lived happily with Zaira for the remainder of his days.[145]

An 'officer has for sale a 16 year old girl, formerly belonging to a poor house, who knows how to knit, sew, iron, starch and dress a lady; she has a nice figure and a pretty face'.[146] This typical newspaper advertisement appeared in St Petersburg in 1797. The selling of girls such as Zaira was part and parcel of the system of serfdom – an institution that bore a great resemblance to that of slavery in America, except that serfs were liable for tax and conscription. Serfs were subject to an autocratic sovereign and the will of their immediate owners. Either in state or private ownership, they accounted for a staggering 90 per cent of Russia's population.[147] Catherine wrote to her Procurator General, Prince Vyazemsky, that serfdom was an 'unbearable yoke',[148] but the empress, being neither democratic nor egalitarian, did little to ameliorate the system. The end of the eighteenth century was a politically volatile period for European powers: there were revolts against taxation without representation in the English colonies, and against the monarchy in France. During her reign Catherine experienced two striking affronts to her authority – one in the form of armed rebellion, the other in print.

The insurrection of the great pretender and ex-soldier Emilian Pugachev, the self-styled Peter III, was unprecedented in scale and violence. Attracting a large number of Yaik Cossacks, Kazakh nomads and Bashkirs, Pugachev's following swelled to 20,000.

His methods were brutal, killing more than 1,500 nobles, including women and children. Some were bludgeoned, many were hanged or shot, and others were stabbed to death or drowned. Pugachev was not the first to proclaim himself Emperor, but he was the most outrageous. Shortly before his eventual capture and execution, he issued an emancipation proclamation: 'We, Peter III, by the Grace of God Emperor and Autocrat of all Russia etc. . . . with our monarchical and fatherly love, grant freedom to everyone who formerly was in serfdom.'[149] When his forces were eventually beaten at Tsaritsyn in August 1774, hundreds of Pugachev's followers were put to death or knouted. As for their leader, he was executed, then quartered.[150]

Some sixty years later, Pugachev was pictured as the villain with a kind heart in the earliest great work of historical fiction in Russian, Alexander Pushkin's novella *The Captain's Daughter.* Its hero, Peter, encounters Pugachev before he becomes the great pretender. Guided through a snowstorm to an inn by a brigand, Peter rewards his guide with a hareskin coat and then they part company. Later, during Pugachev's uprising, they meet again by chance. The rebel leader has not forgotten the young hero's kindness and helps Peter rescue his loved one from the dangers of the insurrection. A complex portrait emerges of the man beneath the brigand, as Peter attempts to save Pugachev. Consequently Peter is convicted of treason. By chance, the heroine explains her loved one's plight to a lady whom she encounters on a bench in the park at Tsarskoe Selo. The lady is none other than the empress herself and she promptly releases the hero from jail. Pushkin's decision to present Pugachev as a loveable tyrant shows he fully understood that, behind the inhumanity of the rebels, stood the inhumanity of their masters. The rebellion may have occurred a long way from the capital, but as a precedent for armed insurrection, Pugachev's revolt would have enormous consequences for St Petersburg. Pushkin's heartfelt plea, 'Heaven send that we may never see such another senseless and merciless rebellion,'[151] reveals that the writer felt what Catherine herself had so clearly understood about serfdom, that if 'we do not agree to reduce this cruelty and moderate a situation intolerable for human beings, then sooner or later they will do it themselves'.[152] Dangerously, she did little to solve the problem.

Nearly twenty years after Pugachev's insurrection, the empress was outraged by a flagrant attack in print. Catherine had taken trips into the heartlands of her domains, where she was cheered by the very peasants for whom she showed such little active compassion. In villages and towns that she visited during her six-month progress to Sevastopol in 1787, with fourteen carriages, 124 sledges and forty other vehicles intended to impress foreign dignitaries, she was met by apparently contented crowds. Although there were probably no 'Potempkin villages' – empty shells with impressive façades, like streets on Hollywood back-lots – Prince Potempkin worked hard to put on a happy show for the empress.[153] But beneath the superficial adoration, labourers were starting to flex their muscles. In that very same year, 400 workers gathered in Petersburg's Palace Square to petition Catherine with their grievances against the pay and conditions imposed by the contractor Dolgov, who was building the granite banks on the Fontanka and the Catherine Canal. Seventeen protesters were arrested and charged with illegal assembly and conspiracy. Orders were issued against such gatherings and an inquiry was set up. However, with winter coming on and the urgent need to complete the job, the charges were dropped, and Dolgov was instructed to improve his working practices.[154] The protest – small as it was – hinted at labour's latent power.

The *St Petersburg Vedomosti* kept its readership up to date with events as they unfolded in post-revolutionary France. The country – which had inspired some of the most outrageous extravagance of the Russian court – was now fashionable as the nemesis of autocratic excess, as revolutionary literature circulated among the burgeoning intelligentsia of St Petersburg. Against

such ferment, Alexander Radishchev – a wealthy young noble
who served at court – took advantage of the 1783 law allowing
people to set up printing presses and in 1790 published a series
of letters recounting *A Journey from St Petersburg to Moscow*.
He thereby became Russia's first great revolutionary writer.

On Radishchev's journey there were no spick-and-span peasants, no cheering crowds to greet him as he travelled to the soul
of the people:

> Look at a Russian; you will find him pensive. If he wishes
> to purge his melancholy, or, as he would say, to have a good
> time, he goes to the tavern . . . A barge hauler who goes to
> the tavern with downcast head and returns blood-splattered
> from blows in the face may help to explain much that has
> seemed puzzling in Russian history.[155]

Radishchev predicted revolution, unless changes were made.
He believed that only sweeping reform could forestall inevitable
catastrophe. Catherine – who had understood as much – accused
Radishchev of being the new Pugachev. Adding philosophical
diatribe to his appraisal of the country, Radishchev included a
Blakean 'Ode to Liberty' in his publication. It was quite possibly
added after he sent *A Journey* to the censor, who, in any case,
imagined from the title that the book was an innocent piece of
travel writing. Catherine's outraged annotations to her copy of the
text reveal that she found the Ode 'manifestly revolutionary'. She
asked: how can power be 'joined with liberty for mutual advantage'?[156] She was not about to find out. As soon as the anonymous
author of *A Journey from St Petersburg to Moscow* had been
identified, he was arrested. Only twenty-five copies of the book
had been sold and Radishchev agreed to destroy the rest, so that
he could be joined by his family during his exile in Siberia. It
was not until 1858 in London that *A Journey* was published in
Russian by that 'father of Russian Socialism', Alexander Herzen.

By then, among writers and thinkers, the journey towards revolution was under way. If Pushkin had been taken by the human side of Pugachev, he was also inspired by Radishchev. In 1817, the poet wrote his own 'Ode to Liberty' and – towards the end of his short life – was busy making notes and beginning to write a return journey from Moscow to St Petersburg.[157]

Radishchev's timing was bad. Russia was fighting the Turks in the south and the Swedish in the north. His attack on absolutism and the social structure of Russia, written against the backdrop of revolution in France, was bound to meet the harshest response. Catherine – physically sickened by the execution of Louis XIV and the bloodbath that ensued – felt that an absolute and iron grip was indispensable. She was interested in consolidating the richness of the Russian state and the power and prestige of its ruler. People threatening the state were put under surveillance. In 1796, a system of formal censorship was introduced, and all private presses – previously supported by the empress – were shut down. The long battle between autocracy and the Russian intelligentsia was under way.[158]

As her principles became increasingly inflexible, Catherine – a fierce guardian of her image – used portraits to evoke a kindly, benevolent ruler.[159] She dressed with dignity. She inhabited a warmer, quieter world and appeared as a matronly Mother Russia, even as she sought lovers who were ever younger, less suited to her intelligence and less loved. As Charles Masson has it in his *Memoirs*, at an 'advanced period of her life' the empress spent her days with three 'young libertines . . . while her armies were slaughtering the Turks, fighting with the Swedes and ravaging Poland'. The empress held masked parties during which the select company 'romped and engaged in all sorts of frolics and gambols'. There was, Masson claims, 'no kind of gaiety which was not permitted'. Furthermore, the empress formed a more

*Vladimir Borovikovsky's* Catherine II Promenading in the Park at
Tsarskoe Selo with the Obelisk to Count Rumyantsev's Victories, *1794.*

mysterious group, the Little Society, of which 'the particulars
are not fit to be repeated'. They were allegedly so scandalous that
Masson burned 'his memoranda which could have afforded any
information on the subject'.[160]

Private lifestyle apart, the extravagant writer of these keyhole
memoirs leaves a chilling assessment of Catherine's reign:

> O Catherine! dazzled by thy greatness, of which I have had
> a near view, charmed with thy beneficence which rendered
> so many individuals happy, seduced by the thousand ami-
> able qualities that have been admired in thee, I would fain
> have erected a monument to thy glory; but torrents of blood
> flow in upon me and inundate my design; the chains of thirty
> millions of slaves ring in my ears, and deafen me; the crimes
> which have reigned in thy name call forth my indignation.[161]

The rhetoric is heightened to such a pitch that Masson's vision
echoes the exultation at Catherine's death expressed by the

young Romantic poet, Samuel Taylor Coleridge. He rejoiced 'as at the extinction of the evil Principle impersonated!' Catherine's crimes were listed – among them 'the poisoning of her husband, her iniquities in Poland . . . the desolating ambition of her public life . . . the libidinous excesses of her private hours!'[162]

The Scottish traveller Andrew Swinton noted that by 1790 St Petersburg had become part of the European Grand Tour and that – except for Constantinople – no city in Europe contained a greater mix of foreigners. Petersburg's energy encouraged the Dutch doctor Pieter van Wonzel to believe that in two centuries it would be 'the first city of the universe'. Diderot, however, found a capital in panic – the inhabitants 'trying to find out if the ground is really firm under their feet'.[163] Casanova was likewise pessimistic about a city that he suggested was 'built with the childish aim of seeing it fall into ruins'. The Venetian, whose native city was similarly under threat, believed that, sooner or later, St Petersburg's 'soil must give way and drag the vast city with it'.[164] Nevertheless, during Catherine's reign there had been a huge consolidation of the architecture, culture and general civility of the capital. In the grand streets, among the palaces and in their parks, space had been dignified. St Petersburg was a magnificent and theatrical city, aspiring to be the crowning capital of Europe.

During the three decades after Catherine's death, its defining buildings would all be completed and the Nevsky Prospekt would become one of the most fashionable and exciting streets in the world. The stage would be set for Petersburg's great nineteenth-century drama. The agitated voices of its writers and thinkers would resonate through the ample spaces and dark byways, turning Peter's port into the 'Petersburg' of Russian literature – glittering, rich, but as dismal and desperate as the underbelly of Dickensian London. The court would still dominate the city, but the city would soon learn to speak for itself.

# 7

# MADNESS, MURDER AND INSURRECTION

## *1796–1825*

St Petersburg was resplendent during the final years of Catherine's reign. On summer days the wealthy enjoyed elegant excursions on the Neva, protected under silk canopies from harsh sun or sudden showers. Crew occupied the forward part of the boat and rowed with such dexterity 'that even English sailors' acknowledged their superiority.[1] Musicians brought on board to entertain the company with their clarinets and tambourines found themselves in competition with the powerful voices of these gaudily dressed oarsmen.[2] When – in the brief heat of the early-summer White Nights – there were nocturnal outings, the Neva resounded with song.

Although distances within the city were considerable and the weather was indecisive, strolling became a popular activity. The gardens of the Cadet Corps buildings were opened to a 'motley throng' on Sundays and – as in the Summer Garden – people paraded their latest finery to the strains of military bands. The islands in the small branch of the Neva had become a popular weekend retreat. There was the 'romantic wildness' of Kamenny Island, on which a summer carnival was held at Count Strogonov's villa. There were tents erected for the food and a wooden pavilion – open at the sides – for dancing. Krestovsky Island offered similar entertainments, with delicacies sold from stalls set up in Count Razumovsky's park. On Yelagin Island and in the rural Vyborg sector there were pleasure gardens with Turkish music, dancing and fireworks.[3] The Russian capital had taken on the buzz of a thriving city – an exciting emporium driven by the demands of a voracious court. On the Nevsky Prospekt it was impossible to move twenty paces without passing a *magasin de modes*, selling silk hats, embroidered waistcoats and assorted trimmings. There were English and German furniture show-rooms, instrument-makers and Russian shops of all kinds in the *gostiny dvor*. Within a century, St Petersburg had achieved what many cities take hundreds of years to accomplish: it had become one of the great capitals of the world.

That disappeared overnight. As it would again. In a significant instance of bad timing, Catherine intended to make a formal statement on the first day of 1797 exiling her son Paul to Lithuania and elevating her grandchild, Alexander, to heir apparent. But only weeks before the date chosen for the announcement, a stroke destroyed Catherine's ability to communicate and she died some hours later.

Paul's first act as emperor was the exhumation of the man he needed to be his father – Peter III, grandson of Peter the Great. This action was not, as one English eyewitness ventured, 'a testimony of Paul's affection for the memory of his father', but rather 'an act of hostility against his mother'. The forty-three-year-old tsar laid Peter's opened coffin beside Catherine's catafalque in the Mourning Room of the Winter Palace and ordered two of the tsar's surviving assassins to stand guard beneath the inscription 'Divided in life, united in death.'[4] Thus the fiasco of Paul's reign began with the spectacle of the new emperor wailing over the remains of his murdered father, who – quite possibly – had played no part in his conception. A rumour circulated that Paul was not even the son of Catherine II, but rather Empress Elizabeth's secret baby: gossip that sought to explain the sovereign's uncharacteristically maternal attitude towards the child. Some historians claim that Paul was 'beyond all reasonable doubt the son of Peter III and Catherine II',[5] others that 'presumptive evidence' suggests he was the offspring of Sergei Saltykov.[6] In a contemporary memorandum to the French Cabinet, the diplomat Gérard de Champeaux noted that Peter was impotent, whereas Catherine was not. One possible motive for the suppression of her *Memoirs* during the nineteenth century was that they suggested Paul was illegitimate.[7] If Paul was not the son of Peter III, then successive tsars would not be Romanovs or Holstein-Gottorps, but simple Saltykovs.[8] Yet pug-nosed Paul resembled Peter III and not the tall and handsome Saltykov. What is more, the courtier Charles Masson suggested that Catherine's hatred for 'the very sight of Paul'[9] was sufficient proof that he was indeed Peter's son.

Stressed and nervous from infancy, Paul had a short fuse. Insomnia and nightmares pestered his childhood and youth. He was kept away from Catherine, surrounded by spies and isolated by his petulance and his explosive tantrums. George Macartney recorded a vivid moment when Paul's paranoia magnified a perfectly rational fear. Upon being invited to a masquerade, the grand duke told his tutor, 'there is a great monster called the small-pox, walking up and down the ball-room and . . . that same monster has very good intelligence of my motions, for he is generally to be found precisely in those very places where I have the most inclination to go'.[10]

In 1776, Paul had married his second wife – the niece of Frederick the Great, Sophia Dorothea of Württemberg – who took the Russian name Maria Feodorovna when she was received into the Orthodox Church. Five years later, the couple went on a European Grand Tour, which included a visit to the house in Zaandam where Peter the Great had briefly lodged.[11] In Paris they purchased drawings from the studio of one of Catherine's favourite artists, Jean-Baptiste Greuze. They bought Sèvres porcelain and furniture from Dominique Daguerre – their enthusiasm provoking a lively interest in the Russian capital for French fixtures and fittings. Travelling with the grand duke and duchess was the connoisseur Prince Nikolay Yusupov, whom Paul later charged with the upkeep of the Hermitage galleries – no easy stewardship, as the tsar, on a whim, decided to split the collection between his various palaces. In Venice the grand duke had attempted to purchase the extensive sculpture collection of Filippo Farsetti, but the republic would not grant an export licence. Years later, after the French annexation of Venice in 1797, the purchase became possible, and 371 crates of sculpture arrived in St Petersburg, which Paul promptly donated to the Academy of Arts.[12]

Returning from their Grand Tour to a cold reception from Catherine, whose court and policies Paul had consistency criticised abroad, the grand duke and duchess settled in Gatchina. When Paul took possession of Rinaldi's austere palace, he employed his favourite architect, Vincenzo Brenna, to embellish the complex. Forty-two kilometres south of the capital and set overlooking ponds and gracious parkland, Gatchina not only provided the grand duke with a base at some remove from his mother, but also allowed him to develop – both positively and negatively. He was a good landlord to the estate's 3,000 inhabitants,

*Carl Shulz's* View of Gatchina Palace *from the mid-nineteenth century.*

concerning himself with the health and education of all classes and aiding people if they encountered financial hardship.[13] The ease created by these measures was, however, compromised by the strict discipline of a life controlled by passports, guard posts, curfews and a demanding dress code. At Gatchina, Paul was able to drill a private army to the highest standard.[14]

In the first year of his short, erratic and unfortunate reign, the city of St Petersburg was subjected to a torrent of rules which overwhelmed the administration and bewildered the inhabitants. State secretary Dmitry Troshchinsky claimed there were 48,000 new orders and laws during that first year.[15] As with estimates for the number of Catherine's lovers, the sum of laws and decrees passed during Paul's four-and-a-quarter-year reign varies wildly, but there is no doubt that excessive legislation poured from the troubled waters of a brain that was desperately seeking structure and precision. Like Peter III, Paul's 'Prussianness' aimed to restrain inchoate 'Russianness' and curb a dangerous cosmopolitanism. His officers looked like German soldiers from the age of Frederick the Great. He built 'barracks, guard houses and, above all things, sentry boxes', although – as Heinrich von Storch observed – these buildings were of timber and would 'scarcely last longer than their builder'.[16] The easy-going pleasures of the well-to-do which had characterised much of Catherine's reign disappeared, as St Petersburg was brought to order by a monarch increasingly held to be off his head.

Paul had a wooden theatre pulled down simply because Catherine had built it.[17] Count Rostopchin suggested that 'one might think he was searching for ways of making himself loathed and detested'. Charles Whitworth, the British Ambassador, showed tolerance for the new emperor – until his patience ran out. Soon after Paul's accession, Whitworth wrote that 'great allowances must be made for the peculiar delicacy of his situation'.

Less than three years later, Whitworth was complaining that his sole occupation – 'to mark the constant turn and change of the Emperor' – was no easy job.[18] By March 1800 Whitworth confirmed that 'the emperor is literally not in his senses . . . His disorder has gradually increased and now manifests itself in such a manner as to fill everyone with the most serious alarm.' While some of the more extreme instances of Paul's lunacy were con-cocted by enemies or exasperated subjects, an English visitor's opinion of the emperor having 'a slight approach to insanity in the organisation of his mind' was clearly nothing but the finest example of British understatement. Impetuous and often rude, Paul was given to making impudent and infantile remarks. Once, deciding to play coachman to the court engraver, James Walker, Paul suddenly tapped on the carriage window and declared, 'Do you know, Squire Walker, if I chose, I could spit in your face.'[19] Again, sense was lurking in this apparently fatuous statement. The emperor was obviously delighted that the glass windows of the coach would protect his guest's face. Nonetheless, Paul's reign was – like one of Paul's own tortured dreams – a nightmare.

The tsar transformed the capital into a fortress. The city was locked down with barriers and guard posts, and there were infan-try, police and Cossacks on every corner. When Casanova had planned to quit Petersburg in 1765 he was obliged to post the information in the *Vedomosti* a fortnight before his departure.[20] It was a procedure that afforded protection to the city's merchants. With Paul on the throne, such an advertisement was required to be placed in the paper on three separate occasions.[21] When Paul demanded that a passport be issued to inhabitants temporarily leaving the city to visit friends or country houses round about, people started to rail. They suffered further from an inconveni-ent and degrading decree, which stipulated that whenever the emperor or a member of the imperial family passed, subjects were required to stop and kneel – dismounting if they were on horse-back, descending if they were in a carriage. In bad weather the duty was unpleasant, but failure to comply resulted in arrest.[22] As the German dramatist Auguste von Kotzbuë arrived in Petersburg after a difficult trip, the Grand Duke Alexander galloped past. Von Kotzbuë, neither recognising him nor being aware of the rule of obeisance, narrowly escaped punishment.[23]

The capital changed colour as Paul ordered the painting of bridges, watch-houses and imperial gates in red, black and white 'harlequin jackets'. These appeared across the city overnight. Another caprice was the placing of the monogram 'Paul I', surmounted with a crown, in every corner and above every window of the palace. When someone attempted to count them all, he 'left off perfectly weary, after he had numbered eight thousand'.[24] As for dress, each day there was some alteration to what was permissible.[25] Associating the whims of fashion with self-indulgence and a flagrant disregard for authority, Paul stipulated old-fashioned breeches, stockings and powdered wigs. Frock coats and round-style French hats were forbidden, and watchmen were despatched with long poles to flick offending hats off the heads of those who persisted in wearing them. French fashion called to mind revolution and republicanism, but when relations with England soured and Paul absurdly despatched a troop of more than 22,000 Cossacks to attack British India, he likewise became hostile towards English dress. Animosity extended to a complete ban on the import of British goods in 1800, further stunting life in what had been a vibrant and cosmopolitan capital. Books were also the target of embargo. In 1800, the emperor forbade the import of foreign titles and sheet music,[26] although it seems readers were able to obtain a good deal of forbidden material – a skill that would serve a repressed and subversive population throughout the nineteenth and twentieth centuries.

Idiocies proliferated. Paul banned some 12,000 nobles, arrested seven field marshals, 333 generals and 2,261 officers.[27] One early-twentieth-century Russian source claims that he commanded prostitutes to wear yellow dresses in order to signal their trade.[28]

Commands were often swiftly followed by countermands, and Paul's reputation as a compulsive and crazy lawmaker was spreading far and wide. A cartoon attributed to the Scot Isaac Cruickshank was published in March 1800, 'The Three Orders of St Petersburg'. Paul holds an 'Order' in his right hand, and in his left is a paper marked 'Counter Order'. Consequently, 'Disorder' is inscribed on the emperor's crown. Another English caricature shows Paul with one foot on St Petersburg, the other in bedlam. Even palace dinners – more restrained than under previous sovereigns – were touched by Paul's folly. When the simple meal was over, the emperor grabbed the plates containing leftover cakes and flung them into the corner of the room, 'apparently finding amusement in watching the pages pushing and shoving each other in their efforts to gather up as many as they could'.[29]

*Isaac Cruikshank's* The Three Orders of St Petersburg.

A French visitor recorded that, one day, Paul visited the docks and watched a sailor caulk the hull of a boat. 'There is a skilful man,' cried the monarch, approaching the spot and examining the work with care. 'This is admirable,' he told the sailor. 'Your skill merits recompense.' The excited man, expecting a couple of roubles, bowed before his sovereign, who said, 'Rise, I name you lieutenant-general.'[30] This incident smacks of one of the most absurd episodes of Paul's reign: the factual life of the fictitious Lieutenant Kijé, made famous in the West after Sergei Prokoviev wrote suitably pompous, comic and catchy music for a 1934 film of the story, shot in Leningrad's Belgoskino studios. The Kijé biography in its earliest guise appeared in *Stories of the Time of Paul I*, published in 1870 by the Russian lexicographer Vladimir Dahl, who got it orally from his father. In the story, a scribe deforms a phrase in a list of promotions and thereby creates a non-existent ensign named Kijé. When the document is shown to Paul, the emperor suggests that this ensign be promoted to the rank of lieutenant, in line with the others on the list. From nothing, Kijé rises rapidly through the ranks. When he becomes a colonel, Paul decides it is time to meet the officer, but no Kijé can be found. Officials trace the origin of the mistake, dare not reveal the bureaucratic blunder and decide to tell the emperor that Kijé is dead, whereupon Paul declares that it is a great pity, as he was such a good officer.

Almost equally odd was the experience of the German dramatist Auguste von Kotzbuë. After his arrival in Petersburg in the spring of 1800, Paul exiled him to Siberia but, after several months, recalled him, gave him an estate and made him the director of St Petersburg's German Theatre. One day, the emperor summoned von Kotzbuë and asked him to translate into French an absurd – almost Arthurian – summons to all European sovereigns to settle their political differences with a single tournament. Although von Kotzbuë left Russia the following year, his association with the country appears to have continued. He was assassinated by a student in Mannheim in 1819, suspected of being a Russian spy.[31]

As Catherine had left Russia in a sorry financial state, Paul attempted to cut costs. Even within the palace, he reduced expenses by refusing to use *traiteurs* and ordering food directly from the market. He put the colleges under the control of a minister answerable to the tsar. He attempted to rationalise the provinces and made nobles liable for the costs of local government. On the delicate subject of serfs, he instructed landlords not to force them to work on Sundays, and suggested that serfs only labour for their masters for three days a week – although this was never written into law.[32]

In the capital there was little new building. A design competition was announced for the projected cathedral of Our Lady of Kazan on Nevsky Prospekt, although Paul – who had been much impressed by the curving colonnades of St Peter's in Rome – determined the overall effect. The Tauride, one of the city's most splendid palaces, fell victim to Paul's military passion and was converted into a barracks, while the tsar's notorious impatience resulted in the old St Isaac's Church being rapidly finished with brick. Paul was understandably exasperated that such a significant structure, right in the centre of St Petersburg, remained unfinished after twenty-six years. Meanwhile, the emperor's acute insecurity resulted in the building of the fortified Mikhailovsky Palace, in which he intended to live. Moated and protected by drawbridges, the castle was designed to afford protection against dangerous plots.

On the site of Rastrelli's old Summer Palace, Vincenzo Brenna constructed a forbidding mass, which suddenly turned red. The colour of a pair of gloves worn by a lady of the court so struck the emperor that – as a contemporary visitor noted – 'the next day it became his favourite tint and he gave instant orders that his new residence should be painted accordingly. Hence it is called the Red Palace and a most frightful, glaring appearance

*Entrance to the moated, martial Mikhailovsky Palace.*

it makes.'[33] Paul laid the foundation stone in February 1797, and the Mikhailovsky Palace was swiftly completed by thousands of builders and decorators working around the clock. The main approach was made between stable buildings along a short avenue that terminated in a square, where Peter sited an impressive snub to the memory of his mother: a copy of Carlo Bartolomeo Rastrelli's unrealised equestrian statue of Peter the Great. In order to disparage Catherine's text on the base of Falconet's *Bronze Horseman*, which linked her with Peter the Great, Paul added a caption below his statue: 'To Great-Grandfather – from his Great-Grandson'.[34] Legitimacy and lineage were proclaimed and the imperial family moved into the Mikhailovsky Palace, against their wishes, on 1 February 1801. The plaster was still damp, the interior clammy.[35]

By then, as Prince Viktor Kochubey wrote, a 'black melancholia' had 'taken possession of everyone'.[36] Presiding over this gloom was the emperor, who was living in perpetual terror and was vividly aware – as he confessed to the Swedish Ambassador – that he was 'insupportable'. By mid-1800 plans for a coup had been conceived by Count Nikita Panin, the nephew of Paul's tutor. The fine-tuning and organisation were undertaken by the military governor of the St Petersburg district, Count Peter von der Pahlen, who persuaded the reluctant grand duke, Alexander, to agree to the ousting of his father. There was no talk of regicide, but the composition of the band chosen to penetrate the Mikhailovsky Palace, and the manner in which they prepared for the attack, suggested that matters would get out of hand. On 11 March 1801, a group of disgruntled soldiers – led by officers of the Preobrazhensky and Semyonovsky Guards, along with senators eager for change – met for supper. Their enthusiasm in toasting the man who was soon to rule over them resulted in inevitable inebriation. Alexander, meanwhile, was dining with his father and a small group of relations and courtiers, in the supposed safety of the Mikhailovsky Palace.[37]

Pahlen covered the main entrance and surrounded the stronghold with soldiers. The last of Catherine's three great favourites, Platon Zubov, along with his mighty younger brother, Nicholas, and General von Bennigsen snuck in through a back entrance and attempted to negotiate the labyrinth of passages designed to bewilder intruders. They overcame sentries manning interior guard posts, and found and forced their way into Paul's apartment. The emperor attempted to hide behind a screen, but – as in almost any farce – his ankles gave him away. Von Bennigsen and Zubov were placing Paul under arrest when a group of about eight rowdy soldiers burst into the room and – thinking the tsar was putting up a fight – set upon him. Paul's jaw was smashed against a marble table and a pair of large hands closed around his throat.

The tsar was dead, and few Russians shed a tear. When it was announced that Paul had died of an 'apoplectic stroke', spontaneous celebrations erupted throughout the capital. As suddenly as

St Petersburg had been converted into an armed camp, it reverted
with jubilation into an easy, elegant and urbane capital. Absurd
dress codes were dropped, the police presence diminished and a
great number of people who had been arrested were released. Furnishings and paintings were rescued from that 'monstrous mass
of red rock', the Mikhailovsky Palace, so that they would not
decay in its deadly atmosphere.[38] The new emperor moved back
to the airiness of the Winter Palace. But in that very moment in
which the city regained its brilliance – with candles of thanksgiving burning brightly in every window – patricide compounded
with regicide in Alexander's perception of the recent coup, and
his concern about his unnatural complicity in the plot would cast
a shadow over his reign.[39]

Four years later, in 1805, a student of Benjamin West arrived in
St Petersburg as historical painter to the Russian court. Robert
Ker Porter found a capital in which almost every joy was beset
with difficulty and annoyance. Kronstadt, where he disem-
barked, was in its habitual state of neglect. Attempting to climb
the 'straggling staircases' leading to the customs and immigra-
tion offices, he found them 'obstructed by heaps of rubbish,
bricks and mortar'. A more splendid welcome was offered by the
orange-sashed, blue-tunicked boatmen who oared him into the
city, low-toned Russian folk songs sounding from beneath their
'well-curled mustachios'.[40]

Upon arrival, Porter beheld what another contemporary visitor
famously called 'a city of columns', with buildings placed in clear
geometrical patterns. That visitor – Theodor von Faber – provided
a compliment and update to the thorough study made by Heinrich von Storch towards the end of St Petersburg's first century.
In 1794, Storch estimated that a family of five people with five
servants and a carriage-and-pair, living in a comfortable part of
the capital, could exist on 3,500 roubles per annum. By 1805, that

had risen to 6,000 roubles, and by the end of the decade 'a very mediocre household' would spend 10,000 roubles a year.[41] Storch caustically suggested that the work of three Russian servants was easily performed by one maid in Germany, although, in St Petersburg, serfs were legion.[42] Casanova claimed that there was no 'better servant in the world than a Russian', who 'works without ceasing, sleeps in front of the door of his master's bedroom to be always ready to fulfil his orders, never answering his reproaches, incapable of theft'.[43] And yet, 'after drinking a little too much he becomes a perfect monster'. The servant hired by Theodor von Faber during his stay certainly indulged. One night, von Faber returned to his lodgings where his soused servant, Fedor, failed to recognise him. Falling against his master repeatedly as he tried to help him undress, Fedor was locked up in his room and threatened with dismissal. The following morning, von Faber was awoken by his apologetic serf, who presented breakfast faultlessly laid out on the table. Thinking Fedor had forced the lock in order to escape from his room, von Faber was furious. After further explanations – it had been Fedor's birthday, he'd drunk with a friend, and he hadn't forced the lock but escaped through the window to perform his duties – von Faber remained adamant. Yet, after musing on the various qualities of Russian servants and on the need for a little pleasure and alcohol in the cold north, von Faber told Fedor that he could stay.[44] A few decades later, Lord Redesdale's coachman would ask his lordship's leave to get drunk. Redesdale would check his engagement book. If he was free that night, he'd let his coachman go.[45]

Among the wealthy and fashionable women of St Petersburg there was a growing tendency towards simplification,[46] which was visible in the high-wasted dress designs. Beside the sobriety of this French Empire style, native Russian dress appeared both exotic and excessive. The over-made-up wives of well-to-do merchants sported brocade and gold lace[47] – to which, in winter, they added velvet capes lined with sable. Among the aristocracy, the display of great swathes of jewels had been replaced by extravagance at the milliners' – but the wives of merchants still decked themselves with pearls. Petersburg fashion was also coloured by decoratively dressed Cossacks, Bashkirs and Armenians, while the smocks of local peasants resembled those worn in England at the time of Richard II.[48] The serfs grew 'great unmerciful patriarchal beards', which made the Irish visitor Catherine Wilmot wonder if they had not been born before the Flood. She was fascinated by peasants crossing themselves incessantly. Even when they were floating 'on timber planks in the river', she witnessed 'men bowing with all their might and main . . . their long beards forking in the wind'. As for the servants of the nobility, Catherine was struck by their 'oddest' appearance – 'as if a Turk had been their Father and a Quaker their mother!'[49]

With Alexander's accession in 1801, the festivities of each season were celebrated once again. Winter arrived with slivers of ice swirling down the Neva, as the beards that Catherine Wilmot saw blowing in the wind began to glitter white with frost.[50] The freeze hardened and thickened. Fir branches marked out carriage tracks across the Neva, along which people drove, oblivious of the great current swirling underneath. Robert Ker Porter found the incessant and rapid movement of so many colourful carriages and sledges skidding about, against the blinding dazzle of the ice, painful to his artist's eye. Yet he was thrilled when the early arrival of winter animated the city and transformed its trees into clumps of white coral dusted with diamonds. The freeze thawed the hearts of the Russians who sung, laughed and wrestled – 'tumbling about like great bears' on the snow. The ever-popular ice-hills on the Neva rose to a height of twelve to fifteen metres, which did not prevent the reckless from skating down their vertiginous slopes.[51]

Approaching Christmas, Porter was invited to a Venetian masquerade at the Winter Palace, where he was able to see and smell 1,500 assorted guests – from members of the court down to the rich merchants and their wives, who appeared like 'magicians and overgrown fairies clad in glittering robes of shining green'. He spent an hour or so among the 'steaming' throng, after which the imperial family made its slow progress through the palace and – along with the grateful historical painter to the court – retired from the 'offensive vapour'. Quarenghi's theatre in the Hermitage had been converted into a banquet hall to enable them to dine to the harmonies of a hidden orchestra. Such balls were frequent during Christmas and carnival, when hordes of masked revellers crowded the streets and as many as 800 carriages could be seen drawn up outside the Winter Palace.[52] Lent was strictly observed and the people prepared 'for abstinence with extravagance'.[53] Porter noted that the extreme cold and 'mad festivity' of carnival led to drunkenness and death.[54]

When the thaw arrived, fragile ice was deliberately broken along the river banks to dissuade pedestrians from trying their luck.[55] Roadways marked out across the frozen river held fast the longest, but were eventually swept away by the vast blocks of ice speeding downriver towards the Gulf, leaving the Neva navigable only by boat once more. John Quincy Adams – who, in 1809, became the first American Minister Plenipotentiary to be recognised by the Russian court – noted that, while his family was breakfasting at about 10 a.m. on 24 April, there was a five-gun salute from the Peter and Paul Fortress, signalling that the river was free. As had been the custom since the city's earliest days, the governor carried a glass of water to the tsar to mark the occasion.[56]

With the onset of spring, melting snow flooded the streets and unlucky pedestrians were doomed – as they were in autumn, with its rains and piercing winds – to be splattered and soaked. When Easter arrived, the festivities resumed. Peasants gave one another hard-boiled eggs dyed with logwood, while sugar, glass, gilded wood, porcelain or marble eggs and boxes full of sugar plums were exchanged among the well-to-do. Fairs were

set up in St Isaac's Square with swings and 'whirligig chairs'[57]–
a four-seat wooden forerunner of the Big Wheel, propelled by a
peasant pushing the back of each chair as it circled down to begin
its ascent. Booths were set up for short performances of raucous
comedies performed by clowns and local amateurs, and larger
temporary wooden theatres holding up to 1,500 spectators were
constructed. There were tightrope-walkers and dancers. Sometimes a dromedary clumped around between the dancing bears
and monkeys.[58] If the gardens on the small Neva islands were
compared with London's eighteenth-century pleasure gardens at
Vauxhall, then these boisterous scenes more closely resembled
London's Bartholomew Fair.

As summer approached and the sun parched the usually
moist St Petersburg soil, thick dust clouds of street dirt coated
hot pedestrians – and those who could do so left the city. By
June, the Petersburg season had ended. Returning from a trip
to Moscow, Porter found the capital particularly deserted and
lacklustre in the summer months.[59] But those who were forced,
by profession or poverty, to stay there did find amusement. Alexander arranged a gravelled walk around the southern perimeter
of the Admiralty, where stalls for amusement and refreshment
were set up. John Quincy Adams enjoyed boating parties and
picnics to the islands.[60] Catherine Wilmot's sister, Martha, saw
the emperor review the Cadet Corps, turned out in their green-
and-scarlet uniforms. On the same day, she had the good fortune
to watch a manned balloon flight over the capital, the two men on
board privileged to see the extensive cityscape of Messrs Trezzini,
Le Blond and Eropkin laid out beneath them, as on a map.[61]

If the Wilmot sisters enjoyed being out and about, Martha
took no joy in Russian dining. In the summer of 1803, she wrote
that two soups were always brought to the table: 'one composed
of herbs . . . ornamented and enriched by lumps of fat', while
the other was dumplinged with '*petit patées* of bad paste'. Next
came 'a fowl smothered in butter and boiled to rags', followed

by a vegetable so well disguised it was impossible to identify it. That was followed by roast meat, wild-boar ham and 'such a train of dishes . . . as keeps one hours at table'.[62] At court, however, Alexander laid less emphasis on interminable banquets and introduced the idea of the buffet supper, which started with hors d'oeuvre, followed by four courses reflecting the emperor's personal love of French cuisine. Drunkenness was not tolerated, and it was rumoured that the emperor removed drunkards from the lists of those in line for promotion.[63] As for the humbler inhabitants of the capital, the 'culture of the kitchen garden' was 'brought to such perfection', and the baking was so good, that Storch suggested it was 'impossible anywhere, even in Paris, to eat better bread'.[64]

The tradition of offering hospitality accounted for a considerable part of the expenditure of great households. Anyone of good manners and appearance who had been presented and accepted by such a household had the right to dine there, uninvited, on any occasion. The custom led to the kind of absurd situations to be found in nineteenth-century Russian novels. A poor foreign officer seeking admission into the Russian service kept himself in St Petersburg for two years, by virtue of Count Razumovsky's hospitality. During that time, Razumovsky noticed the man at his table, spoke with him in his library and found the stranger to be most knowledgeable about military matters. Never once did the count ask his name or enquire about his circumstances. One day, the man disappeared and Razumovsky missed him. Nobody knew who he was or where he lived. At length, the stranger returned and a more personal conversation was struck up between host and guest. At once – after two years and one meeting – the man was commissioned in the Russian Army.[65]

Entertaining in such a multilingual city was not without its difficulties. John Quincy Adams remembered the awkwardness of presenting the US Consul at Arkhangelsk to Count Romanzov. As the latter had no English and the consul scarcely any

French, their exchanges were halting.[66] French had become fashionable Petersburg's lingua franca, although Russian, German, English, Dutch, Italian, Greek, Turkish and Swedish – to name but a few – were also heard. Walking along the Nevsky Prospekt in the first years of the nineteenth century provided an aural mix as varied as that of London's Oxford Street or the Parisian *Grands Boulevards* in the twenty-first century. The Nevsky proclaimed St Petersburg as a city of strangers, and its places of worship testified to that diversity: there were Armenians, Orthodox, Protestants, Catholics, Lutherans, Calvinists and – among the tradesmen in the markets – Muslims.

The city was growing. In the first years of Alexander's reign, the population was floating between 200,000 and 270,000 – that considerable spread flagging the uncertainty of the estimate. What can be established with some confidence is that peasants and military personnel outnumbered merchants and townspeople by three to one, and that the population was volatile. In 1811 – the year before Napoleon's invasion of Russia – St Petersburg was counted the fifth-largest city in Europe, with 336,000 inhabitants. It was divided into eleven parts and fifty-five quarters, of which the First Admiralty Quarter remained the most exclusive.[67] Construction and maintenance continued, using simple, time-honoured procedures. More often than not, the workmen's sole tool was a hatchet and, in place of elaborate scaffolding to repair fractured stucco, an angled beam onto which thin steps of wood were nailed provided access to all levels of a façade. Otherwise, a plasterer sat on a strip of wood tied to a rope dangling from an overhang and bobbed around in mid-air as he smoothed the damaged surface [68] – a procedure still seen in the city today.

William Hastie – a Scot who worked as a stonemason for six years at Tsarskoe Selo and then became its chief architect – was appointed to the Office of Waterways in 1804. Hastie's study of cast-iron bridge-building, which had developed in England and Germany during the 1790s, resulted in designs to replace the wooden bridges over Petersburg's canals. Among them was the twenty-seven-metre-long, twenty-one-metre-wide Police Bridge over the Moika on the Nevsky Prospekt, which opened in late 1806, and the Red Bridge on Gorokhovaya Street with its four granite pillars. The moat around the Admiralty was filled in and its fortifications removed in 1806, and there was a port for galleys at the undeveloped western end of Vasilevsky Island.[69] As the Peter and Paul Fortress now stood in the centre of a sizeable city, it was even less useful for defence than it had been in the early days. However, it was a structure suited to a prison, and it continued to house the imperial mint. Every day 300 workers stripped off as they arrived and were given thin, unpocketed shirts and shorts, which made pilfering almost impossible.

An unskilled worker could earn anything between fifteen and eighty kopeks a day and feed himself well on cabbage soup, dried fish or buckwheat *kasha* for about seven kopeks. The poorest slept for one kopek on one of the hard beds crammed in three huge vaulted basements which stood beneath the Haymarket. A door porter collected admission and took care of security. Close by there was a trader selling leftovers and cuts of meat too putrid to be offered anywhere else. These were chopped into morsels so that they could be eaten easily with a toothpick – all knives were confiscated at the entrance. After a fitful sleep in a rat- and roach-infested stench, 1,000 workers were discharged into the dawning city.[70]

Under Alexander, Petersburg was satisfactorily policed. A Court of Conscience was in place to moderate misguided calumny and the petty delinquencies of youth.[71] The authorities regularly raided taverns, in an attempt to control prostitution and the spread of sexually transmitted diseases. Petty thefts occurred in crowded public places, but crime continued to be low. However, one brutal murder – committed in 1806 – drew the most sensational punishment. The coachman of the allegedly cruel Count Ablenovsky struck his boss with the iron key used to tighten the bolts on carriages, strangled him with the reins, robbed him and then fled to Lake Ladoga, where he was apprehended. Sentenced to be 'knouted without mercy', the guilty man was paraded through Petersburg, then taken to 'an open and muddy plain' near the Neva to be flogged. As a huge crowd of spectators gathered, the executioner bound the murderer to a board and began to beat him. After only a few minutes, 'nothing was heard except the bloody splash of the knout on the senseless body of the wretched man'. The punishment continued for a good hour, before the torturer was instructed to stop. At that point the apparently lifeless body was branded, and gunpowder was rubbed into the wound to mark the man indelibly. After that, an instrument resembling 'monstrous curling irons' were thrust up the man's nose, while two officers tore the nostrils from his head, an act so painful that the prisoner revivified and was carted off towards Siberia. Not surprisingly, at the first staging post on the following day, he expired.[72]

Upon acceding to the throne, Paul had relieved the architect Charles Cameron of all his duties. Although the tsar briefly relented in 1799 and commissioned Cameron to design a bridge at Pavlovsk, it is likely that the Scot went home and returned to St Petersburg only when Alexander summoned him to be Chief Architect of the Admiralty. Approaching sixty, Cameron proved unequal to the task and worked on smaller projects, such as the cathedral at Kronstadt and the repairs to fire-damaged Pavlovsk. He died a recluse in Petersburg in 1812, his architectural library auctioned off by the appropriately named Jean Grabit of 78 Nevsky Prospekt.[73]

The man who replaced Cameron to oversee the building of the new Admiralty was Andreyan Zakharov. A gold medallist from the St Petersburg Academy of Arts, he was appointed chief architect for all naval building in the capital in 1806. The renovation

and restructuring of the 407-metre-long Admiralty with its central tower took seventeen years to complete. A bas-relief runs
around the tower, celebrating the creation of the Russian Navy
under Peter the Great, who is seen receiving a trident from Nep-
tune. At each of the four corners there are statues of classical
warriors, including Alexander the Great: a mistaken nod to the
emperor who was named more for the Russian warrior and saint,
Alexander Nevsky, than for the Greek general. New motifs and
mythologies – discovered when Napoleon invaded Egypt – had
begun to influence European artists and designers. One of the
first instances in Russian architecture was the inclusion of Isis,
the Egyptian god of water and wind, among the twenty-two
statues representing the elements and seasons placed around the
tower above the Admiralty's triumphal arch.[74] Another Russian
architect, Andrei Voronikhin – possibly the illegitimate son of
the great patron of the arts, Count Stroganov – finalised plans for
Kazan Cathedral, which was to stand on the Nevsky Prospekt.
The design merged Paul's beloved colonnades of St Peter's in
Rome with the dome of Soufflot's Eglise Sainte-Geneviève
in Paris. The new cathedral would provide a home for the venerated icon *Our Lady of Kazan*, which was brought to the capital
during the reign of Peter the Great. Kazan's powerful and airy
colonnade embraced a theatrical space which – sixty years on –
would provide a dramatic platform for early socialist orators.

Unlike Cameron, the ageing Quarenghi made an important
contribution to St Petersburg during the early years of Alexander's reign. As well as the Imperial Chancery, there was a new
building for the daughters of the impoverished gentry at the
Smolny Institute, the colonnade of the Anichkov Palace and the
Horse Guards Riding School, or Manège. Built between 1804
and 1807, this last remains one of the finest classical buildings
in the capital. The statues of the horsemen Castor and Pollux,
which are sited in front, are fine examples of the statuary that
appeared all over Alexander's capital.[75]

As for the palaces surrounding the capital, John Quincy Adams found Oranienbaum to be in better condition than Peterhof, but despaired that the furnishings were 'magnificence in all its stages of decay, from the mere change of fashion to the perishing rags and tatters of crimson satin curtains and chair covers'. At Peterhof he found 'once-gilded wainscotting and doors, . . . Chinese lacquering and pictures perished upon the canvas, from the damps of uninhabited apartments'.[76] While Martha Wilmot marvelled at the gardens which displayed 'works as indeed I could not have supposed it possible for art to produce – fountains . . . gladiators with swords of water', Adams found some of the contraptions risible. One such was the fountain with 'three leaden ducks pursued by a dog, which are movable and made to imitate the barking of a dog and the quack of ducks'. The effect, he wrote, besides 'being ridiculous, is very bad.'[77]

Once a year in the summer, when Alexander gave a great public ball, the gardens at Peterhof were illuminated, and the well-engineered causeway from Petersburg became choked with traffic. As dusk fell, the gardens became a blaze of glimmering light, as the soft harmonies of Russian hunting music horned from the depths of the park. Light glinted on the shimmering leaves and struck the white bark of the birch trees. Beyond the jewelled spray of the Grand Cascade, well-lit ships of the line were anchored offshore. A similar, smaller fête was held for the diplomatic corps. Adams attended, marvelling at the 300,000 lamps and the 1,600 servants detailed to illuminate them. As Robert Ker Porter remarked, 'in the luxury of light no country is so lavish as Russia'.[78]

The seemingly gentle, blue-eyed emperor who invited people to these Peterhof celebrations had been born in 1777. Rather as Empress Elizabeth had done with Paul, Catherine whisked Alexander and his younger brother, Constantine, away from their parents and managed their upbringing. Their governor, Count Nikolai Saltykov, was encouraged to teach Alexander to 'learn

while playing' and to foster virtue rather than inculcate knowledge.[79] In any case, this somewhat unconventional education
was interrupted by Alexander's marriage to Catherine's choice
of bride, Princess Louise of Baden, who took the name Elizabeth Alekseevna.[80] It was an unsuccessful marriage, although the
couple were reconciled towards the end of their lives when the
emperor's mysticism led him to break up with his giddy mistress,
Maria Naryshkina.[81]

Alexander expressed his desire to 'govern the nation according
to the laws . . . of the august Catherine the Great, our grandmother'. A university was created in the capital, and the architect
Vasily Stasov was commissioned to add a wing to the imperial
palace at Tsarskoe Selo to house an elite lyceum set up to train
the sons of the nobility for service. The school's first pupils
included future Decembrist conspirators, other radicals and the
poet Alexander Pushkin. Alexander I also lifted the restriction
on publishing and the import of books, but only to introduce
pre-emptive censorship by the government through the newly
formed Ministry of Education.[82] Serf auctions and serf-for-sale
adverts were forbidden and the abolition of serfdom was discussed. In March 1803, the Free Cultivators' Law was passed,
enabling landlords to free serfs and – in return for a 'redemption'
payment – give them a strip of land to cultivate. But the scheme
hardly stimulated widespread change. By 1825, fewer than
50,000 serfs had been freed and, of those, nearly one-third were
on the estates of Prince Alexander Golitsyn.[83]

The man responsible for attempting to deflect Alexander from
Catherine's autocratic regime was the self-made son of a village
priest, Mikhail Speransky, who wished to make Russia both
efficient and humane. Repelled by serfdom, Speransky famously
wrote, 'I find in Russia two classes: the slaves of the sovereign and
the slaves of the landowners. The first call themselves free only
in relation to the second: there are no truly free people in Russia,
apart from beggars and philosophers.' Speransky prepared a

new code of law, which he based on Napoleon's Civil Code of 1804, but his proposals were not adopted. Napoleon intruded on the peaceful processes of the Russian court, and Alexander found himself at war.[84] A decade of his reign was preoccupied with Napoleon, who began his campaign against Russia with the massacre of the Austro–Russian alliance at Austerlitz in December 1805. Alexander – who put himself at the head of his armies and ignored the advice of the venerable General Kutuzov – was humiliated by his defeat at Friedland into making an uneasy truce at Tilsit in June 1807. The treaty was roundly condemned in Russia, and anti-French sentiment ran high. In St Petersburg salons there were rumours of plots against the tsar.[85]

Madame de Staël, the Frenchwoman of letters and fervent opponent of Bonaparte, arrived in the Russian capital in 1811, the year before Napoleon renewed hostilities. She found herself enchanted by a city in which 'a wizard with a wand had conjured all the marvels of Europe and Asia in the middle of a wasteland'. She felt convinced that Petersburg's very existence presented 'proof of the ardent will of the Russians which knows nothing to be impossible'. The house she was renting overlooked Falconet's *Bronze Horseman*. As Madame de Staël gazed at the sober buildings of Senate Square, she reflected on the silence of a city void of brave and raucous young men, who had gone to join the army that the tsar was urgently rebuilding.[86]

When presented to Alexander, she found the beleaguered ruler a fine example of 'goodness and dignity'. She visited his mother, the conservative Maria Feodorovna, in her apartments in the vast Tauride Palace and was much impressed by the white-pillared hall with its indoor garden, where 'the frigid airs of winter never breathe' and 'a luxuriant maze of oranges, myrtles, and clustering vines' was to be found. She studied Petersburg society and concurred with Storch that love – as Europeans understood it – was rarely seen. Storch had observed that men often neglected to pay women 'little attentions', so the ladies, in return, were 'dryness itself'.[87] The poetry and prose were still not in place to instruct and sustain a sentimental or profound love. Many Russians still acted impetuously and were still prompted by lust. Madame de Staël visited the Institute of St Catherine on the Fontanka, where 250 girls were 'brought up under the gaze of the empress', and she found their elegance and grace remarkable. Her only sadness was that St Petersburg's exceptional beauty was soon to be threatened by 'the arrogance of a man who ... like Satan' claimed all the kingdoms of the earth.[88]

In May 1811, when John Quincy Adams was taking his morning constitutional along the Fontanka Canal, he encountered – as he often did – Emperor Alexander out for a stroll. They discussed the growing tension between England and America and the possibility of war. Ten months later, meeting on the quay, a struggle much closer to home was preoccupying the tsar: a 'war is coming which I have done so much to avoid ... we expect to be attacked'. Less than a month later, Alexander told Adams that he was about to leave St Petersburg to join his army.[89] Napoleon had placed his troops in Germany in a state of readiness and arrived in Dresden on 9 May to lead his men into Russia, on to Moscow and thence to the Russian capital, St Petersburg. That was his plan.

On 23–4 June 1812, Napoleon crossed the River Niemen into Russian territory with between 300,000 and 400,000 men. A week later, the *Vedomosti* carried a report of Alexander's vow to Nicholas Saltykov, President of the Imperial Council. He would never surrender as long as the enemy remained on Russian soil. While the *Grande Armée* pressed forward to Moscow, Napoleon's 2nd French Corps and 10th Franco–Prussian Corps advanced in the direction of St Petersburg. Their aim was to cut off Count Peter Wittgenstein, the general defending the capital. But the French were defeated at the Battle of Kliastitzi in mid-July and Wittgenstein became known in the capital as the

'Defender of Petropolis'.[90] By mid-August, Napoleon's main army was 350 kilometres south-west of the old capital, laying siege to Smolensk, which the Russians evacuated and set on fire. As Leo Tolstoy observed, the further the Russian army retreated, the more fiercely blazed 'the spirit of fury against the enemy'.[91]

Kutuzov was in the capital at the head of the St Petersburg militia when Alexander appointed him Commander-in-Chief.[92] He immediately ordered the Russian Army to retreat, thereby luring the French deeper and deeper into unfriendly territory, stretching their supply lines beyond all strategic reasoning. On 26 August, 115 kilometres south-west of Moscow, the bloody Battle of Borodino was fought – much against Kutuzov's will. Artillery action was so intense that, at times, as many as 700 guns were firing from both sides across a sector scarcely one kilometre wide.[93] The Russians lost 50,000 men. Napoleon lost 40,000 and carried the day. By the time the first news arrived in Petersburg, mistakenly presenting Borodino as a great Russian victory, Napoleon was set to enter Moscow.

General Kutuzov's passionate aria in Prokofiev's 1943 opera based on Tolstoy's *War and Peace* leaves the listener in no doubt that, while St Petersburg may have been the fashionable capital, Moscow was the heart of Russia. To the invaders, Moscow was exotic – a Dutch engineer in Napoleon's army thought it appeared like 'a fairy tale city'.[94] It was 'Russian', in marked contrast to that hybrid and still-unfinished European parody, St Petersburg. Napoleon entered the ancient capital on 2 September and set up his HQ in the Kremlin Palace. Much of the population had fled, and those who stayed – most probably encouraged by Moscow's governor, Count Rostopchin – set fire to the city. When a strong wind rose on the night of 4 September the flames became impossible to control and French troops were ordered to shoot on sight any Muscovite suspected of arson.

Tolstoy gives a caustic appraisal of the intricate personal battles which, while Moscow burned, hardly ruffled 'Petersburg's daily round – tranquil, luxurious, concerned only with phantoms and reflections of life'.[95] But when rumours of the fall of Moscow reached the capital, Alexander's popularity plummeted. He took to riding in a closed carriage and ordered the Hermitage collection to be carted off to three remote northern towns.[96] The English prepared to leave. Madame de Staël had already departed.

In western Russia, snow fell early in 1812. On 9 November, as Adams took his morning walk, he noticed that the pontoon bridges on the Neva had been removed and found the river half-full of floating ice.[97] In the deepening cold, Napoleon – whose position in Russia was untenable – had begun his retreat through burnt-out territory, harassed by determined guerrilla warriors. His sappers, who were building bridges to carry the retreating army, were swept away by the freezing water. A Russian officer in pursuit reached the River Berezina and found French horses and men frozen beneath the surface of the ice. The 'anti-Christ' who had come to conquer Russia struggled back across the River Niemen on 13–14 December, his *Grande Armée* decimated by the elements. Emperor Alexander arrived in Vilna on 23 December to declare the end of the war, in the very place it had begun half a year earlier.[98] Napoleon's campaign had been swift but devastating – both to his opponents and to himself. In St Petersburg, the emperor's birthday passed off without celebration, as Alexander forbade expensive winter festivities in the wake of the recent suffering.[99]

The tsar rode at the head of his army across Europe, and Paris fell to the allies at the end of March 1814. Napoleon was exiled to Elba, but escaped to France and gathered around him the very troops sent to check his advance from the south coast. His daring escapade was abruptly curtailed after 100 days when he was beaten by the allies at Waterloo. From less accessible exile on St Helena, he wrote in awe of Russian determination, warning that 'all Europe could be Cossack'. In Paris, however, Alexander declared that he offered France 'peace and commerce'.[100] Seen as the saviour of Europe, he was enormously popular except among the politicians, who distrusted his simplistic notions and his developing mysticism. At the height of his international influence, between the Congress of Vienna in 1815 and the Congress of Aix-la-Chapelle in 1818, Alexander was radiant. Convinced that he was blessed by God, he sought to establish a Holy Alliance to protect and preserve Europe[101] – a kind of Christian EU both ahead of and behind its time. Meanwhile, Russian officers who spent months in Europe with Alexander's army absorbed progressive ideas that were to rattle the foundations of autocracy. Masonic lodges – ridiculed and suppressed by Catherine towards the end of her reign, but tolerated by Alexander when he acceded – gave their members a taste for conspiracy and secrecy that would help pave the way to revolution. The philanthropic tendencies of the Masons placed them in opposition to an emperor who – sanctioned by Divine Will – was growing increasingly reactionary.[102]

St Petersburg had been physically untouched by Napoleon's armies. It was, however, overrun by the Empire style, which – stimulated by Bonaparte's various conquests – drew on Greek, Etruscan, Roman and Egyptian motifs. Sphinxes were placed on the quay of Vasilevsky Island in front of the Academy of Arts; an Egyptian Bridge was built over the Fontanka; Egyptian Gates – designed by Adam Menelaws – were added at Tsarskoe Selo. The neoclassical Empire style transformed interior decoration, furniture design and tableware. Outstanding among Russian designs of the period were the hundreds of variations on classical abstract motifs surrounding the dishes of the Guryev Service, which was produced by the Imperial Porcelain Manufactory.

The pleasurable life of the capital continued much as it had done in the early years of Alexander's reign. There was, however, a feeling of familiarity about everything, a sense of stasis – as if the city was impatient for some new impetus or energy. In his *Memoirs* the journalist O. A. Przhetslavsky complained of the 'monotonous' streets and the 'unfinished' look of the city.[103] Alexander, however, was eager to raise his capital to a 'perfection . . . commensurate with its worth'. Accordingly, St Petersburg's last great homogenous architectural style came to dominate, and thereby rationalise, the centre of the capital. A Committee for Building and Hydraulic Works was created, and among the architects enlisted to fulfil the emperor's dreams were Vasily Stasov, Carlo Rossi and Auguste Ricard de Montferrand, all active between 1816 and the 1840s. After 150 years of stumbling through successive styles and orders of architecture, the neoclassical style predominated, creating a majestic harmony across the façades of a city, which was to be forced – increasingly – to confront its underlying chaos.

One outstanding project was the Stock Exchange, which occupies a prominent position on the spit of Vasilevsky Island. Quarenghi had submitted designs for this, but his scheme was abandoned after plans were provided by a passionately royalist Frenchman, Jean-François Thomas de Thomon, who fled to Petersburg from revolutionary France. Announcing his proposal with great showmanship, the Frenchman invited spectators to a specially constructed amphitheatre, where he dramatically revealed his ideas for a new exchange. Finished in 1810, de Thomon's powerful Doric-columned structure was an unmitigated statement of confidence in the economic future of the capital. Clearly indebted to the Second Temple of Hera at Paestum, the entrance was crowned with a sober Doric frieze. Standing a little apart from the building on the Strelka were Thomon's thirty-two-metre-high Rostral Columns, which were built in 1810 to imitate Roman columns of the third century BC. Stuck like slugs to the terracotta-coloured pillars were the prows of ships and bowls for oil, which were lit on ceremonial occasions. Unlit, they jar with the elegance of the nearby Exchange.[104]

*Ivan Cheskoy's* View of the Spit of Vasilevsky Island with
the Stock Exchange and Rostral Columns, c. *1810*.

*Looking through the gates of the Winter Palace at the base of the Alexander
column and Rossi's arches to the Nevsky Prospekt. In Eisenstein's film*
October, *Bolsheviks pour through those arches and scale these gates.*

Although there was a striking succession of deaths among the great architects of St Petersburg during the second decade of the nineteenth century – Zakharov in 1811, Cameron in 1812, Voronikhin in 1814, Quarenghi in 1817 and de Thomon in 1819 – the great genius responsible for much of the grandeur of the capital was coming to maturity. Carlo Rossi was born in Naples to a ballerina who later married the dancer and choreographer Charles le Picq. Invited to join the Russian imperial ballet in 1787, le Picq brought his wife and stepson to Petersburg, where the latter studied and worked under Tsar Paul's architect, Vincenzo Brenna. Rossi's 500-metre curving façade for the offices of the General Staff of the Army and the Ministries of Finance and Foreign Affairs embrace Palace Square. Yet behind the right-hand axe of this magisterial parabola – in typical Petersburg style – stands a warren of confusing rear courtyards. It was Rossi who determined the sharp left turn towards the bottom of the Nevsky Prospekt into a wide passage of three linked arches, the last of which opens onto Palace Square and is crowned by a sculptural ensemble: Victory drawn by six horses and driving straight for the palace.[105] By creating the passage, Rossi – unwittingly – set up the topography of revolution. It was down the Nevsky Prospekt and into this passage that people from the hidden spaces behind and beyond elegant St Petersburg would stream, in order to challenge autocracy. Rossi, while crowning the imperial capital, was preparing its demise. Meanwhile, his monumental vision produced a good number of gracious and stately buildings, including the second Imperial Library and a new Mikhailovsky Palace. Paul's red fortress became home to the Guards Corps of the Engineers and was thereafter known as Engineers Castle. Rossi also contributed to the planning of twelve squares and thirteen streets in the capital, one of which bears his name. The short Rossi Street, which the architect planned in its entirety – two buildings 220 metres long, on either side of a street twenty-two metres wide – terminates at the back of his own Aleksandrinsky

Theatre, which opened in 1832.[106] It is a street designed by the son of a ballerina, along which Nijinsky, Pavlova, Karsarvina and Nureyev would walk to reach the studios of their school, a street of well-ordered proportions and regular effects – like a perfect corps de ballet.

During Alexander's reign, Ivan Valberg, Russia's first native ballet master, made his mark in St Petersburg. He studied under the Italian choreographer Gaspero Angiolini during Catherine's reign, and danced under Rossi's stepfather, le Picq. In response to Napoleon's aggression, Valberg conceived *Love for the Fatherland*. It was set to music by the Italian composer Catterino Cavos, who lived in Petersburg for more than forty years and was the father of the architect of two of Russia's greatest theatres, the Bolshoi in Moscow and the Mariinsky in the capital. While Catherine II had dabbled in historical opera, it was Cavos who is credited with introducing the genre to the Russian public. He composed *Ivan Susanin* in 1815 – twenty years before Mikhail Glinka wrote his more famous version of the story.[107] The music Cavos produced for Valberg's *Love for the Fatherland* was so stirring that, when it was performed in 1812, young men rushed from the theatre to the recruiting office.

Soon after Alexander's accession, the emperor appointed the collector and bibliophile Count Dmitry Buturlin to run the Hermitage, suggesting that the collection should be opened to the public for a certain period each year. Alexander also noticed that there were gaps in the collection. As Spanish painting was not well represented, canvases were bought from the English banker William Coesvelt. After the Tilsit Treaty, the services of Dominique Vivant Denon, director of the Napoleonic Museum at the Louvre, were secured. When Franz Labenzsky, custodian of the Hermitage, went to Paris in 1808, Denon helped him obtain Caravaggio's *Lute Player*, along with twenty-two other important paintings.[108] After the final defeat of Napoleon, when Alexander was in Paris he delighted in the company of

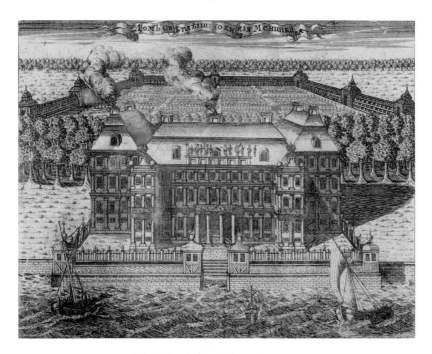

The Menshikov Palace in 1717.

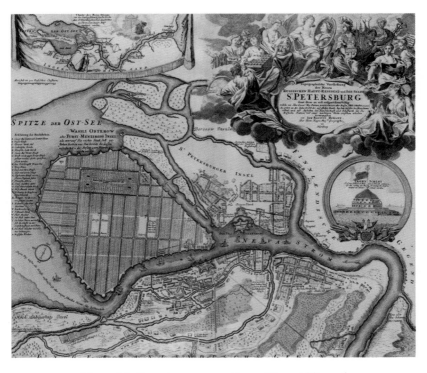

Map of St Petersburg, *c.* 1718–20. The gridding of
Vasilevksy Island was, at that stage, a mere projection.

The evolution from the residual influences of a highly decorative baroque architecture through the early, vigorous phase of neoclassicism and on into more sophisticated variations on the style.

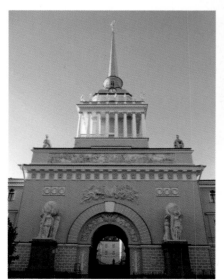

*Anti-clockwise from top*: St. John the Baptist Church at Chesme – now absorbed by southern St Petersburg; the stark Tuscan Doric columns of New Holland Arch; the tower over the central arch of the Admiralty; the Palace of Pavlovsk; the Mikhailovsky Palace's main staircase.

*The Bronze Horseman* in Senate Square, unveiled in 1782.
A print by K. Ludwig after Benjamin Paterssen.

A fair in St Petersburg, *c.* 1803, from *A Picturesque Representation of the Manners, Customs and Amusements of the Russians in One Hundred Coloured Plates* by John Atkinson and James Walker.

The Nevsky Prospekt's Police Bridge over the Moika
with Wolff & Béranger café on the left.

The Mikhailovsky Palace, now the Russian Museum.

A. P. Bogolubov's
*Sledging on
the Neva*, 1854.

Postcard of the
Mariinsky Theatre,
which opened
in 1860.

Pyotr
Vereshchagin, *The
Alexandrinsky
Theatre*, 1870s.

С. Петербургъ
Невскій пр. домъ Елисѣева.

Postcard of the Eliseev building, which went up on the Nevsky Prospekt between 1902 and 1903.

The almost palatial *stil moderne* interior of Vitebsk Station, created between 1902 and 1904.

Невскій проспектъ.                    С.-Петербургъ.

Postcard of the Nevsky Prospekt, *c.* 1909.

That these three items appeared within a year of each other reveals the gulf between the tsarist assertion of the past and the desire of Russia's performers and painters for a revolutionary future.

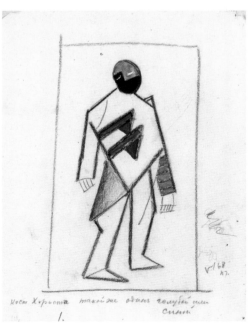

*Above*: menu for the banquet to celebrate the 300th anniversary of the Romanov Dynasty in 1913.

*Top right*: Auguste Rodin's maquette for a sculpture of Nijinsky, *The Dancer*, 1912.

*Right*: Kasimir Malevich's design for the Chorister costume in *Victory Over the Sun*, which premiered in 1913.

International Women's Day, February 1917:
women workers demonstrate on the Nevsky Prospekt.

Lenin speaking in Petrograd, July 1920.

Napoleon's first wife, Empress Joséphine. She was an arbiter of taste and dearly wished to keep her house at Malmaison, with its striking collection of art. Joséphine needed Alexander to look kindly upon her and, to that end, gave him the prized Gonzaga Cameo when they met in the spring of 1814. This fifteen-by-eleven-centimetre gem, dating from the third century BC, is a particularly ugly two-toned sardonyx treasure, with a lineage that makes that of the Maltese Falcon pale. During the sixteenth century it belonged to the Gonzaga Dukes of Mantua.then, in the seventeenth, to the Holy Roman Emperor, Rudolph II. After that, Queen Christina of Sweden possessed it. Then it passed to the Odescalchi family in Rome, on to the Vatican and, ultimately, to Josephine. She – in keeping with her contemporaries – thought the cameo represented Alexander the Great and his mother and thus imagined it to be an apt gift with which to flatter the Russian emperor. When, following one of their delightful picnics, Joséphine contracted a fatal bronchial disorder and died, leaving huge debts, Alexander bought thirty-eight paintings from the Malmaison estate, including Rembrandt's *Descent from the Cross*, and twenty-one canvases which had been looted from the Landgrave of Hesse-Kassel. While the landgrave was able to repossess the paintings stolen from his collection that were hanging in the Louvre, he was appalled to find that those passed on to Alexander would only be returned if the tsar was reimbursed the 940,000 francs they had cost. The landgrave refused to pay twice, and so the canvases stayed in Russia, where they were exhibited in the new Malmaison Hall of the Hermitage.[109]


Against a pan-European drive to limit monarchical power and edge towards democracy, Russia held fast to its autocractic form of government. During the early 1820s, revolts in Spain, Portugal, Greece, Naples and the Piedmont increased Alexander's resolve to resist change, and many enlightened groups among the intelligentsia were bitterly disappointed. Merchants in Moscow complained that they were treated unfairly, and Petersburg shopkeepers felt they would profit greatly from a constitution.[110] The daring young poet Alexander Pushkin wrote epigrams targeting the establishment and short poems celebrating liberty. Groups – some inspired by European secret societies, such as the *Carbonari*, who aimed to overturn the restoration of the French monarchy after the defeat of Napoleon – met for fervid political discussion. Dissent seemed to be growing alarmingly and, in August 1822, despite rumours that he himself was a member of a lodge, Alexander banned all secret societies, including the Freemasons.[111]

It was 'hard to describe the state in which St Petersburg found itself in the spring of 1823', wrote the Russian diarist Filipp Vigel. 'Alexander's gloomy looks, more sorrowing than severe, were reflected on its inhabitants.'[112] The tsar's adjutant likewise suggested that the ruler was now 'increasingly consumed with reticence and suspicion'.[113] When, in November 1824, the capital suffered one of its worst floods – the deluge that Pushkin was to describe in his apocalyptic vision of tsarist power, 'The Bronze Horseman' – it seemed as if nature had joined the rising tide of human revolt. Across the city, hundreds of people were killed and nearly 500 houses were swept away, as the Nevsky Prospekt flooded as far up as the Anichkov Bridge over the Fontanka. Alexander's sister, the Grand Duchess Anna Pavlovna, wrote that 'in the space of one hour the square in front of the Winter Palace' was sunk beneath 'a raging sea'.[114]

Against an ever-deepening gloom, a group of intellectual, aristocratic and military conspirators began to meet. They abhorred serfdom, looked towards Europe for enlightenment and yet were intensely patriotic. Nourished by the ideas published in a handful of Petersburg periodicals with spirited titles such as *Son of the Fatherland* and *Champion of Enlightenment and Philanthropy*,[115] they grew into two important pressure groups,

*Fyodor Alekseyev's* November 7th 1824 in Teatralnaya Square.

one based in a Ukraine garrison town and the other in the capital. After much discontent and debate, three officers – Nikita Muravyov, a senator's son, heir to sizeable estates and thousands of serfs, along with Princes Yevgeny Obolensky and Sergei Trubetzkoy – decided that the time for talking was over. As their accomplice, Lieutenant Bestuzhev-Ryumin, asked: 'Would the Russians, who had freed Europe from Napoleon's yoke, fail to shake off their own?'[116]

The plan, at first, was to assassinate the tsar in May 1826 when he was scheduled to review troops in the south. At that moment, members of the imperial family in St Petersburg would be rounded up and deported, and Bestuzhev-Ryumin would march on Moscow. Fate intervened. On 19 November 1825, Alexander died in Taganrog. Masses were being sung in St Petersburg to celebrate his recovery while messengers were en route to the capital to report his death. Russia was without an emperor for days, and worse confusion was to come. When Alexander's death was announced, Constantine, his younger brother, was proclaimed emperor, in ignorance of the fact that the grand duke had already renounced his claim to the throne, which left his younger brother, Nicholas, as heir apparent. Russia effectively remained without a tsar until Constantine's letter from Warsaw, confirming his position, reached St Petersburg. Even then, Nicholas required Constantine's endorsement before he would agree to ascend the throne.[117] In all this mess, the idealistic architects of the original plan to murder Alexander decided to press on with their revolt, but in the event they proved faint-hearted and disorganised. They wanted to force the Senate to denounce the Romanovs, seize the Peter and Paul Fortress and the Winter Palace and assassinate Nicholas. Everything went wrong. Pyotr Kakhovsky, the man detailed to attack and occupy the Winter Palace, refused at the last minute. The rebel who promised to assassinate Nicholas reneged. Meanwhile, Grand Duke Nicholas – surprised to find himself tsar – exhibited exceptional cool and stole a march on the insurgents.

At the outset of Alexander's reign, to mark the 100th anniversary of the foundation of St Petersburg, the tsar had paraded 20,000 troops – their banners dipping in reverence as they marched past Falconet's statue of Peter the Great.[118] At 11 a.m. on 14 December 1825, on the first day of a new reign, troops in open rebellion against autocracy assembled around that same significant sculpture in Senate Square. But the senators had already sworn allegiance to their new emperor early that morning, and Nicholas was primed. He moved his family from the Anichkov Palace to the greater safety of the Winter Palace, which he then surrounded with the 1st Battalion of the Preobrazhensky Guards. Troops sealed off Carlo Rossi's new passage between Palace Square and the Nevsky Prospekt. Stones and other debris were hurled at government forces by a rabble who promised that, if they were given arms, 'in half an hour' they would 'turn the city upside down'. While loyal troops were ordered to load their firearms, churchmen tried to reason with the 3,000 insurgents. Grand Duke Mikhail was fired upon when he spoke with them.

The governor of St Petersburg, Count Miladorovich, went to appeal to the rebels and was killed by Kakhovsky, who later shot the commander of the Grenadier Guards.

By 3 p.m. dusk was beginning to obscure the scene. A band of rebel grenadiers set out to seize the imperial family from the palace, but were repulsed. Re-joining their comrades, they passed close enough to the new emperor to shoot with precision, but failed to recognise him. With darkness falling, Nicholas knew that the uprising had to be quashed. He gave the mutineers one last chance to lay down their arms and, when they refused, ordered his cavalry to attack. On the icy surface of Senate Square, the charge was not only ineffectual, but dangerous. Riders were thrown, as the horses skeltered. After that, Nicholas trained thirty-six cannon on Senate Square. A few rounds cleared the area, leaving about a hundred bodies bleeding in the snow. Innocent people and mutineers were among the dead, but none of the hard core of sixty conspirators had been touched. Bestuzhev-Ryumin attempted to assemble a group of rebels

*Karl Kolman's* Decembrist Rising, *1825.*

on the frozen Neva in order to march and seize the Peter and Paul Fortress. The tsar merely turned his cannon on the river and attempted to shatter the ice. It was 5 p.m. Night had fallen and the Decembrist uprising was over. General Alexander von Benckendorff – the man who would become the head of Nicholas I's infamous Third Section – was despatched to round up the insurgents.[119]

# PART II

# SUBJECTS

*1825–1917*

# 8

# A NEW KIND OF COLD

## *1825–55*

Within hours of their arrest, core members of the Decembrist uprising were being grilled in the Winter Palace. Nicholas I sat at a desk beneath Carlo Maratta's arresting portrait of Pope Clement IX. Suspects were thus confronted by the rigorous inquisition of the new emperor, quickened by the Pope's icy glare. Ivan Yakushkin – who distracted himself during questioning by focusing on Domenichino's tender *Holy Family*[1] – refused to name names and was clapped in irons so tightly that he could not move. The poet Kondraty Ryleyev had been betrayed and – under questioning – unmasked Trubetzkoy, who begged the tsar for his life. Colonel Bulatov admitted his intention to kill the emperor and was incarcerated in the Peter and Paul Fortress, where he committed suicide by smashing his head repeatedly against the stone wall of his cell.[2]

During the six months in which the Investigating Committee sat through nearly 150 meetings, issued 175 reports and generated one million sheets of legal and bureaucratic rumination, the prisoners – deprived of pen, paper or any reading material – shared dank cells with water rats, mice and cockroaches.[3] When it reported on 30 May 1826, the committee emphasised the smallness of the conspiracy, the vulnerability of its hard core to dangerous foreign ideas, and argued that – overall – the episode revealed widespread and sincere devotion to the emperor.[4] Of the 1,400 Decembrists arrested, only 121 were convicted. Most of the conspirators were exiled to Siberia, but five – Ryleyev, Kakhovsky, Pestel, Muravyov and Bestuzhev-Ryumin – were to be quartered, a sentence that was commuted to hanging on 13 July 1826. When the instant of extinction came, ropes broke and knots slipped, and three of the offenders had to be hanged twice. A memorial service in Senate Square consecrated the punishment, and holy water was sprinkled to purify the ground where autocracy had been challenged. Nicholas claimed that revolution was 'at the gates of Russia' and swore to master it. 'Orthodoxy, Autocracy, Nationality' were the order of the day.[5] All public discussion of the Decembrists was prohibited, but – as there had been no death-sentence under Alexander – the executed leaders rapidly gained status as martyrs. Portraits of the rebels were banned. Talismanic likenesses changed hands under the counter.

Tsar Nicholas – realising that the suppressed rebellion had become a cause célèbre – established the notorious Third Section, a special branch of that power-centre, His Imperial Majesty's Own Chancellery. In the tsar's own words, the functions of the Third Section included the gathering of 'detailed information concerning all people under police surveillance'; the 'exile and arrest of suspicious or dangerous persons', and the tracking of foreigners 'travelling in the country'. From September 1829, the Third Section received all copies of all printed matter. Nearly a decade later, it moved from its sizeable premises at the corner of the Moika Canal and Gorokhovaya Street to the old residence of Prince Kochubey near the Chain Bridge over the Fontanka. Behind forbidding gates, this large house with its warren of detention cells became a very busy interrogation centre. Police wagons clattered in and out of the courtyard under the cloak of darkness.[6] The 'Chain Bridge house' was as notorious in

the Petersburg of Nicholas I as the Leningrad headquarters of
the KGB, the Bolshoi Dom on Liteiny Prospekt, or Moscow's
infamous Lubianka during the Soviet era.

Until the oppressive rule of Nicholas I, the creation of St Petersburg and its culture had been driven by the court. After 1825,
tsars – for as long as they lasted – became reactive. The initiative for change passed on to writers and thinkers – 'little men'
with increasingly big voices. After a century of consolidating
its magisterial cityscape, St Petersburg faced an era of turmoil.
Alexander Herzen, the intellectual dynamo of the mid-nineteenth
century, characterised the reign of Nicholas I as 'a time of out-
ward slavery and inner emancipation'. In a chilling foretaste of
the shape of things to come, poems were circulated without being
printed. Writers and intellectuals – albeit controlled, censored
or incarcerated – began to contour the new character of the city.
Lomonosov had provided them with a solid base by formalising
Russian grammar in 1755, and by the late 1820s many young
Russians had been abroad either to study or to fight and had
returned with explosive ideas. In their search for a new order,
they attempted a reconciliation between Western ideas and a
growing awareness that the road to revolution began with the
simple organisation of the Russian village commune.

Despite a youth of dissipation and flirtation with the high
society that he came to despise, the first great Russian writer
was a product of the Decembrist zeitgeist. Alexander Pushkin
formed friendships with future Decembrists such as the poet
Wilhelm Küchelbecker, who was to die exiled in Siberia. On his
mother's side, and still visible in his own physiognomy, Pushkin
was the great-grandson of an African princeling, whom he identified as 'The Negro of Peter the Great' in an unfinished story of
that name. This tall and well-proportioned man was taken from
Constantinople; the tsar instructed him, promoted him and sent

him off to Paris to acquire knowledge that would be useful to the
development of the new Russian court.[7]

Alexander Pushkin – descendant of this remarkable figure –
burst upon the Petersburg literary scene with poetry that was
epigrammatic, critical of authority and scathing about serfdom.
This resulted in his banishment from the capital in 1820. Permitted to return in 1826 – only to be shadowed by agents of
the Third Section[8] – Pushkin was already well advanced in his
masterpiece, the verse novel *Eugene Onegin*. Only months after
the execution of the Decembrist ringleaders, Pushkin wrote a
subsequently deleted stanza elaborating the politics of his character Lensky who, in the poem, is pointlessly killed in a duel by the
bored Onegin. Had Lensky lived, Pushkin tantalisingly suggests,
he might have been executed like the Decembrist poet Ryleyev.

Uncannily, the killing of Lensky is an eerie portent of Pushkin's own death. Having married a simple yet ambitious beauty,
Natalia Goncharova, Pushkin's inflammable jealousy was
sparked by the tattle of Petersburg socialites. Pestered by feelings
that his position in society did not match his stature as a poet,
perturbed by gossip that linked the emperor to his wife,[9] Pushkin
was taunted into a duel. He was mortally wounded by one of
Natalia's alleged lovers – the adopted son of the Dutch Ambassador, Baron d'Anthès de Heeckeren. The funeral was held in
secret to prevent public disorder. Yet – to the consternation of
the Third Section – Mikhail Lermontov's lyric 'The Death of
a Poet' stirred abundant emotion. In its final lines the writer
painted a venomous picture of court toadies – jibes that earned
him a posting to the Caucasus. Lermontov found St Petersburg
society like a French garden where 'the clippers of the master had
reduced all to uniformity'.[10] Banishment to the provinces happily
provided him with a fresh setting for Russia's first great prose
novel, *A Hero of Our Time*.

Four years before his mortal wounding in the snowy woods
to the north of St Petersburg, Pushkin wrestled with the idea

of Peter the Great's hubris in constructing an absurd, dangerous and oppressive capital. He offered Russian literature – in the character of the humble clerk, Yevgeny – a prototype for the oppressed anti-hero driven mad by the acts and works of despotism. 'The Bronze Horseman: A Petersburg Tale' was inspired by the work of Pushkin's sometime friend, the Polish poet Adam Mickiewicz. In 'Monument of Peter the Great', part of a six-poem cycle, *Digression*, Mickiewicz bemoaned the state of Russia after the suppression of the Decembrists. He also composed a long poem presenting Petersburg as an unnatural and untenable construction devastated by the 1824 flood.[11]

Pushkin commences his 'Bronze Horseman' with a eulogy in the tradition of the architectural odes to St Petersburg by eighteenth-century poets such as Lomonosov and Derzhavin. Celebrating the city just over a century after its founding, Pushkin punctuates his apparent tribute with the repeated declaration, 'I love you.' This litany later irritated the novelist Fyodor Dostoevsky, who curtly addressed Pushkin's passion for St Petersburg, 'I'm sorry, but I don't love it,' and left a substantial body of writing to prove his point.[12] As a young man, when Dostoevsky arrived in St Petersburg to study at the Academy of Military Engineers, his first port of call had been the wood where Pushkin was shot. His second pilgrimage was to the room in the house on the Moika in which Pushkin died.[13]

Although Dostoevsky was such an ardent admirer of the poet, Pushkin's declaration of love to a place Dostoevsky later described as a 'rotting and slimy city' clearly disturbed him. But Pushkin's opening panegyric was merely a springboard for his narrative. The celebration of nature tamed into a city of 'stern and graceful countenance'[14] provides a striking contrast to the tragedy of the downtrodden, humble clerk Yevgeny, which occupies the body of Pushkin's poem. In fact Yevgeny was to act as an inspiration for a character in Dostoevsky's 1846 novel *The Double* – Golyadkin, a 'little man' who is 'snubbed and derided

*Yevgeny imagines that Peter the Great leaps off the thunder rock and pounds after him in pursuit. Alexandre Benois's frontispiece to an edition of Alexander Pushkin's* The Bronze Horseman.

by his superiors in the official hierarchy and in society'.[15] Taken as a whole, Pushkin's 'Bronze Horseman' presents Petersburg as 'a terrible bequest'.[16]

A vivid image of the violence of the city's worst flood, in which more than 500 people perished and hundreds of houses were destroyed, was provided by the Grand Duchess Anna Pavlovna. She described the Winter Palace, during the 1824 deluge, as 'an island battered by the waves'.[17] It was an image that took on a political resonance at the end of the following year, when the Decembrists initiated their rebellion against the palace, which would, at length, terminate in the 1917 October Revolution. It is in the context of the devastating 1824 flood that Pushkin introduces St Petersburg's oppressed clerk, Yevgeny. As the flood rises, this 'nobody' vainly goes in search of his beloved Parasha, who lives on one of the city's more vulnerable outlying islands.

In the post-Decembrist world of the secret police state in which Pushkin was writing, tsarist power is perceived as indomitable. Falconet's *Bronze Horseman* is seen by Yevgeny, poised:

> . . . high above the invaded land,
> above the raging of the flood
> with back to him, and outstretched hand
> in overmastering command . . .[18]

Yevgeny goes wandering among the wreckage thrown up by the water – the first of those modern anti-heroes to negotiate their luckless way among the chaos of a metropolis, attempting to make sense of their anchorless lives. Parasha is drowned and Yevgeny goes mad, obsessed by the figure ultimately responsible for the tragedy, the autocratic tsar. In his demented state, Yevgeny fancies that Peter the Great leaps off the 'thunder rock' and pounds after him in pursuit. In Nicholas I's Russia, Pushkin understood that a tsar would have the last word. Yet – simply by placing a humble clerk centre-stage – the poet allows the 'little man' a presence in what was to be the long struggle against 'the vigilant spirit of autocracy'.[19]

A very different, but equally unfavourable take on the capital was offered by the waspish and often brilliant French homosexual Astolphe de Custine, who visited the city in 1839 – two years after Pushkin's death. Acknowledging St Petersburg as one of 'the marvels of the world', Custine fell into the perennial trap of comparing it to Venice – 'less beautiful but more astonishing'. The comparison is, at best, superficial. Venice is intimate and oozes history, whereas Petersburg is vast and – until well into the nineteenth century – persistent in its desire to be brand-new. But when Custine considers Petersburg's soul – or lack of it – he at once becomes more penetrating. The capital is a freak, built 'for a people which never existed anywhere'. By denying the natural grace of the Russian 'Oriental genius', Peter built a pompous city that was without 'historical meaning'. It was, Custine remarked, 'barely possible to see more of Russia in St Petersburg than in France'. He decried the artless imitation and damned the Russians not 'for being what they are', but for 'pretending to be what we are'. Not only did the rulers who conceived the city betray their soul, but they also – perhaps ambitiously, perhaps pretentiously – built ahead of themselves. 'The magnificence and immensity of St Petersburg,' Custine suggests, 'are tokens set up by the Russians to honour their future power.'. He derides the city as the headquarters of an army, not the capital of a country. 'Magnificent though this garrison town may be, it appears empty to Western eyes.'[20] It was a city for the nobility, sustained by a bureaucracy and the military. Half the capital appeared to be wearing uniforms and, out of a population of nearly 450,000 in the early 1840s, nearly a quarter worked as domestics.[21]

Custine's opinions were shared by many Russians. The dandy libertarian thinker Peter Chaadaev questioned the direction taken by his nation in a series of letters written – ironically – in French. Russian culture was stranded in some no-man's-land between East and West, not having truly learned from the example of the West, and guilty of having contributed no useful ideas to civilisation. The question of national character became a preoccupation for writers and intellectuals during the 1830s and 1840s.[22] The 'true Russian' felt uncomfortable, even odd, in Petersburg's alien cityscape. The sociologist and literary critic Vissarion Belinsky, who moved from Moscow to the capital in 1839, suggested that if 'one suffers in St Petersburg one is a true human being'.[23]

Neoclassicism, Petersburg's prevailing international architectural style, created large and gloomy squares in which Custine counted 'fewer humans than columns'. Alexander Herzen – who, since his early adolescence, was 'against all imposed authority' and for 'the absolute independence of the individual'[24] – wandered the capital's regimented granite pavements 'close to despair'.[25] Meanwhile, the finishing touches of imperial bombast were being added to the 'unrelieved regularity' in the form of the new St Isaac's Cathedral and the Alexander Column in Palace Square. Carlo Rossi had planned a monument to celebrate Alexander's victory over Napoleon. In the event, it was Auguste de Montferrand – a Napoleonic soldier decorated with the *Légion d'honneur* – who eventually designed and erected the 600-tonne column between 1830 and 1834. Mounted on a sizeable plinth, the ensemble stands more than forty-seven metres high. Its single column of red granite, capped with a statue of the militant yet angelic Alexander crushing a serpent, was conceived as an image of Russia triumphant.[26]

Montferrand was also responsible for the winning design to rebuild St Isaac's Cathedral. In fact, the energetic Frenchman submitted twenty-four different proposals in every known style, so it is hardly surprising that he won the commission. The cathedral was eventually completed at a cost of more than twenty-three million roubles in 1857, two years after the death of Nicholas I. This dour, dark grey bastion of a church – its four powerful

*A statue of the militant yet angelic Alexander on top of Auguste de
Montferrand's Alexander Column in Palace Square under snow.*

porticoes supported by huge granite columns – appears as an
architectural testimony to Nicholas's unrelenting rigidity. Its formidable 100-metre-high dome rose to dominate the skyline of a
city in which no civic building was permitted to exceed the height
of the cornice on the Winter Palace. Inside the cathedral – under
the innovative all-metal engineering of the twenty-six-metre-
wide dome – a sumptuous effect was created by 200 oil paintings
and by the generous use of gilt, mosaic, malachite, porphyry,
marble and lapis lazuli.[27]

The column and cathedral were among the last sizeable imperial additions to a capital which 'greatly disappointed' a visiting
Englishwoman. After reading of Petersburg's magnificence, she
found that a half-hour drive was all it took 'to pass through all
the best parts of the city'.[28] In fact, the capital was growing inde-
pendently of the court, which – as Belinsky observed – formed 'a

city within a city, a state within a state'.[29] Much of the expansion was in the poorer quarters, which were still little more than a congeries of shanty towns or villages. In 1844, the Ukrainian poet and essayist Evgeny Grebenka identified the Petersburg Side as the poorest area of the capital. It was home to retired clerks and down-at-heel artists and performers, who lived in long, narrow streets of wooden houses with miserable front yards. Without taverns or entertainment, the quarter contained cheap canteens where the inhabitants could get a meagre meal before returning to their dismal rooms.[30]

A government commission visited 1,000 dwellings occupied by Petersburg workers in the early 1840s and found nearly three-quarters of them to be overcrowded, with up to nineteen workers crushed into a single space.[31] The editor and early champion of Dostoevsky Nikolai Nekrasov wrote 'The Petersburg Corners', a documentary text that penetrated the ugly spaces festering behind the city's grand façades. When Nekrasov enters a yard, he is greeted by 'unbearable smells' and 'all kinds of crying and banging'. Searching for a room, he realises the yard is not purely residential, for there are signs advertising second-hand clothes, a midwife, a coffin-maker and a boarding school of questionable standing. Nekrasov negotiates pigs, puddles and dogs and finds an inner courtyard full of heaped-up refuse. He dodges the waste raining down from above, and attempts to ignore the stench of rank water and rotten cabbage. He takes a room in this slum, in which he finds a welcoming committee of insects keen to inspect his face. In and around his building there is a bulge of pregnant women and down-and-outs, raging drunk.[32] Outside the property there are beggars, flower girls and a lemonade-vendor, selling from a single cup, which is handed-on, unwashed, from customer to customer. In winter, tea-sellers circulate – their kettle kept hot in swaddling bands and a row of glasses hanging from their neck in a leather rack. Impoverished peasants – obliged to pay dues to their old estate while living precariously in the city – could be seen huddled in sunken tea-houses, sluicing hot liquid through lumps of yellow sugar trapped between decaying teeth.[33] Meanwhile, Peter's city encouraged such lowly inhabitants to turn their backs on simple Russian pleasures in pursuit of imported novelties. Vissarion Belinsky noted that the taste for coffee percolated down to the peasants living on the fringes, and that humble girls forgot Russian dances in their enthusiasm for the French quadrille.[34]

Despite the poor quarters and the over-hasty implementation of inappropriate architectural procedures, which necessitated incessant repair work, it is easy to overdo the 'unfinished' or 'under-developed' aspect of the capital in the mid-nineteenth century. In many aspects, St Petersburg was not so very different from the much older cities of Europe. In Camille Corot's 1833 oil of Paris's *Île de la Cité*,[35] there are sandy river banks without granite cladding right in the heart of the French capital. In the early 1850s, Charles Dickens evokes London as a mire of mud and manure, its centre barely visible through impenetrable fog. In his novel *Bleak House*, pedestrians lose their footing at street corners 'where tens of thousands of other foot passengers have been slipping and sliding since the day broke (if this day ever broke)'.[36] Indeed, Nicholas I favourably contrasted the ordered discipline of his capital with the squalor of older cities.[37]

The main thoroughfares in the centre of St Petersburg were occupied by different classes at different times of the day. A typical winter's morning would see the labourers on the streets first. Imperfectly protected from the early hour's icy chill by worn sheepskins, they were heartened by the aroma of hot bread and pastries from the bakeries around which the destitute clustred, hoping for yesterday's stale, unsold bread. Next on the street were the favour-seekers, people fallen on hard times who were on their way to beg for help from high officials or noblemen. Then came the scribes and copyists, the army of 'little men' who were beginning to assume such an important place in the city's literature. They scurried in their thousands through the dwindling darkness, making haste to reach their uncomfortable high-stools in the countless cluttered copying offices of innumerable government departments.

The late morning was the time for hectic business – everybody frantic to get everything done before they dined. People, desperate 'to kill the day',[38] became 'sick' with feverish activity.[39] They were always late, always falling short of their concocted aims. They had become 'modern' men. Pavements were a congestion of conflicting purposes, and carriages thundered about, 'dancing' – as Alexandre Dumas had it – over cobblestones, each as big as a baby's head.[40] In clement weather the frenetic tempo gave way to a more leisurely rhythm, as members of the nobility and the families of high officials, having completed their morning rides, came out to be seen strolling along the tree-bordered wooden walkways of the Nevsky Prospekt. On that most fashionable avenue – amid the extravagant vanity of moustaches, uniforms, frock coats, hats and furs – people shopped. To make the passage smoother for the carriages delivering customers to the doors of boutiques, wooden runways had also been set into the road.

After the frenzy of the morning and the fashionable parade of the forenoon, people dined – either at the increasing number of restaurants lining the Nevsky, such as Talon's where Onegin ate, or at home, at an hour that varied according to the occupation or nationality of the host. Such differing habits allowed itinerant guests to partake of several dinners in one afternoon. Having eaten, some stayed, playing cards until a late supper arrived. After feasting, they trundled home in their clattering carriages during the early hours of the morning, 'their stomachs fevered with the richest food'. Once home, they went directly to sleep in 'bedrooms where an artificial heat, like that of a hot-house' fermented 'their digestion, leaving them at waking, pale, languid and spiritless'.[41]

Those who did not stay on after lunch were out and about. Along the Nevsky, the hours between one and three in the

afternoon were among the busiest. Merchants dined early in order
to be ready for the new onslaught of shoppers. By mid-afternoon,
civil servants in their green uniforms swarmed about – everyone
eager to see and be seen.[42] Belinsky observed that the denizens
of the capital were so smug and vain, so preoccupied with the
trivia of fashion, that they would notice if a button was about
'to fall off one's waistcoat'.[43] As for the Nevsky itself, it was well
turned out. Théophile Gautier called it a 'show street' and likened it to the rue de Rivoli in Paris or London's Regent Street.[44]
He observed that nowhere, except in Berne, were the signboards
so luxurious. Nowhere – without exception – were they painted
in so many languages. Cyrillic characters jostled with Roman letters, signifying the riches of the commercial world in a plethora
of European languages. There were jewellers, *parfumeries*, con-
fectioners, *Buchhändlerin*, *chocolatiers*, *barbieri*, *librairies*,
lithographers, hatters and tailors. Words arced invitingly across
awnings over doorways. But if the strangeness of the language
proved bewildering, painted images on the glass windows depicted what was on offer inside. There were toy shops selling
rocking horses, puppets, drums and Cossack caps. Hairdressers
advertised therapeutic bleeding, or phlebotomy, along with their
tonsorial activities.[45]

The Nevsky was, increasingly, the place where things happened. Engelhardt House was a popular venue for concerts and
masked balls. Mikhail Lermontov's 1835 play, *Masquerade*, was
set there. Not performed until 1852, it was banned by the censor
for – among other things – sullying the reputation of an institution run by the celebrated aristocratic Engelhardt family. At the
Wolff & Béranger café on the corner of the Moika, an informal
literary circle gathered, which included Lermontov, Pushkin and
Nikolai Chernyshevsky. It was there that Pushkin met his second
before his fatal duel.

Along the Nevsky, people were propelled through an endless
onslaught of transitory impressions with such velocity that it was

difficult for them to glean the truth. Nikolai Gogol's *Petersburg Tales* turned the city into an active and important protagonist.[46] The tales centred on the Nevsky, where information distorted and mutated as it passed from person to person. It offered a glimmer of possibility, an alternative. Yet although it proposed hope, so often it delivered despair.

In Gogol's story 'Nevsky Prospekt', Lieutenant Pirogov goes blundering after the wife of a German craftsman, while the artist hero, Pishkarev, falls for a woman who sends his world reeling. Pishkarev's sensation of the animated street acts as a vehicle for his emotional excitement. 'The pavement rushed away beneath his feet . . . the bridge expanded and split at the arch, and houses turned upside down.'[47] But after the hallucinogenic intensity of his experience, the ideal beauty turns out – like so much on this thoroughfare – to be 'for sale'. Unable to reconcile his vision with the fact that she is a prostitute, Pishkarev takes to opium and eventually slits his throat: 'Nevsky Prospect always lies.'

In 1835, the year in which Gogol wrote this startling short story, Vasily Sadovnikov, the son of a household serf and self-trained engraver, produced a fifteen-metre panorama of this avenue, recording the measured elegance of the buildings lining the smart segment of the avenue closest to Palace Square. Unlike his contemporary, Gogol, Sadovnikov displays a gentle sophistication akin to Regency London or Jane Austen's Bath. Nevertheless, Petersburg writers such as Pushkin, Gogol and Dostoevsky were intent on identifying and creating what we call 'the modern'. Moving through their seemingly over-determined yet actually incoherent city, they experienced the collisions of the incompatible, and the desperate confusions and clashes of urban life. They were the direct progenitors of the modernist chroniclers of twentieth-century cities, whose vivid and fractured visions have made such an important contribution to the way we see our world. Andrei Biely in his 1916 novel *Petersburg*, James Joyce in his epic wander through Dublin in *Ulysses*, John Dos Passos in his 1925 engagement with New York in *Manhattan Transfer*, and Alfred Döblin's interwar exploration of the Weimer capital in *Berlin Alexanderplatz* are all heirs of the Nevsky Prospekt.[48]

Walking up the Nevsky Prospekt, away from the palace and the Admiralty, is to head for the lower depths. Custine noted that as soon as you venture 'away from the centre of town, you are lost in a waste land, bordered by huts . . . sheds or warehouses' – the 'splendid prospekt . . . disappears in a horrible confusion of booths and workshops' and 'vast shapeless open spaces'.[49] An Englishwoman who visited in the middle of the nineteenth century was quick to realise that even the elegant portion of the Nevsky Prospekt was suspect. Like 'everything Russian, the showy façade only hides what is mean behind'.[50] This deceptive avenue presented the latest kind of 'Potempkinisation' and, from the 1830s onwards, writers were refusing to be fooled. Petersburg literature, which began by using outworn forms to extol its architectural wonders, was being rescored amid the commercial flotsam of imported dreams. In this alien city, writers began to assert their Russianness, and their literature darkened.

Born into Ukrainian petty nobility in 1809, Nikolai Gogol settled in St Petersburg and worked briefly as a teacher, before becoming a government clerk – a post that offered him considerable insight into the Petersburg malaise. His story 'The Overcoat' concerns Akaky Akakievich, one of the myriad unseen copying clerks who labour away and struggle to cope with the growing pressures of modern urban life. Victims of a system intent on resisting change, such 'little men' were miserably paid – in the low hundreds of roubles per year. The Russian administration under Nicholas I was so opaque that, by comparison, the ineffectual Court of Chancery in Dickens's *Bleak House* appears transparent. Documents generated documents and, by 1850, the Ministry of the Interior dealt annually with up to 165,000 sheets marked 'Urgent'. A simple sale of land spawned 1,351 separate certificates. Any tiny mistake necessitated recopying. It is alleged that it could take months even for the tsar to obtain a response to a routine enquiry, and the backlog of requests by the early 1840s was well over three million.[51] It is hardly surprising that when Gogol arrived in the capital at the end of the 1820s, he commented that 'people have been spreading false rumours' about a city in which, 'everyone is drowned in his trivial meaningless labours at which he spends his useless life'.[52] Gogol's Akaky Akakievich struggles to purchase a splendid new coat, observing that a man 'is esteemed by his overcoat'. With a salary of between 250 and 400 roubles a year, his choice is necessarily humble, and the coat becomes the object of contempt – the very antithesis of what Akaky desires. Maliciously, the overcoat is stolen from him and, after his death, rumours spread that, as a ghost out for revenge, Akaky rips coats of all qualities off assorted backs as he terrorises his tormentors. This tale of repression, madness and revenge was provocative – Joseph Brodsky later noted that 'all Russian writers "came out of Gogol's 'Overcoat'"'.[53]

While authors were beginning to engage with the street, there were painters who began to explore everyday life. Aleksei Venetsianov treated rural Russia, and led the way for succeeding generations of painters. Pavel Fedotov was a social satirist with an eye so keen that he was considered dangerous enough to be banned from official exhibitions. However, the work of three painters in particular demonstrates that the Academy still played an important role in the artistic life of the capital during the reign of Nicholas I. Karl Bryullov, Fedor Bruni and Alexander Ivanov studied at the Academy, served the establishment and produced large-scale academic works touched by Romanticism. As young painters, they found themselves in an insular world – Bryullov, whose father taught woodcarving, was instructed by Ivanov's father. But all three attempted to escape the Petersburg Academy by travelling. Bryullov knew Ingres in Italy, and Ivanov

and Bruni came into contact with the pseudo-medieval circle of
German painters known as the Nazarenes.

   The most forward-looking of the three was Alexander Ivanov,
who damned the Academy as a relic of the eighteenth century.
His small Italian landscapes looked forward to Impressionism,
while his large work *The Appearance of Christ to the People*
(1833–57) was conceived as a celebration of the moment when
the world threw off all forms of slavery – a potent theme in a
country much preoccupied with the need to renounce serfdom.
However, the long gestation period of the painting meant that
Ivanov became prey to the mounting religious scepticism of
the mid-nineteenth century. Worried about the state of Russia,
lonely, homosexual and searching for an art that could appeal to
people from all walks of life, Ivanov died – perhaps of cholera,
perhaps by his own hand – in St Petersburg in 1858.[54]

   Less innovative than Ivanov's *Appearance of Christ* were
Bruni's *Death of Camilla* and the stagey disaster painting that
won the Grand Prix at the Paris Salon of 1834, Karl Bryullov's
*Last Day of Pompeii*, painted between 1828 and 1833.[55] Alexander Herzen saw behind this painting's sensational effects a potent
reflection of the state of Russia: 'Groups of terrified figures are
crowded in confusion . . . They seek in vain for safety . . . They
will be overwhelmed by savage, senseless, ruthless force . . . Such
are the images inspired by the Petersburg atmosphere.'[56]

   At the Winter Palace, disaster struck in December 1837 while
Nicholas and his wife, Alexandra Feodorovna, were attending
a performance of *Dieu et la Bayadère*. The tsar slipped home
to assess the damage. Luckily, the fire had been slow to spread
from its source in a chimney between the Throne Room and the
Field Marshals' Hall. The tsar evacuated his sons, then returned
to supervise guards and servants who were struggling to contain
a blaze which would rage for several days and gut the first and
second floors of the palace.[57] Water was pumped from the Neva
and the Moika, while servants dumped what they could rescue

from the flames into the deep snow in Palace Square. Although newspapers boasted that there was no pilfering, it emerged that 160 pieces of the Sèvres Cameo Service given by Catherine II to her favourite, Potempkin, had gone missing, and in 1865 it became known that the London dealer John Webb was offering for sale more than a hundred items from the service. Alexander II managed to buy back most of these, although six pieces found their way into London's Wallace Collection.[58] As for the Hermitage, the imperial picture collection was saved by guards who worked feverishly to destroy connecting passages and build a barrier between the palace buildings.

A huge reconstruction and restoration project got under way and resulted in an interior that survives to this day. Auguste de Montferrand – whose carelessness some held responsible for the fire – rebuilt the Field Marshals Hall. The architect Alexander Bryullov, brother of the painter of *The Last Day of Pompeii*, designed both the Malachite Hall and the Alexander Hall, and remodelled the rooms facing Palace Square. Director of this vast operation was Vasily Stasov, who restored the main state rooms.

*Fire guts the Winter Palace, December 1837.*

While Stasov sought to reproduce Rastrelli's interiors faithfully, on the imposing Jordan Staircase he replaced the original gilded bronze handrails with white marble, and the old pink columns with polished grey granite. Rastrelli had taken eight years to build the palace.[59] Reconstruction was completed within eighteen months by a workforce of 8,000 men working in shifts around the clock. Custine reported that even when it fell to −30° outside, these builders and decorators worked in extreme temperatures in order to dry the plaster on the walls speedily. They covered their heads 'with a kind of ice-cap, so that they could preserve the use of their senses in the baking heat'.[60] Even then, some died.

One particularly positive consequence of the fire was the decision to build the New Hermitage, which would house the imperial collection. While the palace reconstruction was under way, Nicholas visited King Ludwig I of Bavaria in Munich and was much impressed by the architectural transformation of the city. Nicholas commissioned Ludwig's architect, Leo von Klenze, to design the New Hermitage. Building began in 1839 and the museum eventually opened in 1852. An eclectic combination of classical, Renaissance and baroque styles, the museum's public entrance was a portico supported by ten five-metre-tall granite atlantes. Influenced by von Klenze's Munich Glyptothek, the first floor of the Hermitage would display antiquities. On the second floor the imperial picture collection would be shown. Nicholas appointed three artists to review and rate the paintings owned

*On the Neva from right to left: the Winter Palace, the Small Hermitage, Old Hermitage (New Hermitage hidden behind) and the Winter Palace of Peter I.*

*Leo von Klenze's Greek-style portico at the entrance to*
*the New Hermitage, built between 1839 and 1852.*

by the Crown. Works were to be categorised into four groups:
those worthy of display in the New Hermitage, those suitable
for hanging elsewhere in the imperial palaces, those to be stored
and those of little value. Nicholas liked to interfere and was –
according to Fedor Bruni, director of the Hermitage between
1849 and 1864 – very stubborn. Against advice, the emperor
sold off well over a thousand paintings, including some of the
collection's finest.[61] As for Bruni, he never lived up to his early
promise as a painter. His large canvases lacked the ideological or
political undertones of his contemporaries, Ivanov and Bryullov,
and, among his many decorations for St Isaac's, only *The Flood*
reveals great originality.

Culture in the capital – imported and indigenous – was buzzing.
In 1832, Molière was performed at the French theatre in the presence of Nicholas I, and Carl Maria von Weber's nationalistic *Die
Freischütz* was presented at the German theatre. Shakespeare
was played, but any work treating an attack on authority – such as
*Julius Caesar* – was forbidden. Pushkin's masterpieces were published in the early 1830s, followed by Gogol's *Petersburg Tales*

in 1835. His play *The Revizor* or *The Government Inspector* was performed in the spring of 1836 at Carlo Rossi's magnificent Alexandra Theatre – named in honour of Alexandra Feodorovna, the tsar's wife and 'one of the most marvellous jewels of the Nevsky Prospekt'. *The Government Inspector* seemed an audacious piece to perform in front of a tsar obsessed with disciplining his unruly empire. Watching a revival in the 1850s, an English visitor was astonished that the play was permitted, thinking that 'pride alone would have prevented such an exposure' of the 'extortion and bribery which are . . . truly national'.[62] However, in the 1830s Gogol was played for broad comedy. Corrosive insights were cloaked in buffoonery[63] and Nicholas enjoyed the first performance so much that he laughed loudly and incessantly. This guaranteed a splendid evening for all, as etiquette dictated that no one could laugh aloud until the emperor was heard to laugh.

In that same year, 1836, Mikhail Glinka – wellspring of Russian opera – premiered *Ivan Susanin* under the baton of the man who had treated the same subject twenty years earlier, Catterino Cavos. The opera concerned a peasant who, in 1613, diverted Polish troops and saved the life of the founder of the Romanov dynasty, Tsar Mikhail, grandfather of Peter the Great. It was the first Russian opera without spoken dialogue, and the first tragedy. In the Cavos version, Ivan Susanin survives, whereas Glinka has the peasant die to save the tsar. The emperor attended rehearsals and shaped elements of the opera to underline the politically useful idea that the tsar is the guardian of the nation and that personal happiness is closely tied to the preservation of autocracy. Renamed *A Life for the Tsar* by Nicholas, it was to open the opera season every year.[64]

Musically, St Petersburg established itself as an international venue. Franz Liszt dazzled audiences in April 1842. The pianist was such a showman that he took the novel step of appearing on a stage erected in the centre of the Assembly Hall of the Nobility, from where he played not only pieces written for his instrument, but orchestral and vocal works in bravura piano renditions. He also performed at receptions given by the nobility and was presented to the tsar, who ignored all others present in order to engage the virtuoso in exclusive conversation. Liszt gave six public concerts, including a benefit for a children's hospital. But when he returned to Petersburg one year later – his impact diminished by the renewed craze for Italian music – he was booked in the smaller Engelhardt Hall.[65] Robert Schumann remarked on the dominance of Italian productions and performers when he visited the capital with his wife, Clara, in 1844. More celebrated as a pianist than her husband was as a composer, Clara was invited to perform before the empress. She also entertained the imperial family with a two-hour recital at the Winter Palace and gave a brilliant public concert at the Mikhailovsky Theatre. Hector Berlioz travelled fourteen days through the snows of northern Europe to conduct four concerts in 1847, including two complete performances of his *Roméo et Juliette*. The critic Vladimir Stasov hailed these as 'the most magnificent, most crowded, most brilliant and most deafening concerts'[66] presented in the capital that season, and Berlioz – who was called back countless times by the appreciative audience – wrote in a letter, 'I have to come to Russia to hear my favourite work properly played, it has always been more or less ruined everywhere else.'[67]

Berlioz had met Glinka in Paris three years earlier and was so enthusiastic about his music that he included it in his French concerts and praised it in reviews. Liszt was similarly impressed with this first giant of Russian music.[68] In a scene dominated by foreigners, Glinka's sudden appearance 'caused the whole city of St Petersburg to begin attending Russian performances'. The young Rimsky-Korsakov recorded that *A Life for the Tsar* threw him into 'a veritable ecstasy' – 'there were no bounds to my enthusiasm for and worship of this man of genius'.[69] Gogol was among those impressed: 'What an opera you can make out of our national tunes! Show me a people who have more songs! . . . Glinka's opera is only a beautiful beginning.'[70] Apart from folk idioms and melodies, there were the obvious influences of Donizetti and Mozart, but Glinka himself asserted that composers do not create music, the people do. His first opera was one of the first declarations of the new nationalism which would – through the arguments between 'Slavophils' and 'Westerners' – dominate the intellectual debate between St Petersburg's European modernity and Moscow's traditional Russian soul.[71]

Glinka's second opera, *Ruslan and Lyudmila* – a very free adaptation of Pushkin's witty mock-heroic poem – premiered in 1842. Despite the expectations raised by previews of the score which included piano performances by Franz Liszt, the libretto proved awkward and doomed the opera. The imperial family left the theatre abruptly at the end of the fifth act, and *Ruslan* gradually disappeared from the repertoire – understandably upsetting the composer. Glinka spat on the ground as he left his 'vile' native land to settle in Berlin. After his death, the composer Mily Balakirev gave the first uncut performance of the opera in 1867 and the next generation of Russian composers began to borrow from Glinka. Tchaikovsky called *Ruslan* 'the tsar of operas' and Stravinsky referred to the composer frequently. But in the 1840s, in the climate of growing nationalism, Nicholas surprisingly deserted Russian music and spent large sums on supporting the fashionable Italian opera. Society, so taken with the Italians, turned its back on what it took for boorishness in Glinka. In 1843, the Russian opera lost its theatre to the Italians and was forced to settle in an old circus, which burned down in 1859.

Stimulated by the international talent that was appearing in St Petersburg, ballet was developing swiftly. By the time Théophile Gautier visited in the late 1850s, he observed that it was 'not an easy matter for a dancer to win applause in St Petersburg; the Russians are experts in such matters, and the scrutiny of their opera glasses dreaded'. A leading figure in French ballet during the preceding decades, Gautier found Petersburg theatres to be well equipped with flies and traps capable of changing scene efficiently. He observed that the Imperial Ballet School was training 'remarkable pupils' and their corps de ballet was 'unequalled for the *ensemble* precision'. Russian dancers were skilled and professional, never 'giggling or glancing amorously at the spectators', as they often did in Paris.[72]

The publication of the letters of the French choreographer Jean-Georges Noverre made a great impact on the development of the dramatic nature of Russian ballet. Noverre asserted that technique was only a means to an end and suggested that the stiff, restrictive costumes should be modified. Indeed, the frontiers of visual respectability were being tested by Petersburg's ballet in the early nineteenth century. Heavy, cloaking costumes were replaced by the transparent net used by French companies, and became progressively shorter. Later in the century, Tchaikovsky despaired of the vulgar young dandies who went to the ballet to ogle the legs of the girls.[73] Young male theatregoers fell in love with actresses and dancers, screaming at their favourites, congregating at stage doors and showering their idols with flowers and self-indulgent poetry.[74] Pushkin's Onegin – like the poet himself – was infatuated with the Russian prima ballerina Avdotya Istomina, finding it impossible to disentangle the dancer from the dance.[75]

Training in ballet is very much about the pupil–teacher relationship, and Petersburg was blessed to have a succession of remarkable ballet masters. The 'fiery and unpredictable' Charles-Louis Didelot – ballet master from 1801 to 1811 – trained Istomina. Jules Perrot, who had been a pupil of the celebrated Vestris, came to Petersburg as a ballet master in 1851 and married the Russian ballerina Capitoline Samovskaya. The great giant of Russian ballet, the dancer and choreographer Marius Petipa, arrived in the Russian capital in 1847 and would live on into the twentieth century, providing ballet with some of its greatest and most durable works. Nourishing this developing tradition was the influence of the greatest foreign performers of the age. The ethereal Marie Taglioni, who 'danced as nightingales sang', was first seen in Petersburg in 1837, in *La Sylphide*. Carlotta Grisi – common-law wife of Jules Perrot and the greatest Romantic dancer of the age – became the prima ballerina of the Imperial Theatre in St Petersburg from 1850–53. Gautier co-wrote the libretto of Adolfe Adam's *Giselle* for Grisi, but the initial reaction to her performance in Petersburg was cool. Audiences had initially seen the great Austrian dancer Fanny Elssler in the part. While the story of *Giselle* suggests there are fatal consequences for those who wish to break social ranks, the choreography – forcing dancers to explore the air and defy gravity with their *ballon* – must have provided a welcome vision of freedom in the capital of Nicholas I.

The tsar's love of performance and theatre was reflected in a court that took on renewed splendour after the muted celebrations of Alexander's reign. Nicholas loved chivalry and there were extravagant medieval parades. In 1829, Nicholas celebrated the Festival of the Magic of the White Rose. In 1842, a tournament was held in the Arsenal. His love of dressing-up is recorded in letters of January 1835 and 1836 to his sister, Anna Pavlovna: 'Our winter has only just begun: yesterday a small masked ball was held to celebrate Twelfth Night; everybody appeared at it in the exact costumes of my father's time; very funny and very different, almost unbelievable.' The following year, the guests at the ball numbered between 26,000 and 27,000 and, on that occasion, everybody appeared 'in the costume of Peter the Great's time, and the military men looked as droll as possible with the grotesqueness and strangeness of their dress and turn out'.[76] Themed celebrations included the 'Gods of Mount Olympus', a Chinese masquerade and a Gothic Ball, which made use of the Gothic Banquet Service presented to Nicholas for Christmas

1833. Such festivities were stimulated by the pan-European fad for 'historicism' – an obsession with the art, culture and fashion of past epochs.[77] Less than a year and a half after fire had gutted the Winter Palace, magnificent balls resumed, always opening with the polonaise from Glinka's *A Life for the Tsar*, in which Nicholas led out the wife of the leader of the diplomatic corps, followed by the *tsarina* escorting the head of the diplomatic corps. After this procession, the dancing followed – quadrilles, waltzes and the mazurka, which, according to Gautier's expert eye, was 'danced in St Petersburg with a degree of perfection and elegance unknown elsewhere'.[78]

Nicholas noted that Peterhof continued to grow more beautiful and, when the annual ball occurred on 1 July, there were up to 100,000 guests. Custine recorded that on the *tsarina*'s name-day, '6,000 carriages, 30,000 pedestrians and an innumerable number of boats leave St Petersburg to form a camp around' the palace. During Custine's visit, while guests dined, a sudden tempest sunk boats sailing in the gulf. The authorities admitted to 200 drowned. Others claimed there were up to 2,000. Custine suggested that the truth would never be known, as the newspapers would not mention an accident that 'would distress the *tsarina* and accuse the tsar'. A week later, Custine recorded that the disaster 'exceeded what I had been led to suppose' and commented, 'how little we can be certain of anything' – facts were 'considered of no account in Petersburg, where the past and future, like the present, are at the disposal of the master'.[79]

Adam Menelaws designed a pseudo-Gothic English 'cottage' at Peterhof for Alexandra Feodorovna in which the medieval imagery of the interior decoration celebrated her roles as wife and mother. Nicholas cherished the mid-nineteenth-century ideal of the family, but such sentimentality did not stop the 'tall, athletic' tsar from enjoying other women as he exerted his autocratic right over the daughters and wives of court officials.[80] Neither did this comfortable Christian notion of the family, or the chivalric fantasies of the design, reflect a spirit in tune with the progress that was palpable on St Petersburg streets. At a time when Europe was industrialising, Nicholas ignored the challenge, afraid that a working class that was not tied to the land would undermine Russia's social structure.

When cholera struck in 1831, one victim was the should-have-been tsar, Constantine. Another was the ageing Adam Menelaws, who had worked for forty-seven years in Russia. The disease was first observed in the Ganges delta of British India in 1817 and spread to southern Russia the same year. A pandemic broke out in 1823, which came to a head in 1830–31. St Petersburg was quarantined, but insufficient controls were set up and the first reported case occurred in the capital on 15 June 1831. A cholera commission was set up the very next day. It prohibited people from drinking canal water, but offered no alternative source. Rumours spread faster than the disease, and the epidemic was gossiped about as a police plot or the work of Russia's enemies. Doctors – working hard to contain the disease – were dubbed Polish agents. Intransigence confronted ignorance, as anyone resisting the intervention of the authorities was 'arrested', thrown into the cholera carts and taken off to be quarantined in lazarettos. Crowds began to block the passage of these wagons, shaking and rocking them, until they spilt those arrested onto the street. Violence flared on Vasilevsky Island and in the administrative district of the Admiralty. On 21 June, a huge crowd stormed a lazaretto on Rozhdestvenskaya Street, but was repulsed by the police. The following day, thousands of people converged on the Haymarket, where the crowd swung out of control. A German doctor was pounded to death and – as guards and police fled – the mob surged into the hospital and liberated the sick. Soldiers, backed by artillery, were sent to put down the riot and rounded up 180 offenders. In mourning for his brother Constantine, Nicholas I was quarantined at Peterhof when the news of the violence reached him. Showing a similar presence of mind and fortitude that marked his first act as tsar in Senate Square in December 1825, the emperor arrived in the capital and toured the city, urging calm and restraint. He spoke to the dangerous Haymarket rabble, calmed the mob and quelled the rioting. It passed into folklore that a quasi-divine intervention by God's chosen had halted the spread of the disease. Nevertheless, there was a second Russian pandemic from 1847 to 1851, which resulted in more than a million deaths.[81]

The decade leading up to 1848 – when harvests were bad and protest and revolution rattled the doors of the establishment throughout Europe – was a period of prosperity for St Petersburg merchants. The first railway in Russia, which connected St Petersburg with Tsarskoe Selo, opened in 1838 and, four years later, the Petersburg–Moscow railway was under construction. When it opened in the autumn of 1851, it was the longest double-track railway in the world and carried passengers on a magical overnight journey between the old and new Russias. Currency stabilised in 1843 and, despite Nicholas's misgivings, industry was expanding. But in the spring of the troubled year of 1848, cholera – which had broken out in Kazan and Orenburg a few months earlier – once again reached the capital and killed one out of every thirty-six inhabitants.[82] In the *gostiny dvor* many shopkeepers ceased to trade, and on 4 July a young lady attending the Smolny Institute recorded in her diary that 'during the past two weeks, about 100,000 people have fled . . . There are almost no hackney drivers. The city is empty.'[83] A thriving capital with half a million inhabitants was – within a matter of weeks – deserted. Another eyewitness recorded that cholera seized 'many victims from among the poor. The slightest carelessness in food, the slightest cold was enough to bring it on and after only four or five hours a person would be no more. Terror reigned everywhere throughout the entire summer.' A decade after the pandemic subsided, the 1861–4 health reforms made some impact, but while western Europe had eradicated cholera by the end of the nineteenth century, Russia – revealing a debilitating sluggishness – suffered pandemics in 1893–4, 1908 and 1925, before the Soviet authorities eventually eliminated it.[84]

The rigidity of Nicholas's regime was reflected not only in its slowness to reform but also in its suffocating control of education. Pupils were quarantined from subversive Western influences by limits to the curriculum. At university, philosophy was no longer offered, and religious truth replaced rational thought as the standard by which arguments were tested.[85] Uniforms – which Herzen observed, were 'passionately loved by despotism' – became obligatory, emblematic of the stuffy conformity in the capital. Herzen suggested that if one were to show an Englishman 'the battalions of exactly similar, tightly buttoned frock coats of the fops on the Nevsky Prospekt', he would take them for a 'squad of policemen'.[86]

With the government keeping a tight rein on the capital after the Decembrist uprising, the intellectual initiative and impetus for change moved – temporarily – to Moscow. During the 1830s, the revolutionary thinkers Alexander Herzen, Vissarion Belinsky, Timofey Granovsky and Mikhail Bakunin attended its university. They formed a circle around Nikolai Stankevich, a young philosopher attracted by the idea – proposed by Friedrich von Schiller – that it was in the private arena of the soul that mankind achieved freedom. These young rebels were sensitive, educated members of a class whose days were numbered. They became known as 'superfluous men' who could find no place for themselves in Russia even though they strove, through the printed word, to advance radical thought and action. Attracted by Western ideas and freedom, most of them moved to St Petersburg, which – despite the rigour of the tsar – was always more open than Moscow. Others went into exile abroad, in a search for the freedom to proclaim radical thought.[87]

Belinsky converted to French utopian socialism in the early 1840s and set out – for the rest of his brief life – to expose the social evils of his society through his work as a literary critic and sociological commentator. He was an early champion of Dostoevsky, whose first story, *Poor Folk*, 'revealed the life of the grey, humiliated, Russian minor official as nobody had ever done before'.[88] Famously, Belinsky took Gogol to task for the writer's late conversion to mystical conservatism. In the course of his incendiary letter, Belinsky – protesting against autocracy and serfdom – claimed that Russia needed an awakening of 'human dignity lost for so many centuries amid the dirt and refuse'.[89] Dying of consumption in 1848, he avoided imprisonment or exile for promulgating such unpatriotic ideas.

This generation of thinkers, in its search for solutions to Russia's impasse, split into Slavophils and Westerners – two groups with distinct methods and opinions, but who, nonetheless, shared a good number of ideas. Hating the bureaucracy of the state, the Slavophils sought solutions through the Orthodox Church and in the rejection of European ideas. For them, Peter the Great had been gravely mistaken in turning his back on Moscow and looking westwards. One of their number, Ivan Aksakov, suggested that the only way to revive the nation was to 'spit in the face' of St Petersburg.[90] While the Slavophils were devout, Westerners tended to be atheists. Vissarion Belinsky went so as far as to say that the Orthodox religion was 'the handmaid of despotism'[91] and was infuriated by its desire to block scientific progress with superstition. But there was one traditional structure which attracted both Westerners and Slavophils – the village commune, or *obshchina*, where people met in a high street peace meeting to settle matters.[92]

Herzen was the illegitimate son of a Russian aristocrat and a humble German woman. Frequently in trouble with the authorities, he eventually fled to England, where he set up the Free Russian Press with which to attack the Russia of Nicholas I.

Reacting against idealists such as Hegel and spurning histori-
cists such as Marx, Herzen declared that nature and history
were not subject to schemes and plans. The duty of people was
to the present and to the freedom afforded by 'the labourer's
wage or pleasure in the work performed'. History was an incoherent teacher, a senseless tale of 'chronic madness'. Progress
meant respecting and ameliorating the present. The realisation
of personal potential should triumph over tyranny, and political
freedom should protect human dignity. To sacrifice such dignity
in striving for the ghost of a future was delusional. Increasingly
Herzen came to believe that socialism could be achieved through
the collectivism of the *obshchina*.[93] By virtue of its backwardness, Herzen believed that Russia could avoid capitalism and
succeed in becoming truly socialist – an idea that proved influential to the succeeding generation, the *narodniki*, or 'populists',
of the 1860s and 1870s.[94]

Nicholas Ogarev, Herzen's friend and Bakunin's publisher,
went beyond mere words and freed the serfs on his estate in
1838 – more than twenty years before the botched emancipation
edict of 1861. Sadly, his intention that the village commune
would successfully administer the estate ended in failure, and
Ogarev – coping with his heavy drinking – left Russia in the mid-
1850s to join Herzen.[95] The most extreme of all the 'superfluous
men', Mikhail Bakunin, also fled to Europe after being exiled to
Siberia. Bakunin advocated unreserved destruction in order to
allow fresh ideas to take root. He shared with Herzen a belief in
the supreme importance of individual liberty.

Mikhail Petrashevsky, a young official working in the Ministry of Foreign Affairs, had been stunned by a series of political
economy lectures that explored the ideas of the French utopian socialists Charles Fourier and Louis Blanc. As a result,
in 1845 Petrashevsky initiated his informal Friday gatherings,
where 'everybody spoke loudly about everything, without any
reservation whatsoever'. Three years later, these meetings were

formalised and lectures were given. Some of these proved to be of
an extremely contentious nature. In 1848 – when, from all over
Europe, news arrived of reforms, uprisings and revolts – such
meetings were seen as dangerous. Nicholas I, keeping revolution
at bay by vigilance, placed undercover agents in the Petrashevsky
circle.

One of the most dangerous speakers was a ruthless, strong-
willed and wealthy landowner called Nikolai Speshnev. Having
learned the ways of revolutionaries from European groups,
Speshnev wanted the members of the Petrashevsky circle to produce and circulate propaganda that incited peasants to rise up
against landlords and then to massacre the army units sent to
subdue them.[96] Increasingly anxious about the radicalisation of
the fringes of the circle, the authorities rounded up and questioned more than 250 suspects, exiled fifty-one of them and
sentenced twenty-one – including Fyodor Dostoevsky – to death.
The writer was accused of a conspiracy to overthrow the state.
His crime? Reading Belinsky's letter to Gogol to a meeting of
the circle.

On 22 April 1848, Dostoevsky awoke to find a policeman and
an agent of the Third Section standing in his bedroom. They
had come to arrest him. Along with other members of the circle
who complained of torture while they were in captivity, Dostoevsky was locked up in the Peter and Paul Fortress. At dawn on
22 December 1849, the condemned were led through the gently
falling snow to the place of execution in Semyonovsky Square.
Prisoners who had been kept in solitary confinement were madly
chattering – their sallow faces and straggled black beards ghoulish against the jewel-white snow. As Dostoevsky wrote to his
brother, 'the sentence of death was read to us, we were all made
to kiss the cross, a sword was broken over our heads, and we
were told to don our white execution shirts. Then three of us
were tied to the stakes in order to be shot . . . For me, only one
minute of life remained.'[97] But, strangely, the drum roll beat a

retreat. The sentence of execution delivered in mid-November had been commuted, but in order to impress upon the miscreants the gravity of their crimes, Nicholas insisted that it be kept from them until they had suffered the ordeal of the execution ceremony. Dostoevsky was carted off to penal servitude in Siberia until, in February 1854, he was released to be a soldier. In his sadistic act of clemency, Nicholas made his greatest gift to the arts. One of the world's major writers had been spared.[98]

An official history of the Third Section compiled in 1876 admitted that the Petrashevsky circle had consisted only of 'corrupt youths who dreamed of spreading socialism to Russia'.[99] Nevertheless, the authorities placed further restrictions on reading matter, there were rumours of university closures and increased surveillance – measures that only served to fire the next generation of radicals. Just as Custine, in summarising Russia, suggested that fear was paralysing thought, so the writer and critic Alexander Nikitenko protested that there were 'more censors than books'. There were so many government agents in the press that no story could be given straight. And even these plants were subject to censure. One of the journalists employed by the Third Section, Faddei Bulgarin, was taken to task for complaining about Petersburg weather, for daring to be negative about the climate of the capital of the tsar. For the most part, Bulgarin denounced writers, planted stories in periodicals and – as a steady contributor to the *Vedomosti* – helped turn that publication of the Academy of Sciences into a propaganda sheet for the government. Vissarion Belinsky railed against the 'venal journalism' of Bulgarin, who edited *The Northern Bee*, a publication subsidised by the Third Section in order to provide a rosy picture of life under Nicholas. It proved very popular, with circulation rising from 7,000 in the 1830s to 10,000 during the Crimean War in the early 1850s.[100] As censorship took the bite out of much that was published, Nikolai Chernyshevsky – who would become the mouthpiece of the revolutionary movement

in the next decade – noted that among the writers of the capital in the early 1850s, apathy triumphed. Nikolai Nekrasov,
leader of the literary investigation into Petersburg's middle and
lower depths, lost heart and became addicted to cards. Others,
in order to make money, wrote pornography.[101] In his celebrated
1851 letter to Jules Michelet that same year, Herzen provided
a chilling image of the repressive tsar: 'Nicholas tries to forget
his isolation, but grows gloomier, more morose and uneasy
with every passing hour. He sees he is not loved; the silence that
reigns near him seems all the more deadly because of the distant
murmur of the impending tempest.'[102]

Before Herzen fled to Europe, he was hauled up before the Third
Section. Accused of not 'effacing the stains left from . . . youthful errors', the pretext for his arrest concerned the gossip that
circulated about a sentry on the Blue Bridge, who had allegedly
killed and robbed a passer-by in the middle of the night. But Herzen's was a spurious charge, occasioned by the fact that the tsar
had seen his file, noticed that he had been exiled to Siberia and
thought he should be sent back. Herzen was accused by a secret
force 'outside the law and above the law', which possessed the
'right to meddle in everything'. The Third Section had become
such a part of Russian life that – although its name changed – its
methods persisted in the perennial drive to secure the Russian
state. An English lady visiting in the 1850s noted that it 'is no
exaggeration to say that a Russian subject scarcely dares to utter
his true sentiments, even to his own brother'. She had often
witnessed 'conversations in which perhaps four or five would
be taking part each knowing' – absurdly – 'that his neighbour
was telling a lie'. The visitor ascertained that 'besides the secret
police', there were '80,000 paid agents in the country', including
'some of the French milliners in St Petersburg'. The tsar, quipped
Custine, was 'the only man in his empire with whom one can
converse without fear of informers'.[103] And Derzhavin's lines of
1808 revealed the capital's true character:

Why venture to Petropolis, if uncompelled,
change space for closeness, liberty for locks and latches.[104]


When the London *Times* broke the news of Nicholas I's death in
March 1855, Alexander Herzen broke open the champagne.[105]
The tsar had acted as the 'gendarme of Europe'[106] through three
decades of political unrest and revolution, crushing rebellion in
Poland, revolt in Hungary and forcing Prussia to accept Habsburg
domination. His foreign policy, however, ended with the
miscalculation that Russia could successfully combat an Anglo–
French alliance in the Crimea. When Sebastopol fell, there were
Russians who rejoiced, hoping that defeat would result in the
fall of the Romanovs. [107] Under the tsars, Russia was stagnating.
It was uncompetitive. It was a place – observed Custine – where
people had two coffins, 'the cradle and the tomb'. It was a prison
to which the tsar alone held the key. Writing a few years before
Nicholas died, the Russian historian Timofey Granovsky saw
Russia as 'nothing but a living pyramid of crimes, frauds and
abuses, full of spies, policemen, rascally governors, drunken
magistrates and cowardly aristocrats'.[108]

There were police scams in the capital, such as the slowly
accumulating profit to be made from lighting two, instead of
three, wicks in the city's oil lamps. There was 'disturbing and
unnecessary police brutality' – one visitor regarding the police
'as wolves instead of the watch-dogs of the community'.[109] Yet, as
the population grew, crime increased and during these years the
Petersburg police faced greater challenges. In the early 1840s,
about 20,000 petty criminals and drifters were arrested each
year and carted off in long, squat boxes – most of them being
released within days. In order to curb crime and illegal prostitution, there were raids on suspicious establishments. In 1843,
the regulation of prostitutes began. Medical Police Committees
issued prostitutes with a licence known as the 'yellow ticket' and

impounded their passports.[110] To control infection, prostitutes were instructed to wash their genitals with cold water and to change bed linen between clients. Soliciting when menstruating was forbidden, as blood was thought to transmit disease. With the shift from moral outrage to recognition that prostitution was unavoidable, and hence tolerable, brothels were given strict guidelines. They were to be kept clean, alcohol was to be served with moderation and they were to be closed on Sundays and only opened after the midday meal on holy days. The workers had to be over sixteen, could accept no custom from minors or students and were responsible for inspecting the genitalia of their clients. Nicholas was, of course, happy to tolerate brothels. Madams were well placed to act as agents and informers.[111]

Despite the tone of Nicholas I's reign, in which 'procedure and regularity' ruled, the infrastructure of the capital developed erratically. In late 1850, the Nevsky Bridge – the first permanent structure to span the Neva – was opened. Its 331-metre length made it the longest bridge in Europe. But, while several central streets were lit by gas, others languished in the dim light of two-wick oil lamps. As illumination was necessary as early as three o'clock in the freezing fogs of winter afternoons, the city – away from the Nevsky Prospekt – remained gloomy. The slums of the city remained grimy and unhealthy, while on the Nevsky, where pedestrians were fined for smoking in the street, crinolines fluttered and French was the dominant language. In the houses of the well-to-do there were flowers on the tables and in every alcove so that, while it froze outside, there was an illusion of temperate paradise. For the wealthy, food was plentiful, with fresh produce harvested throughout the year from the numerous hothouses around the city. Gautier described a luncheon of *zakuski* 'taken standing and washed down with vermouth, Madeira, Dantzig brandy' and cognac. Yet there was evidence of a society not quite adapted to the European customs they sought to emulate. Gautier remarked on the fact that halfway through a dinner, people would switch from Bordeaux and champagne to porter, ale and kvas, suggesting that Custine was right to observe that Petersburgers 'confuse . . . luxury with refinement'.[112] There was still a native insecurity when it came to questions of style. The Russian Boris Efremov advertised himself – in French, for credibility – as a Parisian tailor.[113] And while the *gostiny dvor* boasted 'luxurious shop windows', like those seen in London or Paris, the experience of shopping was quite different. An Englishwoman asked for French ribbon. The merchant showed her Russian. She patiently demonstrated that she knew what she wanted and, at length, French ribbon was produced. But that was only the start of the tortuous process. Bargaining ensued, which resulted in her storming out of the shop, only to be recalled by an offer only a few kopeks above what she had proposed. After threatening to go next door, she obtained what she wanted for the sum she expected. But still that was not the end. A shop-keeper never had the correct change. It was his way of recouping the losses of bargaining. But, at the end of it all, the customer prevailed. What should have taken a few minutes, or a couple of sentences to describe, dragged out into a paragraph.[114]

By the time Nicholas I died in 1855, booksellers were routinely being visited by the police. In one bookshop in the capital they discovered more than 2,500 banned books, suggesting the size of the market for revolutionary ideas and their continued availabil-ity, despite the crack-down.[115] As Custine observed, everywhere 'I hear the language of philosophy and everywhere I see oppression as the order of the day'. Indeed, taken all in, Custine perceived Russia as 'a tightly sealed boiler on a mounting fire'. He added, 'I fear an explosion.'[116]

# 9

# DISCONTENT

*1855–94*

In 1850, employees at the Stieglitz cotton factory were denied a wage rise and 700 of them downed tools. The police isolated sixty-six leaders, six of whom were beaten publicly and returned to their villages. St Petersburg was experiencing the first effects of an industrial revolution. The cotton-spinning industry was thriving, and heavy industry was stimulated by the Crimean War. In the middle years of the 1850s, revenue rose by 50 per cent across the city's 367 factories and by 100 per cent in its iron foundries. But expansion was compromised by growing unrest among workers and by the post-war economic crisis of 1857. A questionnaire submitted to manufacturers revealed their exploitation of the 1,282 minors who were employed in the capital's factories – some as young as eight years old. It appeared acceptable that foremen chastised children who were lodged in filthy conditions and forced to work nights.[1] Yet – despite a growing perception of the appalling circumstances under which workers laboured – police generally sided with the owners. When, in 1861, a seventeen-year-old girl was killed by steam-driven machinery in one of the larger cotton mills, the owners installed rails around the machinery – and that was that. Despite nearly 3,000 complaints lodged by workers between 1858 and 1861, reform was left to fester from below, as bread shortages, rising prices and an endless stream of new arrivals from the countryside exacerbated the misery of St Petersburg's working poor.

Although the capital was thriving commercially, with more than 1,700 fruit-sellers, 2,000 butchers and 250 bookshops, its transport system lagged behind that of London or Paris. There were horse trams on Vasilevsky Island, squeakily moving loads from the wharves to the customs storehouse. Trams also ran along the Nevsky, hauling goods between ship and rail, but there were no omnibuses.[2] Passengers without their own carriages travelled in one of the inumerable horse-drawn cabs – the drive through the centre of the city giving the impression of 'slosh and mud and misery'.

The opening of the railways stimulated the *dacha* boom that had begun in the 1830s. While these country residences were once the preserve of the aristocracy, the writer and journalist Faddei Bulgarin now instructed his readers not to bother, during the brief weeks of summer, to go searching for 'a merchant in his shop, an apothecary in his drugstore, a German tradesman in his workshop or a clerk in his office! All of them are at the *dacha*!'[3] Poorer people would pack up bedding, furniture and crockery and go off to enjoy the freshness of the black firs, silver birch and hayfields of the countryside.[4] As the city grew, people were forced to venture further than the increasingly urbanised and industrialised Petersburg and Vyborg areas to the north of the Neva.

Railways were busy, and activity in and around Petersburg stations was hectic. Travelling to the capital by rail at the height of the 1863 Polish insurrection – soldiers everywhere, fellow passengers armed with revolvers – Lord Redesdale recorded his arrival: 'What a crowd it was at the station! Railway officials, Custom House officers, police, hotel touts, droshky drivers, indescribables of all sorts; swearing, chaffing, abusing, howling.' A policeman 'wielding a stout cudgel, with a few blows indiscriminately administered about the heads of the rabble, sent them all flying in various directions'. After this hectic first impression, Redesdale found Petersburg 'deaf and blind to all tragedy. There could be no gayer city in the world; certainly none where the foreign diplomats were so hospitably treated; our lives were a round of festivities in the very home of joyous revelry.'[5]

St Petersburg was flourishing as an international, cultural capital. In 1859, the novelist Alexandre Dumas visited and, rather than adding to the often-repetitive impressions left by endless visitors, was content to write a long, colourful and energetic history of the Romanovs. That same year, Dostoevsky returned to Petersburg, primed by exile in Siberia to explore the underbelly of the city and to excoriate in prose those damp corners 'where an entire family lives in one room, hungry and cold'. The Mariinsky Theatre opened in 1860. Named after Alexander II's wife, Marie Alexandrovna, it was designed by Alberto Cavos and constructed on the site of the burnt-out circus.[6] It was in the Mariinsky that Alexander and Marie Alexandrovna attended the premiere of Giuseppe Verdi's *La forza del destino* in November 1862. The opera had been munificently commissioned, and Verdi – who would substantially revise the work before its Milan premiere seven years later – was present.[7]

To stimulate taste and to educate, the Russian Musical Society was founded. It was sponsored by the forward-looking German-born grand duchess, Elena Pavlovna. The celebrated pianist Anton Rubinstein – who, as a child prodigy, had played before Chopin and Liszt – was appointed director. He exerted an enormous influence on music in the capital and on the young Tchaikovsky who, having graduated from St Petersburg's School of Jurisprudence in 1859, was gravitating towards a musical career. Elena Pavlovna was also eager to found a St Petersburg Conservatoire. She had discussed the project with the Schumanns when they visited in 1844. Nearly twenty years later, in 1862, the Conservatoire opened its doors. The director was, once again, Anton Rubinstein.[8]

Although St Petersburg's great era of palace-building was past, additions were made during the second half of the nineteenth century. The finishing touches were put on the elegant neo-classical Mikhailovsky Palace in the early 1860s, only decades before Alexander III converted it into a museum for Russian art. It was in this palace that the politically engaged Elena Pavlovna held her glittering *salon*, to which she welcomed thinkers, scientists and artists. She had shown sympathy for the Petrashevsky circle, liberated the serfs on her estate at Karlovka in 1856 and would advise Alexander on his 1861 emancipation plans.

The New Hermitage had opened its doors in 1852, but remained without a director until Stephan Gedeonov was appointed in 1863, after outmanoeuvring both the Louvre and the British Museum to acquire Giampietro Campana's important collection of antiquities. This Marchese di Cavelli had assembled thousands of items by using money he embezzled from the Monte de Pietà Bank. When Campana was imprisoned, Gedeonov obtained them from the Vatican. His first act as director of the Hermitage was to shift the imperial book collection to the public library on the Nevsky Prospekt in order to make room for his prodigious acquisition. Under Gedeonov, the museum acquired Leonardo's *Madonna Litta* along with three other paintings from the Milanese collector Count Litta. Gedeonov purchased Raphael's *Conestabile Madonna* for the empress, and it passed into the Hermitage collection after her death. Numerous archaeological items were added, brought from far-flung parts of the Russian Empire that had been opened up by extensive railway and road construction.[9]

In 1863, as Gedeonov took charge of the Hermitage, the selection for the Paris Salon proved so conservative that artists petitioned for an alternative exhibition, and Napoleon III was obliged to sanction the celebrated Salon des Refusés in order to show progressive works such as Manet's shocking *Déjeuner sur l'herbe*. In a similar rejection of stale academicism, St Petersburg students of history painting at the Academy of Arts refused to accept the title set for their examination, 'The Entry of Wotan into Valhalla'.[10] In some ways it was an ill-timed protest, as interest in the historical and mythological was gripping northern Europe – by 1863, Richard Wagner had composed half of his mighty Ring cycle, its plot provoked by the conniving of the doomed Wotan. But although the students may have misjudged the subject's paradoxical topicality, they were justified in demanding a more contemporary Russian subject. Their peers in genre painting had been set the pertinent title 'The Liberation of the Serfs'.

The rebellion of the history-painting students and their decision to set up a kind of cooperative, or *artel*, was merely symptomatic of wider academic unrest. At the outset of the 1860s, a significant number of students at St Petersburg University were badly fed and fell prey to diseases such as typhus and tuberculosis. Returning for the 1861 autumn term, students were greeted by a pamphlet printed by Alexander Herzen's Free Press in London and co-authored by an academic contributor to *The Contemporary*, Nikolai Shelgunov, and by the women's rights activist Mikhail Mikhailov. The pamphlet – *To the Younger Generation* – called for an end to tsarism, demanded elections and criticised the 1861 Emancipation of Serfs Edict as being too little too late.

The governmental reforms of the early 1860s that purported to be progressive were, in fact, ill conceived, badly managed and inadequate. Despite ameliorating the situation of the Jews and permitting Jewish merchants and craftsmen to live in Russia's two largest cities, despite introducing trial by jury and a defence counsel, despite easing censorship of the press and despite creating the *zemstvo* – an elected, multi-class assembly that administered affairs at a local level – the tenor of Alexander II's reign remained repressive.

Nicholas I had identified serfdom as the 'indubitable evil of

Russian life'. To prove the point, during his reign there had been more than 550 peasant uprisings, though nothing on the scale of the Pugachev revolt. Alexander II's celebrated statement that it 'is better to abolish serfdom from above rather than to wait for the time when it will begin to abolish itself from below' resulted in the 1861 Emancipation Edict. Anxious that its publication might spark revolt, loaded cannon and troops on full alert surrounded the Winter Palace and patrolled the streets of the capital. It was a precautionary measure against those – such as the authors of *To the Younger Generation* – who regarded the badly drawn-up reform as 'a bone you throw to an angry dog to save your calves. The emancipation is the last act of a dying despotism. The Romanovs have disappointed the people and must go.'

Enacted two years before Abraham Lincoln's Emancipation Proclamation, the Edict 'freed' 23,000,000 serfs owned by 100,000 landowners, but without granting them free land. Absurdly, peasants were left with less terrain to cultivate and with heavy redemption payments, which shackled them to their lords.

Fired by the call to arms in *To the Younger Generation*, a group of students occupied a lecture theatre and held a protest meeting. The following day – passionate and jubilant in the late-September sun – students swarmed across the city from the university on Vasilevsky Island and swept down the Nevsky. Although French barbers in festive mood emerged from their shops shouting, '*Révolution! Révolution!*'[11] the sight of a chanting mass of long-haired men accompanied by women – their hair cropped short, in true revolutionary style – appeared to many passers-by just as degenerate as anti-Vietnam War protesters would on the streets of the West a century later.

Shouting slogans, the crowd surged towards the home of the university rector. He refused to meet them. In fact he did nothing. So, to increase the pressure for reform, undergraduates disrupted classes and boycotted lectures. Continued agitation resulted in student lockouts, the detention of ringleaders and the

*Nikolai Yaroshenko's* A Student, *1881.*

university being shut down for two years – all of which inspired
sympathy for the student cause among those with any interest in
the conditions of life in Alexander's Russia. During benefits in
aid of the radicals, Dostoevsky read from his novel *The House
of the Dead*, and Rubinstein performed. When the leading
agitators were jailed, Fyodor Dostoevsky and his elder brother
Mikhail – co-editors of the progressive and populist periodical
*Time* – sent them grilled meat, wine and cognac.[12] Government
censorship tightened. *The Contemporary* was closed in 1862,
*Time* a year later.

For the first time since the Decembrist revolt, mass dissension
was on the streets of St Petersburg and pamphlets were scattered
everywhere. Perhaps the most radical of these was *Young Russia*

of May 1862, which called for 'bloody and pitiless revolution'. Penned by a Moscow student, it was pushed through letter boxes across the capital and was even scattered in the chapel of the Winter Palace. *Young Russia* urged people to snatch their axes 'and attack the imperial party with no more mercy than they show us'. With decidedly Churchillian rhetoric, the pamphlet claimed that 'we will kill them in the squares, we will kill them in the houses, kill them in the narrow alleys of towns, in the broad avenues of capitals' and 'unfurl the great flag of the future, the red flag'.[13] The violence of the text led people to suspect that those who produced it were also responsible for the arson attacks that devastated parts of Moscow and St Petersburg in mid-1862. Fires broke out in rapid succession in different quarters of the capital in May. Fanned by high winds, the blazes consumed wooden buildings at an alarming rate. Houses on the left bank of the Fontanka were destroyed, as was the Tolkuchy Market and the Apraksin Arcade. The arsonists were never identified, but their action was dramatic and eminently newsworthy in a country chronically fascinated by fire.[14] In Dostoevsky's *Crime and Punishment*, Rashkolnikov – scouring the newspapers for reports of his own crime – finds only stories of 'a fire in Peski . . . a fire in the Petersburg quarter . . . another fire in the Petersburg quarter . . . and another fire in the Petersburg quarter'.[15] Nobody was interested in the axe-murder of a pawnbroker.

The man who became the mouthpiece of the 1860s generation was positively the worst significant novelist in Russian literature: Nikolai Chernyshevsky. Son of a provincial priest, Chernyshevsky had an empathy with the humbler sections of society and, just like Herzen, believed that the habit of mutual responsibility which guided the peasant commune could be applied to society at large. The example of village communes and craftsmen's cooperatives – functioning autonomously, taking decisions without any central authority – would point Russia's progress towards socialism.[16] More radical than most of his followers,

Chernyshevsky believed that industrial and agricultural labour was entitled to what it produced. Before *The Contemporary* was shut down, Chernyshevsky and Nekrasov had edited the periodical, filling it with socialist propaganda disguised as literature. When the publication was permitted to restart, Nekrasov published Chernyshevsky's tedious but tremendously influential fiction *What Is to Be Done?* which highlighted the radical difference between the pampered reformers of the 1840s and the revolutionaries of the 1860s. That divide was dramatised in Ivan Turgenev's exquisite novel *Fathers and Sons*. The nihilist hero, Bazarov, is a *raznochinets*, one of the sons of impoverished smallholders, merchants, clergy or minor civil servants who were lucky enough to gain an education. *Raznochintsy* were members of a new social category in Russia, the intelligentsia, who took nothing for granted. It is perhaps a tribute to the accuracy of the book's vision that when Turgenev – very much a 'superfluous man' of the 1840s – attempted to engage with radical students in 1860s Petersburg, they appeared bored or contemptuous.[17]

While repressive measures were taken against student revolutionaries, there were limited advances in the education of women. Secondary schools were established for girls of moderate means, offering pupils a wide curriculum, including Russian, religion, history, arithmetic, geometry, physics, geography, natural history, drawing, sewing, modern languages, music and dance. Russia's first Pedagogical Institute for women opened in 1863. The following year, Dostoevsky's future wife was in attendance, preparing herself for what would be her first position – Dostoevsky's stenographer.[18] As women started office jobs and aspired to the professions, the voice of feminism began to be heard, sparked by the late Mikhail Mikhailov's desire to purge women of the scourge of 'femininity'. Mikhailov wanted character traits to be 'neither masculine, nor feminine, but purely human'. Some progressive or 'crop-headed' women – as a character in *Crime and Punishment* describes them[19] – began to train for medicine at the St Petersburg Medical-Surgical Academy. When the university prohibited female students, the more enterprising went off to Zurich to study. Among them was Nadezhda Suslova, daughter of one of Count Sheremetev's serfs, who became Russia's first female doctor. Another student was Mariya Bokova, prototype for Vera Pavlovna in Chernyshevsky's *What Is to Be Done?*[20]

This novel, which inspired decades of Russian revolutionary disruption, nearly failed to make it into print. Chernyshevsky was arrested in July 1862 and it was during his two-year detention in the Peter and Paul Fortress while pending trial that the novel was written. The manuscript was confiscated by the prison authorities and covered with every sort of official stamp by each and every member of a Commission of Inquiry. By the time it arrived in the censor's office, it was assumed that, after such an excess of scrutiny, it had been approved for publication. The manuscript was handed over to the editor of *The Contemporary*, Nikolai Nekrasov who – perhaps in an act of unconscious literary criticism – left it in a taxi. He only managed to recover the subversive text after advertising his loss in – of all places – *The Police Gazette*.[21]

As literature, *What Is to Be Done?* should have been lost. As a radical polemic, it clamoured to be read. Its socialist ideals and feminist vision are as attractive as the prose and plot are awkward and unwieldy. The heroine, Vera Pavlovna, sets up a sewing cooperative in decent premises. Her enterprise is not run for her profit, and she works – like those she employs – for a wage. She pays her seamstresses sick-pay, reads aloud to them, dresses them comfortably and feeds them well. She takes them on outings to Petersburg islands, where they picnic, play games and dance quadrilles. The love plot sees Vera move from man to man, offering a picture of an ambitious, advanced and empowering feminism. In Russia of the 1860s, this was trail-blazing.

Chernyshevsky was a diehard optimist who believed that man was capable of creating a socialist utopia.[22] No such faith in unqualified good was shared by Dostoevsky, who reacted against the utopianism of *What Is to Be Done?* In his novel of 1864, *Notes From Underground*, Dostoevsky's anti-hero – 'a sick man . . . an angry man' – is a creature who spurns the scientific faith of Turgenev's Bazarov or Chernyshevsky's heroine. Heir to the 'little men' of Pushkin and Gogol, Dostoevsky's anti-hero is the victim of the etiquette of Petersburg's public spaces. The Underground Man – one of the countless scribes ingested by the megalosaurean Russian civil service – feels degraded by that street of splendour, the Nevsky Prospekt. He experiences the gulf between what he is and what he wishes to be. The Nevsky lies, and the Nevsky grades and degrades. The avenue – so generous to the wealthy or well known – makes the lowly squirm. When the Underground Man goes to the Nevsky in the afternoon to enjoy a walk in the sun, he confesses, 'I didn't actually enjoy my walk at all: I experienced an endless series of torments, crushing humiliations . . . I darted like a minnow through the passers-by in a most ungraceful fashion, constantly giving way to generals, officers of the Horse Guards and Hussars.'[23]

Joseph Brodsky contended that during the middle years of the nineteenth century, 'Russian literature caught up with reality to the extent that today when you think of St Petersburg you can't distinguish the fictional from the real.'[24] While Chernyshevsky inhabited the abstracted world of the polemic, Dostoevsky moved among the down-and-outs in the broken and unhealthy parts of his challenging city. His narrator encountered the 'rag pickers . . . crowding round the taverns in the dirty stinking courtyards of the Haymarket' and suffered 'the airlessness, the bustle and the plaster, scaffolding, bricks and dust . . . and that special Petersburg stench, so familiar to all who are unable to get out of town in the summer'. The protagonists of *Crime and Punishment* crowd in rooms or live in 'practically a passage', in houses crammed with 'working people of all kinds – tailors, locksmiths, cooks . . . girls picking up a living as best they could'.[25]

The authorities did attempt to further regulate prostitution and make it safer for the workers. Numbers rose. Although many women remained unregistered, the official figures – 1,800 in the early 1860s, rising to nearly 4,500 in 1870 – are undoubtedly underestimated. By the middle of the decade there were about 150 brothels operating. Owners were supposed to keep no more than three-quarters of the earnings and – in return for their hefty cut – provide adequate lodgings and good food for their workers. Brothels were not tolerated within 320 metres of churches or schools, and no image of the imperial family was permitted to grace the interior. Swelling numbers of prostitutes meant that the small charitable shelter caring for them since 1833 was replaced by a larger establishment run by the Sisters of Mercy, which, in turn, was superseded by yet another shelter established in the grounds of the Kalinkin Hospital. From 1857, a *dacha* in the woods to the north of the capital cared for child prostitutes.[26] All these establishments were overcrowded and – at best – inefficient. For most of the girls and women forced into selling their bodies, life was ugly. In *Crime and Punishment*, prostitutes are seen 'covered with bruises', their upper lips 'swollen', their future promising more of the same – or the madhouse and suicide.[27] Meanwhile, confirmed cases of syphilis – identified with considerable difficulty by the medical authorities – rose staggeringly from just over 6,000 in 1861 to nearly 15,000 in 1868.[28]

During the mid-1860s drunkenness – once again – became an issue. The capital boasted 1,840 taverns, 562 inns, 399 shops selling alcohol and 229 wine cellars. Workers, drinking heavily before they started their day, were often disorderly and there were countless arrests. Before he began *Crime and Punishment*, Dostoevsky planned a novel called *The Drunkards* to explore the epidemic. When Alexander II remarked on the rise of 'debauchery, depravity and especially drunkenness', it resulted in the 1867 restrictions on the sale of alcohol on public holidays.

Before the tsar's intervention, 'people's promenades' – not unlike modern outdoor raves – saw thousands of workers moving in a mass around the city getting steadily plastered. After the restrictions were imposed, 100,000 people gathered peacefully in Mars Field during August without a single arrest for drunkenness.[29]

The tsar's anxiety about the rowdiness of his people reflected his own sense of insecurity. In April 1866, there was the first of six unsuccessful attempts on his life. The would-be assassin was a depressed and deranged character, right out of the pages of Dostoevsky. Dmitri Karakozov – expelled from the University of Kazan for student agitation and from the University of Moscow for not paying his fees – journeyed to the capital with the express intention of assassinating the tsar. So demented was the ex-student that he put this plan into print and distributed copies to all and sundry. The police obtained one, but in a city pestered by rowdy workers and radical students, they chose to ignore Karakozov's declaration, imagining – quite rightly, but nearly fatally – that it was penned by a nut. Karakozov had, in fact, joined a radical group with the sensational name of 'Hell'. It was led by a Manson-like fanatic called Nikolai Ishutin, who attracted the wayward and unbalanced. One member of the group contemplated poisoning his own father, in order to contribute his inheritance to the coffers of Hell.[30]

On 4 April 1866, after strolling in the Summer Garden with his mistress, Ekaterina Dolgoruka, the tsar was climbing into his carriage when Karakozov took aim. Whether through vigilance or by chance, a bystander jogged the assassin's arm and the shot missed its target. While this brazen attempt failed, defiance had moved to a new pitch, and the American Congress touchingly sent their regrets that an 'enemy of emancipation' should attempt to take the life of the tsar.[31] Count Muraviev – the scourge of the 1863 Polish Rebellion – was appointed to investigate. Of the thirty-five people brought to trial, Ishutin and Karakozov were sentenced to death, although only the would-be regicide was executed. The sentence of Hell's leader was commuted to the purgatory of hard labour for life.[32]

While the students, writers and revolutionaries of the 1860s were attempting to find ways to ameliorate their situation and change the regime, the social and industrial conditions went from bad to worse. Petersburg's population increased and its industry – by fits and starts – expanded. The authorities began to worry about the adverse effects of the capital's peculiar atmosphere. A good number of the stories set in Petersburg were clouded by depression and melancholia and saturated with images of its choking fog. But blaming sickness and unrest on the climate was dismissed by the doctors working for the city's Archive of Legal Medicine and Social Hygiene. Landlords were to blame. The authorities were to blame. An inspection in 1870 revealed that cellar dwellings were congested, cold and damp – some were even flooded with polluted water. Outside, courtyards were piled with refuse and excrement. The situation had deteriorated since the 1840s, when Nekrasov offered the first eyewitness account of Petersburg slums. Five-floor tenements – constructed by entrepreneurs for profit – added to the crowding, and thus to the pollution and contamination. Typhus struck the capital in 1865, followed by cholera and smallpox in 1870.[33] Thirteen two-storey buildings had risen on land owned by the Viazemsky family between the Fontanka and the Haymarket. Home to about 10,000 lodgers, they provided the depraved backdrop for Vsevolod Krestovsky's popular and sensational novel of 1864, *The Slums of St Petersburg*.[34]

The 1870s saw a marked increase in industrial production, stimulated by the threat of Prussian military might and the rapid expansion of Russia's railways. Factories were built around the capital – in the Petersburg and Vyborg sectors and on parts of Vasilevsky Island to the north, but with the highest concentration in Narvskaya, along the Obvodnogo Canal in the south. The Putilov Iron Works became Petersburg's largest industrial employer with several factories, sixty engineers and more than 12,000 workers. The Arsenal was modernised in 1870, and Ludwig Nobel – cousin to the man who invented dynamite and instituted a Peace Prize – became a major arms manufacturer for the Russian military, working from a small factory on the Vyborg Side. Nobel was only one of the many foreign bosses who complained about the lack of skill among Russian workers and their large number of holidays. Nonetheless, growing confidence resulted in the 1870 'All-Russia Industrial Exhibition', showcasing the country's manufacturing prowess, and the first All-Russian Congress of Manufacturers, which exaggerated the harmonious relationship between workers and owners. Nikolai Putilov's closing speech pushed the image of the factory as one big happy family even though, as the Congress opened, 800 spinners at the Nevsky textile factory had walked out and mounted the first sustained strike in Russian history. Its leaders were tried and punished, but the intransigence of the authorities triggered a decade of intensifying industrial unrest.[35]

*The Catechism of the Revolutionary*, written in Geneva in 1869 by Mikhail Bakunin and Sergei Nechaev, stimulated protest and revolt. Head of a group known as The People's Vengeance, Nechaev was a young extremist who believed that anything which served the revolution – however ruthless or amoral – was acceptable. When a member of his group decided to withdraw, Nechaev had him eliminated. *The Catechism* proposed that revolution could only succeed if it was prepared to destroy 'the entire state apparatus and eliminate all state traditions, orders and social classes in Russia'.[36] Arrested and returned to Petersburg for trial, Nechaev was sentenced to solitary confinement in the Peter and Paul Fortress, where he died of scurvy in 1882. Although his attempt to set up a network of revolutionary cells controlled by an all-powerful centre ended in failure, he had encouraged revolutionaries to spurn the egalitarian communal model. They could learn how to gain control from the methods of their enemies.

Switzerland was a source of printed propaganda and a hotbed of revolutionary thinking. Russian women obliged to obtain an education in Zurich were exposed to the radical ideas of Russian exiles. This potentially dangerous breeding ground for dissent prompted the authorities to create the St Petersburg Medical Institute for Women in 1872. One of the forces behind this was the great and part-time Russian composer Alexander Borodin. In *Fathers and Sons*, Bazarov suggests that a 'decent chemist is twenty times more useful than any poet' – a sentiment obviously shared by Borodin, who never allowed music to displace his work as a Professor of Chemistry at the Medical Academy.[37]

Although female revolutionaries would prove themselves to be every bit as ruthless as their male counterparts, their presence in higher education had an effect on the gentle and defining movement of the early 1870s – the *narodniki* or populists. Rejecting the savagery of men like Ishutin and Nechaev, and taking their inspiration from the ideas of sacrifice and humility expressed by Bakunin's Zurich rival, Peter Lavrov, the populists set out to make contact with rural Russia. They wished to reach out beyond the centres of power and search for a future – as Herzen wanted – derived from the *mir*, or village commune. Even Karl Marx, whose political scheme depended on an urban proletariat seething to revolt, realised that in the agrarian Russian context, the *obshchina* provided a useful starting point for communist development.[38] The *narodniki* went out into the countryside to raise the political consciousness of rural communities and learn their ways, so that the procedures of the peasant commune could be applied to society at large. In the spring of 1874, about 4,000 students – one-fifth of them women – left the cities wearing rough peasant clothes.[39] They travelled in small groups, or sometimes as man and wife. Others went singly, claiming to be travelling

*The meeting of the village commune – one model for socialist revolution.*

craftsmen or itinerant field workers. While they shared broad ideals, there was no coherent approach in their various attempts to educate and instruct. What is more, they encountered a great deal of suspicion and indifference. Although the *narodniki* had come to do good, village priests informed against them and about 1,600 were arrested and brought to trial between 1875 and 1878.[40]

The desire to go out to the people was reflected in a new movement in Russian painting. Inspired by ideas Chernyshevsky had put forward in his Master's dissertation for St Petersburg University in 1855, these painters maintained that art should serve social progress by its choice of relevant subject matter – a concept which re-emerged during the ascendancy of Soviet Realism in the twentieth century.[41] Chernyshevsky had an obvious appeal for the students who had rejected their Academy examination in 1863 and organised themselves into a society to present travelling exhibitions. Innovative in terms of subject matter rather than technique, the Wanderers, or *peredvizhniki*, presented scenes of rural life which neither idealised nor sentimentalised. When, in *Fathers and Sons*, the two young protagonists drive through a landscape described as 'not in the least picturesque', they are in *peredvizhniki* country. The political dimension of the work was clear from canvases such as *Barge-Haulers on the Volga* by Ilya Repin or his two versions of *They Did Not Expect Him* – variously interpreted as a political exile returning home or Christ's second coming.[42]

On 6 December 1876, against the stately curving colonnades of Kazan Cathedral, a vibrant red banner with the slogan 'Land and Freedom' was courageously unfurled before a crowd of angry revolutionaries. Georgy Plekhanov – one of the country's first self-declared Marxists, and later founder of the Social Democrat Movement – gave a rousing speech, which sent the radicals yelling anti-tsarist chants as they marched down the Nevsky, right into a rough mob of feisty, frightened shopkeepers and workmen. Policemen stood aside to watch the demonstrators drubbed and then arrested them. Detentions were unaccountably long. It was March 1877 before fifty of the *narodniki* arrested in 1874 were given a hearing. Later in the year, another 193 agitators – thirty-eight of whom were women – were brought to trial. By that time, ninety-seven others had died, gone mad or committed suicide in prison. One of the defendants, Ippolit Myshkin – later executed for attacking a prison guard – made a stirring speech against the senators trying the case, and roused the crowd in the courtroom to fever pitch. Many defendants were acquitted, only to be rearrested on orders from the tsar. During their trials, the goodness of the students who had gone to the country made a profound impression on the Petersburg public, while the overreactive attitude of the authorities inflamed the challenge to the regime.[43]

The governor of St Petersburg, General Fyodor Trepov – the man who supervised the beating of radicals detained in prison – ordered the public flogging of a political prisoner who, when brought before him, had refused to remove his cap. Outraged by this unnecessary brutality, Vera Zasulich decided to settle the score. An introverted, unhappy orphan whose devotion to Christ had led her to the fanaticism of Nechaev, Zasulich gained admittance to Trepov's office and shot him. An unpractised assassin, she only wounded the governor and was brought to trial. Acquitted by the jury, Zasulich was carried out of the courtroom by a triumphant crowd who fired shots in exultation. Someone was killed and policemen were despatched to rearrest Zasulich, who was swiftly smuggled out of Russia to work in Switzerland with Plekhanov.[44]

After such an exasperating verdict in the Zasulich case, the government suspended trial by jury, and revolutionaries responded with new levels of violence. The head of the Third Section, General Nikolai Mezentsov, was stabbed to death at high noon on a Petersburg street by Sergei Stepniak-Kravchinsky, a *narodnik* escaped from prison. Mezentsov's successor, General Alexander Drenteln, narrowly escaped death when Leon Mirsky – a handsome young aristocrat and member of the Land and Freedom movement – galloped past his carriage and took several shots at him.[45] Provincial officials and governors were assassinated in Odessa, Kharkov and Kiev and, in April 1879, there was another lone-wolf assassination attempt on the tsar in Palace Square. The would-be assassin, Alexander Solovyev, pursued Alexander II with a revolver and fired five times, without – incredibly – hitting his target. The ex-student, obviously untrained in marksmanship, was apprehended and hanged the following month.[46]

Meanwhile, Land and Freedom members were developing the skills and acquiring the necessary equipment for successful subversion. One of nearly 600 women revolutionaries identified during the 1870s was Vera Figner, who had been among those who went off to Zurich to study medicine.[47] After returning to St Petersburg in 1876, she passed her examinations to become a midwife, and was about to move on to higher studies when she gave up everything and plunged into the revolutionary movement. She was outraged that the *narodniki* who 'turned to the people with peaceful propaganda' were met by a government 'with wholesale arrests, exile' and 'penal servitude'. At first Figner performed simple tasks, such as writing coded letters to comrades in prison and working as a typesetter for the group's printing press. She saw clearly that 'the entire life of the nation was at every point subjected to the arbitrary and unrestrained caprice of the administration'. Against such callous indifference, she suggested that terror could only be considered 'a weapon of protection, of self-defence'.[48]

Land and Freedom split in two in late 1879. One group, which was led by Plekhanov and included Zasulich, worked from Switzerland. The other, the deadly *Narodnaya Volya* – the aptly named People's Will – issued a death-threat against Alexander II. Scientists within the group started to experiment with dynamite. It set up safe houses across St Petersburg. Plans were laid, and another formidable woman – the daughter of a governor of St Petersburg, granddaughter of the governor of the Crimea and great-granddaughter of Kyril Razumovsky, the precocious President of the Academy of Sciences under Elizabeth – played a major role in leading operations. Sofia Perovskaya directed a cell detailed to blow up the tsar's trains as they trundled through a Moscow suburb in November 1879. One bomb failed to detonate and the first train passed. The revolutionaries rapidly resolved the problem and wrecked the second train. Unfortunately for Perovskaya and her colleagues, the tsar was in the first.[49] Although the attempt sent shockwaves across the globe, *Narodnaya Volya* felt it necessary to publish a face-saving statement: Alexander deserved to die in payment for all the 'blood he has shed' and 'the pain he has caused'. The seemingly blessed tsar surrounded himself with police and Cossacks when he walked out from the Winter Palace. He drove about his capital in a closed carriage with the blinds drawn down. Increasingly on edge, he was at war with an invisible and ubiquitous adversary. As the Grand Duke Konstantin noted, we 'not only do not see them or know them, but have not the faintest idea of their number'.[50]

Meanwhile, a personable young carpenter named Stephan Khalturin obtained a position in the maintenance team at the Winter Palace and started to smuggle dangerous quantities of nitroglycerine past the lax security at the service entrance. Shortly afterwards, Vera Figner's sister, Evgenia, was arrested with another revolutionary. During a search of their premises, gendarmes found not only dynamite and detonating agents, but also a screwed-up piece of paper on which a floor plan had been sketched and marked with an X. The plan was identified as the Winter Palace, and the X was placed on an area occupied by the Yellow Dining Room. Beneath the dining room were the quarters of the palace guards; beneath them, the rooms where the maintenance team was lodged. A security search of these floors revealed nothing, and Khalturin continued to accumulate explosives.

*Narodnaya Volya* was ready for its next attempt against the tsar. On 5 February 1880, Alexander was hosting a dinner for the empress's brother-in-law, Prince Alexander of Battenberg. Khalturin was given the go-ahead at 6 p.m. He connected a Rumford fuse to the fulminate detonator, lit it and left the palace. At 6.22, just as the imperial party was about to enter the dining room, a blast sent the nauseating smell of nitroglycerine spiralling through the palace. The floor of the dining room sagged. Cracks, like lightning bolts, zigzagged across the walls. The floor held, but windows were blown out and a bitter wind agitated the thick dust of shattered bric-a-brac. None of the imperial party had been hurt, but the floor below, where the guards of the Finland Regiment were quartered, had been blasted to kingdom come. Ten guards were dead and more than fifty lay wounded. Two days later, *Narodnaya Volya* claimed responsibility and expressed their deepest regret for the death of the soldiers.[51]

The attack had been even more impressive than the assault on the train. To strike at the emperor in the very heart of imperial power suggested that the group would stop at nothing and that they were, indeed, everywhere. As one government minister observed, 'the ground is shaking, the house threatens to crash down'. The celebrations in 1880 for the twenty-fifth anniversary of Alexander's accession were muted, with festivities largely centred on the palace.[52] Frightened people left the capital, and there were many empty boxes at the inevitable performance of Glinka's beguiling paean to loyalty, *A Life for the Tsar*. Borodin's *In the Steppes of Central Asia* – a celebration of eastward expansion under Alexander II – was not even performed. Mikhail Loris-Melikov, who had experience of fighting terrorists in the south, was appointed head of the Supreme Administrative Commission. He was welcomed to the position by the bullet of yet another terrorist, who failed to hit his target and was hanged a few days later, before a huge crowd in Semyonovsky Square. Among the spectators was Fyodor Dostoevsky, who watched the execution and commented on the strange sympathy of people for the perpetrators of terrorist crimes.[53] As for Loris-Melikov, he recommended a shake-up of law enforcement and replaced the Third Section with the Department of State Police. While his reforms could not beat the terrorists, some of his methods would be used by those whom they eventually brought to power.

Despite the perpetual threat of terrorism, St Petersburg became a destination for Americans visiting Europe during the post-civil-war tourist boom.[54] European musicians and composers also came. Berlioz returned during the 1867–8 season to conduct six concerts. The Russian composer Rimsky-Korsakov recalled that, despite bad health and signs of age, Berlioz was alert in rehearsal but, on this occasion, appeared indifferent to the wider musical life of the capital. Richard Wagner visited in 1863 and his opera, *Lohengrin*, was performed at the beginning of the 1868 season.[55] Tchaikovsky's 1st Symphony was finished the same year. The chemist Borodin had completed his 1st Symphony a year earlier and was worrying away at a second – work delayed by his generosity to students and by the hospitality he offered to sick friends and poor relations. There was also a great clutter of cats roaming about his apartment, so Borodin's piano was often inaccessible. One tabby – known as 'the fisherman' – was adept at trapping small fish during the freeze by dunking its paw through tiny holes in the ice.[56] Academic commitments and kindness postponed the successful completion of the symphony by a decade, and Borodin drew on melodic material from *Prince Igor*, the opera that he doubted he would ever have time to finish.[57] As Russian music came of age, it looked back to reclaim Russia's legendary past. The composer of *Prince Igor* was 'a pre-muscovite warrior prince'. Sweet-voiced, drunken Modest Mussorgsky wrote *Boris Godunov*, set at the beginning of the seventeenth century, during the Time of Troubles. Rimsky-Korsakov was 'a magician' from a medieval Russian epic. Tchaikovsky alone, was 'a Russian gentleman from the mental and spiritual world' inhabited by Turgenev.[58]

After the death, in 1873, of music's patroness, the Grand Duchess Vera Pavlovna, the Conservatoire and the Russian Musical Society were taken under the wing of the imperial treasury and placed on a more professional footing.[59] Rimsky-Korsakov began to play a vital part in the musical life of the capital. He taught, advised, orchestrated, composed and rescued unfinished scores from the lodgings of dead composers. He even conducted in eternally dilapidated Kronstadt, where concerts were performed by the United Bands of the Navy Department to an audience that never realised – much to Rimsky-Korsakov's consternation – that music 'has such a thing as a composer! . . . "He played that fine" – that is as far as they got in Kronstadt!'[60]

Mily Balakirev, who had once contemplated making an opera out of Chernyshevsky's *What Is to Be Done?*, became a staunchly tsarist Slavophil and something of a religious recluse. He

influenced Tchaikovsky's 2nd Symphony, 'The Little Russian' –
composed in 1872 and revised at the end of the decade – as well
as the peasant song in Tchaikovsky's masterly 1879 opera of
Pushkin's *Eugene Onegin*. The poet's tales had also inspired
Glinka and, with Mussorgsky's 1874 *Boris Godunov*, Pushkin's
influence continued. Revelling in the costumes and rituals of old
Russia, the opera delighted Slavophils and carried a warning for
more progressive members of the audience: Boris is a usurper,
and his end is defeat and death.

Looking backwards provided a comforting aesthetic for a society facing an uncertain future. This was reflected in the historical
eclecticism of Petersburg fashion during the second half of the
nineteenth century. Designers plundered past epochs, using historical fabrics, cuts, patterns, textures and embellishments. The
interiors of the capital's palaces decorated during this period were
subject to a similar historical mix, as the aristocracy sought to take
refuge in the safety of a fantasy past. A Renaissance revival began
to dominate exteriors from the 1860s, visible in palaces such as
Maximilian Messmacher's Admiralty Embankment structure
built for the Grand Duke Mikhail, or his State Council Archive,
which went up facing the New Hermitage. There was, nevertheless, modern utilitarian construction. A second permanent bridge
across the Neva was built between 1875 and 1879, linking the
increasingly industrialised Vyborg Side with Liteiny Prospekt.
But the overwhelming nostalgia in palace building and interior
decoration revealed that the aristocracy had lost touch with the
quickening pulse of the age.

Misjudging the zeitgeist was not the Romanovs' only mistake.
In 1867, Alexander rashly sold Alaska to America for just over
$7 million.[61] Despite the nexus of family ties, the Romanovs were
also staring into the barrel of German militarism. The defeat of
the French at Sedan in September 1870 had unified Germany.
The political fallout in France was the Paris Commune's revolt
against the monarchist National Assembly. Disdaining the signs

of the times, Russia's rulers exhibited a self-absorbed decadence which was eroding respect. They kept the population in thrall and squandered money on the luxuries of a lavish court. The story broke of how Alexander's nephew, the Grand Duke Nicholas Konstantinovich, was caught red-handed stealing the jewels from his mother's icon frame in order to pay his gambling debts. After details began to circulate of his affair with a shameless American adventuress, Henrietta Blackford – who all too gladly dished the dirt, in memoirs published in Belgium in 1875 – there was outrage. When the grand duke brushed off his guilt, claiming that such behaviour was in his genes, the attitude of the aristocracy appeared to have sunk to a cynical low. As for the tsar himself, his foxy eyes kept him in trouble. His unrelenting susceptibility to impressionable women, his habit of strolling with young ladies when he took the air in the Summer Garden and his all-too-visible infidelities were damaging to the image of the 'father' of the Russian people, a monarch anointed by God.[62]

An 1870 revolutionary manifesto addressing women suggested that only in work would they find freedom and cited 'the debaucher, Alexander II, himself' as the worst offender in the conspiracy to keep women down.[63] Matters came to a head in 1880 when the tsar – after an indecently short forty-day mourning period for his deceased empress, Maria Alexandrovna – married his long-term mistress, the unpopular Ekaterina Dolgoruka. She had been with Alexander in the Summer Garden on that afternoon in 1866 when the unstable Karakozov had taken a potshot at autocracy. They were in Paris when another assassination attempt on Alexander II miscarried and, in St Petersburg, the tsar rented a convenient townhouse on the English Quay for Ekaterina. On top of this trail of flagrant self-indulgence, their marriage violated the taboo – in place since the time of Peter the Great – on tsars taking Russian wives and marrying outside the exclusive club of reigning European dynasties. It also rekindled a 200-year-old peasant superstition that predicted death to any

Romanov who dared to marry a Dolgoruky: a superstition given credence by the fact that Peter II died on the very day he was to have married one.[64] But Alexander and Ekaterina were wedded by an inexhaustible lust. She vividly documented their passionate romps, noting that they climaxed only hours before the tsar was blown to pieces.[65]


While a sophisticated plot to kill Alexander II was coming to fruition in January 1881, Fyodor Dostoevsky died. Radical in his youth, the novelist had come to detest socialism and political extremism. In his late novel, *A Raw Youth*, he explored the tensions between the 1840 generation and the nihilists. He also revisited one of his early impressions of St Petersburg. He imagined the capital in the twilight hour, from 'the refuges of the poor' to 'the gilded palaces for the comfort of the powerful of this world', to be a 'fantastic vision of fairyland, like a dream which in its turn would vanish and pass away'.[66] Through the newly industrialised vapours of the tsarist capital, that disintegration was on the horizon. Decades of unrepentant arrogance provoked the ultimate act of anti-tsarist terrorism. Had there ever been so many failed attempts to assassinate a head of state? Five times assassins had failed. It would take two goes to make the sixth attempt succeed.

Vera Figner looked back on late 1880 and early 1881 as a 'brilliant period' when the Military Organisation of *Narodnaya Volya* was at its height. As unrest spread among an increasingly urbanised proletariat, some members of the military were becoming concerned about the state of their country and the immodesty and barbarism of its rulers. Naval officers and midshipmen began to spread revolutionary propaganda among the ranks at Kronstadt. Soldiers in an artillery division stationed in the capital were responding to the complaints of the revolutionaries. On the civilian front, funds were collected through robbery and donation – revolt was expensive. An estimate for three of the attempts on the life of the tsar put the cost at 30,000–40,000 roubles.[67] Having failed so often, the assassins realised the necessity of financing a watertight plan with a backup strategy.

In January 1881, a couple opened a cheese shop in the front room of premises on Sadovaya Street.[68] In the back room, excavations began to undermine the road along which the emperor's carriage drove on his Sunday outing to review the troops at the Mikhailovsky Manège. The police budget in St Petersburg during these dangerous times was a fraction of what it was in contemporary Paris,[69] and when the underfunded force – acting on a tip-off – conducted a cursory inspection of the premises, the odour of the cheese on sale blotted out the stench rising from a wooden sewer that had accidentally been pierced by the tunnellers. The police shot out a question about the damp clay around the cheese barrels in the shop – barrels filled with excavated earth – and were satisfied to be told that sour cream had been spilt. They left it at that.

The plan was to bomb Alexander as he passed above the tunnel that extended from the shop. Should that miscarry, four bomb-throwers – Nikolai Rysakov, Ignaty Grinevitsky, Timofei Mikhailov and Ivan Emelyanov – were to be actioned. If they failed, Andrei Zhelyabov – armed with a dagger – was to stab the tsar. The bomb-throwers would carry six-pound devices comprising nitroglycerine and proxilin packed in empty paraffin cans. Defying detection, they had tested two such bombs in a wood outside the capital, but only one had detonated. The conspirator who acted the part of Vera Figner's husband had three fingers blown off conducting a test.[70]

On 28 February, the bomb-making went on throughout the night. Figner helped, while Sofia Perovskaya – the director of the operation – slept. Mikhailov lost his nerve and went home, leaving three bombers. Grinevitsky prepared a statement: 'It is my lot to die young . . . but I believe that with my death I shall do all it is my duty to do.'

The tsar took one of two possible routes to review the troops. On 1 March 1881 – driving in a bullet-proof carriage presented by Napoleon III – he took the route that did not go via Sadovaya Street. When he returned from the inspection, taking the same route, Sofia Perovskaya signalled as much to the bomb-throwers, who hurried to the Catherine Canal. Just after 2.15 p.m., the tsar's carriage turned right out of Inzhenernaya Street onto the quay. As the tsar approached Konyushenny Bridge, Rysakov hurled a bomb, which rolled underneath the horses' legs and exploded beneath the carriage. It killed a Cossack who was riding in the tsar's guard; it also killed a passer-by. As Rysakov was taken, the tsar emerged from his battered carriage. Security pressed to speed him away, but Alexander wished to confront his would-be assassin. Asked by a member of his staff if he was all right, the tsar answered, 'Thank God.' At this, Grinevitsky yelled out, 'It's too early to thank God,' and threw a second bomb, which mortally wounded the terrorist and smashed the legs of the emperor. Alexander was sledged to his study in the palace, where his doctor saw immediately that the terrorists had – at last – achieved their goal. At a little after 3.30, the flag above the palace was lowered. Armed Preobrazhensky Guards patrolled the corridors. Cossacks encircled the exterior.[71]

*Tsar Alexander II is assassinated, illustration from* The Illustrated London News, *1881.*

With the bad timing of an awards ceremony on a day of national tragedy, Vasily Surikov's *Morning of the Execution of the Streltsy* went on exhibition in St Petersburg on Sunday 1 March.[72] A painting that depicted the savage treatment of Russian subjects at the hands of a Romanov was – depending on your politics – a timely or an unfortunate subject to present at the moment the tsar's blood and body parts stained the white velvet snow of the imperial capital. Peter the Great had built his city on the bones of dead *muzhiks*. Now the oppressed were constructing the road to revolution on the shattered bones of a tsar.

Vera Figner rushed home, weeping for joy, through streets abuzz with gossip. The bomb made 'all Russia tremble' and Figner's prominent role in the success of the endeavour, along with that of her comrade Sofia Perovskaya, set an example to the numerous women who joined the revolution in the succeeding decades.[73] Only days after the assassination, Perovskaya was arrested in the street. The backlash – 'the white terror', as Figner called it – had begun. After being taken into custody, Rysakov had been turned and he squealed. Not that it did him much good. Within a month, under a sunlit spring sky, he was among the six terrorists carted into Semyonovsky Square to be hanged. As priests prepared them for the next world, Perovskaya snubbed the turncoat, but only a short while later they were dumped together in a common grave.[74]

Figner wanted to use the cheese shop and its tunnel for an attempt on Alexander III, but the seven other members of the Executive Council who remained at large disagreed. Despite the palpable support for *Narodnaya Volya* in the capital, it was considered prudent to relocate. Two years later, Figner was arrested in Kharkov and incarcerated for twenty years in the tomb-like void of the fortress at Shlüsselburg. She later observed that a period of reaction had set in and that *Narodnaya Volya* had been ahead of its time, anticipating the political development of the people by a quarter of a century. However, the group gave an impressive and impassioned curtain call. Audaciously, it petitioned Alexander III, explaining the assassination of his father as the upshot of repression. It promised that the revolutionary 'movement will continue to grow . . . A terrible explosion, a bloody hurly-burly, a revolutionary earthquake throughout Russia will complete the destruction of the old order of things.'[75] As if to underline the purity of its motives, when US President Garfield was assassinated at the end of 1881, the Executive Committee of *Narodnaya Volya* declared itself to be 'against such acts of violence'. Violence could be 'justified only when it is directed against violence'.[76]

In May 1881, Alexander III proclaimed his 'faith in the power and truth of absolutism' and enlisted the help of Konstantin Pobedonostsev, procurator of the Holy Synod, to buttress autocracy with orthodoxy. Pobedonostsev – tutor to Alexander's son, the future and final tsar, Nicholas II – hated progress and any form of parliamentary government.[77] His reactionary vision was to be of little benefit to the challenged dynasty.

Surly and shy, Alexander III enjoyed fishing, drinking and hunting big game. After the hunt, all the dead animals were laid out by torchlight outside the palace – those bagged by the emperor being placed in the front row. As the imperial family arrived for the hunt dinner, music was played, with different melodies evoking the various species that had been shot.[78]

The empress – Princess Sophie Frederikke Dagmar, daughter of Christian IX of Denmark, who took the name of Maria Fyodorovna when she married – adored festivities and, at balls, would dance for hours. New Year 1886 saw the first ceremonial ball with the palace lit by electricity. The rooms were filled with exotic plants transported from the Crimea and adorned with thousands of flowers cut from the greenhouses at Tsarskoe Selo. For the New Year ball in 1891, there were 3,700 hyacinths,

1,700 sprays of lily-of-the-valley, 1,600 red and white tulips, 180 yellow tulips, 150 cyclamens and sixteen orchids gracing the public rooms. But apart from such splendid occasions,[79] Alexander preferred to live in the relative simplicity of the Anichkov Palace, away from dining rooms marked with Xs. He had a passion for Fabergé. If Easter eggs were symbolic of Christ's resurrection, then intricate and ostentatious Fabergé eggs – fabricated to the tsar's specifications – suggested the revivification of the imperial family. But that was not about to happen.[80] If Alexander's reign corresponded to a period of peace abroad, it was a time of mounting trouble at home. A scapegoat was sought, and Alexander – a pernicious anti-Semite – blamed the Jews.

Anti-Semitism was a fact of Russian life, part of a wider xenophobia that touched even intelligent and creative people. Dostoevsky held the Jews – with their 'perpetual look of peevish dejection'[81] – responsible for the commercialisation and industrialisation of his country. Rimsky-Korsakov labelled Balakirev 'an implacable Jew-hater',[82] an accusation that could also be levelled against Glinka and Mussorgsky. Nicholas I had not been anti-Semitic, but – driven by his zeal for conformity – wanted Jews to be forced to integrate into Russian life. During the reign of Alexander II, after a pogrom against the Jews in Odessa in 1871, the *St Petersburg Vedomosti* blamed 'Jewish exploitation' for the violence. The anti-Semitic newspaper campaign gathered intensity as the 1870s progressed, and fuelled the violence that was unleashed against peaceful, inward-looking communities.[83] Most dangerously, between the 1860s and the assassination of Alexander II, the number of Jewish revolutionaries had increased. The Jews who crucified Christ had now killed God's anointed tsar. On the tenth anniversary of the 1871 pogrom, violence against the Jews flared in Odessa and Warsaw. A rumour circulated that Alexander himself had provoked the attacks.[84] Nicholai Ignataev, the Minister of the Interior, complained about the Polish Jews who controlled the banks, the judiciary and the press in the capital. The *Vedomosti* reported that St Petersburg was full of foreigners desperate for the break-up of Russia – the subtext, an attack on Jews. When Alexander appointed his younger brother, Sergei, as Governor General of Moscow, the grand duke shut the Great Synagogue and raided Jewish homes, raping, pillaging and burning. He cleared the city of Jews – allowing Jewish women to remain only as registered prostitutes. Between the accession of Alexander III and the outbreak of the First World War, nearly two million Jews emigrated.[85]

When Mikhail Pyliaev, in his impressions of St Petersburg, described the crowd strolling around the picturesque point of Elagin Island in 1889, he unashamedly and insistently revealed his anti-Semitism, his remarks interspersed with quips about high-class and low-class prostitutes: 'There are cavaliers, but also many Jews; there are diplomats, but also many Jews; there are grande-dames, but also demi-dames, and even quarter-dames.'[86] The sentence occurs in a passage in which Pyliaev contrasts the people he sees with a romantic vision of earlier visitors. By 1890 there was a noticeable deterioration of behaviour in city parks. Previously places of calm, they were now disturbed by the raucous behaviour of workmen. As for female factory workers out and about in the city, they were frequently mistaken for prostitutes by the wealthy. Child prostitution was an ongoing problem. In 1889, St Petersburg police arrested twenty-two young girls, aged between eleven and fifteen, for soliciting. Among adult prostitutes, clinic attendance was low, and infected workers often tried to fool the medical examiners by disguising vaginal sores with make-up or silver nitrate. Despite the attempt to keep students away from brothels, the poet Alexander Blok – who was at school in the capital during the 1890s – was infected by venereal disease before he was seventeen.[87]

*

Alexander III's stubborn assertion of old Russian values was responsible for St Petersburg's most egregious cathedral. The Church of the Saviour on the Spilt Blood was deliberately provocative. Its Muscovite style challenged the architecture of Peter's city, which was predominantly European and – by extension – now associated with dangerous, anti-Russian ideas. Alexander II's commission suggested that from now on, tsars would be Russian, tsars would be orthodox – in belief, if not in lifestyle. Between 1881 and 1914 more than twenty churches in the nationalistic style were consecrated in the capital – most of them demolished or converted to other uses during the 1930s. Ironically, the chief architect of the Church of the Saviour on the Spilt Blood was Alfred Parland, an Anglican born in St Petersburg to English parents. He worked in collaboration with the archimandrite Ignaty, abbot of a suburban monastery and a student of old Russian architecture. The opulent and extravagant cathedral – not completed until 1907 – boasted more than 7,000 square metres of mosaic on exterior and interior surfaces, after designs by Viktor Vasnetsov, Mikhail Vrubel and other important artists of the day. There was also a profusion of ceramic tiles on walls and roofs, and two of the cupolas were of gilded copper.[88]

The siting of the church necessitated the installation of the first concrete foundation in St Petersburg and included such innovations as steam heating and electrical lighting.[89] While the tsar looked backwards stylistically, in an attempt to secure autocracy, the country was undergoing technological change. By 1882 there was a telephone system in Moscow, and five years later there were 7,000 subscribers nationally – by 1911, there were more than 56,000 in Petersburg alone.[90] The son of a railway official, Sergei Witte, was appointed Minister of Finance in 1892 and stimulated industrial production with his grand enterprise, the Trans-Siberian Railway. Under Witte, 'state capitalism' was developed to finance projects which, in the West, would have been funded by an investing middle class. Witte also secured much-needed foreign capital. After the formalisation of the military-political Franco–Russian Alliance of 1893, French francs fuelled Russian industrial muscle.[91] Witte and his colleagues may have been forging railways and expanding heavy industry for the power and prestige of the country, but they were also swelling the ranks of a brutalised proletariat – badly paid, overworked and increasingly eager for change.

Long before the completion of Church of the Saviour on the Spilt Blood, there was an attempt on the life of Alexander III. Using bombs containing pellets filled with strychnine, *Narodnaya Volya* intended to attack the tsar's carriage on the Nevsky Prospekt in early 1887. Among the conspirators was a zoology student at St Petersburg University, Alexander Ilyich Ulyanov. Six subversives, including Ulyanov, were caught before they succeeded and were brought to trial and hanged at Schlüsselberg in May 1887. The execution traumatised Ulyanov's younger brother, Vladimir.[92] He read and reread his brother's copy of Chernyshevsky, and when Vladimir published a manifesto in 1902 calling for Marxists to press on to revolution, he borrowed Chernyshevsky's title and published *What Is to Be Done?* by V. I. Lenin. Galvanised by his brother's revolutionary activity and subsequent death, Lenin's text proposed that the struggle against the tsar should merge with the fight against capitalism. After arriving in St Petersburg in 1893, Lenin became a leading figure in the Marxist Russian Social Democratic Labour Party. Arrested for sedition in 1897, he survived a three-year exile to Siberia that initiated two peripatetic decades during which he prepared for the Bolshevik Revolution.

The brutality of the tsarist reaction continued. Against the wishes of his minister, Alexander III insisted that the mortal penalty 100 lashes be inflicted on a weakened female prisoner who had merely insulted a gendarme. In his reaction against the continuing unrest, the tsar was aided by the surveillance of the *Okhrannye Otdeleniia*, or Okhrana – the political secret police.

In a tactic that was to be widely used, its chief turned a prominent member of *Narodnaya Volya*, Sergei Degaev. Subsequent betrayals were so numerous that, when suspicion fell on him, his party demanded proof of Degaev's fidelity. This he provided by meeting the chief of the Okhrana, Grigory Sudeikin, and killing him.[93] Increasingly complex undercover operations involving double and triple agents would complicate the road to revolution.

For a tsar desperate to assert Russian values, it was not surprising that Alexander III was keen to establish a museum in which to display his country's art. The elegant Mikhailovsky Palace, designed by Carlo Rossi, was chosen as its premises. The young Alexander Benois, who was to play such an important role in the St Petersburg art scene, was selected to catalogue Russian works collected by Princess Tenisheva, the wife of the entrepreneur who enjoyed a monopoly on passenger traffic on Russia's vast river network. Opened after the tsar's death by his son, Nicholas II, the museum was known as the Alexander III Museum until the revolution, when it acquired its present name, the Russian Museum. The very fact that such a project was contemplated is a testimony to how much had been achieved by Russian painters during the nineteenth century. But while championing home-grown art, Alexander did not neglect the Hermitage. He bought the Basilewski Collection of medieval and Renaissance art from a Russian living in Paris. He obtained a vibrant *Annunciation* by Cima da Conegliano and the Golitsyn Museum from Moscow, where it had been assembled during the previous century.

The tsar's policy of promoting Russian arts meant that St Petersburg's once-popular Italian opera was closed, although recitals by singers of international calibre continued.[94] The Italian-French soprano and astute businesswoman Adelina Patti came to perform. Pauline Viardot – a singer who had dazzled Turgenev – returned. The Australian soprano, Dame

Nellie Melba, appeared in Gounod's *Roméo et Juliette* at the Mariinsky in the presence of Alexander III in February 1891. In tow, as she toured across Europe, was her lover, Prince Philippe, Duc d'Orléans, the Orléanist claimant to the French throne. During the 1888–9 season, an entire Ring cycle was performed several times, and Rimsky-Korsakov noted how Wagnerian tricks became part of his musical vocabulary, as well as those of the young Alexander Glazunov. Russian music was thriving at the time, despite some significant deaths. Mussorgsky, whose conceit had ballooned after the success of *Boris Godunov*, had gone into a slow alcoholic decay. He was immortalised in his habitually drink-fuddled state a few days before his death in March 1881 in a portrait by Ilya Repin. His last opera, *Khovanshchina*, which Rimsky-Korsakov continued to work on after Mussorgsky's death, was presented when Savva Mamontov's Private Opera Company played St Petersburg to great acclaim in 1886. Months later, on 15 February 1887, Borodin – enjoying a lively evening with invited guests – dropped dead. At once, all the chemist's incomplete scores were taken to Rimsky-Korsakov, who orchestrated portions of the unfinished opera *Prince Igor*, before handing it over to Glazunov, who composed the missing sections. In a rich fortnight for Russian opera, *Prince Igor* was presented at the Mariinsky Theatre on 4 November 1890, just two weeks before the premiere of Tchaikovsky's first opera in ten years, *The Queen of Spades*. Happily for Rimsky-Korsakov – who complained that the directorate of the Mariinsky had butchered the score and under-rehearsed *Prince Igor* – his orchestration of the opera stimulated his own ideas for an orchestral composition inspired by the Scheherazade stories.[95] Orientalism in Russian music – which presented the 'irrational' and erotic East as a powerful temptation to the 'Western' Russian – appeared to argue against the reassertion of pre-Petrine values. At the same time, however, it celebrated the consolidation of the diverse Russian Empire.[96]

Not only was there a ten-year gap between Tchaikovsky's *Eugene Onegin* and *The Queen of Spades*, but there had also been a long interval between the shaky and unsuccessful premiere of *Swan Lake* in provincial Moscow in 1877 and the first performance, during the 1889–90 St Petersburg season, of *The Sleeping Beauty*. This ballet, which, as a celebration of the court of Versailles under Louis XIV, could be seen as the glorification of absolute monarchy, was of considerable significance for at least two young people. Léon Bakst – who would later become one of the great theatre designers of the twentieth century – obtained a ticket for the dress rehearsal. Afterwards the young man had the good fortune to meet the urbane and generous Tchaikovsky and claimed that his 'calling was determined' that night.[97] A little while later, a weak and pale eight-year-old was taken to a performance by her poverty-stricken mother, who scrimped to purchase the tickets. Later, Anna Pavlova remembered that she had been spellbound. When her mother asked if she would like to dance with the performers on the stage, young Anna – revealing the single-minded determination necessary for success – replied, 'I would rather dance by myself, like the lovely Sleeping Beauty. One day I will and in this very theatre.' Two years later, the ten-year-old Pavlova passed the medical examination and was admitted to the Imperial Ballet School. By 1895 she was dancing in school performances with Mikhail Fokine, who would later – amidst his innovative and stellar career in dance – choreograph the lucrative *Dying Swan* for Pavlova's international tours.[98]

The imperial ballet was still considered a hunting ground for rich young aristocrats. The brother of Alexander II's second wife, Vladimir Dolgorukov, gave a son to the ballerina Alexandrova. Pregnancy cut into the short life of dancers. Some, like Vera Legat, were fortunate enough to marry their aristocratic admirer, but others were merely casual playthings for the idle rich. During the 1880s the Italian dancer, Virginia Zucchi, introduced the short tutu to St Petersburg, making performances even more enticing for the young bucks.[99] According to Nijinsky's wife, Romola, there was an old general who 'knew the shapes of the legs of each ballerina far better than his strategy or ballistics'.[100]

During the graduation performance at the Imperial Ballet School in March 1890, Alexander III noticed a pretty and gifted young Polish girl called Matilda Kchessinskaya. When she curtsied before the tsar, he instructed her to become 'the glory and adornment of our ballet' and invited her to sit next to his son, Nicholas, at supper. After Carlotta Brianza – the first Princess Aurora in *Sleeping Beauty* – retired, Kchessinskaya took over the part and became the queen of Russian ballet. She also became the mistress of the *tsarevich*, who – in 1892 – as his father had done before him, rented a house on the English Quay for his lover. When Tchaikovsky's last opera, *Iolanta*, premiered before the court in December of that same year and a baritone began to sing the aria 'Who Can Compare with My Matilda?', Sergei Diaghilev – who was in the audience – recorded that people were beside themselves, chuckling over the affair between Nicholas and Matilda Kchessinskaya.[101]

On the same bill that night was Tchaikovsky's ballet *The Nutcracker*. Despite its origins in the tales of the Prussian polymath, E. T. A. Hoffmann, the opening of the ballet presents a St Petersburg Christmas celebration. As well as taking its young heroine, Clara, from childhood into puberty, the ballet manifests the dream of someone from the cold north being transported to the exotic south – to the palace of the Sugar Plum Fairy, where Arabian and Spanish dances are performed. *The Nutcracker* heightens the magic of both journeys by moving from mime and social dancing at the beginning of Act I to almost uninterrupted ballet and character dancing in Act II.

St Petersburg nobility, with their greenhouses and double glazing, were desperate to outwit the cold. Christmas celebrations were a declaration of success. The tradition of the Christmas tree had been introduced from Prussia in the early nineteenth

*St Petersburg Christmas. The tradition of the tree had been introduced from Prussia.*

century. Baroness Maria Fredericks described the Christmas Eve ritual in the Winter Palace under Nicholas I, during which the 'sovereign and the imperial children each had their own separate table and tree adorned with all kinds of gifts'.[102] The ballerina Tamara Karsavina – a child in the early 1890s – remembers her delight in the Petersburg Christmas markets, which sprung up around churches and along the prospekts with their 'forests of fir trees'. Her father – a dancer in the imperial ballet – loved choosing a tree with his two children and taking it home to the fifth-floor apartment they rented overlooking a curve in the Fontanka, then decorating it with gilded walnuts, Crimean apples and apricots.[103]

With its celebration of Christmas, its militarism and its mice, its love of magic and its stately polonaise, *The Nutcracker* is a St Petersburg ballet. Audiences travelled to the Mariinsky in carriages through a city laced with snow. They swept past street lanterns and warmly glowing windows. They sped along the Nevsky, the Moika and the Fontanka, the embankment of the Neva – streets that played host to glittering aristocratic, official and military elites. A view down the length of any broad avenue in this winter season, with snow icing the cornices, entablatures and pediments of the harmonious buildings as if they were giant cakes, presented scenes redolent of the enchanted fairy-tale world of Tchaikovsky's ballet.

*The Nutcracker* was choreographed by two of the three great ballet masters working in the capital towards the end of the nineteenth century, Marius Petipa and Lev Ivanov. The third was the Italian Enrico Cecchetti who brought strength and gutsiness to the imperial ballet, upsetting the dominance of the more delicate Franco–Danish tradition. When the Russian Nikolai Legat replaced Petipa as ballet master in 1903 he brought both traditions together, thus blending technical expertise with strength and thereby determining the character of twentieth-century Russian ballet. Not that the work of these great choreographers and teachers was much esteemed by the men who wrote the music for the ballets. Rimsky-Korsakov complained that people like

*The 1892 Mariinsky production of* The Nutcracker.

Ivanov and Cecchetti failed to understand any music unless it was 'of the routine ballet type'. The choreography of the ballet masters was, he complained, 'invariably ill suited' to the score.[104]

Only nine days after he conducted the first performance of his 6th Symphony on 16 October 1893, Tchaikovsky died, and the *Vedomosti* reported that the capital was humming with rumour. The composer's nephew, Vladimir Davidov – one source of the whisperings – recalled going to the Leiner restaurant where, if he was slipped a little something, the owner would admit underage students through the back door. Tchaikovsky loved St Petersburg restaurants, often sitting in a circle with fellow composers till three in the morning, drinking prodigiously without manifesting the slightest sign of intoxication. On the occasion of the post-premiere party, which included Davidov, Tchaikovsky had called for water. Being informed there was no bottled water, he had demanded a glass from the tap. With cholera in the city, no one drank tap water, but Tchaikovsky insisted. Days later, the composer was dead. Glazunov asserted it was suicide. Riccardo Drigo, composer and conductor of the imperial ballet, spoke of homosexuality and suicide. When the Norwegian composer Edvard Grieg had met Tchaikovsky some years earlier, he had found the Russian 'melancholic almost to the point of madness'. If indeed it was suicide, was the death prompted by his attraction for the young Davidov or the result of a more general despair? According to a Soviet musicologist, public exposure of Tchaikovsky's homosexuality was imminent and would have stained the reputation of his alma mater. The School of Jurisprudence was vulnerable to scandal, and all the available alumni from Tchaikovsky's student days were supposed to have told him to kill himself in order to preserve the honour of their school. It was a tall story, which paid no heed to the relatively relaxed attitude towards homosexuality that prevailed, nor to the newspaper reports and doctor's bulletins monitoring the progress of the composer's sickness. The scandal – if any – was that cholera was thought to be a disease of the poor.[105] Two years after Tchaikovsky's death from the infection, the first complete and successful performance of *Swan Lake*, with a new story-line written by the composer's brother, Modest, was given in St Petersburg. The essence of the tale – death by love and water.

Alexander III died in 1894. Between 1881 and his death, St Petersburg had become the scene of immense creativity. Industrially, the capital was steaming ahead with an energy worthy of Peter the Great. But St Petersburg was also galloping towards tragedy, and the apogee of its artistic triumph would be short. Meanwhile, some ardent revolutionaries were losing sight of the communal *mir* and were following the dictatorial example of their tsarist adversaries. They were starting to place a political system – an abstraction – above the needs or feelings of the people.

# 10

# DANCING ON THE EDGE

## *1894–1905*

The 1905 Revolution touched everybody. On 'Bloody Sunday' in early January, the promising young dancer Vaslav Nijinsky was coshed by a Cossack rampaging to disperse a crowd. Months later, a law student named Igor Stravinsky was mistakenly arrested with a group of protesters while walking through Kazansky Place.[1] Members of the imperial ballet came out on strike in October – among the leaders, three of the greatest dancers of the age: Tamara Karsavina, Mikhail Fokine and Anna Pavlova. Meanwhile a 'semi-naked young girl . . . in a semi-transparent Greek tunic, giving full freedom to her movements'[2] had astounded St Petersburg. Sergei Diaghilev – a portly man from Perm, with a stylish shock of white hair and a taste for young men – immediately understood that a presentation by the American dancer Isadora Duncan could change the course of dance in Russia. The symbolist poet and novelist Andrei Biely viewed one of Duncan's 'shocking' performances in the company of the woman who had nearly driven him to suicide – the wife of his dear friend, the poet Alexander Blok. Biely saw, in the freedom of Duncan's gestures, 'the symbol of the new, young revolutionary Russia'.[3]

The decade leading up to the year when Russia danced on the edge was dominated by Nicholas II, an intransigent tsar and the last of the species. Stravinsky remembered him as a 'colourless'[4] figure flanked by dour guards whose job it was to keep people at bay. Nicholas refused to consider the idea that an emperor could consult with elected representatives. The rift between autocracy and progressive thought – deepening since the accession of Nicholas I – had become abysmal. Anti-Semitic like his father, Nicholas II considered that pogroms were justified by the high proportion of Jews to be found in revolutionary groups, and so 'brotherhoods' of right-wing thugs were not discouraged from attacking 'kikes' and 'lefties'.

Nicholas II was dominated by his wife, Princess Alexandra of Hesse-Darmstadt. As a granddaughter of Queen Victoria, she spent a good deal of her childhood in the shelter of Kensington Palace in London. Taking the name of Alexandra Feodorovna when she converted to the Orthodox Church, she was introspective, stiff and unpopular. Her intelligence – like that of her husband – was limited, and the couple avoided their terrorised capital as much as possible.[5] Sir Cecil Spring Rice, chargé d'affaires at the British Embassy, sounded a note of exasperation in a letter to his friend, Mrs Theodore Roosevelt, wife of the American president: 'The Empress has a bad ear, the emperor won't attend to business and no one can do anything at all. What becomes of the U.S. when your ear aches?'[6]

Nicholas and his family spent the spring at Tsarskoe Selo and the early summer at Peterhof. A cruise on the imperial yacht was next on the agenda, followed by a sojourn in Crimea at their neo-Renaissance palace at Livadia. This annual progress terminated at their hunting lodges in Poland, before the season of official functions brought them – for the briefest interval – to the capital.[7] They were reluctant hosts. The last costume ball held in the Winter Palace was in February 1903, part of the bicentennial celebrations for the founding of a city that was so soon to shake off its imperial carapace. Three hundred guests dressed in the costume of Peter the Great's father, Alexis. There was a performance of *Boris Godunov*, which had been banned from imperial theatres for political reasons during the reign of Alexander III.[8] After the performance, guests sat down to eat. Dinners were interminable, with up to twelve fatty soups sitting tepid on the table, as if to signal that the whole imperial binge had gone on too long. The 200th anniversary of the founding of the city was celebrated by its 200th flood. Although not on the scale of the city's worst deluge in 1824 – the water rising only half as much – warning guns boomed from the fortress. The wind howled. The Neva rose above the quays. The streets were awash. Throughout the two preceding centuries, flood warnings had tolled with monotonous regularity, and every year winter ice landlocked St Petersburg. Latterly a new threat had settled. In the Romanov capital, a staggering number of people had grown sick and tired of the regime. The one ball held each year in the Great Nicholas Hall of the Winter Palace had an air of tiresome familiarity. Braziers flamed around Palace Square as carriages and open sledges – for 'those officers who did not fear the cold' – arrived. Shortly after 8.30 in the evening, as their majesties came 'in full procession of state, from the Malachite Room, the orchestra plunged into a polonaise'[9] – Glinka's perennial tonic for tone-deaf tsars. But the last court ball ever held in the Russian Empire was in January 1904. Such celebrations seemed less appropriate after the birth of the haemophiliac *tsarevich*, the military disaster in the Far East and the affront of the 1905 Revolution.[10]

As ever, looking back was one way of holding on to a fast-disappearing life, and that was provided in the curious context of an innovative arts magazine, *Mir Istkusstva*, or *The World of Art*. The enterprise began with a rather precious group of young men who quaintly named themselves the Nevsky Pickwickians. Their leader was the painter, theatrical designer, art critic and historian Alexandre Benois. His engagement with the elegance of Petersburg's past was a family affair – which made it an appropriately European affair. On his mother's side, Benois was descended from Catterino Cavos, the Venetian director of music to the imperial theatres

and father of Alberto Cavos, architect of the Mariinsky and
the Bolshoi in Moscow. Alberto's daughter married the half-
French, half-German Nicholas Benois, a gold medallist in
architecture at the St Petersburg Academy of Arts. St Petersburg's history was clearly in Alexandre Benois's blood. The
Nevsky Pickwickians formed in the 1880s, while Benois and
his two friends, Dmitri Filosofov and Walter Nuvel, were
studying at the private May School in the capital. Just before
graduating in 1890, they befriended a Jewish art student,
Léon Rosenberg, who would gain fame as a revolutionary
stage designer under the safely non-Jewish name of Bakst. He
burst upon the scene in 1900 with sets for a ballet presented
so successfully in the Hermitage Theatre that it transferred to
the Mariinsky. Towards the end of that same year, Filosofov's
dynamic cousin, Sergei Diaghilev, arrived in the capital and
took charge of the Nevsky Pickwickians, transforming them
into *Mir Istkusstva*, a group of aesthetes who mounted exhibitions and produced an influential magazine. *Mir Istkusstva*
displaced the social focus of the *peredvizhniki* with a *fin-de-
siècle* 'art for art's sake' mentality – 'a world of art' which was
a world apart. All too aware of the flat philistinism of Nicholas II's reign, *Mir Istkusstva* delighted in the capital's rich
architectural history.[11] In 'Painterly Petersburg', an article he
wrote for their magazine, Benois challenged the familiar epi-
thets 'putrefying swamp', 'absurd invention' and 'regimental
office' with the declaration that he loved the capital.[12]

Published as a large-format magazine, *Mir Istkusstva* was
devoted to St Petersburg architecture as well as to older forms of
Russian building and decorative arts. Well placed in society, the
Nevsky Pickwickians met fascinating figures such as the decadent
scientist Alfred Nurok – devourer of de Sade and erotic verse. He
introduced them to the work of the art-nouveau English illustrator
Aubrey Beardsley, whose subsequent influence on their magazine
and on contemporary Russian graphics was considerable. After

a French diplomat acquainted the group with the latest in French painting, they enthusiastically presented Gauguin, Van Gogh and Cézanne to art lovers in Russia, at a time when these artists were derided or barely known to the public in France. Thus Diaghilev introduced Post-Impressionism to Petersburg and kick-started the short-lived modernist revolution in Russia. He began to organise important exhibitions. 'English and German Watercolours' was presented in the two-floored hall of Maximilian Messmacher's sumptuous and eclectic neo-Renaissance Stieglitz Museum. Diaghilev mounted a show of 'Scandinavian Painters' in 1897 and of 'Russian and Finnish Painters' in 1898, in which contemporary Russian artists such as Isaak Levitan, Valentin Serov, Mikhail Vrubel and Viktor Borisov-Musatov were shown.

Diaghilev capped these important Stieglitz exhibitions with the huge 1905 display of 3,000 Russian portraits at the Tauride Palace. The walls of the exhibition space were specially painted

*Maximilian Messmacher's Stieglitz Museum.*

in deep colours, and Bakst created a garden effect, with statues placed to break up the endless rows of pictures.[13] It proved to be a sensation with privileged sections of society. Benois was, however, astonished by the indifference of the emperor to images of his antecedents. The utter boorishness of the Romanovs was demonstrated when the Grand Duke Nicholas put his foot through a portrait during the hanging of the exhibition. Trying to shrug off his faux pas, the grand duke superciliously suggested that the work needed restoration. As the public poured into the exhibition, Diaghilev sensed a frisson of 'alarm and foreboding' as people passed through the room full of portraits of the unstable Paul I. The great irony was that this extensive celebration of the Romanovs was presented just as the regime was on the point of collapse. Diaghilev sensed as much. Speaking at a Tauride banquet given in his honour, he described the exhibition as a great 'moment of summing-up in history, in the name of a new and unknown culture, which will be created by us and which will also sweep us away'.[14]

Despite the fact that the bulk of Russia's huge population remained illiterate and hopelessly poor, there were parts of the country that were modernising. As it moved into the twentieth century, Russia's commercial isolation was eroded by the ongoing initiatives of the progressive Minister of Finance, Sergei Witte, who secured the rouble by going onto the gold standard and – between 1893 and 1904 – brought Russia into the orbit of international capitalism. Expanding rapidly during the boom years of the 1890s, when industrial growth was high,[15] St Petersburg became the largest manufacturing complex in the Russian Empire, its architectural treasures prey to pollution, its skyline spoilt by belching soot from workshop chimneys. As Biely wrote, a 'many-thousand swarm' plodded towards the factories each morning. Out of a population of 1.5 million, nearly 300,000 worked in industry. Building could not keep pace with the influx of workers from the provinces and rents rose. When boom turned to bust in 1900, labour felt the pinch. Even when the economy bounced back, stimulated by the misguided and highly unpopular Russo–Japanese War of 1904–5, the population had little to celebrate. Russia's intrusion in the Far East was badly timed. In 1898, Port Arthur in southern Manchuria had been seized to secure a naval and trading base. Two years later, the Boxer Rebellion against Western imperialism broke out in China, and the tsar was forced to send 170,000 troops into Manchuria to protect Russia's eastward expansion along the Trans-Siberian Railway. Meanwhile Japan – victim of Western arrogance since the mid-nineteenth century – had colonial dreams of its own. In a tactic that it would repeat in 1942 against the American Navy, Japan launched a surprise attack on Russia's Pacific squadron in Port Arthur in April 1904 and laid siege to the town. As the Japanese army pressed on into Manchuria and defeated a superior Russian force, the tsar's Far Eastern ambitions shrivelled.[16]

Superficially, for the middle classes, life in St Petersburg seemed untouched by all this. Top hats and 'the froth of ostrich feathers' still promenaded on the Nevsky. Art nouveau – or *stil moderne* as it was called in Russia – came to the capital. Never architecturally as exuberant as its Moscow counterpart, Petersburg remained close to the stone-hewn folk world of the Finnish take on the movement. The art-nouveau Eliseev Brothers' Trading House – which sold 'all kinds of fruit and native and foreign dainties'[17] – went up on the Nevsky between 1902 and 1903. The asymmetrical, almost palatial and splendidly detailed interior of Vitebsk Station was created in 1902–4. The American Singer Company constructed the first metal-frame building in the capital, a technique that enabled the use of large windows.[18] But the most accomplished and forward-looking art-nouveau structure was the mansion built by Alexander Gogen between 1904 and 1906 on Kronverksky Prospekt for Matilda Kschessinskaya, the ballerina who had been collecting noblemen and a sizeable fortune. When Prince Radziwill observed that Kschessinskaya

*The top of the Singer Building on the Nevsky –*
*the first metal-frame building in the city.*

*St Petersburg* stil moderne *with echoes of Finnish* art nouveau.

must 'be proud to have two grand dukes' at her feet, she replied that it was not strange – 'I have two feet.'[19] As a result of her considerable talents, Kschessinskaya became so wealthy that she was accompanied by a special bodyguard and held court, entertaining lavishly at her country estate or in her stylish mansion overlooking Troitskaya Square.

In terms of furniture design and decoration, St Petersburg's *stil moderne* was eclectic. Friedrich Meltzer, one of the capital's two leading firms, decorated Empress Alexandra's bathroom in the Winter Palace in 'the English style', its upper walls in white chintz with pale pink irises. Meltzer's rival, Svirsky, designed the children's apartments on the imperial train using a bright floral pattern. The apartments of the empress in the Winter Palace and at Tsarskoe Selo were also decorated in *stil moderne*. Imperial egg-maker Carl Fabergé went through an art-nouveau phase between 1889 and 1902, and Alexandra bought Gallé glassware and instructed the Imperial Porcelain Factory to make unique pieces of fake Gallé exclusively for the royal family. Prince Sergei Shcherbatov and Baron Vladimir von Meck – inspired by the art-nouveau Maison Bing in Paris – set up Contemporary Art on the Bolshaya Morskaya in early 1903 in order to promote *stil moderne*. But despite their energy in organising exhibitions, the prince and the baron only sold one chair and, after eighteen months, shut it down. Nonetheless, *stil moderne* made its appeal to the nouveau riche. Its use of swirling floral motifs[20] – suggesting the gentle play of water on fronds in a clear pool – acted as a palliative to the harsher St Petersburg experience of water.

Nineteenth-century traditions and pleasures were still flourishing in the rapidly changing capital. The novelist Marta Almedingen remembered the fairs held on Vasilevsky Island, with paraffin-smelling sweets, honey-stewed apples, hot waffles and plaster busts of the imperial family for sale. Tamara Karsavina recalled the fire watchtowers, the horse-drawn fire engines and the brass helmets and bugles of the firemen. Stravinsky recalled

the smell of horse and leather from the droshkies, the reek of gas
and paraffin lamps that slowly disappeared as the city electrified,
and the pervasive scent of Mahorka tobacco, which had been
imported from Spain through Holland since the founding of the
capital. Karsavina remembered the enthusiastic, accomplished
and inexpensive Jewish tailors she visited with her parents in
the glass-roofed Alexandrovsky market,[21] while the spoilt young
Vladimir Nabokov recorded the city's ongoing Anglophilia – his
family bought Pears Soap, Golden Syrup, fruitcakes, striped
blazers and smelling salts from the English Shop on the Nevsky
Prospekt. The poet Osip Mandelstam insisted that the streets
of St Petersburg demanded spectacle and that their architecture
inspired him 'with a kind of childish imperialism'. He recalled
the May Parade in the Field of Mars, with its gleaming swords
and bayonets, silver trumpets and bugles. It seemed to him 'that
in Petersburg something very splendid and solemn was absolutely
bound to happen'.[22]

Nevertheless, Nicholas II did much of his official entertaining in the safe and imposing palaces roundabout. The King of
Siam – whose troupe of dancers inspired Fokine and Bakst –
was entertained at Peterhof, as was President Félix Faure of
France and Kaiser Wilhelm of Germany. Karsavina recalled
a gala – *Swan Lake* with Kschessinskaya dancing Odette/
Odile – presented to another French president, Emile Loubet, in
Catherine the Great's Chinese Theatre at Tsarskoe Selo, where
all the lacquer panels, the red and gold rococo chairs and porcelain flowers remained unusually radiant.[23] Splendid as such
occasions may have been, there was something hollow about the
capital, drained of its imperial purpose. St Petersburg had been a
stage erected for the pageant of the Romanovs but, as tsars and
their ministers became increasingly intimidated by revolutionaries, Mandelstam sensed 'the quiet misery . . . of the life that
was dying'. He smelt 'the humid air from mouldy parks' and suffered 'the rubbery aftertaste of Petersburg's boiled water', drawn

from what Biely described as the greenish 'turbid germ-infested waters of the Neva'. It was a city whose streets in autumn were tormented by an icy drizzle which saturated pedestrians until the flu 'crawled under the raised collars' of clerks and students and pursued them indoors, where the Petersburg street flowed in their 'veins like a fever'[24]

It was a divisible city. Indeed, the bridges crossing the Neva could be raised to protect the government from the discontent of the masses in the suburbs. By early 1900 the press began to report on the rise of small gangs of hooligans who distressed respectable passers-by with taunts, obscenities and demands for money. Gangs fought turf wars. Despite the ban on carrying weapons in the street – a measure intended to curb terrorism – uncontrollable mobs of up to a hundred youths swarmed along the Bolshoi Prospekt on the Petersburg Side, smashing shop windows and fighting with knives and knuckledusters. The Narva Gate in the industrial south-west of the city and Harbour Fields on Vasilevsky Island became no-go areas for the bourgeoisie. And, as they began to sense their clout, gangs started to range through Alexandrovsky Park and cross the Neva to rattle the well-to-do who were strolling in Senate Square.[25]

During the late 1890s there was mounting unrest in Petersburg factories. Some weak or ineffectual concessions were made by employers – the promise in 1897 to restrict the working day to eleven and a half hours, the promise in 1903 of medical treatment for accidents at work – but the lot of the Petersburg worker remained dire. At the Putilov Iron Works, most employees earned less than a rouble a day, and in the textile industry wages were even lower. Lenin, the Marxist revolutionary, recognised that tension in the factories 'represented the class struggle in embryo, but only in embryo'. He tried to up the ante by somewhat grandiloquently celebrating a large strike by textile workers as the 'famous St Petersburg industrial war of 1896'. But he also recognised the period as one of 'confusion . . . and vacillation' and argued for a cohesive party run by a professional, centralised leadership.[26] This would prove to be the beginning of a new end. For two more decades, different groups with different aims would stumble towards revolution, as activists struck and the authorities hit back. Cossacks frequently ruptured student demonstrations and their intervention – such as the one in front of Kazan Cathedral in March 1901 – often resulted in heavy casualties. Assassination continued – the Minister of the Interior, Dmitri Sipyagin, was killed by a revolutionary in April 1902. His replacement was the uncompromising Vyacheslav von Plehve, 'the enemy of all reform'. When he was blown up just over two years later, 'Everyone', according to Cecil Spring Rice, 'was delighted'.[27]

During his time in office, von Plehve transformed the Okhrana, the Department for Protecting the Public Security and Order, into a sophisticated secret-police network with a quantity of undercover agents who penetrated terrorist organisations. The Okhrana tapped telephones and practised perlustration, which had been used at least since the reign of Catherine the Great.[28] James Buchanan, head of the American Legation in St Petersburg in the 1830s and later President of the United States, had correspondence opened. In the mid-1860s, Lord Redesdale had been warned by the wife of the British Ambassador to use the diplomatic bag – her children's governess had received two letters from different parts of England. Two envelopes arrived. In one, there were two photographs, and in the other, two letters![29] There was a 'black cabinet' in the Central Post Office responsible for mail intercepts, despite the fact that perlustration without a specific court order was officially illegal.[30]

From 1901 to 1907, St Petersburg Security Section HQ was at no. 12 Moika Embankment – the house where Pushkin died. Never independent, like the earlier Third Section or the later Cheka, it was caught in the departmental labyrinths of the capital. The Special Section located on the Fontanka kept a

50,000-and-growing card index of codenamed suspects. Often using women for surveillance because they were less obvious, and drawing many field officers from the ranks of the city's garrison of 500 mounted gendarmes, the Okhrana also relied heavily on the support of the capital's 6,000-strong police force. But Okhrana detectives and stakeouts were badly paid, compromising efficiency and inviting bribery. They turned uncommitted revolutionaries with ease,[31] but when they recruited dedicated terrorists as double-agents, matters became complicated. Evno Azeff would organise the 'murders of Grand Dukes and Ministers, and at the same time . . . betray perpetrators of these crimes and their accomplices to the secret police'.[32] Double-agent Azeff planned twenty-eight terrorist attacks on officials and was personally involved in the plan to assassinate von Plehve.[33]

It was Von Plehve who promoted the ex-revolutionary Sergei Zubatov to head political investigation in St Petersburg. Astutely understanding that revolutionaries could not succeed in their struggle without the proletariat, Zubatov suggested infiltrating groups of workers and persuading them that the resolution to their problems lay in the amelioration of the existing system. Attempting to establish self-help groups under police supervision, he sought aid from a religious teacher who could speak simply in a language the working masses could understand. Father Gapon was a vain and disturbed Orthodox priest with dangerously unorthodox ideas. From a lowly family in the Ukraine, his life before he arrived in St Petersburg was marked by an unsuccessful marriage and bouts of depression and erratic behaviour. But he harboured 'a genuine concern for the poor' and possessed the charisma to control them. Zubatov's scheme for monitored labour organisations never took off, but soon Gapon had developed a plan of his own. He understood that revolutionaries could not easily influence the masses because they had to work from the shadows, whereas a priest's purpose was to make himself heard. Gapon could develop a direct and open relationship and

so, in the summer of 1903, he opened a clubhouse in Vyborg
for labourers and set up an association the following spring,
which he called the Assembly of the Russian Factory and Mill
Workers of the City of St Petersburg. In their clubhouse, workers
could relax or participate in classes, attend lectures and even sing
in a choir. Gapon started to invite the most intelligent among
them to his home for nicotine-charged, beer-fuelled discussions,
which ranged widely over a host of Russian grievances: freedom
of speech, the need for universal education, equality before the
law, the abolition of the land redemption tax, an eight-hour day,
a minimum wage and the protection of labour by the law.

Gapon's initiative was so successful that workers in other
neighbourhoods clamoured for a clubhouse of their own, and
one was soon opened in an old inn near the Putilov Iron Works
in Narva. Another followed on Vasilevsky Island. With the crudity of his arguments, his rapid speech and touching stammer,
Gapon forged a simple, tight bond with the workers. As Christmas 1904 approached, more clubhouses opened and parties were
planned for the children. When a small group of workers at the
Putilov plant were unfairly dismissed, Gapon put the weight of
his Assembly behind the call to strike. Russia was at war, so
Putilov's important contribution to military hardware made a
strike highly undesirable. After a meeting at the Vasilevsky clubhouse on Sunday 2 January 1905, the sacked workers decided to
confront the management. On Monday 3rd, the director promised that if everybody returned to work, he would investigate the
problem. Too little too late. On Tuesday 4th the strike spread,
and the following day Gapon was calling for a general strike.
He warned the city governor and urged him not to deploy the
Cossacks.[34]

Epiphany, with its annual Blessing of the Waters, was on
5 January and, in 1905, the celebration was marred by a discharge of live ammunition during the gun salute by the horse
artillery. Shrapnel went over the heads of the dignitaries, struck

the roof of the pavilion, wounded a policeman and shattered some windows, penetrating the Nicholas Hall of the Winter Palace, where the court and diplomatic body were assembled. The 'accident' was attributed to carelessness – a shotted cartridge had been left in the breach of a gun after target practice. That was the official explanation, but rumours suggested it was an attempt on the tsar's life.[35]

Gapon sought an interview with von Plehve's successor, Peter Sviatopolk-Mirsky, to insist on how serious the situation had become. Refused an audience on Thursday 6th, Gapon decided to organise a group of workers who would march to the tsar that coming Sunday and petition him, demanding solutions for those grievances that his Assembly had discussed.[36] When he appeared before the workers dressed in a cassock, his eyes bristling, Gapon was incendiary. According to the correspondent of the *Manchester Guardian*, the priest declared that 'factory inspectors were in the pockets of the capitalists'. He read from the petition, 'We are impoverished, overburdened with excessive toil, contemptuously treated. We are not even recognised as human beings . . . O sire . . . We have reached that frightful moment when death is better than the prolongation of our unbearable sufferings.' His audience went wild. Gapon urged them to swear – despite his protestations about the peaceful nature of the march – to come armed on Sunday. 'We swear,' exclaimed the crowd. Gapon issued a threat: 'If the Tsar does not satisfy our demands there will be no Tsar.' The thundering echo of the workers rattled the walls of the clubhouse: 'No Tsar.'[37]

By Friday 7th the city was strikebound, and – afraid of stirring up further unrest – the authorities decided to leave Father Gapon at large. The priest sent the petition to the typist, ordering multiple copies. One would be carried by him and handed to the tsar. Another went out on Reuters' news agency despatch a little before midnight. By then Gapon was off on a tour of the Assembly branches, stirring up the workers into a frenzy of suicidal support. The *Guardian* correspondent noted that Gapon spoke of 'the possibility of his own death or the butchery of his followers'.[38] Meanwhile the commander of the guards, General Vasilchikov, met his officers, instructing them – when the time came – to repulse the workers from the centre of the city. On the evening of Saturday 8 January, the streets were ominously deserted. During the night, troops from Pskov and Revel arrived. There would be twenty-one battalions of infantry, twenty-three squadrons of cavalry and hundreds of Cossacks ready to welcome the workers as they marched to petition the tsar.[39]

It was a bracing January Sunday – a kind of new-dawn day – as workers carrying icons and even portraits of their venerated 'father', Tsar Nicholas II, began to assemble at points in the outlying areas of the poorer parts of town. Workers, wives and children started to move along the right bank of the Neva from Okhta. Others assembled on the Vyborg Side and crossed the short bridge onto Petersburg Island, where they were blocked by a barricade in Troitskaya Square. The official plea was – as Biely put it in his novel, *Petersburg* – 'oh, Russian people! Don't let the crowd of shadows in from the islands!'[40] Detachments of the Pavlovsky and Grenadier Guards were in place to make sure they did not. An officer ordered the petitioners – their numbers augmented by a second march streaming down Kamennoostrovsky Prospekt – to stop. The marchers pulled open their coats to prove they were unarmed, but those at the front were pushed forward by eager protesters piling into the rear. A bugle sounded. A volley of shot shattered the deadlock. The cavalry charged. Sabres flashed and wriggled through the crowd like silverfish. Two more rounds were fired and fifty lay dead, while the groans of the wounded mocked the optimism of Father Gapon's plan.

The Minister of Finance, Count Vladimir Kokovtsov, was sorting papers in his study at about 10 a.m. when he heard rifle fire coming from the direction of the Police Bridge over the Moika. A group of marchers, pushing down the Nevsky, hurling stones and bottles at soldiers, had been ambushed by troops advancing along Bolshaya Morskaya. The soldiers advanced. The crowd retreated, then regrouped and pressed onwards. Kokovtsov was eager to investigate, but the *dvornik* informed him that the front door to his building had been locked on the orders of the police.[41]

The imperial standard was flying over the Winter Palace, suggesting that the tsar – in fact at Tsarskoe Selo – was in residence. A fourth group of protesters assembled in the northern part of Vasilevsky Island and marched down the lines, only to be blocked by soldiers at the bridges across the Neva. More petitioners advanced across the ice and, for all the barricades, fusillades and skirmishes, protesters made it into the troop-infested sweep of Palace Square to lend support to Father Gapon's ominous declaration to the tsar: 'We have only two roads open to us: one leading to freedom and happiness, the other to the grave.'[42]

By two o'clock, Prince Vasilchikov decided that the incursion had lasted long enough and gave orders to clear the area – by firing,

*Massacre in Palace Square on 'Bloody Sunday', 1905.*

if necessary. Bugles sounded. Shots rang out. Children who had merely clambered into trees to get a better view were hit by stray bullets.[43] The cavalry were sent to disperse the crowd in the Alexandrovsky Garden that led through to Senate Square, and Cossacks were despatched to clear the Nevsky Prospekt. That was where Nijinsky, coming from the Imperial Ballet School, was swept up into the crowd, which propelled him towards a Cossack baton charge. A cudgel came down hard on the skull of the dancer – something that did little for the mental stability of *najinka*, 'the tender one'. Nijinsky fingered the blood streaming down his face and wriggled away through the crush of protesters.[44]

Kokovtsov managed to get out by mid-afternoon and noted that the demonstration had been effectively broken up. There were stragglers rioting and looting, but Gapon – still intending to press on to revolution – was in hiding. The official figure was kept low, but the toll of dead or badly wounded on 'Bloody Sunday' was close to 1,000 – the foreign press had 'thousands'. As with the numbers of those who perished while building the city, an accurate figure is difficult to determine.[45] In any case, statistics only tell so much. The tension, hope and despair of Bloody Sunday – the march, the massacre – survive in Dmitri Shostakovich's 11th symphony, 'The Year 1905'.

That Sunday evening there was a benefit performance at the Mariinsky for the ballerina Olga Preobrajenskaya. While the performance went ahead without a hitch, rumours of insurrection rippled through the audience and the theatre began to empty. Karsavina remembered walking home afterwards with her brother and finding the streets strangely 'quiet and empty'. Across the globe, however, the headlines shocked readers, and Kokovtsov – in the process of negotiating loans with Paris and Berlin – faced the difficult task of reviving the market's faith in Nicholas II's Russia. Although the capital swiftly returned to a semblance of normality, a new pitch of protest and suppression had been registered.[46] Spring Rice wrote to Mrs Roosevelt that there was a consensus among courtiers and diplomats that Bloody Sunday had been an inevitable and very good lesson – but one that fell on deaf ears. The emperor played with the baby *tsarevich* 'and will hear nothing but baby talk. If you come with disagreeable truths, he listens but says nothing. His ideas, if he has any, are to maintain the autocracy undiminished and to continue the war until he has gained the "mastery of the Pacific".'[47]

While St Petersburg's theatre world remained largely unruffled by the massacre, it was disturbed by a revolutionary dancer. There was – in certain circles – considerable discomfort with classical ballet. Tolstoy thought it a 'lewd performance'. Chekhov understood nothing about the medium, but could vouch that 'the ballerinas stink like horses' backstage.[48] The young Alexander Benois declared in *Mir Istkusstva* that 'fairies have been the ruin of ballet'.[49] The American dancer Isadora Duncan, who thought ballet 'false, absurd and outside the domain of art',[50] arrived in St Petersburg on 12 December 1904 and gave a benefit for the Society for the Prevention of Cruelty to Children the following day. Diaghilev and Fokine were in the audience, and the impresario claimed that Duncan was 'the foundation' of all Fokine's later creations.[51] Duncan's presentation proved so popular that she gave another performance on the 16th and then left for Germany. When she returned to Petersburg and Moscow the following year, she expressed discomfort at dancing for the rich while strike action and potential revolution rocked the city. The late-January dates for her return suggest that Duncan was fabricating her account, when she claimed that she was welcomed – as her train arrived – by a mass funeral procession for the dead from Bloody Sunday. If, however, the authorities buried the dead discreetly, a few at a time in the deserted hours before dawn, then it is possible that the dancer may have witnessed 'men laden and bent under their loads – coffins – one after another', a city going to its grave.[52]

Meanwhile, workers were bewildered. It seemed almost as if Gapon had led them into a trap. No one could understand why the authorities would massacre peaceful protesters wanting to petition the tsar. The answer lay in the stupefying indifference of an emperor who eventually consented to meet a deputation of carefully selected workers at Tsarskoe Selo in late February, for tea and sympathy and empty gestures, while the suffering capital intensified its efforts to obtain justice.[53] For most of 1905, St Petersburg was in a state of upheaval as revolutionaries, students, workers and professional unions consolidated their attack on autocracy. Doctors who treated the victims of Bloody Sunday were politicised in the process. There was turmoil at the Conservatoire, and Rimsky-Korsakov refused to teach in a building ringed by policemen. After thirty-five years as a professor, he was fired.[54] Support erupted in other higher-education establishments and resulted in closures for the remainder of the academic year. Engineers, lawyers, technicians and writers formed unions – a useful tactic, as professional meetings were the only public assemblies tolerated by the government. A bomb plot to hit the commemoration service for Alexander II in the Peter and Paul Cathedral on 1 March was thwarted when the bombmaker blew himself up in his hotel room and the new head of the Okhrana, General Gerasimov, tumbled twenty suspects.[55] Mrs Roosevelt was informed by Spring Rice that 'anarchy is growing and incidents abound. It would be difficult to give an idea of the disintegration which is taking place. It is like a great animal dead and rotting, with jackals tugging at its tough hide . . . Autocracy has lived by *fear* and seems to have destroyed every other feeling – now it is by fear that Autocracy is being attacked.'[56] Street violence – muggings, knife attacks and brawls – increased after Bloody Sunday. Hooligans invaded the Nevsky Prospekt on balmy spring evenings and, armed with iron bars, spat contemptuously into the faces of the fashionable. The young Nabokov kept a knuckleduster in his pockets.[57]

When the Second Pacific Ocean Squadron was all but wiped out in the Strait of Tsushima in May 1905, more than 4,000 Russians died and 6,000 were captured, forcing the tsar to abandon his pretensions in the Far East and sue for peace. Closer to home, peasants – more politicised than Lenin dared hope – continued to burn out landlords. On 5 July, an aristocratic officer shot dead a deckhand who had dared to complain about the maggoty food on board his ship anchored in Odessa. *The Battleship Potempkin*, Sergei Eisenstein's masterly film of the incident and subsequent revolt, demonstrates how imperial mismanagement sparked rebellion – the *Potempkin* was Russia in miniature. As the oppressed seized the moment, the empire struck back. The steady march of the tsarist military machine down the Odessa Steps, bayonets poised to stamp out mutiny and massacre innocent bystanders, was Bloody Sunday all over again.

The situation deteriorated over the summer. An outbreak of cholera was expected. Riots spread like an epidemic. There were huge political meetings held in Petersburg lecture halls – 2,000 workers and students gathered at the Technological Institute on 1 October, followed by 12,000 at the university on the 5th. Trains were running irregularly. A fatal accident occurred on the overnight Moscow–Petersburg service on 4 October, when carriages were smashed as the locomotive, travelling at full speed, hurtled into a siding. Was it human error or the result of the disruption caused by the railway 'go-slow'? Three days later, the Moscow–Kazan railway came out on strike – a stoppage which swiftly spread across the network.[58] On 13 October, forty revolutionaries met at the Technological Institute to shape uncoordinated rebellion into a general strike, which started four days later under the direction of the newly created St Petersburg 'soviet', or council of workers. On 19 October, freedom of the press was declared by the St Petersburg soviet, and industrialists who refused to shut down their plants were intimidated. The soviet sent orders to the post office and railways, collected money for hungry strikers, negotiated with the city council and formed its own militia. Armed with knives, revolvers and shovels, it numbered 6,000 strong by mid-November. Strikers created self-defence groups, which roamed the night streets in patrols of eight to ten. French bankers, come to put the finishing touches to a loan agreement, didn't recognise the city and returned to France prematurely, without concluding the deal.[59]

Andrei Biely's great modernist novel *Petersburg* is set against the backdrop of the developing crisis between 30 September and 9 October 1905, when the government was losing control. The book centres on a bomb plot to kill Apollon Apollonovich Ableukhov, a fictional character who has much in common with the arch-reactionary procurator of the Holy Synod and sometime tutor to Nicholas II, Konstantin Pobedonostsev. Ableukhov is a self-confessed 'man of the school of Plehve'. When his 'wizened and utterly unprepossessing little figure' is considered in relation to 'the immeasurable immensity of the mechanisms managed by him', it seems hardly surprising that the country is slipping from government control. During the 'entire period when the strike was in progress,' Ableukhov 'appeared in chancelleries, offices and ministerial residences – exhausted, emaciated'. He is terminally out of touch. His carriage cuts him off from 'the scum of the streets' and the 'red covers of the damp trashy rags on sale' at crossings. Meanwhile, Ableukhov's son, Nikolai – a university student who flirts with the revolutionary movement – is selected to bomb a government target. In a world of terrorists like Nechaev and Ishutin and double-agents like Evno Azeff, and in the context of a city splintered and broken up by the novel's modernist vision, it is hardly surprising that the victim selected by Nikolai's controllers is his father.

*Petersburg* never gets close to the strikers. Indeed, Biely observes that from 'the procession of bowlers, you would never say that momentous events were rumbling'. Yet the novel is – in the tradition of St Petersburg itself – murderously concerned with replacing the old with the new. Not only is the son detailed to kill his father, but the great innovator, the *Bronze Horseman*, is also seen to be on the move again, going at full gallop to change Russia. Biely, however, hints to his reader that Russia may yet be stuck in the mud. There is an unresolved tension between the front and back of Peter the Great's bronze horse. The 'two front hooves have leaped far off into the darkness, into the void' while the statue's 'two rear hooves are firmly implanted in the granite soil'. Peter is seen 'racing through the days, through the years, through the damp Petersburg prospekts' and Biely predicts another 'leap across history. Great shall be the turmoil.' He repeatedly presents Petersburg's streets and skies mired by 'slush' and suggests that the city's ultimate vaporisation will be effected by revolution, by the terrorist bomb ticking in the sardine tin given to Nikolai, a bomb 'capable of turning everything nearby . . . into slush'.[60]

In December 1903, Spring Rice observed that when Russians met, they 'discuss how long it will be before the revolution comes. Just as in Japan we always talked about earthquakes.'[61] By October 1905 it was clear that one day soon, tsarism would break up like the frozen Neva at the beginning of spring. There would be a fracturing that would shake the world. Tamara Karsavina recalled the autumn of 1905 as 'a nightmare'. Electricity cut frequently and the horrid clang of Petersburg telephones was silenced. She recorded how the 180 dancers at the imperial ballet, 'so conservative at heart, usually so loyal to the Court . . . succumbed to the epidemic of meetings and resolutions' and walked out. The strike committee, which included Karsavina and Pavlova, met in Fokine's garret. Delegates arrived late because the trams had stopped and the bridges had been raised. Two dancers swept excitedly into the room, making fretting jokes about the plainclothes policemen lurking below – their cover blown by their green coats and standard-issue galoshes. Karsavina and Fokine conferred in private. He was resolute, but she was hesitant, for

her mother had cautioned her not to oppose an emperor who
had given her 'an education, position, means, and livelihood'.
The dancers at the Mariinsky were asked to sign a declaration of
loyalty to Nicholas II. The strike committee refused – except for
one, the original prince in *The Nutcracker*, Sergei Legat. One
night, when the committee was in session, Fokine went to answer
a rap on his door and came back ghost white. Sergei Legat had
slit his throat. Already overwrought by his turbulent relationship
with Petipa's daughter, Legat felt himself a traitor to the tsar and
a Judas to his friends.[62]

Nicholas II was advised by his generals against calling out
the army, on whose loyalty they suggested he could not rely. So,
to defuse what was an alarming situation, Nicholas prepared
a manifesto full of empty promises. While it was stalled at the
printers by an electricity strike, a bomb was thrown at the police.
They shot back. Violence erupted and the authorities pressed to
get the manifesto out. The following morning there were jubilant
processions, with red flags waving to the strains of the 'Marseillaise' as socialists naively imagined that the document signified
a great victory.[63]

Winter 1905 began with a bloody massacre, which was
followed by months of disruption and bloodshed that culminated
in an autumn general strike. The tsar's indifference to political
evolution and fair-mindedness effectively disqualified him from
ruling. As people surged down the Nevsky, demanding a better
world, the numbness of Nicholas II consigned the Romanovs to
history. His October Manifesto was a desperate gesture, which
mendaciously promised that 'no law shall become effective without the confirmation by the State Duma, and that the elected
representatives of the people shall be guaranteed an opportunity of real participation'.[64] It did little to quell revolt. By the end
of the year, fifty-five cities in Russia had soviets; and Gerasimov, head of the St Petersburg Okhrana, was instructed to flush
out revolutionary activity in the capital. On a single evening he

coordinated 350 searches, which uncovered three laboratories for producing explosives, 500 bombs, illegal printing presses and armouries. The following day there were 400 further search-es.[65] There were attacks on police and assassinations, followed by a vigilante backlash against Jews and students as lists were made and houses to be targeted were marked. Jews took refuge in the relative anonymity of the big hotels or fled to Finland. The extreme right-wing Union of Russian People formed the Black Hundred gangs, to combat the subsequent increase in violence after the publication of the Manifesto. Essentially a bunch of thugs, they were welcomed by the regime as providing evidence of mass support for the tsar among the lower orders.[66] The gover-nor of St Petersburg issued the Union and similar 'brotherhoods' with the firepower to combat the armed revolutionary militia.

By early December the St Petersburg streets were full of shop-pers once again and there were few signs that the country had been in the throes of revolution.[67] The statues in the Summer Garden were, as usual, boxed for the harsh winter months. Nevertheless, given the revolutionary preoccupations of his novel, Biely offers this very scene as a potent image of imperilled imperial Petersburg: 'The statues each stood hidden beneath boards. The boards looked like coffins standing on end. The cof-fins lined the paths. Both nymphs and satyrs had taken shelter in them, so that the tooth of time might not gnaw them away with frost.'[68] Although the worst of the crisis appeared to be over, the Mariinsky dancers had played their part in what Lenin later called the 'dress rehearsal' for the real revolution.

# 11

# DAZZLE AND DESPAIR

## *1906–17*

The tsar's 1905 October Manifesto promised a constitutional monarchy with a Duma, a lower house of government intended to have legislative powers. This commitment was immediately broken by the reassertion of Nicholas's unassailable autocratic power in the 'Fundamental Law of Empire', published three months later. However, in March 1906, the Temporary Regulations legitimised trades unions, eased censorship[1] and admitted workers to the first Duma, which was proclaimed on 27 April 1906 in the Georgievsky Hall of the Winter Palace. In this throne room – the very heart of the tsar's empire – the royal family found the ceremony uncomfortably confrontational. There were some familiar delegates in full court dress, but the overwhelming impression created by the assembled members of the Duma was that of an uncouth rabble in working clothes. The conservative Peter Stolypin – appointed prime minister three months later – watched as a workman with high oiled boots insolently inspected the throne and reproachfully eyed the royal family. Stolypin murmured to Count Kokovtsov that he felt the man 'might throw a bomb'.[2] The dowager empress was utterly rattled by the rough faces that communicated 'an incomprehensible hatred for all of us'. The whole experiment seemed untenable. Not long after the assembly started to sit in

*Nicholas II makes a speech to members of the State Council and the Duma on 27 April 1906.*

the Tauride Palace, the English writer Maurice Baring suggested to a Petersburg cabbie that it might be dissolved. 'They won't dare,' replied the driver. 'But if they do dare?' 'Then we shall kill them.' 'Kill whom?' 'Why all the rich.' Baring suggested that the soldiers might intervene – they had shot at protesters in the past. 'Before they did not understand what it was all about. Now they know . . . the people are screaming.'[3]

Lenin had arrived in Petersburg incognito in November 1905 – too late to play an active part in the general strike. He understood that Bloody Sunday had revealed 'the gigantic reserve of revolutionary proletarian energy' and yet – at the same time – a damaging lack of organisation. His 1902 text, *What Is to Be Done?* asserted the need for discipline and centralised management – 'professional revolutionists' living at the expense of the party, who 'would train themselves to become real political leaders' and gain support through a Russian party newspaper.[4] This he reiterated at the Second Party Congress of the Russian Social Democratic Labour Party in London in August 1903, resulting in the split between Lenin, leading the majority of the delegates – who thereby became 'Bolsheviks' – and the minority, who became 'Mensheviks'.[5]

After Father Gapon's credulous attempt to petition the tsar, he fled Russia to make contact with revolutionary exiles in Switzerland. Bored by their studious devotion to Marx, he moved on to Paris, London – and celebrity. He dined out on Bloody Sunday, and speaking engagements followed, accompanied by a sizeable advance on his autobiography. With that money, the priest purchased arms to smuggle to revolutionaries, but the ship transporting them ran aground off the Russian coast. Returning home, Gapon elected to co-operate with the Okhrana but was betrayed to party combatants and hanged in a *dacha* near St Petersburg. Socialist Revolutionaries, or SRs, were suspected of the murder. Operational since 1901 – heirs to the *narodniki*, who believed that communal values lay at the heart of socialism – the SRs denied responsibility, and the killers of the priest have never been positively identified.[6]

In Petersburg during 1906, Lenin collaborated with the Mensheviks, who believed that a bourgeois revolution was the precondition of a successful socialist insurrection. Lenin's own scheme turned out to be more abrupt and brutal. In May 1906, under the bright sky of a White Night, the Bolshevik leader electrified a huge crowd. But with spies on his tail and life becoming too hot in the capital, Lenin decamped to Kaukola in Finland, from where he directed what was left of the revolutionary networks after Gerasimov's crackdown.[7] In one month over the New Year, 1,700 people had been arrested. In the six months to May 1906, more than 70,000 people were imprisoned. A revolt at Kronstadt in July resulted in thirty-six executions.[8]

Soldiers were trigger-happy, the Black Hundreds were out for blood, and revolutionaries revealed their resolve. Baring tells the story of a policeman who rescued a student from a lynch mob. Walking away from danger together, the young radical turned and promptly shot his saviour. With sardonic understatement,

Baring observed that there was 'some danger from the reckless way in which the population toy with Browning pistols'.[9]
Attacks flared across the capital and although some were politically motivated, the disruptions also provided opportunities for
street crime. Petersburg newspapers were so full of violence that
it seemed as if the capital was paralysed by hooliganism. Despite
a determined police effort to drive vagrants from the centre,
Baring was astonished by the number of beggars – nearly 16,000
were picked up each year between 1905 and 1910. They clustered, huddled in doorways or slept flat out against walls, soaked
by the miserable Petersburg weather as rain spattered from the
bent-out ends of outsized downpipes. Abandoned by their parents or fleeing abuse, small children could be found sleeping in
rubbish bins. In 1909, a gang of girls was arrested thieving in the
gostiny dvor; their ages ranged from nine to twelve.[10]

After impotent and turbulent sittings, the Duma was indeed
dissolved on 8 July. Prime minister Stolypin wanted a more conservative body voted in, so that the establishment, rather than the
revolutionaries, would become the instrument of change. Just
over a month later, Stolypin was receiving guests at his dacha on
Aptekarsky Island when three terrorists, shouting, 'Long live the
Revolution,' threw a bomb into the vestibule. They blew themselves up, killed nearly thirty guests and wounded many more,
including the prime minister's children. Kokovtsov, in Paris to
negotiate a loan, was rebuffed. When the French judged that
the Russian government was stronger than the revolution, they
would agree a loan.[11]

Russia's amour propre was rescued somewhat by the timely
triumph of Sergei Diaghilev in the French capital. He not only
organised the Russian section of the 1906 Parisian 'Salon
d'Automne', presenting masterpieces of Russian art to the West,
but followed this with festivals of Russian music. He crowned
the enterprise in 1908, when Fyodor Chaliapin sung the lead
in the imperial theatre production of Boris Godunov at the

Paris Opera. Diaghilev had become an international impresario: 'I am, firstly, a charlatan, though a rather brilliant one; secondly, a great charmer; thirdly, frightened of nobody; fourthly, a man with plenty of logic and very few scruples; fifthly, I seem to have no real talent.'[12] He had chosen the ideal profession. Larger than life, Diaghilev epitomised the defiant and showy nature of the Russian capital. His successful Paris enterprise indicated that the artistic triumph of St Petersburg was of truly international calibre and that, with trouble at home, a good number of the most creative Petersburgers were happy to work abroad.

Igor Stravinsky's father was a Mariinsky baritone, and Borodin and César Cui were frequent visitors to the family apartment overlooking the Kryukov Canal – one floor below Karsavina's and one floor above a manufacturer of secret-police galoshes. Stravinsky was privately taught composition by Rimsky-Korsakov, and his musical apprenticeship was enriched by the number of outstanding concerts given in the capital. The Czech violinist and composer Jan Kubelik performed in the winter of 1904. Pablo Casals was in the midst of a cello recital at the height of the 1905 troubles when the electricity cut. Almost immediately, candles flared from the concert hall's magnificent chandeliers.[13] Gustav Mahler, the harbinger of twentieth-century music – the man who visited Niagara Falls and commented, '*Fortissimo* at last' – came to Petersburg in the autumn of 1907 to conduct his 5th Symphony. Stravinsky was there, waiting in the wings. Just three years later the young Russian enjoyed a breakthrough success with his music for Diaghilev's ballet *The Firebird*. In Paris, Stravinsky found celebrity and continued to work outside Russia for most of the rest of his life. Nine years younger than Stravinsky, Sergei Prokofiev made a sensational debut – aged seventeen – at the Petersburg Evenings of Contemporary Music in December 1908. He would spend a good part of the next three decades abroad and would find his return to a very different Russia difficult. Both composers were given their chance to work in Europe for Diaghilev's remarkable Ballets Russes.

When Alexandre Benois first met Nijinsky, he was surprised to see a 'rather thick-set little fellow . . . more like a shop assistant than a fairy-tale hero'.[14] At the Imperial Ballet School, other students had found the young dancer dull-witted and had ridiculed his Tartar bone-structure. Although Nijinsky's professional debut was striking, his meagre pay at the Mariinsky necessitated giving ballroom dancing lessons to the children of the rich. This precarious situation changed when the homosexual socialite Prince Pavel Lvov took Nijinsky to bed. Suddenly part of a smart set, frequenting nightclubs such as the Aquarium or the Alcazar and after-show parties at Cubat's restaurant on Kamenny Island, Nijinsky was introduced to Diaghilev by Lvov in the autumn of 1908. The dancer's account of the consequences of that meeting were given in his *Diary*, written in 1918, when he was married and on the verge of insanity.[15] Nijinsky remembered that when he was summoned to the Hotel Europe on the Nevsky Prospekt by Diaghilev, 'I allowed him to make love to me. I trembled like a leaf. I hated him, but pretended, because I knew that my mother and I would die of hunger otherwise.' He declared that Diaghilev was 'a bad man' who loved boys, suggesting that one 'must stop men like him by any means'. Nijinsky's disgust erupted into disturbed utterances: 'Gogol: masturbation was his downfall,' 'I am no longer Nijinsky of the Russian Ballet, I am Nijinsky of God,' 'I want the death of the mind'[16] – a desire reflected by the implicit absurdity and spontaneity of the burgeoning Russian avant-garde. However, before Nijinsky was hospitalised with schizophrenia, his artistic collaboration with Diaghilev allowed him to become one of the most celebrated dancers of all time and the physical manifestation of modernism – a tightly wound spring so powerfully captured by Auguste Rodin in a small plaster maquette for a bronze.

Preparing for the 1909 Russian Ballet season at the Châtelet in Paris, Diaghilev ran into difficulties. When Nijinsky appeared onstage at the Mariinsky with the crotch of his tights stuffed with handkerchiefs, the royal family were shocked and Diaghilev was held to account. Up till then his troupe had been allowed to rehearse in the Hermitage Theatre, where Karsavina remembered being served tea or chocolate by liveried servants. The fallout from the Nijinsky scandal, and the displeasure of the mighty Matilda Kschessinskaya over Diaghilev's casting, resulted in the authorities cutting their funding and withdrawing permission to use the royal palace. But the French, wary of investing in revolutionary Russia, were willing to support its revolutionary art. Nijinsky and Pavlova were dancing *Les Sylphides* in Paris that May. The Ballets Russes would return to the French capital over the next years to scandalise and triumph. It was, as Karsavina observed, an 'invasion of Russian art into Europe'.[17] Meanwhile the departure of Diaghilev and his pleiad, the urgent struggle against the regime and the tensions of driving industrialisation left the greying Russian capital decidedly less polished and sophisticated.

Soon after the Second Duma – which included members of the Russian Social Democratic Labour Party – began to sit at the Tauride Palace in February 1907, the ceiling of its debating chamber caved in.[18] The delegates were not in session at the time, but the feisty socialist contingent – with their vigorous attacks on the government – soon brought down the assembly. After weeks of agitation for reform, the police arrived in early June to arrest Bolshevik and Menshevik delegates. New guns were sited on the ramparts of the Peter and Paul Fortress and the Okhrana launched an offensive. The ferocity of the clampdown forced extremists such as Lenin and Grigory Zinoviev to flee to Switzerland, where radical exiles were, nonetheless, kept under the prying eyes of the Paris-based foreign branch of the Okhrana. After dismissing the rebellious Second Duma, the authorities secured a Third Duma stuffed with businessmen and noblemen.[19] As with its predecessors, the speaker's chair was placed pointedly in front of a domineering portrait of the tsar. This Third Duma lasted five years, and Count Kokovtsov claimed it was the only one that made a constructive contribution to government.[20]

With the revolution 'crushed', St Petersburg industrialists went on the offensive. A recession meant that bosses were able to disregard their promised wage rises and forget the eight-hour day.[21] Time sheets were introduced, an hourly wage replaced the daily rate, and time-and-motion studies attempted to increase productivity. Disheartened, membership of the Bolshevik Party dwindled from nearly 7,000 in early 1907 to a mere 500 by 1911, when industrial output rose to satisfy the hunger for modern artillery and, once again, turned St Petersburg into a boom town. Foreign investment poured in, after strike action imploded – walkouts came down from about 1,000 in 1907 to just eleven in 1910.[22] Among the wealthier inhabitants of the city the pace of life accelerated. In the centre of what was now Europe's fifth-largest 'unhealthiest and most expensive capital', there was an increasing number of motor cars. The affluent Nabokovs had a Benz and a Wolseley in the city and an Opel convertible, which shot along country lanes at more than ninety kilometres an hour.[23] A Moscow–St Petersburg–Moscow motorbike rally became popular, along with other sports and gymnastics. The British community enjoyed excellent tennis courts and a yacht club on Krestovsky Island, and an American-style roller-skating rink opened in 1913.[24] Biplanes took off from Kolomiagi Aerodrome in Vyborg, and hydroplanes bump-landed on the choppy Neva. These first aircraft were imported but, by 1913, Igor Sikorksky was designing and assembling them at the Russian-Baltic Aeroplane Factory. There were also electric doorbells, lifts in lacy cages and – most beguilingly – 'electric palaces' or cinemas. A film theatre first opened in May 1896, and fifteen years later there were more than 130 in the city, of which twenty-three were to be found on the Nevsky Prospekt. Electric trams appeared in

September 1907, serving more affluent areas and causing accidents as idling pedestrians underestimated the enthusiasm of the drivers.[25] But passengers living in the suburbs still had to use the antiquated horse-tram network to make the slow commute from their muddy streets and their dwellings, void of sanitation. Already split by extremes of culture and ignorance, enormous wealth and abject poverty, St Petersburg was now divided by the emerging technology of the twentieth century. Pollution was increasing. Marta Almedingen recalled the inhabitants of the Petersburg Side seeming as if 'they had never seen a sunrise in their lives'.[26]

Functionalist principles of design had been championed by the Society of Architects and the Institute of Civil Engineers since the 1880s. By 1910, their triumph over nostalgic neo-Russian building and all the whimsies of *stil moderne* was visible in the emergence of a modern take on neoclassicism. During the first two decades of the new century Kamennoostrovsky Prospekt on the Petersburg Side was developed with fashionable bourgeois multi-storey apartment blocks, which gentrified the street, if not the quarter. The Mertens Trade House on the Nevsky and the

*Trams on the frozen Neva, the spire of the Peter and Paul Fortress Cathedral and factory chimneys beyond.*

Azov-Don Bank offered mighty modern structures worthy of determined capitalism.[27]

There were still some 14,000 street traders in St Petersburg, but increasingly retail trade was conducted in markets or in the new department stores. The *gostiny dvor* traded in quality goods, as did *Passazh*, which boasted sixty individual outlets selling elegant furnishings and high-class fashion. Modelled on the nineteenth-century Parisian *passages couverts*, the gallery included a Café de Paris and a branch of the Crédit Lyonnais bank. Petersburg's new department stores sold all the paraphernalia for an emergent bourgeoisie – many designs confirming that *stil moderne* had gone beyond the boutiques to reach a wider market. Elsewhere along the Nevsky, luxury items replaced the food and consumer goods that were prevalent half a century earlier. Beauty became big business. Countless shops were dedicated to the pursuit of youth and there were interminable adverts in magazines for lotions and potions.[28] But that is to view a troubled capital cosmetically.

There was a new sensationalism and brashness. Hoardings and adverts spread like acne across the elegant buildings of the Nevsky. Men paraded with sandwich boards, providing advertising on the move. Newspapers reduced their content for publicity. The population began to crave tales of sex and violence, and the Petersburg press enthusiastically reported muggings – if the victims were beaten to a pulp. Armed robbery and aggressions against women spiralled during the first decades of the twentieth century and, between 1908 and 1913, there was a steep rise in indictments for murder. Pulp fiction revelled in the erotic. The titillating and sadistic novel *The Sex Market*, of 1908, offered a Temple of Eros where people of all ages met for group sex.[29] As an insight into the mores of the age, Alexei Balabanov's disturbing 1998 sepia film *Of Freaks and Men* – set in the twilight of the imperial capital – captures the sadomasochism, sexual exploitation and fervour of a bourgeois world of fringed standard lamps and antimacassars. The film's fascination with physical aberration also harks back to the obsessions of the city's earliest rulers – Empress Anna's jesters and Peter the Great's collection of curiosities in the Kunstkammer.

Student unrest continued to flare. Agitators intent on revolution used 'noxious gases and other terrorist measures' to disrupt those who wished to study. Female students – derided by reactionaries as 'street girls', and scorned for doing something as 'unfeminine' as studying – were discouraged from mixing with their male counterparts, lest they became radicalised. But they did, and they were. Medicine alone was considered suitable for women and, by 1910, Russia had 1,500 women doctors.[30] They were badly needed in St Petersburg. Despite 'placards with glaring red letters' posted 'on house fronts, inside tram cars' and in most public places, warning people against 'drinking raw water', workmen continued to slake their thirst by scooping it in their greasy caps from the foul canals.[31] In 1907, typhoid struck in the poorer quarters. The following year, a cholera epidemic

*St Petersburg soup kitchen, 1910.*

struck 8,000 people and it was noted that 2,500 victims of the typhus outbreak of 1908 were sleeping rough or were long-term inhabitants of one of the city's thirty-four dosshouses. The capital still lacked an adequate underground sewage system. There were still cesspools and rubbish in the courtyards and streets. St Petersburg was ninety million roubles in debt,[32] awash with vice and corruption and – with its leaders constantly jockeying amongst themselves – little seemed to get done.

The Russian Society for the Protection of Women became one of the city's chief pressure groups against prostitution, but it fought a losing battle and many of the city's 500 brothels remained dangerous for prostitutes and patrons alike, as well as being a constant nuisance to their neighbours. Residents of Kronstadt petitioned the authorities to move a brothel whose clients – loud, crude and drunk – habitually accosted women on the surrounding streets. Punters completely blinded by booze often forced entry to the wrong house, yet no action was taken and the brothel remained open. In fashionable parts of the city, the owners or managers of hotels, shops, bars and restaurants pimped their female staff – often not even paying them a wage, but expecting them to make money by selling their bodies. If the middle-men didn't skim off too much commission, the pay was high. Two girls of nine and eleven, who were rescued by the House of Mercy, were earning five times what a female factory hand earned. But the price they paid was monstrous. Illegal abortions multiplied. White slavers operated.[33] A report to the Congress for the Struggle against the Trade in Women claimed that 13 per cent of the capital's prostitutes killed themselves, and that nearly 40 per cent who registered for the first time in 1909 already suffered from venereal disease. Overloaded clinics meant that thorough inspections were impossible. Sometimes an examination consisted of no more than the lifting of a dress. In two of the city's three damp and dirty clinics there was no access to hot water, and the pressure of work meant that doctors often neglected to clean speculums between inspections. An estimated 50,000 prostitutes contended with police corruption, abuse, alcoholism and enslavement and both suffered from and spread syphilis.[34] Into this world came a monk from the Urals who – far from denouncing and saving this Gomorrah – would revel in its amorality.

After producing four daughters, the empress had given birth to the haemophiliac *tsarevich*, Alexei, in 1904. The condition – which prevented blood from clotting – was passed on from his great-grandmother, Queen Victoria. Distressed and desperate for a solution to the *tsarevich*'s frailty, Nicholas and Alexandra turned to the magical powers of a convicted rapist, horse-rustler and holy man, Grigory Rasputin,[35] who decided it was his mission to save the dynasty and, thereby, the country. Sizeable, strong and increasingly well dressed, Rasputin had an exceptional talent for manipulation, which made fashionable St Petersburg putty in his hands. Despite the fact that he behaved like a peasant, wiping his mouth with his satin blouse and leaving orts stranded in his straggling beard, he was a guest at the most fashionable tables, where he proved capable of manipulating the most sophisticated listener. He held court, controlling the discussion by constantly shifting his attention or changing subject, while his topics of conversation ranged from the risqué to the downright indecent.[36] He was suspected of belonging to the ecstatic sect known as the Kristovovery or Khlysty,[37] who believed they had a hotline to the Holy Spirit. Such power of prayer appeared to help Rasputin staunch the flow of the *tsarevich*'s blood, but it also gave him a licence to debauch. When one of his close associates Chionya Berlatskaya accused Rasputin of raping her on a train, he claimed that he had merely exorcised a devil. Morality – he maintained – was merely a cowardly screen to protect people from temptation. It was only through sinning with passion that a person could repent and hence receive salvation. Rasputin offered himself as the catalyst for sin.[38]

Prime minister Stolypin had Rasputin followed by the Okhrana, but by the summer of 1911 Stolypin was out of the way, murdered at the Kiev opera by a double-agent, Mordko Bogrov, who had been assigned to safeguard him.[39] By the end of the year, the St Petersburg press and city gossips were becoming obsessed with the charismatic spiritual leader, who – it was rumoured – spent bath and bedroom time with the emperor's children and had seduced their nurse. The chairman of the Third Duma circulated hectographed copies of letters written to Rasputin by the empress and her daughters, and it is easy to see why Alexandra's sentiments were questioned: 'I kiss your hands . . . To fall asleep forever on your shoulder, in your arms . . . Come quickly . . . I am torment-ing myself for you.'[40] Meanwhile her younger daughters admitted that they often dreamed about the healer. Young boys who had been hawking pornography up and down the Nevsky for some years added to their stock faked scenes involving Rasputin and the Romanovs. Bolsheviks sold pamphlets detailing lewd encounters, and projected faked pictures in the cinema and onto street-corner cycloramas.[41] When the First World War broke out, German Zeppelins showered images over the Russian trenches of the empress and the holy man, and of Nicholas nesting on Rasputin's genitals. Rasputin vied with reactionary ministers and various Romanovs for the title of the most-loathed figure in the capital.

Count Kokovtsov – anxious that press attention gave Rasputin too much publicity and 'played into the hands of all the revolu-tionary organisations' – summoned the 'Siberian tramp'. During their encounter he was 'shocked by the repulsive expression' in Rasputin's puckered, deep-set eyes, which fixed on the minister as if in an attempt to hypnotise him. When Kokovtsov suggested that the healer disappear, so as not to harm the monarchy, Rasputin screamed, 'It is all lies, calumnies! I do not insist on going to the palace – they summon me.'[42]

The press and the Duma intensified their campaign against Rasputin, and the empress demanded that Kokovtsov silence them. However, when Mikhail Rodzianko, President of the Duma, reported to Nicholas II on 26 February 1912 that 'no revolutionary propaganda could achieve as much as Rasputin's mere presence at court',[43] and provided numerous examples of people corrupted and driven to distraction by his behaviour, the tsar was understandably upset. The Ministry of the Interior plotted an assassination – but the minister lost his nerve. Fleeing the capital, Rasputin returned to Siberia, where he indulged himself sexually and practised distance-healing on the heir to the throne.[44]

With Petersburg agog with scandal and increasingly unstable, many people began to express nostalgia for a world that was fast disappearing. Alexandre Benois – who became Vice-President of the Society for the Protection and Preservation of Russian Monuments of Art and Antiquity – recalled that, as a child, he became delirious whenever he 'heard the loud, nasal cries of the travelling showman, "Here's Petrushka! Come, good people and see the show!"' As an adult, Benois decided to celebrate the magic of the mid-nineteenth-century Butter Week fair, which had enchanted inhabitants and visitors alike. In the 1860s, Lord Redesdale had recorded that, during *Maslenitsa*, the area around the Admiralty was 'entirely taken up by booths, circuses, giants and dwarfs, cheap pantomimes and ballets, boneless contortionists and the inevitable Hercules of the Fair with his weights and clubs'.[45] As that had all vanished by the early years of the twentieth century, Benois was determined to recapture it. Ironically, his evocation of old St Petersburg, with the ballet *Petrushka*, served as a testimony to the city's striking cultural diaspora. He may have conceived and designed the work in the capital, but Stravinsky wrote the music on the Côte d'Azur, Fokine and Diaghilev rehearsed it in Rome, and it premiered in Paris at the Théâtre du Châtelet on 13 June 1911. With western Europe increasingly anxious about the possibility of revolution in Russia, there was an appetite for visions of the old, picturesque St Petersburg, and the ballet was a hit.[46] Stravinsky remembered that Enrico Cecchetti, the legendary ballet master who played the magician, was so old that a long false beard was unnecessary. Nijinsky's Petrushka, was 'the most exciting human being' the composer had ever seen onstage.[47]

Premiering two years later, *The Rite of Spring* had a more complex relationship to St Petersburg. The ballet's folk rituals evoke Russia before Peter opened a window onto Europe. Yet, reinvented through strange choreography and cacophonic sound, the piece helped to forge the musical and choreographic revolutions of the twentieth century. Stravinsky spent the summer of 1911 at Princess Tenisheva's arts-and-crafts establishment at Talashkino, working with Nicholas Roerich on the decor of the ballet. Roerich – a neo-Russian artist – was an acknowledged authority on myth and, for his score, Stravinsky took inspiration from Slavic folk song. But there were also more immediate and personal influences. The first music Stravinsky remembered was the brazen taratantara of a military fanfare from the nearby barracks. But a sound that had made an even deeper impression on the boy was the tympanic noise of ice breaking on the Neva.[48] This mutated, in the composer's mind, into the harangue that bursts on the sad, high-pitched bassoon solo which opens *The Rite of Spring*. Nijinsky's choreography and Stravinsky's score were so revolutionary that, when the ballet premiered at the Théâtre des Champs-Elysées in May 1913, there was cat-calling and booing. Jokers among a shocked audience pretended to summon dentists to treat the obviously stricken dancers. In the fracas, someone was challenged to a duel, and the uproar resulted in a sold-out season. Diaghilev was thrilled and wanted to return home and scandalise the Russian capital, but the only non-imperial theatre that was large enough – the *narodni dom*, or People's Palace – had burned to the ground the year before. When the score alone was eventually performed in St Petersburg and Moscow under Sergei Koussevitzky, it stimulated scant enthusiasm or outrage.[49] That response, coupled with the confiscations and deprivations of the revolution, effectively severed Stravinsky's association with his native land. He had grown up in a city where ballet was part of the fabric of life. Yet, however much he loved it, as he matured he felt that dance would not be a viable medium for any ambitious and serious composer.[50] How wrong he had been. Through the vision of Diaghilev, not only had dance been revivified, but twentieth-century music had also been born.

After Diaghilev took so much Petersburg talent to the West, artists and entrepreneurs who remained in the city took up the challenges that he had initiated through *Mir Istkusstva*. In January 1909, Sergei Makovsky, the publisher of *Apollon*, mounted a huge exhibition of modern Russian art in the Menshikov Palace. Salons featured works by painters as diverse as Benois, Bakst, Alexei von Jawlensky and Vasily Kandinsky. What is striking is the crucial role that some of these artists were to play in the history of modern art. Kandinsky went on to set up the expressionist *Der Blaue Reiter* group in Munich. Of its six founding members, three were Russian: von Jawlensky – who had been stationed in St Petersburg as a young officer – had taken lessons with Ilya Repin; Marianne von Werefkin had been born in Tula; and Moscow-born Kandinsky spent his youth in Russia and Europe and made a significant contribution to developing the all-important non-objective nature of modern art, which was every bit as consequential as Stravinsky's scores were to music.

Theatre in St Petersburg took an exciting turn when the actress Vera Komissarzhevskaya began to promote young dramatists and directors – among them Vsevelod Meyerhold. Her productions pushed back the barriers of taste and morality and, in 1908, her production of *Salomé* – dubbed 'pornographic' by the Holy Synod – was banned. The most spectacular pre-war scandal, however, was presented at the Luna Park Theatre in the same year that *The Rite of Spring* shocked Paris. *Victory Over the Sun* was an avant-garde spectacle presented by artists and writers who belonged to the Union of Youth. A short-lived Petersburg futurist group, Union of Youth mounted six exhibitions between 1910 and the outbreak of the First World War and effectively set the style for art in Russia after the revolution. *Victory Over the Sun* was Dadaist before its time, for it was not until 1916 that the Dada cabaret at Zurich's Café Voltaire declared war on the civilisation that went to war. The café stood – coincidentally – in Spiegelgasse, the same tiny but consequential street where Lenin was in hiding. The Union of Youth – product of a society disrupted by seismic fault-lines – pre-empted Dada. The curtain didn't rise on *Victory*; it was ripped apart. Kasemir Malevich designed the colourful cardboard costumes of the strongmen who set out to conquer the sun. He credited the experience as the beginning of his Suprematist work, which reached its logical conclusion with his painting *White on White* of 1918. This presented a square – a form not found in nature – and whiteness. Malevich shed substance and materiality with his revolutionary vision of infinity: a new heaven that ranged beyond the skies of Marian blue in Western religious art. As with *The Rite of Spring* in Paris, the audience at *Victory Over the Sun* booed and hollered so much that it was difficult to hear if the craziest sounds were coming from the stage or from the spectators.[51]

Filippo Marinetti's provocative *Futurist Manifesto* was translated into Russian in 1909, and Marinetti visited St Petersburg prior to the First World War to scandalise and proselytise. While some Petersburg aesthetes distrusted Marinetti's furious ego, his futurism – with its celebration of the machine – resonated in an electrified capital that was beginning to choke on the exhaust of fossil fuel. There were more than 3,000 private cars and motor taxis on Petersburg's streets. Inhabitants watched as the world's first four-engined aeroplane, designed by Sikorsky, flew over the capital with sixteen people and a dog on board.[52] By the second decade of the twentieth century Russian artists were not just interacting with but were also stimulating the European avant-garde. They created Rayonism, Suprematism and – later – Constructivism. Artists such as Natalia Goncharova, Mikhail Larionov and Kasemir Malevich worked in a climate of danger, excitement and optimism, believing in the promise of a revolutionary tomorrow.

Over the New Year of 1911–12, the Second All-Russian Congress of Artists was held in St Petersburg. The 200 presentations included talks on education and aesthetics, and debates on neo-Russianism versus the avant-garde. The highlight of the congress was a reading and discussion of Kandinsky's seminal *Concerning the Spiritual in Art*. The essay expressed the idea – so fundamental to an understanding of modern art – that, in the attempt to express inner truths, the artist must renounce 'all consideration of external form'. Form, claimed Kandinsky, was 'most often expressive when least coherent' – an idea that ricocheted through the work of Picasso and other giants of the twentieth century. By 1911, Kandinsky had begun to use a kind of shorthand squiggle to hint at figures and objects, and colour sequences to produce 'intervals' and 'harmonies'. Envious of music – the 'most non-material of the arts' – Kandinsky was highly influenced by the Wagnerian desire for *Gesamtkunstwerk*, the synthesis of many arts.[53]

Moscow-born Alexander Scriabin – towards the end of his short life – attempted to synthesise light, dance, music, colour and incense in his compositions, which were produced on a colour keyboard linked to a turntable of coloured lamps. The ever-powerful Orthodox Church used a similar mix of sensation to carry its message and move souls in its 500 churches spread throughout St Petersburg. During these years, symbolism and the search for transcendence touched painters, poets and even – through the paranormal dabbling of Nicholas, Alexandra and Rasputin – Russia's stuffy rulers. Indeed, spiritual fads or exotic enthusiasms were the disorder of the day. Esoteric philosophies, yoga, eurythmics and Eastern religions gripped a giddy and unstable population who were desperate for change. Unlikely edifices appeared. With support from the Dalai Lama, between 1909 and 1915 a Buddhist temple was constructed on Primorsky Prospekt facing Yelagin Island, architected by Gavriil Baranovsky, who also created the *stil-moderne* Eliseev emporium opposite Ostrovsky Square on the Nevsky Prospekt.[54]

Flights of fancy to escape the material world and dislodge rationalism, and attempts to approach the rich mysteries of inner life, were numerous. The symbolist Andrei Biely wrote a prose symphony and people were astounded by Nijinsky's leap offstage in *Le spectre de la rose*. The dancer was seen to go up – but never came down, apparently defying gravity like a Sikorsky aeroplane. If symbolists sought to escape the banality of the terrestrial, then the machine was opening up new worlds of velocity and illumination. Darkness became light on Petersburg's nighttime streets. Cars whisked people down the Nevsky at speeds unknown only a few years earlier and sound recording made voices sing for eternity.

However, as the capital soared from recession to boom, the lot of the worker did not improve. But it was the disproportionately bloody response to a peaceful march of strikers in the Siberian Lena Goldfields in April 1912 that triggered further unrest in the capital and set off a new succession of strikes. At Lena, 172 workers had been killed and 372 wounded and there was, consequently, a heavy police presence at the sizeable 1912 Petersburg May Day parade. One year on, the march would swell to 100,000, according to the police, or 250,000, according to *Pravda*. Deepening disgust with the regime resulted in a growing list of pretexts for anniversary demonstrations by workers and organised by socialists – the bungled serf emancipation of 1864, Bloody Sunday, the Lena massacre – to which were added solidarity with stoppages outside the capital, and sympathy for the fifty-two sailors of the Baltic fleet who were accused of revolutionary attitudes and actions in the summer of 1913.[55] Soon

these manifestations of profound discontent would be augmented by protest marches against Russia's involvement in the
First World War and subsequent food shortages. The right-wing
Duma appeared to do little for the workers, and the pace and
size of stoppages increased at a rate that testified to mounting
grievance and despair. There were nine strikes in 1909, 737 in
1912 and 1,632 in the first half of 1914. Some were merely one-
day walk-outs in response to minor incidents, but a substantial
number lasted between a week and a month. These were largely
disputes over conditions, unfair treatment, wages and working
hours, although strikes inspired by the desire for wider political
change also touched heavy industry[56] – a sector on which the
government would need to depend as Europe descended into war.

Trouble was punching at Petersburg's veneer of affluence and
success, yet among the better-off there was a dangerous indifference to the threat. In places like 'Vaskina Village' on Vasilevsky
Island, slum landlords allowed their tenants to exist in similarly
appalling conditions to those first described seventy-five years
earlier by Nikolai Nekrasov. Attitudes to the poor hardened.
Limited sympathy in certain quarters had now been replaced
by fear, and beggars were increasingly identified as pickpockets
and thieves. Hooliganism underlined the social divide, and the
deployment of destructive 'hooligan tactics' by angry workers
was blamed on the dismal lack of leadership by the tsar and his
government.[57]

There was a helter-skelter of elation, panic and fear. The
novelist Alexei Tolstoy observed the descent of the idle and
depressed nouveau riche into depraved oblivion: 'People doped
themselves with music . . . with half naked women . . . with
champagne'.[58] Even after the war began, British secret agent and
diplomat Sir Robert Bruce Lockhart was appalled by the quantity of champagne drunk by saturated officers stumbling through
the luxurious bars of the Astoria and the Hotel Europe, when
they should have been at the front. On the eve of the revolution,

the American reporter John Reed saw gambling clubs where the fizz flowed, the stakes were outrageous and fur-clad, high-class whores paraded.[59] Yet, from the vantage point of hotel cocktail bars, it was almost possible – through the alcoholic haze – to see the long queues of ill-clad people snaking round the block, waiting 'for the bread that never came'.[60]

With entertaining at court mothballed, the British Ambassador, Sir George Buchanan, recalled only one occasion – apart from the New Year's reception – when he was invited to the Winter Palace, and that was to watch a performance of Wagner's *Parsifal* in the Hermitage. He observed that the interval dinner 'hardly came up to one's expectations after all that one heard of the splendours of such entertainments in the past. Neither from a spectacular nor from a gastronomic standpoint could it compare with a State banquet at Buckingham Palace.'[61] But if the tsar was avoiding his social duties, the St Petersburg elite had stepped into the breach. Baron Rosen remembered the winter season of 1913–14 as 'one of the most brilliant'[62] the capital had ever seen. Fancy-dress and themed balls were fashionable, such as Countess Shuvalova's Coloured Wig Ball, designed by Bakst. The cakewalk, one-step and foxtrot were popular dances, and the tango craze spawned a sub-genre of films in the fledgling cinema industry.[63] Baron Rosen was particularly affected by a dance given during carnival week at the palace of the Grand Duchess Vladimir. Nicholas and Alexandra were invited with their four daughters, who 'rapturously' enjoyed 'their first ball – which alas! was to be their last'.[64]

One rare court celebration was the tricentenary of the Romanovs, and although neo-Russianism was finished as a style, it was appropriately exhumed to celebrate a dynasty about to die. Menus, designed by artists such as Viktor Vasnetsov, were embellished by images drawn from folklore and lettered in archaic script. But compared with what such a celebration would have been in the past, the spectacle was self-conscious and muted. Jubilee Day occurred on 21 February 1913 and, on the eve of the celebration, an unrelenting wind battered and destroyed many of the imperial decorations lining the route between the Winter Palace and the Kazan Cathedral, where Mass was to be celebrated. Mikhail Rodzianko ordered Rasputin – newly back in town – out of the cathedral during the celebration. Conflicting attitudes towards the healer only underlined the administrative chaos in the capital. Rasputin's telephone was tapped by the government while, at the same time, the tsar arranged for the Okhrana to protect him. Police reports catalogued a new intensity of drunkenness and debauchery, and charted Rasputin's degrees of intoxication: 'very', 'absolutely', completely' and 'dead drunk'. One can only wonder how many bottles of vodka stood between each classification.

Rasputin went partying till dawn and beyond, and it was not uncommon for him to leave the sexually charged entertainment of Massalsky's Gypsy Chorus after noon. The popular nightclub Villa Rode was shut down after Rasputin was reported rampaging through the restaurant wearing only a shirt.[65] Given the legends, few shirts would be large or long enough to have rendered the holy man halfway decent. According to the American Ambassador, George Marye, Rasputin's apartments were 'the scene of the wildest orgies'. Society women – bored by life – rushed to experience Rasputin's wham-bam-thank-you-ma'am sexual prowess. The poor servant girls living in his building, became victims, while others offered themselves in return for favours as they queued up at Rasputin's desk for help. Marye found the stories circulating almost too outrageous to be true, but accepted that 'they are too numerous' and 'told by too many credible people not to be believed'.[66] The healer exposed himself, to prove his identity, and boasted intimacy with the empress and her daughter Olga. Rasputin – empowered by his court connections and social skills – entered into an informal partnership with the devious homosexual racketeer Mikhail Andronnikov. Melding

*Cartoon of Rasputin and a Romanov heading for the banya.*

his sexual appetite with the conviction that knowledge is power, Andronnikov targeted messenger boys and invited them to his apartment on the Fontanka. He offered food, plied them with drink and, more often than not, had sex with them beneath the wrought-iron thorns crowning the camp, sybaritic shrine that housed his bed. While the boys rested, Andronnikov scoured their bags to uncover information that would allow him to black-mail, bribe and influence the movers and shakers of the capital. Until Rasputin became distrustful of Andronnikov, they made a dangerous team.[67]

Growing hostility to Alexandra's spiritual guide, increasing resentment at the distance and indifference of the stubborn tsar, and rising distrust of the military ambitions and menace of Germany were spiralling out of control. It was voiced by progressives in the government, by angry workers and even by a composer known for his conservatism. Rimsky-Korsakov's last opera, *Le Coq d'Or*, was unperformable by any imperial theatre. Its vision of the idiot tsar Dodon and his blustering, misguided sons was written in 1906–7 as an embittered response to the intransigence of the regime and its stupidity in waging war in the East. Dodon – an out-of-touch tsar who wants to 'forget peril', 'rule from bed' and has never heard the word 'legal' – is a withering *buffo* portrait of Nicholas II. Impossible material for the censor to approve, it was eventually performed after the composer's death in Moscow and then at a private theatre in St Petersburg, where it became – according to Stravinsky – 'a rallying point for students'.[68]

By the summer of 1914, discontent was seething on the streets of the capital. Among the first impressions registered by the daughter of the British Ambassador, Meriel Buchanan, when she arrived in July, was that of a 'crowd of dirty, evil-looking men gathered at the corners'. Among them stood 'a little boy with a torn red blouse' who 'shouted out some unspeakable insult and threw an old bit of stick at the motor'.[69] During the previous month there had been 118 strikes and these coalesced into a general strike, which coincided with the arrival of the French president, Raymond Poincaré. The visit, along with the Serbian crisis, was the top story in the press, keeping the latest eruption of violence among workers off the front page. Half of St Petersburg's factory labour had now downed tools. Transport ground to a halt. Two hundred tramcars were overturned or vandalised, and telegraph poles were uprooted, breaking lines of communication. The number of Bolsheviks in the capital had increased tenfold between 1910 and 1914 and, by July of that year, they had control of the Petersburg Union of Metalworkers. On 9 July, the Central Electricity Station came out on strike.[70] Meanwhile, French flags fluttered and Poincaré dined at Peterhof, where he presented the tsar with a series of Gobelin tapestries designed by the frothy poster artist Jules Chéret.

The American missionary and theologian Jarred Scudder arrived during the general strike. He was struck by the glut of warships in the Neva delta and found the capital 'like a giant fort with mammoth cannon pointing out to sea'. Since its first days, St Petersburg had been a city full of uniforms – now it was a city mobilised. The 'steady tramp of soldiers could be heard at all hours' and anti-German fever ran high, as Russia was threatened by the expansionist ambitions of the impatient and blustering Kaiser Wilhelm II. Excited mobs rolled through the streets, destroying German shop fronts and looting stock as the authorities turned a blind eye. Scudder was booked into the German-owned Astoria Hotel and was greeted in a profoundly guttural French that would have fooled nobody. A mob sacked the German Embassy, recently designed by Peter Behrens on the far side of St Isaac's Square. They rampaged for two hours before the fire brigade arrived to hose down the crowd. Anxious that the Astoria would be the next target, Scudder decamped to the American Embassy, where he found a mass of hysterical Germans seeking asylum. Having made an important contribution to Peter's city, these inhabitants were losing what it had taken them decades to achieve.[71] As for Yiddish-speaking Jews, they were doubtless treasonous and were therefore arrested and shot.

On 28 June, the Serbian agent Gavrilo Princip assassinated Archduke Franz Ferdinand in Sarajevo. Austria would take revenge and wanted German support, knowing that Russia would intervene. France would help Russia. Britain would help France. European war. The tsar celebrated a *Te Deum* in the Winter Palace, appeared on the balcony, and 25,000 patriots fell to their knees. Having been rent by domestic strife, would Russia now unite in combat against Germany? Production was stepped up. Huge contracts landed on the desks of industrialists such as Putilov, Lessner and Lebedev. Orders for 700 field guns, telephone and telegraphy equipment, aircraft engines and millions of shells sent factories into overdrive.[72] In a powerful and didactic sequence in his masterly celluloid polemic *The End of St Petersburg*, Vsevolod Pudovkin revealed the

interdependence of capital and carnage as exploding shells on
the Russian front sent the stock of Putilov, Lessner and Lebedev
soaring. He left the viewer in no doubt about what Russian soldiers were dying for: 'Tsar, homeland, CAPITAL.' In the smoke
and smog-filled air of St Petersburg, the working day – that is,
every day of the week – was extended to up to twelve hours in
machine plants and thirteen hours in textile mills. Accidents
multiplied in the insufferable heat, and inflation devoured rotten
wages. The German-sounding Peterhof became Petrodvorets,
and Petersburg became Petrograd. Meanwhile – as Nabokov
observed – 'Beethoven turned out to be Dutch.'[73]

In the first five months of the First World War, Russia lost
nearly two million men. During the bitter winter of 1914–15,
shortages of food and fuel at home began to impinge. Meriel
Buchanan remembers that when the hot-water pipes burst in
the British Embassy – housed in a palace built by Catherine the
Great for her favourite, Sergei Saltikov – guests were obliged to
sit wrapped up in their fur coats. They were the lucky ones. On
the streets, the crowds and flags disappeared, lines for bread
and milk lengthened, and wives and parents clustered round
shop windows on the Nevsky where the telegrams of death were
posted.[74] As the Germans advanced in the summer of 1915,
trainloads of soldiers – thousands, daily – were carried to the
front while the wounded, along with countless refugees, flooded
into the capital.[75] Shanty towns sprung up. Petrograd reverted to
the uncertainties of St Petersburg's earliest days.

A soup kitchen was started by the ladies of the British Embassy.
They held sewing parties and started a relief fund.[76] A British
Convalescent Home on Vasilevsky Island and an Anglo–Russian
hospital on the Nevsky were supervised by the ambassador's
wife. The Americans opened an orphanage, and the empress
set up a hospital in the Winter Palace with well over a hundred
beds crammed into the Nicholas Hall. Alexandre Benois visited
the dimly lit wards and saw, elsewhere in the palace, that the

decorations added by Nicholas and Alexandra revealed 'an outstanding lack of taste'.[77]

Fokine remained ballet master at the Mariinsky throughout the war. There were new productions for which people queued long hours in all weather, watching the latest recruits bayonet hay-stuffed dummies as they drilled in Teatralnaya Square. The ballet audience appeared grimmer and greyer – gone were the splendid uniforms and exotic frocks.[78] After a performance, Karsavina recalled that artists congregated at the Stray Dog, a brashly decorated, cramped and clubby cabaret. There was dancing. There were satirical sketches tumbling over one another in anarchic delight. There were talks, discussions and debates. On Monday evenings – continuing the tradition of Nurok and Nouvel's Contemporary Music society – the Stray Dog presented serious concerts.[79] Diaghilev wrote asking Karsavina to join the Ballets Russes in a tour of America. She protested that she neither could nor would: 'In the great sadness of those years I would not of my own accord have missed a day.' As for Diaghilev, he brought everything the Nevsky Prospekt had taught him to a thoroughgoing understanding of Broadway. He chided Americans for their inappropriate nostalgia for European elegance, when he – who helped shape modernism – knew the importance of the flashiness and brashness of the Great White Way: 'It is time the American people realised themselves. Broadway is genuine.' It offered the multitude of absurd impressions that had surprised Gogol on the Nevsky Prospekt: a hairdo, a hat, a nose, a tart, an overcoat, a sign, a jolt, a jostle – speed, rhythm, razzamatazz. Diaghilev loved it: Broadway was the Nevsky run riot. For all its backwardness and incoherence, Russia was making waves in a new age in the new world. Diaghilev spoke to the *New York Times* about his 1905 portrait exhibiition at the Tauride: 'It has always seemed wonderful to me that in the same year the portraits of the nobility went out of the Palais, the Duma, representative of the people, came in.'[80] So Karsavina stayed in

Petrograd, danced and enjoyed the company of artists revitalised by the uncertainties of the future. She was also lucky enough to savour the delights of a rapidly vanishing order. She often dined with Maurice Paléologue, the French Ambassador – on one occasion at an early hour, so guests could enjoy the sunset over the Neva. It was, she recalled 'a charming party; the sunset alone failed'.[81] A few years and a different world later, the poet Osip Mandelstam dreamed that

> We shall meet again, in Petersburg,
> as though we had buried the sun there.[82]

Outside the theatres, palaces and embassies, the warm autumn of 1916 grew 'feverish' with 'richly coloured gossip', food riots grew in 'frequency and scale' and public meetings were forbidden.[83] Meriel Buchanan noted that Empress Alexandra's 'stiffness and aloofness . . . alienated all circles and the court of Russia'. It was rumoured, she wrote, that the 'Empress trafficked with Germans' and 'everywhere the slander spread and ripened . . . The German influence at court! . . . The power of Rasputin!'[84] There was hearsay that the grand duchesses were smuggling gold to Germany in coffins that allegedly contained corpses.[85] In November 1916, the tsar was forced to replace Boris Sturmer, because the prime minister had a German name. There would be a cascade of prime ministers as the country tumbled towards revolution. Sturmer was replaced by Alexander Trepov, whose father had been shot by Vera Zasulich and whose older brother – during the troubles of 1905 – became notorious for instructing his troops not to spare bullets. Infiltrating bread queues, German agents were stirring the hungry and disaffected against the war. The danger of the unholy coalition – the German-born empress and the degenerate Rasputin – pushed the powerful and the responsible into plots. A troika attempted to kill Rasputin.[86] A motor car hit his sleigh and overturned it. He survived. A story circulated that the reprobate was bragging about his sexual encounters with the royal family when a shocked Prince Yusupov offered his pistol, for Rasputin to do the decent thing. Rasputin turned it on Yusupov – but missed. The killing of the healer was, in fact, less spontaneous.[87]

The Yusupov Mansion on the Moika, with its elegant rotunda, its Moresque salon, its jewel of a theatre, its furniture once owned by Marie-Antoinette and its gallery full of paintings by Watteau, Fragonard and Rembrandt, was the home of the fabulously wealthy transvestite Felix Yusupov. Married to the tsar's niece, Irina, the slight Prince Felix was an accomplished cross-dresser. He had been thrilled to be ogled by Edward VII in Paris, and also got his kicks from tarting with Nevsky prostitutes. When he returned from studying at Oxford in 1909, he had consulted Rasputin about his sexuality. The holy man gave Yusupov advice and attempted to debauch him. Seven years later, the prince was in the visitors' gallery of the Duma when he heard the URP leader, Vladimir Purishkevich, railing against Rasputin. Together they hatched a conspiracy.

On 16 December 1916, Yusupov lured the healer to his mansion, perhaps with the promise of pimping his wife. Six cakes containing potassium cyanide, along with poisoned wine, were prepared. At first Rasputin – who was invited for a hot night out – refused this modest hospitality and, in the absence of the beautiful Irina, suggested going to a nightclub. As Yusupov procrastinated, his guest started to nibble the cakes and sip the wine, but they appeared to have no effect, and the impatient Yusupov went to fetch his Browning. Bored by the lack of action, Rasputin insisted, once again, on a night out. Yusupov suggested that he should rather pray, and then shot him. Rasputin slumped, then revived and broke out of the mansion, with Purishkevich hard on his heels, shooting at him. It was 4 a.m. Soldiers passing came to investigate and expressed their relief at the murder. Heavily bound and weighted, Rasputin was dumped through a hole in the ice near the Petrovsky Bridge. As the news spread across the capital, people rejoiced. Strangers embraced. Cabbies refused tips. One of the conspirators was given a standing ovation at the theatre.[88] Then, on the 19th, the body was recovered. In spite of the distress of the empress, the tsar was advised not to punish the assassins. Alexander Kerensky, who would lead Russia's post-imperial Provisional Government, suggested – mistakenly – that the murder would strengthen the monarchy. The British Ambassador thought the assassination, 'though prompted by patriotic motives, was a fatal mistake. It made the Empress more determined than ever to be firm, and it set a dangerous example, for it prompted people to translate their thoughts into action.'[89]

The action had started long ago. It began with Radishchev and Herzen and Chernyshevsky and gathered strength in the salons, garrets and open spaces of St Petersburg. It intensified when Dmitri Karakozov fired six shots at Nicholas II. Vera Figner and her friends raised the pitch of protest to regicide when they blew the emperor to kingdom come. Action simmered on factory floors and rocked the capital with protest and revolution in 1905. It gathered strength as Russia went to war and the empire was abandoned to Alexandra and Rasputin. So it was hardly surprising that, by February 1917, Kokovtsov felt everybody 'sensed that something extraordinary was about to happen but no one had any clear idea what it would be'.[90] Weariness with the war was undermining well-being. Shortages of basic food had become more acute over the previous months. Alexander Kerensky, the lawyer and politician who was soon to play a key role in the first of the two 1917 revolutions, noted that for the women queuing for whatever food was available, hunger was 'becoming the only tsar'. Prices rose steeply and, on the morning of 23 February, workers in a textile mill in the Vyborg district downed tools in desperation. It was International Women's Day, temperatures rose and people took to the streets, clamouring for bread. That evening, bakers were looted in the poorer quarters, and Cossacks went thundering down the Nevsky to protect the celebrated *patisserie* Filipov, which was besieged for its chocolate cakes and tarts.[91] Meriel Buchanan thought it hardly surprising that the Bolshevik promise of 'Bread – Peace – and Freedom' should have tempted a people who were uneducated and untaught, and worn out by three years of untold suffering. David Francis, who had arrived in the capital nearly a year earlier 'as Ambassador from the greatest Republic of the New World to the Court of the mightiest Autocracy of the Old', heard of German agitators stirring unrest among those in the long lines 'waiting to be served small amounts of sugar or meat in the shops where such things are distributed'.

By 25 February, the protest had taken on the dimensions of a general strike – 270,000 workers in 2,000 enterprises had downed tools, and students came out in support. Tram drivers and cabbies, vulnerable to attack by angry mobs, stopped working. The following day, people from all walks of life – from domestics to civil servants – joined the uprising. In Znamenskaya Square tension rose steadily throughout the icy afternoon until, once again, a Sunday became bloody and fifty demonstrators were shot. Nicholas, safely at Tsarskoe Selo with his family, was alerted. But what could he do? The Pavlovsky Regiment of the imperial guard mutinied and the rebellion spread, the following day, to the Semyonovsky Guards.[92]

Posters went up everywhere banning demonstrations – those who did not return to work the following day would be sent to the front. A few streets from the American Embassy, the cook to the commercial attaché was traumatised as he witnessed a sabre severing a policeman's head. Sharp fragments of ice were hurled at the police on the street. Some officers, firing from windows and rooftops, prompted students and soldiers to break into the buildings where they nested and drag the snipers out into the street for public execution.[93] Machine guns spat into the Sunday strollers on the Nevsky, sending them scattering down

Mikhailovskaya Street out of the line of fire. In the rout, as motor cars accelerated and horse-drawn sledges galloped, people were hit and children trampled to death – 'nearly a hundred unarmed people were shot down'.[94]

On Monday 27th, Kokovtsov was walking his dog along Mokhovaya Street in the early afternoon when bullets, once again, began to fly. It proved to be a decisive day. The law courts on Liteiny Prospekt, and police stations across the city, were set ablaze. Cossacks refused to face down the crowds. Meriel Buchanan, arriving back from holiday in Finland, was met by English officers in full uniform. Their embassy car was stopped at a barricade, but was eventually allowed to pass. Once safely home on the banks of the Neva, the ambassador's daughter was not allowed to leave and sat listening to the rattle of machine guns. Her father was at the Ministry of Foreign Affairs when General Alfred Knox telephoned from the embassy with news that a large part of the Petersburg garrison had mutinied and was in control of the Liteiny Prospekt.[95] By the evening, the Duma in the Tauride Palace was occupied by a mob of students, workmen and renegade soldiers, who were joining the people in droves. An announcement was made to the huge crowd outside. A Provisional Executive Committee of the Soviet Workers' Deputies was created, operating from rooms of the Duma Budget Commission. They issued a declaration in *Izvestia Zhurnalistov*, the sole paper published on 27 February, appealing for representatives of workers, soldiers and the people of Petrograd to attend a meeting in the Duma premises that evening. At about midnight, a bedraggled figure in a soiled fur coat wandered in and declared, 'I am the late Minister of the Interior, Protopopov. I desire the welfare of our country, and so I surrender myself voluntarily.' Despite the fact that he was a 'follower of Rasputin and certainly not quite sane',[96] Protopopov's capitulation signalled the end of the old order.

On Tuesday 28 February, fighting continued as prisons were sacked and inmates were liberated. The Admiralty surrendered, under threat of bombardment from soldiers sympathetic to the revolution who were positioned in the Peter and Paul Fortress. The house of Count Fredericks – a close friend to the tsar – was looted and torched. When the servants tried to lead the count's horses from the burning stables, they were ordered to lead them back and barricade the animals inside.[97] On 2 March, Nicholas abdicated in favour of his brother, the Grand Duke Mikhail, who was 'to govern in full union with the national representatives sitting in the Legislative Institutions . . . May God help Russia.'[98] On 3 March, the emperor-of-a-day abdicated, asking people 'to obey the Provisional Government . . . until, within as short a time as possible, the Constituent Assembly, elected on a basis of universal, equal and secret suffrage, shall express the will of the nation regarding the form of government to be adopted'. Colonel Romanov, aka Nicholas II, was placed under guard at Tsarkoe Selo and advised to flee the country. He refused.[99] The long final sequence of Alexander Sokurov's film *Russian Ark* presents a moving requiem. After the most exuberant and spirited Winter Palace ball, the music stops and the guests in their gaudy regalia start down the Jordan staircase, mumbling unintelligible social noise as people do when they leave a party. Some of them are clearly bewildered as if they sense they are about to face a struggle between desperate, sometimes ignorant and often misled people, people who would fumble through the dark aftermath of autocracy. As the camera travels through a palace window to the misty Neva, the observation – 'the sea is all around' – dissolves imperial Petersburg into the marshy shore that preceded its founder.

The British Ambassador noted that the government, 'by ordering the troops to fire on the people . . . fanned the prevailing discontent into a blaze that spread with lightning speed over the whole town'.[100] Socialist propaganda – aided by German agents intent on knocking Russia out of the war – was effective among soldiers in their barracks and workers in their factories.

The violence continued. In early March, soldiers forced entry to the chapel where Rasputin's coffin lay, and measured his penis. Under orders from Kerensky, they were to remove the body and bury it in an unmarked grave. When their lorry broke down and a crowd gathered, it was decided to cremate the corpse without its penis – if later claims are to be believed. As for Prince Yusupov, he fled the revolution with two Rembrandts and a collection of snuff boxes, and charged his coffers with a defamation suit against MGM and their film *Rasputin and the Empress* – a victory that prompted Hollywood's obsessive use of disclaimers. As for Rasputin's daughter, Maria, she became a lion-tamer in the USA.[101]

In Petrograd, old tsarist officials were under guard and under threat. Kokovtsov was abducted on the way to the bank by a group who commandeered a car and paraded him along the Nevsky, shouting that here was 'the former tsarist minister, the thief, Count Kokovtsov caught red-handed dragging from the bank a million roubles with which to rescue the tsar'. After the incident, the Kokovtsovs were assigned live-in guards to monitor them day and night.[102]

At the end of March, the American Ambassador became the first authority to recognise the Provisional Government that had been established on 11 March. The man who came to be its leader after the July disturbances, Alexander Kerensky, was short and of an 'extremely nervous temperament'. By sheer coincidence, he had attended the same school in Simbirsk on the Volga as Vladimir Ilyich Ulyanov.[103] Miscalculating that the soviet movement would implode, Kerensky's short-lived government would be toppled by that childhood acquaintance, who – by October 1917 – had become, as Lenin, the Chairman of the People's Commissars. In the meantime, under the Provisional Government, by early April a semblance of order had returned to the capital. Factories were back at work, but producing less. Dancers and singers at the Mariinsky performed, its auditorium stripped of imperial eagles, its ushers wearing greasy jackets, its audience including workers.

Diaghilev's troupe was performing at the Teatro Constanzi in Rome when Kerensky took power, and the impresario was summoned home to become Minister of the Fine Arts – an offer he refused. A more immediate problem was that the troupe could no longer use the tsarist national anthem as a curtain-raiser, and Stravinsky sat up all night orchestrating that dirge of serfdom, 'The Volga Boatmen', which Mily Balakirev included in his 1860s collection of folk songs. Later, in Paris, when it was sung and the red flag was unfurled onstage before a performance of *The Firebird*, *Le Figaro* took exception. Diaghilev tartly retorted, 'In Russia today the red flag is the emblem of those who recognise that the well-being of the world depends on the freedom of its people.'[104]

As America entered the war, Germany deployed a secret weapon to disrupt the Russian effort. They allowed Lenin and thirty Bolshevik comrades to speed across their territory in a sealed train in order to reach Russia. Arriving in Petrograd on 3 April, Lenin was smuggled in an armoured car to the Kschessinskaya mansion, which he occupied with the help of sympathetic troops. From a small kiosk in the garden, the Bolshevik leader stirred the population against the war and the bourgeois government. He wanted peace and the transfer of power to the soviets. He would no longer accept the Menshevik vision that communism would be achieved through the present bourgeois revolution. In his 'April Theses', Lenin declared his contempt for a Provisional Government that comprised 'capitalists and landlords', and he encouraged Bolsheviks to struggle to transfer power to the soviets. Opposite the mansion was the Cirque Moderne, which could hold up to 10,000 spectators and – although badly lit and gloomy – was ideal for revolutionary meetings.[105] As a result of such gatherings, and of urgent canvassing in factories and on the streets, the Bolsheviks raised their membership fortyfold between the spring of 1917 and the October Revolution. May Day celebrations brought the centre of Petrograd to a standstill, with the peaceful demonstration of thousands of socialists, demanding bread and peace, waving red flags and singing the 'Marseillaise'. But Lenin's strategy of street manifestations failed to deliver these demands, and in early July the streets were, once again, covered in blood. After a peaceful Bolshevik march, the government decided to ban demonstrations and appealed to the Cossacks to disperse the crowds. A lorry full of revolutionary Kronstadt sailors with a machine gun mounted at the rear retaliated by gunning down a cavalcade of Cossacks approaching Liteiny Bridge, scattering bodies over four blocks. In the 'driving rain . . . the street was . . . running with blood'.[106] On 3 July, soldiers of the First Machine Gun Regiment – refusing to be sent to the front – came out on the streets in aid of the soviet cause. Thousands of workers joined them, as did 20,000 Kronstadt sailors. When Kerensky ordered a severe response to the Bolshevik insurrection, Lenin fled to Finland.

*Troops of the Provisional Government firing on peaceful demonstrators, 4 July 1917.*

A sometime Menshevik who had come over to the Bolsheviks was briefly arrested. According to Raymond Robbins, head of the American Red Cross Mission, Leon Trotsky was 'a poor kind of a son of a bitch but the greatest Jew since Christ'.[107] After four days of detention, Trotsky was released and cunningly prepared for a coup under the cover of the first All-Russian Congress of Soviets, which would become the supreme governing body of the country after the socialist revolution. By the time Lenin returned to a Petrograd suburb, bread rations had fallen yet again and sugar was 'a perhaps'. From Catherine the Great's sceptre on the statue fronting the Alexandrinsky Theatre, a tiny red flag waved.[108]

Although Kerensky styled himself the man 'to save Russia', Sir George Buchanan suggested that the Provisional Government 'lost a unique opportunity of putting down the Bolsheviks once and for all after the disturbances' in July. As a measure of how things had changed, when Buchanan and fellow ambassadors were invited to the opera, they were introduced to the surprising occupants of the royal box: Vera Figner and Vera Zasulich – heroines of the long struggle against autocracy.[109]

During August, the Romanov family were removed to Tobolsk in Siberia, in case the Bolsheviks prevailed or the German army pushed through. Red propaganda was making an impact in the trenches, and deserters were streaming into Petrograd. To stop everything falling apart, General Lavr Kornilov – the former tsarist Chief of Staff, whom Kerensky appointed Commander-in-Chief – advanced on the capital to mount a coup. His intention was to set up a military dictatorship or perhaps even restore the monarchy. Railway workers refused to transport his troops, and workers and the Red Guard turned out to defend the city. The attempt disintegrated and Kornilov was placed under arrest. Meanwhile, people worried about the chance of bombardment from the sea. The late-summer German advance on Riga, and its fall, threw Petrograd into panic. Women and children from the British colony were evacuated. State archives were to be moved to Moscow and there was talk of government relocation. Barges were loaded with official documents and ciphers – one was packed with such enthusiasm that it sank under the weight of the infamous tsarist paperwork. More than 800 crates were prepared to ship Hermitage treasures to the safety of the Moscow Kremlin. Two trains departed over the following weeks, but a third was prevented by the upsets of late October.[110]

Kerensky appealed to the people to support his government and, in desperation, on 24 October the printing presses of several Bolshevik papers were seized. But it was too late. The initiative had passed into the hands of the revolutionaries. Soldiers insulted the police. Cossacks killed policemen. A crowd beat a soldier to death in the street for stealing.[111]

On 25 October, at about eight on a raw morning, the cruiser *Aurora* – which had survived the Strait of Tsushima – arrived from Kronstadt, manned by sailors sympathetic to the revolution. On the streets of Petrograd there was sporadic gunfire, but the military were increasingly going over to the Bolsheviks. Motor cars used by members of the government were vandalised or appropriated – though Kerensky, borrowing an American flag from one of the secretaries at the US Embassy, went off under diplomatic cover to muster the troops and master the situation. The following day, 26 October, delegates from the revolutionary committee, backed by armoured cars, came to the Winter Palace to demand an unconditional surrender. There was no reply and at about nine o'clock the *Aurora* fired a blank over the Neva.[112]

Karsavina was performing that night. The audience was sparse and only one-fifth of the company was dancing. Afterwards she was on her way to dine in the Millionnaya when machine guns started to rattle, and the dancer worried that she might get it in the leg. After dinner, while walking home, she saw someone shot and tumble into the gently falling snow.[113] When people awoke on 27 October 1917, the city was white; the government was red.

# PART III

# COMRADES & CITIZENS

*1917–2017*

# 12

# RED PETROGRAD

*1917–21*

I f the city was surprisingly quiet, the Smolny was buzzing.
Quarenghi's gracious Palladian Institute for Noble Maidens had been requisitioned by the Petrograd soviet to function
as the nerve centre of their revolution. Messengers clutching
urgent despatches and porters staggering under large bundles of
propaganda bumped along sporadically lit corridors thick with
cigarette smoke. Crudely lettered placards, slung on doors to
former classrooms, signalled the new scheme of things: 'Union of
Socialist Soldiers', 'Central Committee of the Petrograd Soviet'.
According to eyewitness reporter John Reed, the huge meeting hall – freezing, since fuel ran short – was now baking with
'the stifling heat of unwashed human bodies' in feverish debate.
A Harvard-educated radical with the eagerness of an excited
puppy, Reed was convinced that Petrograd was about to spark
world revolution. His celebrated account, *Ten Days that Shook
the World* – as partisan as Eisenstein's film *October* – offers a
spirited picture of the first days of the revolution.

Reed's wife, fellow reporter Louise Bryant, was also in the
Smolny. She rejoiced at the sound of typewriters clicking in a
hundred rooms and marvelled at the meetings of soviets from
across Russia. Delegates who had never spoken in public before

came mud-covered and blood-spattered from the trenches to make impassioned pleas to the assembly.[1]

The American Embassy in Petrograd 'regarded Mr Reed as a suspicious character and had him watched'. They found out that he was a socialist who 'believes that the workmen can manage the factories themselves'[2] – anathema to the representatives of a robustly capitalist republic. Reed was exultant as he watched the drama of October 1917 gather speed. Kerensky made his last desperate appeal for support from the Russian people on 11 October, the day before the Petrograd soviet formed a Military Revolutionary Committee to direct their insurrection. On the days leading up to the revolution there were pockets of Bolshevik agitation scattered around the country and in Petrograd, on 22 October, there was a major fund-raising drive: the Day of the Petrograd Soviet.[3] On the 23rd, Reed recorded that 'two thousand Red Guards tramped down the Zagorodny Prospekt behind a military band playing the *Marseillaise*', 'blood red flags' held aloft. All the 'business men, speculators, investors, landowners, army officers, politicians, teachers, students, professional men, shopkeepers' and clerks were against them. On 'the side of the Soviets were the rank and file of the workers'.[4]

Overnight on 24 October, the Military Revolutionary Committee instructed Red Guards to seize key institutions: army garrisons, railway stations and Lvov's Central Post Office on Pochtamtskaya Street. Volunteers drawn from factories and the military, the Red Guard were detailed to use force to protect soviet power. They would later become part of the Red Army founded under Trotsky's leadership. A Women's Battalion had been created to to set an example of courage to male troops reluctant to attack the enemy. When they assembled in Palace Square to leave for the front, the Red Guards dispersed them and – like the 1880 bomber, Stephan Khalturin, with his dynamite and detonating agents – wandered into the palace through the service entrance. Apprehending members of the Provisional

Government, they took possession without violence. Some started to pilfer, and both Bryant and Reed recorded the reproaches of optimistic revolutionaries standing at the threshold of decency and fairness: 'Comrades, this is the people's palace. This is our palace.'[5] 'Comrades! Don't take anything. This is the property of the people.'[6] In Pudovkin's 1927 film, *The End of St Petersburg*, the wife of one of the comrades arrives at the palace with what was to have been a hot meal for her husband. She carries an empty pot because she has distributed its contents to other hungry Red Guards. The revolution was more important than family ties.

Others had a different take on the events. Sir George Buchanan recorded that soldiers and workers 'looted and smashed whatever they could lay their hands on'. As for the Women's Battalion, Buchanan sent General Knox to obtain their release from a barracks 'where they were being most brutally treated by the soldiers'.[7] Marta Almedingen heard 'grim stories' about lamp posts 'decorated with policemen'.[8] Anarchists and opportunists armed themselves, seized some of the best houses and lived by

*A Red Guard picket in the Smolny courtyard, 11 October 1917.*

mob rule. Members of the Provisional Government narrowly escaped a lynching as they were escorted from the palace to the Peter and Paul Fortress.[9] Robert Bruce Lockhart recalled that Moisei Uritsky – later chief of the Petrograd Cheka – was 'pulled from his sleigh by bandits, stripped of all his clothes, and left to continue his journey in a state of nudity'. Meriel Buchanan's car was stopped by a shot from Red Guards who wanted to commandeer the vehicle. With a pistol pressed to his temple, an embassy official protested that the car was British. He prevailed and they drove home. Bruce Lockhart never went out alone, never ventured far and kept his finger on the trigger of the pistol in his pocket.[10] People lived in terror of a motor car without lights, which toured the city intermittently, machine-gunning at random. The British Ambassador was told by his doctor that he 'was at the end of his tether' as friends arrived 'to take refuge in the embassy'. Their own cellars had been 'occupied by soldiers who were indulging in indiscriminate firing'. Theft and murder were 'becoming common everyday proceedings'.[11]

During December, wine cellars and storage depots in the city were ransacked. Bolshevik militias were sent to arrest pillaging workers in the Winter Palace. Some of them took to the priceless vintages and became too drunk to carry out their duty. Thousands of bottles were broken or smashed on the Neva's ice, to prevent rioters drowning in alcohol. Armed tenants mounted guard in halls and courtyards twenty-four hours a day. Cashiers and shopkeepers were murdered for the meagre contents of a till, and more and more shops were boarded up. Gangs found rich pickings in the vacant apartments of the bourgeoisie. When sailors, soldiers and police raided the thieves' den near the Obvodnovo Canal, they uncovered a staggering hoard of swag.[12]

Meanwhile, proclamations flew out from the Smolny – a spate of decrees worthy of Paul I. 'TO THE CITIZENS OF RUSSIA!... State Power has passed into the hands of ... the Petrograd Soviet.' They proposed 'a democratic peace, abolition

of landlord property-rights . . . labour control over production'
and the formation of a Soviet government. The Mensheviks challenged Bolshevik claims: 'The promise of immediate peace – is
a lie! The promise of bread – a hoax! The promise of land –
a fairy tale.' Lenin riposted: 'All private ownership of land is
abolished immediately without compensation . . . Any damage
whatever done to the confiscated property which from now
on belongs to the whole People, is regarded as a serious crime,
punishable by revolutionary tribunals.'[13] Until the creation of a
Constituent Assembly – the avowed aim of the revolution – a
provisional worker/peasant government was to function under a
Council of People's Commissars. This included Lenin, Trotsky
and Joseph Stalin, an active Bolshevik since the beginning who
had been exiled to Siberia for his revolutionary activities and had
taken over the editorship of the paper *Pravda* after his arrival in
Petrograd in 1917.

Money was urgently needed by the government to pay the
workers, but bank staff had gone on strike. By mid-December,
civil servants, schoolteachers, the Union of Artists and the staff
at the Alexandrinsky Theatre all came out. The poor continued to be hungry, the rich were still in the happy position of
ignoring government allocations and enjoying restaurants and
crowded cabarets.[14] Across the city, food shops were empty, while
Bryant recalled 'window after window full of flowers, corsets,
dog-collars and false hair!' The hair came from 'emancipated'
women. The corsets were of the 'out-of-date, wasp-waist variety'.[15] The customers for such punishing garments – refusing to be
emancipated – had fled. Street lighting was erratic. Trams broke
down and lay abandoned. Meriel Buchanan witnessed 'disorder
and dirt and neglect' everywhere.[16] In churches, 'nobody prayed'.
Writer Viktor Shklovsky noted that, by the middle of January
1918, Petrograd had grown quiet – there was 'no regular life of
any kind, only wreckage'. Coffee 'was made of rye', people ate
'potato peel gruel'.[17] The painter Yuri Annenkov remembered

'rotten, frozen offal'[18] for sale. Nutrient-deficient women stopped menstruating. Two years later, Princess Wolkonsy recorded the devastating impact of undernourishment on the birth rate.[19] She was a member of one of Russia's oldest aristocratic families, and she courageously returned to post-revolutionary Petrograd from England to rescue her imprisoned husband, who had been a surgeon in the city before the revolution.

Attempts to alleviate misery were often quashed by a zealous excess of revolutionary logic. When the Vyborg soviet tried to establish a free canteen for the unemployed, it was castigated for its 'bourgeois philanthropy'.[20] Slowly, however, the Bolsheviks began to get a grip on the situation. Their priorities included terminating the war with Germany and the formation of the Constituent Assembly. In the last free elections to be held in Russia for more than seventy years, the Bolsheviks lost out to the Socialist Revolutionaries, who had people's welfare rather than state power at heart. But the Bolsheviks were taking bloodthirsty measures to secure their revolution. By the time the Assembly first sat in early January 1918, they had put their troops on the street to subdue opposition and had killed around ten people and wounded dozens.[21] Then – in a clear indication of the shape of things to come – the Bolsheviks closed the Assembly, over which they had failed to gain control in the election.

On 1 February 1918, it was time to blink. Blink and it became 14 February. Out with tsarism went Peter the Great's antiquated Julian Calendar, and Russia – just as it began to turn its back on the West and look inward – adopted the Gregorian Calendar, which was in use almost everywhere else. St Petersburg had been created by Peter the Great to deflect history. The Bolshevik Revolution erupted in the city, not only because it was the seat of industry and power, but because it was also a cradle of change. But when, in early 1918, the Germans once again advanced towards Petrograd and even attempted – unsuccessfully – to bomb the city from the air, it became apparent that Petrograd was too

Anna Ostroumova-Lebedeva, *First Snow*, 1917 –
a view of Senate Square from the University Embankment.

Nikolai Terpsikhorov, *The First Slogan*, 1924 –
turning their backs on antiquity, artists worked for the revolution.

*Clockwise from top left:* Alexander Rodchenko's colourful revolutionary library was never more than an installation at the 1925 Exhibition of Decorative Arts in Paris; Vavara Stepanova's design for unisex sportswear, 1920s: function and simplicity above all; women and men fight for the revolution in Alexander Deineka's *The Defence of Petrograd*, 1928.

Alexander Deineka, *Construction of New Workshops*, 1926.

During the Siege.
The poster reads, 'Death
to the Child Murderers'.

'We Defended Leningrad!
We Will Restore It!'

Intourist buses parked in front of the Headquarters of the General Staff, 1979.

Alexei Sundukov, *Queue*, 1986.

Private enterprise on the Nevsky during the White Nights, 1993.

Desperate selling, early 1990s.

The pop art city.
The Nevsky Prospekt, 2016.

Temporary city heating pipes on Vasilevsky Island making way for pedestrians and traffic.

The Nevsky Prospekt is full of surprises. Kazan Cathedral in the background.

A glut of traffic, tourists and cables obscuring the city.

A statue of Trezzini looks proudly out on all the might and the mess –
on what has become of the city that Peter-the-Great engaged him to build.

*The Bronze Horseman.*

vulnerable to remain the capital, and the Bolsheviks moved their government to Moscow. Vissarion Belinsky called St Petersburg 'a new city in an old land'.[22] Ironically, when that old land was shaken by a new vision, its power centre retreated to its old capital and absolutism prevailed.

The German threat to Petrograd was removed when the government signed the Treaty of Brest-Litovsk on 3 March 1918 – an act that prompted the British to send an expeditionary force to Arkhangelsk and Murmansk. By then the relocation of the administration had already emptied Petrograd of much of its purpose. The unappealing, high-pitched speech-maker and member of the Bolshevik Central Committee, Grigory Zinoviev, took charge of the city's Council of Commissars. But Zinoviev divided his time between Petrograd and Moscow, where he also headed the powerful engine of world revolution, the Third International, founded in March 1919. His frequent absences hardly endeared him to his diminished city, where telephonists sat in vain waiting for news of revolutionary outbreaks across the globe.[23]

The Cheka was set up at no. 2 Gorokhovaya, the building where Vera Zasulich had attempted to assassinate Fyodor Trepov. The Extraordinary Commission with Responsibility for Counter-Revolution and Sabotage was headed by Felix Dzerzhinsky, who had served as Lenin's bodyguard. Under 'paralysed' lids, noted Bruce Lockhart, Dzerzhinsky's eyes 'blazed with a steady fire of fanaticism'.[24] His Cheka would terrorise the unwilling into accepting the revolution, executing them in the evening and disposing of the bodies during the night. Various crimes were dealt with, such as espionage, speculation and counterfeiting, but by far the bulk of the executions carried out by the Petrograd Cheka punished counter-revolution and banditry – just over 1,000 executions were officially recorded in the eighteen-month period from its founding in December 1917.[25]

When Cheka headquarters also moved to Moscow, Anatoli Lunacharsky's education and arts department of the government

remained in Petrograd until the spring of 1919.[26] A gentle yet
persuasive cosmopolitan, Lunacharsky dubbed himself 'an
intellectual among Bolsheviks and a Bolshevik among intellectuals'.[27] Believing that it was not for a government to interfere too
vigorously with the arts, he wanted to preserve the best of the old
order, yet facilitate revolutionary expression. Lunacharsky was
the leader of Proletkult, the body dedicated to the development of
culture for the masses. It organised cells in factories and studios
where workers could practise art, and lecture rooms where they
could begin to encounter literature.[28] It also promoted choral
music with a new cannon of revolutionary hymns.[29] Lunacharsky
was also commissar of Narkompros, the unwieldy People's
Commissariat for Education, which controlled all aspects of
pedagogical, intellectual and artistic life. Wireless was in the
first stages of development, so Narkompros turned to cinema as
a medium for popularising soviet ideals. There were screenings
for workers in the Nicholas Hall of the Winter Palace. Agit-trains
and agit-boats – gaudily decked out in revolutionary red –
travelled throughout the country, spreading the word. On board
were libraries, printing presses and darkened spaces in which
to show films.[30] The Academy of Fine Arts was closed and
Narkompros set up the Petrograd Free Studios, open to anyone
over sixteen years of age. Among a host of other activities, young
soviet women prepared themselves for athletics by imitating the
poses of the Greek statuary in the collection.

Working from the old apartments of the royal children in the
Winter Palace, Lunacharsky insisted that only rooms with no
artistic interest should be used for social or administrative purposes. The rest of the palace should become a state museum,
part of the Hermitage, in which a Museum of the Revolution had
been installed by staff working in such icy conditions that they
were 'streaked with blue blotches, their hands frost-bitten'. After
months of operating in this appalling environment, 'severe cases
of rheumatism and tubercular infections' broke out among them.

As for the presentation of more traditional museum exhibits, in Petrograd alone there was so much to expropriate that the museums promised to be even richer than they had been in the past.[31] With the best of the imperial collection moved to Moscow's Kremlin for safe keeping, curators devoted their energies to cataloguing the rich private collections. Property and movables, accumulated over the centuries, were to be owned by the people. A photograph of peasants getting their first glimpse of a palatial interior shows them dumbstruck. Wide-eyed, it seemed as if they had arrived in heaven. Or – if they were well instructed in Bolshevik thinking – in hell.

The playwright Maxim Gorky was the 'Noah of the Russian intelligentsia',[32] determined to protect culture in post-revolutionary Russia. He warned Lenin that shops were springing up across northern Europe selling antiques smuggled out of Russia, and the leader issued a decree in September 1918 prohibiting the export of art treasures. Gorky petitioned Lenin after the Cheka arrested the poet and first husband of Anna Akhmatova, Nikolai Gumilev, for harbouring anti-Bolshevik sentiments and participating in a trumped-up monarchist conspiracy. Gorky obtained a reprieve from Lenin in Moscow but, by the time he returned to Petrograd, Gumilev had been executed along with sixty others. In December 1919, Gorky converted the Eliseev mansion into the House of Arts, a meeting place and refuge for intellectuals and creative people.[33] Princess Wolkonsy was offered a room in what had been Eliseev's study, with family photos still hanging on the wall. She remembered the shock of hardly recognising figures like Andrei Biely and 'the cream of the Russian intelligentsia . . . dirty and lice-ridden, silently devouring their miserable dinner' in the communal refectory. Despite such conditions, the House of Arts provided a bolthole in difficult times.[34]

Facing what Lunacharsky called 'the agonising process of reducing its economic and political significance', Petrograd set about changing street names. Anything with a Romanov association was replaced with the name of a socialist luminary.[35] Monuments went up to Radishchev and Herzen. Marx was given pride of place in front of the Smolny. Among these new tributes, it was an angular and distorted futurist monument to the regicide Sofia Perovskaya whose 'misshapen face' challenged notions of what was an apt style for socialist art.[36] 'Individualistic' and self-indulgent, modernism was already under threat. Nevertheless, those relics of 'bourgeois individualism' – the futurists – were usefully employed to provide an arresting spectacle for Petrograd's May Day holiday. In October, for the first anniversary of the revolution, Nathan Altman swathed 16,000 metres of canvas painted with cubist and futurist designs all around Palace Square.[37] It was almost tsarist in its excess and inappropriate amid the hardships of civil war. Two years later, the event became even more spectacular, but even less – in aesthetic terms – revolutionary. In an unashamed demonstration of Bolshevik hyperbole, 8,000 Red Army soldiers 're-enacted' the storming of the palace into which their comrades had strolled, unopposed, in October 1917.[38]

Aside from such extravagant celebrations, Petrograd had become a ghost town. Cholera returned in the spring of 1918, as efforts to repair sanitation stagnated. The perilous economic situation was aggravated by the termination of the war with Germany, which resulted in 200,000 factory workers being laid off during the spring and summer. So bad was the situation that the unemployed were offered free passage on the railways to allow them to escape to the countryside in search of food.

By June, armed opposition to the Bolsheviks had coalesced into a White Army in the south, comprising Russians nostalgic for the monarchy and commanded by tsarist generals. Ex-allies intervened in the civil war: the French navy was in the Black Sea, the Americans arrived in the Far East and the British in Murmansk, all eager to crush the socialist revolution and protect their interests. With the Red Guard moving off from Petrograd to fight the civil war, the Cheka – licensed to kill – policed the city. They raided SR strongholds and moved against the bourgeoisie. As the *Krasnaya gazeta* put it, 'The *cheka* for the bourgeoisie, boiling water for lice!'[39] In August, Moisei Uritsky, Petrograd Commissar for Internal Affairs, was assassinated at his desk in a revenge killing. Days later, Lenin was shot in the lung and the neck by a near-blind young SR, Fanya Kaplan. Such violent threats by Bolshevik opponents provoked the Red Terror – a campaign of intense repression, in the form of torture and execution, unleashed against counter-revolutionaries. In six weeks, between 500 and 1,300 were killed and 6,000 arrested by the Cheka. Bolsheviks began to use institutional violence as a political tool. It became a basic strategy of the Soviet state.[40] During the Red Terror the official number of prisoners killed by the Cheka was 12,773, but some unofficial estimates reached 300,000 people killed between September 1918 and 1920.

One piece of unfinished business was Colonel Romanov and family, who – when moved to Ekaterinburg in April – were greeted by a crowd yelling, 'Hang them!' It sounded merely like the excited clammerings of a mob, but it was the fanfare announcing the end of the Romanov dynasty. On 17 July 1918, first the tsar, then the empress, then the *tsarevich* and his sisters were shot. The assassins boasted that they chased the grand duchesses round the cellar, firing at them.[41] Their spree was an effortless and pleasurable massacre – like that enjoyed by the hunters in Empress Anna's *Jagdwagen*.

Paul Dukes studied music in St Petersburg before the war. As he spoke Russian and knew the country, he was asked by the British government to observe the revolution. Inducted into Britain's fledgling MI6 – then known as the SIS – Dukes returned to Petrograd in November 1918 to gather high-quality, unbiased information and estimate the chances for regime change. His forged identification papers were relatively easy to use, given the illiteracy of many Red Guards. Dukes knew a man who travelled from Petrograd to Moscow using his English tailor's bill as a pass. With twenty disguises at his disposal – one as a Cheka employee called Joseph Ilyich Afirenko, another as a Red Army soldier – Dukes monitored events and attempted to spring tsarist sympathisers from jail. Through the darkest part of the night, he would drift in a fishing skiff in the mouth of the Neva, waiting for a Royal Navy torpedo boat to slip past the Kronstadt watch and collect whatever material he had to offer. His reports confirmed the breakdown of the self-styled 'Metropolis of the World Revolution'. The uncollected residue of the first-anniversary celebrations – 'shreds of washed-out red flags' – were strung over the streets from house to house. Skeletal horses lay dead where they fell. There were books for sale, many of them looted from private libraries, but it was necessary to obtain a licence to purchase anything other than the ubiquitous soviet propaganda. Rotten vegetables in the markets, 'bits of herring on microscopic pieces of black bread' and a 'liquid of tea-substitute' in the bar of the Finland railway station all testified to the 'stagnation of normal life'.[42] With good reason, Dukes called his book about his time in Russia not *Red Dawn*, but *Red Dusk*.

On Vasilevsky Island where she was living, Marta Almedingen remembered haggard people haunted by the fading painted panels on bakeries long since shut.[43] Ghosts of plump rolls and ochre loaves mocked a population without butter, and condemned to make do with one – often rotten – egg per week.[44] When the American anarchist Emma Goldman asked to try the ration of bread given to workers at the Putilov factory, they told her to 'Bite hard.'[45] Determined people pretended they had no use for food[46] – mind over absence of matter. The desperate sold anything, from clothes and knick-knacks to gangrenous bread patties, which customers sniffed before they purchased. Citywide communal eateries with free food for children under fourteen were not up and running until the middle of 1919. When they did open, people found the cooking unappetising at best. There were, as Emma Goldman put it, 'rude awakenings in the Soviet Arcadia'.[47]

Arriving in 'the metropolis of Cold, of Hunger, of Hatred, and of endurance' in the winter of 1919, the revolutionary Victor Serge found the façades of imperial residences 'painted over in ox-blood red'. Lilina Zinoviev, wife of the Petrograd soviet leader, told him that 'we are besieged people in a besieged city. Hunger riots may start, the Finns may swoop on us, the British may attack.'[48] A spate of strikes erupted as workers watched the party privileged eating well, while their promised increase of rations did not materialise. Holidays were cancelled. The Cheka fired on hungry strikers.[49] The revolution was clearly under threat.

British agent Sidney Reilly was trying to coordinate a 1919 counter-revolution. Mercenaries would apprehend Lenin and Trotsky, 60,000 Whites would march on Moscow and General Yudenich would simultaneously attack Petrograd. In August, an English torpedo boat sunk the cruiser *Memory of Azov* during a raid on Kronstadt. In early October, General Yudenich captured Gatchina and, days later, was at the outskirts of Petrograd. Workers were mobilised to defend the deserted city, canal by canal, bridge by bridge. With little more than cabbage to eat, a tired and betrayed population erected street barricades. Yudenich tried to encircle the city, but failed to capture the Moscow–Petrograd railway. Shells burst over the Neva, the Cheka rounded up 300 suspects and the Red Army arrived by rail to defeat Yudenich at the Battle of Pulkovo Heights, sixteen kilometres south of the city.[50] As Trotsky put it in *Pravda* on 30 October, 'a victory for us in the Petrograd duel will mean a crushing blow for Anglo–French imperialism, which has wagered too highly on the Yudenich card. In fighting for Petrograd we are not only defending the cradle of the proletarian revolt but are also fighting in the

most direct way for the extension of this revolt all over the world.'
Yudenich's forces retreated towards the Estonian border.[51]

Given the disruption and deprivation, the English writer
H. G. Wells was astonished by Petrograd's theatrical activity –
both popular and high-brow – with up to forty performances
given in an evening. Large theatres, subsidised by Narkompros as they had been under the tsars, thrived.[52] Louise Bryant
recorded that Karsavina was dancing to a packed Mariinsky,
the audience dressed in rags.[53] Chaliapin demanded a huge fee
to sing but, when the going got tough, he performed for flour
and eggs.[54] In 1920 – in an early example of outreach – he sang
*Boris Godunov* at the Putilov Iron Works. The unpopular
futurist Theatre of the Noisy Present proved to Lunacharsky that
avant-garde work was inaccessible to the workers. More suitable
was the simple didacticism of the *Legend of the Communard*.
Written in 1919 by a Red Army infantryman, its socialist message appealed to a population that was hoping against hope that
things could work out.[55]

By the early autumn of 1920, after a series of significant Red
Army victories, the civil war was abating. In November, with
Petrograd secure, many Hermitage paintings were returned from
Moscow. By the end of the month the Rembrandt room was open,
followed by the Dutch and Italian rooms in December – just in
time for the pipes to burst.[56] An Expertise Commission had
taken up residence in the former British Embassy to catalogue
the artefacts confiscated from palaces and mansions. H. G. Wells
thought it resembled 'some congested second hand art shop in
the Brompton Road'. Wells had been in St Petersburg in 1914
and was in Petrograd six years later, clearly disappointed by most
of what he saw. His host was his old friend Maxim Gorky, who –
despite the importance of his position – possessed only the suit he
wore. Across the city, wooden pavements had been torn up and

wooden houses smashed for firewood. Petrograd's roads were lined with 'dead shops'. If Bryant found only corsets and false hair, Wells saw only 'tea, cigarettes and matches' – necessities such as crockery were nowhere to be found. His lament for a failing revolution sounds a note of domestic despair, 'There is no replacing a broken cup.' Wells contended that a city is nothing but 'shops and restaurants and the like. Shut them up, and the meaning of a street has disappeared.' When he shared this insight with Lenin, he was told that the purpose of towns had largely ceased. They were obsolete.[57]

Similarly disappointed with the direction of the revolution was the Russian-born American, Emma Goldman. Frequently imprisoned in and subsequently deported from the USA, she was welcomed by Gorky, who lauded her revolutionary credentials. Arriving in the wake of the Yudenich threat, she found Petrograd tense. Her first glimpse of soviet inequality was provided by her lodgings in the grand Hotel Astoria, requisitioned for ranking party officials and known as the First House of the Petro-Soviet. Criticism of official corruption was already widespread. Rations were graded, and Goldman wondered why – when certain stores sold butter, meat and eggs to the privileged – workers and women stood 'long hours in endless queues for their ration of frozen potatoes, wormy cereals and decayed fish'. Zinoviev retorted that they could do little else during a civil war and an allied block-ade. Goldman toured the comfortably appointed hospitals for important communists, and visited other clinics where, by con-trast, equipment was non-existent and medicine rare.[58] For most comrades, the best diet they could expect was buckwheat *kasha* and an unappetising salt-water fish called *vobla*, with bones that splintered easily and, if ingested, could damage the intes-tines.[59] Oats distributed by the authorities were often consumed unwashed and uncooked, completely clogging the digestive tract. As purgatives and enemas proved useless, Princess Wolkonsky was forced to watch her patients perish in terrible torment.[60]

Hygiene was a major problem. There had been eighty-eight *banya* in 1916. By 1921 only about twenty remained.[61] Many bathers arrived covered in a 'thick grey coat of dirt and lice', which, once washed away, revealed huge boils and the red scars of scabies. People took to drugs to obliterate their misery. Bought from barbers and hairdressers, cocaine was freely used by people from all walks of life. Those wishing to avoid conscription could buy 'typhus lice' from beggars on the Nevsky Prospekt in order to infect themselves.[62] When Victor Serge was sent to search for suitable apartments for party staff, he found 'whole rooms plastered with frozen excrement'.[63] As winter thawed into spring, floors were awash and – in the true spirit of socialism – clearance squads were organised. The pro-revolutionary correspondent for the *Manchester Guardian*, Arthur Ransome roomed with Karl Radek of Lenin's inner-circle and ran off with Trotsky's secretary, but was forced to acknowledge the 'appalling paralysis' and the immanent 'collapse of civilisation'.[64]

In February 1921, a proclamation was issued by disgruntled workers in Petrograd claiming freedom from the Bolsheviks and, the following month, sailors from Kronstadt mutinied against the fall in living standards and set out to put the revolution back on-course. But the now-sizeable Red Army was commanded by many officers who had been expertly trained in the imperial military schools. The man they sent to quash the Kronstadt rebellion, General Tukhachevsky, was one of them.[65] His mid-March attack on the island was made by men camouflaged in white, moving over the frozen gulf. The sailors fired on the advancing troops, and in places the ice started to crack. Hundreds were killed before Tukhachevsky suppressed the rebellion, after which Chekist repression intensified and a new terror reigned in Petrograd. Emma Goldman met sailors from Kronstadt and workers from the forges and the mills, the 'very brawn of the revolutionary struggle . . . crying out in anguish and bitterness' against the Bolsheviks whom they had helped to power. As for

the Cheka, Goldman put it to John Reed that she never understood that revolution could allow 'indifference to human life
and suffering'. Reed had returned to Russia three years after the
October Revolution, which he had greeted with such enthusiasm.
He was no longer so sure. Nevertheless, he died a hero and was
buried in Moscow's Kremlin wall. Shortly afterwards, Emma
Goldman left Russia with all her 'dreams crushed'.[66]

Many artists and writers believed that revolutionary approaches
in their respective disciplines could serve the new order, but they
were considered out of touch with the workers. Experimentation
in theatre and art was questioned by philistine party chiefs, and
many modernist artists began to realise that Bolshevism would
never accept their ideas.[67] Proletkult urged the development of a
collective, proletarian art that ignored traditions and movements
which meant nothing to the workers. But if modernists were seen

*V. Panov as 'The Worker' in a dramatization of* We Grow From Iron
*on the opening night of The Proletkult Arena Theatre.*

*Vladimir Tatlin standing with an assistant in front of a model*
*for* Monument to the Third International *in a Petrograd studio.*

to fail the revolution, so the revolution would fail its visionaries.
A prime example was Vladimir Tatlin's 1919 commission for
a *Monument to the Third International*, which was intended
to straddle the Neva and soar to twice the height of the as-yet-
unbuilt Empire State Building. The tower was designed to suspend
a giant glass cylinder, cube and cone. The cylinder would rotate
over a period of a year and contain a conference centre. The cone
would turn once a month and contain administrative offices. The
cube would rotate daily and contain broadcast equipment such
as screens and radio speakers. Tatlin's vision ranged way beyond
the limits of soviet skill and it was never built.

By 1920, there were more than 600,000 members of the
Communist Party, with a Central Committee of nineteen out

of which, Arthur Ransome calculated, there were only five who mattered. There were the Jews, Trotsky, Kamenev and Zinoviev. There was the Pole, Dzerzhinsky and the Georgian, Stalin.[68] The ailing Lenin was in charge. The Bolsheviks had won the civil war, but needed to stay in power. Nabokov suggested that Lenin and his cronies – rather like the tsars before them – 'subordinated everything to the retention of power'.[69]

In the mid-nineteenth century, Alexander Herzen had asked, 'Who will finish us off? The senile barbarism of the sceptre or the wild barbarism of communism; the bloody sabre or the red flag?' He also hinted that it might be worse than that: 'after the Christians were torn and tortured by wild beasts, they themselves, in their turn, began to persecute and torture one another'.[70]

# 13

# A CITY DIMINISHED

## *1921–41*

Petrograd's population of 2.5 million in 1917 had fallen to around 740,000 by the early 1920s.[1] Almost 170,000 worked, like the clerks of tsarist Russia, in the already-bloated Soviet state administration. Others – estimates stand at 156,000 for 1919 – were illiterate. The city was more extensive than Berlin or Paris but, in those capitals, populations were on the increase and, after the recent war, heading for the boom of the jazz age. Petrograd was an abandoned, half-ruined museum, which few had the time, money or inclination to curate. Mandelstam's expectation of 'something very splendid' was no longer about to happen. The red staining the imperial palaces was a colour – according to Biely's Ableukhov – 'emblematic of the chaos that was leading Russia to its doom'.[2] The tram count had fallen from 724 cars in 1918 to 227 in 1921. Passengers hung on to the running boards for dear life or were pushed off, sometimes losing it. Industry was idle. A quarter of the city's apartments were empty. Such was the upshot of seven years of war, revolution and civil strife.

Considering the city in the mid-1920s, the religious philosopher Georgy Fedotov suggested that there was 'something insane in the idea of it, something that has predetermined its demise . . . A Titan rose up against Earth and Heaven and is now suspended in space, poised on a granite rock.'[3] While the younger generation in Peter's city witnessed impressive efforts in education and a drive to improve standards of living, the period between the end of the civil war and Hitler's downfall was one of turmoil and trauma. According to Arthur Koestler, 'within the short span of three generations the Communist movement had travelled from the era of the Apostles to that of the Borgias'.[4] The period saw the socialist vision of Marx's co-author of the Communist Manifesto, Friedrich Engels – that government should slowly work itself out of a job – harden into the worst kind of totalitarian bureaucracy. In Russia's capital, Moscow, a new tsarism was driven by the paranoia of Joseph Stalin. For two centuries Peter's city had dictated change. Now it was the victim of change – or, rather, of stagnation.

Immediately after the civil war there had been glimmers of hope. In 1922, Viktor Shklovsky observed that spring came early. Professionals returned from the south, and private traders were once again accepted, as Lenin's economic compromise of 1921 tolerated controlled capitalism. This was forced upon him by the appalling conditions of war and famine and was voted in at the Xth Party Congress, while General Tukhachevsky was putting down the Kronstadt revolt.[5] The temporary New Economic Policy (NEP) returned something of St Petersburg to Petrograd. There were restaurants, shops, cinemas showing Hollywood films and galleries hanging avant-garde art. There was a freedom in the press, and opportunity for public discussion. Popular entertainers and con-men were jubilant, as the Nevsky sprang to life again with the gaiety and vice that had reigned before the First World War.[6] But while it offered some respite for the bourgeoisie, the NEP was anathema to hard-line Bolsheviks, who viewed 'NEPmen' as mobster capitalists. However, when Lenin's tactical economic retreat was terminated by Stalin in 1928, the 'NEPman' mentality went underground. Black markets persisted throughout the Soviet era and morphed – after the break-up of the USSR – into Russia's racketeering way to get rich quick.[7]

*Alexander Deineka,* NEPmen, *1927.*

On 22 April 1922, Joseph Stalin – Lenin's choice – was elected as Party General Secretary. He was a no-nonsense pragmatist, an energetic Bolshevik organiser who had done time in tsarist camps in Siberia. Ten months later, Lenin changed his mind and wanted Stalin out. As with Catherine the Great and her intention to disinherit Paul, Lenin should have spoken sooner – before a third stroke left him incoherent. When, on 21 January 1924, he died of a fourth seizure, Stalin dramatically vowed to complete Lenin's work and thereby consolidated himself as the natural heir.[8] Petrograd, a city that Lenin never much liked, was renamed Leningrad. Local leaders argued that the seedbed of the revolution should become the capital once again. Others – including a few elderly ex-aristocrats still seen walking their dogs – suggested that the city should make a stand against the drabness of life in Soviet Russia.[9] Old imperial splendour could become a beacon against the shabbiness of Soviet life. But Peter's city was instead consigned to oblivion and, in late September,

was overwhelmed by its second-largest flood. Water peaked at
380 centimetres – forty centimetres below the level of the worst
flood 100 years earlier.

Felix Dzerzhinsky's Cheka had become the Political Directorate of the State, the GPU, which kept expanding in order to
satisfy Stalin's ruthless campaigns against his fellow country-
men. With the leader's mesmerising contempt for human life, it
took less than the nod of a head in the wrong direction to trigger
his distrust. Obtaining false confessions under torture became an
efficient way to purge suspected enemies – only a handful from
thousands of victims had the will to resist. Complete conformity,
Stalin observed, was achieved only at the cemetery. Extermin-
ation was his solution: 'No man, no problem.'[10] In 1923, the
GPU became the OGPU, the United Political Directorate of the
State. In 1934, this evolved into the dreaded NKVD, the People's
Commissariat for Internal Affairs, which developed through the
MGB and the MVD to become the KGB in 1954, the year after
the dictator's death. Much of what was baleful in Stalin's regime
had been created by Lenin in the brutalising turmoil of the civil
war. Surveillance, detention, exile and terror were part of Lenin's
scheme of things. The first death-camp became operational in
1922. Stalin merely intensified the campaign against enemies of
the revolution – both real and imagined. The OGPU and then the
NKVD became the vital instruments of terror. Behind the smiling
face of 'Father' Stalin stood Saturn devouring his children. So
thorough were his methods that, by the end of the 1920s, he was
the only member of the original leadership who remained in the
central executive committee, the Politburo.[11]

By the time Stalin adopted the plan to improve the economy in
October 1928, he was in full control of the party, the army and
the secret police. His drive to modernise was manic. Workers
were compelled to 'donate' their *sobotnik*, or day off, in order to
speed up the plan.[12] *Pravda* crowed about achieving a Five-Year
Plan in four. It was a dangerous acceleration worthy of Peter the

Great. In 1929, profiteering *kulaks* – wealthy peasants accused of hoarding grain while cities starved – became 'class enemies'. Some were murdered by gangs despatched from the towns, while others were exiled to Siberia, their farms confiscated and merged into huge collectives. By 1930, more than half of Russia's peasants had been collectivised, but only half the promised number of tractors rolled off the production lines. When they did arrive, many lay idle, as farm workers had no idea how to operate them.[13] To escape the threat in the countryside, embattled peasants slaughtered their cattle, burned down their barns and houses in protest and streamed into the cities at the rate of 50,000 a week. Leningrad found itself facing a housing shortage.

Amid the disarray there was excitement, confusion and crisis in the arts. Proletkult, buffeted by conflicting aims, hardly survived the civil war.[14] Its desire to provide the workers with their own comprehensible art mutated into Stalin's cultural terror. Narkompros took over publishing houses, and all manuscripts had to be approved by Glavit, the Main Administration for Literary and Publishing Affairs. The intellectual and artistic purge gathered speed. While some classic writers such as Pushkin and Tolstoy remained popular, Dostoevsky's late, anti-socialist ideas kept his works from publication. The verses of Sergei Yesenin, hip alcoholic poet, singer and sometime husband of Isadora Duncan, were filled with raw life and rough weather. In 1925, Yesenin found himself in such an uncongenial climate that he killed himself. The poet Anna Akhmatova lived with mirrors that did not 'expect smiles'.[15] Her work was disparaged by Vladimir Mayakovsky. Trumpeting the value of socialist art, he claimed that Akhmatova's 'indoor intimacy' held no meaning for a 'harsh and steely age'.[16] Mayakovsky's satire on 'NEPmen', *The Bedbug*, was presented in 1929. Its form and content were attacked and its author subsequently driven to suicide. *The Bedbug*'s director, Vsevelod Meyerhold, was later tortured and shot in 1940 on a spurious charge of spying for foreign powers.

Prokofiev's ballet for Diaghilev, *Le Pas d'acier* – intended as a
tribute to the artistic possibilities of socialism – was censored for
'dissonance' when it was performed in the Soviet Union. Shostakovich's first opera, *The Nose*, treated the increasingly prevalent
fear of power. After its 1930 Leningrad premiere, it was attacked
for its 'anti-soviet escapism'.

The 'red detective story' became a popular genre in the
Twenties. Among the most successful was Marietta Shaginyan's
*Mess-Mend: or a Yankee in Petrograd*, which was serialised
and given a Constructivist photomontage cover by Alexander
Rodchenko. Such an avant-garde cover on a popular novel reveals
something of the artistic potential of the early 1920s. The book
treats capitalism's collapse into fascism, pictures a socialist revolution in America, champions the Soviet way of life and the
triumph of science – a theme reflected in the contemporary vogue
for science fiction. Eugene Zamyatin's futuristic novel *We* was
the most powerful of that genre because it undercut misplaced
scientific optimism with a searing attack on mass-surveillance
and conformism, in which every last detail of life was planned
and monitored. One of the first books banned by communist censors, it remained unpublished in the Soviet Union until 1988.[17]

Indecision over what kind of art was appropriate for a
working-class revolution was reflected in the programme of the
Institute of Artistic Culture, Inkhuk, which initially embraced
everything from Kandinsky's pure painting to Tatlin's 'laboratory' or factory art. Originating in Moscow, Inkhuk was
established in Petrograd in 1921 under Tatlin and, in Vitebsk,
under Malevich. But when Kandinsky departed for Germany[18] –
one of the numerous artists, intellectuals and writers who left or
were deported from Soviet Russia – easel-painting went with him.
The artists who remained were technicians exploring utilitarian designs that could be manufactured and could serve society.
But their socialist vision was not allowed to thrive. Oil painting
returned, depicting sentimental scenes full of propaganda.

While the NEP witnessed the re-emergence of the private
tailor, as inside legs were measured up and down the Nevsky,
socialist artists such as Aleksandra Exter, Malevich, Rodchenko,
Lyubov Popova and Vavara Stepanova were busy exploring fashion possibilities – both international and anonymous – that
would be cheap to produce, hygienic and suited to the activities of
the workers. Stunning designs were produced, but projects were
hampered by economic constraints or curtailed by a hardening
of the leadership against innovation.[19]

Great success was achieved in typography and photomontage.
At Vitebsk, under El Lissitzky, Malevich and Marc Chagall,
modern typographical design developed from its futurist origins. Constructivists conceived arresting agitprop posters and
emblems for trade unions. Impressive interior designs for clubs
offered workers light, bright places for recreation and learning.
But Rodchenko's colourful revolutionary library was, sadly, never
more than a Silver Medal installation at the Paris Exhibition of
Decorative Arts in 1925. So many ambitious schemes were never
realised. Although Popova and Stepanova did some fashion work
in textile plants, Vladimir Tatlin was the only 'artist-engineer'
who spent much time in a factory. But during his sojourn at
Petrograd's Lessner metallurgical plant he learned little. His
ambition to build a stove intended to give out maximum heat
using minimum fuel was important, but Tatlin could not make
his designs work. The stove and the gigantic *Monument to the
Third International* – like the fledgling Soviet state itself – were
remarkable but unrealisable dreams.[20]

The artist, architect and engineer El Lissitzsky introduced his
constructions or 'prouns' in 1921. Defining a proun as 'a station
where one changes trains between painting and architecture',
he set about trying to conceive buildings that would serve a
population ravaged by hunger and war. The private client,
he declared, had been replaced by the 'social commission'.[21]
Surveying early Soviet architectural ideas – plans by El Lissitzky,

*Statue of Felix Dzerzhinsky against the reality of the Soviet world he helped to create.*

the 1923 Ladvoski Atelier designs for a Moscow skyscraper, Barkhin's first proposal for the *Izvestia* Building, Varentsov's Utopian City – it is clear that the country was being offered a future for which it was not prepared. It was Peter the Great all over again.

Lenin clearly understood film as a most efficient propaganda tool through which to spread the revolutionary message.[22] However, the films that came to be recognised as masterpieces of Soviet cinema were not appreciated by a public used to the cheap, sensational and sexy flicks pumped out by a slapdash industry. A typical production featured the adventures of Rasputin. Six shorts could be filmed in two days on the same set, with the props merely repositioned. The public, worn down by deprivation, had an understandable hunger for excitement and glamour. Of the 183 new films shown in Leningrad between late 1924 and mid-1925, only twenty-five were Soviet, while 103 came from America.[23] Sergei Eisenstein's revolutionary *Battleship Potempkin* caused a sensation abroad and was banned in Berlin in 1926, although in Russia itself American movies proved more popular. *Potempkin* was prematurely replaced by Douglas Fairbanks's *Robin Hood* at a *kino* in Moscow. In Leningrad, it played in only two major cinemas.[24]

Eisenstein maintained that he was opposed to constructing unconvincing sets, in the manner of the shoddy Rasputin producers. He shot his tenth-anniversary celebration of the revolution, *October*, in that most striking of locations, Peter's capital. Many of his extras had served as Red Guards. For the massacres on the streets of Petrograd, Eisenstein commented that 'no rehearsal was necessary; the workers knew too well' how it had happened.[25] A triumph of propaganda and hagiography, *October* merges images inspired by newspaper photographs and agit-prop posters to create the seething excitement of the revolution through montage. The technique empowers moments such as the impassioned, quasi-religious manifestation of Lenin outside the Finland Station. It also charges intimate scenes of horror, such as the sequence in which a frocked bourgeoise viciously kills a Red with the point of her frilly umbrella while his copy of *Pravda* sinks slowly into the Neva. Lev Kuleshov, Pudovkin's teacher and the man responsible for developing montage, faced a shortage of film stock when he came to make his first full-length feature film, *The Unusual Adventures of Mr West in the Land of the Bolsheviks,* in Leningrad in 1924.[26] He resolved the problem by cutting strictly, in order to tell the story economically, and montage was born.

As the Twenties progressed, Stalin's watchdogs kept their eye on serious film-makers. Alexandr Dovshenko's *Zvenigora*, with its exploration of human nature in relation to the land, was criticised for being 'bourgeois' and 'nationalistic'. By contrast, *Earth* – the final film of Dovshenko's *War Trilogy* – combined the kinetic thrill of early Soviet cinema with a positive vision of the Five-Year Plan. Dovshenko's message was that if you give the right tools to the working class, it can oust rich, drunken *kulaks* who are too idle to compete with technological and ideological advances. In the film, the workers instinctively know how to use the tractors.

While Lenin was keen to proselytise through film, Stalin was alert to the emotional pull of music. In 1926, the Leningrad Philharmonic premiered Dmitri Shostakovich's 1st Symphony. Originally offered as his diploma composition for the Leningrad Conservatoire, the symphony – allowing the first glimpse of the composer's disquiet – was recognised as remarkable and was taken up by the Leningrad Philharmonic. During the period of the NEP, before the Soviet Union turned inwards, it was possible for a musician like Shostakovich to hear the work of foreign composers such as Berg or Hindemith conducted by a rich array of visiting conductors, including Otto Klemperer and Bruno Walter. In 1926, the composer Boris Asafiev formed the Leningrad Circle for New Music and, two years later, Shostakovich's first opera, *The Nose*, based on Gogol's short story, was accepted by the MALEGOT, or Leningrad Maly State Theatre of Opera and Ballet. But during rehearsals there were signs of intolerance towards a piece that was described as 'individualistic' or 'modern'. It was not the kind of music that would serve Stalin, who was in the process of compromising Russia's capacity for technological advance and artistic excellence by replacing intelligence and expertise with ignorance and inexperience. At Leningrad's Conservatoire, party members with no musical training were put in charge. The aim of the institution was redirected to the production of rousing songs to motivate farm and factory workers. Under RAPM, the Russian Association of Proletarian Musicians, music likely to fall on deaf ears was discouraged. Simplicity was the goal. Folk song – 'proletarian in content, national in form' – became dominant.[27] During the First Five-Year Plan, RAPM launched an attack on the 'narcotic' nature of Western popular music, which encouraged 'man to live not so much by his head as by his sexual organs'. Although RAPM was disbanded in 1932 in the cultural volte-face that accompanied the successful conclusion of the First Five-Year Plan, its simplistic attitudes towards music persisted.

The equivalent body in literature, RAPP – the Russian Association of Proletarian Writers – campaigned against authors who were not prepared to ignore individuality by making a pact with Soviet platitude. In painting, Socialist Realism mendaciously celebrated the achievements of the people. Yet, among the early work of Kuzma Petrov-Vodkin and Alexander Deineka – social realists before Socialist Realism – there were striking images that were politically pointed and gently modernist. Later, Socialist Realism descended into idealised, painted propaganda in the work of painters like Alexander Gerasimov.

While the West was living through a Great Depression that called capitalism into question, it still had Fred and Ginger and open argument. In Soviet Russia the drabness, deprivation and danger were paralysing. During Stalin's tyrannical drive for modernis-ation, the standard of living declined and about 44 per cent of household income went on food, which, in 1929, was rationed once again.[28] Leningrad, however, remained something of a case apart. Enjoying a remarkably high literacy rate compared with other Russian cities, it was also home to more than sixty institutes of higher education. There was a marked increase in the number of women studying – not only subjects such as medicine and law, but also construction, transport and industry. Yet in many ways socialism had let women down. Post-revolution party meetings had urged them to imagine a brighter future. The Family Code of 1918 awarded eight weeks' paid maternity leave to women before and after giving birth. But, all too soon, the state cut back on supportive institutions such as childcare, forcing Zhenotdel, the Women's Bureau, to struggle hard for women's rights. Thousands lost their jobs to soldiers returning from the war. Only in the traditionally female and worst-paid sectors, such as textiles and food-processing, did they continue to dominate. What is more, although there was a considerable number of women doctors, in the 1930s, there were only four female chief physicians in Leningrad hospitals. The Commissariat of Labour – allegedly committed to equality of opportunity – favoured men during the First Five-Year Plan, and large numbers of women were left unemployed. In desperation, 700 Leningrad women falsely registered as diseased prostitutes merely to get into the 'labour clinic' where 100 places had been set up to prepare 'fallen women' for work.[29] As for prostitution, the Bolsheviks failed to eradicate it and simply drove it underground.

The New Family Code of the mid-Twenties sought to protect women, but the ease of divorce created a situation in which men became serial husbands, leaving a trail of wives with dependent children as they moved on to the next amusement.[30] Upping the cost of divorce on each successive occasion was an attempt to curb the problem – as was abortion. Legalised from 1920, the numerous *abotaria*, or termination clinics, had long waiting lists of women, often in the advanced stages of pregnancy. Eight or nine terminations were not uncommon, and some women had as many as sixteen.[31] When, in an attempt to strengthen the family, Stalin made abortion a criminal offence in 1937, 'quantities of cheap contraceptives made of metal, celluloid and composite rubber' were put on sale.[32] Against the backdrop of Stalin's terror, the stable, cosy – almost bourgeois – family was promoted in Russia and brandished abroad by Willi Münzenberg's Comintern propaganda magazines. Using faked photographs, they presented the well-dressed 'family Filipov' enjoying a hearty meal at a table crowned by a gleaming samovar. The Filipovs became the laughing stock of the embattled Soviet housewife who, if she managed to get hold of a smoked fish that didn't make the gums bleed, or decent herring, or sausage made from anything but horse meat, was hailed as a veritable 'Mrs Filipov' – a figure with obvious connections.[33]

Successful socialism promised adequate supplies of basic foods, shoes and suitable clothing for everybody. The wait to purchase such items – if they materialised – could be endless and was largely the lot of women, employed or otherwise. When rationing ended, prices rose, outstripping wage increases, and 'repulsive' goods of decreasing quality were produced to match diminished purchasing power.[34] The gulf between the poor and the party elite widened. Glavosobtorg, set up in 1930, served privileged customers in its bakeries, food shops and department stores. The flagship Gastronom shops in Moscow and Leningrad sold live carp from a fish tank and greenhouse-grown strawberries. Priced well beyond the means of the average household, their forty-one varieties of canned or frozen fish and assortment of sixty-seven different kinds of smoked fish and caviar were sold to people who were well placed within the system. From 1930 Torgsin shops, where the cash-strapped went to offload heirlooms, sold to tourists and the Soviet elite. Cooperatives that were exclusive to the NKVD offered what was simply unobtainable elsewhere – newspapers began to include advertising for products that most people couldn't afford. When a department store opened in *Passazh* on the Nevsky Prospekt in the early Thirties, there were speeches, bunting and orchestras to celebrate the event. But, behind the foofaraw, clothing departments had neither fitting rooms nor mirrors.[35]

To bolster pride in a regime that was badly organised and increasingly unfair, schoolchildren were fed antiquated notions of capitalist countries, where – it was suggested – boys under ten lived in squalor and worked the mines for capitalists who preferred cheap, expendable labour to expensive machines. Extracts of the texts they studied were taken from writers such as Charles Dickens, Mrs Gaskell and Upton Sinclair.[36] When André Gide visited Russia in the mid-1930s, he found the population 'in an extraordinary state of ignorance concerning other countries' – workmen actually asked him if they had schools in France.[37] Meanwhile, the developing cult of Stalin, which originated with his fiftieth-birthday celebrations in 1929, attempted to sugar-coat a bitter pill. Busts of Stalin's smug face were churned out for mass adoration, and images of the mass murderer became increasingly saccharine.

From the earliest days of his leadership, Stalin's venom and vindictiveness had been patently apparent, but it was the assassination of the First Secretary of the Leningrad Party, the enormously popular Sergei Kirov, that marked the threshold of an abyss. On the afternoon of 1 December 1934, a troubled young drifter called Leonid Nikolaev was unaccountably admitted to Leningrad Party headquarters in the Smolny. Possibly Stalin's hit-man, Nikolaev proceeded to murder Kirov. Hours later, Stalin boarded a train for Leningrad in order to investigate. The following day, Kirov's apparently negligent bodyguard also died. Some claimed it was an NKVD murder, others that the terrified man had thrown himself from the back of the lorry to avoid interrogation by Stalin. Within a week, Nikolaev and the alleged 'co-conspirators' had been executed and the head of the Leningrad NKVD sacked.[38]

Kirov's lifestyle, evident in his flat on the smart Kamennoostrovsky Prospekt, offers some insight into the minimal sacrifice expected of the socialist elite. The portraits of Kirov's communist superiors and heroes, his 20,000-volume glassed-in library, his extensive desk with the array of phones so beloved of communist bureaucrats, his 'red star' hotline to Moscow – all seem fitting accessories for an important local party leader. Otherwise, the flat appeared altogether bourgeois, with its large kitchen range, refrigerator and ample pantry. Kirov's passion for hunting – his trophies, his skin rugs, his exquisitely made equipment – recall the hunting expeditions so beloved of the late-nineteenth-century tsars. Yet Kirov was an accomplished orator who came across as a man of the people, a champion of the workers who did much to improve standards of welfare in Leningrad.[39] Recklessly independent, he worked with whoever he considered best for the job – party veterans or even those whom Stalin disliked or distrusted. During the XVIIth Party Congress in the winter of 1934, Kirov was solicited by prominent party members as a possible replacement for the General Secretary. Seen as a threat, the hunter became the prey to someone who distrusted his successful popular touch – perhaps Stalin himself.

More than half of Leningrad filed past Kirov's body, lying in state in the Uritsky Palace. They proposed to name streets and build statues in his honour. The Mariinsky had been renamed GATOB – the State Academic Theatre of Opera and Ballet. Anxious to rid the city of at least one ugly acronym, comrades wished to rename the theatre the Kirov, which happened in 1935.

If Stalin did arrange the killing, he needed to cover his tracks. If he did not, then a purge would curb dissent.[40] With zeal, he set to work on the Leningrad party and the city's residual nobility and bourgeoisie. There was a trial of twelve Leningrad NKVD chiefs, who were committed to concentration camps for negligence. Nearly 850 associates of the former Leningrad party leader, Grigory Zinoviev, were arrested early in 1935, and 11,000 Leningraders were sent off to Corrective Labour Camps, or *gulags*, where they worked in appalling conditions to help achieve Stalin's ambitious industrial targets. Kamenev and Zinoviev were sentenced to imprisonment and – in 1936 – retried and executed. By the end of 1938, the 'old communists', including Karl Radek, Nikolai Bukharin and Alexei Rykov, had been purged. Abroad, the NKVD was eliminating Trotskyites fighting in the Spanish Civil War and was tracking Leon Trotsky himself. In Russia, torture became a standard mode of questioning. The new Leningrad party leader, Andrei Zhdanov, dismantled Kirov's power-structures – of the 154 Leningrad delegates to the

XVIIth Party Congress of 1934, only two were re-elected to the next congress in 1939.

In the years following Sergei Kirov's murder, Stalin used the assassination of the Leningrad party leader as a pretext for unrestrained terror. Under the close, unrelenting control of the Soviet leader, the NKVD effectively waged war against the party and the population. Victims were rounded up in vans marked 'Milk' or 'Vegetables' and herded in cattle-trucks to camps where they perished from cold, malnutrition, disease or despair, while Stalin chortled, 'Life has become better, life has become merrier.' Shostakovich had a private toast – 'Let's drink to life not getting any better.' Of nearly 2,000 delegates to the XVIIth Party Congress, 1,100 were shot over the following years. Between 1934 and 1938, 1.5 million party members were purged. Those who aided and abetted Stalin – the notorious security chiefs – fell like dominoes, along with thousands of NKVD operatives who knew too much. Like the monster who vacuums up everything around him, Stalin would soon have no victims left, no population to celebrate his great leadership. Every day, at the height of the Terror, an average of 1,500 people were shot. Official records admit that 681,692 people were executed in 1937–8, while so many of the three million who were incarcerated died in prisons and labour camps.[41] Countless Soviet citizens were put to death for their alleged part, however remote, in the so-called conspiracy surrounding what was, for Stalin, the politically useful murder of Kirov. Arthur Koestler remembered how the party taught him to watch his step, guard his words and thoughts, in the knowledge that anything he said could, one day, be turned against him. He learned to 'avoid any original form of expression, any individual turn of phrase . . . nuances of meaning were suspect. Language, and with it thought, underwent a process of dehydration.'[42]

Shostakovich – cunning, courageous and po-faced – sailed very close to the wind. His second opera, *Lady Macbeth of Mtsensk*, was based on Nikolai Leskov's 1865 novella about a highly sensual woman forced into an unsuitable marriage by brutes. It was to have been the first in a tetralogy, intended to celebrate the liberation of women in Russia. The second was meant to focus on Sofia Perovskaya, who led the plot to assassinate Alexander II, but Shostakovich abandoned the project. A scene in *Lady Macbeth* set in a police station was taken as a satire on Stalin's NKVD and rattled the dictator when he attended a performance. In January 1936, the opera was attacked in *Pravda* as 'a petit-bourgeois formalist attempt to produce originality'. In such an unfavourable climate, it was surprising that the composer's 4th Symphony was accepted by the Leningrad Philharmonic. Indeed, after ten distressing rehearsals under a frightened conductor, Shostakovich withdrew the work, excusing it as a 'failure', and it remained unperformed until 1961. When the composer courageously premiered his 5th Symphony under Yevgeny Mravinsky at the Philharmonic Hall in November 1937, the audience wept during the performance and cheered after it was over, giving what they suspected to be a covert criticism of Stalinism a resounding thirty-minute ovation. When interviewed, Shostakovich disarmingly claimed that the 5th was about 'man in all his feelings'.[43] Earlier in the year, the composer had been summoned to the 'Big House' – NKVD Leningrad headquarters on Liteiny Prospekt. Shostakovich had been friendly with General Tukhachevsky since the mid-1920s and he was interrogated about the general's alleged plot to kill Stalin. Surely, after his bumpy relationship with the state, Shostakovich's implication in the trumped-up charges meant that his luck had run out. He was instructed to return to the 'Big House' several days later. He duly bid goodbye to his family and prepared for exile. But when he arrived at NKVD headquarters, he was dismissed. In the intervening days the investigator in charge of his case had himself been arrested.[44]

Although Shostakovich was obviously as lucky as he was cunning and courageous, it is remarkable that he got away with

*The 'Big House': NKVD Leningrad headquarters on Liteyny Prospekt.*

so much, when everybody else around him did not. Perhaps he was saved by the international success of *Lady Macbeth* – the composer had become a celebrity abroad. His spirited music for Soviet cinema probably also played a part. As a young man, Shostakovich had worked as a pianist for silent films in Leningrad cinemas and the experience, combined with his love of jazz, served him well. When he produced the huge hit 'Song of the Counterplan', for a 1932 film about the way in which Soviet workers dealt with a bunch of 'wreckers' in a Leningrad factory, Stalin – like Napoleon with the 'Marseillaise' – knew he had a cultural weapon worthy of a thousand cannon. Shostakovich, despite erring in the direction of obscurity and 'formalism' in his serious work, could be relied upon to deliver a damned good tune that would rouse the nation.[45]

After its popularity during the NEP years in the early Twenties, jazz came back into fashion during the 1930s. Against the backdrop of the purges and developing terror, people were encouraged to be merry.[46] Gramophones appeared in shops. But none of this disguised the fact that fear was taking its toll on mental stability, as people became suspicious and confused, living in perpetual fright. Any semblance of ordinary life was illusory when people feared the midnight knock of the NKVD. To add to their distress, Leningrad's poor were crammed into communal apartments, or *kommunalki*, in which families shared kitchens and bathrooms and everybody knew what everybody else was up to. Forced into living public lives, people were reduced to a state of paralysing isolation and loneliness. Victor Serge remembered that, from the late Twenties, 'the lie in the heart of all social relationships' became 'even fouler'.[47] People sold out to the authorities in order to stay alive. If two people were talking, there was a strong chance one of them might be from state security. In this climate of distrust and betrayal, the twelve-year-old Pavlik Morozov became a national hero for denouncing his own father. The incident may well have been apocryphal but, through the poems, songs and plays that it spawned, it served Stalin. When accusing someone, evidence was not necessary – it was simply fabricated to suit the situation. The phrase 'he lies like an eyewitness'[48] became a common simile.

The need for money pressed hard on the Bolsheviks. In February 1920, GOKHRAN had been set up to collect precious metals and jewellery. There were thirty-three depositories for such items in Petrograd, and Maxim Gorky was put in charge of the eighty experts evaluating them. His team amassed 120,000 pieces for the first wave of selling from 1920–24. A second wave, from 1928–31, offered paintings that included masterpieces from the Hermitage. The museum had taken possession of a huge number of new treasures after private collections were nationalised in 1923 and Petrograd's Stieglitz Museum was shut down.[49]

Given the financial instability in the West at that time, it was not the most propitious moment to sell, but the scheme was considered unavoidable. The Commissariat for Foreign Trade and the somewhat shifty Soviet trade delegations in several foreign capitals contacted interested buyers. A sensational auction fetching miserable prices was held in Berlin in May 1931 – just over $600,000 was obtained for 256 lots, including important Van Dyck portraits, an *Adam and Eve* by Cranach, and Rembrandt's *Christ and the Samaritan at the Well*. In America, Victor and Armand Hammer became the agents selling Fabergé jewels in New York. Andrew Mellon, First Secretary to the American Treasury, bought twenty-one canvases from the Hermitage, including Jan van Eyck's *Annunciation* and two important Rembrandts. When Mellon founded the National Gallery of Art in Washington, these were among the paintings he donated to the collection. Other interested parties also came forward. The Philadelphia Museum of Art acquired Poussin's *Birth of Venus* through the Soviet–New York trade delegation, AMTORG. The British-Armenian head of Iraq Petroleum, Calouste Gulbenkian, acquired a Rembrandt portrait for a mere $30,000.

In a move to increase the prestige of the new Soviet capital, 400 paintings were transferred from the Winter Palace to the Pushkin Museum of Fine Arts in Moscow. By way of compensation, the Hermitage received 100 works from the fabulous Impressionist, Post-Impressionist and early-twentieth-century paintings collected by the Moscow merchants Sergei Shchukin and Ivan Morozov. These included important canvases by Van Gogh, Gauguin and Cézanne, along with Matisse's large and sublimely affirmative masterpiece *The Dance*. In 1932, these new acquisitions were re-contextualised. Post-Impressionists were exhibited as examples of art from the 'era of rotting capitalism'. Picasso and Matisse – appropriately given the visual vocabulary borrowed from exoteric cultures – were examples of painting in 'the era of imperialism'. It was all part and parcel of the museum's Marxist restructuring, in which early-eighteenth-century French art was seen as painting from the 'era of the disintegration of feudal society and the bourgeois revolution'.[50]

During the Stalin era, Leningraders were denied the vitality of a flourishing literary scene. Of the 700 people who attended the First Congress of Soviet Writers in 1934, only fifty were alive to attend the Second, twenty years later. Disease, old age and war played their part – but so did the dictator. Osip Mandelstam wrote a withering poem about a man for whom 'every killing is a treat', whose laws are 'flung, like horseshoes at the head, the eye or the groin', whose sycophants circle as the 'cockroach whiskers leer' and words, 'final as lead weights, fall from his lips'. It was circulated on scraps of paper – or, more safely, by word-of-mouth.[51] But the NKVD had eyes and ears everywhere, and Mandelstam was arrested. Saved from immediate execution, he was exiled to a *gulag* in 1938, where he attempted suicide and eventually died. Mikhail Bulgakov's writing was banned. Boris Pasternak wrote in secret. Anna Akhmatova, like Shostakovich, managed to survive, while speaking out against the 'voiceless terror'. Meanwhile, comrades were regaled by Five-Year Plan pulp, such as *People of the Stalin Tractor Works* or Alexei Tolstoy's *Peter the First*, which recast the founder of St Petersburg in Stalin's image. By 1939, however, adult male literacy stood at an impressive 94 per cent, and print runs of permitted reading – *Pravda* and *Izvestia* – rose from just under ten million in 1927 to thirty-eight million by 1940.[52]

Horseracing had been the only popular sport in St Petersburg before the revolution. During the 1930s gymnastics flourished, adding grace and muscle to the great parades flaunting Soviet might. Football, along with fencing and rowing, became popular.[53] Sports clubs opened and entertainment thrived, to beguile an embattled population. The circus, attacked in the first days of the revolution as vulgar, cruel and demeaning, had been nationalised in 1919 and became very popular. At the Kirov Theatre – where conductors still appeared in white waistcoats and tails[54] – the audience of white-collar workers and the party elite was able to watch one of Russia's greatest ballerinas. Both her parents had been dancers, and she remembered watching one Mariinsky performance of *The Sleeping Beauty* when she was four. When the Lilac Fairy came onstage, she had screamed, 'That's Mama, my Mama.' She also remembered that when she was about seven and the revolution was in full swing, her parents gave free recitals to film audiences before the screening started, in an effort to introduce their art to the people. Galina Ulanova was taken into the ballet company in 1928 and made her debut as Princess Florinda, following that with a sensational performance as Odette/Odile in *Swan Lake*. Her mother was in the audience. She didn't scream, but when it came to the infamous thirty-two *fouettés* in the third act, she left her seat and went to the rear of the box to say a silent prayer for her daughter. Ulanova went on to a great career, first at the Kirov and then at Moscow's Bolshoi.[55]

Despite attempts to displace religion with Soviet festivals, the Church still made a powerful claim on people's embattled souls. St Isaac's had been turned into an 'anti-God' museum, and the cathedral at Peterhof was used as a cinema, yet a variety of Christian denominations still exerted their spell over Leningrad's population. Socialist May Day celebrations fought hard against the opulence of Easter Mass in 1937, when the festivals clashed.[56] More than 80,000 people crushed into Leningrad's remaining churches, with up to a 100,000 disappointed believers gathering outside. The state became intolerant of such a popular rival, and Stalin not only demolished churches, but also exiled or imprisoned priests.

Russia's highest concentration of urban Jews was to be found in Leningrad and, just as they had been denounced as revolutionaries by the last tsars, Stalin targeted them – incredibly – as Hitler's spies. Forming a significant portion of the party elite, intellectual Jews were resented and figured as high-profile victims in the show trials that continued until Stalin's death.[57] Anti-Semitism accounted for Stalin's strange scheme to purge western Russia of Jews by

transforming a segment of Far Eastern Siberia into a 'Jewish Auton-
omous Region'. Birobidzhan, the designated area, was about half
the size of England and was located in a harsh region, vulnerable to
possible attack from China or Japan. In the event, Stalin took care
of the Jews – almost all of those who were settled in Birobidzhan
were killed during the purges of 1937–8.[58]

Towards the end of the Thirties, the incessant hiss of outdoor loudspeakers spewing uninterrupted party propaganda
and muzak polluted the Leningrad streets. Juvenile crime had
increased and hooliganism persisted. The Australian visitor
Betty Roland spoke of organised criminals emptying entire
apartments. Otherwise, she was enchanted by the continued use
of the frozen Neva as a thoroughfare and a place for pleasure. She
watched Red Army soldiers doing manoeuvres on skis while, on
land, floodlit tennis courts were transformed into skating rinks.
She noticed how, in the depths of winter, astute Leningraders
would stand on the steam vents of the city's heating system while
waiting for trams, in order to keep warm. She also witnessed one
event that was redolent of old St Petersburg. A fur auction for
foreign buyers took place in the Winter Palace, where there was
a good deal of 'drinking, toasting, guzzling and gorging' before
the visitors inspected the pelts of ermine, sable, mink and fox laid
out in the ballroom.[59]

*Central part of the frieze on the House of Soviets, built between 1936–41,
fronting Moskovskaya Square in southern Leningrad.*

As the terrible Thirties moved towards a combustible future, Leningrad was listed as a special area for defence purposes, and foreigners – including diplomats – were no longer permitted to live there. Una Birch, Dame Pope-Hennessy, was one of the last to arrive before the embargo. She was on a visit to Lady Muriel Paget, who had administered the Anglo-Russian Hospital in Petrograd from 1915 to 1918. Dame Pope-Hennessy dined well with Lady Paget on 'red brown crayfish, slices of grey bread, a jar of sour cream, some butter and a bowl of small thick-set cucumbers'. She marvelled at the brightly coloured mosque on the Petrograd side and at Gavriil Baranovsky's Buddhist temple overlooking the northern branch of the Neva. But she found, to her dismay, that the famous Nevsky Prospekt had been renamed, and what little was left of fashion was obliged to stroll down 'The 25th of October Street'. In de la Mothe's sumptuous Yusupov Palace, rows of iron beds filled the rooms and corridors, making a dormitory for visiting engineers working in the city. Schlüsselberg Fortress had been allowed to crumble. Rather than restoring it as a testimony to tsarist tyranny, workers protested that they had suffered too much themselves to bother. There were 'aggressive, persistent' flies everywhere, and muslin was used to cover food. Yet – despite new and perennial inconveniences – Dame Una summed it up: 'Leningrad, one is glad to see, is still Petersburg, poorer, shabbier, but in outline unchanged.'[60]

# 14

# DARKEST AND FINEST HOUR

*1941–4*

'For 23 years we have all been on death row . . . but we have reached the epoch's grand finale.' That diary entry was written by the puppeteer Liubov Shaporina a few days after the Nazis started shelling Leningrad in September 1941.[1] In her early sixties, Shaporina had lived through famines, wars, revolution, civil war and Stalin's terror. One of the most self-destructive aspects of that terrifying purge was Stalin's execution of 512 members of the Soviet high command, among them the civil-war hero who had suppressed the Kronstadt rebellion, Marshal Tukhachevsky – tortured and then executed for allegedly plotting a *coup d'état*.[2] Accused in a fabricated document purchased from the Germans with forged marks, Tukhachevsky was clearly framed. Hitler's immediate objective was to cripple the Russian military through the inevitable purge that would follow the exposure of the alleged coup. Hitler could dominate eastern Europe without Russian interference.

Released in 1937, the year that Tukhachevsky was executed, Sergei Eisenstein's historical epic *Alexander Nevsky* told the story of the thirteenth-century invasion of Teutonic knights and acted as an explicit, unremitting warning of the dangers of German aggression, laced with a celebration of Soviet virtues and a rousing spur to resist invasion. Stalin – without the caution of generals who knew better – signed the Soviet–German Non-Aggression Pact on 23 August 1939. It came as a thunderbolt for communists and fellow travellers across the globe. *Humanité*, official organ of the French Communist Party, claimed that it demonstrated Stalin's supreme effort to prevent war. For Arthur Koestler, it was 'the funeral of his illusions'. Squealer, in Orwell's *Animal Farm*, would have called it 'Tactics, comrades, tactics.' But for once, Stalin's overweening paranoia deserted him. Alexander Solzhenitsyn claimed that during his 'suspicion-ridden life', Stalin 'only trusted one man . . . Adolf Hitler'.[3]

Between November 1939 and March 1941, Stalin fought the territorial Winter War against Finland. Leningrad proved an unreliable arsenal, its factories frequently crippled by power outages. Food shortages continued. People clamoured for rationing and were rewarded with price rises. Work conditions became terrifying, as bosses struggled to meet impossible quotas proposed by the Third Five-Year Plan. Employees arriving a few minutes late for work were sent for trial. During an eight-month period in the year before the Nazi invasion, more than 140,000 Leningraders were sentenced to corrective labour in a misguided effort to curb absenteeism.[4]

During the Winter War between 125,000 and 200,000 Russian soldiers lost their lives and the Finns lost territory between Lake Ladoga and the Gulf of Finland.[5] While Stalin was thus preoccupied, Hitler was planning his attack. In the spring of 1941, the Nazis massed enormous forces on Stalin's western frontier. Churchill warned the Kremlin about Hitler's intentions. Soviet agents sent incontestable evidence of impending invasion. German soldiers defected to warn the Russians. But Stalin trusted Hitler. The defecting German soldiers were shot as spies.

At 3.15 a.m. on 22 June 1941, the Germans crossed the River Bug. Operation Barbarossa was under way. Russian border guards were surprised. Stalin – despite the warnings, despite Luftwaffe sorties over Russian air space – was surprised. Habitually over-quick to react, the Soviet leader hid in the Kremlin and made no official statement until 3 July. He had been stunned by the largest invasion ever mounted: 5,000 aircraft, 3,000 tanks and five and a half million troops sweeping into Soviet territory along a 3,000-kilometre front,[6] capturing towns, cities and taking three million prisoners of war in the first sixth months of the campaign. The one man Stalin trusted intended to enslave the Slavic people and exile them to the wastes of Siberia. He wanted the rich farmlands of southern Russia, the oil fields at Baku, a Black Sea port and *Lebensraum* – space for the expansion of the Third Reich. The shipyards, industry and arms manufacturers of Leningrad would be a prize, but with characteristic fanaticism, Hitler wanted to wipe the cradle of the communist revolution off the face of the earth.

In the early hours of 22 June – the night after Wagner's *Lohengrin* was given at the Kirov – Russian ships were torpedoed in the Baltic and foreign planes were in the skies above Leningrad. It was a lucid White Night, during which the city's high-school students celebrated their graduation. At 4 a.m. a Soviet squadron scrambled from the Vyborg Sector to chase off the Luftwaffe. At 5 a.m. the German Consul announced that Germany was at war with Russia. Stalin's protégé, Molotov, was on the radio claiming there had been no warning. Patriotic songs played all day and, within twenty-four hours, 100,000 Leningraders had volunteered to defend the motherland.[7]

Guide books, maps and cameras were confiscated by the authorities. Street signs and direction panels were dismantled or painted over. Civil defence was swiftly mobilised. The deportation of 'enemies of the people' – Germans and Finns, ethnic minorities, old bourgeoisie – combined with conscription and the evacuation of nearly 650,000 inhabitants, of which nearly two-thirds were children, reduced Leningrad's population to around 2.5 million by the beginning of September, when the siege closed around the city. There was chaos and danger in the evacuations. Some of the chosen destinations lay in the direct line of the German advance, and trains were harassed by Stuka dive bombers.[8]

Throughout the summer, thousands of old men, women and teenagers dug trenches and tank-traps to protect the south-western approaches to Leningrad. Also under construction was a second line of defence stretching from Peterhof south-east to Gatchina, and then north-east to Kolpino. A third, last-ditch defence was prepared at the city limits. Despite the summer storms that bogged the German advance, Novgorod fell. Then Chudovo, on the Leningrad–Moscow railway line. Along the gulf coast to the west of the city, only the sixty-kilometre-wide 'Oranienbaum Pocket' held out against the invaders. To the north, the Finns reached Lake Ladoga. After weeks of defeat and heavy losses, Stalin ordered the catastrophic naval withdrawal from Tallinn in the last week of August. Many ships were sunk, numerous lives were lost, and Leningrad was left almost defence-less. On 8 September, the Nazis reached the southern shore of Lake Ladoga, and Schlüsselberg was taken.[9] As the siege ring closed around Leningrad, Nazi intentions were perfectly clear: 'Any requests for surrender . . . will be categorically rejected since the problem of maintaining and feeding the population should not and cannot be solved by us . . . We have no interest in saving any party of the civilian population of this large city.'[10]

Evacuation of industrial machinery began in the first weeks of the invasion and, by the time rail and road links were cut, nearly 100 ordnance factories and well over 150,000 workers had been moved east. Plans to destroy nearly 60,000 strate-gic targets were put in place, should the Nazis break through. Guns were taken from ships at Kronstadt to defend the city and contingency procedures to scuttle the fleet were prepared. Win-dows were taped, then boarded. Falconet's *Bronze Horseman*, the proud symbol of the energy of the city, was sandbagged and boarded up.[11] The Alexander Column was sheathed in wooden scaffolding, but the sculpture of the militant, yet angelic Alexander atop the column – the image of Russia triumphant – was left to stand out against the sky. Rollers of wooden logs were used to slide the equestrian statues off the four corners of the Anichkov Bridge over the Fontanka and trundle them to the nearby Alexandrinsky Gardens for burial. A Gutenberg Bible, an early Greek Old Testament and Pushkin's letters were removed from the library on the Nevsky. The most valuable manuscripts were transfered from the Academy of Sciences. At the Hermitage, the curator started to move paintings to the security of the reinforced jewellery room, immediately after Molotov spoke to the nation on 22 June. Six days and six nights of hectic packing began. Small pictures were placed in crates with cloth dividers, and large canvases were rolled. On 1 July, nearly half a million treasures were carried out of the city in twenty-two freight wagons with an armoured car harbouring the most valuable items. A second train followed on 20 July, with twenty-three freight wagons and a million objects. But before a third train was loaded with 350 packed crates, the Germans had gained control of the railways and so the boxes remained in the Winter Palace.[12]

Owing to the swiftness of the German advance, the evacuation of the surrounding palaces was not so successful. At Gatchina, they buried sculptures in the park and bricked up treasures in the extensive cellars. But many furnishings had to be left in place. An alert curator, on the point of departing, saved a portfolio of drawings by the architects Quarenghi, Rossi and Voronikhin. Later in the siege, an article published in *Leningradskaya Pravda* reported how the invaders were looting the gilded statues at Peterhof, dismantling the Amber Room panels in Rastrelli's palace at Tsarskoe Selo and trashing the palaces.[13] Swastikas were cut into tapestries and hung in German bunkers.

The streets of Leningrad were savaged. Not, at first, by the Germans. Inhabitants scarred its prospekts and open spaces with sharp concrete pyramids and clusters of short girder tank-blockers. They dug trenches, crevices and dugouts two metres deep for gun emplacements. Six anti-aircraft batteries were mounted in the Field of Mars. Barrage balloons were inflated in open spaces and were walked like giant sausage-dogs along streets that were empty but for army lorries, antique trams and trolley buses. During the first weeks of the invasion, more than 320 balloons were deployed at heights of two and four kilometres above the city. Also escorted through the streets were German POWs, eliciting both curiosity and incomprehension. Every so often, someone drew close to spit in their faces.[14]

One of the strangest sights was the batteries of 'listeners' – quartets of huge cubist tubas that were used to scan the skies for the sounds of approaching bombers. Air-raid sirens were tested, sending people scurrying towards imperfect shelters and fracturing sleep in the middle of the night. On 4 September – the first day of shelling – German gunners demonstrated their knowledge and uncanny accuracy by hitting railway stations and factories. Two days later the first bombs dropped on the Nevsky Prospekt, damaging buildings and bursting a water pipe. The

*Air defence sound receivers mounted on a bastion of the Peter and Paul Fortress.*

major food-storage depot – the Badaev warehouses – were hit on the 8th and the 10th.[15] Clouds mushroomed in the sky, gloriously amber, then bronze in the dying rays of the early autumn sun. Then a sinister helix pierced the splendour and obscured the scene. Oil depots had been set on fire.[16] On the 9th, Luftwaffe attacks became more sustained and shells pounded the city, shaking the ground. Smothering smoke spiralled through burnt-out buildings. Yellow flames licked black walls. On 19 September, *gostiny dvor* was hit, killing 100 shoppers. Hospitals and markets were targeted, along with the dense concentration of factories in the southern part of the city, close to the German front line. During the first months the university on Vasilevsky Island and the Academy of Arts were hit. A shell took a bite out of the Kirov theatre, and the vital Elektrosila power plant was hit again and again.[17]

First you heard 'the whirr of an enemy shell, then a whistle, a crack, the thunderclap of a building collapsing', followed by a rumbling echo. On 14 September, teenage Lena Mukhina

*An air-raid hits the Nevsky Prospekt.*

*A bombed-out Leningrad street.*

recorded that already-familiar sequence in her diary.[18] As tenements tumbled, they left bathtubs stranded in space and doors to nowhere. Human chains formed to salvage what was still intact. After a bombardment, as the chemical-thick clouds dispersed, odd assortments of pianos, lamps and sewing machines were heaped in the street beside their bewildered and homeless owners. A couple seemed to embrace. Then one lowered the other to the ground. Buildings burned for days. Volcanoes mocking the gaining cold.

People stumbled across unsteady hillocks of tumbled bricks, past forests of charred beams and futuristic explosions of smashed wood and jagged, shattered glass. Their eyes fixed firmly on the ground in front of them, in order to avoid unfamiliar hazards – rubble, shell-holes, corpses. In the following months, survivors would come to negotiate such obstacles without so much as a second glance. People deprived of fats and sugar became prone to vertigo[19] and – like blitzed buildings – seemed on the point of teetering. In her diary, Lydia Ginzburg noted how easy it was to lose one's balance, even in the simple act of tying up a shoe. The body 'slithered out of control' and wanted 'to fall like an empty sack into some incomprehensible abyss'.[20] People found themselves short

of breath and wondered – slowly – why the simplest thing took
a deal of effort. They gradually lost interest in what had always
fascinated them. Some complained of a constant droning in the
ear: the buzz of the radio, the drone of aircraft, the wail of the
air-raid sirens or some relentless tension drumming an inexplica-
ble tinnitus. Gums started to swell. In food queues, racoon-eyed,
swollen-faced survivors waited patiently for a bread ration that
had been reduced five times since the introduction of rationing
in July. An understandable crumbling of resolve occurred as a
quite reasonable idea gnawed at the spirit: the Germans might be
preferable to Stalin. Painted images of their leader's face gloated
from walls – with that smile that doesn't smile – on the mess
of his own making. Swastikas splashed across the crumbling
walls of tenements. But Leningraders' familiarity with sacrifice and deprivation helped strengthen their resolve. The poet
Olga Berggolts, who had been arrested in the 1930s and beaten
until she miscarried, read comforting, uplifting poetry on the
local radio.[21]

Snow fell in mid-October – about the time the power stations
ran low on fuel. The dancer Vera Kostrovitskaya observed that
people became 'aware of days and dates only by means of small
square paper coupons with the number 125', which signified
the next ration of 'a small piece of greenish-brown bread, half
wood shavings'.[22] Bakers were obliged to find all kinds of alternatives. Flour was eked out with dust scraped from the walls
and from beneath floorboards at the mills. Nearly half the quantity of flour needed to make a loaf of bread was substituted by
bran, the pressed seeds of oil-producing plants and wood-cel-
lulose extracted from pine shavings.[23] *Kasha* kept many people
alive. An ersatz 'meat jelly' was fabricated from carpenter's glue.
It tasted authentic because wood-glue was manufactured by
boiling the hooves and horns of animals. Industrial glue, dex-
trin, was less tasty and tended to stick people's teeth together.
At home, people scraped the dried glue from peeling wallpaper.

They gouged dusty crumbs from table cracks, scurf from hats, softened leather from the inside of worn belts. Medicine was drunk, cosmetics consumed. People gnawed their furniture and chewed their clothes. Lena Mukhina, a pupil at Leningrad's School no. 30 on Vassilevsky Island, was 'so terribly hungry. There's a horrible emptiness in my stomach. I'm so desperate for bread. I want it so badly. Right now I feel as though I would give anything to fill my stomach.'[24] The going price for a Bechstein piano was 'a few loaves of bread'. By late October, corpses were being put out on the streets.[25]

Paraffin ran out and people burned solvents and insecticides. Home-made metal stoves were fuelled by wood taken from bombed-out buildings or by antique books or broken furniture. By mid-November low-wattage bulbs were used in those institutions that were allowed electricity. By the end of the month, home use was forbidden during the day.[26] The water supply and sanitation had been hit. Abandoned rooms were used as toilets. Indispensable was a long-handled cylindrical ladle capable of scooping water from the holes cut in the thickening ice. Also useful, as the snow compacted, was a child's sledge. Everybody on the streets seemed to drag bundles behind them: water, fuel, a few possessions gathered from a bombed-out life, a body. Everyone seemed on the move and yet there was nowhere to go.

Some people – raw and hungry – just sat down in the middle of a short journey and could not, or did not want to, get up and froze to death. Vera Kostrovitskaya passed a man who, 'on his way to the Finland Station, got tired, and sat down. For two weeks while I was going back and forth to the hospital, he "sat", without his knapsack, without his rags, in his underwear, naked, a skeleton with ripped-out entrails'.[27]

The winter of 1941–2 was severe and – in one week in December – almost 850 people died in the street. More than 50,000 people perished of starvation that month and mortality in the city peaked at over 100,000 in January and then

again in February, before falling back gradually in March and
April. Medical orderlies were working around the clock. Valentina Gorokhova remembered that her hospital was completely
unprepared. 'The temperature in the wards was below zero. The
medicines froze . . . The wounded were put two to a bed.' Instead
of uniforms, 'staff and doctors worked in their winter coats' and
used a covering sheet as a lab tunic, secured 'at the back, on the
arms, and at the wrist with surgical instruments'.[28]

In mid-January 1942, with temperatures at −30°, Lena
Mukhina despaired. The 'shops are empty, the lights don't work,
there's no water and the lavatory won't flush'. Some corpses scattered in the streets were wrapped up for burial, others stared
with glazed eyes, their yellowing faces ghosted under settling
snow.[29] In a bleak echo of Peter the Great's funeral cortège, isolated individuals sledged a coffin or a corpse across the frozen
Neva to a communal grave, where workers fish-hooked corpses
into parallel lines to ensure maximum capacity. New morgues
were set up and, in February, 25,000 bodies piled up at the
Piskarevskoye cemetery, stacked in rows 200 metres long and
two metres high.[30] With so many dead, it was almost possible to
imagine how Stalin could hold life so cheap.

Without the usual pollution – 270 factories closed, and others
barely functioning – the winter became shockingly beautiful,
with the crispness that had delighted and dazzled the eyes of
court artist Robert Ker Porter. Snow lay like Gautier's 'crushed
marble'.[31] The unused spiders' webs of tramlines were gently
fuzzed by frost. But, for all the beauty, Ginzburg noted that, in
the cold, 'fingers tended to double up and freeze in some chance
attitude and the hand lose its ability to grasp. Then it could only
be used as a paw, like a stump or club-like implement.'[32]

Everything took so long. Elza Greinert described the wait to
get a coffin for her late husband. On 14 January 1942, she 'went
to the clinic to register a certificate, stood in line from 8.30 to
2.00'. On the 17th, she couldn't 'get a coffin since there were

fist fights over them and you had to stand in line'. At last she found someone in her building who made a coffin from her own material 'for 400 gms of bread and 50 roubles cash'.[33] Against the frustrations and delays, Ginzburg insisted on the importance of strategies for acting, rather than merely reacting.[34] The absolute ordinariness of much that happened seemed almost ghoulish beside the boundless suffering and death. When air raids started, people having their hair permed would not budge. Life went on as best it could.

Horses dropped dead in the street and crowds gathered to hack off meat and scoop out offal. If you loved your cat or dog, you kept it indoors. But that might prove a murderous temptation. When members of the militia went to collect the dead from apartments, they sometimes found limbs missing. A teenager axed his grandmother to death to eat her innards. Another scavenged an unburied body to mince it. A black market opened up for human flesh.

The Russian language makes a very important distinction between *trupoedstvo*, the eating of already-dead human flesh, and *lyudoedstvo,* the consumption of people killed on purpose. When survival was at stake – in sieges, famines and shipwrecks – the former could be justified. But there were abuses and arrests: more than 2,000 from the late autumn of 1941 to December 1942.[35] Many of the culprits were uneducated or illiterate. Olga Berggolts heard of a couple who ate their own child, then trapped and killed three more. Elsewhere, a one-year-old was slaughtered to feed her two-year-old sister.

Not everyone needed to resort to such extremes. The cafeteria at party headquarters in the Smolny served cutlets and small pies throughout the first winter of the siege.[36] Recuperation clinics for party leaders offered choice food and decent medical treatment. City leaders had a resthouse in the woods to the north of city, where lamb, chicken and fish were available.[37] The NKVD ate well and, in 1943, while the city was still under siege, the council arranged for ranking officials to receive, annually, 5,000–6,000 roubles worth of subsidised goods.[38] Throughout the siege, corrupt bosses arranged unfair food distribution and – in a scam right out of Gogol's *Dead Souls* – people obtained ration cards in the names of those departed for the front or evacuated to the east. People even hoped that if a member of their family had to die, they would do so after 1 January, the date on which a new ration card was issued.[39] Bakery staff were bribed outrageously. Food-industry workers stole huge quantities of provisions. Three chiefs from one shop were arrested for stealing 700 kilos. Teenagers – orphans mostly – snatched purchases as people left bakeries. Some stole from stealers by threatening to report them.[40] People killed for groceries or ration cards and, in the first half of 1942, there were 1,200 related arrests. The NKVD asked Moscow for reinforcements. Food crime was demanding a good deal of their time and they had other concerns.[41] Between the beginning of the siege and the summer of 1943, nearly 4,000 civilians were convicted of counter-revolutionary crimes.

During the first winter of the siege 'the road of life' helped save those who were left to be saved. By the beginning of November, barge traffic across the southern end of Lake Ladoga was halted as the water began to freeze. The last railway line into the city was cut as Tikhvin fell to the Germans. The only way in and out of the city was by air. On 17 November, the ice on Lake Ladoga was ten centimetres thick – too thin for any kind of traffic. But, with temperatures falling, sledges and even lorries would soon be able to attempt a crossing. At −5°, fifteen centimetres of ice – capable of supporting a horse and sledge with a load of one tonne – takes six days to form. For a lorry carrying a similar load, a thickness of twenty centimetres was necessary.

On 20 November, at −12° and with ice eighteen centimetres thick, sledges drawn by worn horses pulled out of Kabona

*A convoy of lorries forming the 'Road of Life' across frozen Lake Ladoga.*

and started the twenty- to thirty-kilometre journey through the arctic white-out to Osinovets. Traffic controllers and prisoners were spread along the way, testing the ice, maintaining the track and receiving the necessary vodka to sustain them. Horses too weak to complete the journey were shot for meat to feed the city. Two days later, the ice was thick enough for sixty lorries to set off across Lake Ladoga and onwards – overland through the block of Soviet-held territory between the Finnish and the German front lines – into the starving city. Lorries kept a good distance between them and hauled sledges, in order to spread their load. With freezing fog and blizzard squalls, visibility was often down to a few metres. German bombs rained down, plummeting through the ice to detonate at the bottom of the lake. When the ice fractured, controllers modified the route. But with the drifting snow, cracks were often covered and lorries were lost when they sagged into splintered ice. When a German attack force set out on skis from Shlüsselburg to sabotage the 'road of life', they were beaten back. For all this effort and endurance, in the last third of November only flour sufficient to feed the city for two days had been delivered. Moscow ordered women, children and the elderly to be evacuated in empty trucks returning across the lake. Despite the grim situation in the city, many were reluctant to leave. The journey was arduous. The fifty-kilometre rail trip to Osinovets could take several days. In their severely weakened condition, many evacuees simply fell from the lorries as they zigzagged across the lake. Each morning, infant corpses were collected by the traffic patrols. Many of those who did make it across died during the hardships of the onward journey.[42]

With Stalin's campaign to destroy or convert churches, it was the Nazi invasion that saved Leningrad's flamboyant Church of Christ the Saviour on the Spilt Blood. A good number of the city's other churches were still intact, and priests offered hope and urged defiance. Powerful appeals by the clergy from the earliest days of the invasion forced the dictator to realise that the church was a useful ally in the struggle against Hitler. Every day of the siege, the Metropolitan, Alexei, processed around Leningrad's baroque Cathedral of St Nicholas, holding an icon high to protect his population and defy German bombers.[43] But with beetroot juice substituting for holy wine at mass, it seemed that nothing short of a miracle could transubstantiate the fate of Peter's city.

People were starving to death, the Nazis were pounding the city, but the weather was improving. With the spring came the thaw, and severely weakened bodies banded together in an effort to clear rubble, corpses, excrement and all the broken traces of damaged lives. There were outbreaks of typhoid and dysentery, and many died in the aftermath of the cruellest winter of all the cruel winters they had known. For those left alive, a new determination burgeoned as Leningrad's green spaces were turned into vegetable patches. Seedlings were distributed and hoes and wheelbarrows provided. In Catherine the Great's hanging

*Proud harvesters. Cabbages grown in St Isaac's Square during the siege.*

*Clearing snow and rubble from the Nevsky Prospekt.*

garden on the first floor of the Small Hermitage, beet, spinach, cabbage and carrots were planted.[44] As spring grew into summer, cabbages – like aliens from a distant planet – took over St Isaac's Square. By the autumn of 1942 the city had cultivated, on its own embattled turf, enough food to keep itself alive for up to four months. People started to eat normally – some so enthusiastically that they made themselves severely ill. Markets opened, attracting speculators and high prices. The syncopated rattle of passenger trams was heard again, but for a population strung out on its nerves, the freight trams were unsettling. Lydia Ginzburg noted that they came screeching around curves in the track, sounding like 'anti-aircraft sirens'.[45] Evacuation resumed over Lake Ladoga by barge, and more supplies were brought in. With cables and an oil pipeline laid across the bottom of the lake, life was looking more possible as the city entered the second year of the siege.

The aural bombardment of a radio metronome ticked constantly from the city's 1,500 street speakers, quickening its rhythm when bombers were on their way, slowing it down as they departed.[46] In apartments across the city 400,000 speakers had been installed to keep inhabitants almost up-to-date, or partially informed, through twice-daily news bulletins.[47] Otherwise, radio broadcasts of patriotic song and classical music sustained the spirit of the city. Two musical giants responded to events. The first finished an opera which was premiered in Moscow in 1957 – too late for the war. The other composed a symphony that trumpeted Leningrad's plight to the world.

Under suspicion for having spent so much time abroad, Sergei Prokofiev had redeemed himself as a Soviet composer with the rousing cantata he produced as a soundtrack to Eisenstein's patriotic epic *Alexander Nevsky*. This was followed by his ballet *Romeo and Juliet*, premiered at the Kirov during the dark days of the Winter War, with Galina Ulanova, somewhat reluctantly, dancing the lead. Although she famously declared,

'Never was there a tale more of woe, than Prokofiev's music for Romeo,' Juliet was one of her most expressive creations. It was while working on a follow-up ballet, *Cinderella*, that Prokofiev first thought of writing an opera based on Tolstoy's *War and Peace*. The composer felt that the story of 'the expulsion of Napoleon's army from Russian soil' was 'particularly relevant'. To be sure, the novel was republished with a wartime print run of half a million copies in Leningrad alone.[48] Prokofiev's powerful opera, with its choruses of defiance and Kutuzov's declaration before the Battle of Borodino that 'there is no people greater than ours', was written for a wartime audience.[49] Finished in Perm in 1943, it would have been a tonic to the nation, but the resources needed to perform such a work proved too considerable.[50] Even a symphony – Shostakovich's 7th – barely made it onto the platform in the city to which it was dedicated.

Shostakovich finished the third movement of the symphony during the autumn of 1941, when he was working as a fireman in the Civil Defence Brigade. In October, he and his family were forced to evacuate to Kuibyshev on the Volga River where he finished the work. It was premiered by the Bolshoi Theatre Orchestra in Kuibyshev on 5 March 1942 and broadcast across the Soviet Union. Three weeks later, it was performed in Moscow and the score was microfilmed and transported via Persia and Cairo, to be flown to London and New York. Henry Wood premiered the symphony in London in June, and Arturo Toscanini – whose performance displeased the composer – gave its American premiere at Radio City in New York in July. Sixty-two further performances were given across the United States before the end of the year. In the composer's native city, deprived of food and power, the 7th Symphony's passage to performance was challenging.

The Leningrad Philharmonic had been evacuated, so when the score was flown in, posters went up across the city appealing for performers. The oboist Ksenia Matus wanted to participate, but found her instrument rotten. When she took it to be repaired, the charge was a cat. The man declared he had already eaten five. The distraught instrumentalist replied that there were no cats or dogs or birds left, so the craftsman repaired the oboe for cash. Musicians arrived from villages outside the city with passes declaring, 'Permission to enter Leningrad to perform the Seventh Symphony.'[51] Players arrived with grimy faces or crawling with lice, and the conductor, Karl Eliasberg, was disappointed by the response. The orchestra that assembled was below the number of players specified in the score, and each time they arrived for rehearsal they would be greeted by 'How many violins do we have left?' or 'We've just lost a bassoon player.' Yet the symphony was given its Leningrad premiere on 9 August 1942, the very day that Hitler had planned to celebrate the city's fall at the Astoria Hotel. The invitations had been printed. On the day of the concert, German artillery positions were bombarded, in an attempt to secure the quiet needed to relay the performance by loud-speaker across the city. It was even blared out beyond Leningrad's defences, to the Nazis camped close to the city. Several years after the end of the war, Eliasberg was thanked by some German soldiers who had been sitting in those siege trenches in 1942. They had listened to the symphony and burst into tears, realising they would never be able to capture Leningrad.[52]

By the time the siege moved into its second winter, shell damage had disfigured the cityscape. The glass dome of the old Stieglitz Museum had been hit. A bomb shattered the façade of the Small Hall of the Philharmonic. The Winter Palace was hit. When a one-tonne bomb fell in Palace Square, glass was blown out and there were gaping holes in the Hall of Columns and on the Jordan staircase. One of the most surreal spectacles of the siege was the guided tours given to soldiers from the front through the freezing galleries of the Hermitage. They were stopped in front of faded rectangles and empty frames on bare walls, while their guides lovingly described the composition and quality of the paintings that had been taken away for safe keeping.[53]

The Kirov Ballet had been evacuated to Perm. Ulanova was touring, frequently dancing for Red Army audiences. Many of the young ballet students left behind at the school were too ill and undernourished to dance.[54] But a good number of cinemas and theatres remained open. Lena Mukhina remembered seeing the 1937 American film *Champagne Waltz* at the Koloss cinema and revelling in its world of 'sparkling shops, gleaming cars, adverts, adverts, endless adverts. Adverts here, there and everywhere. Glittering, whirling, clamouring adverts.' Many of her peers loved what they knew of American popular culture, and it would be hard for those who survived the war to cope with the strengthened censorship of Soviet peace.[55] Leningrad Zoo, on the Petrograd Side, evacuated many animals before the Germans surrounded the city. The creatures that remained were fooled into eating paltry vegetable substitutes by spiking their rations with splashes of blood or bone-broth. But the zoo had been hit in an early raid, and a much-loved elephant from Hamburg was among the casualties.[56] The National Public Library on the Nevsky Prospekt was able to make a significant number of acquisitions during the siege, as the apartments of the dead were emptied and private libraries came onto the market. All in all, they added to their collection '58,892 books, 112,640 prints' and over 48,000 roubles worth of manuscripts. The library never closed, and people came to consult treatises on pressing topics such as vitamin deficiency and edible wild plants.[57]

Part of the Hermitage was opened as a convalescent centre – and a morgue – for the staff of Leningrad's museums.[58] In the hospitals, conditions slowly improved with the arrival of medicines and new materials. For New Year 1943 the staff managed a small party, and wrapped little bags of toys or sweets for the patients, who were also given fifty grams of vodka to welcome what people hoped would be a better New Year.[59]

Although German shelling had become so accurate that tram stops frequently had to be moved, by the winter of 1943 conditions were definitely better.[60] The winter was less cold than the previous one, and the food and fuel supply improved when the Red Army regained enough territory to enable the building of a railway to the city – the first train arriving on 7 February. During the rest of the year – with the track repaired 1,200 times – heavily shelled trains continued to get through. That summer, the city's vegetable harvest was twice as large as the previous year and, by late autumn 1943, the birth rate exceeded the number of deaths.[61] In September, the Germans began their retreat. Peterhof, Pushkin and Pulkovo were liberated.

On 23 January 1944, the last German shell fell on Leningrad and a new light filled the night sky – the safe, joyous sparkle of fireworks. The war had not yet been won, but Leningrad had been saved. Survivors could stare at the explosions snowing down on them, without scattering for cover. Blanks fired from ships and gun salutes discharged from the fort were a disturbingly joyous

The 'overmastering' Bronze Horseman, *uncovered after the war.*

echo of the deafening explosions that had wrecked their lives for 900 days and 900 nights. In the fighting around Leningrad, two million Russians had been killed. Civilian deaths in the city stood at one million. As liberated prisoners of war started to trickle back, they were interrogated. Had they been turned by Western Intelligence? One and a half million were carted off to camps.[62]

Today, rival clubs taunt Petersburg's Zenit football team, calling them 'Blockade Rats' and their grandparents 'cannibals'.[63] Those grandparents bravely faced down the Nazi terror. Yet, with the return to peace, they were once again forced to confront the omnipresent threat of their Comrade General Secretary. Shostakovich later declared that his 7th Symphony was 'about Leningrad that Stalin has systematically been destroying'.[64]

# 15

# MURMURS FROM THE UNDERGROUND

## *1945–91*

There are two museums in St Petersburg dedicated to Leningrad's suffering and resistance in the Great Patriotic War. It was not always so. Stalin's incompetence before and during the early stages of the conflict resulted in strict censorship after the end of hostilities. The siege became taboo. Three victory arches appeared, then disappeared. The first attempt to show what life had been like – the Museum of the Heroic Defence of Leningrad – was closed down and its directors arrested.[1] Meanwhile the priority for survivors was to plant trees and restore the parks and open spaces that were such an important aspect of Leningrad life. Extensive damage to the city required building on a scale unseen since the days of Peter the Great, and architects saw, in Leningrad's post-war reconstruction, an opportunity to emphasize what they held to be the city's defining style: the austere order beloved by Catherine and Alexander I – neoclassicism. Since the second quarter of the nineteenth century, construction serving the changing needs of life had resulted in a cityscape that was increasingly functional and eclectic. Railway stations, stores, apartment and office blocks generated a grab-bag of neo-Renaissance, neo-baroque, *stil-moderne*, modernist and Soviet-empire style. To allow neoclassicism to dominate, after the war the façades of certain ruined buildings constructed in other styles were modified, thus altering the architectural balance of the city centre. No. 68 Nevsky Prospekt, beside the Anichkov Bridge over the Fontanka, was one such building. Local architects organised training in plastering, moulding and marble-cutting as young people returned from evacuation. The Herculean task of reviving the city was underpinned by giving a number of important streets and squares their pre-revolutionary names.[2]

In October 1945, the Hermitage welcomed back the paintings sent off to Sverdlovsk for safe keeping. Less than a week later, trains from Germany began to deliver some of the two million artworks taken from German museums and private collections in retaliation for the Nazi invasion. One and a half million of these were returned to Soviet satellite countries in the 1950s, but hundreds of thousands of artefacts were kept hidden and remain in Russia as 'moral and not . . . financial compensation'[3] for the 110 million books and documents destroyed, the 427 Russian museums and 4,000 libraries devastated by the Nazis.[4] As the Hermitage collection was to be rehung, repairs to the damaged interior of the Winter Palace were a priority and, by November 1945, sixty-nine rooms and galleries were open to the public. Renovations to the city's palaces also went ahead. The Yusupov Palace functioned as the base of the Union of Workers in Education, the Anichkov Palace as the headquarters of the Leningrad Young Pioneers, the Tauride Palace as the Leningrad Communist Party High School.[5] By 1950, a substantial number of buildings had been restored, although Leningrad's outlying palaces lay in ruins for years.

People were swift to realise that the war, for all its terrors, had offered some respite from the unremitting fear of Stalin's Russia. After their new-found camaraderie, many were loath to return to suspicion and treachery and pined for the collapse of the regime. But with only one communist candidate standing for each seat in the 1946 elections, there seemed little chance. That same year, as a poor harvest resulted in a famine that killed yet another one

*Ruins of Peterhof Palace after the German occupation.*

million Soviet citizens, Stalin set about securing the good life
for the party elite. The Gastronom network of special shops had
reopened, with luxury goods offered at prices well beyond the
means of ordinary workers. Fees had been introduced to cover
the last three years of school and university, so that the chance for
advancement was placed beyond the means of modest families.[6]
Special hospitals and holiday homes rewarded the party faithful,
and Stalin waited for his reward – Shostakovich's victory symphony. If the composer had sustained the nation with his 7th
Symphony, and in his 8th had targeted totalitarianism – which
Moscow understood as fascism – then Stalin expected a musical
tribute to his leadership, a surging, triumphant, victorious 9th.
Daring as ever, Shostakovich produced an energetic, often-happy
work – but happy in the boisterous, vulgar manner of post-war
ebullience in the streets. The 9th Symphony contained no glorious paean to the man who had crushed the Nazis. Once again
Shostakovich seemed to be the only person who could humiliate
Stalin and live to tell the tale. The composer simply offset his
insult with scores to soundtrack the mawkish adulation of the

Comrade General Secretary in films such as the 1949 *Fall of Berlin*. 'That's the reason,' wrote Shostakovich, 'I survived.'[7]

The first movement of the 9th Symphony is impish and capricious. Stalin, at the time, was increasingly gripped by fear – fear of rivals, plots, Jews, foreigners and foreign achievements. An encyclopaedia was produced. Forget Marconi, Edison and the Wright brothers. Alexander Popov invented the radio. Alexander Lodygin switched on the first electric light. Alexander Mozhaisky was the first to fly.[8] Apart from indicating that 'Alexander' was a sterling choice of name for ambitious parents to give their child, the entries suggested that Stalin's paranoia was spinning out of orbit. His fear of opposition from intellectual Leningrad ran at least as far back as 1925, when the city's leader, Grigory Zinoviev, dared oppose the Central Committee in Moscow.[9] After the war, among the protégés of Andrei Zhdanov, Kirov's successor as local party leader, there had been talk of an increasingly important and independent role for Leningrad. When the city warmly welcomed a delegation from that wayward satellite, Marshal Tito's Yugoslavia, it seemed as if it was intent on flouting Stalin. Zhdanov – who had been transferred to Moscow in 1944 – was detailed to attack cultural deviation in his old city. The journals *Zvezda* and *Leningrad* were criticised for publishing Akhmatova and the satirist Mikhail Zoshchenko.[10] Stalin personally wrote an article criticising 'hooliganlike representations of our reality' and 'anti-Soviet attacks'.[11] Most ominously, the article declared that 'the transgressions could not have taken place without a deplorable lack of vigilance on the part of local Party organs.'

A new purge started: the 'Leningrad Affair' of 1949–50, targeting Zhdanov's associates, Nicholai Voznesensky, Alexei Kuznetsov and Peter Popkov – ironically, all supporters of Stalin. After a meteoric career, the economist Voznesensky became a member of the Politburo and received the Stalin Prize for his book *The War Economy of the USSR*. On closer reading, however, Stalin decided

*Leningrad workers are told of the execution of Zinoviev and others*
*for complicity in the Kirov murder.*

that the text criticised his handling of the war, and Voznesensky
was imprisoned, then shot. Kuznetsov – more effective in the management of Leningrad during the war than Zhdanov – had been
promoted to First Secretary when his boss was moved to Moscow.
After refusing to confess to trumped-up charges in a closed trial
of 1950, he was executed. A hook was slammed into the back of
his neck. Accused of turning the city into a nest of 'un-Bolshevik'
opponents who were plotting against Moscow's Central Committee, 2,000 Leningraders lost their jobs. By 1952, sixty-nine had
been executed, imprisoned or exiled.[12]

Zhdanov was already dead from drink and the suppression
was directed by Lavrenti Beria and Georgy Malenkov, Stalin's
new favourites.[13] Once again, the purge demonstrated that
following Stalin was the only option. The leader – glorified in
increasingly magisterial parades and mushy films – had become
so paranoid that he surrounded himself with *gulag*-like security.
His isolation was almost total. Fond of commenting that one
death is a tragedy, but a million deaths are a statistic, he listened,
misty-eyed, to his favourite song, 'Suliko' – touched by a tale of
the search for a loved one's grave. Most of Stalin's victims had no
grave. By the time he himself became a 'tragedy' – choking slowly
to death at his maximum-security *dacha* in March 1953 – Stalin
had realised a good number of statistics.

At the XXth Party Congress in 1956, Nikita Khrushchev denounced his predecessor, and the long Stalin winter began to thaw. Totalitarianism eased into authoritarianism, and between Stalin's death and the end of the decade, two million people returned from the *gulag*s and a further two million from special settlements. But the world outside the Soviet Union appeared increasingly dangerous. The threat of nuclear war and Western imperialism resulted in cultural lockdown at home, just as young Soviets were showing even greater enthusiasm for Western film and fashion.

One way of undermining foreign influences was to give the products of Western culture a new ideological slant. John Ford's classic western, *Stagecoach* – the story of personal tensions in a vehicle under threat of attack – was presented as the dramatic struggle of an indigenous population against imperialist invaders.[14] Nonetheless, new ideas and influences did begin to infiltrate with gathering speed. Foreign tourists started to arrive, wearing different styles of clothing. Sailors returning to Leningrad brought back Western records, although their impact was slow and slight, compared with that of the American singles that Liverpool merchant seamen carried home with them, thereby changing the course of popular music. When Leningraders listened to the Voice of America and Radio Free Europe, intimations of the easy-going and genial life in the West only added to their disenchantment and impatience with the party. Workers continued to be lodged in overcrowded factory hostels, and handled industrial equipment that was obsolete. Others were crammed into communal flats, where the kitchen, bathroom and toilet were shared. Many Leningrad *kommunalki* had been built as sizeable apartments for the pre-revolutionary bourgeoisie and had deteriorated after 1917. Many more had been damaged during the siege. In the single room that lodged a family, screens and wardrobes were arranged to secure a modicum of privacy for each generation.

Such inconveniences and deprivations did not square with the party vision offered in *Leningradskaya Pravda* in 1961, which bragged that 'mutual assistance and friendship have strengthened . . . apartment squabbles have disappeared'.[15] Yet it was true that conditions in the city were improving. The Leningrad metro – driven deep because of the soft clays – became operational in October 1955. The late Fifties welcomed enterprise-based housing cooperatives. As there was nothing much to buy, workers had cash surpluses. These could be used to place a deposit of 40 per cent to help fund new building, which – after a while – delivered the investor a flat of up to sixty square metres.[16] Crash building programmes began in 1957, the year of preparations for the overdue 250th anniversary celebrations for the foundation of the city. Chocolate factories went into overdrive. Resembling sludge dredged from the Neva, over-sweet fillings oozed from their huge mixers. Chocolate medallions were struck with the image of *The Bronze Horseman*. Special packaging with kitsch ballerinas, or a united nations of ethnic costumes, was produced. The anniversary was going to satisfy Leningrad's sweet tooth.[17]

Despite the city's political marginalisation under the Soviets, many people felt that Leningrad was the true capital. Russian literature and music had developed in the city, and its constellation of distinguished buildings and collections of art were magnificent. There was continued determination to repair and maintain historical buildings. Vallin de la Mothe's *gostiny dvor* on the Nevsky Prospekt needed attention, and Oleg Lialin, the architect in charge of restoration, scrutinised the city archives in order to renovate the exterior faithfully, while restructuring the interior to suit modern-day demands. In the event, the *gostiny dvor* was divided into unattractive stalls resembling those sad perimeter kiosks in stadiums. The wish to turn the lower reaches of the Nevsky into a kind of architectural museum, where commerce was forbidden, was prompted by the desire to rid it of such tattiness and hide the fact that small shops – so many of which seemed to have sunk into the ground for shame – were empty. On the fringes of the city centre there was no such drive for preservation: modern buildings were thrown up amid eighteenth- and nineteenth-century edifices. Starkly visible structures, such as the new Finland Station and the Maltsevsky Market, appeared either outrageous or misconceived among their elderly neighbours.[18]

Much of the artistic activity of these years was not so visible. When Vasily Grossman submitted his long novel *Life and Fate* to a literary magazine, the KGB seized copies and notebooks from his apartment and tore the ribbon from his typewriter. Comparisons between Stalinism and fascism, such as those made by Grossman, were unacceptable. Boris Pasternak's *Dr Zhivago* was read in *samizdat* – or secretly circulated – copies. Perhaps the most interesting forbidden copy of this novel was the one printed in Holland for the CIA, who had obtained the Russian text on film supplied by British intelligence. They produced an edition that could be slipped secretly to Russian visitors to the Vatican Pavilion at the 1958 Brussels World's Fair. As for Alexander Solzhenitsyn's terrifying portrait of the camps, *One Day in the Life of Ivan Denisovitch*, that only made it into the literary journal *Novy Mir* because Khrushchev agreed. Five years later, its author was under attack as an ideological enemy of the state and, in 1974, he was deported.[19] Truth – or, at least, a version of events that did not toe the party line – was doomed to remain a murmur from the underground.

In painting, the 'Potempkinising' Social Realist par excellence, Alexander Gerasimov, was Chairman of the Artists' Union of the USSR from 1958 to 1963. No friend to modernism, he broke into fits of laughter when he unrolled Matisse's *Dance* to amuse apparatchiks. As for non-representative art, it was 'individualistic' and frowned upon. When, in 1964, the Hermitage celebrated its 200th anniversary, Mikhail Artamonov – the museum's director since 1951 – was sacked for tolerating abstraction in an exhibition. But despite Khrushchev's celebrated assessment of abstract art – 'dog shit' – there were signs of an artistic thaw. The Sixties began with the British Council's exhibition 'Painting in Great Britain 1700–1960', which went on view at the Hermitage and the Pushkin Museum. In 1963, American graphic art was presented at the Russian Museum, and examples of American architecture went on display two years later at the Academy of Arts. The decade also witnessed important retrospectives of early twentieth-century Russian revolutionary artists. Meanwhile, Leningrad painters, who tended to be more mystical and gloomy than their card-carrying Moscow counterparts, were having a frustrating time. Cut off from art in the West – a tradition to which Russian painting had been yoked, from the eighteenth century to the revolution – they were thrown back on old notions or compromising attempts to gain official approval.[20]

Contemporary theatre was likewise moribund. Audiences in the 1950s and early 1960s were treated to plays like *Rural Evenings*, a 1954 lyrical comedy about life on a collective farm, or Dmitri Gordunov's *It Was Once So*. Unloading the coal that the protagonists have been waiting for is the play's central drama, and the arguments that are raised sound like the tedious 'demarcation disputes' of late-Sixties Britain. But when a wise comrade begins, 'Listen to what Lenin told me over a cup of tea,' the entire cast kneels in awe. The play ends with the declaration that 'It may be hard at first . . . but nobody will help us unless we help ourselves.' To thunderous applause from the audience, the characters rush off to unload the coal.[21]

Music and dance often focused on Leningrad's past. In Vano Muradelli's *October* – which stands somewhere between an epic musical and *Aïda* – misty-eyed Kronstadt mariners sing about the revolution. The 1949 Kirov ballet *The Bronze Horseman* was choreographed to music by Reinhold Glière and the Stalin Prize-winning score was resurrected for a new production of the ballet at the Mariinsky in 2016. In 1961, tribute was paid to the fortitude of Leningraders at war when Igor Belsky – later artistic director of the Kirov – choreographed *Sedmaya Sinfoniya* to the first movement of Shostakovich's 7th Symphony.

By 1958 times were changing: Shostakovich was going Broadway. His capacity to function as a popular composer had been in evidence since *Tahiti Trot* of 1927 – an exuberant variation on the Vincent Youmans hit 'Tea for Two' from the show *No, No, Nanette*. Begun in 1957, the year that *West Side Story* premiered in New York, Shostakovich's *Cheryomushki* bridges the gap between Soviet operetta and the American musical. Satirical and full of self-quotation, it is an absurdly delightful tale of love, set among the sub-Le Corbusier dream-blocks of an ambitious Soviet housing project. Inevitably, the enterprise is plagued by corruption, but it promises to change the lives of people used to disappointment. One character sings excitedly of – at last – 'having his own window', until neighbours, mistaken for cohabitants in what will be a new and tiny *kommunalka*, arrive for a house-warming. The musical is endlessly playful: another new tenant introduces himself with a parody of that fateful moment in Tchaikovsky's opera – 'Your neighbour, Onegin.' It is understandable why *Cheryomushki* is often dismissed, but it stands as a more evocative reminder of the guarded optimism of an era of mass building than today's decaying relics of the many 'cherry towns' that ring Moscow and St Petersburg.[22]

As part of a cautious opening up to the West, the individualistic twenty-four-year-old Canadian pianist Glenn Gould performed in Moscow, and then in Leningrad on 13 May 1957. Playing works unheard in Russia, by composers of the Viennese school, Gould was considered a visitor from Mars by the more conservative members of the audience. But the excitement of his playing was infectious, and news travelled fast. A concert that was half empty in the first half subsequently filled to overflowing in the second. Gould played Leningrad's Philharmonic

*Rossi's 'Theatre Street' in the late Soviet period.*
*The Vaganova is towards the end on the right.*

Hall and then the Maly, where the regulation 1,400 capacity was augmented by a further 1,100 enthusiasts crushed in the aisles.[23] In the audience on 13 May was a young Tartar who had arrived in September 1955 to study at the Leningrad State Academic Vaganova Choreographic Institute. Training as a dancer, he was soaking up every drop of culture in the capital. As his piano-playing improved, he tested scores on the piano in the sheet-music shop next to Dom Knigi on Nevsky Prospekt. He would often start an evening by watching the first act of a ballet at the Kirov, then dash to the Philharmonic to catch the second part of a concert. Rudolf Nureyev and his fellow students absconded from their dormitory during the White Nights in order to claim the expansive, theatrical spaces of the city for exuberant declarations of their art. On one occasion he and his pals circled the Alexander Column in Palace Square with *grands jetés en tournant.* Nureyev later remembered that he found Gould's performance 'weird', 'upsetting', but dynamic. He could almost have been describing his own Leningrad debut in *Giselle* two years later. Nureyev's Albrecht was not an idle aristocrat toying with the emotions of a delightful peasant girl. The ballerina, Irina Kolpakova, noted that when he came onstage in *Giselle*, Nureyev was like a 'hooligan boy' with ragged hair. Although he showed no interest in contemporary rock'n'roll, he caught the mood of the times. Offered a place in Moscow's brasher Bolshoi company, he opted to stay with the Kirov, after the star of the company, Natalia Dudinskaya, invited him to partner her in *Laurentia* in November 1958. The success of this partnership created a precedent for his electrifying work with the much older Margot Fonteyn.

Touring Russia with a production of *My Fair Lady*, American actress Lola Fisher was bowled over by Nureyev's performance in *Giselle*. When she invited the dancer to breakfast, the entire cast of the musical rose to welcome Nureyev with a standing ovation as he arrived at the restaurant in the Grand Hotel Europe. Soon he would enjoy such acclaim in the West, where he became the essential 'Russian' – wild and unpredictable.

As a young Kirov dancer, he was in competition with Yuri Soloviev who was already famous for his tremendous elevation. 'Cosmic Yuri' was Nureyev's roommate on the Kirov Ballet's 1961 tour to Paris. The grace and opulence of the French capital made a huge impression on Nureyev, who sensed that the Soviet authorities had begun to cramp his style. When the KGB agent who posed as deputy director of the Kirov asked him why he had not joined the Komsomol, the Soviet youth organisation, Nureyev snapped back, 'I've far more important things to do with my time than waste it on that kind of rubbish!'[24] He decided to defect. In Leningrad, that left the field clear for Soloviev – at least until he suffered a serious injury; the dancer struggled on, but his frozen body was found shot in his *dacha* in January 1977, in what appeared to have been suicide.

Despite the continued presence of state-sponsored mass song, traditional dance and balalaika orchestras, there was no way that ballads like 'My little Water Meadow, where have you been?' could hold the attention of young people, who listened to records smuggled from the West and made copies for their friends on the sound-carrying emulsion of X-ray plates – *roentgenizdat*, or 'discs on the bones'. The Soviet leadership, however, remained deaf to Western music. Waddling Nikita Khrushchev, in his clownish baggy pants, declared that jazz made him feel as if he 'had gas on the stomach'. As for the dances imported with rock'n'roll, the First Secretary observed with distaste that they involved an indecent wiggling 'of a certain section of the anatomy'.[25]

Although many youngsters still dreamed of joining the Young Pioneers and Komsomol and of marching together singing spirited Soviet anthems, at the 1957 Youth Festival, when foreign rock was played, the teenagers went wild. The authorities dismissed it as a waste of energy, which could – in the words of one MVD agent – 'be put into the building of a hydro-electric power station'.[26] Nonetheless, children of the Soviet elite clamoured for Camel cigarettes, Coca-Cola and 'Love Potion No. 9'. Perhaps it was the beginning of the end – or the beginning of a new beginning. Guitar poetry became a potent force among students and intellectuals, circulated by *magnitizdat* – songs that were privately tape-recorded. Singers like Alexander Galich and Bulat Okudzhava, whose work was not unlike the French *chansons à texte* of George Brassens and Barbara, became popular, as a counter-culture developed to urge change.

Competitive sport was becoming glamorous. Soccer became enormously popular with factory workers, and players were given pride of place in Physical Culture Day parades. Skilled sportsmen began to be treated to the same privileges as the artistic elite. Sport was also developing into a weapon in the propaganda war. In ice hockey, the Russians reigned supreme by playing with consummate grace. When they were in North America, musical or balletic images were applied to the ease and elegance with which they continually passed the puck to and fro: the Russians were playing a 'Soviet symphony'. North America's beaten and dejected hockey fans were confused – they were not at a game 'to see the Bolshoi', remarked one commentator. But Red Army ice-hockey team trainers studied dancers in rehearsal and turned a potentially brutal sport into something deft. Ice skaters likewise made use of dance in their long and often punishing training, and children as young as four would begin lessons in the small rink of Leningrad's Palace of Sport. Meanwhile, in the early Sixties, Vladimir Putin – a pupil at Leningrad High School 281 – spent a good deal of his time perfecting the art of judo.[27]

In the late Fifties and early Sixties the Russian economy was booming. Natural gas had been discovered in Siberia, technology for industry developed, and great strides were temporarily made in agricultural production, under ever-larger collectives. Sputnik was launched in 1957 and then, in April 1961, another 'Cosmic Yuri' became the world's first astronaut. Not surprisingly, after Yuri Gagarin orbited the earth, rocket fins suddenly vanished from new designs for American Cadillacs and, in Leningrad, a song club opened called Vostok, named after Gagarin's spaceship, *Vostok 1*. By the middle of the 1960s robots were being shown on TV, helping in the home: rousing a comrade from sleep and pouring his morning glass of milk.[28] Clever, early-rising robot – shops ran out of milk and other basics soon after opening.

While the Soviet scientific future looked bright, people were complaining that new housing estates on the outskirts of Leningrad mocked the idea of a city famed for its 'theatres, museums, gardens and parks',[29] for they had no such facilities. Inhabitants had nothing else to do but sit at home, watching the endless outpouring of party rhetoric. On screen, an over-rehearsed Comrade Shulpin pledged that his team would deliver an exceptional eighty tonnes of steel by election day, while Comrade Kirsanov pledged a tonne of steel a day above his shift target. Similarly, when a particularly heavy goods train arrived twenty minutes

ahead of schedule, a local newspaper reported the event as a triumph of Soviet will.[30] Museums were set up to record and glorify
transport, utilities and production, although industrial discipline
was weak and workmanship was often shoddy.

Yet, for the ordinary citizen, the years 1955–75 were arguably
the most congenial period under communism. There was peace.
The state offered educational sessions on 'social behaviour' in
which they promoted weak aromatic aperitifs, instead of marriage
and liver-destroying vodka. As cars were seen increasingly on the
streets – more than 27,000 in Leningrad in 1963 – loudspeakers
were mounted on mobile traffic-control units, urging pedestrians
to take care. Offices remained austere, without personal decoration or family snaps, but living standards rose. It didn't matter
that pensions and wages were low; what counted was access and
influence, or *blat* – the connections necessary to obtain scarce
goods or elusive services. Presents, not money, were useful, in
order to obtain things 'under the table'. A 'little something'
might persuade an official to take a little extra care.[31]

By 1964 Khrushchev was losing support. His erratic buffoonery was
beginning to wear thin. When he was invited to stay at Camp David
during his American visit, the First Secretary and his team were so ignorant on the subject of presidential dwellings that they thought it a snub.
In the States, Khrushchev's playing to the gallery went down well, but
the celebrated shoe-banging episode at the United Nations – exploited
by Khrushchev, although probably apocryphal – did little for his reputation among dour colleagues at home. It also reinforced the vision of
barbaric Russianness that was cultivated in the West. Insight into the
impression that Khrushchev created, and the way in which communism was perceived in America, comes in a comic sketch on Vaughn
Meader's best-selling 1962 LP satirising the Kennedy White House,
*The First Family*. When Kennedy proposes an everyday, office-style
takeout lunch to the assembled heads of state and asks Khrushchev
what he would like to eat, the First Secretary replies, 'Oh, you don't
have to order a special for me, I'll have a bite of everybody else's.' When

the West German Chancellor orders a 'Western Sandwich', Khrushchev interjects, 'If Adenauer has a Western Sandwich, then I'll have an Eastern Sandwich.' When Kennedy informs him that there is no such thing, Khrushchev tells Adenauer, 'Then I'll have the eastern portion of your Western Sandwich.'[32]

After the Cuban Missile Crisis of 1962, and a series of bad harvests, the Politburo lost confidence in their leader and Khrushchev was suddenly removed from power in 1964. The lacklustre Stalin protégé, Leonid Brezhnev, became Soviet leader and presided over eighteen years of gathering stagnation. It was a period during which, quipped Russians, 'the difficulty of growth turned into the growth of difficulties'.[33] People old enough to remember the siege persisted in mopping crumbs from the table with a moistened finger. In 1970, there were still 200,000 people living in nearly 1,000 hostels scattered about Leningrad. Although the majority were in their twenties and their tenancy lasted no more than a few years, they endured a cramped, unhealthy environment, and tensions resulted in hard drinking and fighting. As for *kommunalki*, in 1970 40 per cent of Leningrad's population still suffered the irritations and indignities of living in one room with paper-thin walls and sharing limited facilities with many other people. The percentage continued to fall, but by the time the regime collapsed twenty years later, nearly a quarter of the city's population still lived in *kommunalki*. For those who were lucky enough to move into their own apartments, life was far from idyllic. As in Britain during the 1960s, Soviet housing of the period was often cheaply or badly built. Apartment blocks and prefabs of between five and fourteen floors were low-ceilinged constructions of numbing monotony, surrounded by untouched scrubland. Attempts at landscaping – such as occurred in London's Robin Hood Gardens – were unknown. In response to the inevitable public disregard for such unfriendly environments, the party set up committees of parents and neighbourhood foot patrols. The tensions in *kommunalki*, the emptiness of the new neighbourhoods void of recreational facilities, pushed teenagers out onto the street where the boys acted tough and the girls were provocative.[34]

Ground floors of new buildings were noisy, the top floors leaked, and undecorated brutalist stairwells invited littering and syringes. If a flat came with a telephone – bugged, of course – that was fine. If you wanted to obtain one, forget it. But a private apartment was a blessed release from communal living. The kitchen became the place to welcome friends. Over vodka and *zakuski* – nibbles concocted from ingredients often stored for a special occasion – people talked. And talked. And talked. If you put a pillow over the telephone or jammed it by turning the dial to the last hole, then trapped it with a pencil and took the precaution of speaking at least two metres from the receiver, you could speak freely. At the end of the 1960s the KGB employed 166,000 people to tap, bug and perlustrate, in order to amass huge amounts of often-useless information about their comrades.[35]

The New Family Code of 1968 made it illegal for a man to divorce his wife without her consent during pregnancy. It also defined forced intercourse in the home as rape, yet society remained riddled with strong sexism – one repulsive pearl maintained that 'A wife isn't a jug, she won't crack if you hit her a few.'[36] Abortion remained high, as barrier contraception and intrauterine devices were scarce and Soviet condoms were as thick as the Iron Curtain. From 1960, terminations outnumbered births, and as many as six abortions were performed in a single room at the same time. Messy and humiliating – but cheap.[37]

The first supermarkets opened in Leningrad in 1954, but much of the available food was basic and unappetising. In the 1960s and '70s many Leningraders were able to grow vegetables on small allotments in vast garden settlements. In summer and early autumn the diet was augmented by mushroom-picking, berry-gathering and fishing – all activities associated with the gentle, simple pleasures of the *dacha*. Otherwise, a tedious system of queuing remained a part of everyday life. In shops, customers would join different queues for different items. Then they would queue to pay, before joining a queue to retrieve their purchases.[38] Diminishing into the distance, the queue became an image for ever-receding improvement. In Petrograd, bread queues had provoked revolution. The revolution delivered yet more queues. Something was wrong. People could wait up to ninety minutes to buy a pineapple, and would queue overnight to get on a list to buy a car that would not be delivered for eighteen months – perhaps a Zhiguli 1 or 2, Soviet imitations of the Fiat 124 and 125.[39] Different-coloured passes helped people from the higher echelons of the party or those with valued jobs beat the queues but, for most people, the procedure was inescapable. During the Seventies the Soviet press estimated that the nation spent thirty million hours queuing each year. Customers avoided items produced in the last ten days of any month – they were worse than usual, as factories rushed to complete quotas. Products from the satellite countries were preferred to Soviet goods: Polish bras, East German electrical fittings, Bulgarian toothpaste or Hungarian shampoo.[40] Why could a country the size of the Soviet Union, with such resources, not do better? And still can't. As President Obama remarked, in his final press conference of 2016, Russia 'doesn't produce anything that anybody wants to buy, except oil and gas and arms. They don't innovate.'[41]

Dining out in Leningrad was often marred by long queues to obtain a table, and by rude staff who overcharged. Slowly the number of restaurants grew from about forty at the beginning of the Brezhnev era to more than eighty at the time of *perestroika* in the late 1980s,[42] when Georgian restaurants began to offer diners new tastes – spinach and pomegranate timbales instead of the inevitable herring; coriander-flavoured *lobio* instead of the standard meat in aspic; char-grilled lamb instead of the ubiquitous *kotletta*. Hard on sweet-tooths, Leningrad cafés in the late

Seventies still offered a negligible selection of cakes and pastries. Milk bars, clubs and cafés where guitar poets performed became the haunt of young people. Earlier, in the Sixties, youth and student clubs had been places where films were shown, poetry read and photographs exhibited. At that time, students only dared to talk politics outdoors and were denied what their revolutionary forebears had – to a limited extent – enjoyed under the tsars. They were not permitted to demonstrate.[43]

In the late Sixties and Seventies, thousands of young people became what the authorities defined as 'inner immigrants'. They listened to Radio Luxembourg and struggled to buy or copy Western records. 'Inner immigrants' lived in the Soviet Union, but mentally and emotionally inhabited the unfamiliar world of what they knew of Western pop. They listened to The Beatles and learned English from their lyrics. Photos of the pop group were difficult to come by, and young Leningraders couldn't tell a Lennon from a McCartney. In the late 1970s, disco invaded Russia with films such as *Saturday Night Fever* and groups including Abba and Boney M followed. Imported LPs cost one-third of a monthly wage, so they were rare and home-grown singers filled the gap. At the commercial end, on the frontiers of variety, there were figures like Valery Leontov and the publicity-hungry, red-haired celebrity Alla Pugacheva. Yet Leningrad was not, at the time, a late-night city. Gone were the after-theatre revelries of the Diaghilev era. The city was pretty quiet by 11 p.m. Ownership of televisions stood at more than forty million nationwide in 1970, so people stayed in and watched Pugacheva on TV. The Russian band Mashina Vremeni – Time Machine – likewise enjoyed a huge following, with a sound veering from folk to hard rock.[44] The group started in the late Sixties and has exhibited, like many of Russia's top groups and singers, great staying power. Deep Purple fan and Russian president Dmitri Medvedev saw Time Machine in concert in Washington DC in 2010. 'Russia's Bob Dylan', Boris Grebenshchikov, sang in the short 1982 university film *Ivanov*. It celebrated a *kommunalka* on the Petrograd Side where friends drank wine, made music and dreamed of imported cigarettes. *Ivanov* became a beacon for the youth counter-culture of which Grebenshchikov, rightly, became a star. One of Grebensh-chikov's recent songs – his voice gravelled by imported ciggies – was prompted by the violence in the Ukraine in 2014.

Exhibitions from abroad continued to weaken cultural isolation. In 1974, the highly successful Tutankhamen exhibition from London and New York was presented at the Hermitage, followed by '100 Paintings from the Metropolitan' in 1975 and treasures from the Louvre and the Prado in subsequent years.[45] The increased number of foreign visitors carefully shepherded by Intourist guides, checked by hotel tea-ladies and quizzed by KGB plants contributed to the cultural thaw. Leningraders may not have had much chance to speak with the visitors, but they could see what they were wearing and how they behaved. Tourist guides had a loaded cultural agenda and a certain amount of contempt for the Western obsession with Fabergé and the riches of the tsars. In the Hermitage, groups were swiftly marched through the centuries and civilisations. Guides hurried past the Cézannes and Matisses and lingered in front of earlier examples of Western decadence. Instructions were brusque: 'Hurry up, please, we've got another floor to get through,' adding under the breath, 'I've got a lot more – uh – fairy tales to tell you.'[46] At the Kirov, tourists were amused by the gold, blue and white hammer and sickle placed tastefully above the proscenium amid the sumptuous nineteenth-century decor. Gently interrogated by their KGB plant, posing as a member of the group, tourists were asked to offer opinions on whether the Kirov productions were tatty, compared with those they saw at home. They were. What did they feel about the Russian Melodiya record label, the food, the hotel comfort? Almost every answer confirmed that the USSR was unable to satisfy the average expectations of a Westerner.

During the Sixties a spirited version of Christian Dior's 1950s New Look was produced by Soviet designers, but everyday clothing remained drab. Nevertheless, people in Leningrad tended to be fashion-conscious, and jeans soon became the ultimate fashion statement. Dmitri Medvedev – the son of university teachers who lived in the far-flung suburb of Kupchino – coveted a Pink Floyd album and jeans.[47] Meanwhile, the Russian language slowly kitted itself out with Western conveniences, concepts and fads that had no equivalent in Russian: *kredit*, *press relis*, *kheppening* and *mass mediya*.[48] Russia was on a crash course with the tail-chasing earn-and-spend of capitalism.

By the late 1970s, half of Soviet families had a refrigerator and more than 60 per cent owned a washing machine, and yet the technology gap between East and West was not closing. The frames and lenses of Soviet glasses were heavier than their Western counterparts. The electrical consumption of appliances was seven times that of European models. Two-fifths of the hard currency earned was spent on importing food.[49] Leningrad leaders were so concerned with the city's industrial and military supremacy, and with its heritage, that healthcare and infrastructure suffered. Corruption was rife. Violence resulting from alcoholism was pandemic. Writing in 1979, Joseph Brodsky observed that at 9 a.m. 'a drunk is more frequently seen than a taxi'. But, as he went on to point out, vodka was a huge source of state revenue: 'its cost is five kopecks and it's sold to the population for five roubles. Which means a profit of 9,900%.'[50] Alcoholism accompanied widespread demoralisation among the male population in the late Brezhnev era. It fell to women to hold house and home together.[51] They would earn all day, queue for food or shoes in every spare moment, look after their children and cook for a husband, if they still had one. Not unlike in the West – just worse.

Yet some Leningrad institutions functioned successfully, as they had done for years. At the Leningrad Choreographic Academy the number of pupils grew from 170 to 500. The

*A class at the Vaganova Academy given by the legendary Natalya Dudinskaya.*

school, which considered seven – the age at which children had started at the Imperial Ballet School – too young for developing bones, accepted pupils from the age of nine.[52] They ate well on a vitamin-and-protein diet of fruit, vegetables, eggs and meat. Training was long and arduous, and the institute tried to involve parents to enable them to understand what their child was going through. There were academic subjects beside ballet, and training included historical dance from the first year, character dance from the third, *pas de deux* from the sixth, and piano right through to their penultimate year. Very few pupils were taken into the Kirov and most would look for work elsewhere. Still, the system was working well, although by 1990 Kirov dancers would be complaining about low wages and malnutrition.

Perhaps the most impressive addition in the 1970s was the monument to the 900-day siege at Moskovsky in the south of the city. The memorial is flanked on either side by statues of people who endured the siege. They are remarkable by the standards of the figurative sculpture of the period. City leaders, some of whom mismanaged the siege, are notably absent and the ensemble celebrates the female workers, barricade-makers, snipers, guards, soldiers and sailors whose fortitude helped the city to survive.

*The monument to the siege looking towards Moskovsky Prospekt
and Soviet-era building complexes.*

A vast forty-eight-metre-high central obelisk, standing as tall as
the Alexander Column in Palace Square, has 'the victors' – again,
anonymous citizens – standing near its base. The visitor then
descends through a broken ring, representing the blockade, to
an underground chamber of sombre polished granite in which
900 dim lamps symbolise the days and nights of the siege. In a
deliberately muted exhibit, the visitor chances upon a fragment
representing the bread ration, a violin played in the performance
of Shostakovich's 7th Symphony, a few simple tools that constructed trenches, buckets that fought fires and carried water: the
ensemble adding up to a powerful, dignified and stirring tribute
to the city under siege.[53]

Towards the end of the Brezhnev era, social equality still seemed
remote. Information continued to be rationed – telephone direc-
tories, for instance were only available at information kiosks.
Hard-line communist devotees were increasingly ashamed of the
empty shops: no milk, no meat.[54] They were fed up with the

stale leadership jangling their endless rows of medals. Brezhnev himself – chest ablaze with decorations – was overweight and ailing. He smoked too much, drank to excess and was addicted to downers. By the time he died in November 1982, the resources of the USSR were being severely stretched by the government's support for the communist regime in Afghanistan, fighting against the mujahideen. The Soviet Union passed through the brief rule of the ageing ex-KGB chief Yuri Andropov, and the even briefer leadership of Konstantin Chernenko, to Mikhail Gorbachev.

Shortly after becoming leader, Gorbachev visited Leningrad in May 1985. During his visit, he did something unusual. He broke away from the official party paying its respects at a war memorial and started talking to the crowd. By that gesture, made in a city of uncertainty and perpetual change, Gorbachev demonstrated his desire for a novel approach. The malaise of the early 1980s resulted from a paucity of new ideas. At the XXVth Party Congress in February 1986 – thirty years exactly after Khrushchev's secret speech denouncing Stalin – Gorbachev put forward some ideas which determined *perestroika*, or 'restructuring'.[55] This was to be accomplished by *glasnost*: greater openness of discussion, out of which new ideas would emerge. In April 1986, after the Chernobyl disaster, there was a degree of openness hitherto unknown in the USSR. Gorbachev campaigned against corruption and alcoholism, but many people used to rigour and hardship were suspicious, rather than welcoming. Subservience to the state had been a staple for decades, and now there were hints that entrepreneurial self-advancement was not wrong.

The lively underground Leningrad art scene of the 1970s grew and spilled out into the open. Private exhibitions and concerts in people's homes went public. Young people were less afraid of the KGB than their parents.[56] In the 1986 underground jazz film *Dialogues* there was obvious criticism of the party. Songs were sung with American accents, the lyrics – Fats Domino-style – being slurred so as not to be entirely clear. It was a useful way to criticise. To be and not to be heard. There was a pounding beat, wild dress and a new sense of freedom. David Goloshchekin ran the popular Leningrad Jazz Club, packing the house five nights a week.[57] Akhmatova was read openly, yet the new freedoms were not uncontested. In 1987, when students protested against plans to destroy Leningrad's historic Angleterre hotel, some were arrested.[58] At the time Yuri Shevchuk was a restaurant cleaner by day and a protest rock-singer by night. Looking a little like John Lennon during his spell of Indian meditation, Shevchuk and his group, DDT, used a mix of electric and traditional instruments to pump out 'anti-Soviet' songs. He was summoned to sign a paper agreeing not to sing or write. The authorities called him an 'enemy of the people', a mouthpiece for America and – of all things – for 'the Vatican'.[59] Demonstrations were not tolerated, but his fans went out onto the streets to petition support for the band. Shevchuk is another survivor on the Petersburg music scene, despite being highly critical of Vladimir Putin's Russia – one of his lyrics suggesting that the president will die when the oil runs dry.

On 14 February 1988, the library of the Academy of Sciences was ravaged by a major fire in its main stack room. Some of the books destroyed belonged to Peter the Great, and many volumes and manuscripts were hurled into the courtyard and bulldozed into rubbish heaps. The official response merely noted that an insignificant portion of the deposits had been lost. But that kind of party cover-up was, in the future, going to prove more difficult. There was a new kid on the block. In 1987, ex-stuntman-turned-investigative-journalist and shit-stirrer Alexander Nevzorov exploded onto Soviet television screens with his inflammatory programme 600 Seconds. He went around Leningrad seeking out, or making, trouble. Contacts with the police got Nevzorov to crime scenes with an immediacy that enabled his TV cameras to reveal the underbelly of city life with a frankness never seen before. With an audience of sixty million viewers, he changed the

Soviet population's perception of what was going on. Nevzorov had a cocksure, cheeky approach. On one occasion, holding up a radiated chicken for his audience to see, he stated in a dead-pan voice that the good news was that 'levels of radiation vary through its body'. Whether he was covering violence between emerging gangs, between prison inmates or between rival lovers, Nevzorov was there barging into the ugliness of people's lives. At first a fresh-faced advocate of *glasnost*, he hardened into an ardent champion of the old KGB. He filmed shootings with gruesome intimacy, catalogued the inadequacy of the police with disturbing frequency, and gaily paraded the malfunctioning of every department of the state with such zest and enthusiasm that it seemed as if his programme was nothing other than a self-serving personal pitch for public office. When, in May 1990, the foundations of Trinity Cathedral flooded and paintings were lost, Nevzorov was on the scene to inform sixty million people – in complete contrast to the Academy of Sciences cover-up two years earlier.[60]

A less extreme example of the drive to redress injustice was the Soviet Women's Committee. In 1987, it was able to claim openly for the first time since 1930 that Soviet authorities discriminated against or ignored women. In industry, women were left to shift loads in excess of what was medically safe, and they were often forced to work in toxic conditions. By 1990, Leningrad's 'Reading for Women' movement had started, and certain progressives began to question stereotypes.[61] Yet life was not getting easier, but tougher. By the end of the 1980s, Soviet state retailers had run out of basics such as tea, coffee and soap. Aspirin and toilet paper were hard to come by and,[62] at the beginning of 1990, the Leningrad city authorities issued ration cards for the first time since 1947. Among the first items to be rationed was meat. By the summer, alcohol and sugar were added, and then butter, eggs and flour in December. Violent crime was on the increase. Alcoholics and runaways lived in squats in damp basements.

*The elderly chat during the time of upheavals.*
*The sign painted on the wall reads 'No Parking!'*

Glue-sniffing was the favoured cheap and easy high used by the young.[63] Everywhere there were signs of breakdown. There were two philosophy graduates from Leningrad State University. She worked as janitor, he was a boiler stoker, and in their leisure time they enjoyed reading books. He reflected that with '*perestroika* everything came crashing down'. His ninety roubles a month became ten dollars, and the couple were forced to become street vendors, selling melting ice cream that they obtained from a factory because they had no fridge on their market stall. 'The discovery of money,' he commented, 'hit us like an atom bomb.'[64] In a documentary from that time, *Third Class Carriage*, someone is heard on the overnight train from Leningrad to Moscow saying, 'It's hard to believe this country could put rockets into space.'[65]

The millennium of Russia was celebrated in 1988, and Gorbachev used the occasion to assert that Orthodox believers had a right to worship. The Orthodox religion had not been outlawed under communism, but it was barely tolerated, and many churches had been destroyed or converted into sports clubs or swimming pools. After 1988, monasteries were opened and services were even televised. The exultation of the huge congregation at the Alexander Nevsky Monastery was palpable. When the Metropolitan emerged from behind the iconostasis and came down into the congregation, there was a surge of worshippers, radiant with the spirit of miracle and wonder: God was among them.

The May Day parade of 1988 was notable for the snow falling in Palace Square as people – feeling the first flush of freedom – carried placards with slogans such as 'Remember the victims of Stalin in Leningrad.' Gorbachev was airing ideas that paved the way for a democratic future, and in the elections of the following year the Communist Party lost control. Still, people wondered what had happened to *perestroika*. They thought it a flash-in-the-pan, like Lenin's NEP. Gorbachev had undermined the basic elements of communism – the one-party state, atheism, state economic monopoly and a centralised administration. The Soviet Union was fracturing, as regions such as the Ukraine, Uzbekistan and Byelarus declared their sovereignty. When Gorbachev refused to use force against the rebellious Soviet Bloc, the Soviet empire fell apart.[66] By the spring of 1991, Leningraders – a doomed species – were facing two elections: one for the newly created post of president of their country, the other for a mayor. Scheduled for the same day, 12 June, there was also a referendum to determine whether or not their city should remain 'Leningrad' or become, once again, 'St Petersburg'.

# 16

# BROKEN WINDOW ONTO THE WEST

## *1991–2016*

The referendum asked, 'Do you want our city to return to its original name of St Petersburg?' Would that hint at past glory? Or was the name Leningrad sufficient testimony to a great vision? The dismal march of a troubled twentieth century argued against that. It was the moment, perhaps, for its inhabitants to mark their dissatisfaction with the nightmaring of the socialist dream. But what about the spirit of Leningraders who had kept their city on the face of the earth? Behind closed doors, warmly gathered about tables scattered with scraped-together *zakuski*, the debates continued late into the night:

– The place is filthy. How can we call it Petersburg?

– If you knew how many fine dresses had—

– We need communism.

– We need food.

– We don't need Yeltsin.

– Who needs another souse?

– It should stay Leningrad. The world knows Leningrad.

– When did anything ever change around here?

On 12 June 1991, Boris Yeltsin was elected president. Anatoly Sobchak was elected Mayor of Leningrad . . . or St Petersburg? By a vote of 54.9 per cent to 35.5 per cent, Sobchak found himself mayor of the newly renamed St Petersburg. It was a signal moment, like the blank fired from the *Aurora* in October 1917. And – as with 1917 – things went from bad to worse.[1]

Many felt it was too soon to go back. Others suggested returning to St Petersburg via Petrograd. Mayor Sobchak cited the Patriarch of Russia, who suggested that Leningrad had been an 'ideological construct imposed upon the name of St Peter in whose honour the city was named'. Upbeat, the mayor insisted on his city's renewed importance. After the loss of the Baltic countries, St Petersburg was Russia's 'door to Europe'.

On 7 November 1991, the official day chosen for the renaming, flames burned from the Rostral Columns on Vasilevsky Island and Mayor Sobchak spoke in Palace Square, requesting a minute's silence for all the Leningraders who fell in the siege. Grand Duke Vladimir, heir to the Romanov throne, flew from Europe for the ceremony. Thereafter, the old communist holiday of 1 May was replaced by 'City Day', commemorating the founding of St Petersburg in May 1703.[2]

Yet again, a new vision gave way to immediate disappointment. The planned economy was in ruins, industrial output fell,[3] the government printed money and a mighty empire was breaking up. Meanwhile, people had voted 'St Petersburg' and now had to set about remaking a city that lived up to that talismanic name. Peter the Great had designed his city to showcase the most worthy and progressive aspects of European Enlightenment. Newly renamed St Petersburg imported cut-throat capitalism and extortion. It was like 1918 all over again, with desperate people out on the streets selling what little they had. A plague of desperation plastered the walls around the Haymarket with small ads. There were five million scared, pale faces in the metro; and hustlers and druggies living out on the street or working the hotels. The Hotel Moskva, opposite the Alexander Nevsky Monastery, was a cat-house and casino. Gamblers lay sprawled on sofas in the lobby, while prostitutes prowled the long, bare corridors, trawling for valuable foreign trade. Prostitution was

*Lucky Strike vs. the hammer and sickle – St Petersburg of the early 1990s.*

one sector of the economy that was flourishing. With employment precarious and wages tumbling, it was regarded in some quarters as a 'prestigious occupation', providing access to foreign currency and exceptional opportunities for clothes and travel. A 1989 Soviet film, *Intergirl*, treated the subject of a Leningrad nurse unable to survive on her wages, who turns to prostitution and secures the opportunity of escaping to Sweden by marrying a client. Apart from revealing the blunt facts of late-Soviet life, Pyotr Todorovsky's film – which topped the Russian ratings in the year of its release – also provided a close-up of the drabness of Leningrad.[4]

The mafia were in control of the markets. On the opposite side of the Neva from the Smolny there was heavy drug-dealing. Pulkovo Airport was gang-controlled, and suitcases were frequently opened or stolen. Apartment blocks near the centre had dope-scented staircases, where unemployed teenagers sprawled smoking. Living conditions were still basic, with dangling bare bulbs or, at best, Fifties-style lampshades. The bathroom shower and the sink – where you had to hit the pipes to encourage the arrival of the ferric water – were often in a curtained-off area of the kitchen. There seemed to be no way forward, and understandably – as they had lived as communists all their lives – many comrades felt an agonising sense of defeat. As George Smiley says of the Russians in John Le Carré's *The Secret Pilgrim*, 'The Bear is disgusted with his past, sick of his present and scared stiff of his future.'[5] As Galina, a character in Malcolm Bradbury's *To the Hermitage*, puts it, 'You can see how Russia is now. Now the bad times are over, the worse times come.'[6]

The year 1992 began with a catastrophe – deregulation of the markets, which turned many people into paupers overnight. For most, deprivation and shortage were much worse than they had been under communism. Half a century had passed since the cruel first winter of the Nazi siege and life was, yet again, grim. By March, the rouble stood at 125 to the US dollar. A teacher earned 500 roubles a month – £2.30 – the cost of the ingredients for a celebration meal of meat, *smetana*, potatoes, oranges and flowers.[7] A pensioner on 342 roubles just wouldn't celebrate. Fake was available: 'foreign' perfume, 'Danish' beer made in Greece and well past its sell-by date. By September, the Russian deficit stood at 716 billion roubles and inflation was high. By the end of the following month the rouble stood at 627 to the pound: enough to buy a loaf of bread, a couple of pounds of potatoes, a kilo of butter and a litre of milk for eight days, and that was that. Figures also showed that unprecedented unemployment was beginning to grip Russia, with more than 900,000 people registered as out of work on 1 October and another two million on part-time work or temporary leave.

Prices were swinging wild. The cost of a toilet roll – wise to keep one with you at all times – was fifteen roubles. That was the price of a comfortable seat for an orchestral concert beneath the eight magnificent chandeliers of the sensibly sized

Philharmonic Hall. Both were a steal beside the price of one orange: 350 roubles, an enormous sum, given pensions and salaries. I was told, but still find it hard to believe, that three scoops of Häagen-Dazs ice cream cost as much as an Aeroflot flight from Petersburg to Vladivostok. In *Passazh* a pair of badly made, plain cotton panties cost 185 roubles – nearly one-third of the monthly earnings of a scientist. Tampons were plentiful there, but the price was prohibitive. The cost of electrical goods like Western stereos and VCRs was exorbitant. Only those with access to foreign currency – people working in the tourist industry, wheeler-dealer import–export syndicates – were able to afford such things or offer serious help to their kin.

Moving offices to the Smolny, Anatoly Sobchak was mayor from 1991 to 1996 and presided over the city in an authoritarian manner. He appointed ex-KGB officers to important posts such as the directorship of the Vaganova Ballet School, simply because, he claimed, 'they were experienced in administration'. The day-to-day running of the city at a time of mounting violence and corruption was in the hands of two deputies: Sobchak's successor, Vladimir Yakovlev, and ex-KGB officer and future President of the Russian Federation, Vladimir Putin.

In the early 1990s, a friend wrote to me describing 'a pervasive cynicism. We have been exploited and lied to. We don't need any politicians.' The young needed 'dollars and . . . a Western standard of living' and began to look for little subterfuges in order to make a buck. Some would rise early to secure a place near the front of a shopping queue. Hours later they would sell their place and take the money to buy some vodka and obliterate the day.[8] Vodka offered rescue through death, before a worse fate intervened. Post-millennium statistics reveal that the average Russian male consumption was a bottle a day. Others had grander and bloodier schemes to get rich. Fraud was part of the warp and weft of Russian life. Stealing from the state existed before Prince Menshikov made it such an art. Under communism, dishonesty and fraud had intensified, and bribe-taking, asset-stripping and embezzlement were to become the staples of Russia's post-Soviet establishment. In the raw, post-communist world the easiest way to thrive was to lie to the taxman, buy mafia 'protection', bribe the local bureaucrats and pay workers late – if at all. Since May 1988 authorised 'cooperatives' had bought just about anything and everything from the state at knock-down prices, then sold them on at the market rate. They split the difference with the official who had facilitated the scam. When a twenty-eight-year-old banker was asked how to make money in Russia, he replied, 'You kill somebody, you steal, you bribe.'[9]

Privatisation of industry was under way by 1992 and millions of workers found that conditions changed for the worse. Between 1992 and 1994, a staggering 70 per cent of state assets, including natural resources, were sold.[10] Many of the party elite, along with regional administrators and directors, kept hold of power by the appropriation of goods and resources. Some had even begun to transfer Soviet property to themselves before privatisation became widespread. New companies were helped by sympathetic local authorities, as interests converged. In 1992, the first deputy of the Executive Committee of St Petersburg was head of the governing body of the tourism company, Nord. He was therefore in a position to provide his firm with two buildings on the Nevsky Prospekt, charging just 174,000 roubles each, at a time when a single apartment in the same area would sell for more than a million.[11] There were anomalies in city finances, as fraudulent accounting lined the pockets of officials. In fact the system continued to work through *blat*, as officials in high places aided – for a cut – the setting-up of enterprises. By the early 2000s the *baksheesh* required to mobilise a sizeable building project stood at about $1 million. The state, at first weak, just became compliant.[12]

As wealth shifted into private hands, fortune was flaunted on the streets of Moscow where its Disneyfying mayor, Yuri

Luzhkov, was adding glitz and sparkle. Mellow St Petersburg tended to hide its wealth behind the genteel shabbiness of interminable decay or in the woods of its islands, where the new elite built extravagant, eclectic post-modern *dachas* with a little dash of neo-Gothic here and a little bit of *stil moderne* there. Strikingly, just fifty kilometres beyond such luxury dwellings, with their state-of-the-art Western mod cons – say, in a little village on the road to Novgorod – peasant women could still be seen carrying a milkmaid's yoke to transport buckets of water. Between the nouveau riche, the urban poor and the villagers beyond, Russia was living in dramatically different ages.

Cold-blooded initiative and chutzpah, backed by persuasive firepower, developed business during the 1990s. Rival gangs vied for control and blocked the evolution of a fair yet competitive free market. Oligarchs sprung from Soviet caricatures of cut-throat capitalists. Backed by security services that behaved more like private armies, few of them had any sense of responsibility towards their country, and pillaged state assets, paid no tax and left Russia's

*Early 1990s desperation. Walls plastered with small-ads.*

economy devastated.¹³ With hucksterism everywhere, nationalism and even fascism began to seem like attractive alternatives. As the 1990s dragged on, there was a further increase in gang warfare in St Petersburg, with drug-trafficking and, at the higher end of the scale, arms-dealing. The city took on the atmosphere of Prohibition Chicago. Leningraders who worked for aspiring entrepreneurs – people 'in business' – carried guns.

A good insight into how business was conducted at the time is afforded by Alexei Balabanov's powerful 1997 film, *Brat*,¹⁴ in which a Chechen gangster gets out of jail and muscles in on the protection racket in St Petersburg markets. The hit-man employed to take care of the Chechen is visited by his brother, Danila, a disarming young man who – more often than not – uses might for what he believes to be right. A child of his times, Danila doesn't like Jews or the insolent Armenian fare-dodgers on Petersburg trams. His passion is Russian pop, played by the instrumentally inventive new-wave Nautilius Pompilius band, Grebenshchikov, Shevchuk and Konstantin Kinchev's band Alisa, whose hard-rock protest became, in the late 1990s, increasingly nationalist. Danila listens obsessively to his Discman, which he keeps strapped around his belly. Blasted to pieces by an assassin, it – significantly – softens the blow of the bullet. *Brat* presents St Petersburg as a squalid city spattered with blood and mud. The shells of crippled cars litter the streets. Paint bubbles like skin disease on the interiors of public buildings. The depot on Vasilevsky Island is a graveyard for ailing trams, from what was once the largest network in the world. Shortly after Danila arrives from the country, an elderly German, sleeping rough in a cemetery, tells him that 'The city is a frightening force . . . it sucks you in.' It also spits out the unwanted. At the end of the film, when things get too hot and he has made a pile, Danila hitch-hikes to Moscow – with his gun.

Fast forward six years to *Progulka*, released in 2003 – the year St Petersburg put on its Sunday best for its 300th-birthday celebrations. The film finds the protagonists strolling in a sunny, bright world, able to enjoy the city without fear of intimidation. Yet the irresponsibility – or is it infantility? – of the central character spikes her apparent easy-going freshness with edginess and deceptiveness.

As the youngsters stroll down the Nevsky and around the city, there is much evidence of preparatory restoration for the tercentennial. The city 'Potempkinised' for its very special birthday, ignoring the 'inner spaces' – those Petersburg courtyards that were fetid from the time of Nekrasov and Dostoevsky. Behind the increasingly primped façades, the old grime persisted. In public buildings, utility installations that would be shielded from visitors in the West remained 'on show'. In the Kunstkammer, in a corridor between well-ordered exhibition spaces and displays, wires, pipes and badly painted walls all hinted at a vulnerability,

*'Hidden spaces' of St Petersburg, 1990s.*

a hazardous reality. After the collapse of the Soviet Union, apartment blocks suffered. The 'staircase elder', who was responsible
for cleanliness and order, no longer existed and residents took
to pasting complaints about cleanliness and hygiene on tene-
ment walls.

By August 2002, the city was largely under scaffolding. The
spire of Trezzini's cathedral in the Peter and Paul Fortress and
St Isaac's were shrouded. Palace Square was being resurfaced.
Nearly 2,500 'monuments of history and culture', 300 'monumental sculptures' and 600 'decorative sculptures' were in need
of repair.[15] The Palace at Strelna, which had been an orphanage
in the 1920s and was later occupied by the Nazis, was turned
into the sumptuous National Congress Palace by Vladimir Putin.
The president has always shown generosity towards improving
the look and increasing the status of the city where he grew
up in a *kommunalka*, not far from the KGB's 'Big House' on
Liteiny Prospekt. Money from the federal budget was allocated
to St Petersburg during the tenure of Putin's protégé, Mayor

*Peter and Paul Fortress before and after restoration for 2003.*

Valentina Matvienko, who energetically presided over a number of high-profile projects between 2003 and 2011.[16]

For the tercentennial celebrations, St Petersburg's bus station was overhauled. Streets were paved. The potholed old Nevsky was smoothed over, and life in the city – so hard throughout the 1990s – was gentrified. Big events were planned: promenade concerts in the Summer Garden, a laser show on the Neva, where coloured fountains played and jets of water sprayed. There was a regatta, an ice-cream festival. Flames blazed again from the Rostral Columns. There was a Peter the Great exhibition at the Hermitage, the reopening of the Mikhailovsky Palace after extensive restoration, and the inauguration – by President Putin and the German chancellor, Gerhard Schröder – of the Amber Room at Tsarskoe Selo, after twenty-four years of restoration. There was a $1,500-a-ticket ball. Top Russian bands played the rock festival 'Open the Window'. A performance of Donizetti's little-known opera, *Peter the Great*, was given. There was the White Nights Swing Jazz Festival and the 6th International Early Music Festival. James Levine visited with the orchestra of the Metropolitan Opera, and a gala concert from the Mariinsky was broadcast worldwide by the BBC.[17]

The dynamic workaholic Valery Gergiev, who has been at the helm of the Mariinsky since 1996, transformed the institution into a powerhouse of creativity. It employs about 1,000 people – 180 in the orchestra, 200 dancers, 80 singers, 300 techies, along with administrators and doctors. Giving up to 100 performances at the Mariinsky each year, Gergiev frequently comes off the podium, bundles into a car to Pulkovo Airport and jets off to conduct in Europe. Among his many directorial tasks are the gala dinners held after performances. It is hard to step from the realm of Glinka or Tchaikovsky and plunge into the world of millionaire diners who may just become valuable sponsors, yet for Gergiev today it is part of the process of turning the Mariinsky into a world-famous brand that people are willing to buy into. Like the Hermitage, the name alone sells, as visitors come as much for what the institution represents in the cultural top-sights league-table as for the artistic treasures it offers.[18]

Indeed, the anniversary celebration was seen as an opportunity to sell the city. Residents who had been looking west found a renewed pride in Russian brands. Peter the Great was put to work promoting products and services. The Petrovsky Bank on the Nevsky displayed a bust of the great Westerniser over its entrance. Peter I cigarettes claimed to contain a superior type of tobacco sold at the tsar's court. Petrovskoe Beer with its *Bronze Horseman* logo and Peter the Great Vodka – brewed and distilled in the city – appealed to resident and tourist alike. But the celebrations were not, of course, entirely without pain or difficulty. Survival websites were set up to suggest ways for residents to cope with the influx of tourists: how to escape the deafening spiel from the bullhorns hawking canal cruises or hydrofoils to Peterhof; how to negotiate the clusters of frilly-bonneted maidens and giant Peter the Great photo-ops.[19] Above and beyond all those nuisances was the familiar shadow of corruption, casting its sombre and familiar light. Funds had gone missing. There were suspicious misallocations of huge sums.[20]

Yet the city learned the lesson of 2003 and continued to present attractions that would add to the already-rich array of sights and keep the tourists coming. A large but dubious item, another fragment of St Petersburg flotsam, was added to the historical curiosities that fill the city. At the Museum of Erotica in Furshtatskaya Street a thirty-centimetre-long preserved penis, which reputedly once belonged to the orgiastic Grygory Rasputin, went on display in 2004 – its authenticity understandably questioned. Resembling one of the eerie pickled oddities on show in the Kunstkammer, the object has been identified variously as a sea cucumber or the penis of one of the larger quadrupeds. The item was purchased by Igor Knyazkin, the director of the museum, for $8,000 from a French antiquarian who had obtained it from a Californian who, in turn, had acquired it from Rasputin's daughter, who had wrested it from a circle of Russian émigrés in Paris, who treasured it as a holy relic.

Banned by the Soviet regime in 1964 as a member of The Beatles, Paul McCartney played to 60,000 fans in St Petersburg forty years later, in June 2004. Although it was his first concert in the city, it was McCartney's 3,000th concert, in a career spanning more than half a century, and tickets changed hands for up to $500.[21] The stage was set up facing the Alexander Column, with its back to the Moika, and McCartney sang to generations for whom his early songs had been like a 'road of life' to the West. The Rolling Stones played in July 2007. On the set list was 'Sympathy for the Devil', which includes references to the regime change of 1917 that occurred in the Winter Palace only a few metres from their stage.

The previous winter, another temporary tourist attraction had appeared in Palace Square. The company Ice Studio made a glacial replica of Empress Anna's Ice Palace. Such attractions were useful to an industrial city that had lost much of its manufacturing base. Inhabitants were increasingly white-collar, working hard in private marketing firms, import–export or public relations. By the end of the first decade of the new millennium, the civil service had grown to positively tsarist proportions. Housing was increasingly expensive, and although the rise in owner-occupiers impacted positively on the environment, many people commuted to work as apartment prices in the centre – where 40 per cent of the population worked – were particularly high. Yet behind the new prosperity, there was still old St Petersburg, dilapidated and wild. Police blackmailed drivers with faked felonies, in order to make a bit on the side. At length the city responded with a hotline for the denunciation of corruption, bribery and scams. Prostitutes, many of them working to feed their drug habits, were rounded up by a local police official, driven to the outskirts of the city and made to 'lick his car clean'. Little was done about the

patently racial attacks on African students studying in the city –
five were shot or stabbed between 2000 and 2006. Freedom of
speech was under attack, as democracy was edged out by the
Putin machine. One of his first acts as president was to silence
independent television. In April 2015, a building on Shavush-
kina Street in north-west Petersburg was pinpointed as the HQ
of Russia's Internet trolls, who spend their days slipping praise
for Putin and defamation of Western democracy across Internet forums and social networks. While the strengthening state
successfully restrained the gang culture of a decade earlier, its
own officials engaged in protection and extortion.[22]

In 2007, a survey conducted in three cities – including
St Petersburg – returned the staggering statistic that 71 per cent
of people thought Stalin had been a positive influence, and even
more believed that Felix Dzerzhinsky had preserved order.[23] It
offered a carte blanche to the leadership. Putin's KGB training
had taught him that what was not controlled remained a threat.
Action against Chechnya and Georgia, as well as the annexation
of Crimea – as shown on Russian television – did much to push
the idea of a renewed, restrengthened Russia. Many citizens were
persuaded that the president was the best man to defend them.
He was a judo black belt, caught big fish, hunted big game and
sent his soldiers to quash any challenge to the Russian nation.
Wars reported through state-controlled media – live broadcasts
had been banned – were as useful as chemically enhanced sportsmen or enormous propaganda budgets, in proclaiming Russian
prowess. Putin, aching from the humiliation of Russia by the
West in the 1990s, wanted his country to be great again, but
somewhere along the line he marginalised the quest for national
greatness in his drive to amass personal wealth. It was Catherine
the Great all over again. Troublesome journalists were silenced.
Alexander Litvinenko accused the reincarnated KGB – the FSB –
of planting the murderous 'Chechen' bombs that ripped through
Moscow apartment blocks, thereby justifying a war against the

alleged perpetrators. Litvinenko, a former FSB agent who tackled organised crime, also accused Putin of involvement in the 2006 murder of the human-rights journalist Anna Politkovskaya, who opposed the president's policy in the Second Chechen War. By 2010 Robert Gates, the US Secretary of Defence, suggested that the idea of democracy in Russia had all but vanished. And hours before he was shot in February 2015, only a stone's throw from the Kremlin, Boris Nemtsov – who had been an idealistic and honest member of Yeltsin's government and was intensely optimistic about the changes in Russia – sadly declared that Russia was becoming a fascist state.[24]

Post 2010, the St Petersburg city authorities listed 660,000 people as still inhabiting the remaining 105,000 *kommunalki* in the city, although many of these were temporary or even illegal migrants.[25] The financial crisis of 2008 had led to a renewed government subsidy on basic foods, and the old and poor were stranded with the perennial peasant diet of grains and pulses, while the rich seemed even better off. Some were very much better off. Krestovsky Island became fashionable. Housing developments sprang up in the neighbourhood near

*Video watchdogs guard new money in St Petersburg 2016.*

the Tauride Palace. Property developers – with a little help
from the authorities – would evict people from desirable buildings that were conveniently declared uninhabitable, in order to
create luxury apartments. Prices were commensurate with those
in other major cities in Europe and America. However, some
controversial developments were blocked by local resistance.
Gazprom planned to build a 400-metre-high tower in Okhta, on
the land where the Swedish fort at Nyenskans had stood. Apart
from being an archaeological site, its proximity to the Smolny
Monastery and the Smolny Institute on the other side of the
Neva was considered an intrusion on the historical city. Local
pressure, stimulated by the St Petersburg intelligentsia, managed
to sway Dmitri Medvedev – president during Putin's tactical
interregnum – to urge Gazprom to move their projected tower
to the less historical Lakhta,[26] and become the silver-needle
centrepiece of a steel-and-glass development on the waterfront:
St Petersburg meets Singapore.

Passing the Lakhta site, driving along the A181, you soon
join the 142-kilometre St Petersburg Ring Road, which con-
nects Kronstadt with the shore. It runs along the flood barriers

*Kronstadt's empty canals and warehouses.*

begun in the late 1970s, interrupted by the political turmoil of the 1990s and finally completed under Putin's initiative between 2005 and 2011. Kronstadt, suffering from its demise as a naval base, became a St Petersburg suburb that was accessible by bus. The barrier should protect the city from the flooding which has threatened its survival since the year it was founded. That is, if leaders across the world agree to cut back on fossil fuels. But gas and oil are Russia's biggest exports. In 2009, as six million Russians became poverty-stricken, the country became the world's biggest oil producer. And Putin – like a tsar – became enormously wealthy.[27]

Another exciting project was the redevelopment of Peter the Great's old maritime timber yard on New Holland Island. The powerhouse director of the Mariinsky, Valery Gergiev, had plans for a huge glass-cube opera house to be suspended over the island. The design, submitted by Los Angeles architect Eric Owen Moss, was vetoed by city planner Oleg Kharchenko, who had no enthusiasm for 'formless glass structures' – a sentiment backed by the Kremlin. The concept of a floating glass cube harked back to one of the city's most exciting, yet unrealised architectural dreams – Tatlin's *Monument to the Third International*. The decision was thus unhistorical, and was damaging to the city's capacity to attract tourists. The plan was replaced by a more conservative scheme by the British architect Norman Foster, which in turn, foundered when the consortium behind it encountered financial difficulties. The oligarch and Chelsea Football Club owner, Roman Abramovich, stepped in with a welcome 400-million-euro donation. The resulting complex, phase one of which was finished in 2016, includes studios, bookshops, galleries and a park, but lacks that magnificence of vision associated with the daring architectural tradition of St Petersburg.[28]

At the nearby Mariinsky, Gergiev made do with a new concert hall of modest size and a new auditorium. The concert hall is well disposed and the acoustics warm, but the Mariinsky II is neither architecturally nor acoustically innovative. As for Mariinsky performances, some are brilliant, while others appear to be a victim of the St Petersburg time-warp. A recent performance of *Swan Lake* was somewhat soulless – although the corps de ballet, as befits St Petersburg tradition, was adept. The production dated from 1950, but apart from strangely outsized swans gliding across the backdrop – swans which also made a guest appearance in the 2017 production of Rimsky-Korsakov's *Sadko* – the effect was contemporary. This is not the case with all the older Mariinsky productions. A *Nozze di Figaro* dating from 1998 – lumpen, leaden, lacking wit and brio – should have been mothballed long ago.

Today, the Mariinsky seems obliged to present certain ballets and operas again and again, in an obvious pitch to tourist audiences. Elsewhere in the city, the theatre offers a gamut of entertainment. In late 2016, these ranged from the French farce *Boeing-Boeing* to a powerful and brilliant adaptation of Yuri Grossman's novel *Life and Fate* at the Maly Drama Theatre. As for the city itself, St Petersburg has always provided a magnificent set for its own drama. Whether it is a break-dancer who bursts into a metro carriage and begins to gyrate as the train starts to move, a ghostly street artist promenading the night-time Nevsky or the architecture renovated for the tercentennial celebrations, St Petersburg remains truly theatrical. Sometimes the architecture is difficult to appreciate through the spiders' webs of overhead trolley-bus lines, but the buildings are a grand testimony to a huge, if short, past. Standing by the Blagoveshchensky Bridge on Vassilevsky Island, the statue of Trezzini looks proudly out on all the might and the mess – on what has become of the city that Peter the Great engaged him to build.

# 17

# MIRAGE

## *2017*

This book began with a walk down the Nevsky Prospekt in the strange twilight of the post-communist decade. The going was – for St Petersburg – about to get rougher. In one way or another, for one section of the community or another, it has always been tough. Peasant, tsar, intellectual, bourgeois, comrade, the quiet person going about his or her business – they've all struggled for a vision of the city and a decent life.

On 31 October 2015, a terrorist bomb downed a Russian passenger jet killing 224 people en route from the Egyptian resort of Sharm El Sheikh to Petersburg's Pulkovo Airport. Seventeen months later, on 3 April 2017, a terrorist bomb killed and injured travellers on the Petersburg metro. Both tragedies hurt the city and shocked the world.

Peter's dream capital was majestic but crumbling, even as it was built. Workmen spent their summers restoring what winter destroyed.[1] The city that was an eruption of otherness became a nightmare of endurance. The sum of all the misery sustained in its 300-year history weighs heavily in the balance against its myriad joys and triumphs. Yet, through the drama of St Petersburg, a mighty territory became a mighty nation. The city's vitality proceeded from its rootlessness. Like New York, St Petersburg was a construct of strangers who brought with them a mix of traditions

*St Petersburg: a fort, a port and a centre of enlightenment learning.*

and capacities that created a new and particular cultural identity. Certainly more like New York than Brasilia – another self-consciously constructed capital built in the middle of nowhere, which nobody wanted to inhabit – St Petersburg forged, in record time, the complex character of one of the most artistically rich and politically volatile cities in the world. But how can any city thrive in a country that is corrupt from the top down?

St Petersburg has spawned monsters and monstrous ideas. The city seemed bizarre and 'different' enough to prompt Mary Shelley to begin the story of *Frankenstein* in this northern capital. Captain Walton's voyage to Arkhangelsk and beyond to discover 'a thousand celestial observations' in 'unexplored regions' begins in St Petersburg. During Walton's expedition, he encounters Frankenstein tracking his hideous monster.[2] St Petersburg's promise is mysterious, unsafe. Dostoevsky described it as 'the most fantastic city with the most fantastic history of all cities on this planet'.[3]

St Petersburg was an antidote to Moscow – the 'true Russian,' observed Casanova, was 'a stranger to St Petersburg'.[4] A Frenchman in the early nineteenth century considered that it was 'not the city of Russians', but a 'city of foreign artists paid by Russia'.[5] That impression of the capital was offered again by an American visiting in the communist era. Playwright Lillian Hellman came to Leningrad and was delighted by the imagination that had placed 'pale, delicate southern-yellow buildings' in a 'cheerless, damp northern climate'. It was clear to her that the city was built by 'people who had no connection with Moscow or Kiev.'[6] Yet so much of the glory of Russia has been created in Peter's city – its literature, its music, its dance – and even, between the 1820s and 1918, its political vision. For three centuries there has been a struggle between life and death, and the miserable weather has always played its part.

Looking at a map of the Neva delta, there seems something pharyngeal. The estuary is an open maw exposed to cold winds. Vulnerable inhabitants – like siege victims – are hostage to the

*A Rastrelli-like sequence of downpipes deals with the weather.*

weather. Dostoevsky shivered and suffered 'a terrible night, a
November night, damp, foggy, rainy, snowy, fraught with agues,
catarrhs, colds, quinsies, fevers of every possible species and
variety, in short . . . a St Petersburg November'.[7] He wrote of
a terrain so wet that gravediggers could not bury a dry body.[8]
And yet, when you step off the train from hard, driven, dressy
Moscow, although a bitter sleet may cut you to the quick, there's
a palpable warmth. You move through a more relaxed, studenty
kind of atmosphere. Big-city busy people still barge and scowl –
they've had to fight their corner – but there is a relative ease that
is elusive in chic and edgy Moscow.

St Petersburg was an unwanted upstart. Moscow became a
brash usurper. In Petersburg restaurants today, people appear
to relax informally. In Moscow, I round the corner of a restaurant and walk straight into the combat-kitted unit of a small
private army. Like mercenaries in some banana republic, operatives lounge against jeeps and bulletproofed, dark-windowed
limos, while others patrol, cradling weapons of size and power.
I'm happy not to have a reservation, in case a rival clan comes
to call. The establishment is a curious choice for someone who
needs protection. But the outing must be about ostentation if
the boss, flanked by Armani-suited associates and cleavaged
women, chooses to occupy a window seat. The top dog nibbles
voraciously, as if he hasn't quite recovered from impecunious
provincial origins. His plateau of *fruits de mer* includes species
that – at a glance – I believe I have never seen. I want to linger
and investigate but, as a minder two metres tall approaches me, I
decide to hasten off in the direction of the Kremlin. The enormous
department store, Gum – lit up like Harrods – screams out at
Lenin's mausoleum on the far side of Red Square. The recently
revamped St Basil's Cathedral looks so brand-new that it would
outshine any over-radiant Las Vegas imitation. 'What did we
want?' mused a construction worker who was interviewed here
in Red Square in 1991. 'Gentle socialism, humane socialism . . .

What did we get? . . . bloodthirsty capitalism. Shooting. Show-downs.'[9] Twenty-five years on, I know that St Petersburg has at least settled somewhat, after the violence of the Nineties, into a new attempt to find, if not a 'humane socialism', then at least a smoother, more palatable kind of life – as far as that is possible in the kleptocracy of Putin's Russia. The president is known to be richer than Abramovich. It's Kremlin Inc., with oligarchs for boyars. Putin, the Leningrad kid, is heir to Menshikov rather than Peter the Great. Yet, just as Peter did, Putin needs the West – it's where his pals stash their cash.[10]

St Petersburg is not a flawless museum where every Rastrelli flourish and Rossi sweep is perfect. Ten to fifteen historical buildings – from among the 15,000 pre-1914 edifices in this Unesco World Heritage site – are lost to developers or disintegration each year. As with Venice, dilapidation is woven into every fibre of the city's being. Its life has been short and damaged. Like a starlet – the casualty of ambition, fame and infamy – the city enters rehab and emerges with a new lease of life time and time again. Elizabeth's shimmering palaces, Paul's harlequin fortress, schooners swept by flood waters against the sides of baroque

*Land versus sea – the Western Rapid Diameter bridge system and the core of the Lakhta Gazprom Tower under construction beyond.*

churches, Gogol's double-dealing Nevsky Prospekt and the cabbage patch in St Isaac's Square: all become different kinds of absurdity in the bright business noon of the modern city. Understandably, St Petersburg authorities want to make of their metropolis more than the magnificent utterances of its past. City planners insist that people must want to live in St Petersburg. It must compete with other modern centres. Hence initiatives such as the Lakhta Centre and the Zenit Arena, which will feature in the 2018 World Cup. Typically, its construction workers are living in appalling conditions and some are owed back-pay.[11]

Petersburg brags and boasts to tourists. But, seen from a certain angle, Falconet's *Bronze Horseman* appears puny. Custine dismissed his compatriot's statue; it was 'excessively praised because it happens to be in Russia'.[12] The Horseman has nothing of the power of, say, Andrea del Verrocchio's equestrian Colleoni Monument, which dominates Venice's Campo SS Giovanni e Paolo. Youthful, spirited, but dwarfed by the immensity of Senate Square and the expanse of the Neva, Falconet's Peter seems hardly up to the job. If he dismounted, he'd stagger off – like a drunkard trying to walk the straight line, his dubious legacy 300 years of murderous desire.

Modern St Petersburg struggles to thrive, determined – after all the mismanagement – to find viable solutions to possibly insoluble problems, such as geological risk. Most of the centre is rated as high, which is why they built the metro low. The lowest station is Admiralskaya, at nearly ninety metres. The metro system works very well. Trains are frequent and the distances covered at high speeds are considerable. The stations don't have the imperial swagger of their Moscow counterparts, but they are impressive and very clean. The problem is that the stops are sparsely located and the city's trolley-bus network and its privately run, rattling and bouncing *marshrutki* minibuses are consequently overloaded. Another problem with the metro is that escalator rides take between two minutes fifteen seconds and two minutes fifty seconds. A worker going to the office every day – with two descents and two ascents – clocks up nearly an hour a week on escalators, without counting pleasure trips. Some commuters sit on the moving steps, while the daring run, and most stand – often reading. St Petersburgers are still voracious readers. The older generation remembers the time of treasuring words; mimeographed *samizdat* copies of forbidden works were as prized as an extra ration or a weapon that could change the world.[13]

Areas of the city are strangled by the ugliness of a cheapskate or ageing infrastructure. On Vasilevsky Island or on the Vyborg Side, huge, temporary, cladded tubes run above ground to deliver heat. On the outskirts, cat's cradles of overhead electricity lines blight the sky. Vast tracts of potholed terrain flag incomplete or abandoned building projects. Unprofitable scrubland stands bleakly between brash shopping centres. The new perimeter of the city is under siege by a commercial ring of Auchan, H&M, Castorama, Decathlon, Ikea – the list is growing. The only sparkling dose of Anymall, Planet Earth plumped in the centre of the city is Galeria, which was opened in 2010 on Livorsky Prospekt near the Moskovsky railway station. But, as Western-style or Western-owned enterprise installs itself, the city's sense of difference and identity is eroded. Yet St Petersburg has always been disturbed by novelties imported from beyond Russia's borders, promising something tantalising, something out of reach. With average salaries in 2016 running at between 40,000 and 50,000 roubles a month – around £650 – it is difficult to see how ordinary people easily afford the scarves and woolly hats for sale in middle-range shops like Zara, let alone have enough for a down-payment on one of the modestly sized new apartments discreetly advertised in the metro.

Inhabitants under twenty-five don't have a memory of the really hard times. The *gulag* is a distant epoch. This shows in their tendency to smile and in their capacity to enjoy life. Students dress casually. They kiss, hold hands, expect to be met

*The present past: Petersburg in 2017.*

by friendly staff in coffee bars and wonder – as students do in Europe – what kind of prospects are open to them, post-degree. Resisting the brash intrusion of anonymous globalisation, there are pockets of great charm where intimate cafés resemble some of the cosier haunts found in Europe or America. The architectural eclecticism of the late nineteenth century – as it is brought back from years of neglect – echoes certain gracious parts of venerable American cities. Rubinsteyna Street, with its cafés and restaurants, glows, as do streets in Chicago or New York built during the same period. Rubinsteyna even has an American-style open parking lot. The elegantly restored Maly Konyushennaya is reminiscent of smart streets found in northern European cities. At the Mariinsky and the Philharmonic, tickets remain inexpensive and the public passion for the performing arts runs high. Yet lurking behind the impressive façades remain dark entranceways, drab staircases and creaky lifts. Soviet-era bureaucracy is lodged stubbornly in the psyche – form-filling, stamping, registering – and often occludes even a simple commercial transaction.[14] Will the Nevsky Prospekt ever reassert itself against the most fashionable thoroughfares of the West – this time round, with good Russian products for sale – or will it stay fractured and rough? Darker than any doorway is the regime that stops Russia from realising its vast potential. The kleptocrats – Menshikov redivivus – pocketing the riches. Any decent *mir* would know what to do with Gazprom profits.

I am watching the waters of the choppy Neva splash against the shore not far from where Peter's log cabin stands, not far from where the *Aurora* is moored, and I'm thinking about murderous desire – desire for a frontier fort, an imperial capital, revolutionary success, communism, gangsterism, capitalism, the non-capital that remains a cultural capital – the desire for the splendour worthy of a capital, the desire for freedom, openness and life. It is 100 years since that blank, fired from the *Aurora*, triggered a nightmare vision of a good dream. Seventy-five years since genocidal Stalin stood against holocaustic Hitler. Twenty-five since Gorbachev dissolved the Soviet Union. Oligarchs echo Romanovs. Revolution was a good idea that went horribly wrong. Look back behind the chaos and slaughter, and see Alexander Herzen gazing on the shores of utopia.

An image I first saw painted on a wall in Vilnius has gone viral: the new American president and the familiar, old, ongoing president of the Russian Federation are kissing. Dangerously erotic – power. If one thinks of the Nazi-Soviet Pact and all the deception that entailed, it's true that strange bedfellows have played their part in Russian strategy. Who – one asks – is playing who? How will it pan out, when the misspelt impetuous tweet meets the calculated smirk of the KGB? The weight of Russia's past – a terrible howl of mistreatment and misfortune – presses heavily on human rights and happiness. Does the future promise to prove Chaadaev's celebrated statement that Russia exists simply to alert the world that its way of doing things should be avoided, whatever the cost? In the film *Russian Ark* the visitor asks, 'What system is there now?' The reply comes back, 'I don't know.'

I cross a long bridge over the Neva. Night falls. Between the Alexandrinsky Theatre and the Anichkov Palace an operatic moon – the kind that so often gloats low in the Petersburg sky – is suddenly eclipsed by a gusting cloud. The city is, in many of its guises, incredible: the Summer Garden in autumn, winter buildings laced with snow, the islands in late spring. There are unexpected architectural details, fanciful effects in no-nonsense spaces. The lighting of palaces and public buildings enchants the darkness. The city surprises. You can walk along the Moika in the early hours and catch sight, through an unexpectedly lit window, of a corner of Matisse's *Dance*, one of the simplest, most powerful and most positive paintings ever made. Above all – in hope for the future – there is potential in the number of gracious buildings waiting to be restored. The city has a capacity to astound. For the moment, looking back through its changing faces, I feel it as a mirage, a magnificent Atlantis, an impossible metropolis risen from the mists, which the mud and the mire keep trying to reclaim.

Peter wanted a window onto Europe. He aspired to Western style – he was left with Russia. Now the riches of that country are all tied up in offshore accounts, and 143 million citizens have been buried in the enterprise.

'We'll *build a city here, a port*' – *Pushkin*, The Bronze Horseman

# ACKNOWLEDGEMENTS

As usual, my greatest debt is to Katiu, whose loving contribution has been of an incredible calibre. Marjotte, my daughter, has been most sensitive – her enthusiasm and intelligence are treasures.

I should like to thank my previous agent, John Saddler, for his help on *St Petersburg* in its earliest stages; also George Lucas at InkWell in New York for a similar contribution. Great thanks are due to my agent, Julian Alexander, for judiciously placing the book with Hutchinson, whose staff I thank heartily for their tremendously warm response to the project. Particularly I would like to mention the avid, supremely sensitive and truly collaborative editor Sarah Rigby. I should also like to thank the eagle-eyed Mandy Greenfield, who copy-edited and made some astute suggestions; Melissa Four, who produced a dazzling jacket; Lindsay Nash for her elegant book design; and Najma Finlay for her energetic publicity push.

Many influences stand behind this work. A significant debt is owed to the late Marshall Berman, whose *All That's Solid Melts Into Air* provides moving and provocative insights on the subject of the city and modernism. But there are so many people – the scholarship on Petersburg that has been achieved in recent years has been voluminous and penetrating, augmenting a rich record provided by the multitude of wonderful 'eyes on the ground'. The scholars who have excoriated often obscure aspects of the city's past are too numerous to mention but they are to be found in the bibliography.

I would like to thank Karen Hewitt and the Oxford Russia Fund, the wonderful staff of that superlative library, the Bibliothèque Nationale in Paris, the very helpful staff of the Bodleian Library in Oxford, as well as the staff of museums, palaces and theatres in St Petersburg, Moscow, both Novgorods, and other Russian cities, including Perm, where the children at the lycée gave me a tour of what was once Sergei Diaghilev's natal house and is now their school. Also, a big thank you to the very giving Russians I have met both in their country and abroad, among them dancers at what was then the Kirov, academics from all over Russia, as well as Nadia Boudris and her family, Olga Kolatina, Lyudmila Kadzhaya, Marina Koreneva and Anatoli Fetisov. Thanks also to Vladimir Malakoff, Virginie Aubry at the Cinémathèque de la Danse in Paris for obtaining rare footage of Pavlova, Ulanova and Nureyev, and to Laurence and Chadi Chabert for their help and thoughtfulness and for the magical Bret. Also, much gratitude to a whole host of understanding friends, to the very supportive Amélie Louveau, and to my patient, kind and ever lovely mama, Claire.

# LIST OF ILLUSTRATIONS

INTEGRATED ILLUSTRATIONS

## PLATE ILLUSTRATIONS

# NOTES

## 1 TWILIGHT ON THE NEVSKY

1   Dumas, Alexandre, *En Russie – Impressions de voyage* (1859), Paris: Editions François Bourin, 1989, p. 163.

2   Arnold, Sue, 'Human Warmth Amidst the Ice and the Ashes', *Observer*, 3 January 1993.

3   De Custine, Astolphe, *Letters from Russia*, trans. Robin Buss (1991), London: Penguin, 2014, p. 105.

4   Gide, André, *Back From the USSR*, London: Secker and Warburg, 1937, p. 32.

5   Brodsky, Joseph, 'A Guide to a Renamed City', in *Less Than One: Selected Essays*, London: Viking, 1986; Penguin Classics, 2011, p. 88.

## 2 HAVOC IN LONDON

1   Schuyler, Eugene, *Peter the Great – Emperor of Russia*, Vol. I, New York: Charles Scribner's Sons, 1884, pp. 287–8.

2   Gilbert Burnett, Bishop of Salisbury, qtd in Cross, Anthony, *Peter the Great Through British Eyes – Perceptions and Representations of the Tsar since 1698*, Cambridge: Cambridge University Press, 2000, p. 11.

3   Alexei Tolstoy, *Peter the First*, qtd in Shrad, Mark Lawrence, *Vodka Politics – Alcohol, Autocracy, and the Secret History of the Russian State*, New York: Oxford University Press, 2014, p. 404.

4   Warner, Elizabeth, *Russian Myths*, London: British Museum Press, 2002, pp. 18–19.

5   Schuyler, *Peter the Great*, Vol. II, pp. 9–10.

6   Shrad, *Vodka Politics*, pp. 37–8.

7   Massie, Robert K., *Peter the Great – His Life and World*, New York: Knopf, 1980; UK: Head of Zeus pbk, 2013, pp. 39–50.

8   Prince Boris Ivanovich Kuratkin, Tsar Peter's brother-in-law, from his notes for a projected life on the tsar, in Vernadsky, George, senior ed., *A Source Book for Russian History From Early Times to 1917*, Vol. II, New Haven, CT, and London: Yale University Press, 1972, p. 311; Massie, *Peter the Great*, pp. 66–70.

9   Hughes, Lindsey, *Russia and the West, The Life of a Seventeenth-Century Westernizer, Prince Vasily Vasilevich Golitsyn (1643–1714)*, Newtonville, MA: Oriental Research Partners, 1984, pp. 96, 98; Hosking, Geoffrey, *Russia and the Russians – A History*, Cambridge, MA: Belknap Press of Harvard University Press, 2001, pp. 179–80.

10   Shrad, *Vodka Politics*, p. 46.

11   Prince Kuratkin, in Vernadsky, *A Source Book for Russian History*, p. 312.

12   Schlafly Jr, Daniel L., 'Filippo Balatri in Peter the Great's Russia', in *Jahrbücher für Geschichte Osteuropas*, Neue Folge, Bd. 45, H. 2, 1997, pp. 181, 188–9.

13   Schuyler, *Peter the Great*, Vol. I, p. 286.

14   Deschisaust, Pierre, *Description d'un voyage fait à Saint Petersbourg*, Paris: Thiboust, 1728, pp. 4–5; Prak, Maarten, *The Dutch Republic in the Seventeenth Century*, trans. Diane Webb, Cambridge: Cambridge University Press, 2006, p. 101.

15   Schuyler, *Peter the Great*, Vol. I, pp. 287–8, 291; Massie, *Peter the Great*, p. 200.

16   Bruijn, Jaap R., *The Dutch Navy of the Seventeenth and Eighteenth Centuries*, Columbia, SC: University of South Carolina Press, 1993, p. 101; Schama, Simon, *The Embarrassment of Riches*, London: William Collins, 1987, pp. 301–2.

17   Prak, *The Dutch Republic*, pp. 222–4.

18   Ibid., pp. 223–4; Albedil, M. F., *Peter the Great's Kunstkammer*, St Petersburg: Museum of Anthropology and Ethnography of the Russian Academy of Sciences, Alfa-Colour Publishers, 2002, pp. 6, 14, 17.

19   Schama, *The Embarrassment of Riches*, pp. 151, 180, 265.

20   Shrad, *Vodka Politics*, p. 39.

21   *Post Boy*, No. 371, Saturday 18 September–Tuesday 21 September 1697, qtd in Cross, *Peter the Great*, p. 12.

22   Boulton, Jeremy, *Neighbourhood and Society – A London Suburb in the Seventeenth Century*, Cambridge: Cambridge University Press, 1987, pp. 1, 293; McKellar, Elizabeth, *The Birth of Modern London – The Development and Design of the City 1660–1720*, Manchester: Manchester University Press, 1999, pp. 3, 12–13.

23   McKellar, *The Birth of Modern London*, p. 219; Cracraft, James, *The Petrine Revolution in Russian Architecture*, Chicago, IL and London: University of Chicago Press, 1988, p. 6.

24   Hawksmoor, qtd in McKellar, *The Birth of Modern London*, p. 30.

25   Ibid., pp. 30, 204.

26   Cross, *Peter the Great*, p. 29.

27   Ryan, W. F., 'Peter the Great and English Maritime Technology', in Hughes, Lindsey, ed., *Peter the Great and the West – New Perspectives*, London and New York: Palgrave Macmillan, 2001, p. 145.

28   Perry, Captain John, *The State of Russia under the Present Czar*, London: Benjamin Tooke, 1716, p. 166.

29  Cross, *Peter the Great*, pp. 21–2.
30  Perry, *The State of Russia*, p. 166.
31  Cross, *Peter the Great*, pp. 20–23.
32  Shrad, *Vodka Politics*, p. 40.
33  Perry, *The State of Russia*, p. 229.
34  Cross, *Peter the Great*, pp. 18–20.
35  Hughes, Lindsey, 'Images of Greatness: Portraits of Peter the Great', in Hughes, *Peter the Great and the West*, pp. 253–4.
36  Anderson, M. S., *Peter the Great*, London: Thames and Hudson, 1978, p. 42; Ryan, 'Peter the Great and English Maritime Technology', in Hughes, *Peter the Great and the West*, p. 138.
37  Cross, *Peter the Great*, pp. 20, 28; Shrad, *Vodka Politics*, p. 41.
38  Evelyn, John, *The Diary of John Evelyn Esq. F.R.S. from 1641 to 1705–6*, London: Gibbings, 1890, p. 571.
39  Cross, *Peter the Great*, pp. 30–31.
40  Perry, *The State of Russia*, p. 165.
41  Cross, *Peter the Great*, pp. 26–7.
42  Hughes, 'Images of Greatness', in Hughes, *Peter the Great and the West*, p. 254.
43  Hoffman, qtd in Schuyler, *Peter the Great*, Vol. I, pp. 307–8.
44  Kollmann, Nancy S., '27 October 1698: Peter Punishes the Streltsy', in Cross, Anthony, ed., *Study Group on Eighteenth-Century Russia – Days from the Reigns of Eighteenth-Century Russian Rulers*, Part I, Proceedings of a workshop dedicated to the memory of Professor Lindsey Hughes held at the Bibliotheca di Storia Contemporanea, 'A. Oriani', Ravenna, 12–13 September 2007, Cambridge: Fitzwilliam College, 2007, pp. 23–6, 29–31.
45  Korb, Johann Georg, *Diary of an Austrian Secretary of the Legation at the Court of the Czar Peter the Great*, trans. Count MacDonnell, London, 1863, qtd in Dmytryshyn, Basil, ed., *Imperial Russia – A Source Book 1700–1917*, 2nd edn, Hinsdale, IL: Dryden Press, 1974, pp. 1–11.

## 3 DANGEROUS ACCELERATION

1  Chaadaev, Peter, 'Philosophic Letters', 1829, published 1836, qtd in Hare, Richard, *Pioneers of Russian Social Thought*, Oxford: Oxford University Press, 1951, p. 9.
2  Peter the Great, *Decree on a New Calendar*, December 1699, in Dmytryshyn, *Imperial Russia*, p. 13.
3  von Strahlenberg, Philip John, *An Historico-Geographical Description of the North and Eastern Parts of Europe and Asia*, London, 1738, p. 27.
4  Ryan, 'Peter the Great and English Maritime Technology', in Hughes, *Peter the Great and the West*, pp. 146–7.
5  Schlafly, 'Filippo Balatin in Peter the Great's Russia', p. 187; Cross,

Anthony, *By the Banks of the Neva – Chapters from the Lives and Careers of the British in Eighteenth-Century Russia*, Cambridge: Cambridge University Press, 1997, p. 166.

6   Deane, John, 'A Letter from Moscow to the Marquess of Carmarthen Relating to the Czar of Muscovy's Forwardness in his Great Navy', London, March 1699, p. 1.

7   Vigor, Mrs, *Letters from a Lady who Resided Some Years in Russia to her Friend in England*, London: Dodsley, 1775, pp. 14–16.

8   Voltaire, *Histoire de Charles XII* (1731), in *Œuvres historiques*, ed. R. Pomeau, Paris: Gallimard, 1957, p. 193.

9   Anisimov, Evgenii V., *Five Empresses – Court Life in Eighteenth-Century Russia*, trans. Kathleen Carroll, Westport, CN, and London: Praeger, 2004, pp. 9–11.

10  Whitworth, Lord Charles, *An Account of Russia as it Was in the Year 1710*, Strawberry Hill, 1758, pp. 82–3; Jones, Robert E., 'Why St Petersburg?', in Hughes, *Peter the Great and the West*, pp. 190–91.

11  Marsden, Christopher, *Palmyra of the North – The First Days of St Petersburg*, London: Faber and Faber, 1942, pp. 46–7.

12  La Mottraye, Aubry de, *Voyages en Anglois et en François D'A. de La Motraye en diverses provinces et places*, London, 1732, p. 71; Milner-Gulland, Robin, '16 May 1703: The Petersburg Foundation-Myth', in Cross, *Study Group on Eighteenth-Century Russia*, pp. 37–9, 40–41.

13  Shvidkovsky, Dmitry, *Russian Architecture and the West*, trans. Anthony Wood, New Haven, CT, and London: Yale University Press, 2007, p. 194.

14  Anon. (Weber, Friedrich), *The Present State of Russia in Two Volumes, The Whole Being the Journal of a Foreign Minister who Resided in Russia at the Time*, trans. from the High Dutch, London, 1723, pp. 333–4.

15  Bell, John, *Travels from St Petersburg in Russia to Various Parts of Asia*, Vol. 1, Edinburgh, 1788, pp. 2–3.

16  Cracraft, *The Petrine Revolution in Russian Architecture*, p. 176.

17  *The Present State of Russia*, pp. 299–300.

18  Peter the Great, letter to Menshikov of 4 September 1704, qtd in Jones, Robert E., *Bread Upon the Waters – The St Petersburg Grain Trade and the Russian Economy, 1703–1811*, Pittsburgh, PA: University of Pittsburgh Press, 2013, p. 21.

19  Qtd in Schuyler, *Peter the Great*, Vol. II, pp. 5–6.

20  *The Present State of Russia*, pp. 300–301.

21  Hosking, *Russia and the Russians*, p. 228; Dukes, Paul, *The Making of Russian Absolutism 1613–1801*, Harlow and New York: Longman, 1982, p. 83.

22  Cracraft, *The Petrine Revolution in Russian Architecture*, pp. 182, 184.

23  Schönle, Andreas, *The Ruler in the Garden – Politics and Landscape Design in Imperial Russia*, Bern and Oxford: Peter Lang, 2007, p. 41.

24  Keenan, Paul, *St Petersburg and the Russian Court 1703–1761*, London and New York: Palgrave Macmillan, 2013, pp. 14, 21-2.

25  Giroud, Vincent, *St Petersburg – A Portrait of a Great City*, New Haven, CT: Yale University – The Beinecke Rare Book and Manuscript Library, 2003, p. 20.

26  Shvidkovsky, *Russian Architecture and the West*, p. 202; Deschisaux, *Description d'un voyage*, p. 21.

27  Schönle, *The Ruler in the Garden*, pp. 39-41.

28  Shrad, *Vodka Politics*, pp. 39, 45.

29  Hughes, Lindsey, '"For the Health of the Sons of Ivan Mikhailovich": I. M. Golovin and Peter the Great's Mock Court', in *Reflections on Russia in the Eighteenth Century*, ed. Klein, Dixon and Fraanje, Cologne: Böhlau Verlag, 2001, p. 44.

30  Anderson, *Peter the Great*, pp. 60–61; qtd in Jones, in Hughes, *Peter the Great and the West*, p. 194.

31  *The Present State of Russia*, pp. 312-13.

32  Whitworth, *An Account of Russia*, p. 136.

33  Cracraft, *The Petrine Revolution in Russian Architecture*, pp. 88, 175.

34  *The Present State of Russia*, pp. 302-303, 306.

35  Ibid., p. 323.

36  Vigor, Mrs, *Letters from a Lady*, p. 38.

37  Shrad, *Vodka Politics*, pp. 43, 45-6.

38  Alexander, John, 'Catherine I, Her Court and Courtiers', in Hughes, *Peter the Great and the West*, p. 233.

39  Ibid., pp. 234-5.

40  Kratter, Franz, *The Maid of Marienburg – A Drama in Five Acts. From the German of Kratter*, London, 1798, p. 7.

41  Rousset de Missy, Jean, *Memoires du Regne de Catherine, Imperatrice et Souveraine de toute la Russie &c. &c. &c.*, Amsterdam, 1728, pp. 15ff; Anisimov, *Five Empresses*, p. 20.

42  Engel, Barbara Alpern, *Women in Russia 1700–2000*. Cambridge: Cambridge University Press, 2004, pp. 11-12.

43  Kratter, p. 207.

44  *The Present State of Russia*, pp. 263, 329.

45  Charles Whitworth, Britain's first regular ambassador to Russia, qtd in Cracraft, *The Petrine Revolution in Russian Architecture*, p. 195.

46  *The Present State of Russia*, p. 191.

47  Keenan, *St Petersburg and the Russian Court*, pp. 17-18; Cracraft, *The Petrine Revolution in Russian Architecture*, p. 177.

48  *The Present State of Russia*, p. 4.

49  Ibid., pp. 26-7.

50  Algarotti, Francesco, *Lettres du comte Algarotti sur la Russie*, London, 1769, p. 65.

51  *The Present State of Russia*, p. 9.

52  La Mottraye, *Voyages*, p. 241.

53  Keenan, *St Petersburg and the Russian Court*, pp. 20, 120.

54  Peter Henry Bruce, in Vernadsky, *A Source Book for Russian History*, p. 323; *The Present State of Russia*, pp. 89–90, 109.

55  Peter the Great, declaration to Tsarevich Alexei of October 1715, in Dmytryshyn, *Imperial Russia*, pp. 21–4.

56  Whitworth, *An Account of Russia*, p. 128; *The Present State of Russia*, pp. 102, 320.

57  Dixon, Simon, '30 July 1752: The Opening of the Peter the Great Canal', in Cross, *Study Group on Eighteenth-Century Russia*, p. 94.

58  Hughes, Lindsey, 'Architectural Books in Petrine Russia', in *Russia and the West in the Eighteenth Century – Proceedings of the Second International Conference Organized by the Study Group on Eighteenth-Century Russia and Held at the University of East Anglia*, Norwich 17–22 July 1981, p. 103.

59  Cracraft, *The Petrine Revolution in Russian Architecture*, pp. 156–7, 180; Brumfield, William Craft, *A History of Russian Architecture*, New York: Cambridge University Press, 1993, p. 205.

60  *The Present State of Russia*, pp. 315–16.

61  Ibid., pp. 179–80, 318.

62  La Mottraye, *Voyages*, p. 240.

63  *The Present State of Russia*, pp. 318–19.

64  Ibid., pp. 317, 319.

65  Jones, *Bread Upon the Waters*, pp. 24, 27, 29–31, 33.

66  La Mottraye, *Voyages*, pp. 185, 253, 254.

67  Wortman, Richard S., *Scenarios of Power – Myth and Ceremony in Russian Monarchy*, Vol. I, Princeton, NJ: Princeton University Press, 1995, p. 49.

68  Cracraft, *The Petrine Revolution in Russian Architecture*, p. 190; Hughes, 'Images of Greatness', in Hughes, *Peter the Great and the West*, pp. 259–60.

69  Dmytryshyn, *Imperial Russia*, p. 16.

70  Bird, Alan, *A History of Russian Painting*, Oxford: Phaidon, 1987, pp. 41–2.

71  Hughes, 'Architectural Books in Petrine Russia', in *Russia and the West in the Eighteenth Century*, p. 103.

72  Albedil, *Peter the Great's Kunstkammer*, pp. 26–7.

73  La Mottraye, *Voyages*, p. 248.

74  Qtd in Anisimov, *Five Empresses*, p. 24.

75  Shvidkovsky, *Russian Architecture and the West*, p. 204.

76  Buckler, Julie A., *Mapping St Petersburg – Imperial Text and Cityshape*, Princeton, NJ: Princeton University Press, 2005, p. 160.

77  *The Present State of Russia*, pp. 93–4.

78  Richardson, William, *Anecdotes of the Russian Empire in a Series of Letters Written a Few Years Ago from St Petersburg*, London, 1784, pp. 222–3.

79  Keenan, *St Petersburg and the Russian Court*, pp. 125, 131, 136; Cracraft, *The Petrine Revolution in Russian Culture*, pp. 228–32.

80  Bagdasarova, Irina, 'Official Banquets at the Russian Imperial Court', in *Dining with the Tsars*, Amsterdam: Museumshop Hermitage Amsterdam, 2014, p. 18.

81  Qtd in Engel, *Women in Russia*, p. 14.

82  Wortman, *Scenarios of Power*, Vol. I, p. 59.

83  Bernstein, Laurie, *Sonia's Daughters – Prostitutes and Their Regulation in Imperial Russia*, Berkeley and Los Angeles: University of California Press, 1995, pp. 13–14.

84  Keenan, *St Petersburg and the Russian Court*, pp. 120–21.

85  *The Present State of Russia*, pp. 31–2.

86  Pososhkov, Ivan, 'A Book on Poverty and Wealth', in Dmytryshyn, *Imperial Russia*, pp. 30–36.

87  Lewitter, L. R., 'Ivan Tikhonovich Pososhkov (1652–1726) and "The Spirit of Capitalism"', in *The Slavonic and East European Review*, Vol. LI, No. 125, October 1973, London: University College London, pp. 537, 539, 552–3.

88  Keenan, *St Petersburg and the Russian Court*, pp. 35, 40.

89  Cracraft, *The Petrine Revolution in Russian Architecture*, pp. 175, 180–81.

90  Mottley, John, *The History of the Life and Reign of the Empress Catherine*, Vol. I, London, 1744, pp. 366–7.

91  Hughes, '"For the Health of the Sons of Ivan Mikhailovich"', in *Reflections on Russia in the Eighteenth Century*, p. 48.

92  Alexei's 'Confession' of June 1718, in Dmytryshyn, *Imperial Russia*, pp. 26–7.

93  Official Condemnation of Alexei, June 1718, ibid., p. 28.

94  *The Present State of Russia*, p. 305.

95  Peter Henry Bruce, in Vernadsky, *A Source Book for Russian History*, p. 341.

96  Cracraft, *The Petrine Revolution in Russian Architecture*, pp. 19–21.

97  *The Present State of Russia*, p. 307.

98  Ibid., p. 27.

99  Shvidkovsky, *Russian Architecture and the West*, pp. 202–203.

100 Leibniz to Peter the Great, 16 January 1712, in Vernadsky, *A Source Book for Russian History*, p. 366.

101 Dukes, *The Making of Russian Absolutism*, p. 75.

102 Shvidkovsky, *Russian Architecture and the West*, pp. 197–8; Cracraft, *The Petrine Revolution in Russian Architecture*, pp. 158, 161, 163.

103 Hosking, *Russia and the Russians*, p. 202.

104 Dashwood, Sir Francis, 'Sir Francis Dashwood's Diary of his Visit to St Petersburg in 1733', ed. Betty Kemp, *The Slavonic and East European Review*, Vol. XXXVIII, No. 90, London: University of London, Athlone Press, December 1959, p. 204.

105 Qtd in Giroud, *St Petersburg*, p. 10.

106 Bird, *A History of Russian Painting*, p. 41.

107 Cracraft, *The Petrine Revolution in Russian Culture*, p. 56.

108 Hughes, '"For the Health of the Sons of Ivan Mikhailovich"', in *Reflections on Russia in the Eighteenth Century*, pp. 448, 50; *The Present State of Russia*, pp. 242–3.

109 Cross, *By the Banks of the Neva*, pp. 33–4.

110 Baehr, Stephen L., 'In the Re-Beginning: Rebirth, Renewal and *Renovatio* in Eighteenth-Century Russia', in *Russia and the West in the Eighteenth Century – Proceedings of the Second International Conference Organized by the Study Group on Eighteenth-Century Russia and Held at the University of East Anglia*, Norwich 17–22 July 1981, p. 153.

111 Wortman, *Scenarios of Power*, Vol. I, p. 48.

112 Hosking, *Russia and the Russians* pp. 205, 213.

113 Duc de Saint-Simon, qtd in Hughes, 'Images of Greatness', in Hughes, *Peter the Great and the West*, p. 255.

114 Anisimov, *Five Empresses*, pp. 25, 34.

115 Marker, Gary, 'Godly and Pagan Women in the Coronation Sermon of 1724', in Bartlett and Lehmann-Carli, eds., *Eighteenth-Century Russia: Society, Culture, Economy – Papers from the VII International Conference of the Study Group on Eighteenth-Century Russia, Wittenberg, 2004*, Berlin: Lit Verlag, 2008, pp. 211–19; Alexander, 'Catherine I, Her Court and Courtiers', in Hughes *Peter the Great and the West*, p. 229.

116 Alexander, 'Catherine I, Her Court and Courtiers', in Hughes *Peter the Great and the West*, p. 229; Galitzin, Le Prince Augustin, *La Russie au XVIIIe siècle*, Paris, 1863, pp. 252–3.

117 La Mottraye, *Voyages*, p. 203.

118 Dixon, Simon, '30 July 1752: The Opening of the Peter the Great Canal', in Cross, *Study Group on Eighteenth-Century Russia*, p. 93; Cross, Anthony, *By the Banks of the Neva*, p. 174.

119 Qtd in Anisimov, *Five Empresses*, pp. 40–41.

120 Rousseau, Jean-Jacques, *A Treatise on the Social Compact*, London, 1764, qtd in Cross, *Peter the Great*, p. 82.

121 Sokurov, Alexander, dir., *Russian Ark*, The State Hermitage Museum, Ministry of Culture of the Russian Federation et al., 2002.

122 Cracraft, *The Petrine Revolution in Russian Architecture*, p. 177.

123 *The Present State of Russia*, p. 300.

124 Dashwood, 'Diary', p. 203.

125 Brodsky, *Less Than One*, p. 74.

## 4 OBLIVION AND REBIRTH

1 Alexander, 'Catherine I, Her Court and Courtiers', in Hughes, *Peter the Great and the West*, p. 229.

2 Anisimov, *Five Empresses*, p. 355 n.1.

3 Qtd in Proskurina, Vera, *Creating the Empress – Politics and Poetry in the Age of Catherine II*, Brighton, MA: Academic Studies Press, 2011, p. 14.

4   Mottley, *The History of the Life and Reign of the Empress Catherine*, Vol. II, p. 48.

5   Wortman, *Scenarios of Power*, Vol. I, p. 67.

6   Galitzin, *La Russie au XVIIIe siècle*, pp. 179–80.

7   Shrad, *Vodka Politics*, p. 54.

8   Mottley, *The History of the Life and Reign of the Empress Catherine*, Vol. II, p. 49.

9   Qtd in Massie, *Peter the Great*, p. 769.

10  Gogol, Nikolai, *Dead Souls*, trans. Christopher English, Oxford: Oxford World's Classics, 1998, p. 245.

11  Smith, Hedrick, *The Russians*, New York: Ballantine Books, revised edn 1984, p. 134.

12  Vernadsky, *A Source Book for Russian History*, p. 377.

13  Dukes, *The Making of Russian Absolutism*, p. 113.

14  Alexander, 'Catherine I, Her Court and Courtiers', in Hughes, *Peter the Great and the West*, p. 230.

15  Deschisaux, *Description d'un voyage*, p. 21.

16  Galitzin, *La Russie au XVIIIe siècle*, p. 330.

17  La Mottraye, qtd in Cracraft, *The Petrine Revolution in Russian Architecture*, p. 218.

18  Deschisaux, *Description d'un voyage*, pp. 16–17, 21.

19  Galitzin, *La Russie au XVIIIe siècle*, pp. 180, 201.

20  Bolkhovitinov, Nikolai Nikolaevich, *Russia and the United States – An Analytical Survey of Archival Documents and Historical Studies*, trans. J. D. Hartgrove, Soviet Studies in History, Vol. XXV, No. 2, pp. 38, 40.

21  Dashwood, 'Diary', p. 205.

22  Keenan, *St Petersburg and the Russian Court*, p. 30.

23  Albedil, *Peter the Great's Kunstkammer*, p. 24.

24  La Mottraye, *Voyages*, pp. 248–9.

25  Keenan, *St Petersburg and the Russian Court*, pp. 30–31.

26  Anisimov, *Five Empresses*, p. 49.

27  Shrad, *Vodka Politics*, p. 54.

28  Galitzin, *La Russie au XVIIIe siècle*, p. 194.

29  Warner, *Russian Myths*, pp. 73–7, ill. p. 77.

30  Mottley, *The History of the Life and Reign of the Empress Catherine*, Vol. II, p. 2.

31  Smith, Alexandra, 'Pushkin's Imperial Image of Saint Petersburg Revisited', in Reid and Andrew, eds, *Two Hundred Years of Pushkin*, Studies in Slavic Literature and Poetics, Vol. XXXIX, Amsterdam and New York: Editions Rodopi, 2003, p. 125.

32  Dukes, *The Making of Russian Absolutism*, p. 103.

33  Manstein, General, *Memoirs of Russia, Historical, Political and Military*, London, 1770, pp. 8–9, 21.

34  Proskurina, *Creating the Empress*, p. 26.

35  Gerasimova, Julia, *The Iconostasis of Peter the Great in the Peter*

*and Paul Cathedral in St Petersburg* (1722–9), Leiden: Alexandros Press, 2004, pp. 4, 33, 49, 53, 146, 191–2, 194.

36 Galitzin, *La Russie au XVIIIe siècle*, pp. 312–13.

37 Manstein, *Memoirs of Russia*, p. 22.

38 Vigor, *Letters from a Lady*, p. 30.

39 Manstein, *Memoirs of Russia*, p. 26.

40 Dukes, *The Making of Russian Absolutism*, pp. 104–105.

41 Vigor, *Letters from a Lady*, pp. 63–4.

42 Keenan, Paul, '23 December 1742: Elizaveta Petrovna's Ceremonial Entry into St Petersburg', in Cross, *Study Group on Eighteenth-Century Russia*, pp. 80–81.

43 The 'H' form being an 'N' in Russian, it spells ANNA.

44 Marker, Gary, *Publishing, Printing and the Origins of Intellectual Life in Russia, 1700–1800*, Princeton, NJ: Princeton University Press, 1985, p. 48.

45 von Strahlenberg, An Historico-Geographical Description, p. 183, n.22.

46 Algarotti, *Lettres*, p. 107; Dashwood, 'Diary', p. 204.

47 Keenan, *St Petersburg and the Russian Court*, pp. 144–5.

48 Gregory, John, and Ukladnikov, Alexander, *Leningrad's Ballet*, Croesor, Gwynned: Zena Publications, 1990, p. 9.

49 Rosslyn, Wendy, 'The Prehistory of Russian Actresses: Women on the Stage in Russia (1704–1757)', in Bartlett and Lehmann-Carli, eds, *Eighteenth-Century Russia: Society, Culture, Economy*, pp. 69–81, 75.

50 Longworth, Philip, *The Three Empresses – Catherine I, Anne and Elizabeth of Russia*, New York: Holt, Rinehart and Winston, 1972, pp. 80–81.

51 Qtd in Soloviev, Sergei M., *A History of Russia, Vol. 34: Empress Anna, Favorites, Policies, Campaigns*, trans. Walter J. Gleason, Gulf Breeze, FL: Academic International Press, 1984, p. 27.

52 Vigor, *Letters from a Lady*, p. 71.

53 Münnich, Comte Ernest de, *Mémoires sur la Russie de Pierre le Grand à Elisabeth Ire* (1720–42), trans. Francis Ley, Paris: Harmattan, 1997, p. 129.

54 Dashwood, 'Diary', p. 200; Algarotti, *Lettres*, p. 72.

55 Dashwood, 'Diary', pp. 203, 206.

56 Ibid., p. 202.

57 Vigor, *Letters from a Lady*, p. 4.

58 Justice, Elizabeth, *A Voyage to Russia: Describing the Laws, Manners and Customs of That Great Empire as Governed at This Present by That Excellent Princess, the Czarina*, York, 1739, p. 35.

59 Ibid., pp. 16, 35.

60 Ibid., pp. 15–17.

61 Ibid., pp. 15, 22–5, 35.

62 Anisimov, *Five Empresses*, p. 96.

63 Manstein, *Memoirs of Russia*, pp. 43–6.

64 Longworth, *The Three Empresses*, p. 122.

65 Anisimov, *Five Empresses*, p. 95.

66  Manstein, *Memoirs of Russia*, p. 251.
67  Vigor, *Letters from a Lady*, p. 19.
68  Qtd in Soloviev, *Empress Anna*, p. 26.
69  Ibid.; Longworth, *The Three Empresses*, p. 122.
70  Richard, John, *A Tour from London to Petersburgh*, London, 1780, p. 18.
71  Anisimov, *Five Empresses*, pp. 89, 91; Longworth, *The Three Empresses*, p. 121. The incident has been attributed to both Catherine and Anna – in 1726 and 1735. Both would have been capable.
72  Münnich, *Mémoires*, p. 129.
73  Qtd in Soloviev, *Empress Anna*, p. 72.
74  Vigor, *Letters from a Lady*, pp. 102–103.
75  Ibid., pp. 93–4.
76  Manstein, *Memoirs of Russia*, p. 249.
77  Anisimov, *Five Empresses*, p. 115.
78  Justice, *A Voyage to Russia*, p. 14.
79  Rosslyn, in *Eighteenth-Century Russia*, pp. 74–5.
80  Manstein, *Memoirs of Russia*, p. 51.
81  Anisimov, Evgeny V., *Empress Elizabeth – Her Reign and Her Russia 1741–61*, trans. John J. Alexander, Gulf Breeze, FL: Academic International Press, 1995, p. 184.
82  Ibid., pp. 19, 20, 200, 203.
83  Qtd in Longworth, *The Three Empresses*, p. 127.
84  John Cook, *Voyages and Travels through the Russian Empire, Tartary and the Empire of Persia*, Vol. I, Edinburgh, 1770, pp. 96–7.
85  Longworth, *The Three Empresses*, pp. 133–4.
86  Shvidkovsky, *Russian Architecture and the West*, p. 207; Anisimov, *Five Empresses*, p. 112.
87  Shvidkovsky, *Russian Architecture and the West*, pp. 209–210.
88  Giroud, *St Petersburg*, p. 16.
89  Manstein, *Memoirs of Russia*, p. 258.
90  Algarotti, *Lettres*, p. 106.
91  Vigor, *Letters from a Lady*, pp. 119–120; Anisimov, *Five Empresses*, p. 101.
92  Dukes, *The Making of Russian Absolutism*, pp. 107–108.
93  Anisimov, *Five Empresses*, pp. 105–106.
94  Charles Cottrell, qtd in Cross, *By the Banks of the Neva*, p. 337.
95  Anisimov, *Five Empresses*, pp. 145–6, 148–50, 153; Anisimov, *Empress Elizabeth*, pp. 4, 7.
96  Soloviev, *Empress Anna*, p. 42.
97  Vockerodt, Prussian Secretary, qtd in Schuyler, *Peter the Great*, Vol. II, p. 11.

## 5 DANCING, LOVE-MAKING, DRINK

1   Leichtenhan, Francine-Dominique, *Élisabeth Ire de Russie*, Paris: Fayard, 2007, p. 20.

2   Anisimov, *Empress Elizabeth*, pp. 11, 166.
3   Soloviev, Sergei M., *History of Russia, Vol. 37: Empress Elizabeth's Reign 1741–44*, trans. Patrick J. O'Meara, Gulf Breeze, FL: Academic International Press, 1996, p. 19.
4   Soloviev, *Empress Elizabeth's Reign*, p. 44.
5   Dukes, *The Making of Russian Absolutism*, p. 109.
6   Soloviev, *Empress Elizabeth's Reign*, p. 30.
7   Manstein, *Memoirs of Russia*, pp. 319–20.
8   Hanway, Jonas, *An Historical Account of the British Trade Over the Caspian Sea with a Journal of Travels*, Vol. I, London: Dodesley, 1753, p. 82.
9   Shvidkovsky, *Russian Architecture and the West*, pp. 210–13, 219–26.
10  Benois, Alexander and de le Messelier, qtd in Anisimov, *Empress Elizabeth*, pp. 184, 186.
11  Gautier, Théophile, *The Complete Works – Vol. VII: Travels in Russia*, trans. and ed. S. C. De Sumichrast, Athenaeum Press, reprinted by Forgotten Books, n.d., p. 293.
12  Dukes, *The Making of Russian Absolutism*, p. 110; Dixon, Simon, *Catherine the Great*, New York: HarperCollins, 2009, p. 72.
13  Cross, *By the Banks of the Neva*, p. 19; Anisimov, *Empress Elizabeth*, p. 183.
14  Nisbet Bain, R., *The Daughter of Peter the Great*, London: Constable, 1899, p. 139.
15  Anisimov, *Empress Elizabeth*, p. 172.
16  Catherine the Great, *The Memoirs of Catherine the Great*, trans. Mark Cruse and Hilde Hoogenboom, New York: Modern Library, 2005; pbk 2006, p. 143.
17  Nisbet Bain, *The Daughter of Peter the Great*, p. 141.
18  Richard, *A Tour from London to Petersburgh*, p. 44.
19  Richardson, *Anecdotes of the Russian Empire*, p. 218.
20  Anisimov, *Empress Elizabeth*, p. 168, quoting Pauzié, p. 173.
21  Shrad, *Vodka Politics*, p. 52.
22  Qtd in Nisbet Bain, *The Daughter of Peter the Great*, p. 134; Richard, *A Tour from London to Petersburgh*, p. 17.
23  Qtd in Anisimov, *Empress Elizabeth*, p. 176.
24  Dukes, *The Making of Russian Absolutism*, p. 109; Richardson, *Anecdotes of the Russian Empire*, p. 81.
25  Anisimov, *Empress Elizabeth*, p. 180.
26  De Madariaga, Isabel, *Catherine the Great – A Short History*, New Haven, CT, and London: Yale University Press, (1990) 2002, p. 12.
27  Cross, *By the Banks of the Neva*, p. 338.
28  Qtd in Nisbet Bain, *The Daughter of Peter the Great*, p. 136.
29  Ibid., p. 138.
30  Soloviev, *Empress Elizabeth's Reign*, p. 29.
31  Manstein, *Memoirs of Russia*, p. 319.
32  Anisimov, *Empress Elizabeth*, pp. 57–60, 73, 204–205, 209.

33   Elizabeth I's decree of 30 August 1756, in Vernadsky, *A Source Book for Russian History*, p. 390.

34   Keenan, *St Petersburg and the Russian Court*, p. 100.

35   Toomre, Joyce S. 'Sumarokov's Adaptation of Hamlet and the "To Be or Not to Be" Soliloquy', in *Study Group on Eighteenth-Century Russia – Newsletter*, No. 9, Leeds, September 1981, pp. 3–20, 17.

36   Ospovat, Kirill, 'Alexandr Sumarokov and the Social Status of Russian Literature in the 1750s–60s', in *Study Group on Eighteenth Russia – Newsletter*, No. 33, Cambridge, November 2005, pp. 24–30, 34.

37   Atkinson, John Augustus, and Walker, James, *A Picturesque Representation of the Manners, Customs, and Amusements of the Russians in One Hundred Coloured Plates*, London, Vol. I, 1803; Vols II and III, 1804, text facing 'Horn Music' plate.

38   Buckler, *Mapping St Petersburg*, pp. 124–5.

39   Nisbet Bain, *The Daughter of Peter the Great*, p. 151.

40   Rosslyn, in *Eighteenth-Century Russia*, p. 76.

41   Keenan, *St Petersburg and the Russian Court*, p. 80.

42   Nisbet Bain, *The Daughter of Peter the Great*, p. 140.

43   Bilbassov, Vasily A., 'The Intellectual Formation of Catherine II' (St Petersburg, 1901), reprinted in Raeff, Marc, ed., *Catherine the Great – A Profile*, London: Macmillan, 1972, p. 25.

44   Catherine the Great, *Memoirs*, pp. 48, 52, 91, 138.

45   Ibid., pp. xiv–xvi, 110, 179.

46   Ibid., p. 182; McGrew, Roderick E., *Paul I of Russia 1754–1801*, Oxford: Clarendon Press, 1992, pp. 24–7.

47   Proskurina, *Creating the Empress*, p. 57.

48   Bagdasarova, in *Dining with the Tsars*, pp. 22–4.

49   Proskurina, *Creating the Empress*, p. 16.

50   Qtd in Nisbet Bain, *The Daughter of Peter the Great*, p. 153.

51   Jonas Hanway on Elizabeth, qtd in Vernadsky, *A Source Book for Russian History*, p. 386.

52   Catherine the Great, *Memoirs*, p. 93.

53   D'Eon de Beaumont, Charles, *The Maiden of Tonnerre – The Vicissitudes of the Chevalier and the Chevalière d'Eon* (containing *The Great Historical Epistle by the Chevalière d'Eon, Written in 1785 to Madame the Duchesse of Montmorenci-Bouteville*), trans. and ed. Champagne, Ekstein and Kates, Baltimore and London: Johns Hopkins University Press, 2001, pp. ix, 20–21.

54   Taylor, D. J., 'The Chevalier d'Éon de Beaumont in Petersburg 1756–60: An Observer of Elisaveta Petrovna's Russia', in *Study Group on Eighteenth-Century Russia – Newsletter*, No. 6, Norwich, September 1978, pp. 40–54, 50.

55   Anisimov, *Empress Elizabeth*, p. 191.

56   Blakesley, Rosalind P., '23 October 1757: The Foundation of the Imperial Academy of Arts', in Cross, *Study Group on Eighteenth-Century Russia*, pp. 109–120.

57  Keenan, *St Petersburg and the Russian Court*, pp. 131–4.
58  Catherine the Great, *Memoirs*, p. 110.
59  De Custine, *Letters*, p. 54.
60  Dukes, *The Making of Russian Absolutism*, p. 110.
61  Keenan, *St Petersburg and the Russian Court*, pp. 55–6.
62  Atkinson and Walker, *A Picturesque Representation*, Vol. I, text facing 'Milkwomen' plate; Vol. II, text facing 'Zbitenshik' plate.
63  Storch, Henry, from the German of *The Picture of Petersburg*, London, 1801, p. 182.
64  Jones, *Bread Upon the Waters*, pp. 35–7.
65  Atkinson and Walker, *A Picturesque Representation*, Vol. III, text facing 'Fish Barks' plate.
66  Munro, George E., *The Most Intentional City – St Petersburg in the Reign of Catherine the Great*, Cranbury, NJ: Associated University Presses, 2010, p. 39.
67  Catherine the Great, *Memoirs*, pp. 4–6, 148–9, 183.
68  Neville, Peter, *Russia: A Complete History – The USSR, the CIS and the Independent States in One Volume*, London: Phoenix, 2003, p. 87.
69  Catherine the Great, *Memoirs*, pp. 37, 82, 152.
70  Ibid., pp. 104, 120.
71  Shrad, *Vodka Politics*, p. 52.

## 6 THE CITY TRANSFORMED

1  Catherine, qtd in Buckler, *Mapping St Petersburg*, p. 18.
2  Richardson, *Anecdotes of the Russian Empire*, pp. 51, 78, 153.
3  Swinton, A., *Travels into Norway, Denmark, and Russia in the Years 1788, 1789, 1790, and 1791*, London, 1792, pp. 212–13, 335.
4  Ibid., pp. 219–22.
5  Dixon, *Catherine the Great*, p. 256.
6  Casanova de Seingalt, Jacques, *The Memoirs*, London, 1894, trans. Arthur Machen, to which have been added the chapters discovered by Arthur Symons, 'Russia and Poland', Vol. XXV, Minneapolis, MN: Filiquarian Publishing, n.d., pp. 14–15.
7  Storch, *The Picture of Petersburg*, London, p. 444; Atkinson and Walker, *A Picturesque Representation*, Vol. II, text facing 'Ice Hills' plate; Vol. III, text facing 'Race Course' plate.
8  Swinton, *Travels into Norway, Denmark and Russia*, pp. 224–5.
9  Casanova, *The Memoirs*, p. 9.
10  Atkinson and Walker, *A Picturesque Representation*, Vol. III, text facing 'Dvornick' plate.
11  Ibid., Vol. II, text facing 'Boutoushniki' plate.
12  Hartley, Janet M., 'Governing the City: St Petersburg and Catherine II's Reforms', in Cross, ed., *St Petersburg 1703–1825*, Basingstoke and New York: Palgrave Macmillan, 2003, pp. 100, 102, 105.
13  Munro, *The Most Intentional City*, pp. 93–4, 96, 107, 122.

14  Atkinson and Walker, *A Picturesque Representation*, Vol. III, text facing 'Cooper' plate and text facing 'Kalachniks' plate.

15  De Madariaga, Isabel, *Russia in the Age of Catherine the Great*, New Haven, CT, and London: Yale University Press, 1981, p. 555.

16  Atkinson and Walker, *A Picturesque Representation*, Vol. III, text facing 'Gardeners' plate.

17  Anon., *A Picture of St Petersburgh: Represented in a Collection of Twenty Interesting Views of the City, the Sledges, and the People*, London, 1815, pp. 20–21; Swinton, *Travels into Norway, Denmark and Russia*, p. 241.

18  Porter, Robert Ker, *Travelling Sketches in Russia and Sweden during the Years 1805, 1806, 1807, 1808*, Vols I and II, London: Richard Phillips, 1809, pp. 22, 121.

19  Van Wonzel, Pieter, *État Présent de la Russie*, St Petersburg and Leipzig, 1783, pp. 128–9; de Madariaga, *Catherine the Great*, p. 159.

20  Munro, *The Most Intentional City*, pp. 154–5, 218–19.

21  Cross, *By the Banks of the Neva*, pp. 18, 20.

22  Cross, Anthony, 'Mr Fisher's Company of English Actors in Eighteenth-Century St Petersburg', in *Study Group on Eighteenth-Century Russia – Newsletter*, No. 4, Norwich, September 1976, pp. 49–56, 49–50.

23  Cross, *By the Banks of the Neva*, pp. 34–5.

24  Catherine the Great, Letter to Poniatowski, July 1762, in Dmytryshyn, *Imperial Russia*, pp. 59–60.

25  Catherine the Great et al., *Authentic Memoirs of the Life and Reign of Catherine II, Empress of all the Russias. Collected from the Authentic MS's. Translations, &c. of the King of Sweden, Right Hon. Lord Mountmorres, Lord Malmesbury, M. de Volney, and other indisputable authorities*, London, 1797, pp. 23–4.

26  Ibid., p. 34.

27  Anisimov, *Five Empresses*, p. 164.

28  *Authentic Memoirs of the Life and Reign of Catherine II*, pp. 40–41.

29  Proskurina, *Creating the Empress*, p. 117.

30  Keenan, *St Petersburg and the Russian Court*, p. 71; Dixon, *Catherine the Great*, p. 8.

31  Catherine the Great, *Memoirs*, pp. xix–xx.

32  Wortman, *Scenarios of Power*, Vol. I, pp. 111–13.

33  Bagdasarova, in *Dining with the Tsars*, pp. 27, 31; Proskurina, *Creating the Empress*, pp. 41, 118–22.

34  De Madariaga, *Catherine the Great*, p. 206.

35  Schönle, *The Ruler in the Garden*, p. 318.

36  De Madariaga, *Catherine the Great*, p. 206.

37  Casanova, *The Memoirs*, pp. 9, 22; Proskurina, *Creating the Empress*, p. 29.

38  Atkinson and Walker, *A Picturesque Representation*, Vol. II, text facing 'Public Festivals' plate.

39  Qtd in introd. to Catherine the Great, *Memoirs*, p. xxv.

40  Casanova, *The Memoirs*, p. 32.

41  Qtd in Cross, *By the Banks of the Neva*, p. 377.

42  Anon. (Masson, Charles François Phillibert), *Memoirs of Catherine II and the Court of St Petersburg During her Reign and that of Paul I by One of her Courtiers*, London: Grolier Society, n.d., pp. 289–90.

43  Richard, *A Tour from London to Petersburgh*, p. 46.

44  Masson, *Memoirs of Catherine II and the Court of St Petersburg*, p. 101; Neville, *Russia: A Complete History*, p. 93.

45  Catherine the Great, *Memoirs*, p. 147; de Madariaga, *Catherine the Great*, pp. 2–3.

46  De Madariaga, *Catherine the Great*, pp. 209–11.

47  Qtd in Dixon, *Catherine the Great*, pp. 27–8.

48  Catherine the Great, *Memoirs*, pp. 57–8.

49  Alexander, John T., *Catherine the Great, Life and Legend*, New York: Oxford University Press, 1989, p. 79.

50  Munro, *The Most Intentional City*, pp. 235, 237, 247–8; Munro, George E., 'Compiling and Maintaining St Petersburg's "Book of City Inhabitants": The "Real" City Inhabitants', in Cross, ed., *St Petersburg 1703–1825*, p. 87.

51  Swinton, *Travels into Norway, Denmark and Russia*, p. 391.

52  Munro, *The Most Intentional City*, pp. 89, 202–203, 211–12, 215.

53  De Madariaga, *Catherine the Great*, pp. 105–107, 110–112.

54  Marker, *Publishing, Printing and the Origins of Intellectual Life in Russia*, pp. 105–106.

55  De Madariaga, *Catherine the Great*, pp. 92–7.

56  Catherine the Great, *Memoirs*, pp. xxix, 100.

57  Munro, *The Most Intentional City*, p. 83.

58  Bilbassov, Vasily A., in Raeff, *Catherine the Great*, pp. 36–7; Richardson, *Anecdotes of the Russian Empire*, p. 97.

59  Berman, Marshall, *All That Is Solid Melts into Air*, New York: Simon and Schuster, 1982, p. 182, Verso pbk, 1983, p. 18, discussing Rousseau, Jean-Jacques, *Julie, ou la nouvelle Héloïse*, 1761, Part II, Letters 14 and 17.

60  Storch, *The Picture of Petersburg*, p. 541. See also Lermontov, Mikhail, *A Hero of Our Time* (1840), trans. and introd. by Paul Foote, Harmondsworth: Penguin, 1966, p. 54, 'My imagination knows no peace, my heart no satisfaction.'

61  Wilson, Arthur M., *Diderot*, New York: Oxford University Press, 1972, pp. 91, 623, 628, 637, 641, 645.

62  Ibid., p. 512.

63  Anisimov, *Empress Elizabeth*, p. 51.

64  Qtd in Wortman, *Scenarios of Power*, Vol. I, p. 134.

65  McBurney, Erin, 'The Portrait Iconography of Catherine the Great: An Introduction', in *Study Group on Eighteenth-Century Russia – Newsletter*, No. 34, Cambridge, July 2006, pp. 22–7.

66   Schenker, Alexander M., *The Bronze Horseman – Falconet's Mon-
     ument to Peter-the-Great*, New Haven, CT, and London: Yale
     University Press, 2003, pp. 285–6.
67   Ibid., p. 278.
68   Giroud, *St Petersburg*, pp. 36, 38.
69   Masson, *Memoirs of Catherine II*, p. 89.
70   Wilmot, Martha and Catherine, *The Russian Journals of Martha and
     Catherine Wilmot – 1803–08*, ed. Marchioness of Londonderry and
     H. M. Hyde, London: Macmillan, 1934, p. 30.
71   Porter, *Travelling Sketches in Russia*, pp. 35–6.
72   Richardson, *Anecdotes of the Russian Empire*, p. 178.
73   Qtd in Wortman, *Scenarios of Power*, Vol. I, p. 135.
74   Cavanagh, Eleanor, letter of 20 August 1805, in Wilmot, Martha and
     Catherine, *The Russian Journals*, p. 181.
75   Jukes, Peter, *A Shout in the Street – The Modern City London*,
     London: Faber and Faber, 1990, p. 162.
76   Storch, *The Picture of Petersburg*, p. 236.
77   Hoare, Prince, *Extracts from a Correspondence with the Acade-
     mies of Vienna and St Petersburg on the Cultivation of the Arts of
     Painting, Sculpture and Architecture in the Austrian and Russian
     Dominions*, London: White, Payne and Hatchard, 1802, pp. 38–9,
     41–6.
78   Rice, Tamara Talbot, 'Charles Cameron', in *Charles Cameron c.1740–
     1812*, London: Arts Council, 1967–8, p. 7.
79   Wraxall, N., Jun., *A Tour Through Some of the Northern Parts of
     Europe Particularly Copenhagen, Stockholm and Petersburg in a
     Series of Letters*, 3rd edn, London: Cadell, 1776, p. 258.
80   Qtd in Cross, *By the Banks of the Neva*, p. 389.
81   Loukomski, George, *Charles Cameron (1740–1812)*, London: Nich-
     olson and Watson, Commodore Press, 1943, pp. 55–61, 78.
82   Shvidkovsky, Dmitry, 'Catherine the Great's Field of Dreams: Architec-
     ture and Landscape in the Russian Enlightenment', in Cracraft, James,
     and Rowland, Daniel, eds, *Architectures of Russian Identities 1500
     to the Present*, Ithaca, NY, and London: Cornell University Press,
     2003, pp. 51–65.
83   Ibid., p. 78.
84   Cross, *By the Banks of the Neva*, pp. 246–7, 289.
85   Schönle, *The Ruler in the Garden*, p. 43.
86   Catherine the Great, letter to Voltaire of 25 June 1772, qtd in Schönle,
     *The Ruler in the Garden*, p. 48.
87   Shvidkovsky, in Cracraft and Rowland, *Architectures of Russian
     Identities*, p. 61.
88   Schönle, *The Ruler in the Garden*, p. 51.
89   Gautier, *The Complete Works – Vol. VII: Travels in Russia*, p. 200.
90   Wedgwood, Josiah, letter to his partner of March 1773, qtd in Jones,
     W. Gareth, 'Catherine the Great's Understanding of the "Gothic"', in

*Reflections on Russia in the Eighteenth Century*, ed. Klein, Dixon and Fraanje, p. 239.

91 Liackhova, Lydia, 'Items from the Green Frog Service', in *Dining with the Tsars*, pp. 74–5.

92 Schönle, *The Ruler in the Garden*, p. 59.

93 Shvidkovsky, *Russian Architecture and the West*, p. 260.

94 Maes, Francis, *A History of Russian Music*, trans. Arnold J. Pomerans and Erica Pomerans, Berkeley, CA: University of California Press, 2002; pbk 2006, p. 15.

95 Shvidkovsky, *Russian Architecture and the West*, p. 262.

96 Qtd in de Madariaga, *Catherine the Great*, p. 101.

97 Dixon, *Catherine the Great*, p. 194.

98 Piotrovsky, B. B., and Suslov, V. A., 'Introduction', in Eisler, Colin, *Paintings in the Hermitage*, New York: Stewart, Tabori and Chang, 1990, p. 25.

99 Qtd in Dixon, *Catherine the Great*, p. 193.

100 Piotrovsky and Suslov, in *Paintings in the Hermitage*, pp. 24–5.

101 Ahlström, Christian, 'The Empress of Russia and the Dutch Scow the Vrouw Maria', in *The Annual Report*, Nautica Fennica, Helsinki: National Board of Antiquities, 2000; Leino, Minna, and Klemelä, Ulla, 'Field Research of the Maritime Museum of Finland at the Wreck Site of Vrouw Maria in 2001–2002', in *Moss Newsletter*, Helsinki, 2003, pp. 5–8; Piotrovsky and Suslov, in *Paintings in the Hermitage*, p. 26.

102 Wilson, *Diderot*, p. 601.

103 Piotrovsky and Suslov, in *Paintings in the Hermitage*, pp. 9–10, 26; Gray, Rosalind P., *Russian Genre Paintings in the Nineteenth Century*, Oxford: Clarendon Press, 2000, pp. 15–18.

104 Norman, Geraldine, *The Hermitage – The Biography of a Great Museum*, London: Jonathan Cape, 1997, p. 33.

105 Piotrovsky and Suslov, in *Paintings in the Hermitage*, p. 12.

106 Shapiro, Yuri, *The Hermitage*, Moscow: Progress Publishers, 1976, p. 7.

107 Van Wonzel, *État Présent de la Russie*, p. 63.

108 Cross, *By the Banks of the Neva*, p. 323.

109 Piotrovsky and Suslov, in *Paintings in the Hermitage*, p. 26.

110 Norman, *The Hermitage*, pp. 36–7.

111 Dixon, *Catherine the Great*, p. 44; Munro, *The Most Intentional City*, p. 272.

112 Seaman, Gerald, 'Catherine the Great and Musical Enlightenment', in *Study Group on Eighteenth-Century Russia – Newsletter*, No. 19, Cambridge, September 1991, pp. 13–14.

113 De Madariaga, *Russia in the Age of Catherine the Great*, p. 534.

114 Jones, *Bread Upon the Waters*, p. 23.

115 Munro, *The Most Intentional City*, pp. 224, 229.

116 De Madariaga, *Catherine the Great*, pp. 78–9.

117 Wraxall, N., Jun., Letter of 20 July, 1774, in *A Tour Through Some of*

*the Northern Parts of Europe*, p. 245; Storch, *The Picture of Petersburg*, p. 133; Munro, *The Most Intentional City*, p. 113.

118 Munro, *The Most Intentional City*, pp. 46, 255.

119 Qtd in Schönle, *The Ruler in the Garden*, p. 64.

120 Storch, *The Picture of Petersburg*, p. 159.

121 Dixon, *Catherine the Great*, pp. 257–8.

122 Munro, *The Most Intentional City*, p. 127.

123 Hittle, Michael J., *The Service City – State and Townsmen in Russia 1600–1800*, Cambridge, MA: Harvard University Press, 1979, p. 106.

124 Dixon, Simon, '30 July 1752: The Opening of the Peter the Great Canal', in Cross, *Study Group on Eighteenth-Century Russia*, Part 1, p. 93.

125 Glendenning, P. H., 'Admiral Sir Charles Knowles in Russia 1771–1774', in 'Synopses of Papers Read at the 12th Meeting of the Study Group – University of Leeds, 15–16 December 1973', in *Study Group on Eighteenth-Century Russia – Newsletter*, No. 2, Norwich, 1974, p. 10.

126 De Madariaga, *Russia in the Age of Catherine the Great*, pp. 574–5.

127 Richard, *A Tour from London to Petersburgh*, p. 25; Munro, *The Most Intentional City*, p. 191.

128 Qtd in de Madariaga, *Catherine the Great*, pp. 146–7.

129 Munro, *The Most Intentional City*, pp. 27, 74, 121–2.

130 Richardson, *Anecdotes of the Russian Empire*, p. 33.

131 Qtd in Proskurina, *Creating the Empress*, p. 96.

132 Qtd in Bartlett, R. P., 'Russia and the Eighteenth-Century European Adoption of Inoculation for Smallpox', in Bartlett, Cross and Rasmussen, *Russia and the World of the Eighteenth Century*, pp. 193–5, 204; Alexander, *Catherine the Great, Life and Legend*, p. 146.

133 Dixon, *Catherine the Great*, p. 191.

134 Munro, *The Most Intentional City*, pp. 128–9; Alexander, *Catherine the Great*, pp. 158–9.

135 Storch, *The Picture of Petersburg*, p. 201.

136 De Madariaga, *Catherine the Great*, p. 78.

137 Munro, George E., 'Politics, Sexuality and Servility: The Debate Between Catherine the Great and the Abbé Chappe d'Auteroche', in *Russia and the West in the Eighteenth Century*, pp. 124–34, 128, 130.

138 Munro, *The Most Intentional City*, pp. 76–7.

139 Storch, *The Picture of Petersburg*, p. 205; Alexander, *Catherine the Great*, p. 148.

140 Qtd in Bernstein, *Sonia's Daughters*, p. 15.

141 Keenan, *St Petersburg and the Russian Court*, p. 57; Engel, *Women in Russia*, p. 64.

142 Tooke, William, *View of the Russian Empire during the Reign of Catherine the Second and to the Close of the Eighteenth Century*, Vol. I, London: Longman and Rees, 1800, pp. 7–11.

143 Wraxall, *A Tour Through Some of the Northern Parts of Europe*, pp. 248–9.

144 Masson, *Memoirs of Catherine II*, p. 293.

145 Casanova, *The Memoirs*, pp. 16–17, 18, 20, 39–40.
146 Newspaper advert of 1797, in Dmytryshyn, *Imperial Russia*, p. 127.
147 Dukes, *The Making of Russian Absolutism*, p. 166.
148 Qtd in de Madariaga, *Catherine the Great*, p. 54.
149 Pugachev's 'Emancipation Decree' of July 1774, in Dmytryshyn, *Imperial Russia*, p. 96.
150 Neville, *Russia: A Complete History*, pp. 97–9; de Madariaga, *Catherine the Great*, p. 63.
151 Pushkin, Alexander, *The Queen of Spades and Other Stories*, trans. Rosemary Edmonds, London: Penguin, 2004, pp. 250, 285, 292, 300–304.
152 Qtd in de Madariaga, *Catherine the Great*, p. 54.
153 Wortman, *Scenarios of Power*, Vol. I, pp. 139–40.
154 Alexander, *Catherine the Great*, p. 261.
155 Radishchev, Alexandr Nikolaevich, *A Journey from St Petersburg to Moscow*, trans. Leo Wiener, ed. Roderick Page Thaler, Cambridge, MA: Harvard University Press, 1958, p. 43.
156 Catherine's annotations to Radishchev, *A Journey from St Petersburg to Moscow*, p. 247.
157 Introduction to Radishchev, *A Journey from St Petersburg to Moscow*, pp. 34–5; Neville, *Russia: A Complete History*, p. 95.
158 De Madariaga, *Catherine the Great*, pp. 200–201.
159 Proskurina, *Creating the Empress*, pp. 185–7; McBurney, 'The Portrait Iconography of Catherine the Great', in *Study Group on Eighteenth-Century Russia – Newsletter*, No. 34, pp. 22–3, 25.
160 Masson, *Memoirs of Catherine II*, pp. 117–18; Storch, *The Picture of Petersburg*, p. 31.
161 Masson, *Memoirs of Catherine II*, pp. 95–6.
162 Coleridge, Samuel Taylor, *Collected Poetical Works*, Oxford: Oxford University Press, 1978, p. 162.
163 Swinton, *Travels into Norway, Denmark and Russia*, pp. 229–30; Richardson, *Anecdotes of the Russian Empire*, p. 412; van Wonzel, *État Présent de la Russie*, p. 132.
164 Casanova, *The Memoirs*, p. 23.

## 7 MADNESS, MURDER AND INSURRECTION

1 Storch, *The Picture of Petersburg*, p. 445.
2 Atkinson and Walker, *A Picturesque Representation*, Vol. I, text facing 'Pleasure Barges' plate; van Wonzel, *État Présent de la Russie*, p. 118.
3 Storch, *The Picture of Petersburg*, pp. 438–9.
4 Porter, *Travelling Sketches in Russia*, pp. 66–7.
5 Dukes, *The Making of Russian Absolutism*, p. 175.
6 McGrew, *Paul I of Russia*, p. 24.
7 Catherine the Great, *Memoirs*, pp. xxiii–xxiv.

8   McGrew, *Paul I of Russia*, pp. 24–7; Rappoport, Angelo S., *The Curse of the Romanovs*, London: Chatto and Windus, 1907, pp. 26–7.

9   Masson, *Memoirs of Catherine II*, p. 120.

10  Qtd in Alexander, *Catherine the Great*, p. 145.

11  Rappoport, *The Curse of the Romanovs*, p. 141.

12  Norman, *The Hermitage*, pp. 50–51,54, 308.

13  Dukes, *The Making of Russian Absolutism*, p. 176.

14  McGrew, *Paul I of Russia*, pp. 152–7, 182.

15  Ibid., p. 206.

16  Storch, *The Picture of Petersburg*, p. 79.

17  Rappoport, *The Curse of the Romanovs*, p. 194.

18  Qtd in Cross, Anthony, '"Crazy Paul": The British and Paul I', in *Reflections on Russia in the Eighteenth Century*, ed., Klein, Dixon and Fraanje, pp. 7, 11.

19  Walker, James, *Paramythia or Mental Pastimes*, London, 1821, pp. 27–152 of *Engraved in the Memory*, ed. Anthony Cross, Providence, RI, and Oxford: Berg, 1993, pp. 40–41.

20  Casanova, *The Memoirs*, p. 12.

21  Storch, *The Picture of Petersburg*, p. 139.

22  McGrew, *Paul I of Russia*, pp. 210, 213.

23  Kotzbuë, Auguste de, *L'année la plus remarquable de ma vie*, Paris, 1802, pp. 79–81.

24  Porter, *Travelling Sketches in Russia*, p. 39.

25  Walker, *Paramythia*, p. 77.

26  Marker, *Publishing, Printing and the Origins of Intellectual Life in Russia*, p. 231.

27  Norman, *The Hermitage*, p. 55.

28  Bernstein, *Sonia's Daughters*, p. 15; Rosslyn, 'Petersburg Actresses On and Off Stage', in Cross, *St Petersburg 1703–1825*, p. 140.

29  Mikhail I. Pylyaev, *Old St Petersburg. Tales from the Capital's Former Life*, St Petersburg, 2004, pp. 370–73, qtd by Bagdasarova, in *Dining with the Tsars*, p. 32.

30  Breton, M., *La Russie, ou mœurs, usages, et costumes des habitans de toutes les provinces de cet empire*, Vol. I, Paris, 1813, pp. 136–7.

31  Kotzbuë, *L'anée la plus remarkable*, p. 151; Giroud, *St Petersburg*, p. 59.

32  Dukes, *The Making of Russian Absolutism*, p. 178.

33  Porter, Robert Ker, *Travelling Sketches in Russia*, p. 40; Anon., *A Picture of St Petersburgh*, p. 5.

34  Shvidkovsky, *Russian Architecture and the West*, p. 295; Proskurina, *Creating the Empress*, p. 137.

35  McGrew, *Paul I of Russia*, p. 345.

36  Qtd in Hartley, Janet M., *Alexander I*, London and New York: Longman, 1994, p. 24.

37  McGrew, *Paul I of Russia*, pp. 323, 327, 330, 333, 349.

38  De Raymond, Damaze, *Tableau historique, géographique, militaire et moral de l'empire de Russie*, Vol. II, Paris, 1812, p. 132.

39  McGrew, *Paul I of Russia*, pp. 335, 354; Neville, *Russia: A Complete History*, p. 109.

40  Porter, *Travelling Sketches in Russia*, pp. 16, 18; Faber, Gotthilf Theodor von, *Bagatelles. Promenades d'un désœuvré dans la ville de S.-Pétersbourg*, Vols I and II, Paris: Klosterman and Delaunay, 1812, p. 33.

41  Faber, *Bagatelles*, Vol. I, pp. 241–2.

42  Storch, *The Picture of Petersburg*, pp. 500, 506–507.

43  Casanova, *The Memoirs*, p. 21.

44  Faber, *Bagatelles*, Vol. II, pp. 174–80.

45  Redesdale, Lord, *Memories*, Vol. I, London: Hutchinson, 1915, p. 270.

46  Storch, *The Picture of Petersburg*, p. 505.

47  Atkinson and Walker, *A Picturesque Representation*, Vol. II, text facing 'A Merchant's Wife' plate.

48  Porter, *Travelling Sketches in Russia*, pp. 113–14, 163–5.

49  Wilmot, Martha and Catherine, *The Russian Journals*, pp. 169, 176.

50  Anon., *A Picture of St Petersburgh*, p. 23.

51  Porter, *Travelling Sketches in Russia*, pp. 107–109, 154–6.

52  Faber, *Bagatelles*, Vol. I, p. 157.

53  Breton, *La Russie*, Vol. I, p. 53.

54  Porter, *Travelling Sketches in Russia*, pp. 115–16, 149–54.

55  Storch, *The Picture of Petersburg*, p. 163.

56  Adams, John Quincy, *Memoirs – Portions of his Diary from 1795–1848*, Vol. II, ed. C. F. Adams, New York: AMS Press, 1970, p. 256.

57  Ibid., pp. 121–2.

58  Atkinson and Walker, *A Picturesque Representation*, Vol. I, text facing 'Katcheli' plate.

59  Porter, *Travelling Sketches in Russia*, Vol. II, p. 1.

60  Adams, *Memoirs*, p. 279.

61  Wilmot, Martha and Catherine, *The Russian Journals*, pp. 27–8.

62  Ibid., pp. 30–31.

63  Bagdasarova, in *Dining with the Tsars*, pp. 32–3.

64  Storch, *The Picture of Petersburg*, pp. 113, 118.

65  Ibid., pp. 556–7.

66  Adams, *Memoirs*, p. 280.

67  Storch, *The Picture of Petersburg*, p. 29; Jones, *Bread Upon the Waters*, pp. 23, 25.

68  Faber, *Bagatelles*, Vol. I, pp. 40, 43.

69  De Raymond, Damaze *Tableau historique*, p. 152; Cross, *By the Banks of the Neva*, pp. 305–306.

70  Storch, *The Picture of Petersburg*, pp. 122–3; Faber, *Bagatelles*, Vol. II, pp. 153–8.

71  Storch, *The Picture of Petersburg*, p. 129.

72  Porter, *Travelling Sketches in Russia*, Vol. II, pp. 20–24.

73  Shvidkovsky, in Cracraft and Rowland, *Architectures of Russian Identities*, p. 33.

74  Shvidkovsky, *Russian Architecture and the West*, pp. 299–301.

75  Wortman, *Scenarios of Power*, Vol. I, pp. 211–14.

76  Adams, *Memoirs*, pp. 171, 397–8.

77  Wilmot, Martha and Catherine, *The Russian Journals*, p. 33; Adams, *Memoirs*, p. 172.

78  Storch, *The Picture of Petersburg*, p. 460; Adams, *Memoirs*, p. 268; Porter, *Travelling Sketches in Russia*, p. 148.

79  De Madariaga, *Catherine the Great*, p. 108.

80  Hartley, *Alexander I*, p. 15.

81  Faibisovich, Viktor, 'If I Were Not Napoleon, Perhaps I Would Be Alexander...', in *Alexander, Napoleon and Joséphine*, Amsterdam: Museumshop Hermitage Amsterdam, 2015, p. 31.

82  Marker, *Publishing, Printing and the Origins of Intellectual Life in Russia*, pp. 231–2.

83  Hartley, *Alexander I*, p. 48; Faibisovich, in *Alexander, Napoleon and Joséphine*, pp. 32–5.

84  Hartley, *Alexander I*, pp. 83–4, qtd on pp. 86–7.

85  Ibid., pp. 73–6, 78–9.

86  de Staël, Madame, *Mémoires – Dix années d'exil* (first published 1818), Paris: 1861, pp. 431–3, 455, 456.

87  Ibid., pp. 442, 447; Storch, *The Picture of Petersburg*, p. 518.

88  De Staël, *Mémoires*, pp. 462, 463.

89  Adams, *Memoirs*, pp. 268, 352, 356.

90  Ermolaev, Ilya, 'Napoleon's Invasion of Russia', in *Alexander, Napoleon and Joséphine*, Amsterdam: Museumshop Hermitage Amsterdam, 2015, p. 68.

91  Tolstoy, Leo, *War and Peace* (1869), trans. Rosemary Edmonds, Harmondsworth: Penguin, 1975, p. 977.

92  Ermolaev, in *Alexander, Napoleon and Joséphine*, pp. 74, 76.

93  Hartley, *Alexander I*, pp. 112, 114–15; Ermolaev, in *Alexander, Napoleon and Joséphine*, p. 85.

94  Aart Kool, qtd in Spruit, Ruud, 'In the Service of Napoleon – Experiences of Dutch Soldiers', in *Alexander, Napoleon and Joséphine*, Amsterdam: Museumshop Hermitage Amsterdam, 2015, p. 147.

95  Tolstoy, *War and Peace*, p. 1,107.

96  Hartley, *Alexander I*, p. 115; Norman, *The Hermitage*, p. 59.

97  Adams, *Memoirs*, p. 420.

98  Spruit, in *Alexander, Napoleon and Joséphine*, pp. 147, 149; Ermolaev in *Alexander, Napoleon and Joséphine*, pp. 90, 100.

99  Adams, *Memoirs*, p. 435.

100 Qtd in Hartley, *Alexander I*, p. 124.

101 Hartley, *Alexander I*, pp. 7, 119, 139; Faibisovich, in *Alexander*,

*Napoleon and Joséphine*, p. 40; Rappoport, *The Curse of the Romanovs*, pp. 357, 359, 365–7.

102 Seton-Watson, Hugh, *The Russian Empire 1801–17*, Oxford: Clarendon Press, 1967, pp. 184–5; Hartley, *Alexander I*, p. 194.

103 Qtd in Buckler, *Mapping St Petersburg*, p. 30.

104 Shvidkovsky, *Russian Architecture and the West*, p. 297.

105 Solovyov, Alexander, 'St Petersburg – Imperial City', in *At the Russian Court – Palace and Protocol in the 19th Century*, Amsterdam: Museumshop Hermitage Amsterdam, 2009, p. 176; Shvidkovsky, *Russian Architecture and the West*, pp. 310–11.

106 Solovyov, in *At the Russian Court*, p. 176.

107 Maes, *A History of Russian Music*, pp. 16, 22.

108 Norman, *The Hermitage*, pp. 58–9, 62.

109 Rappe, Tamara, 'Alexander at Malmaison. Malmaison in Russia', in *Alexander, Napoleon and Joséphine*, Amsterdam: Museumshop Hermitage Amsterdam, 2015, pp. 104–115, with the Gonzaga heritage provided by Elena Arsentyeva, p. 112; Norman, *The Hermitage*, pp. 61–2.

110 Yarmolinsky, Avrahm, *Road to Revolution – A Century of Russian Radicalism*, Princeton, NJ: Princeton University Press, 1986, pp. 20–21.

111 Seton-Watson, *The Russian Empire*, p. 185.

112 Qtd by Faibisovich, in *Alexander, Napoleon and Joséphine*, p. 53.

113 Alexander Mikhaylovsky-Danilevsky, qtd by Faibisovich, in *Alexander, Napoleon and Joséphine*, p. 50.

114 Pavlovna, Anna, Letter to Mlle de Sybourg of 10 November 1824, in S. W. Jackman, *Romanov Relations – The Private Correspondence of Tsars Alexander I, Nicholas I and the Grand Dukes Constantine and Michael with their Sister Queen Anna Pavlovna*, London: Macmillan, 1969, p. 103; Solovyov, in *At the Russian Court*, p. 178.

115 Hare, *Pioneers of Russian Social Thought*, p. 2; O'Meara, Patrick, '*Vreden sever*: The Decembrists' Memories of the Peter and Paul Fortress', in Cross, *St Petersburg 1703–1825*, p. 165.

116 Yarmolinsky, *Road to Revolution*, pp. 26, 32.

117 Lincoln, W. Bruce, *Nicholas I: Emperor and Autocrat of All Russias*, London: Allen Lane, 1978, pp. 20–21, 28–31.

118 Solovyov, in *At the Russian Court*, p. 166.

119 Yarmolinsky, *Road to Revolution*, pp. 37–8, 40–43; Lincoln, *Nicholas I*, pp. 41–6, 75.

## 8 A NEW KIND OF COLD

1 Norman, *The Hermitage*, p. 68.

2 Yarmolinsky, *Road to Revolution*, pp. 49–50.

3 O'Meara, in *St Petersberg 1703–1825*, pp. 173, 176, 183.

4 Wortman, *Scenarios of Power*, Vol. I, p. 276.

5    Yarmolinsky, *Road to Revolution*, pp. 52-3; Wortman, *Scenarios of Power*, Vol. I, p. 277; Neville, *Russia: A Complete History*, p. 123.

6    Monas, Sidney, *The Third Section – Police and Society in Russia under Nicholas I*, Cambridge, MA: Harvard University Press, 1961, pp. 62-3, 72-4, 91-2, 146-7.

7    Pushkin, Alexander, *Eugene Onegin – A Novel in Verse*, trans. Stanley Mitchell, London: Penguin, 2008, pp. xiv, 235 n.1.

8    Monas, *The Third Section*, p. 204.

9    Ibid., pp. 215, 219.

10   Qtd in Kelly, Laurence, *Lermontov – Tragedy in the Caucasus*, London: Constable, 1977, p. 51.

11   Schenker, *The Bronze Horseman*, pp. 296-7, 319 n.9; Monas, *The Third Section*, p. 219.

12   Buckler, *Mapping St Petersburg*, p. 258 n.58.

13   Frank, Joseph, *Dostoevsky – A Writer in His Time*, ed. Mary Petrusewicz, Princeton, NJ, and Oxford: Princeton University Press, 2010, pp. 19, 38.

14   Pushkin, Alexander, 'The Bronze Horseman: A Petersburg Tale', in *The Penguin Book of Russian Poetry*, Part One, trans. Stanley Mitchell, ed. Chandler, Dralyuk and Mashinski, London: Penguin Random House, 2015, p. 89.

15   Dostoyevsky, Fyodor, *Notes From Underground/The Double*, trans. Jessie Coulson, Harmondsworth: Penguin, 1972, p. 137, Coulson introd. p. 8.

16   Pushkin, Alexander, 'The Bronze Horseman: A Petersburg Tale', p. 90.

17   Pavlovna, Anna, letter to Mlle de Sybourg of 10 November 1824, in Jackman, *Romanov Relations*, pp. 103-104.

18   Pushkin, Alexander, 'The Bronze Horseman: A Petersburg Tale', p. 95.

19   Jukes, *A Shout in the Street*, p. 162; Berman, *All That Is Solid*, pp. 181-9.

20   De Custine, *Letters*, pp. 55, 56, 64, 93, 103, 108-109, 170, 253.

21   Gooding, John, *Rulers and Subjects – Government and People in Russia 1801-1991*, London: Arnold, 1996, p. 55.

22   Seton-Watson, *The Russian Empire*, pp. 257-8; Monas, *The Third Section*, p. 133.

23   Qtd in Buckler, *Mapping St Petersburg*, p. 18.

24   Herzen, Alexander, letter of September 1850 to Mazzini, qtd in Berlin, Isaiah, *Russian Thinkers* (1978, revised 2008), London: Penguin, 2013, p. 93.

25   Qtd in Buckler, *Mapping St Petersburg*, p. 20.

26   Wortman, *Scenarios of Power*, Vol. I, p. 319.

27   Shvidkovsky, Dmitry, *St Petersburg – Architecture of the Tsars*, New York, London and Paris: Abbeville Press, 1996, p. 134; Solovyov, in *At the Russian Court*, pp. 179, 182; Shvidkovsky, *Russian Architecture and the West*, p. 317.

28   Anon., *The Englishwoman in Russia; Impressions of the Society and*

*Manners of the Russians at Home by a Lady Ten Years Resident in that Country*, London: John Murray, 1855, p. 51.

29 Belinsky, Vissarion, 'Petersburg and Moscow', in *Petersburg: The Physiology of a City*, ed. Nikolai Nekrasov, trans. Thomas Gaiton Marullo, Evanston, IL: Northwestern University Press, 2009, p. 37.

30 Grebenka, Evgeny, 'The Petersburg Quarter', 1844, in Nekrasov, *Petersburg: The Physiology of a City*, pp. 103–105, 110–16.

31 Zelnik, Reginald E., *Labor and Society in Tsarist Russia – The Factory Workers of St Petersburg 1855–1870*, Stanford, CA: Stanford University Press, 1971, p. 52.

32 Nekrasov, Nikolai 'The Petersburg Corners', in Nekrasov, *Petersburg: The Physiology of a City*, pp. 131–4.

33 *The Englishwoman in Russia*, pp. 57–9, 62.

34 Belinsky, in Nekrasov, *Petersburg: The Physiology of a City*, pp. 47–8.

35 Corot, Camille, *Le quai des Orfèvres et le pont Saint-Michel*, Paris, Musée Carnavalet.

36 Dickens, Charles, *Bleak House* (1853), Harmondsworth: Penguin, 1971, p. 49.

37 Monas, *The Third Section*, p. 2.

38 From Nikolai Ogarev's, poem 'Iumor', qtd in Buckler, *Mapping St Petersburg*, pp. 76–7.

39 Belinsky, in Nekrasov, *Petersburg: The Physiology of a City*, p. 49.

40 Dumas, *En Russie*, p. 154.

41 Storch, *The Picture of Petersburg*, pp. 510–12; Anon., *A Picture of St Petersburgh*, p. 18.

42 Gogol, Nikolai, 'Nevsky Prospekt', in *Petersburg Tales.*, trans. Dora O'Brien, Richmond, Surrey: Alma Classics, 2014, pp. 4–7, 9.

43 Belinsky, in Nekrasov, *Petersburg: The Physiology of a City*, p. 50.

44 Gautier, *The Complete Works*, pp. 112–13, 116.

45 *The Englishwoman in Russia*, p. 70.

46 Berman, *All That Is Solid*, p. 195.

47 Gogol, Nikolai, 'Nevsky Prospekt', in *Diary of a Madman, The Government Inspector and Selected Stories*, trans. Ronald Wilks, London: Penguin, 2005, p. 87, and *Petersburg Tales*, trans. Dora O'Brien, p. 16 – my variation on both, and passage qtd by Berman, *All That Is Solid*, p. 203.

48 Berman, *All That Is Solid*, p. 198.

49 De Custine, *Letters*, pp. 103, 105.

50 *The Englishwoman in Russia*, pp. 51–2.

51 Lincoln, Bruce W., 'The Daily Life of St Petersburg Officials in the Mid Nineteenth Century', in *Oxford Slavonic Papers*, ed. Fennell and Foote, New Series, Vol. VIII, Oxford: Clarendon Press, 1975, pp. 82–100, 92, 95, 98.

52 Gogol, Diary 1828, qtd in Jukes, *A Shout in the Street*, p. 120.

53 Brodsky, *Less Than* One, p. 78.

54 Bird, *A History of Russian Painting*, pp. 86–91.

55  Ibid., pp. 77–9.
56  Herzen, letter to Michelet of 22 September 1851, in Dmytryshyn, *Imperial Russia*, p. 248.
57  Solovyov, in *At the Russian Court*, p. 182.
58  Vilensky, Jan, 'Cameo Service – 1778–9', in *Dining with the Tsars*, pp. 100–101.
59  Norman, *The Hermitage*, pp. 66–71.
60  De Custine, *Letters*, pp. 43–4.
61  Norman, *The Hermitage*, pp. 67, 72–6, 78–9.
62  *The Englishwoman in Russia*, pp. 89–90.
63  Belinsky, Vissarion, 'The Alexander Theatre', in Nekrasov, *Petersburg: The Physiology of a City*, p. 198.
64  Wortman, *Scenarios of Power*, Vol. I, pp. 391–3.
65  Stasov, Vladimir Vasilevich, *Selected Essays on Music*, trans. Florence Jonas, London: Cresset Press, 1968, pp. 118, 120, 122, 130.
66  Ibid., pp. 23, 132, 142–3.
67  Qtd in Macdonald, Hugh, *The Master Musicians – Berlioz*, Oxford: Oxford University Press, 1982; pbk 2000, pp. 47, 67.
68  Maes, *A History of Russian Music*, pp. 27–8.
69  Rimsky-Korsakov, Nikolai Andreyevich, *My Musical Life*, trans. from the 5th revised Russian edition by Judah A. Joffe, London: Eulenburg Books, 1974, pp. 12, 175.
70  Gogol, in *The Contemporary*, 1836, qtd in *The Wordsworth Dictionary of Musical Quotations*, ed. Derek Watson, Ware, Hertfordshire: Wordsworth Editions, 1994, p. 145.
71  Maes, *A History of Russian Music*, pp. 20–22.
72  Gautier, *The Complete Works*, p. 226.
73  Herman Laroche, in Brown, David, *Tchaikovsky Remembered*. London: Faber and Faber, 1993, p. 236.
74  Rosslyn, in *St Petersburg 1703–1825*, p. 123.
75  Pushkin, *Eugene Onegin*, p. 15.
76  Nicholas I, letters to Anna Pavlovna of 7 January 1835 and 7 January 1836, in Jackman, *Romanov Relations*, pp. 252, 273.
77  Meshikova, Maria, 'Chinese Masquerade', in *At the Russian Court*, p. 269; Korshunova, 'Whims of Fashion', in *At the Russian Court*, p. 241.
78  Tarasova, Lina, 'Festivities at the Russian Court', in *At the Russian Court*, p. 111; Gautier, *The Complete Works*, pp. 209–10, 214.
79  De Custine, *Letters*, pp. 120–24, 264.
80  Wortman, *Scenarios of Power*, Vol. I, pp. 334–5, 338.
81  McGrew, Roderick E., *Russia and the Cholera 1823–1832*, Madison and Milwaukee, WI: University of Wisconsin Press, 1965, pp. 3–4, 18, 108–13.
82  Lincoln, *Nicholas I*, pp. 270, 273.
83  Qtd Ibid., pp. 273–4.
84  McGrew, *Russia and the Cholera*, p. 10.

85  Yarmolinsky, *Road to Revolution*, pp. 58, 79.

86  Herzen, Alexander, *My Past and Thoughts – The Memoirs of Alexander Herzen*, trans. Constance Garnett, revised Humphrey Higgens, New York: Knopf, 1973, p. 255.

87  Berlin, *Russian Thinkers*, p. 303.

88  Belinsky, qtd in Berlin, *Russian Thinkers*, p. 196.

89  Belinsky's letter to Gogol of July 1847, in Dmytryshyn, *Imperial Russia*, p. 222.

90  Bird, *A History of Russian Painting*, p. 149; Berlin, *Russian Thinkers*, p. 244.

91  Qtd in Seton-Watson, *The Russian Empire*, p. 262; Berlin, *Russian Thinkers*, p. 204.

92  Atkinson and Walker, *A Picturesque Representation*, Vol. I, text facing 'The Village Council' plate.

93  Berlin, *Russian Thinkers*, pp. 98–9, 102, 104–105, 114, 241–2.

94  Seton-Watson, *The Russian Empire*, p. 259; Yarmolinsky, *Road to Revolution*, pp. 62–7, 79, 82.

95  Hare, *Pioneers of Russian Social Thought*, pp. 29–31.

96  Lincoln, *Nicholas I*, pp. 308–309; Frank, *Dostoevsky*, pp. 148–9.

97  Qtd in Lincoln, *Nicholas I*, p. 310.

98  Frank, *Dostoevsky*, pp. 174–8, 180.

99  Monas, *The Third Section*, p. 259.

100 Ibid., pp. 108, 118, 120, 134, 146, 259–60; Wortman, *Scenarios of Power*, Vol. I, p. 303.

101 Lincoln, *Nicholas I*, p. 323.

102 Herzen, letter to Jules Michelet of September 1851, qtd in Dmytryshyn, *Imperial Russia*, pp. 244, 253.

103 Herzen, Alexander, *My Past and Thoughts – The Memoirs of Alexander Herzen*, trans. Constance Garnett, rev. Humphrey Higgins, NYC: Knopf, 1973, pp.257–65; *The Englishwoman in Russia*, pp. 79–80; de Custine, *Letters*, p. 101.

104 Gavrila Derzhavin, 'To Eugene: Life at Zvanka', trans. Alexander Levitsky in Chandler, Dralyuk and Mashinski, eds, *The Penguin Book of Russian Poetry*, London: Penguin Random House, 2015, p. 14.

105 Yarmolinsky, *Road to Revolution*, p. 85.

106 Lincoln, *Nicholas I*, p. 47.

107 Yarmolinsky, *Road to Revolution*, p. 84.

108 De Custine, *Letters*, pp. 118, 251; qtd in Neville, p. 131.

109 *The Englishwoman in Russia*, pp. 53, 61.

110 Bernstein, *Sonia's Daughters*, pp. 2, 25.

111 Engel, *Women in Russia*, p. 64; Bernstein, *Sonia's Daughters*, pp. 21–3, 26–8, 302.

112 Gautier, *The Complete Works*, pp. 192, 195–6, 202–203; de Custine, *Letters*, p. 70. *Zakuski* are little snacks eaten before a meal and originally offered to people upon arrival after a journey.

113 Korshunova, Tamara, 'Whims of Fashion', in *At the Russian Court*, p. 244.
114 *The Englishwoman in Russia*, pp. 53–6.
115 Monas, *The Third Section*, p. 195.
116 De Custine, *Letters*, pp. 115–16.

## 9 DISCONTENT

1   Zelnik, *Labor and Society in Tsarist Russia*, pp. 47, 74–5, 109, 126–80, 163.
2   Bater, James H., *St Petersburg – Industrialization and Change*, London: Edward Arnold, 1976, pp. 119, 123–4, 127.
3   Bulgarin, Faddei, 'Dachas', an article of 1837, qtd in Buckler, *Mapping St Petersburg*, pp. 169–70.
4   Pavlova, Anna, 'Pages of My Life', in Franks, A. H. ed., *Pavlova – A Collection of Memoirs*, a reprint of *Pavlova: A Biography*, London, 1956; New York: DaCapo, n.d., p. 114; Nabokov, Vladimir, *Speak Memory* (1947), London: Penguin, 2000, p. 173.
5   Redesdale, *Memories*, Vol. I, pp. 204–205, 232–3.
6   Solovyov, in *At the Russian Court*, p. 186.
7   Giroud, *St Petersburg*, p. 118.
8   Stasov, *Selected Essays on Music*, p. 144; Brown, *Tchaikovsky Remembered*, p. 22; Maes, *A History of Russian Music*, pp. 35–7.
9   Piotrovsky and Suslov, in *Paintings in the Hermitage*, p. 13; Norman, *The Hermitage*, pp. 86, 89, 91–2.
10  Bird, *A History of Russian Painting*, p. 130.
11  Frank, *Dostoevsky*, p. 332; Yarmolinsky, *Road to Revolution*, pp. 103–104, 109–110; Stites, Richard, *The Women's Liberation Movement in Russia – Feminism, Nihilism and Bolshevism 1860–1930*, Princeton, NJ: Princeton University Press, 1978, p. 46.
12  Frank, *Dostoevsky*, p. 334.
13  Qtd in Yarmolinsky, *Road to Revolution*, pp. 111–12; Frank, *Dostoevsky*, pp. 336–8.
14  Frierson, Cathy A., *All Russia Is Burning! A Cultural History of Fire and Arson in Late Imperial Russia*, Seattle and London: University of Washington Press, 2002, pp. 41–2; Buckler, *Mapping St Petersburg*, p. 235.
15  Dostoevsky, Fyodor, *Crime and Punishment*, trans. Constance Garnett, Ware, Hertfordshire: Wordsworth Editions, 2000, p. 138.
16  Berlin, *Russian Thinkers*, p. 256; Service, Robert, *The Penguin History of Modern Russia – From Tsarism to the Twenty-First Century*, London: Penguin Random House, 4th edn 2015, p. 5.
17  Berlin, *Russian Thinkers*, pp. 234, 337.
18  Frank, *Dostoevsky*, pp. 510–11.
19  Dostoevsky, *Crime and Punishment*, p. 445.
20  Stites, *The Women's Liberation Movement in Russia*, pp. 55, 61.
21  Berman, *All That Is Solid*, p. 216.

22  Berlin, *Russian Thinkers*, p. 261.
23  Dostoyevsky, Fyodor, *Notes From Underground/The Double*, pp. 15, 55, 137; Frank, *Dostoevsky*, p. 103.
24  Brodsky, *Less Than One*, p. 80.
25  Dostoevsky, *Crime and Punishment*, pp. 4–5, 22, 55.
26  Bernstein, *Sonia's Daughters*, pp. 191–2.
27  Dostoevsky, *Crime and Punishment*, pp. 137, 275.
28  Zelnik, *Labor and Society in Tsarist Russia*, p. 251.
29  Ibid., pp. 247, 249, 255–6.
30  Frank, *Dostoevsky*, p. 467.
31  Babey, Anna Mary, *Americans in Russia 1776–1917*, New York: Comet Press, 1938, p. 11.
32  Yarmolinsky, *Road to Revolution*, pp. 138–41; Frank, *Dostoevsky*, p. 465.
33  Zelnik, *Labor and Society in Tsarist Russia*, pp. 241–3, 245, 268–72.
34  Buckler, *Mapping St Petersburg*, pp. 172–3.
35  Zelnik, *Labor and Society in Tsarist Russia*, pp. 212–14, 233, 292, 300–302, 337–9, 341, 372.
36  Mikhail Bakunin and Sergei Nechaev, 'The Catechism of the Revolutionary', in Dmytryshyn, *Imperial Russia*, p. 308; Stites, *The Women's Liberation Movement in Russia*, p. 122; Figner, Vera, *Memoirs of a Revolutionist*, DeKalb, IL: Northern Illinois Press, 1991.
37  Turgenev, Ivan, *Fathers and Sons*, trans. Rosemary Edmonds, Harmondsworth: Penguin, 1965, p. 39; Rimsky-Korsakov, *My Musical Life*, p. 194; Stites, *The Women's Liberation Movement in Russia*, p. 85.
38  Yarmolinsky, *Road to Revolution*, p. 337.
39  Stites, *The Women's Liberation Movement in Russia*, pp. 128, 139.
40  Figner, *Memoirs of a Revolutionist*, p. 57; Berlin, *Russian Thinkers*, p. 247; Yarmolinsky, *Road to Revolution*, pp. 189, 205.
41  Gray, Camilla, *The Russian Experiment in Art 1863–1922* (1962), revised and enlarged by Marian Burleigh-Motley, London: Thames and Hudson, 1986, p. 10; Berlin, *Russian Thinkers*, p. 262; Yarmolinsky, *Road to Revolution*, p. 93.
42  Bird, *A History of Russian Painting*, pp. 129–32, 142–3; Turgenev, *Fathers and Sons*, p. 25.
43  Yarmolinsky, *Road to Revolution*, pp. 207–209, 215–16; Neville, *Russia: A Complete History*, p. 143: Frank, *Dostoevsky*, p. 732.
44  Stites, *The Women's Liberation Movement in Russia*, pp. 143–4; Frank, *Dostoevsky*, pp. 764–5.
45  Radzinsky, Edvard, *Alexander II – The Last Great Tsar*, trans. Antonina W. Bouis, New York: Free Press, 2005, pp. 283–5.
46  Frank, *Doestoevsky*, p. 779.
47  Stites, *The Women's Liberation Movement in Russia*, p. 148.
48  Figner, *Memoirs of a Revolutionist*, pp. xiv–xv, 44–5, 72–3, 75.
49  Ibid., p. 80.
50  Grand Duke Konstantin, diary, qtd in Frank, *Dostoevsky*, pp. 804–805.

51  Figner, *Memoirs of a Revolutionist*, pp. 78, 81–2; Yarmolinsky, *Road to Revolution*, pp. 257–60.
52  Wortman, *Scenarios of Power*, Vol. II, pp. 149–50.
53  Berlin, *Russian Thinkers*, p. 351.
54  Babey, *Americans in Russia*, p. 15.
55  Rimsky-Korsakov, *My Musical Life*, pp. 81-2, 101; Maes, *A History of Russian Music*, p. 41.
56  Rimsky-Korsakov, *My Musical Life*, p. 195.
57  Maes, *A History of Russian Music*, p. 69.
58  Alexander Glazunov, qtd in Brown, *Tchaikovsky Remembered*, p. 100; Rimsky-Korsakov, *My Musical Life*, p. 127.
59  Maes, *A History of Russian Music*, p. 48.
60  Rimsky-Korsakov, *My Musical Life*, p. 181.
61  Neville, *Russia: A Complete History*, p. 133.
62  Wortman, *Scenarios of Power*, Vol. II, pp. 115–17, 119.
63  Stites, *The Women's Liberation Movement in Russia*, pp. 124–5.
64  Wortman, *Scenarios of Power*, Vol. I, p. 58; Vol. II, p. 154.
65  Montefiore, Simon Sebag, *The Romanovs 1613–1918*, London: Weidenfeld and Nicolson, 2016, p. 447.
66  Dostoevsky, qtd in Frank, *Dostoevsky*, p. 298; Berlin, *Russian Thinkers*, p. 17.
67  Yarmolinsky, *Road to Revolution*, p. 244.
68  Figner, *Memoirs of a Revolutionist*, pp. 84, 92.
69  Wortman, *Scenarios of Power*, Vol. II, p. 155.
70  Yarmolinsky, *Road to Revolution*, pp. 273–6.
71  Ibid., pp. 278–80.
72  Bird, *A History of Russian Painting*, p. 149.
73  Stites, *The Women's Liberation Movement in Russia*, p. 153.
74  Figner, *Memoirs of a Revolutionist*, pp. 97, 99–101, 104; Yarmolinsky, *Road to Revolution*, pp. 283–9.
75  *Narodnaya Volya*, letter to Alexander III of March 1881, in Dmytryshyn, *Imperial Russia*, p. 314.
76  Figner, *Memoirs of a Revolutionist*, p. 7.
77  Read, Christopher, *Culture and Power in Revolutionary Russia*, Basingstoke: Macmillan, 1990, pp. 2–3.
78  Printseva, Galina, 'The Imperial Hunt', in *At the Russian Court*, pp. 314, 316.
79  Tarasova, Lina, in *At the Russian Court*, pp. 121, 130.
80  Wortman, *Scenarios of Power*, Vol. II, pp. 280–81.
81  Dostoevsky, *Crime and Punishment*, p. 430; Frank, *Dostoevsky*, p. 745.
82  Rimsky-Korsakov, *My Musical Life*, p. 266.
83  Seton-Watson, *The Russian Empire*, p. 273; Klier, John Doyle, *Imperial Russia's Jewish Question 1855–1881*, Cambridge: Cambridge University Press, 1995, pp. 361–2, 371, 373; Aronson, I. Michael, *Troubled Waters: The Origins of the 1881 Anti-Jewish Pogroms in Russia*, Pittsburgh, PA: University of Pittsburgh Press, 1990, p. 228.

84  Yarmolinsky, *Road to Revolution*, p. 247; Neville, *Russia: A Complete History*, pp. 147–8; Montefiore, *The Romanovs 1613–1918*, p. 463.
85  Aronson, *Troubled Waters*, pp. 228–9, 234.
86  Qtd in Buckler, *Mapping St Petersburg*, p. 168.
87  Bernstein, *Sonia's Daughters*, pp. 44, 52, 59, 62, 86.
88  Shvidkovsky, *St Petersburg – Architecture of the Tsars*, p. 188.
89  Solovyov, in *At the Russian Court*, pp. 186–7.
90  McKean, Robert B., *St Petersburg Between the Revolutions*, New Haven, CT, and London: Yale University Press, 1990, p. 1.
91  Neville, *Russia: A Complete History*, p. 148.
92  Yarmolinsky, *Road to Revolution*, pp. 331–3.
93  Zuckerman, Frederic S., *The Tsarist Secret Police in Russian Society, 1880–1917*, Basingstoke: Macmillan, 1996, pp. 24–5; Montefiore, *The Romanovs 1613–1918*, p. 464.
94  Fedorov, Vyacheslav, 'Theatre and Music in Court Life', in *At the Russian Court*, p. 210.
95  Rimsky-Korsakov, *My Musical Life*, pp. 144, 147, 282–3, 291, 309.
96  Maes, *A History of Russian Music*, pp. 80–81, 183.
97  Qtd in Brown, *Tchaikovsky Remembered*, pp. 82–3.
98  Franks, *Pavlova – A Collection of Memoirs*, pp. 12–13.
99  Gregory and Ukladnikov, *Leningrad's Ballet*, p. 14.
100  Nijinsky, Romola, *Nijinsky*, London: Victor Gollancz, 1940, pp. 68–9.
101  Buckle, Richard, *Diaghilev*, New York: Atheneum, 1984, pp. 13, 23.
102  Tarasova, Lina, in *At the Russian Court*, p. 135.
103  Karsavina, Tamara, *Theatre Street* (1948), London: Columbus Books, 1988, pp. 7, 30, 32.
104  Rimsky-Korsakov, *My Musical Life*, p. 321.
105  Ibid., p. 308; Grieg, qtd in Brown, *Tchaikovsky Remembered*, p. 77; Maes, *A History of Russian Music*, p. 134; Brown, *Tchaikovsky Remembered*, pp. 207, 211, 223–4.

## 10 DANCING ON THE EDGE

1  Buckle, Richard, *Nijinsky*, Harmondsworth: Penguin, 1980, p. 29; Stravinsky, Igor, and Craft, Robert, *Memories and Commentaries*, London: Faber and Faber, 1960, p. 27.
2  *Teatr i Iskusstvo*, December 1904, qtd in Blair, Fredrika, *Isadora – Portrait of the Artist as a Woman*, Wellingborough, Northampton: Equation, 1987.
3  Qtd in Blair, *Isadora*, p. 113.
4  Stravinsky, Igor, and Craft, Robert, *Expositions and Developments*, London: Faber and Faber, 1962, p. 24.
5  Neville, *Russia: A Complete History*, pp. 151–2, 155–6; Fitzlyon, Kyril, and Browning, Tatiana, *Before the Revolution*, Harmondsworth: Penguin, 1977, pp. 16–17.
6  Letter of 25 November 1903, in Spring Rice, Sir Cecil, *The Letters*

*and Friendships of Sir Cecil Spring Rice*, Vol. I, ed. Stephen Gwynn, Boston and New York: Houghton Mifflin, 1929, p. 368.

7   Montefiore, *The Romanovs 1613–1918*, p. 494.

8   Tarasova, in *At the Russian Court*, p. 156; Maes, *A History of Russian Music*, p. 184.

9   Benois, qtd in Buckle, *Diaghilev*, pp. 31–2.

10  Tarasova, in *At the Russian Court*, p. 156.

11  Gray, *The Russian Experiment in Art*, pp. 37–40; Buckle, *Diaghilev*, pp. 10–11; Bird, *A History of Russian Painting*, pp. 180–81.

12  Buckler, *Mapping St Petersburg*, p. 35.

13  Gray, *The Russian Experiment in Art*, pp. 44–5, 48, 50, 54; Buckle, *Diaghilev*, pp. 29, 31.

14  Buckle, *Diaghilev*, pp. 85–7.

15  Wcislo, Francis W., *Tales of Imperial Russia – The Life and Times of Sergei Witte 1849–1915*, Oxford: Oxford University Press, 2011, p. 139; Gooding, *Rulers and Subjects*, pp. 82–3.

16  Neville, *Russia: A Complete History*, pp.159–62.

17  Dobson, George, *St Petersburg*, London: Adam and Charles Black, 1910, p. 121.

18  Solovyov, in *At the Russian Court*, p. 190.

19  Qtd in Buckle, *Diaghilev*, pp. 46–7.

20  Bowlt, John E., *Moscow and St Petersburg in Russia's Silver Age*, London: Thames and Hudson, 2008, pp. 133–6, 151; Guseva, Natalya, 'The "New Style" in Russian Interiors', in *Art Nouveau – During the Reign of the Last Tsars*, Aldershot: Lund Humphries, 2007, pp. 72–4, 76–9; Rappe, Tamara, 'Art and Diplomacy in the Reign of Alexander III and Nicholas II', in *Art Nouveau – During the Reign of the Last Tsars*, pp. 38, 44; Anisimova, Elena, 'European Artistic Glass of the Age of Art Nouveau', in *Art Nouveau – During the Reign of the Last Tsars*, p. 64.

21  Almedingen, E. M., *Tomorrow Will Come*, Woodbridge, Suffolk: Boydell Press, 1983, p. 14; Stravinsky and Craft, *Expositions and Developments*, pp. 30–31; Karsavina, *Theatre Street*, pp. 8, 115.

22  Nabokov, *Speak Memory*, p. 53; Mandelstam, Osip, *The Noise of Time*, trans. Clarence Brown, London and New York: Quartet Books, 1988, pp. 73–4; 'The Egyptian Stamp', in Mandelstam, *The Noise of Time*, p. 133.

23  Karsavina, *Theatre Street*, p. 113.

24  Mandelstam, *The Noise of Time*, p. 69, 'The Egyptian Stamp', in Mandelstam, *The Noise of Time*, p. 134; Biely, Andrei, *Petersburg* (1916), trans. Robert A. Maguire and John E. Malmstad, Harmondsworth: Penguin, 1978, pp. 9, 17, 29.

25  Neuberger, Joan, *Hooliganism – Crime, Culture and Power in St Petersburg, 1900–14*, Berkeley, CA: University of California Press, 1993, pp. 25, 26, 29, 31.

26  Lenin, V. I., *What Is to Be Done?* (1902), New York: International Publishers, 1929, pp. 32, 157–8.

27  Letter to Mrs John Hay of 13 September 1904, in Spring Rice, *The Letters and Friendships*, Vol. I, p. 428.

28  Paul Jones, John, *Memoirs of Rear Admiral Paul Jones*, Vol. I, Edinburgh and London, 1830, p. 101; Lauchlan, Iain, *Russian Hide-and-Seek – The Tsarist Secret Police in St Petersburg 1906–14*, Helsinki: SKS-FLS, 2002, p. 63.

29  Redesdale, *Memories*, Vol. I, p. 206; Bater, *St Petersburg – Industrialization and Change*, p. 83.

30  Lauchlan, *Russian Hide-and-Seek*, pp. 115–16.

31  Ibid., pp. 78, 105; Zuckerman, *The Tsarist Secret Police* pp. 25–6, 35–40, 149.

32  Rosen, Baron, *Forty Years of Diplomacy*, Vol. I, London: George Allen and Unwin, 1922, p. 284.

33  Lauchlan, Iain, *Russian Hide-and-Seek*, p. 49.

34  Sablinsky, Walter, *The Road to Bloody Sunday – Father Gapon and the St Petersburg Massacre of 1905*, Princeton, NJ: Princeton University Press, 1976, pp. 34, 45, 52, 55–7, 68–9, 74–6, 81–5, 100–103, 111, 126, 142, 146, 148, 158–9, 162–3.

35  Rosen, *Forty Years of Diplomacy*, Vol. I, pp. 253–4.

36  Sablinsky, *The Road to Bloody Sunday*, pp. 170–71.

37  *Manchester Guardian*, Friday, 27 January 1905; Sablinsky, *The Road to Bloody Sunday*, pp. 188–9.

38  *Manchester Guardian*, Friday, 27 January 1905.

39  Sablinsky, *The Road to Bloody Sunday*, pp. 171, 191, 192, 229–30.

40  Biely, *Petersburg*, p. 13.

41  Kokovtsov, Count, *Out of my Past – The Memoirs of Count Kokovtsov*, trans. Laura Matveev, Stanford, CA: Stanford University Press, 1935, pp. 37–8.

42  Father Gapon's Petition to the Tsar, in Dmytryshyn, *Imperial Russia*, p. 383.

43  Nabokov, *Speak Memory*, p. 139; Sablinsky, *The Road to Bloody Sunday*, p. 250.

44  Buckle, *Nijinsky*, pp. 29–32; Nijinsky, *Nijinsky*, p. 49.

45  Rosen, *Forty Years of Diplomacy*, Vol. I, p. 255; Montefiore, *The Romanovs 1613–1918*, p. 521.

46  Kokovtsov, *Out of my Past*, p. 93.

47  Letter of 13 March 1905, in Spring Rice, *The Letters and Friendships*, Vol. I, p. 458.

48  Tolstoy and Chekhov, qtd in Watson, *Dictionary of Musical Quotations*, p. 258.

49  Qtd in Buckle, *Diaghilev*, pp. 82–3.

50  Karsavina, *Theatre Street*, p. 170; Duncan, from her 1928 autobiography, *My Life*, qtd in Watson, *Dictionary of Musical Quotations*, p. 258.

51  Qtd in Blair, *Isadora*, p. 116.

52  Blair, *Isadora*, pp. 105, 111; Buckle, *Nijinsky*, pp. 31–3, quoting Duncan, p. 31; Buckle, *Diaghilev*, pp. 82–3.

53  Kokovtsov, *Out of my Past*, pp. 39–40.

54  Ascher, Abraham, *The Revolution of 1905 – Russia in Disarray*, Stanford, CA: Stanford University Press, 1988, pp. 94–5.

55  Zuckerman, *The Tsarist Secret Police*, p. 151.

56  Letter of 29 March 1905, in Spring Rice, *The Letters and Friendships*, Vol. I, pp. 465–6.

57  Neuberger, *Hooliganism*, pp. 33, 77; Nabokov, *Speak Memory*, p. 177.

58  Maguire and Malmstad, notes to Biely, *Petersburg*, pp. 343–4.

59  Gooding, *Rulers and Subjects*, p. 103; Zuckerman, *The Tsarist Secret Police*, p. 159; Kokovtsov, *Out of my Past*, p. 70.

60  Biely, *Petersburg*, pp. 5, 10, 64, 213, 217, 240–41, 289.

61  Letter to Francis Villiers of 9 December 1903, in Spring Rice, *The Letters and Friendships*, Vol. I, pp. 371–2.

62  Karsavina, *Theatre Street*, pp. 158–62; Franks, *Pavlova*, pp. 17–18; Buckle, *Nijinsky*, p. 37.

63  Letters to Mrs Roosevelt of November 1905, in Spring Rice, *The Letters and Friendships*, Vol. II, pp. 7, 12.

64  Nicholas II, 'October Manifesto', in Dmytryshyn, *Imperial Russia*, p. 385.

65  Zuckerman, *The Tsarist Secret Police*, pp. 169–70.

66  Gooding, *Rulers and Subjects*, pp. 96–7.

67  Baring, Maurice, *A Year in Russia*, London: Methuen, 1907, p. 45.

68  Biely, *Petersburg*, p. 97.

## 11 DAZZLE AND DESPAIR

1  McKean, *St Petersburg Between the Revolutions*, p. 46; Neville, *Russia: A Complete History*, p. 165.

2  Kokovtsov, *Out of my Past*, pp. 129–30.

3  Baring, *A Year in Russia*, p. 236.

4  Lenin, *What Is to Be Done?*, p. 149.

5  Service, *The Penguin History of Modern Russia*, pp. 19, 71; Figes, Orlando, *Revolutionary Russia – 1891–1991*, London: Penguin, 2014, p. 25. 'Bolshevik' from 'bolshinstvo' – 'one of the majority', and 'Menshevik' from 'menshinstvo' – 'one of the minority'.

6  Sablinsky, *The Road to Bloody Sunday*, pp. 293–4, 299–300, 318–19; Krupskaya, Nadezhda K., *Memories of Lenin*, trans. E. Verney, New York: International Publishers, 1930, pp. 127–8.

7  Krupskaya, *Memories of Lenin*, pp. 166–7, 171.

8  Zuckerman, *The Tsarist Secret Police*, p. 173; Kokovtsov, *Out of my Past*, p. 560 n. 15.

9  Baring, *A Year in Russia*, pp. 50, 67.

10  Neuberger, *Hooliganism*, pp. 170–74.

11  Rosen, *Forty Years of Diplomacy*, Vol. II, pp. 27–8; Kokovtsov, *Out of my Past*, p. 93.

12  Sergei Diaghilev, letter to his mother of 1895, qtd in Gadan, Francis, and Maillard, Robert, *A Dictionary of Modern Ballet*, London: Methuen, 1959, p. 120.

13  Stravinsky and Craft, *Expositions and Developments*, p. 14; Swann, Herbert, *Home on the Neva: A Life of a British Family in Tsarist St Petersburg – and after the Revolution*, London: Victor Gollancz, p. 30.

14  Qtd in Buckle, *Diaghilev*, p. 123.

15  Buckle, *Diaghilev*, pp. 123, 125; Stravinsky and Craft, *Expositions and Developments*, p. 24.

16  Nijinsky, Vaslav, *The Diary of Vaslav Nijinsky*, ed. Romola Nijinsky, Berkeley, CA: University of California Press, 1968, pp. 16, 30, 49, 77, 90.

17  Karsavina, *Theatre Street*, pp. 189, 192; Nijinsky, *Nijinsky*, pp. 80–81.

18  Kokovtsov, *Out of my Past*, p. 170.

19  Montefiore, *The Romanovs 1613–1918*, pp. 541–2; Lauchlan, p. 103; Service, *The Penguin History of Modern Russia*, p. 16.

20  Spring Rice, *The Letters and Friendships*, Vol. II, p. 40; Kokovtsov, *Out of my Past*, p. 459.

21  Letter to Mrs Roosevelt of 4 January 1906, in Spring Rice, *The Letters and Friendships*, Vol. II, p. 23; McKean, *St Petersburg Between the Revolutions*, p. 478.

22  Kokovtsov, *Out of my Past*, p. 464; McKean, *St Petersburg Between the Revolutions*, pp. 11, 53, 76; Bater, *St Petersburg – Industrialization and Change*, p. 218.

23  Nabokov, *Speak Memory*, pp. 137–8.

24  Swann, *Home on the Neva*, p. 30; Clark, Katerina, *Petersburg, Crucible of Cultural Revolution*, Cambridge, MA: Harvard University Press, 1995, p. 56.

25  Stites, Richard, *Russian Popular Culture – Entertainment and Society Since 1900*, Cambridge: Cambridge University Press, 1992, p. 30; Bater, *St Petersburg*, pp. 270–71, 277, 332; Bowlt, *Moscow and St Petersburg in Russia's Silver Age*, pp. 46, 51, 109, 113, 120–22.

26  Almedingen, *Tomorrow Will Come*, p. 55.

27  Bowlt, *Moscow and St Petersburg in Russia's Silver Age*, p. 110.

28  Bater, *St Petersburg – Industrialization and Change*, pp. 264–5; Bowlt, *Moscow and St Petersburg in Russia's Silver Age*, pp. 278–9.

29  Dobson, *St Petersburg*, p. 122; Neuberger, *Hooliganism*, pp. 221–2, 226; Stites, *The Women's Liberation Movement in Russia*, p. 187.

30  Stites, *The Women's Liberation Movement in Russia*, pp. 169, 171, 175.

31  Dobson, *St Petersburg*, pp. 110–11.

32  Bater, *St Petersburg – Industrialization and Change*, p. 351; McKean, *St Petersburg Between the Revolutions*, pp. 38–9.

33  Bernstein, *Sonia's Daughters*, pp. 44, 47, 178, 182; Stites, *The Women's Liberation Movement in Russia*, pp. 181, 184.

34  McKean, *St Petersburg Between the Revolutions*, p. 41; Bernstein, *Sonia's Daughters*, pp. 44, 58–9, 78, 178, 182.

35  Marye, George Thomas, *Nearing the End in Imperial Russia*, London: Selwyn and Blount, 1928, pp. 447–8.

36  Fuhrmann, Joseph T., *Rasputin – A Life*, New York: Praeger, 1990, pp. 34–6.

37  Report of M. V. Rodzianko, President of the Duma, to Nicholas II, in Dmytryshyn, *Imperial Russia*, p. 448.

38  Fuhrmann, *Rasputin*, pp. 26–9, 42–3, 61.

39  Buchanan, Sir George, *My Mission to Russia – and Other Diplomatic Memories*, Vol I, London: Cassell, 1923, p. 156.

40  Moynahan, Brian, *Rasputin: The Saint Who Sinned*, New York: Random House, 1997, p. 157; Kokovtsov, *Out of my Past*, p. 290.

41  Fuhrmann, *Rasputin*, p. 192.

42  Kokovtsov, *Out of my Past*, pp. 291, 296–7.

43  Report of M. V. Rodzianko, President of the Duma, to Nicholas II, in Dmytryshyn, *Imperial Russia*, p. 440.

44  Fuhrmann, *Rasputin*, p. 95.

45  Redesdale, *Memories*, Vol. I, p. 270.

46  Buckle, *Diaghilev*, pp. 179–80, 195; Maes, *A History of Russian Music*, pp. 221–2.

47  Stravinsky and Craft, *Memories and Commentaries*, pp. 33, 38.

48  Stravinsky and Craft, *Expositions and Developments*, p. 21; Stravinsky and Craft, *Memories and Commentaries*, p. 30.

49  Buckle, *Diaghilev*, pp. 214, 252–4; Maes, *A History of Russian Music*, p. 228.

50  Stravinsky and Craft, *Memories and Commentaries*, p. 32.

51  Bowlt, *Moscow and St Petersburg in Russia's Silver Age*, pp. 266–7, 321–4.

52  Bird, *A History of Russian Painting*, pp. 203, 210–11; Moynahan, Brian, *Rasputin*, p. 181.

53  Kandinsky, Vasily, *Concerning the Spiritual in Art*, trans. M. T. H. Sadler, New York: Dover Publications, 1977, pp. 1, 29 n.7; Bird, *A History of Russian Painting*, pp. 191–2.

54  Bowlt, *Moscow and St Petersburg in Russia's Silver Age*, pp. 67, 73, 78, 307.

55  McKean, *St Petersburg Between the Revolutions*, pp. 88, 102–103.

56  Ibid., pp. 193, 241, 266–7.

57  Neuberger, *Hooliganism*, pp. 239–40, 242, 277.

58  Qtd in Moynahan, *Rasputin*, p. 181.

59  Reed, John, *Ten Days that Shook the World* (1919), London: Penguin, 1977, p. 61.

60  Lockhart, R. H. Bruce, *Memoirs of a British Agent*, London: Putnam, 1934, p. 160.

61  Buchanan, Sir George, *My Mission to Russia*, Vol. I, pp. 173–4.

62  Rosen, *Forty Years of Diplomacy*, Vol. II, p. 153.

63  Stites, *Russian Popular Culture*, pp. 14, 21.
64  Rosen, *Forty Years of Diplomacy*, Vol. II, p. 153.
65  Fuhrmann, *Rasputin*, pp. 118–19.
66  Marye, *Nearing the End in Imperial Russia*, pp. 445–6.
67  Fuhrmann, *Rasputin*, pp. 121, 140–44, 164, 192.
68  Stravinsky and Craft, *Expositions and Developments*, p. 63; Maes, *A History of Russian Music*, p. 178.
69  Buchanan, Meriel, *Petrograd – The City of Trouble 1914–18*, London: Collins, 1919, p. 12.
70  McKean, *St Petersburg Between the Revolutions*, pp. 268, 297, 307–308; Neuberger, *Hooliganism*, pp. 258–9, 263.
71  Scudder, Jared W., *Russia in the Summer of 1914*, Boston: Richard Badger, 1920, pp. 18, 21, 161–6.
72  McKean, *St Petersburg Between the Revolutions*, p. 324; Montefiore, *The Romanovs 1613–1918*, p. 577.
73  Nabokov, *Speak Memory*, p. 27.
74  Buchanan, Meriel, *Petrograd*, pp. 46–7.
75  Francis, David R., *Russia from the American Embassy – April 1916– November 1918*, New York: Charles Scribner's Sons, 1921, p. 11.
76  Buchanan, Meriel, *Petrograd*, pp. 46, 48.
77  Qtd in Norman, *The Hermitage*, p. 136.
78  Karsavina, *Theatre Street*, pp. 222, 252; Buchanan, Meriel, *Petrograd*, pp. 113–14.
79  Bowlt, *Moscow and St Petersburg in Russia's Silver Age*, pp. 84, 278.
80  Qtd in Buckle, *Diaghilev*, p. 300.
81  Karsavina, *Theatre Street*, p. 258.
82  Osip Mandelstam, '118' of 25 November 1920, in *Osip Mandelstam Selected Poems* (1973), Harmondsworth: Penguin, 1977, trans. Clarence Brown, p. 55.
83  Almedingen, *Tomorrow Will Come*, p. 89.
84  Buchanan, Meriel, *Petrograd*, pp. 62, 70, 74.
85  Almedingen, *Tomorrow Will Come*, p. 92.
86  Fuhrmann, *Rasputin*, p. 192.
87  Francis, *Russia from the American Embassy*, pp. 35, 43.
88  Fuhrmann, *Rasputin*, pp. 118, 198–208; Figes, *Revolutionary Russia*, p. 86.
89  Buchanan, Sir George, *My Mission to Russia*, Vol. II, pp. 38–9.
90  Kokovtsov, *Out of my Past*, p. 480.
91  McKean, *St Petersburg Between the Revolutions*, p. 460; Moynahan, *Rasputin*, p. 349.
92  Buchanan, Meriel, *Petrograd*, pp. 91–2, 35–6.
93  Francis, *Russia from the American Embassy*, p. 63.
94  Buchanan, Meriel, *Petrograd*, p. 92; Norman, *The Hermitage*, p. 135.
95  Kokovtsov, *Out of my Past*, p. 481; Buchanan, Meriel, *Petrograd*, pp. 94–5, 97; Buchanan, Sir George, *My Mission to Russia*, Vol. II, p. 63; McKean, *St Petersburg Between the Revolutions*, p. 476.

96  Buchanan, Meriel, *Petrograd*, p. 87.
97  Ibid., p. 105.
98  Abdication of Nicholas II, in Dmytryshyn, *Imperial Russia*, p. 478.
99  Kokovtsov, *Out of my Past*, p. 481; Buchanan, Sir George, *My Mission to Russia*, Vol. II, pp. 72–3; Montefiore, *The Romanovs*, p. 627.
100 Buchanan, Sir George, *My Mission to Russia*, Vol. II, p. 62.
101 Moynahan, *Rasputin*, pp. 355, 357–8; Fuhrmann, *Rasputin*, pp. 214, 224–5.
102 Kokovtsov, *Out of my Past*, pp. 482, 484.
103 Buchanan, Sir George, *My Mission to Russia*, Vol. II, p. 91; Francis, *Russia from the American Embassy*, pp. 102, 104.
104 Buckle, *Diaghilev*, pp. 326, 328–9.
105 Shklovsky, Viktor, *A Sentimental Journey – Memoirs 1917–22*, trans. Richard Sheldon, Ithaca, NY, and London: Cornell University Press, 1970, p. 20; Buchanan, Sir George, *My Mission to Russia*, Vol. II, p. 116; Service, *The Penguin History of Modern Russia*, pp. 47–8; Reed, *Ten Days*, p. 45.
106 Francis, David R., *Russia from the American Embassy*, p. 137.
107 Lockhart, *Memoirs of a British Agent*, p. 225, quoting Raymond Robins.
108 Pipes, Richard, *The Russian Revolution*, New York: Alfred A. Knopf, 1990, p. 385; Bryant, Louise, *Six Red Months in Russia – An Observer's Account of Russia Before and During the Proletarian Dictatorship*, London: William Heinemann, 1918, p. 45.
109 Buchanan, Sir George, *My Mission to Russia*, Vol. II, pp. 113, 165.
110 Ibid., p. 176; Buchanan, Meriel, *Petrograd*, p. 181; Norman, *The Hermitage*, pp. 141–2.
111 Reed, *Ten Days*, p. 61.
112 Buchanan, Sir George, *My Mission to Russia*, Vol. II, pp. 205–207.
113 Karsavina, *Theatre Street*, pp. 264–5.

## 12 RED PETROGRAD

1   Bryant, *Six Red Months in Russia*, p. 48; Reed, *Ten Days*, pp. 54–5.
2   Francis, *Russia from the American Embassy*, pp. 168–9.
3   Ibid., p. 171; Reed, *Ten Days*, p. 65.
4   Reed, *Ten Days*, p. 219.
5   Bryant, *Six Red Months in Russia*, p. 88.
6   Reed, *Ten Days*, p. 108.
7   Buchanan, Sir George, *My Mission to Russia*, Vol. II, p. 208.
8   Almedingen, *Tomorrow Will Come*, p. 108.
9   Pipes, Richard, *The Russian Revolution*, p. 496.
10  Lockhart, *Memoirs of a British Agent*, p. 242; Buchanan, Meriel, *Petrograd*, pp. 225, 229–330, 235.
11  Buchanan, Sir George, *My Mission to Russia*, Vol. II, pp. 239–40.

12  McAuley, Mary, *Bread and Justice – State and Society in Petrograd 1917–22*, Oxford: Clarendon Press, 1991, pp. 51–2.

13  Qtd in Reed, *Ten Days*, pp. 105, 134.

14  Almedingen, *Tomorrow Will Come*, p. 90; Reed, *Ten Days*, p. 197; McAuley, *Bread and Justice*, pp. 7–31, 50, 285.

15  Bryant, *Six Red Months in Russia*, p. 37.

16  Buchanan, Meriel, *Petrograd*, p. 227.

17  Shklovsky, *A Sentimental Journey*, pp. 133–4, 145.

18  Qtd in Norman, *The Hermitage*, p. 159.

19  Shklovsky, *A Sentimental Journey*, p. 175; Wolkonsky, Princess Peter, *The Way of Bitterness: Soviet Russia, 1920*, London: Methuen, 1931, p. 163.

20  McAuley, *Bread and Justice*, p. 124.

21  Figes, *Revolutionary Russia*, p. 134.

22  Belinsky, 'Petersburg and Moscow', in Nekrasov, *Petersburg: The Physiology of a City*, p. 31.

23  McAuley, *Bread and Justice*, pp. 31–2, 40; McAuley, Mary, *Soviet Politics – 1917–19*, Oxford: Oxford University Press, 1992, p. 27

24  Lockhart, *Memoirs of a British Agent*, p. 257.

25  Dukes, Sir Paul, *Red Dusk and the Morrow – Adventures and Investigations in Red Russia*, London: Williams and Norgate, 1923, p. 102; McCauley, *Bread and Justice*, p. 390.

26  McAuley, *Bread and Justice*, p. 142.

27  Qtd in Fitzpatrick, Sheila, *The Commissariat of Enlightenment – Soviet Organization of Education and the Arts under Lunacharsky, October 1917–1921*, Cambridge: Cambridge University Press, 1970, pp. 1–2.

28  Ibid., pp. 98–9.

29  Maes, *A History of Russian Music*, p. 238.

30  Norman, *The Hermitage*, p. 164; Taylor, Richard, 'The Birth of the Soviet Cinema', in Gleason, Kenez and Stites, eds, *Bolshevik Culture: Experiment and Order in the Russian Revolution*, Bloomington, IN: Indiana University Press, 1985, pp. 190, 195.

31  Goldman, Emma, *Living My Life*, Vol. II, London: Pluto Press, 1988, p. 783; Norman, *The Hermitage*, p. 149.

32  Shklovsky, *A Sentimental Journey*, p. 188.

33  McAuley, *Bread and Justice*, pp. 331, 335.

34  Wolkonsky, *The Way of Bitterness: Soviet Russia, 1920*, pp. 148, 156.

35  Buckler, *Mapping St Petersburg*, p. 240.

36  McAuley, *Bread and Justice*, p. 364.

37  Norman, *The Hermitage*, p. 163.

38  McAuley, *Bread and Justice*, p. 356.

39  Qtd in McAuley, *Bread and Justice*, p. 378 and see pp. 66–8, 88–9, 110.

40  Holquist, Peter, 'Violent Russia, Deadly Marxism? Russia in the Epoch of Violence 1905–21', in Kocho-Williams, Alastair, ed., *The Twentieth Century Russia Reader*, Abingdon: Routledge, 2011, p. 115; Service, *The Penguin History of Modern Russia*, pp. 107–108.

41 Plotnikova, Yulia, 'Children of the Emperor', in *At the Russian Court*, p. 307; Montefiore, *The Romanovs 1613–1918*, p. 636.

42 Dukes, *Red Dusk and the Morrow*, pp. 7–10, 21–2, 33–4, 114; Knightley, Phillip, *The Second Oldest Profession – Spies and Spying in the Twentieth Century*, London: Pimlico, 2003, pp. 69–73.

43 Almedingen, *Tomorrow Will Come*, p. 123.

44 Buchanan, Meriel, *Petrograd*, pp. 225–6.

45 Goldman, *Living My Life*, Vol. II, p. 790.

46 Almedingen, *Tomorrow Will Come*, p. 109.

47 Goldman, *Living My Life*, Vol. II, p. 779.

48 Serge, Victor, *Memoirs of a Revolutionary*, trans. Peter Sedgwick, Oxford: Oxford University Press, 1975, pp. 70–71.

49 Goldman, *Living My Life*, Vol. II, pp. 873–6; McAuley, *Bread and Justice*, p. 252.

50 McAuley, *Bread and Justice*, p. 389.

51 'The Fight for Petrograd', *Pravda*, No. 250, 30 October 1919, transcribed for the Trotsky International Archive by David Walters, Marxists.org; Serge, *Memoirs of a Revolutionary*, pp. 90, 94.

52 Wells, H. G., *Russia in the Shadows*, London: Hodder and Stoughton, n.d., pp. 9, 14–35; McAuley, *Bread and Justice*, p. 352.

53 Bryant, *Six Red Months in Russia*, p. 44.

54 Wells, *Russia in the Shadows*, p. 37.

55 McAuley, *Bread and Justice*, pp. 354–5.

56 Norman, *The Hermitage*, p. 167.

57 Wells, *Russia in the Shadows*, pp. 9, 14–16, 21, 51, 134.

58 Goldman, *Living My Life*, Vol. II, pp. 727, 732, 735, 742.

59 Poretsky, Elisabeth K., *Our Own People: A Memoir of 'Ignace Reiss' and His Friends*, London: Oxford University Press, 1969, p. 102; McAuley, *Bread and Justice*, p. 293.

60 Wolkonsky, *The Way of Bitterness*, p. 163.

61 Cattell, David T., 'Soviet Cities and Consumer Welfare Planning', in Hamm, Michael F., *The City in Russian History*, Lexington, KY: University of Kentucky Press, 1976, p. 272.

62 Wolkonsky, *The Way of Bitterness*, pp. 166–7, 184.

63 Serge, *Memoirs of a Revolutionary*, p. 117.

64 Ransome, *The Crisis in Russia 1920*, London: George Allen and Unwin, 1921, p. 11; Harding, Luke, *The Mafia State*, London: Guardian Books, 2012, p. 103.

65 Holquist, Peter, in *The Twentieth Century Russia Reader*, pp. 114, 117.

66 Serge, *Memoirs of a Revolutionary*, pp. 130, 149; Service, *The Penguin History of Modern Russia*, p. 108; Goldman, *Living My Life*, Vol. II, pp. 733, 740, 849, 927.

67 Stites, *Russian Popular Culture*, pp. 39–40.

68 Ransome, *The Crisis in Russia*, p. 40.

69 Nabokov, *Speak Memory*, p. 183.

70 Herzen, qtd in Berlin, *Russian Thinkers*, pp. 103, 226.

## 13 A CITY DIMINISHED

1 Davies, Sarah, *Popular Opinion in Stalin's Russia*, Cambridge: Cambridge University Press, 1997, p. 18.

2 Biely, *Petersburg*, p. 112.

3 Fedotov, qtd in Schenker, *The Bronze Horseman*, p. 294.

4 Koestler, Arthur, *The Invisible Writing – The Second Volume of an Autobiography 1932–40* (1954), London: Random House, 2005, p. 33.

5 Goldman, *Living My Life*, Vol. II, pp. 886–7.

6 Stites, *Russian Popular Culture*, p. 61.

7 Hessler, Julie, *A Social History of Soviet Trade – Trade Policy, Retail Practices and Consumption – 1917–1953*, Princeton, NJ: Princeton University Press, 2004, p. 7; Service, *The Penguin History of Modern Russia*, pp. 144–5, 196.

8 Neville, *Russia: A Complete History*, pp. 191–2.

9 Clark, *Petersburg, Crucible of Cultural Revolution*, p. 3; McAuley, Bread and Justice, p. 400.

10 Stalin, qtd in Brendon, Piers, *The Dark Valley – A Panorama of the 1930s*, London: Jonathan Cape, 2000, p. 419.

11 Conquest, Robert, *The Great Terror – A Reassessment*, London: Pimlico, 2008, p. 114; Andrew, Christopher, and Mitrokhin, Vasili, *The Sword and the Shield. The Mitrokhin Archive and the Secret History of the KGB*, New York: Basic Books, 1999, pp. 38–9.

12 Poretsky, *Our Own People*, p. 91.

13 Engel, *Women in Russia*, pp. 166–7; Figes, *Revolutionary Russia*, pp. 208, 210, 213; Service, *The Penguin History of Modern Russia*, pp. 6, 179–81.

14 Stites, *Russian Popular Culture*, p. 40.

15 Akhmatova, Anna, from 'White Flock', trans. D. M. Thomas, *You Will Hear Thunder*, p. 45, qtd in MacDonald, Ian, *The New Shostakovitch*, new ed. revised by Raymond Clarke, London: Pimlico, 2006, p. 96.

16 Qtd in MacDonald, *The New Shostakovitch*, p. 38.

17 Stites, *Russian Popular Culture*, pp. 43–4.

18 Gray, *The Russian Experiment in Art*, pp. 234–5.

19 Bowlt, John E., 'Constructivism and Early Soviet Fashion Design', in *Bolshevik Culture*, pp. 203–4.

20 Gray, *The Russian Experiment in Art*, pp. 248, 253.

21 Lissitzky, El, *Russia: An Architecture for World Revolution*, Cambridge, MA: MIT Press, 1984, p. 27.

22 Taylor, in *Bolshevik Culture*, p. 190.

23 Clark, *Petersburg, Crucible of Cultural Revolution*, p. 345 n.60; Stites, *Russian Popular Culture*, p. 214 n.30.

24 Stites, *Russian Popular Culture*, p. 56; Miles, Jonathan, *The Nine Lives of Otto Katz*, London: Bantam Press, 2010, p. 80.

25 Eisenstein, Sergei, *Film Essays and a Lecture*, ed. Jay Leyda, Princeton, NJ: Princeton University Press, 1982, p. 31.

26  Taylor, in *Bolshevik Culture*, p. 194.

27  Maes, *A History of Russian Music*, pp. 245, 251

28  Davies, *Popular Opinion in Stalin's Russia*, pp. 24–5.

29  Engel, *Women in Russia*, pp. 142–3, 152–4, 156, 175; Davies, *Popular Opinion in Stalin's Russia*, p. 60.

30  Engel, *Women in Russia*, p. 154.

31  Pope-Hennessy, Dame Una Birch, *The Closed City: Impressions of a Visit to Leningrad*, London: Hutchinson, 1938, p. 37.

32  Davies, *Popular Opinion in Stalin's Russia*, p. 68.

33  Miles, *The Nine Lives of Otto Katz*, p. 94.

34  Gide, *Back From the USSR*, pp. 36, 48.

35  Hessler, *A Social History of Soviet Trade*, pp. 201–202, 207; Davies, *Popular Opinion in Stalin's Russia*, p. 30.

36  Pope-Hennessy, *The Closed City*, pp. 177–8.

37  Gide, *Back From the USSR*, pp. 50–51.

38  Service, *The Penguin History of Modern Russia*, pp. 214–15; Davies, *Popular Opinion in Stalin's Russia*, p. 117.

39  Conquest, *The Great Terror*, pp. 12, 35, 215, 218; Davies, *Popular Opinion in Stalin's Russia*, pp. 127, 178.

40  Thurston, Robert W., *Life and Terror in Stalin's Russia 1934–1941*, New Haven, CT, and London: Yale University Press, 1996, pp. 19–23; Davies, *Popular Opinion in Stalin's Russia*, p. 164.

41  Brendon, *The Dark Valley*, p. 399; Service, *The Penguin History of Modern Russia*, p. 222; Figes, *Revolutionary Russia*, p. 266; Conquest, *The Great Terror*, pp. 310–11; Dmitri Shostakovich, qtd by Karen Khachaturian in Weinstein, Larry, dir., *Shostakovich Against Stalin – The War Symphonies*, Rhombus Films, 1997.

42  Koestler, *The Invisible Writing*, pp. 32–3.

43  MacDonald, *The New Shostakovitch*, pp. 111, 124, 148–9; Shostakovich, quoting a *Pravda* article attributed to Stalin, in Weinstein, *Shostakovich Against Stalin*.

44  Story told by Veniamin Basner in Weinstein, *Shostakovich Against Stalin*. Also the interview with Mariana Sabinina.

45  MacDonald, *The New Shostakovitch*, pp. 35, 74, 86; Stites, *Russian Popular Culture*, p. 77.

46  Stites, *Russian Popular Culture*, pp. 73–4.

47  Serge, *Memoirs of a Revolutionary*, pp. 279–80.

48  Russian saying, qtd in Conquest, *The Great Terror*, p. 109.

49  Norman, *The Hermitage*, pp. 155, 168, 182.

50  Ibid., pp. 176, 179, 190–97.

51  Osip Mandelstam, poem about Stalin, November 1933, passed by word of mouth.

52  Stites, *Russian Popular Culture*, pp. 68, 71; Service, *The Penguin History of Modern Russia*, pp. 190–91.

53  Service, *The Penguin History of Modern Russia*, pp. 140, 247; Stites, *Russian Popular Culture*, p. 51.

54  Pope-Hennessy, *The Closed City*, pp. 102–103.

55  Kahn, Albert E., *Days with Ulanova*, London: William Collins, 1962, pp. 115, 132, 202.

56  Pope-Hennessy, *The Closed City*, p. 159; Davies, *Popular Opinion in Stalin's Russia*, p. 76.

57  Davies, *Popular Opinion in Stalin's Russia*, pp. 83–7.

58  Miles, *The Nine Lives of Otto Katz*, p. 175.

59  Roland, Betty, *Caviar for Breakfast*, Melbourne: Quartet Books, 1979, pp. 98–9, 114, 128–9.

60  Pope-Hennessy, *The Closed City*, pp. 7, 16, 43, 78, 136–7, 140, 214, 248.

## 14 DARKEST AND FINEST HOUR

1  Liubov Shaporina, diary, 10 September 1941, qtd in Simmons, Cynthia, and Perlina, Nina, *Writing the Siege of Leningrad – Women's Diaries, Memoirs and Documentary Prose*, Pittsburgh, PA: University of Pittsburgh Press, 2002, p. 23.

2  Service, *The Penguin History of Modern Russia*, p. 220; Conquest, *The Great Terror*, p. 182.

3  Koestler, Arthur, *Scum of the Earth*, trans. Daphne Hardy, London: Victor Gollancz, 1941, p. 24; Service, *The Penguin History of Modern Russia*, p. 256; Orwell, George, *Animal Farm*, London: Penguin, 2008, p. 39; Solzhenitsyn, Alexander, *The First Circle*, pp. 196, 134, qtd in Neville, *Russia: A Complete History*, p. 205; Conquest, *The Great Terror*, pp. 195, 196.

4  Davies, *Popular Opinion in Stalin's Russia*, pp. 41, 43–5.

5  Service, *The Penguin History of Modern Russia*, p. 257.

6  Ibid., pp. 260–61.

7  Mukhina, Lena, *The Diary of Lena Mukhina – A Girl's Life in the Siege of Leningrad*, London: Pan Macmillan, 2016 pp. 51–2.

8  Mukhina, *Diary*, p. 2; Reid, Anna, *Leningrad – Tragedy of a City Under Siege*, London: Bloomsbury, 2011; pbk 2012, pp. 3, 52, 95–7, 99.

9  Simmons and Perlina, *Writing the Siege*, p. xiii.

10  German Naval Command, qtd in Mukhina, *Diary*, p. 3.

11  Reid, *Leningrad*, pp. 96, 115; Mukhina, *Diary*, p. 3; Schenker, *The Bronze Horseman*, p. 296.

12  Norman, *The Hermitage* pp. 243, 246–7; Reid, *Leningrad*, pp. 62–3.

13  Mukhina, *Diary*, p. 171; Reid, *Leningrad*, pp. 118–19.

14  Much of the visual description of what follows in this chapter is inspired by a documentary compilation by Sergei Loznitsa, *Blockade*, using footage found in Soviet archives. St Petersburg Documentary Film Studios, 2005.

15  Mukhina, *Diary*, pp. 57, 105, 114.

16  Liubov Shaporina, diary, 8 September 1941, in Simmons and Perlina, *Writing the Siege*.

17  Reid, *Leningrad*, pp. 144–5.

18  Mukhina, *Diary*, p. 125.
19  Anna Likhacheva, diary, 16 May 1942, qtd in Simmons and Perlina, *Writing the Siege*, p. 59.
20  Ginzburg, Lydia, *Blockade Diary*, trans. Alan Myers, London: Harvill Press, 1995, p. 10.
21  Yevtushenko, Yevgeny, 'The City With Three Faces', in *Insight Guides – St Petersburg*, ed. Wilhelm Klein, Hong Kong: Apa Publications, 1992, p. 38.
22  Vera Kostrovitskaya, diary, n.d., qtd in Simmons and Perlina, *Writing the Siege*.
23  Reid, *Leningrad*, pp. 164–5.
24  Mukhina, *Diary*, pp. 5, 10, 159, 220; Dmitri Tolstoy, interview in Weinstein, *Shostakovich Against Stalin*.
25  Yevtushenko, 'The City With Three Faces', in *Insight Guides – St Petersburg*, p. 40; Reid, *Leningrad*, p. 236.
26  Reid, *Leningrad*, pp. 180–81; Mukhina, *Diary*, p. 8.
27  Vera Kostrovitskaya, diary, April 1942, qtd in Simmons and Perlina, *Writing the Siege*, pp. 50–51.
28  Valentina Gorokhova, 'memoir', n.d., qtd in Simmons and Perlina, *Writing the Siege*.
29  Mukhina, *Diary*, pp. 6, 223.
30  Reid, *Leningrad*, p. 230.
31  Ibid., pp. 219–20; Gautier, *The Complete Works*, p. 163; Porter, *Travelling Sketches in Russia*, p. 108.
32  Ginzburg, *Blockade Diary*, p. 14.
33  Elza Greinert, letter of 25 January 1942 to her children, qtd in Simmons and Perlina, *Writing the Siege*, pp. 34–5.
34  Ginzburg, *Blockade Diary*, p. 76.
35  Mukhina, *Diary*, p. 5.
36  Simmons and Perlina, *Writing the Siege*, p. xvi.
37  Mukhina, *Diary*, p. 7: Reid, *Leningrad*, p. 264.
38  Hessler, *A Social History of Soviet Trade*, p. 302.
39  Mukhina, *Diary*, pp. 200–201.
40  Simmons and Perlina, *Writing the Siege*, pp. xviii.
41  Reid, *Leningrad*, pp. 280–85.
42  Pavlov, Dmitri V., *Leningrad 1941 – The Blockade*, trans. John Clinton Adams, Chicago, IL: Chicago University Press, 1965, pp. 136–8, 151, 153, 161–2, 164, 166.
43  Reid, *Leningrad*, pp. 248–9; Simmons and Perlina, *Writing the Siege*, p. xx.
44  Norman, *The Hermitage* p. 258.
45  Ginzburg, *Blockade Diary*, pp. 12, 58.
46  Mukhina, *Diary*, p. 8.
47  Reid, *Leningrad*, p. 246.
48  Stites, *Russian Popular Culture*, p. 102.

49  Prokofiev, Sergei, *War and Peace*, conducted by Valery Gergiev, Kirov/ Opera Bastille, 1991.
50  Robinson, Harlow, 'Composing for Victory – Classical Music' in Stites, Richard, ed., *Culture and Entertainment in Wartime Russia*, Bloomington and Indianapolis, IN: Indiana University Press, 1995, pp. 63, 66.
51  Interview with Ksenia Matus, in Simmons and Perlina, *Writing the Siege*, pp. 147–9.
52  MacDonald, *The New Shostakovitch*, pp. 179–80; interview with Ksenia Matus, in Simmons & Perlina, *Writing the Siege*, p. 151, and in Weinstein, *Shostakovich Against Stalin*. Also in that documentary: the interview with Dmitri Tolstoy.
53  Yevtushenko, 'The City With Three Faces', in *Insight Guides – St Petersburg*, p. 41.
54  Gregory and Ukladnikov, *Leningrad's Ballet*, p. 25; Vera Kostrovitskaya, diary, n.d., qtd in Simmons and Perlina, *Writing the Siege*, p. 51; Kahn, *Days with Ulanova*, p. 118.
55  Mukhina, *Diary*, pp. 163, 311.
56  Reid, *Leningrad*, pp. 140, 226.
57  Lila Solomonovna Frankfurt, memoir, n.d., qtd in Simmons and Perlina, *Writing the Siege*, pp. 164–7.
58  Norman, *The Hermitage*, pp. 253–4.
59  Valentina Gorokhova, memoir of 1946, qtd in Simmons and Perlina, *Writing the Siege*, p. 94.
60  Reid, *Leningrad*, p. 377.
61  Simmons and Perlina, *Writing the Siege*, p. xxiii.
62  Service, *The Penguin History of Modern Russia*, p. 300.
63  Kelly, Catriona, *St Petersburg – Shadows of the Past*, New Haven, CT, and London: Yale University Press, 2014, p. 4.
64  Shostakovich, *Testimony*, qtd in Weinstein, *Shostakovich Against Stalin*.

## 15 MURMURS FROM THE UNDERGROUND

1  Reid, *Leningrad*, p. 399; Simmons and Perlina, *Writing the Siege*, p. xxvi.
2  Buckler, *Mapping St Petersburg*, p. 240; Kirshchenbaum, Lisa A., *The Legacy of the Siege of Leningrad 1941–1995: Myth, Memories and Monuments*, Cambridge and New York, 2006, pp. 124–6.
3  Irina Antonova, Director of Moscow's Pushkin Museum, 'Politicians Come and Go, But Art Is Eternal' in *Der Spiegel*, 13 July 2012.
4  Norman, *The Hermitage*, pp. 261–2.
5  De Madariaga, *Catherine the Great*, p. 155.
6  Hessler, *A Social History of Soviet Trade*, pp. 5, 302; Service, *The Penguin History of Modern Russia*, pp. 237, 298, 314.
7  Shostakovich, qtd in Weinstein, *Shostakovich Against Stalin*.
8  Smith, *The Russians*, p. 416.

9   Kirshchenbaum, *The Legacy of the Siege*, p. 141; Davies, *Popular Opinion in Stalin's Russia*, p. 18.

10   Simmons and Perlina, *Writing the Siege*, p. xxv.

11   Qtd in Ulam, Adam B., *Stalin – The Man and his Era*, London: Allen Lane, 1974, p. 644.

12   Ibid., pp. 706–707; Simmons and Perlina, *Writing the Siege*, p. xxv–vi; Reid, *Leningrad*, pp. 401–404.

13   Service, *The Penguin History of Modern Russia*, p. 303.

14   Stites, *Russian Popular Culture*, p. 125; Service, *The Penguin History of Modern Russia*, pp. xxxii, 331, 338–9.

15   *Leningradskaya Pravda*, qtd in Steven E. Harris, 'Soviet Mass Housing and the Communist Way of Life', in Chatterjee, Ransel, Cavender and Petrone, eds, *Everyday Life in Russia Past and Present*, Bloomington and Indianapolis, IN: Indiana University Press, 2015, p. 187; Kelly, *St Petersburg*, p. 70.

16   Kelly, *St Petersburg*, p. 71.

17   Harrison, Mark, prod., *The Last Days of Leningrad*, BBC Bristol, 1991, extracts of newsreels about chocolate-making for the 250th anniversary, and 'Summer Comes Soon' of 1987.

18   Kirshchenbaum, *The Legacy of the Siege*, pp. 125, 127; Kelly, *St Petersburg*, p. 170.

19   Ostrovsky, Arkady, *The Invention of Russia – The Journey from Gorbachev's Freedom to Putin's War*, London: Atlantic Books, 2016, pp. 32–3, 47; Harding, Luke, 'How MI6 Helped CIA to Bring Doctor Zhivago in from Cold for Russians', *Guardian*, 10 June 2014.

20   Norman, *The Hermitage*, pp. 285, 300–301, 311; Kelly, *St Petersburg*, p. 232.

21   'Rural Evenings', a 1954 lyrical comedy about life on a collective farm, and *It Was Once So* by Dmitri Gordunov – extracts in Sergei Loznitsa, *Revue*, Federal Agency for Culture and Cinematography and St Petersburg Documentary Film Studios, 2008.

22   Shostakovich, Dmitri, *Cheryomushki*, dir., Paul Rappaport, Lenfilm, 1963, DVD – Decca 2007.

23   Feyginburg, Yosif, dir., *Glenn Gould – The Russian Journey*, documentary, Atlantic Productions, 2002.

24   Kavanagh, Julie, *Rudolf Nureyev – The Life*, London: Penguin, 2008, pp. 37, 40, 46, 51, 52, 56–7, 83, 90, 112.

25   Krushchev, qtd in Stites, *Russian Popular Culture*, p. 132.

26   Qtd in ibid., p. 133.

27   Polsky, Gabe, *Red Army*, documentary, Weintraub and Herzog, 2014; 'Patience and Labour' (1985 – not released until 1991 because of disturbing images of training young ice-skaters), extract in Harrison, *The Last Days of Leningrad*.

28   A 1966 newsreel about robots in the home in Harrison, *The Last Days of Leningrad*; Kelly, *St Petersburg*, p. 258; Figes, *Revolutionary Russia*, p. 363.

29  Harris, 'Soviet Mass Housing and the Communist Way of Life', in *Everyday Life in Russia Past and Present*, pp. 194–5.

30  Loznitsa, *Revue.*

31  McAuley, *Soviet Politics*, p. 78; Kelly, *St Petersburg*, pp. 5, 142; Smith, *The Russians*, p. 8; 'To Drink or Not to Drink' (1977), extracted in Harrison, *The Last Days of Leningrad.*

32  'The Working Lunch', in Meader, Vaughn et al., *The First Family*, LP, New York: Cadence Records, November 1962; McAuley, *Soviet Politics*, p. 72.

33  Qtd in Ostrovsky, *The Invention of Russia*, p. 50.

34  Harris, 'Soviet Mass Housing and the Communist Way of Life', in *Everyday Life in Russia Past and Present*, p. 190; Smith, *The Russians*, pp. 97–8; Stites, *Russian Popular Culture*, p. 124; Kelly, *St Petersburg*, pp. 65, 70.

35  Alexievich, Svetlana, *Second-Hand Time – The Last of the Soviets*, trans. Bela Shayevich, London: Fitzcarraldo Editions, 2016, p. 84; Figes, *Revolutionary Russia*, p. 380; Smith, *The Russians*, p. 97.

36  Qtd in Smith, *The Russians*, p. 171; Engel, *Women in Russia*, pp. 242, 245.

37  Pope-Hennessy, *The Closed City*, pp. 37–8; Engel, *Women in Russia*, pp. 245–6.

38  Kelly, *St Petersburg*, p. 384 n.4; Hessler, Julie, *A Social History of Soviet Trade*, p. xiii.

39  Smith, *The Russians*, pp. 8, 83, 92.

40  Kelly, *St Petersburg*, p. 189; Smith, *The Russians*, pp. 80–81.

41  Obama, Barack, in final press conference of 2016, qtd in Jacobs, Ben, 'Obama Says he Warned Russia to "Cut it Out" Over Election Hacking', *Guardian*, 16 December, 2016.

42  Kelly, *St Petersburg*, pp. 251, 257.

43  McAuley, *Soviet Politics*, pp. 67–8.

44  Stites, *Russian Popular Culture*, pp. 152, 156–7, 160.

45  Norman, *The Hermitage*, p. 311.

46  Intourist guide, overheard in 1979.

47  Harding, *The Mafia State*, p. 215.

48  Smith, *The Russians*, pp. 571–2.

49  Engel, *Women in Russia*, p. 243; McAuley, *Soviet Politics*, p. 5; Service, *The Penguin History of Modern Russia*, p. 467.

50  Brodsky, *Less Than One*, pp. 92–3.

51  Engel, *Women in Russia*, p. 246.

52  Pope-Hennessy, *The Closed City*, p. 210.

53  Kirshchenbaum, *The Legacy of the Siege*, pp. 48, 217, 221–3, 225.

54  Service, *The Penguin History of Modern Russia*, pp. 420, 472.

55  Ostrovsky, *The Invention of Russia*, pp. 58–9, 62.

56  McAuley, *Soviet Politics*, p. 60.

57  'Dialogues', 1986 jazz film from Leningrad Film Documentary Studios,

extracted in Harrison, *The Last Days of Leningrad*; Stites, *Russian Popular Culture*, p. 196.

58  McAuley, *Soviet Politics*, p. 95.
59  'Rock' (1988), extracted in Harrison, *The Last Days of Leningrad*.
60  Nevzorov, Alexander, *600 Seconds*, 22 May 1990 and 4 January 1991, Leningrad Chanel/St Petersburg Television, various emissions shown in Harrison, *The Last Days of Leningrad*.
61  Engel, *Women in Russia*, pp. 251, 256.
62  Hessler, *A Social History of Soviet Trade*, p. xiii.
63  Kelly, *St Petersburg*, p. 274.
64  Alexievich, *Second-Hand Time*, pp. 42–3.
65  'Third Class Carriage' (1988), extracted in Harrison, *The Last Days of Leningrad*.
66  Service, *The Penguin History of Modern Russia*, pp. xxiv, 485; Alexievich, *Second-Hand Time*, p. 85.

## 16 BROKEN WINDOW ONTO THE WEST

1   Comments based on remarks made by Leningraders in Harrison, *The Last Days of Leningrad*.
2   Kelly, *St Petersburg*, p. 2; McAuley, *Soviet Politics*, p. 7.
3   Service, *The Penguin History of Modern Russia*, p. 495.
4   Clark, Katerina, 'Not for Sale: The Russian/Soviet Intelligentsia, Prostitution and the Paradox of Internal Colonization', in *Slavic Studies*, Vol. 7, 1993, pp. 188–9; Bernstein, *Sonia's Daughters*, p. 22.
5   le Carré, John, *The Secret Pilgrim*, London: Sceptre 1991; pbk 2009, p. 392.
6   Bradbury, Malcolm, *To the Hermitage*, London: Picador 2002, p. 395.
7   Womack, Helen, 'The Cost of Living in Cloud Cuckoo Land', *Independent on Sunday*, 26 March 1992.
8   Vladimir Malakoff, letter of January 1992 to Jonathan Miles.
9   Ledeneva, Alena V., *Russia's Economy of Favours: Blat, Networking and Informal Exchanges*, Cambridge: Cambridge University Press, 1998, pp. 191, 196.
10  Ostrovsky, *The Invention of Russia*, p. 147.
11  *Izvestia*, 25, 1992, qtd by Ledeneva, in *Russia's Economy of Favours*, pp. 188–9.
12  Ledeneva, *Russia's Economy of Favours*, p. 189; Kelly, *St Petersburg*, pp. 162–3.
13  Ledeneva, *Russia's Economy of Favours*, pp. 191–2; Ostrovsky, *The Invention of Russia*, pp. 188, 229, 240; Robert Cottrell, 'Russia: The New Oligarchy', *New York Review of Books*, 27 March 1997.
14  The English title is *Brother*.
15  Buckler, *Mapping St Petersburg*, p. 249; Kelly, *St Petersburg*, p. 101.
16  Walsh, Nick Paton, 'The Other St Petersburg', *Guardian*, 12 July 2006; Parfitt, Tom, 'Fewer Tramps, More Plumbers: St Petersburg Goes European', *Guardian*, 31 August 2006.

17  russialist.org, 11 May 2003; Kelly, *St Petersburg*, p. 29.

18  Van den Berg, Rob, dir., 'Catching Up with Music' with Valery Gergiev, bonus feature on Glinka, *Ruslan and Lyudmila*, conducted by Valery Gergiev, Kirov Opera and Chorus, Decca 1996.

19  Buckler, *Mapping St Petersburg*, pp. 248–51; Kelly, *St Petersburg* p. 205.

20  Walsh, Nick Paton, 'City Scandal: St Petersburg Renovation Money Dissapears', *Guardian*, 25 February 2003.

21  BBC News, 20 June 2004.

22  Kelly, *St Petersburg*, pp. 87, 116, 125, 163–4; Walsh, Nick Paton, 'The Other St Petersburg', *Guardian*, 12 July 2006; Shaun Walker, '"Salutin" Putin: Inside a Russian Troll House', *Guardian*, 2 April 2015; Harding, *The Mafia State*, p. 11.

23  Figes, *Revolutionary Russia*, p. 420.

24  Ostrovsky, *The Invention of Russia*, pp. 2, 261, 278, 320, 334; Harding, *The Mafia State*, pp. 11, 177.

25  Utekhin, Ilya, 'The Post-Soviet *Kommunalka*: Continuity and Difference', in *Everyday Life in Russia Past and Present*, p. 240.

26  Ransel, David L., '"They Are Taking that Air from Us": Sale of Commonly Enjoyed Properties to Private Developers', in *Everyday Life in Russia Past and Present*, p. 154.

27  Harding, *The Mafia State*, p. 153.

28  Wrathall, Claire, 'New Holland: St Petersburg's New Cultural District', *Telegraph*, 7 September 2016; Glancy, Jonathan, 'Foster to lead £184m Project to Transform the Ancient Heart of St Petersburg', *Guardian*, 15 February 2006.

## 17 MIRAGE

1   de Custine, *Letters*, p. 78.

2   Shelley, Mary, *Frankenstein* (1818), Ware: Wordsworth Editions, 1993.

3   Dostoevsky, *Winter Notes on Summer Impressions*, p. 23.

4   Casanova, *The Memoirs*, p. 25.

5   De Raymond, Damaze, *Tableau historique*, qtd in Giroud, *St Petersburg*, p. 62.

6   Hellman, Lillian, *An Unfinished Woman*, London: Macmillan, 1969, pp. 208–9.

7   Dostoyevsky, 'The Double', in *Notes From Underground/The Double*, p. 165.

8   Dostoyevsky, *Notes From Underground*, p. 88.

9   Qtd in Alexievich, *Second-Hand Time*, pp. 210–11.

10  Harding, *The Mafia State*, pp. 22, 25, 224.

11  Luhn, Alec, 'Construction Workers at Russian World Cup Stadium Complain of Not Being Paid', *Guardian*, 31 August 2015.

12  De Custine, *Letters*, p. 43.

13  Alexievich, *Second-Hand Time*, p. 240.

14  Viz. Miriam Elder dealing with the dry-cleaners, 'The Hell of Russian Bureaucracy', *Guardian*, 23 April 2012.

# BIBLIOGRAPHY

Adams, John Quincy, *Memoirs – Portions of his Diary from 1795–1848*, Vol. II, ed. C. F. Adams, New York: AMS Press, 1970.

Ahlström, Christian, 'The Empress of Russia and the Dutch Scow the Vrouw Maria', in *The Annual Report*, Nautica Fennica, Helsinki: National Board of Antiquities, 2000.

Albedil, M. F., *Peter the Great's Kunstkammer*, St Petersburg: Museum of Anthropology and Ethnography of the Russian Academy of Sciences, Alfa-Colour Publishers, 2002.

Alexander, John T., 'Catherine I, Her Court and Courtiers', in Hughes, *Peter the Great and the West*, pp. 227–49.

—— *Catherine the Great, Life and Legend*, New York: Oxford University Press, 1989.

Alexievich, Svetlana, *Second-Hand Time – The Last of the Soviets*, trans. Bela Shayevich, London: Fitzcarraldo Editions, 2016.

Algarotti, Francesco, *Lettres du comte Algarotti sur la Russie*, London, 1769.

Almedingen, E. M., *Tomorrow Will Come*, Woodbridge, Suffolk: Boydell Press, 1983.

Anderson, M. S., *Peter the Great*, London: Thames and Hudson, 1978.

Andrew, Christopher, and Mitrokhin, Vasili, *The Sword and the Shield. The Mitrokhin Archive and the Secret History of the KGB*, New York: Basic Books, 1999.

Anisimov, Evgeny V., *Empress Elizabeth – Her Reign and Her Russia 1741–61*, trans. John T. Alexander, Gulf Breeze, FL: Academic International Press, 1995.

—— *Five Empresses – Court Life in Eighteenth-Century Russia*, trans. Kathleen Carroll, Westport, CT, and London: Praeger, 2004.

Anisimova, Elena, 'European Artistic Glass of the Age of Art Nouveau', in *Art Nouveau – During the Reign of the Last Tsars*, Aldershot: Lund Humphries, 2007.

Anon., *L'Art du ballet en Russie 1738–1940*, exhibition catalogue, Paris: Opéra de Paris Garnier, September–December 1991.

Anon., *The Englishwoman in Russia; Impressions of the Society and*

*Manners of the Russians at Home by a Lady Ten Years Resident in that Country*, London: John Murray, 1855.

Anon. (Masson, Charles François Phillibert), *Memoirs of Catherine II and the Court of St Petersburg During her Reign and that of Paul I by One of her Courtiers*. London: Grolier Society, n.d.

Anon., *A Picture of St Petersburgh: Represented in a Collection of Twenty Interesting Views of the City, the Sledges, and the People*, London, 1815.

Anon. (Weber, Friedrich), *The Present State of Russia in Two Volumes, The Whole Being the Journal of a Foreign Minister who Resided in Russia at the Time*, trans. from the High Dutch, London, 1723.

Arnold, Sue, 'Human Warmth Amidst the Ice and the Ashes', *Observer*, 3 January 1993.

Aronson, I. Michael, *Troubled Waters: The Origins of the 1881 Anti-Jewish Pogroms in Russia*, Pittsburgh, PA: University of Pittsburgh Press, 1990.

Ascher, Abraham, *The Revolution of 1905 – Russia in Disarray*, Stanford, CA: Stanford University Press, 1988.

Atkinson, John Augustus, and Walker, James, *A Picturesque Representation of the Manners, Customs, and Amusements of the Russians in One Hundred Coloured Plates*, 3 vols, London, Vol. I, 1803; Vols II and III, 1804.

Babey, Anna Mary, *Americans in Russia 1776–1917*, New York: Comet Press, 1938.

Baehr, Stephen L., 'In the Re-Beginning: Rebirth, Renewal and *Renovatio* in Eighteenth-Century Russia', in *Russia and the West in the Eighteenth Century – Proceedings of the Second International Conference Organized by the Study Group on Eighteenth-Century Russia and Held at the University of East Anglia*, Norwich, 17–22 July 1981, pp. 152–66.

Bagdasarova, Irina, 'Official Banquets at the Russian Imperial Court', in *Dining with the Tsars*, Amsterdam: Museumshop Hermitage Amsterdam, 2014.

Baring, Maurice, *A Year in Russia*, London: Methuen, 1907.

Bartlett, R. P., 'Russia in the Eighteenth-Century European Adoption of Inoculation for Smallpox' in Bartlett, Cross and Rasmussen, *Russia and the World of the Eighteenth Century – Proceedings of the Third International Conference Organized by the Study Group on Eighteenth-Century Russia*, September 1984, Columbus, Ohio: Slavica Publishers.

Bater, James H., *St Petersburg – Industrialization and Change*, London: Edward Arnold, 1976.

Belinsky, Vissarion, 'The Alexander Theatre', in Nekrasov, *Petersburg: The Physiology of a City*.

—— 'Petersburg and Moscow', in Nekrasov, *Petersburg: The Physiology of a City*.

Bell, John, *Travels from St Petersburg in Russia to Various Parts of Asia*, Vol. 1, Edinburgh, 1788.

Berlin, Isaiah, *Russian Thinkers* (1978, revised 2008), London: Penguin, 2013.

Berman, Marshall, *All That Is Solid Melts into Air*, New York: Simon and Schuster, 1982; Verso pbk, 1983.

Bernstein, Laurie, *Sonia's Daughters – Prostitutes and Their Regulation in Imperial Russia*, Berkeley and Los Angeles: University of California Press, 1995.

Biely, Andrei, *Petersburg* (1916), trans. Robert A. Maguire and John E. Malmstad, Harmondsworth: Penguin, 1978.

Bilbassov, Vasily A., 'The Intellectual Formation of Catherine II' (St Petersburg, 1901), reprinted in Raeff, Marc, ed., *Catherine the Great – A Profile*, London: Macmillan, 1972.

Bird, Alan, *A History of Russian Painting*, Oxford: Phaidon, 1987.

Blair, Fredrika, *Isadora – Portrait of the Artist as a Woman*, Wellingborough, Northampton: Equation, 1987.

Blakesley, Rosalind P., '23 October 1757: The Foundation of the Imperial Academy of Arts', in Cross, *Study Group on Eighteenth-Century Russia – Days from the Reigns of Eighteenth-Century Russian Rulers*, Part 1, Cambridge: Fitzwilliam College, 2007, pp. 109–20.

Bolkhovitinov, Nikolai Nikolaevich, *Russia and the United States – An Analytical Survey of Archival Documents and Historical Studies*, trans. J. D. Hartgrove, Soviet Studies in History, Vol. XXV, No. 2.

Boulton, Jeremy, *Neighbourhood and Society – A London Suburb in the Seventeenth Century*, Cambridge: Cambridge University Press, 1987.

Bowlt, John E., 'Constructivism and Early Soviet Fashion Design', in *Bolshevik Culture*, Bloomington, IN: Indiana University Press, 1985.

—— *Moscow and St Petersburg in Russia's Silver Age*, London: Thames and Hudson, 2008.

Bradbury, Malcolm, *To the Hermitage*, London: Picador, 2002.

Brendon, Piers, *The Dark Valley – A Panorama of the 1930s*, London: Jonathan Cape, 2000.

Breton, M., *La Russie, ou mœurs, usages, et costumes des habitans de toutes les provinces de cet empire*, Vol. I, Paris, 1813.

Brodsky, Joseph, 'A Guide to a Renamed City', in *Less Than One: Selected Essays*, London: Viking, 1986; Penguin Classics, 2011.

Brown, David, *Tchaikovsky Remembered*, London: Faber and Faber, 1993.

Bruijn, Jaap R., *The Dutch Navy of the Seventeenth and Eighteenth Centuries*, Columbia, SC: University of South Carolina Press, 1993.

Brumfield, William Craft, *A History of Russian Architecture*, New York: Cambridge University Press, 1993.

Bryant, Louise, *Six Red Months in Russia – An Observer's Account of Russia Before and During the Proletarian Dictatorship*, London: William Heinemann, 1918.

Buchanan, Sir George, *My Mission to Russia – and Other Diplomatic Memories*, Vols I and II, London: Cassell and Company, 1923.

Buchanan, Meriel, *The Dissolution of an Empire*, London: John Murray, 1932.
—— *Petrograd – The City of Trouble 1914–18*, London: William Collins, 1919.
Buckle, Richard, *Diaghilev*, New York: Atheneum, 1984.
—— *Nijinsky*, Harmondsworth: Penguin, 1980.
Buckler, Julie A., *Mapping St Petersburg – Imperial Text and Cityshape*, Princeton, NJ: Princeton University Press, 2005.
Calland, Deborah, 'The Tsar of Operas', pp. 11–16, notes to Glinka, *Ruslan and Lyudmila*, and Valery Gergiev, in an interview, 'Introducing Ruslan' (bonus feature), Decca DVD, conducted by Valery Gergiev, 1996.
Casanova de Seingalt, Jacques, *The Memoirs*, London, 1894, trans. Arthur Machen, to which have been added the chapters discovered by Arthur Symons, 'Russia and Poland', Vol. XXV, Minneapolis, MN: Filiquarian Publishing, n.d.
Catherine the Great, *The Memoirs of Catherine the Great*, trans. Mark Cruse and Hilde Hoogenboom, New York: Modern Library, 2005; pbk 2006.
Catherine the Great et al., *Authentic Memoirs of the Life and Reign of Catherine II, Empress of all the Russias. Collected from the Authentic MS's. Translations &c. of the King of Sweden, Right Hon. Lord Mountmorres, Lord Malmesbury, M. de Volney, and other indisputable authorities*, London, 1797.
Cattell, David T., 'Soviet Cities and Consumer Welfare Planning', in Hamm, Michael F., *The City in Russian History*, Lexington, KY: University of Kentucky Press, 1976.
Chandler, Robert, Dralyuk, Boris, and Mashinski, Irina, eds, *The Penguin Book of Russian Poetry*, London: Penguin Random House, 2015.
Chernyshevsky, Nikolai, *A Vital Question; or What Is to Be Done?*, trans. Nathan Dole and S. S. Skidelsky, New York: Crowell, 1886.
Clark, Katerina, 'The Russian/Soviet Intelligentsia, Prostitution and the Paradox of Internal Colonization', in *Slavic Studies*, vol. 7, 1993.
—— *Petersburg, Crucible of Cultural Revolution*, Cambridge, MA: Harvard University Press, 1995.
Coleridge, Samuel Taylor, *Collected Poetical Works*, Oxford: Oxford University Press, 1978.
Collins, Samuel. *The Present State of Russia – In a Letter to a Friend at London, Written by an Eminent Person Residing at the Great Czar's Court at Moscow for the Space of Nine Years*, London, 1671, facsimile reprinted in Poe, Marshall, *Early Exploration of Russia*, London and New York: Routledge Curzon, 2003.
Conquest, Robert, *The Great Terror – A Reassessment*, London: Pimlico, 2008.
Cook, John, *Voyages and Travels through the Russian Empire, Tartary and the Empire of Persia*, Vol. I, Edinburgh, 1770.

Cracraft, James, *The Petrine Revolution in Russian Culture*, Cambridge, MA, and London: Belknap Press of Harvard University Press, 2004.

Cross, Anthony, *By the Banks of the Neva – Chapters from the Lives and Careers of the British in Eighteenth-Century Russia*, Cambridge: Cambridge University Press, 1997.

—— '"Crazy Paul": The British and Paul I', in *Reflections on Russia in the Eighteenth Century*, ed. Klein, Dixon and Fraanje, Cologne: Böhlau Verlag, 2001, pp. 7–18.

—— 'The English Embankment', in Cross, ed., *St Petersburg 1703–1825*, Basingstoke and New York: Palgrave Macmillan, 2003.

—— 'Mr Fisher's Company of English Actors in Eighteenth-Century St Petersburg', in Cross, ed., *Study Group on Eighteenth-Century Russia – Newsletter*, No. 4, Norwich, September 1976, pp. 49–56.

—— *Peter the Great Through British Eyes – Perceptions and Representations of the Tsar since 1698*, Cambridge: Cambridge University Press, 2000.

—— ed., *Study Group on Eighteenth-Century Russia Newsletter – Days from the Reigns of Eighteenth-Century Russian Rulers*, Part 1, Proceedings of a workshop dedicated to the memory of Professor Lindsey Hughes held at the Bibliotheca di Storia Contemporanea, 'A. Oriani', Ravenna, 12–13 Sept September 2007, Cambridge: Fitzwilliam College, 2007.

D'Eon de Beaumont, Charles, *The Maiden of Tonnerre – The Vicissitudes of the Chevalier and the Chevalière d'Eon* (containing *The Great Historical Epistle by the Chevalière d'Eon, Written in 1785 to Madame the Duchesse of Montmorenci-Bouteville*), trans. and ed. Champagne, Ekstein and Kates, Baltimore and London: Johns Hopkins University Press, 2001.

Dashwood, Sir Francis, 'Sir Francis Dashwood's Diary of his Visit to St Petersburg in 1733', ed. Betty Kemp, *The Slavonic and East European Review*, Vol. XXXVIII, No. 90, London: University of London, Athlone Press, December 1959, pp. 194–222.

Davies, Sarah, *Popular Opinion in Stalin's Russia*, Cambridge: Cambridge University Press, 1997.

de Custine, Astolphe, *Letters from Russia*, trans. Robin Buss (1991), London: Penguin, 2014.

de Madariaga, Isabel, *Catherine the Great – A Short History*, New Haven, CT, and London: Yale University Press, (1990) 2002.

—— *Russia in the Age of Catherine the Great*, New Haven, CT, and London: Yale University Press, 1981.

de Raymond, Damaze, *Tableau historique, géographique, militaire et moral de l'empire de Russie*, Vol. II, Paris: 1812.

de Staël, Madame, *Mémoires – Dix années d'exil* (first published 1818), Paris: 1861.

Deane, John, 'A Letter from Moscow to the Marquess of Carmarthen

Relating to the Czar of Muscovy's Forwardness in his Great Navy', London, March 1699.

Deschisaux, Pierre, *Description d'un voyage fait à Saint Petersbourg*, Paris: Thiboust, 1728.

Dickens, Charles, *Bleak House* (1853), Harmondsworth: Penguin, 1971.

Dixon, Simon, '30 July 1752: The Opening of the Peter the Great Canal', in Cross, *Study Group on Eighteenth-Century Russia – Days from the Reigns of Eighteenth-Century Russian Rulers*, Part 1, Cambridge: Fitzwilliam College, 2007, pp. 93–107.

—— *Catherine the Great*, New York: HarperCollins, 2009.

Dmytryshyn, Basil, ed., *Imperial Russia – A Source Book 1700–1917*, 2nd edn, Hinsdale, IL: Dryden Press, 1974.

Dobson, George, *St Petersburg*, London: Adam and Charles Black, 1910.

Dostoevsky, Fyodor, *Crime and Punishment*, trans. Constance Garnett, Ware, Hertfordshire: Wordsworth Editions, 2000.

—— *Notes From Underground/The Double*, trans. Jessie Coulson, Harmondsworth: Penguin, 1972.

Dukes, Paul, *The Making of Russian Absolutism 1613–1801*, Harlow and New York: Longman, 1982.

Dukes, (Sir) Paul, *Red Dusk and the Morrow – Adventures and Investigations in Red Russia*, London: Williams and Norgate, 1923.

Dumas, Alexandre, *En Russie – Impressions de voyage* (1859), Paris: Editions François Bourin, 1989.

Eisenstein, Sergei, *Film Essays and a Lecture*, ed. Jay Leyda, NJ: Princeton University Press, 1982.

Engel, Barbara Alpern, *Women in Russia 1700–2000*, Cambridge: Cambridge University Press, 2004.

Ermolaev, Ilya, 'Napoleon's Invasion of Russia', in *Alexander, Napoleon and Joséphine*, Amsterdam: Museumshop Hermitage Amsterdam, 2015.

Evelyn, John, *The Diary of John Evelyn Esq. F.R.S. from 1641–1705–6*, London: Gibbings, 1890.

Faber, Gotthilf Theodor von, *Bagatelles. Promenades d'un désœuvré dans la ville de S.-Pétersbourg*, Vols I and II, Paris: Klosterman and Delaunay, 1812.

Faibisovich, Viktor, 'If I Were Not Napoleon, Perhaps I Would Be Alexander...', in *Alexander, Napoleon and Joséphine*, Amsterdam: Museumshop Hermitage Amsterdam, 2015.

Fedorov, Vyacheslav, 'Theatre and Music in Court Life', in *At the Russian Court – Palace and Protocol in the 19th Century*, Amsterdam: Museumshop Hermitage Amsterdam, 2009.

Figes, Orlando, *Revolutionary Russia – 1891–1991*, London: Penguin, 2014.

Figner, Vera, *Memoirs of a Revolutionist*, DeKalb, IL: Northern Illinois Press, 1991.

Fitzlyon, Kyril, and Browning, Tatiana, *Before the Revolution*, Harmondsworth: Penguin, 1977.

Fitzpatrick, Sheila, *The Commissariat of Enlightenment – Soviet Orga-nization of Education and the Arts under Lunacharsky, October 1917–1921*, Cambridge: Cambridge University Press, 1970.

Francis, David R., *Russia from the American Embassy – April 1916–November 1918*, New York: Charles Scribner's Sons, 1921.

Frank, Joseph, *Dostoevsky – A Writer in His Time*, ed. Mary Petrusewicz, Princeton, NJ, and Oxford: Princeton University Press, 2010.

Frierson, Cathy A., *All Russia is Burning! A Cultural History of Fire and Arson in Late Imperial Russia*, Seattle and London: University of Washington Press, 2002.

Fuhrmann, Joseph T., *Rasputin – A Life*, New York: Praeger, 1990.

Galitzin, Le Prince Augustin, *La Russie au XVIIIe Siècle*, Paris, 1863.

Gautier, Théophile, *The Complete Works – Vol. VII: Travels in Russia*, trans. and ed. S. C. De Sumichrast, Athenaeum Press, reprinted by For-gotten Books, n.d.

Gerasimova, Julia, *The Iconostasis of Peter the Great in the Peter and Paul Cathedral in St Petersburg (1722–9)*, Leiden: Alexandros Press, 2004.

Gide, André, *Back From the USSR*, London: Secker and Warburg, 1937.

Ginzburg, Lydia, *Blockade Diary*, trans. Alan Myers, London: Harvill Press, 1995.

Giroud, Vincent, *St Petersburg – A Portrait of a Great City*, New Haven, CT: Yale University – The Beinecke Rare Book and Manuscript Library, 2003.

Glendenning, P. H., 'Admiral Sir Charles Knowles in Russia 1771–1774', in 'Synopses of Papers Read at the 12th Meeting of the Study Group – University of Leeds, 15–16 December 1973', in *Study Group on Eigh-teenth Century Russia – Newsletter*, No. 2, Norwich, 1974, pp. 8–12.

Gogol, Nikolai, *Dead Souls*, trans. Christopher English, Oxford: Oxford World's Classics, 1998.

—— 'Nevsky Prospekt', in *Diary of a Madman, The Government Inspec-tor and Selected Stories*, trans. Ronald Wilks, London: Penguin, 2005.

—— 'Nevsky Prospekt', in *Petersburg Tales*, trans. Dora O'Brien, Rich-mond, Surrey: Alma Classics, 2014.

Goldman, Emma, *Living My Life*, Vol. II, London: Pluto Press, 1988.

Gooding, John, *Rulers and Subjects – Government and People in Russia 1801–1991*, London: Arnold, 1996.

Gray, Camilla, *The Russian Experiment in Art 1863–1922 (1962)*, revised and enlarged by Marian Burleigh-Motley, London: Thames and Hudson, 1986.

Gray, Rosalind P., *Russian Genre Paintings in the Nineteenth Century*, Oxford: Clarendon Press, 2000.

Grebenka, Evgeny, 'The Petersburg Quarter' (1844), in Nekrasov, *Peters-burg: The Physiology of a City*.

Gregory, John, and Ukladnikov, Alexander, *Leningrad's Ballet*, Croesor, Gwynned: Zena Publications, 1990.

Guseva, Natalya, 'The "New Style" in Russian Interiors', in *Art Nouveau*

– *During the Reign of the Last Tsars*, Aldershot: Lund Humphries, 2007.

Hanway, Jonas, *An Historical Account of the British Trade Over the Caspian Sea with a Journal of Travels*, Vols I and II, London: Dodesley, 1753.

Harding, Luke, *The Mafia State*, London: Guardian Books, 2012.

Hare, Richard, *Pioneers of Russian Social Thought*, Oxford: Oxford University Press, 1951.

Harris, Steven E., 'Soviet Mass Housing and the Communist Way of Life', in Chatterjee, Ransel, Cavender and Petrone, eds, *Everyday Life in Russia Past and Present*, Bloomington and Indianapolis, IN: Indiana University Press, 2015.

Hartley, Janet M., *Alexander I*, London and New York: Longman, 1994.

—— 'Governing the City: St Petersburg and Catherine II's Reforms', in Cross, ed., *St Petersburg 1703–1825*, Basingstoke and New York: Palgrave Macmillan, 2003.

Herzen, Alexander, *My Past and Thoughts – The Memoirs of Alexander Herzen*, trans. Constance Garnett, revised by Humphrey Higgens, New York: Knopf, 1973.

Hessler, Julie, *A Social History of Soviet Trade – Trade Policy, Retail Practices and Consumption – 1917–1953*, Princeton, NJ: Princeton University Press, 2004.

Hittle, Michael J., *The Service City – State and Townsmen in Russia 1600–1800*, Cambridge, MA: Harvard University Press, 1979.

Hoare, Prince, *Extracts from a Correspondence with the Academies of Vienna and St Petersburg on the Cultivation of the Arts of Painting, Sculpture and Architecture in the Austrian and Russian Dominions*, London: White, Payne and Hatchard, 1802.

Holquist, Peter, 'Violent Russia, Deadly Marxism? Russia in the Epoch of Violence 1905–21', in Kocho-Williams, Alastair, ed., *The Twentieth Century Russian Reader*, Abingdon: Routledge, 2011.

Hosking, Geoffrey, *Russia and the Russians – A History*, Cambridge, MA: Belknap Press of Harvard University Press, 2001.

Hughes, Lindsey, 'Architectural Books in Petrine Russia', in *Russia and the West in the Eighteenth Century – Proceedings of the Second International Conference Organized by the Study Group on Eighteenth-Century Russia and Held at the University of East Anglia*, Norwich, 17–22 July 1981, pp. 101–8.

—— '"For the Health of the Sons of Ivan Mikhailovich": I. M. Golovin and Peter the Great's Mock Court', in *Reflections on Russia in the Eighteenth Century*, ed. Klein, Dixon and Fraanje, Cologne: Böhlau Verlag, 2001, pp. 43–51.

—— 'Images of Greatness: Portraits of Peter the Great', in Hughes, *Peter the Great and the West*, pp. 250–70.

—— ed., *Peter the Great and the West – New Perspectives*, Basingstoke and New York: Palgrave, 2001.

—— *Russia in the Age of Peter the Great*, New Haven, CT, and London: Yale University Press, 1998.

—— *Russia and the West, The Life of a Seventeenth-Century Westernizer, Prince Vasily Vasilevich Golitsyn (1643–1714)*. Newtonville, MA: Oriental Research Partners, 1984.

—— *Sophia, Regent of Russia 1657–1704*, New Haven, CT, and London: Yale University Press, 1990.

Ilchester, the Earl of, and Mrs Langford-Brooke, eds and trans., *Correspondence of Catherine the Great when Grand-Duchess with Sir Charles Hanbury-Williams and Letters from Count Poniatowski*, London: Thornton Butterworth, 1928.

Irwin, David, *Neoclassicism*, London: Phaidon, 1997.

Jackman, S. W., *Romanov Relations – The Private Correspondence of Tsars Alexander I, Nicholas I and the Grand Dukes Constantine and Michael with their Sister Queen Anna Pavlovna*, London: Macmillan, 1969.

Johnson, Emily D., *How St Petersburg Learned to Study Itself*, University Park, PA: Pennsylvania State University Press, 2006.

Jones, Robert E., *Bread Upon the Waters – The St Petersburg Grain Trade and the Russian Economy, 1703–1811*. Pittsburgh, PA: University of Pittsburgh Press, 2013.

—— 'Why St Petersburg?', in Hughes, *Peter the Great and the West*, pp. 189–205.

Jones, W. Gareth, 'Catherine the Great's Understanding of the "Gothic"', in *Reflections on Russia in the Eighteenth Century*, ed. Klein, Dixon and Fraanje, Cologne: Böhlau Verlag, 2001, pp. 233–40.

Jukes, Peter, *A Shout in the Street – The Modern City London*, London: Faber and Faber, 1990.

Justice, Elizabeth, *A Voyage to Russia: Describing the Laws, Manners and Customs of that Great Empire as Governed at this Present by that Excellent Princess, the Czarina*, York, 1739.

Kahn, Albert E., *Days with Ulanova*, London: William Collins, 1962.

Kandinsky, Vasily, *Concerning the Spiritual in Art*, trans. M. T. H. Sadler, New York: Dover Publications, 1977.

Karsavina, Tamara, *Theatre Street* (1948), London: Columbus Books, 1988.

Kavanagh, Julie, *Rudolf Nureyev – The Life*, London: Penguin, 2008.

Keenan, Paul, '23 December 1742: Elizaveta Petrovna's Ceremonial Entry into St Petersburg', in Cross, *Study Group on Eighteenth-Century Russia – Days from the Reigns of Eighteenth-Century Russian Rulers*, Part 1, Cambridge: Fitzwilliam College, 2007, pp. 79–91.

—— *St Petersburg and the Russian Court 1703–1761*, London and New York: Palgrave Macmillan, 2013.

Kelly, Catriona, *St Petersburg – Shadows of the Past*, New Haven, CT, and London: Yale University Press, 2014.

Kelly, Laurence, *Lermontov – Tragedy in the Caucasus*, London: Constable, 1977.

Kirshchenbaum, Lisa A., *The Legacy of the Siege of Leningrad 1941–1995:*

*Myth, Memories and Monuments*, Cambridge and New York: Cambridge University Press, 2006.

Kizevetter, Alexandr A., 'Portrait of an Enlightened Autocrat' (Berlin 1931), in Raeff, Marc, ed., *Catherine the Great – A Profile*, London: Macmillan, 1972.

Klier, John Doyle, *Imperial Russia's Jewish Question 1855–1881*, Cambridge: Cambridge University Press, 1995.

Knightley, Phillip, *The Second Oldest Profession – Spies and Spying in the Twentieth Century*, London: Pimlico, 2003.

Koestler, Arthur, *The Invisible Writing – The Second Volume of an Autobiography 1932–40* (1954), London: Random House, 2005.

—— *Scum of the Earth*, trans. Daphne Hardy, London: Victor Gollancz, 1941.

Kokovtsov, Count, *Out of my Past – The Memoirs of Count Kokovtsov*, trans. Laura Matveev, Stanford, CA: Stanford University Press, 1935.

Kollmann, Nancy S., '27 October 1698: Peter Punishes the Streltsy', in Cross, *Study Group on Eighteenth-Century Russia – Days from the Reigns of Eighteenth Century Russian Rulers*, Part 1, Cambridge: Fitzwilliam College, 2007, pp. 23–35.

Korb, Johann Georg, *Diary of an Austrian Secretary of Legation at the Court of the Czar Peter the Great*, trans. from the Latin by the Count MacDonnell, London: Bradbury and Evans, 1863; facsimile edn, London: Routledge Curzon, 2003.

Korshunova, Tamara, 'Whims of Fashion', in *At the Russian Court – Palace and Protocol in the 19th Century*, Amsterdam: Museumshop Hermitage Amsterdam, 2009.

Kotzbuë, Auguste de, *L'année la plus remarquable de ma vie*, Paris, 1802.

Kratter, Franz, *The Maid of Marienburg – A Drama in Five Acts. From the German of Kratter*, London, 1798.

Krupskaya, Nadezhda K., *Memories of Lenin*, trans. E. Verney, New York: International Publishers, 1930.

La Mottraye, Aubry de, *Voyages en Anglois et en François D'A. de La Motraye en diverses provinces et places*, London, 1732.

La Neuville, F. de, *An Account of Muscovy as it Was in the Year 1689*, London, 1699.

Lauchlan, Iain, *Russian Hide-and-Seek – The Tsarist Secret Police in St Petersburg 1906–14*, Helsinki: SKS-FLS, 2002.

le Carré, John, *The Secret Pilgrim*, London: Sceptre, 1991; pbk 2009.

Ledeneva, Alena V., *Russia's Economy of Favours: Blat, Networking and Informal Favours*, Cambridge: Cambridge University Press, 1998.

Leichtenhan, Francine-Dominique, *Élisabeth Ire de Russie*, Paris: Fayard, 2007.

Leino, Minna, and Klemelä, Ulla, 'Field Research of the Maritime Museum of Finland at the Wreck Site of Vrouw Maria in 2001–2002', in *Moss Newsletter*, Helsinki, 2003.

Lenin, V. I., *What Is to Be Done?* (1902), New York: International Publishers, 1929.

Lermontov, Mikhail, *A Hero of Our Time* (1840), trans. and introd. Paul Foote, Harmondsworth: Penguin, 1966.

Lewitter, L. R., 'Ivan Tikhonovich Pososhkov (1652–1726) and "The Spirit of Capitalism"', in *The Slavonic and East European Review*, Vol. LI, No. 125, October 1973, London: University College London, pp. 524–53.

Liackhova, Lydia, 'Items from the Green Frog Service', in *Dining with the Tsars*, Amsterdam: Museumshop Hermitage Amsterdam, 2014.

Lincoln, W. Bruce, 'The Daily Life of St Petersburg Officials in the Mid Nineteenth Century', in *Oxford Slavonic Papers*, ed. Fennell and Foote, New Series, Vol. VIII, Oxford: Clarendon Press, 1975, pp. 82–100.

—— *Nicholas I: Emperor and Autocrat of All Russias*, London: Allen Lane, 1978.

Lissitzky, El, *Russia: An Architecture for World Revolution*, Cambridge, MA: MIT Press, 1984.

Lockhart, R. H. Bruce, *Memoirs of a British Agent*, London: Putnam, 1934.

Longworth, Philip, *The Three Empresses – Catherine I, Anne and Elizabeth of Russia*, New York: Holt, Rinehart and Winston, 1972.

Loukomski, George, *Charles Cameron (1740–1812)*, London: Nicholson and Watson, Commodore Press, 1943.

McAuley, Mary, *Bread and Justice – State and Society in Petrograd 1917–22*, Oxford: Clarendon Press, 1991.

—— *Soviet Politics – 1917–19*, Oxford: Oxford University Press, 1992.

McBurney, Erin, 'The Portrait Iconography of Catherine the Great: An Introduction', in *Study Group on Eighteenth-Century Russia – Newsletter*, No. 34, Cambridge, July 2006, pp. 22–7.

Macdonald, Hugh, *The Master Musicians – Berlioz*, Oxford: Oxford University Press, 1982; pbk 2000.

MacDonald, Ian, *The New Shostakovitch*, new edn revised by Raymond Clarke, London: Pimlico, 2006.

McGrew, Roderick E., *Paul I of Russia 1754–1801*, Oxford: Clarendon Press, 1992.

—— *Russia and the Cholera 1823–1832*, Madison and Milwaukee, WI: University of Wisconsin Press, 1965.

McKean, Robert B., *St Petersburg Between the Revolutions*, New Haven, CT, and London: Yale University Press, 1990.

McKellar, Elizabeth, *The Birth of Modern London – The Development and Design of the City 1660–1720*, Manchester: Manchester University Press, 1999.

Maes, Francis, *A History of Russian Music*, trans. Arnold J. Pomerans and Erica Pomerans, Berkeley, CA: University of California Press, 2002; pbk 2006.

Mandelstam, Osip, *The Noise of Time*, trans. Clarence Brown, London and New York: Quartet Books, 1988.

—— *Osip Mandelstam Selected Poems* (1973), trans. Clarence Brown, Harmondsworth: Penguin, 1977.

Manstein, General, *Memoirs of Russia, Historical, Political and Military*, London, 1770.

Marker, Gary, 'Godly and Pagan Women in the Coronation Sermon of 1724', in Bartlett and Lehmann-Carli, eds, *Eighteenth-Century Russia: Society, Culture, Economy – Papers from the VII International Conference of the Study Group on Eighteenth-Century Russia, Wittenberg, 2004*, Berlin: Lit Verlag, 2008, pp. 207–20.

—— *Publishing, Printing and the Origins of Intellectual Life in Russia, 1700–1800*, Princeton, NJ: Princeton University Press, 1985.

Marsden, Christopher, *Palmyra of the North – The First Days of St Petersburg*, London: Faber and Faber, 1942.

Marye, George Thomas, *Nearing the End in Imperial Russia*, London: Selwyn and Blount, 1928.

Massie, Robert K., *Peter the Great – His Life and World*, Knopf, 1980; Head of Zeus pbk, 2013.

Meshikova, Maria, 'Chinese Masquerade', in *At the Russian Court – Palace and Protocol in the 19th Century*, Amsterdam: Museumshop Hermitage Amsterdam, 2009.

Milner-Gulland, Robin, '16 May 1703: The Petersburg Foundation-Myth', in Cross, *Study Group on Eighteenth-Century Russia – Days from the Reigns of Eighteenth Century Russian Rulers*, Part 1, Cambridge: Fitzwilliam College, 2007, pp. 37–47.

Monas, Sidney, *The Third Section – Police and Society in Russia under Nicholas I*, Cambridge, MA: Harvard University Press, 1961.

Montefiore, Simon Sebag, *The Romanovs 1613–1918*, London: Weidenfeld and Nicolson, 2016.

Mottley, John, *The History of the Life of Peter I, Emperor of Russia*, Vol. II, London, 1739.

—— *The History of the Life and Reign of the Empress Catherine*, Vols I and II, London, 1744.

Moynahan, Brian, *Rasputin: The Saint Who Sinned*, New York: Random House, 1997.

Mukhina, Lena, *The Diary of Lena Mukhina – A Girl's Life in the Siege of Leningrad*, London: Pan Macmillan, 2016.

Münnich, Comte Ernest de, *Mémoires sur la Russie de Pierre le Grand à Elisabeth Ire (1720–42)*, trans. Francis Ley, Paris: Harmattan, 1997.

Munro, George E., 'Compiling and Maintaining St Petersburg's "Book of City Inhabitants": The "Real" City Inhabitants', in Cross, ed., *St Petersburg 1703–1825*, Basingstoke and New York: Palgrave Macmillan, 2003.

—— *The Most Intentional City – St Petersburg in the Reign of Catherine the Great*, Cranbury, NJ: Associated University Presses, 2010.

—— 'Politics, Sexuality and Servility: The Debate Between Catherine the Great and the Abbé Chappe d'Auteroche', in *Russia and the West in the Eighteenth Century – Proceedings of the Second International*

*Conference Organized by the Study Group on Eighteenth-Century Russia and Held at the University of East Anglia*, Norwich, 17–22 July 1981, pp. 124–34.

Nabokov, Vladimir, *Speak Memory* (1947), London: Penguin, 2000.

Nekrasov, Nikolai, ed. Thomas Gaiton Marullo, *Petersburg: The Physiology of a City (Fitziologiia Peterburga)* (1845), trans. Thomas Gaiton Marullo, Evanston, IL: Northwestern University Press, 2009.

—— 'The Petersburg Corners', in Nekrasov, *Petersburg: The Physiology of a City*.

Neuberger, Joan, *Hooliganism – Crime, Culture and Power in St Petersburg, 1900–14*, Berkeley, CA: University of California Press, 1993.

Neville, Peter, *Russia: A Complete History – The USSR, the CIS and the Independent States in One Volume*, London: Phoenix, 2003.

Nijinsky, Romola, *Nijinsky*, London: Victor Gollancz, 1940.

Nijinsky, Vaslav, *The Diary of Vaslav Nijinsky*, ed. Romola Nijinsky, Berkeley, CA: University of California Press, 1968.

Nisbet Bain, R. *The Daughter of Peter the Great*, London: Constable, 1899.

Norman, Geraldine, *The Hermitage – The Biography of a Great Museum*, London: Jonathan Cape, 1997.

O'Meara, Patrick, '*Vreden sever*: The Decembrists' Memories of the Peter and Paul Fortress', in Cross, ed., *St Petersburg 1703–1825*, Basingstoke and New York: Palgrave Macmillan, 2003.

Ospovat, Kirill, 'Alexandr Sumarokov and the Social Status of Russian Literature in the 1750s–60s', in *Study Group on Eighteenth Russia – Newsletter*, No. 33, Cambridge, November 2005, pp. 24–30.

Ostrovsky, Arkady, *The Invention of Russia – The Journey from Gorbachev's Freedom to Putin's War*, London: Atlantic Books, 2016.

Parkinson, John, *A Tour of Russia, Siberia and the Crimea*, London: Routledge, 1971.

Paul Jones, John, *Memoirs of Rear Admiral Paul Jones*, Vol. I, Edinburgh and London, 1830.

Pavlov, Dmitri V., *Leningrad 1941 – The Blockade*, trans. John Clinton Adams, Chicago, IL: Chicago University Press, 1965.

Pavlova, Anna, 'Pages of My Life', in Franks, A. H., ed., *Pavlova – A Collection of Memoirs*, a reprint of *Pavlova: A Biography*, London, 1956; New York: DaCapo, n.d.

Perry, Captain John, *The State of Russia under the Present Czar*, London: Benjamin Tooke, 1716.

Piotrovsky, B. B., and Suslov, V. A., introduction, in Eisler, Colin, *Paintings in the Hermitage*, New York: Stewart, Tabori and Chang, 1990.

Pipes, Richard, *The Russian Revolution*, New York: Alfred A. Knopf, 1990.

Plotnikova, Yulia, 'Children of the Emperor', in *At the Russian Court – Palace and Protocol in the 19th Century*, Amsterdam: Museumshop Hermitage Amsterdam, 2009.

Pope-Hennessy, Dame Una Birch, *The Closed City: Impressions of a Visit to Leningrad*, London: Hutchinson, 1938.

Poretsky, Elisabeth K., *Our Own People: A Memoir of 'Ignace Reiss' and His Friends*, London: Oxford University Press, 1969.

Porter, Robert Ker, *Travelling Sketches in Russia and Sweden during the Years 1805, 1806, 1807, 1808*, Vols I and II, London: Richard Phillips, 1809.

Prak, Maarten, *The Dutch Republic in the Seventeenth Century*, trans. Diane Webb, Cambridge: Cambridge University Press, 2006.

Printseva, Galina, 'The Imperial Hunt', in *At the Russian Court – Palace and Protocol in the 19th Century*, Amsterdam: Museumshop Hermitage Amsterdam, 2009.

Proskurina, Vera, *Creating the Empress – Politics and Poetry in the Age of Catherine II*, Brighton, MA: Academic Studies Press, 2011.

Pushkin, Alexander, 'The Bronze Horseman: A Petersburg Tale', in *The Penguin Book of Russian Poetry*, ed. Chandler, Dralyuk and Mashinski, London: Penguin Random House, 2015.

——— *Eugene Onegin – A Novel in Verse*, trans. Stanley Mitchell, London: Penguin, 2008.

——— *The Queen of Spades and Other Stories*, trans. Rosemary Edmonds, London: Penguin, 2004.

Radishchev, Alexandr Nikolaevich, *A Journey from St Petersburg to Moscow*, trans. Leo Wiener, ed. Roderick Page Thaler, Cambridge, MA: Harvard University Press, 1958.

Radzinsky, Edvard, *Alexander II – The Last Great Tsar*, trans. Antonina W. Bouis, New York: Free Press, 2005.

Raeff, Marc, *Origins of the Russian Intelligentsia*, San Diego, New York and London: Harcourt Brace, 1966.

Ransome, Arthur, *The Crisis in Russia 1920*, London: George Allen and Unwin, 1921.

Rappe, Tamara, 'Alexander at Malmaison. Malmaison in Russia', in *Alexander, Napoleon and Joséphine*, Amsterdam: Museumshop Hermitage Amsterdam, 2015.

——— 'Art and Diplomacy in the Reign of Alexander III and Nicholas II', in 'Russian Interiors' in *Art Nouveau – During the Reign of the Last Tsars*, Aldershot: Lund Humphries, 2007.

Rappoport, Angelo S., *The Curse of the Romanovs*, London: Chatto and Windus, 1907.

Read, Christopher, *Culture and Power in Revolutionary Russia*, Basingstoke: Macmillan, 1990.

Redesdale, Lord, *Memories*, Vol. I, London: Hutchinson, 1915.

Reed, John, *Ten Days that Shook the World* (1919), London: Penguin, 1977.

Reid, Anna, *Leningrad – Tragedy of a City Under Siege*, London: Bloomsbury, 2011; pbk 2012.

Rice, Tamara Talbot, 'Charles Cameron', in *Charles Cameron c.1740–1812*, London: Arts Council, 1967–8.

Richard, John, *A Tour from London to Petersburgh*, London, 1780.

Richardson, William, *Anecdotes of the Russian Empire in a Series of Letters Written a Few Years Ago from St Petersburg*, London, 1784.

Rimsky-Korsakov, Nikolai Andreyevich, *My Musical Life*, trans. from the 5th revised Russian edition by Judah A. Joffe, London: Eulenburg Books, 1974.

Robinson, Harlow, 'Composing for Victory – Classical Music', in Stites, Richard, ed., *Culture and Entertainment in Wartime Russia*, Bloomington and Indianapolis, IN: Indiana University Press, 1995.

Roland, Betty, *Caviar for Breakfast*, Melbourne: Quartet Books, 1979.

Rosen, Baron, *Forty Years of Diplomacy*, Vols I and II, London: George Allen and Unwin, 1922.

Rosslyn, Wendy, 'Petersburg Actresses On and Off Stage (1775–1825)', in Cross, ed., *St Petersburg 1703–1825*, Basingstoke and New York: Palgrave Macmillan, 2003.

——— 'The Prehistory of Russian Actresses: Women on the Stage in Russia (1704–1757)', in Bartlett and Lehmann-Carli, eds, *Eighteenth-Century Russia: Society, Culture, Economy – Papers from the VII International Conference of the Study Group on Eighteenth-Century Russia, Wittenberg, 2004*, Berlin: Lit Verlag, 2008, pp. 69–81.

Rousset de Missy, Jean, *Memoires du Regne de Catherine, Imperatrice et Souveraine de toute la Russie &c. &c. &c.*, Amsterdam, 1728.

Ryan, W. F., 'Peter the Great and English Maritime Technology', in Hughes, *Peter the Great and the West*, pp. 130–58.

Sablinsky, Walter, *The Road to Bloody Sunday – Father Gapon and the St Petersburg Massacre of 1905*, Princeton, NJ: Princeton University Press, 1976.

Sadovnikov, Vasily, reproductions by Ivanov I., Ivanov, P., *Panorama of Nevsky Prospekt. First published by A. Prévost between 1830–5*, Leningrad: Aurora Art Publishers, 1974.

Schama, Simon, *The Embarrassment of Riches*. London: Collins, 1987.

Schenker, Alexander M., *The Bronze Horseman – Falconet's Monument to Peter-the-Great*, New Haven, CT, and London: Yale University Press, 2003.

Schlafly Jr, Daniel L. 'Filippo Balatri in Peter the Great's Russia', in *Jahrbücher für Geschichte Osteuropas*, Neue Folge, Bd. 45, H. 2, 1997, pp. 181–98.

Schönle, Andreas, *The Ruler in the Garden – Politics and Landscape Design in Imperial Russia*, Bern and Oxford: Peter Lang, 2007.

Schuyler, Eugene, *Peter the Great – Emperor of Russia*, Vols I and II, New York: Charles Scribner's Sons, 1884.

Scudder, Jared W., *Russia in the Summer of 1914*, Boston: Richard Badger, 1920.

Seaman, Gerald, 'Catherine the Great and Musical Enlightenment', in *Study Group on Eighteenth-Century Russia – Newsletter*, No. 19, Cambridge, September 1991, pp. 13–14.

Serge, Victor, *Memoirs of a Revolutionary*, trans. Peter Sedgwick, Oxford: Oxford University Press, 1975.

Service, Robert, *The Penguin History of Modern Russia – From Tsarism to the Twenty-First Century*, London: Penguin Random House, 4th edn 2015.

Seton-Watson, Hugh, *The Russian Empire 1801–17*, Oxford: Clarendon Press, 1967.

Shapiro, Yuri, *The Hermitage*, Moscow: Progress Publishers, 1976.

Shklovsky, Viktor, *A Sentimental Journey – Memoirs 1917–22*, trans. Richard Sheldon, Ithaca, NY, and London: Cornell University Press, 1970.

Shrad, Mark Lawrence, *Vodka Politics – Alcohol, Autocracy, and the Secret History of the Russian State*, New York: Oxford University Press, 2014.

Shvidkovsky, Dmitry, 'Catherine the Great's Field of Dreams: Architecture and Landscape in the Russian Enlightenment', in Cracraft, James, and Rowland, Daniel, eds, *Architectures of Russian Identities 1500 to the Present*, Ithaca, NY, and London: Cornell University Press, 2003, pp. 51–65.

—— *Russian Architecture and the West*, trans. Anthony Wood, New Haven, CT, and London: Yale University Press, 2007.

—— *St Petersburg – Architecture of the Tsars*, New York, London and Paris: Abbeville Press, 1996.

Simmons, Cynthia, and Perlina, Nina, *Writing the Siege of Leningrad – Women's Diaries, Memoirs and Documentary Prose*, Pittsburgh, PA: University of Pittsburgh Press, 2002.

Smith, Alexandra, 'Pushkin's Imperial Image of Saint Petersburg Revisited', in Reid, Robert, and Andrew, Joe, eds, *Two Hundred Years of Pushkin*, Studies in Slavic Literature and Poetics, Vol. XXXIX, Amsterdam and New York: Editions Rodopi, 2003.

Smith, Hedrick, *The Russians*, New York: Ballantine Books, revised edn 1984.

Soloviev, Sergei M., *A History of Russia, Vol. 34: Empress Anna, Favorites, Policies, Campaigns*, trans. Walter J. Gleason, Gulf Breeze, FL: Academic International Press, 1984.

—— *A History of Russia, Vol. 37: Empress Elizabeth's Reign 1741–44*, trans. Patrick O'Meara, Gulf Breeze, FL: Academic International Press, 1996.

Solovyov, Alexander, 'St Petersburg – Imperial City', in *At the Russian Court – Palace and Protocol in the 19th Century*, Amsterdam: Museumshop Hermitage Amsterdam, 2009.

Solzhenitsyn, Aleksandr, 'The City on the Neva', in *Stories and Prose Poems*, trans. Michael Glenny, New York: Farrar, Straus and Giroux, 1971.

Spring Rice, Sir Cecil, *The Letters and Friendships of Sir Cecil Spring*

*Rice*, Vols I and II, ed. Stephen Gwynn, Boston and New York: Houghton Mifflin, 1929.

Spruit, Ruud, 'In the Service of Napoleon – Experiences of Dutch Soldiers', in *Alexander, Napoleon and Joséphine*, Amsterdam: Museumshop Hermitage Amsterdam, 2015.

Stasov, Vladimir Vasilevich, *Selected Essays on Music*, trans. Florence Jonas, London: Cresset Press, 1968.

Steinberg, Isaac N., *In the Workshop of the Revolution*, London: Victor Gollancz, 1955.

Stites, Richard, *Russian Popular Culture – Entertainment and Society Since 1900*, Cambridge: Cambridge University Press, 1992.

—— *The Women's Liberation Movement in Russia – Feminism, Nihilism and Bolshevism 1860–1930*, Princeton, NJ: Princeton University Press, 1978.

Storch, Henry, from the German of *The Picture of Petersburg*, London, 1801.

Stravinsky, Igor, and Craft, Robert, *Expositions and Developments*, London: Faber and Faber, 1962.

—— *Memories and Commentaries*, London: Faber and Faber, 1960.

Swann, Herbert, *Home on the Neva: A Life of a British Family in Tsarist St Petersburg – and After the Revolution*, London: Victor Gollancz, 1968.

Swinton, A., *Travels into Norway, Denmark, and Russia in the Years 1788, 1789, 1790, and 1791*, London, 1792.

Tarasova, Lina, 'Festivities at the Russian Court', in *At the Russian Court – Palace and Protocol in the 19th Century*, Amsterdam: Museumshop Hermitage Amsterdam, 2009.

Taylor, D. J., 'The Chevalier d'Éon de Beaumont in Petersburg 1756–60: An Observer of Elisaveta Petrovna's Russia', in *Study Group on Eighteenth-Century Russia – Newsletter*, No. 6, Norwich, September 1978, pp. 40–54.

Taylor, Richard, 'The Birth of the Soviet Cinema', in Gleason, Kenez and Stites, eds, *Bolshevik Culture: Experiment and Order in the Russian Revolution*, Bloomington, IN: Indiana University Press, 1985.

Thurston, Robert W., *Life and Terror in Stalin's Russia 1934–1941*, New Haven, CT, and London: Yale University Press, 1996.

Tolstoy, Leo, *War and Peace* (1869), trans. Rosemary Edmonds, Harmondsworth: Penguin, 1975.

Tooke, William, *View of the Russian Empire during the Reign of Catherine the Second and to the Close of the Eighteenth Century*, Vols I and II, London: Longman and Rees, 1800.

Toomre, Joyce S., 'Sumarokov's Adaptation of Hamlet and the "To Be or Not to Be" Soliloquy', in *Study Group on Eighteenth-Century Russia – Newsletter*, No. 9, Leeds, September 1981, pp. 3–20.

Turgenev, Ivan, *Fathers and Sons*, trans. Rosemary Edmonds, Harmondsworth: Penguin, 1965.

Ulam, Adam B., *Stalin – The Man and his Era*, London: Allen Lane, 1974.

Van Wonzel, Pieter, *État Présent de la Russie*, St Petersburg and Leipzig, 1783.

Vernadsky, George, ed., *A Source Book for Russian History From Early*

*Times to 1917*, Vol II, New Haven, CT, and London: Yale University Press, 1972.

Vigor, Mrs (married to Claudius Rondeau), *Letters from a Lady who Resided Some Years in Russia to her Friend in England*, London: Dodsley, 1775.

Vilensky, Jan, 'Cameo Service – 1778–9', in *Dining with the Tsars*, Amsterdam: Museumshop Hermitage Amsterdam, 2014.

Voltaire, *Histoire de Charles XII* (1731), in *Œuvres historiques*, ed. R. Pomeau, Paris: Gallimard, 1957.

von Strahlenberg, Philip John, *An Historico-Geographical Description of the North and Eastern Parts of Europe and Asia*, London, 1738.

Walker, James, *Paramythia or Mental Pastimes*, London, 1821, pp. 27–152 of *Engraved in the Memory*, ed. Anthony Cross, Providence, RI, and Oxford: Berg, 1993.

Warner, Elizabeth, *Russian Myths*, London: British Museum Press, 2002.

Wcislo, Francis W., *Tales of Imperial Russia – The Life and Times of Sergei Witte 1849–1915*, Oxford: Oxford University Press.

Wells, H. G., *Russia in the Shadows*, London: Hodder and Stoughton, n.d.

Whitworth, Lord Charles, *An Account of Russia as it Was in the Year 1710*, Strawberry Hill, 1758.

Wilmot, Martha and Catherine, *The Russian Journals of Martha and Catherine Wilmot – 1803–08*, ed. Marchioness of Londonderry and H. M. Hyde, London: Macmillan, 1934.

Wilson, Arthur M., *Diderot*, New York: Oxford University Press, 1972.

Wolkonsky, Princess Peter, *The Way of Bitterness: Soviet Russia, 1920*, London: Methuen, 1931.

Wortman, Richard S., *Scenarios of Power – Myth and Ceremony in Russian Monarchy*, Vols I and II, Princeton, NJ: Princeton University Press, 1995 and 2000.

Wraxall, N., Jun., *A Tour Through Some of the Northern Parts of Europe Particularly Copenhagen, Stockholm and Petersburg in a Series of Letters*, 3rd edn, London: Cadell, 1776.

Yarmolinsky, Avrahm, *Road to Revolution – A Century of Russian Radicalism*. Princeton, NJ: Princeton University Press, 1986.

Yevtushenko, Yevgeny, 'The City With Three Faces', in *Insight Guides – St Petersburg*, Hong Kong: Apa Publications, 1992.

Zelnik, Reginald E., *Labor and Society in Tsarist Russia – The Factory Workers of St Petersburg 1855–1870*, Stanford, CA: Stanford University Press, 1971.

Zuckerman, Frederic S., *The Tsarist Secret Police in Russian Society, 1880–1917*, Basingstoke: Macmillan, 1996.

## FILMS

Balabanov, Aleksei, writer and dir., *Brat (Brother)*, Kinokompaniya CTB, Gorky Film Studios, Roskomkino, 1997, DVD 2003, Tartan Video.

—— writer and dir., *Of Freaks and Men*, CTB Film Company, 1998.

Dovzhenko, Alexander, dir., *War Trilogy (Zvenigora, Arsenal, Earth)*, 1928–30.

Eisenstein, Sergei, dir., *Alexander Nevsky*, 1938.

—— *The Battleship Potempkin*, First Goskino Production, 1925.

—— *October 1917 (Ten Days That Shook the World)*, Sovkino Productions, 1928.

*Ivanaov*, Mosfilm, 1982, viewable on YouTube.

Khrzhanovskiy, Andrei, dir., *A Room and a Half*, Yume Pictures, 2008.

Pudovkin, Vsevolod, dir., *The End of St Petersburg*, Mezhrabpom, 1927.

—— *Storm Over Asia*, Mezhrabpom, 1928.

Sokurov, Alexander, dir., *Russian Ark*, The State Hermitage Museum, Ministry of Culture of the Russian Federation et al., 2002.

Uchitel, Alexei, dir., *Progulka*, Ministry of Culture of the Russian Federation/Roskinoprokat, 2003, DVD 2005, Madman Cinema.

### SHORTS, DOCUMENTARIES AND TELEVISION

Feyginburg, Yosif, dir., *Glenn Gould – The Russian Journey*, documentary, Atlantic Productions, 2002, DVD 2013, Major Entertainment.

Haefelli, Mark, dir. and prod., *Paul McCartney in Red Square*, DVD Documentary, produced by MPL Communications, 2005.

Harrison, Mark, prod., *The Last Days of Leningrad*, BBC Bristol, 1991.

Loznitsa, Sergei, dir., *Blockade*, using footage found in Soviet archives, Federal Agency for Culture and Cinematography and St Petersburg Documentary Film Studios, 2005.

—— *Revue*, using footage found in Soviet archives mainly from the Krushchev era, Federal Agency for Culture and Cinematography & St Petersburg Documentary Film Studios, 2008.

Nevzorov, Alexander, dir., *600 Seconds*, Leningrad Chanel/St Petersburg Television.

Polsky, Gabe, dir., *Red Army*, documentary, Weintraub and Herzog, 2014.

van den Berg, Rob, dir., 'Catching Up with Music' with Valery Gergiev, bonus feature on Glinka, *Ruslan and Lyudmila*, conducted by Valery Gergiev, Kirov Opera and Chorus, Decca, 1996.

Weinstein, Larry, dir., *Shostakovich Against Stalin – The War Symphonies*, documentary, Rhombus Films, 1997.

### OPERAS, MUSICALS AND DANCE

Borodin, Alexander, *Prince Igor*, conducted by Gianandrea Noseda, DVD Deutsche Grammophon, 2014.

Glinka, Mikhail, *A Life for the Tsar*, conducted by Alexander Lazarev, DVD NVC ARTS, 1992.

—— *Ruslan and Lyudmila*, conducted by Valery Gergiev, DVD Decca, 1995.

*Paris Dances Diaghilev*, Paris Opera Ballet; VHS NVC ARTS, 1991.

Prokofiev, Sergei, *War and Peace*, conducted by Valery Gergiev, Kirov/ Opera Bastille, 1991, Arthaus Musik, 2015.

Rimsky-Korsakov, *Le Coq d'Or*, conducted by Kent Nagano, DVD Arthaus Musil, 2011.

Shostakovich, Dmitri, *Cheryomushki*, dir. Paul Rappaport, Lenfilm, 1963; DVD Decca 2007.

Tchaikovsky, Peter Ilyich, *Eugene Onegin*, conducted by Sir Georg Solti, dir. Petr Weigl, DVD Decca, 1990.

### DISCS

Meader, Vaughn et al., *The First Family*, LP, New York: Cadence Records, November 1962.

# INDEX

Places and institutions in St Petersburg are indexed under themselves and not under the city. References in italics are to illustrations.